Strategies for Counseling with Children and Their Parents

Strategies for Counseling with Children and Their Parents

GERALDINE LEITL ORTON
Gannon University

Brooks/Cole Publishing Company

I**(T)**P® An International Thomson Publishing Company

Pacific Grove • Albany • Belmont • Bonn • Boston • Cincinnati • Detroit
Johannesburg • London • Madrid • Melbourne • Mexico City • New York • Paris
Singapore • Tokyo • Toronto • Washington

Sponsoring Editors: *Claire Verduin, Eileen Murphy*
Marketing Team: *Deborah Petit, Jean Thompson*
Marketing Representative: *Mark DeWeese*
Editorial Assistant: *Lisa Blanton*
Production Editor: *Nancy L. Shammas*
Manuscript Editor: *Barbara Kimmel*
Permissions Editor: *May Clark*

Interior Design: *Terri Wright*
Interior Illustration: *Susan Horovitz*
Cover Design: *E. Kelly Shoemaker*
Art Editor: *Lisa Torri*
Indexer: *James Minkin*
Typesetting: *Aksen Associates*
Cover Printing: *Lehigh Press Lithographers*
Printing and Binding: *Quebecor/Fairfield*

For more information, contact:

BROOKS/COLE PUBLISHING COMPANY
511 Forest Lodge Road
Pacific Grove, CA 93950
USA

International Thomson Editores
Seneca 53
Col. Polanco
11560 México, D. F., México

International Thomson Publishing Europe
Berkshire House 168-173
High Holborn
London WC1V 7AA
England

International Thomson Publishing GmbH
Königswinterer Strasse 418
53227 Bonn
Germany

Thomas Nelson Australia
102 Dodds Street
South Melbourne, 3205
Victoria, Australia

International Thomson Publishing Asia
221 Henderson Road
#05-10 Henderson Building
Singapore 0315

Nelson Canada
1120 Birchmount Road
Scarborough, Ontario
Canada M1K 5G4

International Thomson Publishing Japan
Hirakawacho Kyowa Building, 3F
2-2-1 Hirakawacho
Chiyoda-ku, Tokyo 102
Japan

Printed in the United States of America

10   9   8   7   6   5   4   3   2   1

THIS BOOK IS PRINTED ON ACID-FREE RECYCLED PAPER

Library of Congress Cataloging-in-Publication Data
Orton, Geraldine Leitl [date]
   Strategies for counseling with children and their parents /
Geraldine Leitl Orton
      p.   cm.
   Includes bibliographical references and index.
   ISBN 0-534-23280-9 (case)
      1. Counseling.   2. Children—Counseling of.   3. Family counseling.
   I.   Title
8F637.C6078   1996
618.92'89—dc20
                                                                    96–41264
                                                                    CIP

This book is dedicated to the memory of my mother, Virginia Traska Leitl, whose enduring example of love, faith, and hope is reflected in these pages.

ABOUT THE AUTHOR

Geraldine Leitl Orton, a former grade school teacher and elementary school counselor, has been involved with children and their parents for the past 35 years. Currently she is a professor and director of an undergraduate program in mental health counseling at Gannon University and is a member of the graduate faculty in counseling psychology. In 1988, she established a play therapy clinic—one of four in the state of Pennsylvania—that provides a practicum experience for students and assists area youngsters and their families. From 1992 to 1995, Dr. Orton was chair of the Department of Human Services, which included programs in criminal justice, gerontology, human services, mental health counseling, and social work. She holds memberships in the American Counseling Association and the American Psychological Association and is an associate member of the National Association of Social Workers. In addition to teaching, Dr. Orton has given numerous presentations and workshops on counseling children and their parents. She lives with her husband, Guy, on an apple farm overlooking beautiful Lake Erie and enjoys collecting antiques, especially children's toys and books.

CONTENTS

CHAPTER 5

Individual and Group Counseling with Children 172

CHAPTER 6

Play Therapy 211

CHAPTER 7   *Art Therapy*   253

CHAPTER 10 · *Safeguarding Children's Rights*   352

PREFACE

Somehow, by a quirk of nature and quite paradoxically, while combating and arguing over the labeling of the child's counseling problem, many of us have become very attached to our own labels, oftentimes making the child's problem fit our particular counseling model. In trying to analyze *parts*, sometimes we miss the *whole* picture. This text is an attempt to look at the whole picture—specifically, to look at the whole child and to propose a holistic counseling process that best speaks to and nurtures the child's wholeness.

Our world and its problems are growing ever more complex, and these complexities are certainly capable of deeply wounding our children. However, in the midst of these complexities, a simple truth remains: Against the backdrop of individual circumstances and differences, children require love, time, and attention to become healthy adults. This text recognizes the need for understanding both the complexity and diversity of the child's world and universal needs.

The title of this text, *Strategies for Counseling with Children and Their Parents*, was chosen because it reflects my own philosophy. There is more than one strategy for counseling the same child. Furthermore, no self-aware counselor should apologize for modifying strategies within the guidelines of ethical and legal professional practice. The counselor's experience and value orientation are positive, not negative, forces in helping children change unhealthy behaviors and in encouraging their parents to contribute to and support the desired healthy changes.

We, as counselors and soon-to-be counselors working with children, need to recognize and appreciate not only the often negative way that parents contribute to a child's problems but also the parents' positive intent and personal worth. The reality is that some parents are, in fact, negatively affecting their children's lives; however, many parents are capable of exerting positive influences, and many can identify and understand their children's problems but are unable to evoke change. This text recognizes this reality, and its recurring theme is parent participation in the counseling process. The text also offers parent support group strategies that (1) focus on the positive contributions parents make to their children's lives and (2) build on the strengths of both parent and child. This text has evolved from an anabolic approach, combining and integrating counseling skills with the therapeutic process, emphasizing how the counselor relates to the child and parent, and including the parent as a fully participating partner in the process.

Conceptual Framework

In keeping with my objectives in writing this text, counseling theory—although included—is not the focus. Instead, the focus is on process and practice specifically applied to the counseling of children and their parents. It is assumed that the reader already possesses a basic theoretical foundation and may have developed an affinity for a particular theoretical framework. It is my hope that this text will challenge the reader to be expansive, flexible, and interpretive in his or her approach to the counseling of children and their families.

Admittedly, however, a certain dominance or favoritism in theoretical approaches often emerges in any text. In *Strategies for Counseling with Children and Their Parents*, the Adlerian perspective is somewhat thematic in the conceptualization of cases and in Part 3. This particular theoretical philosophy was selected not entirely out of my own orientation but also because it seems most compatible with the philosophy underlying the text. The Adlerian approach to counseling focuses on strengths; gives equal weight to thoughts, feelings, and actions; addresses developmental as well as remedial concerns; and emphasizes prevention. It is a holistic approach related to the development of the child's "self."

Certain terms used frequently in this text require some clarification. The term *approach* refers to theoretical framework (humanistic, behavioral, psychodynamic); *strategy* refers to the counseling plan or method designed to bring about specific change; and *technique* is used to denote the implementation of the plan—specifically, a manipulative method (play therapy, art therapy, bibliotherapy). The terms *counselor* and *therapist* are used interchangeably.

Text Organization

This text is organized into three parts. Part 1, "Understanding Today's Children and Their Families," sets the stage for understanding the child and family of today and tomorrow—their personas and the social, cultural, educational, and spiritual environment that helps shape them. In particular, these influences may make the child vulnerable to the wounding that ultimately brings the child and his or her family to counseling.

Part 2, "Counseling and Therapy with Children," explores, explains, and describes the drama of child counseling. Identifying what obstacles lie in the child's path to healthy development is the process of assessment, the essential precursor to the counseling and treatment plan. In this section, a framework is presented that enables the counselor to integrate process and skills to facilitate changes in the child's thoughts, feelings, and behaviors. Within this flexible framework, counselors are able to select those counseling techniques that are uniquely appropriate for each child. These techniques include play therapy, art therapy, and bibliotherapy, which can be used with children individually and in groups. Special attention is given in Chapter 9 to behavioral approaches and strategies because of their historical popularity, time- and cost-effectiveness, and often the very nature of the presenting problem. This approach, with its greater emphasis on the presenting behavior and less focus on causative factors, differs from the therapeutic process illustrated in the other chapters—a process that places more emphasis on analysis, insight, and relationship factors. The final chapter in Part 2 discusses ethical and legal concerns related to counseling children and families, balancing the child's participation in the plan, the child's rights, and the counselor's responsibilities to the child and the parents.

Part 3, "Counseling Parents and Families to Effect Behavioral Changes in Children," focuses on improving and strengthening the parent-child relationship. The purpose of this Adlerian counseling intervention is to facilitate and support positive changes in the child's behavior. In addition, guidelines and strategies are presented for using parent support groups as a way to help parents help their children build more cooperative relationships with others.

Practical Application

Each chapter presents opportunities for practical application. Case studies and accompanying dialogues illustrate how the technique presented in each chapter can be applied in practice. Numerous individual and group strategies and activities are also presented to aid the counselor in utilizing a variety of techniques in counseling with children and their parents. A student manual is also available that is designed to help you shape your own counseling strategies.

Acknowledgments

This text would not have been possible without the contributions of a number of professionals in various fields of study. Specifically, I would like to thank the following: my colleague and dearest friend, Mary Ann Frew, for providing her expertise, experience, and encouragement when it was most needed; LeAdelle Phelps for graciously agreeing to contribute the chapter on behavioral therapy; Helen Bolton of the James Prendergast Library Association of Jamestown, New York, and the Chautauqua-Cattaraugus Library System for supplying over 100 children's books and writing many of the summaries that appear in the chapter on bibliotherapy; and G. Christopher Orton, Esquire, for accessing, summarizing, and referencing all the court cases included in the chapter on safeguarding children's rights.

I would also like to acknowledge those experts in the field who reviewed the text and ultimately made it better. Special thanks to: Joan T. England, University of South Dakota; Larry Golden, University of Texas at San Antonio; Elaina Rose Lovejoy, St. Mary's College of California; and Timothy Sewall, University of Wisconsin—Green Bay.

Grateful appreciation is extended to the administration and faculty of Gannon University, specifically to Philip Kelly, former Dean of Humanities, Business and Education, for approving a sabbatical leave and for his continuous support throughout the writing of this text; Carlos Mamani and Mary Lou Scalise for translating the consent forms into Spanish; and Holly Nishimura for her contribution to the section on cultural diversity. Special thanks go to John Pennsy of the Gannon University Library and Sandy O'Neill, Pat Ring, and Sue Sveda of the McCord Memorial Library for checking numerous references and ordering hundreds of books and articles through the inner-library loan program.

Among those deserving special credit are the students who contributed ideas, activities, and counseling cases to the textbook and accompanying manual and to my student assistants, Jennifer Davis and Elizabeth Akers, for reading each chapter, providing thoughtful input, and making countless trips to the library to access information and order journal articles and books. Most important, special love and appreciation is extended to all the children and parents who shared their stories and gave me permission to use them.

Special thanks go to my editor, Eileen Murphy, for her skill, enthusiasm, and warm support, and to Nancy Shammas, production editor, for her expertise and assistance. Heartfelt appreciation is expressed to Barbara Kimmel, an outstanding and invaluable manuscript editor with a wonderful sense of humor; to Kelly Shoemaker and Lisa Torri for the superb interior design and artwork; to May Clark for careful attention to permissions; and to Patricia Vienneau, Lisa Blanton, and Mark DeWeese for all their help and encouragement. Special appreciation and affection is reserved for Claire Verduin, former editor and publisher at Brooks/Cole, without whom this book would not be possible. Thank you, Claire, for believing in the project and helping me do my best.

Finally, my deepest appreciation is extended to my husband and best friend, Guy, for his patience, understanding, and encouragement; and to our children, Alisa and Chris, and our grandchildren, Meghan, Douglas, and Michael, for their immeasurable love and sustained support.

—Geraldine Leitl Orton

Strategies for Counseling with Children and Their Parents

PART 1　Understanding Today's Children and Their Families

All parents must struggle to value children enough to discipline them, spend time with them, be decent role models for them, and fight for what they need from our community and our nation.
—Marian Wright Edelman

CHILDHOOD IS A TIME TO LEARN, EXPERIENCE, AND GROW. It is a time to play, have fun, imagine, explore, and trust in a world that is safe, secure, and friendly. It is a time to be nurtured, valued, and protected by a caring family. It is a time to make mistakes and learn from them and to develop a sense of right and wrong. It is a time to discover and appreciate the person within. It is a time to show initiative, experience success, and develop a sense of responsibility and control over one's own behavior. It is a time to discover one's special talents and abilities and to learn the skills necessary to find a place in the adult world. It is a time to acquire the necessary attitudes, values, and behaviors to become a good person, spouse, parent, - co-worker, and citizen. Happily, many children in America have such a childhood; regrettably, many do not. It is for all children, especially those who need help to have a happier, healthier childhood, that this book is written.

Chapter 1 describes the need for children to be cared for and nurtured in their homes, schools, and communities in order to become caring, confident, and capable adults. It is in these settings that children learn to appreciate themselves and others and to develop a sense of responsibility and control over their behavior. However, the American family, because of its changing structure, function, roles, and attitudes, is undergoing unprecedented stresses and cannot always meet children's needs. In greater numbers than ever before, children are being raised by single mothers, foster mothers, teenage mothers, stepmothers, mothers who work outside the home, and grandmothers. Many children have stepfathers, grandfathers, weekend fathers, absent fathers, and teen fathers. The roles of fathers and mothers as nurturers and providers are blurring and blending, and many parents feel increasingly overworked.

With the decline in the "traditional" nuclear family and the rise in nontraditional family structures, parents are struggling to provide their children with love, nurturance, and guidance, often without adequate parenting models themselves and without the support of spouses and extended family members. Rather than label families "dysfunctional" because they do not fit the traditional model, we as human services professionals have to seek out the strengths in families. We must develop relationships with parents that will encourage them to build on the positive attributes they see in their children and in themselves. To accomplish this task, practitioners must have a thorough understanding of the factors affecting the lives of children and their families and must view these factors within the context of the larger society. Chapter 1 contributes to this understanding by painting a statistical portrait of societal factors that have an impact on children and families.

We live in a society affected by poverty—poverty in the real sense of inadequate financial resources to provide the basic necessities of life and poverty of tolerance, time, togetherness, nurturing, values, and vision. Dramatic increases in reported child abuse and neglect; rising child poverty and hunger; lack of affordable health care; increased risk of school failure; pervasive drug and alcohol abuse; and violence in our homes, schools, and streets are consequences of this poverty. The seeds of poverty, sown in the lives of young children, have produced a bitter harvest for teens, as evidenced by the decreasing number of high school graduates, vanishing employment opportunities for young people, rising teenage birth rates, and soaring juvenile crime arrest rates. All these factors have profound implications for the children of tomorrow as this generation's children become parents.

Chapter 2 provides a developmental framework for counseling that permeates the entire text. This chapter chronicles the familial social, economic, and political forces that have shaped our attitudes toward children throughout the centuries. The historical analysis is followed by a brief overview of child development that focuses on healthy children from birth to age 12. This summary features important developmental milestones including gross and fine motor movement; language acquisition; imagination, humor, and play behaviors; cognitive or thinking skills; emotional development; and social interaction. Because counselors and educators are most likely to work with preschoolers and school-age children, more time and attention has been devoted to these developmental stages than to the period between birth and age 2. This chapter on child development is intended to reinforce concepts learned in child development courses, not to be a substitute for them.

An understanding of the healthy growth and development of children is a prerequisite to understanding those influences that might interfere with continual developmental progress. In the normal course of growing up, most healthy children encounter problems that might cause them to pause or take a few steps back. These stumbling blocks to healthy development might include problems with dependency and attachment, fear and its related responses, or anger as expressed by aggression or jealousy and rivalry. Children who express these common developmental problems might need some help resolving them before they can continue on their journey toward health and growth. Guidelines for referral are included at the end of the chapter to assist parents and professionals in determining the severity of these developmental problems and whether help is needed.

Chapter 3 tells the story of vulnerable children and their fragile families. This vulnerability is portrayed in the stories of children who have experienced the crises of violence and loss. Case studies of abused and neglected children assist the reader in identifying and helping youngsters who are both victims and observers of family violence. One of the contributing factors to violence in the family is substance abuse. Because children of alcoholics may be victims of abuse, may witness family violence, and may have a parent who is unavailable to meet their needs, these children often experience both violence and loss. And because children of alcoholics rarely confide the family "secret," this chapter provides guidelines to assist the reader in recognizing and counseling the child of an alcoholic parent.

Loss is a central theme in divorce, just as it is in death. Children of divorced and separated parents experience the loss of daily contact with one or both parents and, if forced to relocate, may have to leave old friends, familiar schools, and comfortable neighborhoods behind. Common emotional reactions to these events are discussed and strategies are included for helping children cope not only with their parents' divorce but also with a subsequent remarriage.

A more profound loss is the terminal illness of the child or the death of a parent or sibling. Children with AIDS face additional losses because many have parents who are either ill or have already died from the disease. These children have many fears, not only for themselves but also for those they will leave behind. Children have different reactions to the death of a parent or sibling and have different styles of coping. The section on children in mourning details these different styles of coping and gives strategies for helping children through the grieving process. A list of support services for children and their parents is included at the end of Chapter 3.

CHAPTER 1 · Growing Up in the 21st Century

Single-parent families are not simply "growth experiences"; latchkey children are often frightened and lonely; divorce is not merely a hiccup in anyone's life; the difficulties of working parents are very real and fall with special severity on working mothers.
— STEPHANIE COONTZ

CHILDHOOD IN THE 21ST CENTURY

Many opportunities as well as many problems await the children of the next century. Although tomorrow's children will enjoy the benefits of an industrialized society—the advantages of space age technology, new medical discoveries to cure and treat disease, improved agricultural practices to make food abundant and safe, and access to computers and electronic media to put learning at their fingertips—all will not share these benefits equally. A wide range of problem indexes that measure the physical and emotional health and well-being of children, such as prenatal care, immunizations, child health and nutrition, poverty levels, educational achievement, safety, and family stability, indicate that as a nation we are falling short of our goal. We are not protecting many of our children, nor are we ensuring their basic rights to love and understanding, adequate food and health care, quality education, fun, and a sense of identity.

A statistical portrait of childhood in the United States in the 21st century, illustrated in Figure 1-1, reveals some disturbing trends that affect children's health. In one of the richest countries on earth, more than 14 million children live in poverty: 1 in 8 under the age of 12 actually goes hungry—and almost 100,000 are homeless every night. More than 8 million children—1 in 8—had no health insurance at all in 1992; 1 in 4 did not have prenatal care during the first 3 months of life; and the U.S. record for vaccinating children age 2 years and under is worse than in any country in the Western Hemisphere except Bolivia and Haiti. (Center for the Study of Social Policy, 1993; Children's Defense Fund [CDF], 1994; Coontz, 1992).

Many American children from impoverished, violent, drug-filled environments are at risk for developmental delays before they are even born. In Chicago alone, 10,000 babies born addicted to crack cocaine who have reached school age are expected to cost the state between $50 and $100 million a year for foster care and special education (Griffin & Waltz, 1991). As America's crack problem worsens, health and human services professionals have but two choices: get mothers into preventive and treatment programs in time to protect their babies or prepare to deal with a steady stream of troubled children in the future (Kantrowitz & Wingert, 1990).

Compared to white children, black children are four times as likely to be poor, more likely to have low birth weights, and twice as likely to die before their first birthday (CDF, 1994; Center for the Study of Social Policy, 1993). Sadly, "a black baby born in the shadow of the White House is now more likely to die in the first year of life than a baby born in Jamaica or Trinidad" (Hewlett, 1991, p.15). A U.S.

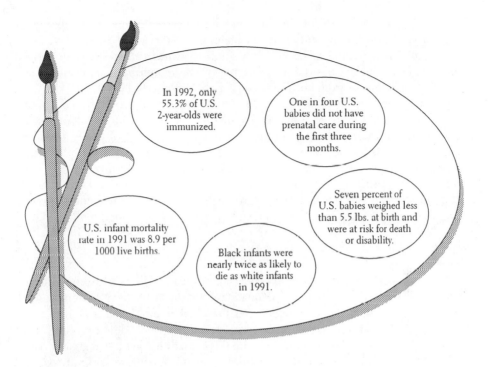

In 1992, only 55.3% of U.S. 2-year-olds were immunized.

One in four U.S. babies did not have prenatal care during the first three months.

Seven percent of U.S. babies weighed less than 5.5 lbs. at birth and were at risk for death or disability.

U.S. infant mortality rate in 1991 was 8.9 per 1000 live births.

Black infants were nearly twice as likely to die as white infants in 1991.

FIGURE 1-1   *Painting a Statistical Portrait of Child Health in America*
SOURCE: Children's Defense Fund (1994).

Department of Education study found that every year spent in poverty adds two percentage points to the chances that a child will fall behind in school (as cited in CDF, 1994). Williams (1992) estimates that 30% of the school population is at risk for failure and that in some city schools nearly 50% of the young people drop out of school.

"Poverty's chief victims have been children and *their* victims. *Delinquency* now seems too quaint a term to describe juvenile crime, which has more than doubled since 1960" (Roberts, 1993, p. 190). After a period of decreased crime rates between 1980 and 1985, crime is on the rise again (U.S. Department of Justice, 1991). The increasing savagery of the crimes and the decreasing ages of the offenders has captured the public's attention and shifted the national emphasis from "children having children" to "children killing children" (CDF, 1994). According to the Center for the Study of Social Policy 1993), the family risk factors that contribute to juvenile violent crime offenders are greater in (1) extremely poor families, (2) families where violence and adult discord are common, (3) families where a male authority figure is often absent, and (4) families who live in isolated and impoverished communities where there are few chances for children to succeed.

Violence in our homes, schools, and society at large imperils the lives and futures of U.S. children and teenagers in countless ways. Consider that homicide and suicide rates have tripled since 1960; every 14 hours, a child younger than age 5 is murdered;

in Chicago's inner city, 74% of the children have witnessed a shooting, stabbing, or robbery. A child growing up in the United States is 15 times more likely than a child living in Northern Ireland to be killed by gunfire. Three million children witness parental violence each year; every 13 seconds a child is reported abused or neglected; each day 3 children die from child abuse (CDF, 1994, Roberts, 1993).

Current trends reveal how vulnerable young people really are, especially young teens who are giving birth to tomorrow's children. Although national attention has been diverted to the problems of crime and violence, millions of children will be affected by what is happening to teenage mothers in the United States today. After reaching a high point in the late 1950s, teen birth rates dropped steadily until the 1980s and then began rising again (National Center for Health Statistics, as cited in CDF, 1994). In 1991, there were 1.1 million teen pregnancies; 30,000 pregnancies were to young women under age 15 and 2/3 of teen births were to unmarried mothers (CDF, 1994). "Murphy Brown, notwithstanding, it's all but impossible for a high school dropout who gives birth to her first baby at 19 to be anything but poor" (Besharov, as quoted in Roberts, 1993, p. 176).

Many of these young women will succeed, but many will lack the supports and security necessary to provide an adequate future for their own families. Often unprepared for motherhood, undereducated, unskilled, unemployed, and unmarried, the teen mother is at serious risk for becoming poor and dependent on public assistance to survive. Young families created with these disadvantages are at greater risk of instability and of breaking up, placing children at risk for future disadvantage and hardship (Center for the Study of Social Policy, 1993).

The National Research Council (NRC) reported in *Losing Generations: Adolescents in High Risk Settings* that 7 million children and youth between the ages of 10 and 17 "are growing up in circumstances that limit their development, compromise their health, impair their sense of self, and thereby restrict their futures" (as cited in CDF, 1994, p.55). These alarming trends are depicted in Figure 1-2. Ten million children are affected by their parents' substance abuse, almost 1.2 million run away from home each year, and suicide is a leading cause of death among teenagers (CDF, 1994; Rosewater, 1989). Almost 10 million children are in need of mental health services (Tuma, 1989), 3 million have serious emotional disturbances, and an estimated two-thirds don't get care appropriate to their needs (CDF, 1994). The National Commission on Children (1991) reported that the proportion of youngsters receiving psychological assistance rose 80% between 1981 and 1988, a reflection of increased need for and availability of help.

Middle-class children, once thought to be immune to the problems poor children experience are becoming increasingly at risk. Hewlett (1991) concluded that "compared to a previous generation, these children are more likely to: underperform at school; commit suicide; need psychiatric help; suffer a severe eating disorder; bear a child out of wedlock; take drugs; be a victim of a violent crime" (p. 81). According to a 1990 National Commission report, even privileged youngsters are overwhelmed "by drugs, pregnancy, bad grades and bad jobs" (as quoted in Hewlett, 1991, p. 81).

The Council on Families in America concluded that "the evidence is strong and growing that the current generation of children and youth is the first in our nation's history to be less well off—psychologically, socially, economically and morally—than their parents were at the same age" (as cited in Roberts, 1993, p. 190). Marian Wright Edelman, in the forward of *The State of America's Children Yearbook* (CDF, 1994,

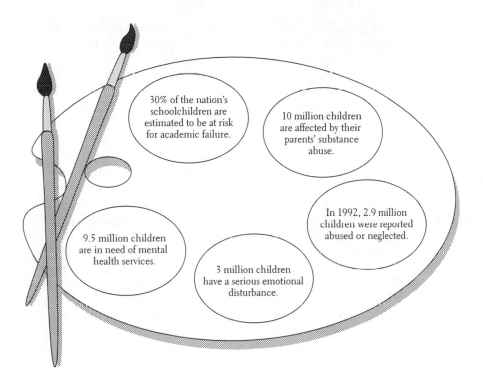

FIGURE 1-2 *Painting a Statistical Portrait of American Children at Risk*
SOURCE: Children's Defense Fund (1994); Tuma (1989); Williams (1992).

p. xxii), stated that unless we do something to curb current trends, the following projections are likely to characterize childhood in the 21st century.

- If economic and social trends of the past 20 years persist over this decade, 17 million children, or 24% of all children under age 18, will be poor by the year 2001.
- If the proportion of births to unmarried women continues to climb over the next 7 years (now 101,000 a month) at the rate it has for the last 7 years, more than 40% of all babies born in 2001 will go home from the hospital to a single-parent family.
- In 1990, the United States spent more than $100 per person on prisons and only $6.22 on Head Start programs. If the trends between 1971 and 1990 persist until 2001, the country will be spending $358 per person to lock up youths, and only $13 to prepare them to benefit from school and stay out of prison.
- If current national trends persist, 1 million babies will be born into poverty every year, 44,000 teen mothers will give birth every month, and 37,000 children will be arrested every week.

We have unleashed a Pandora's box of problems on our children. However, we still have hope that we can counteract the tremendous difficulties children face. There is no single entity in U.S. society that can solve these problems alone: not the government, not the family, not the schools, not the communities. The secret is that we all have to work together, and what better people to tackle the job than the human services professionals who work with children and their families?

A PORTRAIT OF THE CHANGING AMERICAN FAMILY

At the beginning of the 20th century, children lived in large families surrounded by extended family members. Family roles and functions were well defined. Fathers were the providers, mothers were the nurturers, and grandparents were the children's companions, confidantes, and advisors. Children had meaningful work to do within the family and looked after one another. Educational, career, social and marriage choices were limited and expectations were clear. Opportunities for recreation were found through kinship relations and community networks.

By mid-century, the influence of extended family was waning, and the 1950s was the heyday of the "traditional nuclear family." Young couples were taking their children and moving to the suburbs, leaving grandparents and extended family members behind in city neighborhoods and on family farms. Men worked primarily in business and industry, and women made housework and children their life. "Whatever else it may have been, the decade of the '50s was certainly an era of high birthrates, high marriage rates, low divorce rates and general family 'togetherness' and stability" (Popenoe, 1993, p. 528).

The idealized version of the post-war family, as portrayed on television, in books, magazines, and children's readers, is filled with images of serenity and stability. In *The New Friends and Neighbors*, a second-grade reader published by Scott-Foresman in 1952, families lived on Pleasant Street in neat houses with lawns surrounded by white picket fences. Children were met after school by a neatly aproned mom holding a tray of milk and cookies. In these stories, mom spent unhurried days with the children, seeing to their needs for attention, education and recreation. Dad, pictured in his suit and carrying a briefcase, worked downtown. He was greeted home from the office by laughing, happy children and the family dog. Grandmother and Grandfather lived nearby and the children visited them often. During summer vacations, they all visited extended family members in the city and on the farm. The milkman, the policeman, and Zeke, a handyman who builds fences and rakes leaves, all appeared in the stories but didn't live in the neighborhood.

All the families on Pleasant Street were white, middle class, had a father who was a white-collar worker, a mother who was a housewife, and two or three children. These images have some basis in fact. The 1950 census data indicate that 80% of married couple households consisted of a male breadwinner and a female housewife. Popenoe (1993), summarizing family research, stated that "by mid-century a higher proportion of American children were growing up in stable, two-parent families than at any other time in American history" (p.528). However, the families on Pleasant Street did not represent all the families of the 1950s. Working-class families, minority families, poor families, and single-parent families did not live on Pleasant street. Women who felt limited by the "wash on Mondays, iron on Tuesdays" routine and men who were stressed by the burden of being sole provider were not portrayed either.

Tales of alcoholic parents, battered women, and abused children make us wonder how pleasant things really were for some of the families on Pleasant Street, but the image of child-centered family life still endures.

If we paint a mythical portrait of a neighborhood today, we would include both traditional and nontraditional families of all sizes, colors, and combinations. Children on Reality Street might be living with two parents who work, a single parent, a teen parent, a stepparent, a never-married parent, grandparents, adoptive parents, gay parents, or foster parents. Today's young, dual-income family that can afford a single-family home surrounded by a white picket fence might be too harried to enjoy life in the backyard. Instead of greeting the children at the door, working moms or dads scurry to pick them up from day care, the baby-sitter, or an after-school program. Latchkey children, home alone after school, anticipate their single mother's return from work and hope she brings a pizza for dinner. Instead of visiting grandparents often, some of the children on Reality Street live with their grandparents. Some dual-career families hire someone to care for and play with their children, and only a dwindling number of families have homemaker moms who fulfill a more "traditional" role.

Times and families are changing, but one thing seems certain—the 1950s-style family, though not quite extinct, is on the endangered list. After analyzing the 1990 census data, Roberts (1993), concluded that only 3 in 100 households conform to the stereotypical family made up of a working husband, his homemaker wife, and their two biological children. A recent survey found that some 79% of adult Americans agreed that "it takes two paychecks to support a family today," and only 27% favored a return to "at least one parent raising children full-time" (Massachusetts Mutual, 1989).

In the last 35 years, the American family has undergone enormous shifts in roles, structures, finances and attitudes. As we approach the 21st century, the nuclear family, the last vestige of the traditional family unit, is breaking up. According to the report *The Diverse Living Arrangements of Children* (U.S. Bureau of the Census, 1994a), barely more than half of American children live in a traditional nuclear family consisting solely of a mother, father, and full brothers and sisters. The nuclear family is slowly being replaced by the childless family, the single-parent family, the blended family, and the intergenerational family. Even the definition of *family* is evolving. According to Roberts (1993), the word *family* comes from the Latin, *famulus* or "servant," and includes a man's wife, children, and household helpers. In 1950, the census described family as "two or more people related by blood, marriage or adoption"; but in a 1990 survey, three-fourths of the respondents chose "A group of people who love and care for each other" as their definition of "family" (Roberts, 1993, p. 32).

Sam Roberts, in his book *Who We Are: A Portrait of America* (1993), highlighted the changing American family using the latest U.S. Census Bureau data:

> The nuclear family fizzled in the 1980s: for the first time, the number of married, childless couples surpassed the number of couples with children; fewer than three in four children are being raised by two parents; only one in seven families includes a married couple with two children; women, with and without children, began working outside the home and marrying later than at any time in a century; the ratio of divorces to marriages set a record; and the decline in household size halted. (p. 4)

The United Nations declared 1994 to be the International Year of the Family, and sociologists and family scholars debated whether the American family was changing or collapsing. No matter which view the reader takes, many profound changes have occurred in family life since the 1960s that have many serious consequences for children. Some of these changes are listed in Figure 1-3.

Sketching a Mother's Perspective

We continue to praise middle-class women who leave the work force for child-raising. No leaders worth their re-election would demean these women or preach that they are somehow "irresponsible." But we insist that poor women leave their children for work.

—ELLEN GOODMAN (1995), commenting on Congress' efforts to put recipients of AFDC to work without adequate support for child care

Mothers Who Work Outside the Home

Perhaps the biggest change affecting the American family is the massive influx of women into the workforce. The Children's Defense Fund, using 1993 data from the U.S. Bureau of Labor Statistics, reported that nearly 60% of mothers with children under age 6 held paying jobs, an increase of about 50% since 1975. In 1993, employed mothers with very young children were in the majority for the first time. Fifty-four percent of mothers with children younger than 3 years, and 64% of those with children ages 3 to 5 were in the civilian labor force (CDF, 1994).

The feminist movement has been credited with freeing women from full-time housework, opening up new career and educational opportunities for women, and narrowing the wage gap between men and women. Critics blame feminist influences for the demise of the "milk and cookies mom" of the 1950s and the emergence of the "super mom" of the 1970s and 1980s, and they decry the impact of maternal employment on the stability of the family. The fact is that the shift from homemaker to employee was driven by a variety of factors, many of them economic. The need for a second wage earner as salaries lost ground to inflation, and the increasing numbers of women who were single either by divorce, death, or design helped fuel the increase in the number of women in the labor force (Roberts, 1993).

Analyzing data from the U.S. Bureau of Labor Statistics, Roberts (1993) concluded that 73% of all women aged 25 to 34 were in the labor force in 1990, and nearly 62% of single mothers maintaining families worked outside the home. In addition, many women in the work force were older mothers who delayed childbirth until they completed their education and established themselves in their professions.

Many career women with a "take this job and love it" philosophy work for job satisfaction as well as for salaries, and they make tremendous sacrifices to balance work and family life. Many feel stressed in the process. In a survey of 5000 women listed in *Who's Who of American Women,* 36% felt they were under constant stress, and 56% felt stressed part of the time. Fully 50% said they sometimes neglected their marriage, and 46% reported sometimes putting their work ahead of their children (Collins, 1993).

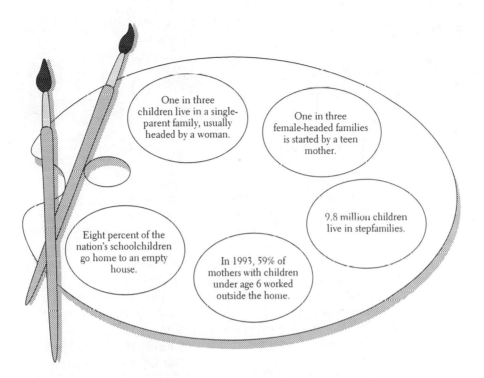

FIGURE 1-3   *Painting a Statistical Portrait of the Changing American Family*
SOURCE: Center for the Study of Social Policy (1993); U.S. Bureau of the Census (1994a, 1994b).

Work outside the home has provided women with greater opportunities, financial independence, and increased self-esteem; but it has created tremendous stress and much guilt about child care. In 1990, more than 6.5 million children under the age of 5 were cared for by someone other than a parent. Another 4.2 million children went to family child care homes and day care centers (CDF, 1994).

The quality of day care centers varies widely; legislation establishing minimum standards of care is lacking and most good day care centers are beyond the resources of the working poor (Hewlett, 1991). Many employed mothers have to settle for substandard care because they can't afford better. However, even mothers who can afford a "Mary Poppins" feel troubled about leaving their children. Whatever the arrangement, child care is often a source of worry, stress and guilt for many mothers who work outside the home.

Recent research suggests that women who work outside the home get more help from their husbands than do women who work at home (Almeida, Maggs, & Galambos, 1993). Although increasing numbers of men—particularly those in dual-career families with young children—are helping with child care and housework (Papalia & Olds, 1996), women are still responsible for the lion's share. Citing national data, Schor (1992) determined that "Twenty-four percent of employed wives are still

For Better or For Worse®   **by Lynn Johnston**

saddled with all the household work, and an additional 42 percent do "the bulk' of it" (p.104). Arlie Hochschild, in her book, *The Second Shift* (1989), concluded that when outside work, housework, and child care are added together, American women work approximately 15 hours a week longer than men do; over the course of a year, this adds an extra month of 24-hour days to their workload.

It is fair to say that the time squeeze for both men and women leaves less time to spend with children and to see to the children's needs for attention, education, and recreation. However, regardless of income, social, or marital status, working women experience the greatest time crunch. Many working mothers, even in two-parent families, are still in the untenable position of having two jobs, countless responsibilities, and exhausting workloads at a time when they should be enjoying their families.

Latchkey Kids

Many of the changes that families have undergone—divorce, single parenthood, women in the workforce—have essentially emptied houses during the day. In *Who's Minding the Kids?* the U.S. Bureau of the Census (1994b) reported that 8% of the nation's school children in 1991 went home to an empty house. Leaving children home alone stresses working parents, contributes to lost production at work as parents "phone home," and increases the likelihood that emergencies at home may develop. Consider the anxiety of a mother whose child phones her at work to say, "I'm bleeding!"

Peterson (1989) concluded that without parents in the home, children may engage in such unhealthy activities as watching too much television, eating too much junk food, and postponing or forgetting to do homework, household chores, and other self-care routines. Some latchkey kids experience loneliness, anxiety, fear, and worry, whereas others may experiment with high-risk behaviors involving drugs, alcohol, and delinquent behavior (Padilla & Landreth, 1989). A 1989 study of eighth-graders in Los Angeles and San Diego conducted by the American Academy of Pediatrics raised parental anxiety by reporting that latchkey children were twice as likely to try marijuana at least once, smoke cigarettes, and drink alcohol, regardless of whether they came from one- or two-parent families or what their grades were in school (Richardson et al., 1989).

Although some researchers report that latchkey kids are more independent and self-disciplined, Elkind (1988) believes that being home alone is a stressful experience for young people. Because the experiences of latchkey children vary widely from family to family, much depends on the child's age, developmental level, and emotional maturity. The safety, effectiveness, and impact of latchkey arrangements is dependent to a large extent on the location of the home, the type of neighborhood, and the availability of family, friends, or neighbors to watch over the children. In any event, although the latchkey arrangement is far from ideal for most parents, it is often the only alternative available.

Profiling Different Kinds of Families

Jack lives with his mom and visits his dad on weekends.
Jill lives with her mother and stepfather and visits her dad in the summer.
Manuel's mom and dad share him; he switches houses every two months.
Niki lives with her grandmother; her mom is on crack.
Joel's dad is gay; he visits him and his new roommate every month.
Yoshi never knew her dad; she lives with her aunt and uncle.
Masood lives with his dad; he visits his mom on holidays and in the summer.

—Sample family situations

Single-Parent Families

Lifestyles have changed dramatically in the decades since the 1960s. Today, 1 million children a year watch their parents split up; an equal number are born out of wedlock. There are 10.9 million single parents, 9.3 million women and 1.6 million men, raising children; 1 in 3 of these children is being raised by the mother. Two disturbing trends account for this statistic: the birthrate for unwed mothers has jumped 82% in the past 10 years, and the number of divorced Americans has increased almost 4 times since 1970 (U.S. Bureau of the Census, 1994a).

Couples in earlier generations may have thought about divorce, but because of social and economic taboos, many stayed married. Today, however, with the advent of no-fault divorce laws, dual incomes, less commitment, and weakened stigmata, approximately half of all marriages eventually dissolve. Census demographers found that although the divorce rate appears to have plateaued during the 1980s, the number of divorces and the rate itself have doubled since the 1960s (Roberts, 1993).

Divorce often plunges mothers and children into poverty. Because women generally earn only 60% of what men earn and because only 32% receive any child support (Center for the Study of Social Policy, 1993), the standard of living for many women declines. Roberts (1993) reported that single mothers who were not poor when they were married were living in poverty within a year after the divorce. The financial desperation in the aftermath of divorce often forces the family into a lower standard of living, necessitating a move to less expensive neighborhoods, taking children away from schools, family and friends. Diminished contact between children and mothers who have an extra job just to make ends meet contributes to the crisis.

Of all of the losses that children experience when their parents divorce, the most devastating are the loss of safety and security the intact family provided and the loss of daily contact with a parent, usually the father. Diminished contact with fathers is one of the heartbreaks of approximately 10 million children who live in homes fractured by separation and divorce (U.S. Bureau of the Census, 1989). In a study of 1000 youngsters made between 1976 and 1987, Furstenberg and Harris found that 42% of children whose father had left the marriage had not seen him in the past year (as cited in Hewlett, 1991).

These losses, combined with the emotions attached to parental separation and divorce, create distress that is associated with a variety of short- and long-term negative outcomes for children. Wallerstein and Blakeslee (1989) concluded that "almost all of the children of divorce regard their childhood and adolescence as having taken place in the shadow of divorce....Almost half of the children entered adulthood as worried, underachieving, self-deprecating, and sometimes angry young men and women" (pp. 298–299).

According to Wallerstein and Blakeslee (1989), some children from divorced families experience difficulties in their interpersonal relationships, school behavior, academic achievement, self-esteem, and in their future outlook on love, marriage, and work. Other studies found that some children become strengthened in one or more areas as a result of coping with their parents' divorce, and they develop competencies or grow psychologically as a result. Growing maturity as a result of greater levels of responsibility and increased self-esteem from successfully performing new tasks have also been reported (Gately & Schwebel, 1992).

Small but growing numbers of fathers are contributing more to raising their children largely as a result of increased joint custody arrangements, the blurring of roles between nurturer and provider, and fathers' desire to be more actively involved in their children's lives. "Given the number of divorces, remarriages and single mothers, children of some single fathers may see more of their dads than most children do" (Roberts, 1993, p. 53).

Thirty-nine percent of parents are single through divorce (Roberts, 1993); but, according to the most recent Census Bureau report (1994a), 30% of all births in 1991 were out-of-wedlock. Five million American children are growing up without fathers (U.S. Bureau of the Census, 1989), and the number of out-of-wedlock births is increasing. Some experts are predicting the figure may hit a staggering 40% by the year 2001 (CDF, 1994). The out-of-wedlock birthrate is growing much faster among whites than among African Americans and some experts are predicting that, if the current trend continues, nearly half of all babies born to both blacks and whites will be to unmarried women (Roberts, 1993).

Although these statistics are troubling, they don't tell the whole story. Many young couples who live together but have chosen not to marry are counted in the statistics. Many of these young, unmarried couples will marry sometime in the future; but even if they don't, many are able to provide their children with warm, loving, and nurturing environments. A choice not to get married, particularly for young college students, is often a very practical one. Financial aid may be jeopardized, a separate apartment may be unaffordable, and live-in grandparents may be needed to help care for the child. Many students cannot raise a baby, work, and complete school at the same time; others can and do.

Luke, a beautiful 10-pound boy, arrived while his parents were preparing for their final exams. All through her pregnancy, his lovely young mother ate all the right foods, neither smoked nor drank alcohol and got plenty of exercise. It was a surprise to our whole class that Luke weighed so much because his mom was so petite. We all teased her that she was "all baby." Luke's mom and dad decided not to get married right now; but they have their own apartment, work, and continue studying toward their degrees. Dad works during the day and goes to night classes; mom goes to day classes and cares for Luke at night; Grandpa cares for him during the day. The result is a smiling, happy, well-cared-for baby.

Teen-Parent Families

One million teens get pregnant every year, and nearly half of these, mostly unmarried, adolescents give birth to babies who will also be at risk for pregnancy as teens. Roberts (1993), citing data from the National Center for Health Statistics, reported two out of three teens who gave birth in 1990 were unmarried. Among black teenagers, nine in ten were unmarried when they had their first child. Although the rate for black teens remains higher than for whites, white teenagers, because they represent a larger percentage of the population, are having two-thirds of the babies (Roberts, 1993).

How does having a baby affect a teen of any race? A composite drawn from a variety of sources (CDF, 1994; Center for the Study of Social Policy, 1993; Roberts, 1993) illustrates some of the obstacles a teen mother faces. Compared to the general population, a teenage mother is less likely to complete her education, less likely to be employed, and more likely to be poor. She is also less likely to get prenatal care and more likely to have premature babies. Her child is more likely to have developmental delays and behavior problems and by high school, is more likely to fail academically or become delinquent. The teenage mother may get married, but she is more likely to subsequently separate or divorce and is more likely to live at home or move back home and get help from her parents. She may head her own family (one out of three female-headed families is started by a teen mother) and is likely to be dependent on welfare and other government benefits.

The direct economic cost of adolescent childbearing is staggering. Benefits to teen families cost the country about $34 billion dollars a year (Waldman, 1994), but there are social, medical, and psychological consequences as well. The consequences of early childbearing to the health and well-being of adolescent mothers and their children is a major concern. Lack of an adequate diet, use of drugs and alcohol, limited funds for vitamins and prenatal care, and problems associated with early sexual activity continue to be a concern for health care providers. For many mental health care providers, a major concern is the teen's lack of knowledge about child development, lack of self-esteem, and difficulty in fulfilling the important role of parenting. Many teen parents succeed but others cannot both grow up and raise a child at the same time. Although there is no single reason for the increase in teen births, experts conclude that there is less stigma against and more pressure to engage in early sexual activity, there is inadequate supervision by families—particularly when both parents work or single mothers are the sole support—and there are fewer job and educational opportunities for teens today. Some of the psychological reasons are highlighted in the box "Pregnancy Is for Your *Real* Girl!"

> ### PREGNANCY IS FOR YOUR *REAL* GIRL!
>
> *Quotes from teen fathers about sex, babies, and marriage*
> "Pregnancy is, like, for your *real* girl."
> "Marriage is a big step....I haven't found Miss Right".
> "I felt like if I had a kid, it would settle me down."
> (He imagines the child saying) "Oooh! That's my father—I'm proud of him."
>
> *Quotes from teen fathers about the responsibilities of fatherhood*
> "I want to be there for my baby."
> (If the mother lost her welfare benefits) "I'd have to get another job." "I'd step up."
> "I want to live long enough to see (my daughter) grow up."
> SOURCE: Waldman, (1994).

The psychological reasons for teen pregnancy are varied and complex, and prevention will require programs for young people before they reach childbearing age. In interviews with teenage fathers in the inner cities, Waldman (1994) found that in this peer culture, "sex happens when you're a kid, babies when you're a teen and weddings—maybe—when you're an adult" (p. 34). The teen fathers and mothers Waldman interviewed wanted their babies, and for them having babies had far less to do with welfare payments than with a deep psychological yearning to be loved and esteemed. They were counting on their children to love them, value them, provide a sense of purpose in their lives, and fill in the emotional gaps left by their own inadequate nurturing. These young fathers, who admitted being abandoned physically, financially, and emotionally by their own fathers, face uncertain futures and dim job prospects. They are confident of their ability to be good parents despite the fact that they do not live with their children and have few resources to support them. Ironically, these teen fathers have internalized the notion that marriage is a serious matter, yet have failed to see that parenting is.

Intergenerational Families

When parents are unable or unwilling to care for their children, grandparents often assume the role of primary caregivers. Sometimes the personal and sociological reasons for this trend are divorce, unemployment, teen pregnancy, the illness or death of a grandchild's parent, incarceration, substance abuse, and the growing number of AIDS cases. According to the U.S. Bureau of the Census (1994a), almost 3.3 million children live in a home maintained by a grandparent. Nearly 1 million, about 1.3% of the nation's youth, are being raised by grandparents in homes where neither parent is present.

With the startling increase in never-married mothers, particularly teenagers, more grandparents are raising their grandchildren, often while rearing their own adolescent children. And according to the 1990 census, grandparents now represent a new type of "extended family" that will need additional resources and support (Roberts, 1993). This dramatic trend often strains the physical emotional and financial resources of older people, who may have declining health, resources, and energy to bring to their "new family." In addition, grandparents may not have legal custody and therefore cannot give consent for routine and preventive medical treatment; they may violate the terms of their housing lease if grandchildren stay with them; and they may qualify for less government support than that given to foster parents (Lehrmann, 1995).

Although circumstances vary, the love and commitment of grandparents is an obvious benefit to the children in their care. Nevertheless, these second-time parents need support and information, which according to the American Association for Retired Persons (AARP) was hard to come by until 1993. Now AARP, together with the Brookdale Foundation Group, has launched a Grandparent Information Center to link grandparents to the resources available to help them care for their grandchildren (Lehrmann, 1995).

Because grandparents need support to strengthen their determination and give direction to their love, it is essential that they be included in the same types of counseling and therapy that parents would be involved in if they were present. Both individual counseling and parent groups can provide useful and practical help for grandparents who are coping with the demands of childrearing. Sharing childrearing experiences and having the opportunity to talk about their concerns is a great help to all parents, regardless of age.

Blended Families

In a report released in 1994, the U.S. Census Bureau estimated that nearly 10 million children live in so-called "blended" families, which include either a stepparent, a stepsibling, or both. The 9.8 million children in blended families had a variety of living arrangements depending on whether the blend involved a stepparent, stepsibling, half-sibling, or some combination. The most common situation was for a child to have a half-brother or half-sister, which is true for slightly more than half of the young people in blended families (U.S. Bureau of the Census, 1994a).

Although it might seem that remarriages would be more successful as a result of the couple's past experience, greater maturity, and heightened motivation to avoid a second family rupture, statistics indicate that the redivorce rate is even higher than the divorce rate for first marriages (Pill, 1990). The increased likelihood of divorce with each successive marriage increases the possibility that stepchildren will be involved. Nearly 20% (17.4) of all families with children under 18 were stepfamilies, and 40% are expected to become stepfamilies before the youngest child reaches 18 (Glick, 1989).

Children in stepfamilies may experience hostility, anger, and sibling rivalry, as well as discipline and loyalty conflicts. As one child in a blended family put it, "It's not like the Brady Bunch." On balance, despite images of Cinderella's stepsisters and Snow White's stepmother, children may come to have genuine love and respect for stepparents, especially when their own parent is unavailable to them. Stepfamilies are here to stay, and practitioners must find ways to meet their special needs. (The needs of children in blended families are addressed in more detail in Chapter 3.)

Assessing the Situation

Many family scholars are divided over whether the American family is disappearing or just changing. Popenoe (1993) notes that "family instability has come to be a dominant characteristic of our time" (p. 532). He believes that the traditional American family is disappearing because the number of intact, two-parent families is declining, and only a minority of today's children will grow up to form and maintain similar family structures. Coontz (1992), on the other hand, argues that nuclear families have not been the norm throughout history and that no particular family type guarantees success. No matter which side of the debate the reader takes, it is fair to say that the dramatic social, demographic, and economic changes of the past 30 years have transformed the American family and altered family life for millions of children.

Current family life mirrors some of the problems in the larger society. A return to a more "traditional" family structure, even if that were possible, would not solve our problems. Instead, we, as human service professionals, must work to accept and strengthen all families—regardless of color, size or configuration—and help them to be "a group of people who love and care for one another."

SOCIETY FROM A CHILD AND FAMILY PERSPECTIVE

The problems that plague many of today's children and their families are reflected in the social, economic, and political portrait of our society. Poverty, crime and violence, child abuse, unemployment, homelessness, and even drug abuse are not new to the 21st century landscape. However, statistics compiled by the Children's Defense Fund (CDF) in *The State of America's Children* (1994) are alarming. Twenty-seven children, enough to fill a classroom, die from poverty each day; 3 die of child abuse; 9 are murdered. Nearly 2 million children under 18 are arrested each year; more than 200 children are arrested each day for drug offenses; and the increased number of child victims of violence, as well as youthful offenders, has prompted Marian Wright Edelman, to identify "children killing children" as the latest national tragedy (CDF, 1994). A few indicators of the crisis in American society today are illustrated in Figure 1-4.

How do we explain these tragic statistics? Experts have differing views about what causes some of society's worst problems such as crime, drug use, unemployment, and homelessness. However, poverty and inequality are central themes in studies that explore how society, increasingly polarized between the haves and the have-nots and divided along racial lines, impacts on the lives of millions of children and their families. The causes most often cited for crime, drug abuse, domestic violence, and child abuse all share the common thread of poverty, unequal distribution of social rewards, poor housing, unemployment, minimal ties to mainstream society, and personal despair and hopelessness. All these factors have eroded the positive influences of the family and strengthened peer pressure on preteens and adolescents. Evidence of this erosion can be seen in the increase of gang membership, early and out-of-wedlock childbearing, and the reliance on drugs, guns, sex, and possessions as a way to solve problems, feel powerful, or be entertained (CDF, 1994; Center for the Study of Social Policy, 1993; LaGrange, 1993; Roberts, 1993).

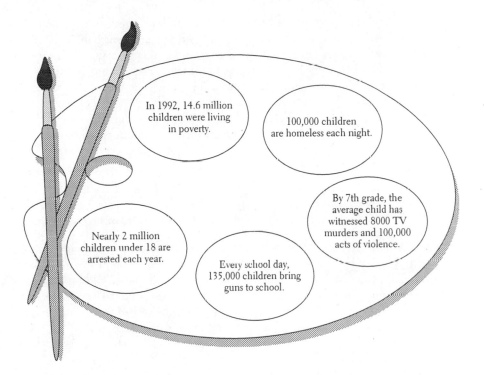

FIGURE 1-4 *Painting a Statistical Portrait of American Society in Crisis*
Source: CHILDREN'S DEFENSE FUND (1994).

Depicting the Many Faces of Poverty

Poverty of Resources

Family income is a far more powerful correlate of a child's IQ at age five than maternal education, ethnicity, and growing up in a single-parent family.
—CHILDREN'S DEFENSE FUND (1994)

Despite welfare, Aid to Families with Dependent Children, food stamps, medicaid, medicare, and social security, there are "more poor people with—or against —us than ever before" (Roberts, 1993, p. 189). Poverty has always existed and despite all the wars fought against it, its chief victims are the 14 million children who confront it in their daily lives. One in every 4 children younger than 6 and 27% of children younger than 3 were poor in 1992 (CDF, 1994). What does this poverty and its accompanying hunger, poor housing, unemployment, homelessness and hopelessness mean to children, their families, and society? Poor children are more susceptible to disease, death, and poisoning; they are more apt to have health problems, nutritional deficits, lower IQs, and lower test scores and more behavior problems in school. Impoverished children are more likely to fail in school, drop out, and become delinquent (CDF, 1994).

Parents, stressed by poverty, are less effective in guiding and nurturing their children, who in turn may not be able to provide for and nurture their babies. Children and parents in poverty lack adequate food, shelter, medical care, toys, and books and often are forced to live in crime-ridden neighborhoods or drift into homelessness. Minton (1994) captured the feelings of Joanne, a 14-year-old homeless unwed mother as she worried about her own homeless, unwed, mother: "My mother is really depressed. Because of being homeless and...going through so much. And she can't work, because she's sick" (p. 32). Despair, dreams, reality, and hope all have a place in Joanne's story.

YOU GET TIRED

Joanne, Age 14, Homeless Teen Mother

Joanne is 14, an unwed mother of a 5-month-old daughter, and she is homeless. When Joanne did have a home, it was a rat-infested apartment with holes in the floor and leaking pipes. When big rats climbed on the bed and the toilet didn't work, Joanne and her baby, along with her mother and 16-year-old brother, were forced to move in with her grandmother. There were often ten people living under one roof at any given time, and the frustration sparked many family fights. According to Joanne, many fights centered around the lack of food. "If you're hungry and that's yours and somebody else comes and eats it, you're going to get mad. Because, what if there isn't anything else to eat?"

For a while, the family lived with their mother's friend, but she had a boyfriend and every time her boyfriend came over, she would ask them to leave. Since then, they have gone from one shelter to another. Now they are in a nice clean shelter with two rooms of their own and plumbing that works. Joanne dreams of a home of her own, with her own room. Beyond that, she cannot say what she wants out of life. Instead she says, "I don't know what to do with my life anymore. You get tired."

Joanne worries about her mother. She thinks that her mother is sick and can't work and that being homeless has added to her depression. "My mother makes us happy when she can. But sometimes she can't. It's not her fault. It's hard to be homeless. It's like a grand pain in your heart. You might look happy, but deep inside, you're not."

When asked about her dreams, Joanne says that if she had a lot of money, she would buy her mother a house. She would also get her daughter whatever she needs because the child's father cannot help her much. He is only 16, doesn't have a job and lives with his own mother. Most of all, Joanne wants her daughter to have a better life than she has had. She wants to finish high school and maybe go on to college. Someday, if she succeeds, she will tell her daughter, "I finished school. I got a job for you. You could do it too."

—SOURCE: Minton (1994).

In a society characterized by a poverty of vision, we spend more money to keep a criminal in prison than to educate a child (Henry, 1993). Half of all high school seniors cannot read well enough to follow even moderately complex directions; our children's achievement test scores lag behind those of children of our leading global competitors; the dropout rate in America is 27% compared to 5% in Japan and 2% in Russia (Rosewater, 1989). The dropout rate for young blacks is slightly above the national average, and the rate for young Latinos is three times as great—35.3% in 1991 (CDF 1994). The connection between the lack of basic skills, unemployment, and poverty is well established, and job prospects for unskilled and uneducated workers remain grim.

Many teens face the "four Ds" in their job search: declining job prospects and wages, discrimination because of their race or age, disinterest, and discouragement. Roberts (1993) noted that in 1990, one-half of America's teens were not even looking for work: "The combination of fewer available jobs and less inclination to find them reduced the employment rate among black teenagers to less than one in four" (p. 183). The consequences of poverty and unemployment on juvenile crime rates, neighborhood stability, youth alienation, and the "American work ethic" are well documented. Without excusing it, Marian Wright Edelman linked teenage unemployment and crime: "Our market culture tells them (young people) that they must have designer sneakers, gold chains and fancy cars to be somebody while denying them jobs to buy them legally" (CDF, 1994, p. xi). It seems safe to speculate that some teens may be unable or unwilling to delay gratification, something they may have learned from the "me" generation. Perhaps there is little incentive to pass up making a lot of money illegally for making a little money for asking, "Do you want fries with this?"

In the past few years, the unemployment rate has been around 8 million, with nearly 5 million more employed only part time. Millions of Americans worry as jobs are lost to increasing global competition, corporate downsizing, and business and industry restructuring. Parents fear, with some justification, that their children will not be as well off financially as they are, and there is guarded optimism about the future. Owning your own home, once a symbol of the American dream, has become an increasingly elusive goal for many young couples. Half of the nation's families cannot afford a median-priced house in their area, and many have had to settle for a mobile home instead. National priorities are reflected in the fact that the fastest growing category of housing in the decade of the 1980s was prisons (Roberts, 1993).

Poverty of Tolerance

Staggering numbers only begin to suggest the lines that corrosive racism and its consequences have etched in American society.
—SAM ROBERTS (1993)

In this portrait of the poverty of tolerance in America, the black child faces major inequities and barriers. Black children are more likely than white children to get poor prenatal care, to die prematurely, to go to inferior schools in deteriorating neighborhoods, and to live in substandard housing in drug- and crime-infested neighborhoods. Unless one has experienced the kind of hopelessness born of poverty and discrimination, it is difficult to imagine how a young boy living in a welfare hotel felt when his 10-month-old sister died, weighing less than 7 pounds. The following account describes how this ghetto child and his brother tortured a pigeon a few weeks after their baby sister, a victim of a condition known as "failure to thrive," finally died (Hayes, 1989, p. 68).

When our baby die we start to sit by the window. We just sit an' sit, all wrapped up quiet in old shirts an' watch the pigeons. That pigeon she fly so fast, move so fast. She move nice. A real pretty flyer.

She open her mouth and take in the wind. We just spread out crumbs, me and my brother. And we wait. Sit and wait. There under the windowsill.

She don't even see us till we slam down the window. And she break. She look with one eye. She don't die right away. We dip her in, over and over, in the water pot we boils on the hot plate.

We wanna see how it be to die slow like our baby die.

The 1990 U.S. Census Bureau data tell us that black children are 3 times more likely than whites to live in poverty and will die approximately 6 years earlier. Black men are 7 times as likely to be murdered than whites and 3 times as likely to die from AIDS. The rewards for staying in high school and graduating from college are less for black men; their earnings total three-fourths of the white male graduates' (Roberts, 1993).

Of course, the poverty of tolerance extends beyond African American children to other minority populations, including Native American, Asian American, and Hispanic American children as well as the children of recent immigrant populations, and is most acutely felt in states where large concentrations of a particular minority reside. The struggle over paying for the children of illegal immigrants has been well publicized, particularly in California and other states with sizable illegal immigrant populations. Recent proposals to restructure welfare cite *legal* immigrants as one group that will not be eligible for welfare benefits. These proposals will seriously affect the poorest of the poor—children.

Intolerance extends to other social issues as well, such as AIDS and homosexuality. Finding ways to combat the ignorance and fear that surround these issues will help children and their parents deal with them in a way that does not destroy self-esteem. Increasing numbers of children are being infected with HIV as a result of their parents' lifestyle, and they are most at risk of contracting the virus in utero or through their mothers' breast milk (Landau-Stanton & Clements 1993). It is estimated that by the year 2000, somewhere between 80,000 and 125,000 children will have lost a mother to AIDS (CDF, 1994). Unless we all work toward combating the fear and ignorance that surrounds this disease, children and their parents will be seriously affected by the intolerance of others. Although there are no accurate census figures on the number of children who might have a gay parent either living with or apart from the family, the fact that children do have parents who are gay cannot be overlooked. These children, like those with AIDS, often fear discrimination by adults and peers at school, and in the community and they keep their secrets well hidden.

Poverty of Time

Hi, remember me? I'm your Dad.

—Father commenting on how overwork affects his relationship with his children

As we approach the year 2000, American families seem more fatigued than ever; the pace of life is too fast, the demands too great. In a recent television interview, Juliet

Schor, author of *The Overworked Americans* (1992), summed up the dilemma as "a choice between a life and a job." Workers in the 1980s spent long hours to get ahead, but in the 1990s they worked long hours just to keep their jobs. Extra jobs and long hours added to women's stress of "balancing" paid work, housework, and child care, and it created new risks for families and their children. In a PTA/*Newsweek* National Education Survey (Finney, 1993), 40% of the parents surveyed felt they weren't devoting enough time to their child's education; approximately one-fourth of all employed parents had problems attending school activities, caring for a sick child, attending parent-teacher conferences, and receiving calls from their child at work.

Coontz (1992) reported that "employed fathers living with their children shared, on the average, only two hours of activity with them per week" (p. 222). While parents struggle to provide children with material things, children value the presence of their parents more. David Elkind (1988, p.130) cited this exchange that occurred during a visit to his own son's preschool class:

CHILD A: My daddy is a doctor and he makes a lot of money and we have a
           swimming pool.
CHILD B: My daddy is a lawyer and he flies to Washington and talks to the
           president.
CHILD C: My daddy owns a company and we have our own airplane.
MY SON (with aplomb, of course):   My daddy is here! (with a proud look in
           my direction).

Elkind (1988) believes that children regard the presence of their parents as a sign of caring and connectedness that is far more significant than material support. Unfortunately, because growing financial insecurity forces many parents to work longer hours and the proportion of youngsters living in single-parent homes is rising, many children are seeing less and less of their parents. The National Commission on Children (1991) concluded that "regardless of family income, parents and children spend less time together" (p. 16).

Poverty of Values

Any discussion of poverty in terms of money and time for nurturing children and family togetherness would not be complete without a discussion of a poverty of values. In a society that claims to value children, we pay teachers in some cities less than we pay garbage collectors, we pay child care workers less than we pay household cleaning help (Henry, 1993), and we entrust our children to a baby-sitter for $1 an hour per child. In a recent national poll on American morality, 25% of the respondents said that for $10 million, they would abandon their entire family (as cited in Coontz, 1992). Apparently, some parents are willing to do the same for a lot less, as indicated by the following news items reported in a single month in 1994.

A Pittsburgh couple left their four children, ages two to ten, with a 14-year-old baby-sitter for 16 days in order to work in another state.

A man left an 11-month-old baby in the path of traffic at a busy intersection while the child's mother watched from the curb. He said he was "just horsing around."

> A 23-year-old woman "sold" her 7-month-old son to a couple she barely knew for a six-pack of beer and a carton of cigarettes.

The current epidemic of crime and violence is another indication that something is terribly wrong with the way Americans value one another and their children. The headlines scream of murders, rapes, and robberies; TV news is dominated by reports of crime; television's tabloid journalists portray violence in its most graphic detail. The current push to increase the public's exposure to crime and its consequences and the relentless coverage of celebrity trials feed America's obsession and fascination with violence, the topic we turn to next.

Painting a Portrait of the Violent American Landscape

Crime transcends the direct and immediate harm done to the victim just as ripples transcend a pebble's entry into water...
No one escapes crime.
—Randy LaGrange (1993)

Contemporary criminologists and historians sound a message that is painfully clear. Crime is rooted in the American way of life, and violence is something that has always defined us and our history (Gilmore, 1994a; LaGrange, 1993). People lock their doors and fear they will be robbed, mugged, raped, or murdered. They view other people and other people's children with suspicion. Americans seem preoccupied with the "stranger danger," and with good reason. Using statistics from the National Crime Survey, LaGrange (1993) reported that the likelihood of being murdered is 1 in 133, and the murder rate among young black urban males is so high that it has become their leading cause of death. Equally chilling are the odds that 1 out of every 12 females, age 12 and over, will be forcibly raped at some time during her lifetime.

Gilmore (1994b), author of *Shot in the Heart*, asks: "Where are all these dangerous strangers coming from, why are they filling our streets and making our private lives so fearful? They are coming from somewhere and that somewhere is our homes, where this violence is learned" (pp. 14–15). Each day, four women are killed by their male partners, and in 1989 more women were abused by their husbands than were married in the same period. These data prompted the U.S. surgeon general to declare that "the home is actually a more dangerous place for American women than the city streets" (as quoted in Coontz, 1992, p. 3). A little over 100 years ago, some communities had laws prohibiting a man from beating his wife after 10:00 P.M. or on Sundays, so as not to annoy the neighbors (LaGrange, 1993).

And what about the 3 million children (CDF, 1994) who witness parental violence every year? Mikal Gilmore, whose brother Gary Gilmore was executed in 1977 for two murders, described the violence of his home life:

> I saw horrible forceful acts of violence by my father against my brothers....My brothers had to deal with that all the time. They were beaten terribly, and witnessed my mother's beatings, and lived with the violent temperament of

our house....I remember watching the anger of my parents, and Gary's anger
in particular, turn into rage, something I always found terribly frightening.
(1994b, p. 13)

Every 13 seconds, a child is reported abused or neglected at the hands of someone
who is supposed to love and care for them. An estimated 1200 children die each year
from such abuse or neglect, and those who survive are often damaged for life (CDF,
1994). Experiencing physical abuse as a child, for example, increases an adult's risk
of chronic aggressive behavior patterns by almost 300% (Coontz, 1992). Some
researchers (Blume, 1990) estimate that as many as 50% of adult women are survivors
of childhood sexual trauma, and Coontz (1992) cited a national poll in which "one in
seven Americans claimed to have been sexually abused as a child while one in six
reported being physically abused" (p. 2).

The reasons some abused children vent their rage on other people and society
whereas others channel it into acceptable outlets are not fully understood. Although
the causes and outcomes of violence are complex and there are no simple answers,
some child victims of violence do become perpetrators.

A Child Becomes a Murderer

Murder very rarely occurs as a single solitary response born of the moment. The
seeds were sown long before, in the murderer's family and environment and in
some ways we are all a part of it.
—MIKAL GILMORE (1994b)

Consider the following stories of three victims of violence who later became perpetrators. Two of the young people had experienced a great deal of brutality at home,
and one had experienced it in his everyday environment. They all had different reasons for pulling the trigger: Jack acted out of anger, Jose out of fear, and Kyung out of
hatred.

> Jack was 15 when he killed a boy he believed was threatening him. He says he
> fired the gun out of "anger." He is serving a 25-year sentence. In detailing his
> childhood, he said his father beat him with a baseball bat. He suffered three
> cracked ribs, a broken jaw, and bruises too numerous to mention. He says that
> family counseling helped him understand his father, who had it rough after his
> mother left, but did not help him deal with his anger.
>
> Jose was 16 when he killed a police officer. Jose says that violence was not in his
> home, but it was in the streets and in the neighborhood where he lived. He fre-
> quently witnessed fights and knifings. He learned to fear and distrust the police.
> He is serving a 30-year sentence and says he fired the gun out of "fear." He had
> never been offered or received any help.
>
> Kyung was 14 when she shot and killed her alcoholic stepfather, ending two years
> of beatings and abuse. Her mother didn't protect her and was beaten too. Kyung,
> who may not get out of prison until she is 40, says she fired the gun out of "pure
> hatred." Did anyone try to help? Yes, her probation officer did, but it didn't stop
> the sexual abuse.

The combination of factors that predispose one child in the family to violence and not another is not fully understood. Violence affected the Gilmore boys in very different ways. Gary became a murderer; Frank, who also suffered greatly, went to prison for refusing to carry a gun; Gaylen was inexplicably murdered; and Mikal, never beaten, came to grips with the past by writing about it (Gilmore, 1994a). They all coped in different ways, but their lives were all affected by a brutal alcoholic who unleashed his rages on his wife and sons. Gary, always rebellious, received the worst of it.

All the Gilmore boys' lives were damaged to some extent by the brutal forces that shaped their home life, but why did one become a murderer? There are no simple answers. In any violent home, certain children, higher on the pecking order, receive more physical and psychological abuse than others. Children also have different temperaments and different interactions with their abusers and other family members. They have different perceptions of abuse and different degrees of guilt about it. Some children turn their rage on others; some turn it on themselves. Some abused children find outlets for their feelings of rejection, anxiety, and anger by abusing drugs and alcohol and engaging in other self-destructive behaviors. Stone (1993) found that abused children are at risk for developing depression and have a higher incidence of suicidal behavior.

Reading, Writing, and Weapons

It's not to say there is a tremendous trend or a time to panic.
But I think the police and school district are alarmed.

—Police lieutenant on an increase in the incidence of students possessing guns in a small suburban school

The violence that is seen, experienced, and reinforced in our homes and our culture has spilled out onto the streets and seeped through our school doors, taking with it the health and well-being of young people, families, schools and communities. Every day, 135,000 children bring guns to school (CDF, 1994), and during the 1990s, cash-strapped school districts had to spend money on crime control instead of academics. Going back to school still means new clothes, new classes, and old friends; unfortunately, it also means metal detectors, surveillance cameras, book-bag bans, and locker searches.

In 1995, the results of a national survey of 16,000 adolescents in grades 9 through 12 found that 11.8% had carried a weapon on school property during the preceding 30 days. In the year before, 7.3% of the students were threatened or injured with a weapon on school property, and 16.2% had been in a physical fight on school property (National Center for Injury Prevention and Control, [NCIPC] 1995). Some of the destruction wrought by these gun-toting youngsters is reflected in the following stories (Dvorchak, 1994):

In 1993, a 10th-grader pulled a gun from his book bag and killed a classmate during first period biology class in a city school. He explained to police, "He punches me and kicks me and makes me look like a jerk."

In 1994, an 11-year-old boy was killed in a Montana schoolyard by a 10-year-old classmate who fired a gun at another youth following an argument.

⋮ A teacher was shot and wounded in 1994 by a student who brought his father's
⋮ police service revolver to school in an attempt to sell it.

"Shot in the line of duty," a phrase once reserved for police officers and soldiers, now applies to teachers in some districts, and the cost to children and their families is staggering. Violence robs children of a positive learning environment, reduces the quality of life for child victims and perpetrators alike, limits the earning and learning potential of incarcerated children, stresses the families of both victims and perpetrators, and forces good teachers out of the profession.

In 1994, Congress required the states to enact legislation to ensure gun-free schools. States that do not comply with the requirement will no longer be eligible to receive federal funding under the Elementary and Secondary Education Act (ESEA). The Improving America's Schools Act of 1994 stated that by October of 1995, each state education agency receiving ESEA funds must pass a law requiring local school districts to expel from school, for not less than 1 year, a student who brings a firearm to school. In addition, the law requires that the offending student be referred to either the criminal or the juvenile justice system. Expulsion from "regular school settings" does not preclude students from receiving education in an alternative setting (Information Legislative Service, 1995).

Some school districts have expanded the mandate by suspending any child who brings a toy gun to school. Other districts, though complying with the law, realize that just conducting weapons searches, turning schools into fortresses, and expelling students will not solve the problems of violence in the schools. Although programs that focus on conflict resolution are needed to teach children to talk instead of shoot, most experts recommend investing in preventive programs for children and their parents. Programs that improve parents' access to and interactions with a variety of supporting social systems such as the school, community, and health and child care services, are seen as more durable solutions than expelling problem children (see Zigler, Taussig, & Black, 1992).

Violence in the Streets

Mostly how you turn out depends on who influences you.
There are a lot of bad influences here.

— 15-year-old girl from Chicago's south side

No one can argue against the fact that juvenile crime is increasing and that young people, especially those under 17 years of age, account for a disproportionate number of both homicide victims and perpetrators. A 1992 Northeastern University report found that the arrest rates for criminal homicide committed by juveniles between 1985 and 1991 increased dramatically. Fifteen-year-olds had the largest increase—a startling 217%—followed by the 13- to 14-year-olds with 140% (as cited in CDF, 1994).

Parents of all races and incomes recognize the growing threat of violence to their children. In a 1993 *Newsweek*/CDF poll of 10- to 17-year-olds and their parents, nearly three-quarters of the parents and more than half of the children said they "fear that a loved one will be the victim of a violent crime"; more than 1 in 10 reported "being personally victimized by violent crime" (CDF, 1994).

Many inner-city children, regularly exposed to violence, develop defense mechanisms that inhibit their ability to learn and that may predispose them to aggression. Children forced to cope with chronic violence may adopt street behaviors that are inappropriate in other settings. For example, a child who becomes hyperaggressive as a way of coping with neighborhood gang members and threats of violence may be rejected, reprimanded, or expelled for displaying the same aggressiveness at school. Conversely, a child who withdraws emotionally may be able to cope in the short run but may have difficulty giving and receiving affection as an adult (Garbarino, Kostelny, & Dubrow, 1991).

The same responses to danger and trauma children exhibit may be evident in their parents' behavior. Fearing shooting incidents, parents, may not allow their children to go out to play, participate in after-school activities or athletic contests, or even visit other children. In a well-intentioned and often necessary attempt to protect children from assault, parents instill fear in children and deny them opportunities for socializing and play. Furthermore, desperate and fearful parents may resort to very restrictive and punitive styles of discipline (including physical punishment) to keep their children from the negative influences of gangs, drug dealers, and purveyors of violence in the streets. Unfortunately, this approach is likely to result in heightening the children's aggression, making it more difficult for the children to succeed in other school and work settings (Garbarino et al., 1991).

In a review of the developmental challenges faced by children in situations of chronic danger, Garbarino and associates (1991) concluded that inner-city violence "is likely to produce a situation in which hopelessness and despair translate into within-group violence, depression, and self-hatred" (p. 382). These authors cited a growing body of evidence that children may use fear, violence, and hatred as socialization models. From living in an environment that instills fear, children may learn to distrust parents, identify with aggressors, model the violent behavior they witness, and exact revenge later in life. More important for future generations, many of these children may have difficulty showing empathy, minimizing hurt, and nurturing, sustaining, and repairing relationships as adults and as parents.

Influence of the Media

The truth remains that the most destructive people in this land learn about violence and find rage in the settings of their everyday lives, not from a TV program or a movie.
—CARL ROWAN (1993)

Television, that electronic marvel that puts us in touch with the world, has both positive and negative influences on children. However, there is growing concern about the number of programs that offer violence as a solution to problems. Most experts agree that television alone does not cause violent behavior, but many believe that it encourages and magnifies it. The Children's Defense Fund reported that, by the seventh grade, the average child witnesses 8000 simulated murders and 100,000 acts of violence on television (CDF, 1994). Children are exposed often and early to television messages, music, and movies that glamorize violence, sex, alcohol, tobacco, and amassing material possessions, often without a parent available to provide the "parental discretion" that the entertainment industry advises.

Postman (1991) argues that television contributes to the demise of childhood because it "sells" adult images and ideas to children who are not yet ready for a full dose of the mysteries, contradictions, violence and tragedies of adult life. The adult world is available to children at ages and timetables that are not in sync with their development. What image does the preschooler get of life when a steady diet of soap operas teaches him or her that adults drink all day, never scrub a toilet, and have no visible job but lots of money? What do they think when television characters poison, shoot and hit one another or hop into bed with everyone and anyone? Many argue that television mirrors life—an even scarier thought.

Others take the position that children are more influenced by the adult models and events in their everyday lives than they are by the fictional characters on television. Carl Rowan (1993, p. 2B) in *Blaming TV for Violence Is Too Easy*, argues that ghetto children learn every four-letter word and racial slur in their own neighborhoods and that television's primary contribution to the rage of ghetto children is that "it shows them how cheated they are compared with other American youngsters." Like Gilmore (1994a), Rowan believes that the violence children witness in their own homes and the physical and sexual abuse they endure at the hands of people who are supposed to love and care for them is what crushes their spirit. It is the violence that surrounds children in their homes, schools, and neighborhoods that is robbing them of their childhood, not any television program they might watch.

Applying an Ounce of Prevention

What we're doing here is picking up babies that are floating downstream and trying to save them. But unless somebody is stopping the people from throwing them in upstream, our job is never going to end.

—Juvenile Court Judge Fred Anthony, Erie County, Pennsylvania, on the worsening problem of violence among teenagers

"Take back our streets" has become a battle cry of sorts for aspiring politicians because it plays on Americans' fear of the "stranger danger." However, as Pogo in the comic strip of the same name once said, "We have met the enemy and they are us." These dangerous criminals we have to lock up and punish were once children who, for a variety of reasons, did not become productive adults. Although we have no choice but to incarcerate many hardened criminals for the safety of communities and the children who live in them, we have to work to prevent the violence in our homes, schools, and streets from creating new generations of criminals.

Gilmore (1994b), commenting on the current national push for more prisons, more police, and stiffer sentences, noted:

I have seen up close what prison does to people; it does not bring people out humbled or better, it brings them out hardened and deadlier. There is no question in my mind that Gary became a much deadlier man, a man much more capable of ruining people, because of his experiences in reform school and prison. I think he came out with more pride and passion about his identity as a criminal as a result. (p. 12)

In 1993, leading legal and criminal justice experts underscored the importance of early intervention to reduce crime and violence. The U. S. attorney general concluded that expanded child care, parenting education, and child support payment enforcement are as important to crime control as prisons. The American Bar Association and the National Council on Crime and Delinquency (NCCD) acknowledged that current corrections and enforcement policies have failed and recommended improvements in health care, child care, education, and employment as crime prevention efforts. NCCD also supported the development of alternatives to detention for young offenders that would offer supportive services to the youths and their families (as cited in CDF, 1994). The most effective childhood intervention programs provide health care, involve parents, and offer specific services to families. Such programs embrace the view that it is more effective to treat the child as a member of a family, school, and community than to focus on one isolated intervention (Zigler et al., 1992).

All these experts provide powerful support for the work that members of the helping professions do in the interest of children and their families. Although there are no magical solutions to the problem of crime and violence, there are many things that human service professionals can do, including establishing early intervention programs, family support programs, and school and community interventions.

Early Intervention Programs

Programs are needed that care for children even before they are born, ensuring adequate nutrition and a healthy start. Parent education programs that teach expectant adolescent mothers about child development and how to nurture their newborns, secure prenatal care, and finish their education all contribute to less poverty, abuse, and delinquency. Providing greater access to and more funding for child care and Head Start programs for preschoolers helps youngsters build self-esteem at an early age. Lay counseling, mother-to-mother programs, and home visits have shown great promise in helping prevent potential abuse by "staying the unkind hand." In studies reported by Zigler and associates (1992), the reduction of child abuse was one of the most striking outcomes of a program for teenage mothers that featured in-home visits providing practical help in child care, good models, and emotional support. Early intervention programs have been found effective in reducing antisocial behavior by enhancing motivation, aspiration level, and self-confidence, thereby lessening aggression, temper, and poor conduct.

Family Support Programs

Even under the best circumstances, parents can't do the whole job. Compelling evidence suggests that children in trouble come from troubled families. But more children can be saved from future incarceration by supporting them and their families through counseling, frequent home visits, and cooperation with juvenile justice programs. According to the Children's Defense Fund (1994), both family support and family preservation programs focus on the family as a unit, work with families in their homes and communities, and build on families' strengths. Family support programs offer parents and children some of the help that once came from the extended family and the community. Home-school and community-based programs help families toward health and togetherness by providing access to a wide range of preventive and support services such as parent education, prenatal classes, and GED preparation.

Family preservation services are generally for families already in crisis, including those at risk of having children removed from the home. In these programs specially trained staff work with families, usually in their homes, for four or six weeks. They offer suppport and services designed to improve family functioning and keep children safe and families together (see CDF, 1994 for examples of successful programs).

Preventive Guidance in the Schools

Developmental guidance programs in elementary schools that attend to the needs of all children are effective ways to prevent problems before they begin. Elementary school guidance programs are essential if we are to teach young children how to resolve their conflicts without violence, detect and prevent child abuse, and help all parents cope with childrearing in these increasingly stressful times. Teachers can be powerful, positive forces in children's lives, and they need to be valued for their contributions and be included in activities that involve both children and their families. Part of the work of school counselors is to work with teachers and administrators to develop policies that will keep troublesome youngsters in school. So often there is little or no tolerance for young people who evidence problems with socialization and with controlling aggression. Alternate programs need to be developed that will keep children growing and learning and will help them get back on course.

Community Intervention.

Members of the community who want to give something back by being role models and mentors for young children are essential prevention workers. Organizations such as Big Brothers and Big Sisters, The Boys and Girls Club of America, and countless community organizations that link caring adults with at-risk children and their families can rescue the child who has a disturbed home or school life. New evidence is emerging that such groups are highly effective in helping children and adolescents. A study of participants in the New York City Big Brothers/Big Sisters programs indicated that within a year after joining, 84% of the adolescents did better in school, 83% kept out of trouble, 90% improved their relationships with their friends, and 96% showed higher self-esteem (Ryan, 1995).

INSIGHTS AND IMPLICATIONS

The three most important environments for children are the home, the school, and the community. Ideally, children should be nurtured in all three environments and should experience acceptance, protection, and opportunities to grow. However, if children are thwarted in their attempts to gain acceptance and are not offered protection and opportunities for growth they are at risk for maladaptive behavior. For example, if a child has a troubled home life and nothing can be done to improve it, warmth and acceptance at school and in the community can help reduce the risk. Conversely, if a child leaves a nurturing home or program and ventures into a drug-infested neighborhood and a crime-plagued school, the risk increases.

The family is the greatest source of love and protection for the growing child. Some families, however, because of a poverty of money, time, nurturing, togetherness, or values, have been unable or unwilling to meet their children's needs. And even under the best circumstances, parents don't raise their children in a vacuum. Society's values, government's priorities and congressional legislation, with all their accompanying biases, can either help or thwart parental efforts. Many situations are beyond parental control and have negative influences on children. Economic stress, chronic unemployment, increasing poverty, poor housing and unequal distribution of social rewards have made the American dream increasingly illusive for many of our children. And as the future unfolds, it seems likely that obstacles to the healthy development of children will only increase.

WISDOM ACCORDING TO ORTON

- *All children, not just troubled children, need as many caring adults in their lives as possible.*
- *Because you cannot help every troubled child, do what you can to touch the lives of a few.*
- *Sometimes when you think you aren't reaching a child, try harder.*
- *Sometimes a child will return years later to say "thanks," but most of your joy will come from seeing the child grow up happy and productive.*
- *Be careful about finding fault with a child's parents, for they are the greatest source of love and affection for the child. Nurture this bond at every opportunity.*
- *Accept parents and children equally and try to help both, for in helping the one, you help the other.*

ORTON'S PICKS

Coontz, S. (1992). *The way we never were: American families and the nostalgia trap.* New York: Harper & Row.

In *The Way We Never Were*, Stephanie Coontz demolishes the notion that everything was better "in the good old days" and reminds the reader that historically there have been a variety of family forms and childrearing arrangements. She places current concerns about children and their families in the context of past and present economic, political, and demographic changes. This book sheds new light on such issues as parenting, division of labor along gender lines, the myth of black family collapse, and the influence of feminism.

Hewlett, S.A. (1991) *When the bough breaks: The cost of neglecting our children.* New York: Basic Books.

In this meticulously researched study, Sylvia Hewlett identifies the risk factors for rich, middle-class, and poor children and outlines a multifaceted plan of action. Some of her recommendations include making the workplace more family-friendly, improving the quality of child care, reforming tax laws to support families with children, and increasing volunteer efforts on behalf of children. Using poignant true stories and a wealth of statistics, this book presents a critical view of America's childcare practices.

Roberts, S. (1993). *The way we are: A portrait of America.* New York: Random House.

Using the latest census data, Sam Roberts weaves statistics into a story about Americans that is difficult to put down. In one powerful chapter after another, he addresses how and where we live, our changing complexion, what we are worth, and where we are going. He addresses the corrosive racism that has fed into poverty and crime. *The Way We Are* is a story of our values, our economy, our country, and the kind of future that our children will inherit.

CHAPTER 2   *The Developing Child*

AROUND AND AROUND—LOVE

Love, Love, Love
Given and found, it's all around—
Love.

It's hard to tell about,
Easy to show.
One sure thing—
When you feel it,
You know it.

Hugs and caring,
Working and sharing
Are love.

You can't grab it
Or take it;
When you give it,
You make it.

Love doesn't stay the same.
It changes as people change,
Grows as people grow.
You can come and go,
Say goodbye or hello,
Hold—
Or let go.
Love.

You can't use it up.
Love is always around.
Like the sound of the beat of our heart,
Like sun in the sky,
Love is part of your life until you die.

Love can make you feel so glad,
Love is a comfort when you feel bad.
But love can make you angry,
Troubled and sad.
Sometimes you can't believe it,
Have to doubt it,
Try to keep it from your mind.
Most times, you find love is kind.

When you feel it and know it,
Tell it and show it.
Whisper it,
Shout it,
Feel good about it!

Given and found,
It's all around.
Around and around and around and around—
Love.
—BETTY MILES

A DEVELOPMENTAL PERSPECTIVE FOR COUNSELING

A basic understanding of the physical, emotional, social, and intellectual development of children, coupled with a sensible and flexible approach to its changing nature, is essential for parents who nurture children, professionals who work directly with children, agencies that provide for children, and legislators who pass laws that affect children. The parent who expects a child to be toilet trained at age 5 months, the nursery school teacher who ties a toddler in a chair to serve a 10-minute "time out," the teacher who injures a child's left hand in a misguided effort to foster right-handedness, the counselor who expects a 6-year-old to know *why* she wets the bed, and the politician who proposes funding cuts for programs that provide prenatal care and food for pregnant women all need to know more about child development.

Misunderstandings about the nature of childhood can lead to both overestimating and underestimating what children are capable of physically, emotionally, socially, and intellectually. Overestimating their developmental level may give rise to unrealistic expectations, which can result in child abuse. For instance, a parent who believes that spanking an infant will force it to stop crying doesn't recognize and understand the physical and emotional development of infancy. Even when abuse is not a factor, overestimating a child's capabilities can place an inordinate amount of pressure on a child. Examples abound of "pee-wee" sports leagues where children, who are little more than toddlers, take their lumps for the greater glory of their parents and coaches—all before an understanding of team competition is developmentally possible or appropriate.

Underestimating what a child is capable of thinking and understanding may encourage parents and professionals to "protect" children by not discussing bad news such as divorce or death, by refusing to talk about sex because "it might give them ideas," and by preventing youngsters from having a say in important decisions, such as their own medical treatment. Decisions that underestimate a child's capacity to understand rob youngsters of an opportunity to develop coping and problem-solving skills and convey a lack of respect for the child's abilities.

The normal course of development is at times very rocky, and even well-adjusted children sometimes pause to indulge in behavior that is not in keeping with their age and developmental level. During these slight regressions, children may exhibit problem behavior that demands both attention and solutions before they can continue on the path to healthy development. As children grow, they learn ways to handle the jealousy they feel when a sibling gets a new bike or a better grade, they learn to rein in their aggression so that it is within socially acceptable limits, and they realize there aren't any monsters under their beds. Some children are more successful than others at managing their emotions, and some children have more family support. If children have not yet learned to manage their emotions, particularly aggression, by the time they reach first grade, they are likely to come to the attention of a member of the helping professions.

In the search to find the source of the child's behavior problem, counselors and educators may discover a crisis in the child's life. Children often show signs of behavior problems as a reaction to a crisis of loss, as in the case of separation, divorce, or death in the family, or a crisis of violence, as in the case of child abuse. The child who receives a lot of negative feedback or who is neglected or abused may have difficulty achieving in school, developing meaningful relationships, conforming to the moral standards of the community, and obeying the laws of the land. These children require special intervention by a caring, concerned professional who will involve the children's families in the education and counseling process.

In this chapter on the developing child, we will trace the course of child development through the ages and come to understand some of the family, social, economic, and political forces that have shaped our attitudes toward children through the centuries. A brief overview of the healthy development of children from birth to age 12, gleaned from the study of children in the previous century, is intended to reacquaint the reader with important milestones in child development. Common developmental problems that result when development does not go smoothly are introduced, and guidelines for referral are given so that parents and professionals can judge the severity of the problem and determine whether intervention is needed.

Childhood Through the Ages

Our forebears lived and died for hundreds of thousands of years without showing more than a glimmer of interest in children as children.
—WATSON & LINDGREN (1979)

In their review of attitudes toward children through the ages, Watson & Lindgren (1979) noted that the Greeks and Romans had a rather enlightened view of childhood compared to what was to follow during the Middle Ages. Children, especially in middle- and upper-class families, were accorded fairly specific rights and responsibilities.

They were valued for themselves, as members of the family group, and as future citizens. Loving memorials to children uncovered in ancient burial grounds near Greek and Roman cities testify to their significance in ancient civilizations.

With the advent of medieval Christianity, however, a different view of childhood came to prevail. Because of the belief in Adam's fall and Eve's culpability, life became more adult-male-centered and women and children lost status. All of humankind was thought to be born in sin, and children, bearing the mark of original sin, were thought to be innately depraved. "The idea that original sin could be beaten out of a child came to dominate child care for many centuries" (Watson & Lindgren, 1979, p. 4).

Childhood in the Middle Ages was almost nonexistent. Infanticide was commonly practiced and mothers tended to distance themselves from their babies because so many died in infancy. Children were not necessarily unloved, but those who survived became adults quickly so they could be contributors to, rather than burdens on, society. Children were treated as miniature adults, dressed in adultlike clothing, and required to work at an early age. There was a great disparity between the classes and the sexes; girls and working-class boys shared the same status as adult women and were servile to upper-class men. Girls went directly from swaddling clothes into adult female dress; did not go to school; and were married around age 10 or 12, usually to older men (Aries, 1960–1962).

The Dark Ages of Europe smothered childhood for hundreds of years, and the unique needs of children were lost until the Renaissance (the 15th and 16th centuries), when increasing literacy and cultural advancement set the stage for the study of child development in the 1600s. In the 17th century, John Locke (1632–1704) disagreed with the notion that children were merely miniature adults who would simply "grow up." He believed that children needed special care, should express their feelings, and should be restrained only when necessary. Instead of apprenticing children or farming them out to other families, as was commonly practiced, Locke advised parents to spend time with their children and influence them by setting a good example. A century later, Jean Jacques Rousseau (1712–1778), who also rejected the idea of original sin and the natural depravity of childhood, expressed a strong faith in the innate goodness of children. Interestingly, Rousseau disagreed with Locke's idea that parents should be interested in and close to children, and he placed all five of his own infants in a foundling hospital (Boswell, as cited in Coontz, 1992). But the first person to recognize the importance of understanding child behavior was Johann Henrich Pestalozzi (1746–1827). His observations of his own 4-year-old son formed the basis of his belief that the mother is the child's first and most significant teacher (Watson & Lindgren, 1979).

Despite the influences of Locke, Rousseau, and Pestalozzi on prevailing methods of child care, life for most children, especially poor children, remained wretched. Throughout the early 1700s, childrearing practices were often cruel and unforgiving, and parents believed in "beating the devil out" of their children. In colonial America, puritanical parents sanctioned the beating and whipping of their children as legitimate forms of punishment. They believed it was important to inspire fear in their children, and they considered watching the public executions of criminals to be a vital part of the moral education of children of all classes (Gibson, 1978). Unquestioned obedience to the father's authority was considered the most important factor in the children's development, and the penalty was death if a person at least 16 years of age and of "sufficient understanding" were to swear or talk back to a parent (Bremner, 1970–1974).

The idea that parents had to "break the will" of their children in order to train them to be acceptable social beings carried into the early 19th century. The following excerpt says a great deal about what was known about child development in the 1800s:

> A middle-class American mother, writing in a woman's magazine in 1834, described her husband's procedure when their sixteen-month-old daughter refused to say "Dear Mama" on command. The infant was placed alone in a room, where she screamed wildly for ten minutes; then she was brought out and again commanded to say "Dear Mama." When the child still refused, she was whipped and the demand made again. This went on for four hours, until the child finally obeyed. (Sunley, as cited in Watson & Lindgren, 1979, p. 8)

There was a great disparity in the way children of different social classes were treated in the 18th and 19th centuries. Rich children learned the avocations of the leisure class, had dancing and riding lessons, were taught proper manners, and learned to give orders to underlings. Slave children labored in the fields and learned to wait on their masters and mistresses. Poor children labored in mills, mines, factories, and crowded tenement workshops (Coontz, 1992; Gibson, 1978). Of the 4000 workers in the cotton mills in 1809, 3500 were women and children. Children as young as 6 or 7 were working 12-hour shifts for 50 cents per week (Bremner, 1970–1974).

Children of middle-class Victorian families of the 1830s and 1840s enjoyed a prolonged childhood at the expense of the poor and powerless children of the lower classes. Slave, immigrant, and poor children were forced to give up a large portion of their own childhoods to produce the goods and services that enabled privileged children to be sheltered in warm and comfortable homes, be shielded from exploitation by employers, and have time to enjoy playing with their exquisite toys.

While middle- and upper-class children were safe in a dull schoolroom studying Homer, the children of the poor were laboring in the mills, mines, and factories. In 1900, 120,000 children worked in Pennsylvania mines and factories and a third of all girls between the ages of 13 and 16 labored in the silk mills (Schneiderman, as cited in Coontz, 1992). Children were given special protection through child labor laws, but exploitation of children through dangerous jobs and long hours continued well into the first half of the 20th century.

The 19th-century English novelists, particularly Charles Dickens, captured the plight of poor children in an increasingly industrialized society. The harsh attitude toward children, the code of absolute obedience, and the "seen but not heard" philosophy carried over to the schools that began to form during the Industrial Revolution. "Children were commonly beaten by schoolmasters and other adults, a practice so often described by Dickens that giving a child a beating became known as giving him the dickens" (Chase, 1975, p.17). Gradually, parents as well as employers began to realize that schooling was necessary for children of all classes, not just for the privileged. More enlightened schoolmasters realized the need for textbooks designed for children, rather than adults, and that beating a child into submission didn't necessarily make him or her learn. Initially schooling was voluntary and available only to the middle and upper classes, but by the latter part of the 19th century a significant number of states passed laws making school attendance compulsory.

In America, acknowledgment of the special needs of children and recognition of childhood as a special and separate part of development came very gradually throughout the 19th century. Books intended just for children and special clothing designed for their activities began to appear. Child care manuals that documented the prevailing views of child development were made available to parents and families, advocating specialized roles for the care of children.

As we approach the 21st century, many of our children are still not being protected from poverty, exploitation, and abuse. Even though much has been written about child development, there are still parents and professionals who do not understand its impact on children's lives. The data cited in Chapter 1 indicate that we have fallen short of being "child-centered" and that there is still much to be done to ensure the health and happiness of all our children. Developing children need the love of their families, the kindness and respect of their teachers, and the interest and support of their communities.

Influences on Development

Our descendants will regard as one of the great accomplishments of our age the discovery of the nature of childhood and the attempt to put this knowledge to work in the upbringing of our children.
—MARGARET MEAD

In most texts on the subject, child development is described as an always changing, never ending process. Children are constantly moving forward, gaining new readiness, and acquiring different competencies. Some do it quite rapidly, others more slowly. Some children grow and develop in positive surroundings, whereas others must adapt to more negative ones. Significant others such as parents, siblings, peers, and teachers influence the child's development and are influenced by the developing child as well. Because development occurs in a specific social context, a lot depends on the type of home and family environment children are exposed to, the type of interactions they have with their families, and the influences of the larger society and culture. "The emphasis is no longer simply on how the child constructs the world but also on how the world constructs the child. And the adult" (Kegan, as cited in Lefrancois, 1990, p. 9).

Although the first and most important influence on children is the family, children and their families interact with a broad system of social institutions that have an impact on children's development (Zigler et al., 1992). In addition, a worldview concept holds that child development is also influenced by "the interaction of social, cultural, political, moral and economic forces that shape ideas about environment during a specific time in history" (Lauter-Klatell, 1991, p. 1).

Many of the same influences that negatively affected children in the past— poverty, inequality, and maltreatment—are seriously impeding the development of millions of children today, particularly poor and minority children. Poor and minority parents lack political clout and are often powerless to negotiate with the system on their children's behalf. Poor nutrition, no prenatal care, and the lack of affordable health care for childhood illness seriously threaten a child's physical and intellectual development. Expectant mothers' substance abuse, high-risk behavior, and overwhelming stress during pregnancy may have various negative effects on the developing fetus. After birth, children cannot reach their full potential without stimulating toys and opportunities to play outdoors, and without bright and comfortable classrooms. In violent homes, decaying schools, and crime-filled neighborhoods where discrimination and hopelessness prevail, children are shortchanged in all areas of development.

Children's unique innate abilities, coupled with their daily experiences and their perceptions of these experiences, are important factors in determining how much their development will be affected by negative influences in the culture and in society. Whether or not children believe they are deprived is an important variable to future adjustment. Some adults who spent their childhoods in the ghettos report that they didn't feel poor or disadvantaged because everyone else was in the same position; they all had their tennis shoes held together with duct tape.

To understand the problems that children bring to counseling, we must have some knowledge of the healthy development of children. The following section provides a brief overview of child development from birth to age 12.

HEALTHY DEVELOPMENT IN CHILDHOOD

The brief summary of child development presented here is meant to reacquaint readers with the highlights of healthy development from birth to age 12. These developmental milestones are explained in terms of gross and fine motor movement, language acquisition, cognitive or thinking skills, emotional development, and social interaction. Imagination, humor, and play behaviors are discussed as part of overall development. Included are landmark studies on child development as well as recent research that both confirms and challenges the work of the early pioneers. Because only a brief review is presented here, I recommend reading further on motor development (Santrock, 1994), cognitive and language development (Bjorklund, 1995), emotional development (Lane & Swartz, 1987), and psychosocial development (Erikson, 1950).

The beginning child counselor will need to know a great deal about normal development before he or she will be able to determine whether a child's behavior is serious enough to require intervention. The brief overview presented here is not sufficient for counselor preparation in child development but serves only to reinforce and refresh. Readers are encouraged to consult a number of excellent child development textbooks (for example, Papalia & Olds, 1996; Santrock, 1994; Vasta, Haith, & Miller, 1995).

The Infant (Birth to Age 2)

Stages of Development

The immediate world of the infant is one of sensations and actions. During what Piaget called the *sensorimotor period,* the baby acts upon and interacts with what it can see, smell, taste, feel, or hear. The early months of life are a time to suck thumbs, feel the warmth of a mother's breast, smell baby powder, watch colored balls dance on mobiles hung high above a crib, and listen to lullabies. During this time the infant begins to reach for things, grasping them in tiny hands and hanging on for dear life. An infant can grip a rattle, shake it, and promptly smack itself in the face with it. Needless to say, motor coordination is not well developed in the first months of life.

Motor development   During the latter part of the first year, children acquire more skill. They can put a bottle in and out of their mouths, temporarily hold a cup, and reach for the spoon being used to feed them. Later, the infant learns to beat a spoon on the table to make a noise, finds blocks hidden under a blanket, and uses a spoon for its intended purpose. After learning to reach, grasp, and hold, the infant learns to sit and later to creep, stand, and climb. Before babies can walk, they can climb upstairs (but usually cannot get back down). After babies reach about 18 months, they begin to perfect their walking skills. Before age 2, they can walk sideways and backward and stand on one foot with help. Once toddlers can walk, their hands are free to explore their environment further and to gain a sense of control over their world.

Cognitive development   At the same time that infants are mastering motor skills, they are beginning to acquire the concept of *object permanence*. For young infants "seeing is believing"; if the infant can't see, touch, hear, or chew on it, it doesn't exist. At about age 6 months, babies begin to look for hidden objects; if the caregiver first displays a rattle and then hides it behind her or his back, the infant will look for it (although not vigorously). By 7 or 8 months, the baby begins to develop a fear of new faces and places and cries when the caregiver leaves the room. Toward the end of the first year, the child will search for blocks hidden under a blanket and, near the end of the second year, will search for and find things that are missing. It is only toward the end of the second year that children realize that objects still exist even when they are out of sight. It is this sense of object permanence, coupled with the acquisition of language, that helps the child progress from "a sensorimotor to a *symbolic* intelligence" (Lefrancois, 1990, p. 68).

Language development   Even before they reach their first birthdays, babies discover the importance of the ability to communicate with others. Discovering that their early attempts to communicate are not always understood gives them a strong motivation to learn to speak. During the first $1\frac{1}{2}$ to 2 years, babies use crying, babbling, gestures, and emotional expressions as a way of communicating. From age 12 to 18 months, children use single-word sentences to express whole ideas (Dale, 1972); expressions such as "milk" indicate the idea that a child wants a drink. Two-year-olds combine words into short sentences such as "Hold doll" or "Go bye-bye."

Emotional development   The emotional responses of interest, distress, and disgust are present at birth and precede the social smile, which appears sometime in the first 4 to 6 weeks of life. Other emotions develop gradually and are characterized by an increasing number of responses as infants get older. Anger, surprise, and sadness emerge at about 3 to 4 months, and the child is capable of expressing fear between 5 and 7 months of age. Shame and shyness make their appearance somewhere between age 6 and 8 months, although contempt and guilt do not appear until the child is about 2 years old (Izard, as cited in Santrock, 1994).

Before infants learn to speak, they use emotion, especially smiling and crying, as a way to communicate. Infants' smiles communicate delight to parents and help ensure that more love and attention will be forthcoming. On the other hand, cries may communicate distress in the form of hunger, pain, or anger. Lefrancois (1990) cited examples of cultures where mother-infant communication occurs through physical contact. In these cultures, where the infant is carried about constantly by the mother and is warm, well-fed, and constantly embraced, crying is interpreted as a sign of illness. In Western cultures, parental responses to crying vary, but Santrock (1994) argues that many developmentalists now believe that an infant cannot be spoiled in the first year. Therefore, a quick parental response to an infant's cries serves to heighten trust and increases the likelihood that the child will form a secure attachment with the caregiver.

Social development According to Erikson (1950), a sense of *trust versus mistrust* develops in the first year as the child faces an uncertain world. If the caregiver, usually the mother, is loving and meets the child's needs for predictability, safety, and love, the child develops a sense of trust. If, however, the infant lives in an unpredictable world with a rejecting caretaker, he or she may grow up to be anxious and mistrustful of others.

From about age 18 months to 3 years, children learn that they are the masters of their own destinies. This is the period Erikson (1950) called the *autonomy versus shame and doubt* stage of psychosocial development. Instead of simply reacting to the world through their senses, children realize that they can act on it as well. Children develop a sense of autonomy by learning that they can carry out their intentions; this is why the word *no* pops up so much around the second and third year. It is at this crucial time that parents need to both encourage the child's attempts to explore and provide opportunities for independence. The child who is too protected at this stage of development may grow to doubt his or her ability to deal with the world.

In summary, infants between birth and age 2 are in the here-and-now stage of development. They explore and understand their world through their senses and through motor activity. Their motor development accelerates rapidly from grasping and reaching to walking and running, and they develop the ability to communicate their wants and needs through language. In the beginning of this period, the child has an "out of sight, out of mind" view of objects; but by the end of the second year, the child has a developing sense that objects exist even when they aren't seen (object permanence). This intellectual realization accompanied by the acquisition of language helps the child to slowly acquire the ability to use mental images, imagination, and symbolic thought. Hopefully, infants will develop a bond of trust with their caregiver during the first months of life, and toward the second year a sense of autonomy will develop as they learn to control their behavior. By controlling their own body movements and the objects in the world around them, healthy infants evolve from helpless creatures with limited mobility and communication skills to alert, verbally and socially adept children, poised on the brink of the next stage of development.

The Preschool Child (Ages 2 to 6)

In the preschool years from ages 2 to 6, children use their increasing skills to interact with and understand an expanding world of people and things. They seek to find out who they are, determine what they can do, and construct a sense of self. Increasingly skillful, preschoolers push out into the world, first striving for autonomy and control of self and others and later using their emerging language, cognitive, motor, and social skills to gather information about the world. If successful, the preschooler uses this information to find new ways to reason, make decisions, and solve problems.

Stages of Development

Motor development   Rapidly developing motor skills make it possible for preschoolers to do more and more for themselves. Having mastered the art of using utensils, holding a glass, and pouring from a pitcher, 6-year-olds are able to feed themselves almost as well as adults. These children, who as 2-year-olds struggled with unbuttoning shirts and working large zippers, are now 5- and 6-year-olds able to unbutton and button shirts and tie their shoes. The skills of walking steadily, running, and climbing, so thrilling to the 2-year-old, have now evolved into walking on tiptoe, hopping, jumping, tricycling, and agile climbing by the graceful 5-year-old. Most 6-year-olds can run fast, climb trees, ride a bicycle, walk a balance beam, learn to skate, and climb a ladder into a treehouse. Balls once chewed on, kicked, and thrown clumsily can now be thrown and caught between the palms of the hands by most 6-year-olds.

All children in this stage of development love creative expression and enjoy drawing, coloring, and making things from play dough. Such activities are both fun and useful for strengthening their developing fine motor skills. Mastery of activities such as coloring within the lines helps prepare 5-year-olds for the rigors of kindergarten. As fine motor skills develop, the kindergartner is able to cut and fold paper; draw a square and a triangle; and copy designs, letters, and numbers. The random circular scribbles of the 2-year-old combined with the straight lines drawn at 3 and the attempts at geometric designs, letters, and numbers at 5 prepare the first-grader to learn to print and later for handwriting. Some of the milestones of motor development are summarized in Figure 2-1.

Language development   As children fine-tune their motor skills, they also increase their ability to communicate with others through language. Children become increasingly verbal during early childhood and can follow simple and direct verbal instruction. However, young children still make extensive use of nonverbal skills like gesturing, even when they are able to use words. During the preschool years, language changes from one-word utterances to highly complex speech and grammar. Many 4-year-olds continue to struggle with pronunciation, and grammatical errors are commonplace. When a rule of grammar is first grasped, it may be applied too widely, because the child rarely allows for exceptions (Bjorklund, 1995; Smart & Smart, 1977). For example, if the rule is to make the past tense by adding *ed*, the child may say, "I goed out and bringed my truck." If *himself*, *herself*, and *myself* are used, why not

FIGURE 2-1 *Landmarks in Motor Development from Age 2 to 6 Years*
SOURCE: Based on Smart & Smart (1977, p. 212), Santrock (1994, p. 164).

hisself? Often when the child applies *s* to form plurals, the result is *deers, mouses,* and *gooses.* Parents should not fuss over these developmental glitches in language. Instead, they should strive to be good speech role models because "children literally pick up the pronunciation of words from people with whom they associate" (Hurlock, 1978, p. 172).

As children grow and develop, the meaning and content of language change, keeping pace with the children's personal growth in social skills and their developing understanding of the world. Two-year-olds make many references to self in their immature language, such as "Me too" or "I go too." Three-year-olds make statements of joining and collaborating, showing increasing social maturity: "Let's play house" and "Give me some more, Mommy." By the time children are 4 and 5 years old, they adapt their speech much more to the listener and increase their verbal interaction with others: "You be the baby, I'll be the Daddy"; "Can I have a candy for my sister?" Before children are old enough to go to school, they are speaking in complex sentences with almost infinite variations of word combinations.

Preschool children love to crawl up on a parent's lap and be read to. Some 4- and 5-year-olds memorize the words to their favorite stories so well that they can "read" to adults. They are also keenly aware when adults alter a known story, as any weary adult who has tried to shorten a long bedtime story can testify.

Play development   Play combines cognitive, imaginative, and motor activities, using them all and weaving them together in development. It is through the early, largely symbolic and nonverbal pretend play that children first use symbols to represent objects in their world and to imitate what they see happening around them. By the time children are 4, they can sustain long periods of pretend play, which is an ideal age to begin play therapy. In *Evolutions End*, Pearce (1992) noted that "play is the foundation of creative intelligence" (p. 154). A preschool child might make "tasty" dishes of play dough and cook them on a pretend stove or bathe a "baby" doll in a sink, washing its hair until the whole room is wet. A 4-year-old can find an old dusty case, make it into a doctor's kit, and possess great healing powers. By putting bandages on all the teddy bears, the child experiences what it is like to *be* the doctor. In this way, the child can move away from egocentric thought and begin to adopt another's viewpoint.

Children love activities that tickle their senses such as finger painting and playing in water, sand, and mud. To watch children play in mud puddles, letting the mud ooze up between their toes as they make footprints, or to see them carve an entire town into the side of a creek bank is to observe the wonder and magic of childhood. Through these experiences the child first explores, comprehends, and then masters the environment.

Cognitive development Intellectually, the preschool child has left the here-and-now thinking of the sensorimotor period behind and is entering the *preoperational* or *prelogical* stage of development (Piaget, 1950; see Table 2-1 for an overview of Piaget's model of cognitive development). This means that preschoolers can think about and represent objects, people, and actions that are not present. Children at this stage use signs and symbols to represent their world through imitation, symbolic play, drawing, mental imaging, and language. Whereas the 2-year-old pretends that dolls are babies and that stuffed animals will bite you, the 3-year-old can use imagination to represent thought and make graphic representations through art. As children approach ages 4 and 5, they construct mental images in the form of internalized imitation in order to act on past events or plan for the future. For example, the child who gives teddy a "shot" from a pretend needle and then soothes the bear with words and hugs may be anticipating an upcoming visit to the doctor. At this stage, language becomes a powerful tool, as children are able to use words to represent objects and events.

Young children organize their experiences into concepts of classes, time, space, number, and causality; but because they cannot quite conceptualize until around age 4, their early thinking is labeled *preconceptual*. Children in the *intuitive* stage of thought (ages 4 to 7) are better able to classify and use more complex representations. They often solve problems correctly by using intuitive mental images rather than logic. For example, when Piaget placed three balls—one blue, one red, and one yellow—in a clear upright tube, the children could tell which colored ball was on top. However, when it was turned a half rotation, a full rotation, or two rotations, the children had to imagine the position of the balls in order to answer correctly. They could not connect the number of rotations with the position of the balls using logical thinking (Lefrancois, 1990).

Children in the preoperational stage have difficulty deciding what to include in a class or category, and their thinking is illogical, egocentric, and dominated by perception. Whereas the child's earliest concepts are rooted in concrete personal experience, conceptualizing in the intuitive stage becomes more objective and

TABLE 2-1 • Jean Piaget's Model of Cognitive Development in Childhood

Stage	Abilities	Age Span
Sensorimotor: Infancy		
1. Reflex Activity	Preverbal Uses natural reflexes Tracks objects in field of vision	0–1 month
2. Primary Circular Reactions	Activities involve the child's body Pleasant activities are repeated Stares at disappearing objects	1–4 months
3. Secondary Circular Reactions	Repeats interesting activities Manipulates objects in the environment Searches for disappearing objects	4–8 months
4. Secondary Schemata	Begins using signs to anticipate events Attempts to coordinate events for a purpose Recognizes familiar objects and people Searches for concealed objects	8–12 months
5. Tertiary Circular Reactions	Explores new situations through trial and error Searches and finds concealed objects Imitates actions of others	12–18 months
6. Mental Combinations	Growing ability to imitate Develops mental images to solve problems Anticipates consequences Knows objects exist after they disappear from sight (object permanence)	18–24 months

Preoperational thought: Childhood	Mastery of symbols, especially language
	Uses mental images, imagination, and
	    symbolic thought
	Cannot conserve (thinks same amount of
	    candy in different size jars isn't the same)
	Has trouble with reversible thinking
		2–7 years

1. Preconceptual	Develops concepts that are not complete
	    or logical
	Reason is dominated by perception
	Inability to consider more than one aspect
	    of a situation
	Egocentric social communication
		2–4 years

2. Intuitive	Intuitive rather than logical solutions Considers more than one aspect of a situation	4–7 years

Concrete operations: Middle childhood	Uses logic to make sense of things and
	    relationships
	Has ability to conserve (knows it's the same
	    amount of candy in different size jars)
		7–11 years

Stage	Activities	Age Span
	Develops understanding of number—groups and series	
	Concrete rather than abstract thinking	
	Reversibility of thought (flat clay can be reshaped as a ball)	
	Develops empathy for another's position	
	Greater capacity for attention, concentration, and memory	
Formal operations: Adolescence		11–15 years
	Capable of abstract thought	
	Has ability to deal with the hypothetical	
	Can generalize thought, make inferences, and use deductive reasoning	
	Capable of flexibility and creativity	
	Develops higher levels of empathy and idealism	

TABLE 2-1 • (continued)

abstract. As children gain more experience, they can interact with others to verify their thoughts and conclusions. For example, Sam believes that rocks sink because they are "stronger," and he tests this perception by fishing with lead sinkers, which his grandfather explained are heavier.

Growth in conceptualizing occurs when young children make simple *classifications* and organize their experiences into concepts of space, time, quantity, and causality. Young children often classify things they have experienced together and sort them according to similarity. For example, 3-year-olds put a doll with a crib, whereas 6-year-olds group a crib, chair, and table together as furniture. Children younger than 4 are more likely to group things by color rather than form (such as putting red trucks, red balls, and red crayons together); older children group by form. A 2-year-old calls all furry animals "doggy," but a 5-year-old can distinguish between dogs and cats and between chickens and ducks.

In Piaget's view (Piaget & Inhelder, 1969) the young child judges the duration of time in terms of content rather than speed. Any parent who has listened to "Are we there yet?" for the last 100 miles of a trip has some idea of a preschooler's notion of time. Two-year-olds have little understanding of the concept of tomorrow and yesterday; 3-year-olds understand yesterday but also interpret it to mean any time other than today: "I'm going to take a nap yesterday." After age 4, children understand the sequence of daily events and express broader concepts such as month, next summer, and last summer (Ames & Learned, 1946). However, unless you want the child to ask you every day, it is usually not a good idea to tell preschoolers that they will be going on vacation in "two weeks"!

At first, young children do not differentiate between time and space, and they relate space to their own bodies, movements, and perceptions. From this egocentric viewpoint, the body is a reference point in judgments of up and down, left and right, near and far, and here and there. Four- and 5-year-olds are able to copy the order of a set of objects, but they still overlap the concepts of big, tall, and high. They tend to think that an object placed *higher* on a table is also *bigger* (Smart & Smart, 1977).

Through experience and discussion, the child builds *quantity* concepts of more or less and of one, some, and all. Concepts of number, like those of time and space, are first derived from concrete experiences; 2-year-olds know what "another" piece of candy is, and 3-year-olds do not need to know how to count to choose the plate with four cookies instead of two. Recent research (Gelman, 1982; Gelman, Meck, & Merkin, 1986) suggests that 4- and 5-year-olds are capable of number abstraction, evidenced through counting behaviors such as how, what, and in what sequence and in the reasoning used in operations like adding to and taking away.

In early childhood, explanations of events (causality) tend to be in concrete and personal terms, much as the concepts of space, time, and number are. The events of the outer world are closely linked to the child's inner world and his or her needs. During the preschool and school years, causality becomes less subjective and less personal. The child evolves from thinking that events were caused by his or her own actions or the actions of people nearby to seeing natural events as caused by forces in themselves. Progress in understanding cause is from concrete to abstract, and preschool children are unable to consider several factors at a time or to come to general conclusions about a particular concept.

Preschoolers are greatly influenced by what they see, hear, or experience, and it is this "seeing is believing" mentality that enables them to conclude that magicians really do pull rabbits out of hats and that by waving a magic wand one can make a bird disappear. Because thought is dominated by *perception*, preschoolers are not only fooled by magicians, they are also unable to *conserve* when solving problems; that is, they are not able to account for the quantity of something when it changes shape. In one of Piaget's (1950) experiments, beads are poured from a short and fat glass into another, tall and thin glass. When asked if there are more or fewer beads in the tall glass, preschoolers usually answer more because the level of the beads has risen. Young children do not understand that simply putting the beads into a different size container, without adding or taking any beads away, does not change the amount. This inability to conserve indicates that preschoolers cannot comprehend the two dimensions of the problem at the same time (such as the height and width of the glass) and that reasoning is still bound by perception and not the rules of logic. Because children cannot replay their earlier understanding of the problem (visualize the beads being poured back into the container), they lack the concept of reversibility that characterizes the concrete operations stage as defined by Piaget. Recently, the neo-Piagetians have noted that, in certain situations, 4- and 5-year-olds are able to solve conservation tasks involving more than one dimension (Donaldson, 1978) and that it is misleading to think of the preschool child's mind as preoperational or prelogical (Flavell, 1985).

Piaget concluded that because preschoolers are quite egocentric in their thinking, they consider only one dimension or perspective at a time; for example, the child cannot consider both the height and the width of the container in the preceding conservation problem. Piaget believed that egocentrism also applies to both the physical and emotional viewpoints of preschoolers, but recent evidence suggests that preschoolers are not egocentric in all situations. Borke (1975) conducted a set of clever experiments in which the character Grover of *Sesame Street* drove his car along a road and stopped to look at scenes mounted on a turntable. Children as young as 3 and 4 years were capable of moving the turntable to match the scene to the way Grover saw it. The process of pretend play enables children to explore the behavior of others and to experience a different emotional viewpoint by taking on the role of another.

Emotional development   Emotionally, the preschool child is capable of love and has the capacity to be affectionate, kind, and helpful as well as selfish and aggressive. When preschoolers have a warm and nurturing model, they accept love as the foundation of their world and can be taught to care for and help one another. Sidel (1973) found that Chinese children as young as 3 years could be taught to love, care for, and help one another through example, stories, pictures, slides, song, dance, dramas, and cooperative activities. Even very young children can recognize another child in distress, feel sympathy, and want to help. However, because they do not have the cognitive ability to experience the hurt from the other child's viewpoint, they cannot be expected to empathize. As children mature, they are able to identify their feelings and relate them to specific events. For example, 3-year-olds are able to tell the difference between happy and unhappy reactions in stories (Borke, 1973); and, with their increased language ability, 4- and 5-year-olds can communicate their feelings to others.

Young children express the primary emotions of anger and fear in both positive and negative ways. Anger in the form of assertiveness is an essential ingredient of initiative and contributes to achievement and problem solving, and fear in the form of mild anxiety acts as a motivator. Anger is also expressed as *aggression*, usually provoked over toys and space, and *jealousy*, seen in the form of sibling rivalry. Fear is another primary emotion and can be expressed as a specific fear, the object of which varies with age. Fear can also be expressed as worry and as anxiety.

Preschoolers express only one emotion at a time and are not yet capable of mixed emotions or the feelings of ambivalence characteristic of later stages of development (Lane & Swartz, 1987). Consequently, many youngsters disguise their emotions or do not have sufficient language capabilities to articulate what is bothering them. Play, art, and storytelling are therefore effective treatment strategies for use with preschoolers age 3 and older.

Social development   Emotional and social development are linked by a common thread and are influenced by the preschool child's increasing cognitive and language skills. As preschool children mature, they get a clearer picture of themselves as unique individuals. Although this sense of self begins to emerge in the sensorimotor period when infants first see themselves as separate from their environment, it continues with the development of a sense of autonomy at ages 2 to 3 and a sense of initiative at ages 4 to 5 (Erikson, 1950). As children grow, they continue to define the feelings, actions, and relationships that make them unique. Erik Erikson's eight-stage model of psychosocial development includes five stages that apply to childhood; those five are illustrated in Figure 2-2.

With their developing sense of autonomy, 2-year-olds have the power of doing and deciding what to do with their emerging abilities. Having mastered the motor skills needed to explore and armed with about 400 words (Smart & Smart, 1977) to represent a great many things, activities, people, and ideas, the 2-year-old can concentrate on gaining a sense of control over self and others. The greatest satisfaction is in the use of the word *no*, for this word helps the child decide whether or not to cooperate with others: whether or not to "give kisses," to "like liver," to "hate day care," and to "go potty" on the toilet. If the child's efforts at autonomy are punished, feelings of shame and worthlessness may result. Shame develops when parents, who conclude that children are doing too many things wrong or are causing too many problems, tell the children how "bad" they are or punish them. Some parents use shame as a method of control, which might result in what Erikson, (1950, p. 252) describes as "rage turned against the self," often expressed as stubbornness, defiance, and compulsive behaviors. Children who are successfully guided through this stage of development emerge as more independent, capable, and cooperative youngsters.

At age 4 or so, the sense of initiative claims the spotlight as preschoolers actively seek to discover who they are and what they can do. As 4- and 5-year-olds push vigorously out into the world, they seek a wide range of information about people and the environment by asking questions and pretending through play. Through imaginative play, children model adult behavior. At first, they model the parent of the same sex—trying the role on for size, exploring what the parent does, and imagining themselves as the parent. Between the ages of 3 and 6, the child takes on the parent's voice and forms a conscience that hopefully is strong enough to regulate behavior without too much punishing guilt. Guilt is a necessary result of the sense of initiative and occurs when the child's wishes and exuberance for growth clash with the parent's push for self-regulation (Erikson, 1950). Here again imaginative play comes to the rescue, as children are able to appease excessive amounts of guilt by creating fantasy characters to take care of the "bad guys."

Healthy growth at this stage requires a delicate balance between initiative and restraint and depends to a large extent on parental warmth and confidence in the child. If the parents believe that the child is basically good, is capable of good behavior, is able to live up to the family's expectations, and can improve as he or she grows, then the child will believe these things also. Because preschoolers seek the love and approval of their families and model after significant others, they try to conform to the standards set by their family and the larger society. Through consistent, loving, and firm handling, parents can encourage children in their quest for independence and self-reliance, thus laying the groundwork for the development of the sense of competence that comes in the next stage.

In summary, preschoolers are increasingly skillful, adventurous, and imaginative. As they grow toward independence, healthy 2- and 3-year-olds gain a sense of self through actions and decisions that promote autonomy and avoid shame and doubt. Four- and 5-year-olds use all their emerging abilities to discover what they can and cannot do, hoping that their actions do not have disastrous consequences that bring

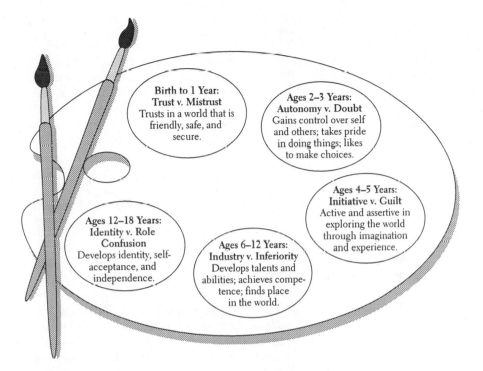

FIGURE 2-2 *Erik Erikson's Stages of Psychosocial Development That Apply to Children and Adolescents*

punishing guilt. Phenomenal growth in language enables preschoolers to carry on conversations with any adult willing to listen, and their growing cognitive capabilities provide unlimited opportunities for exploration and mastery. Play serves as a way to represent the world through symbols, to model the behavior of parents and others, to solve problems, and to learn socialization skills. Although preschoolers may appear "grown up" in their thinking and communication, they cannot yet link events in a logical way, nor can they consider more than one aspect of a problem at a time. Very young children in the preconceptual stage have bits and pieces of knowledge they have not yet been able to weave into a conceptual framework. By age 4 or 5, most preschool children begin to think more rationally and are able to conceptualize and organize their ideas, but they still cling to the "seeing is believing" stage of intuitive reasoning. Emotionally, they are capable of love and kindness, aggression and selfishness, and they have fears that change as they grow. Their imagination, not yet dampened by formal schooling, courses through all that they do and helps strike a balance between initiative and restraint that eases the burdens of guilt. Although words to describe their thoughts and feelings may not be available to them, they use play as a means of self-expression, communication, and problem solving. Therefore, this is an ideal stage of development to engage children in play, art, and storytelling as a means of maintaining good adjustment or helping overcome deficits.

The School-Age Child (Ages 6 to 12)

The healthy school-age child who has mastered the developmental tasks of the first 5 years of life is now entering a new phase of development that will last until age 12 or so. As children enter school, their small circle of family and neighbors expands to include both peers and adults at school and in the community. These broader social contacts, coupled with rapidly developing motor, language, and cognitive capabilities, help youngsters meet the physical and academic challenges of middle childhood. Their developing cognitive abilities allow children to think logically and apply rules to obtain new information, solve more difficult problems, and become interested in achievement. By creating, achieving, and producing, the child gains a sense of accomplishment and adds an image of competence into his or her evolving self-portrait.

Stages of Development

Motor development The physical activity of play and games helps alleviate the *couch potato syndrome*, a term coined to describe the effects of too much television watching, as well as the new *mouse potato syndrome*, spawned by the age of computers. Using new coordination skills coupled with growing stamina and strength, school-age children engage in and enjoy individual, group, and team play. They perfect their running skills in games of tag and hide-and-seek and practice their jumping in leap frog and jump rope. Balancing and fancy footwork are central to activities such as hopscotch, gymnastics, ladder climbing, and skating. Whether they live on a farm, in a suburb, or in the city, school-age children love experiences that challenge gross motor skills and are just plain fun. Children make use of whatever is available to them in their play: trees are for climbing, building houses, and providing leaves to play in; snow is for making angels, snowballs, forts, and snowmen and for sliding; sidewalks are for skipping rope and playing hopscotch; cardboard boxes or scraps of wood make forts or clubhouses; and playgrounds, backyards, and community centers are used for countless play activities.

During the school years, basic motor skills are integrated into games that have social meaning. Team sports gain popularity as children acquire the ability to understand game rules and have a desire to interact and to compete with peers. However, if adults pressure children into competing before they are ready, or if only the most talented children (those with specialized training) get to play, or if the emphasis is on winning at all costs, organized sports teams can have a negative impact on child development and diminish self-esteem (Elkind, 1988; Santrock, 1994). Teams that give everyone, rather than a talented few, an opportunity to play and that emphasize fun and sportsmanship over severe competition can help children practice both physical and social skills and can enhance self-esteem. Performing well, playing by the rules, and being considerate of other players all contribute to recognition and approval by peers and give children a sense of mastery or control over their social and physical environment.

Intellectual games like checkers and chess that integrate cognitive and social skills within a framework of rules are favorites of children in the upper grades. Fourth-graders, now able to plan their strategy and ponder the consequences of their next move, organize chess tournaments to challenge themselves and others. Other forms of internal challenge occur singly and also serve the goal of self-mastery. The ancient game of not stepping on cracks, thought to work magic, helps the school-age child achieve control over the environment. Similarly, when a child challenges himself or herself by setting up an obstacle to be overcome and experiences anxiety and then the burst of exhilaration that comes with success, mastery has been achieved! Imaginative play is also used in the service of self-mastery, for by expressing fear, hostility, or fantasies of grandeur through dramatic play, the child gains control and is able to distinguish between imagination and reality.

Increasing sophistication in fine motor skills makes it possible for the school-age child to learn to print neatly and to begin cursive writing at the end of the second grade. Activities such as drawing and artwork are done more skillfully and with greater attention to detail. Refinements in fine motor skills, as well as increasing eye-hand coordination, make it possible for some children to learn to play musical instruments or excel at a particular sport or physical activity.

Language development   The child's language world is filled with reading, talking, and listening, all of which provide countless opportunities to learn vocabulary and grammar. At age 6, vocabulary is exploding at the rate of 22 new words a day (Miller, 1981), and children make fewer grammatical errors as they learn to apply the rules. By age 7, when *concrete operations* begin to be established, children are able to analyze words that are outside the realm of their personal experience. For example, whereas preschoolers associate the word *cat* with its color or its meow, school-age children classify it as an animal and are able to expand the context to include *lion* or *zoo*. Compared to the preschooler, the school-age child has made a quantum leap in understanding both semantics (meaning) and syntax (sentence structure). For example, when "I sawed the tree" is announced, the preschooler has just looked at the newly planted tree; the school-age child has already cut it down.

As children hear new words in different contexts and learn to extract the meaning of unfamiliar words used in sentences, they rely less on context and more on syntax to determine meaning. Using syntax, school-age children are able to construct longer and more complex sentences. The most basic use of syntax is in constructions like "Jack kissed Jill" or "Jill was kissed by Jack." The fact that Jill was the one being kissed is easily understood by the school-age child. However, in the early school-age years, children might interpret "Jill asked Jack to quit kissing" to mean only that Jack quit kissing. Similarly, children are confused by the sentence "Jack slapped by Jill ran down the hill" and may interpret it to mean that Jill is the one who ran. Correct interpretation requires knowledge of the association between objects and actions when sentence structures do not follow the subject-verb-object rule (Kopp & Krakow, 1982). The ability to interpret meaning in such sentences is usually not present until age 10 or beyond (Chomsky, as cited in Smart & Smart, 1977).

Much of the humor of childhood finds its origins in language and is linked to the child's developing social and cognitive skills. As children learn new words, meanings, and structures, they begin to understand metaphors ("He is a hard teacher") and figurative speech ("Go jump in the lake"). Children from ages 7 to 11 are able to understand riddles and jokes that are based on double meanings, because they can fit the word into two different classifications and are able to do it quickly enough to keep both meanings in mind at the same time. The appreciation of a riddle such as "Q: What do you call a witch doctor's mistake? A: A voodoo boo boo!" requires that the child first associate *mistake* with *boo boo*, which is easy enough; but then the child must understand the term *witch doctor* and associate it with *voodoo*. This ability to shift from one meaning to another, essential to understanding jokes, is made possible by the concept of reversibility, one of the cornerstones of operational thought.

Brian Sutton-Smith (1976) found that children in middle childhood enjoy jokes and riddles that model their experiences in school and allow them to play the role of the adult. Jokes and riddles that disparage adults enable children to release, through laughter, the tensions they feel over their own inadequacies and their relationships with authority figures. By asking a riddle, children are able to reverse roles and be the authority. In his study of children in grades 1 through 8, Sutton-Smith (1976) collected and classified riddles and jokes as either pre-riddles, riddles, or parodies. About one-third of the first- and second-graders submitted pre-riddles, which were funny to them but would not amuse older children. Most of the riddles submitted required some sort of reclassification of a central word or idea. About 60% required implicit reclassification. A smaller number were classified as riddle parodies, in which an expectation is upset by a straightforward answer. The balance were riddles in which patterns between relationships were reversed. For example, *pre-riddles* are actually not riddles but are funny to younger children.

> Q: Why did the man chop down the chimney?
> A: He needed the bricks.

Implicit reclassifications are riddles in which a central word or idea is presented in one way but is then reclassified in another way to produce a climax. In the following riddles, *dog* and *sheet* have to be reclassified.

> Q: Why did the dog go out into the sun? *or*   Q: What sheet can't be folded?
> A: He wanted to be a hot dog.   A: A sheet of ice.

Riddle parodies do not involve reclassification but are humorous because an expectation is upset by a straightforward answer. Instead of the expected complicated answer, a direct one is given.

> Q: If you threw a brown rock into the Red Sea, what would it become?
> A: Wet.

Inverted riddles are those in which the patterns between relationships are reversed. Ordinarily we expect dogs to have fleas, but we don't expect fleas to have dogs.

> Q: What does one flea say to another as they go strolling?
> A: Shall we walk or take a dog?

Another form of riddle is a *pun*, which is a play on words that resemble one another but have a different meaning.

> Q: What is the difference between a tunafish and a piano?
> A: You can't tune a fish.

Easy to understand *knock-knock* jokes remain the perennial favorites of primary school children. Older children who are more cognitively advanced are able to enjoy riddles and jokes that play not only on words but also on unexpected interpretations. The following are some favorites:

LINDA: Last week my brother shot an elephant in his pajamas.
MAXINE: How did an elephant get in his pajamas?

CHRIS: How is a baseball team like a pancake?
BRYAN: I don't know, how?
CHRIS: They both depend on the batter.

GERRI: I was born in Pennsylvania.
HELEN: What part?
GERRI: All of me!

CUSTOMER: Would you mind if I tried on that dress in the window?
CLERK: I would prefer that you use one of our dressing rooms.

Imagination and creativity are central to children's development in middle childhood and find expression in fantasy, daydreaming, and the arts. Although school-age children have increased cognitive and language abilities to deal with their environment and are able to pay closer attention to the tasks at hand, they still continue to daydream and fantasize. Through imagination, children produce unique and original work and find creative solutions to problems.

Cognitive development   Intellectually, children in the concrete operations stage of development are able to think more logically and apply rules systematically in order to obtain new information. As was noted in the section on language and joke telling, the school-age child is now able to consider more than one dimension at a time and can shift rapidly from one thought to another. In addition, the school-age child can add and subtract, classify, and conserve.

According to Piaget, the ability to conserve substance is an indication of the child's growing ability to apply three rules of logic: identity, reversibility, and compensation. When beads are poured from a short, narrow container into a tall, wide container, the child reasons that because nothing has been added or taken away, the quantity is the same and therefore *identity* has been preserved. Similarly, the child is able to reason that if the action were *reversed*—if the beads were poured from the tall, narrow glass back into the short, wide glass—the amount would remain the same. Finally, the child is able to reason that the height of the narrow glass *compensates* for the width of the short glass and that therefore they hold the same quantity of beads.

With this increasing cognition, children are capable of planning strategy in their game playing and can solve mathematical problems that involve logical reasoning. However, they are still not capable of the kind of abstract thinking they will begin to acquire at the end of this period. In the formal operations period (Piaget, 1950), children at about age 12 will be able to form hypotheses, use inference and deductive reasoning to arrive at the solution to problems, and generalize their conclusions to similar problems. These cognitive abilities vary from child to child and are developed and refined throughout the formal operations period.

Emotional development Although school-age children have the same range of emotion preschoolers have, increasing cognitive skill allows for different expression. School-age children are able to experience more than one emotion at a time and are able to experience different emotions simultaneously (Lane & Swartz, 1987). For example, a 10-year-old might express excitement about a trip to an amusement park while at the same time expressing dread at getting carsick during the trip. At this age, children learn to conceal certain emotions—for example, boys don't cry for fear of being labeled "sissies."

Emotionally, school-age children have the ability to show caring and concern for others (empathy) because their increasing cognitive ability makes it possible to take another person's role or perceive his or her point of view. To perceive another person's thoughts and feelings, a child must first get information from the behavior of the other person through verbal and nonverbal clues.

Selman (1980, 1981) distinguished different levels of social role taking. Unlike preschoolers, school-age children between age 6 and 8 are aware that others have different emotional and intellectual points of view; at ages 8 to 10, they can perceive what other people are thinking and feeling; and at 12 and beyond, they are able to analyze and evaluate their own perspectives as well as those of others, paving the way for a deeper level of empathy. For example, Maria sees her brother break the neighbor's window. Maria, age 6, thinks that her father will be very angry with Julio and might spank him, which will hurt. When the same situation happens when Maria is 8 or so, she thinks that Julio should explain it was an accident, and she hopes her father understands because she doesn't want her brother hurt by a spanking. At age 10, Maria understands that Julio didn't mean to break the window; she thinks her father will see it that way too, if only Julio would explain. It would be unfair if Julio got spanked. At age 12, Maria thinks that her brother should explain and offer to pay for the window. After all, a broken window is not worth a broken heart!

Moral thought and judgment are linked to social, emotional, and cognitive development. The school-age child's sense of right and wrong is defined by the rules of family, school, community, and peers, and as children mature they shape their own beliefs within the broader social and cultural framework. According to Piaget, children age 6 and 7 know the rules, view them as unchangeable, and think in terms of consequences (punishment) for breaking the rules. By age 10 and older, children consider intention as well as consequence and realize that there are different ways of viewing any given act. They realize that rules are changeable with consensus and compromise. Lawrence Kohlberg's theory of moral development proposed that children at the conventional level of moral reasoning are able to internalize rules, separate an act from its consequences, seek approval from and avoid disapproval by their families, and conform to society's rules (as cited in Santrock, 1994).

Social development Middle childhood has its own culture (Smart & Smart, 1977). Children apparently teach their rhymes, riddles, chants, and "magic-making" words to one another, bestowing these treasured rituals on younger children and then forgetting them as they move toward adolescence. Chants and "magic words" are part of this unique peer culture of middle childhood and are passed from one generation of children to the next. Believing that words give them power over reality, children use the chants of childhood to bestow good luck, cement the bonds of friendship, and make wishes come true. Favorites include:

Making a Promise

Cross your heart and hope to die?
Stick a needle in your eye?
Put a dagger in your thigh?
Eat a cow manure pie?

Making a Wish

Star light, star bright
First star I've seen tonight
I wish I may, I wish I might
Have the wish I wish tonight.

Bestowing Good Luck

Lucky, lucky, white horse
Lucky, lucky lee
Lucky, lucky, white horse
Bring your luck to me.

Even the name-calling chants of childhood are said half in earnest, half in jest. Examples include:

Fatty, fatty, two by four,
Can't get through the kitchen door.
Fatty, fatty, two by eight,
Can't get through the garden gate.

Liar,
Liar,
Pants on fire!

Sometimes the chants of childhood involve references to emerging sexual interest, such as:

I wish I was a little bar of soap.
I wish I was a little bar of soap.
I'd slippey and I'd slidey
Over everybody's hidey.
I wish I was a little bar of soap.

Meghan and Mike
Sitting in a tree
K-I-S-S-I-N-G

Some of the chants are used in interaction with peers during physical activities such as jumping rope:

Down in the valley where the green grass grows
There sat Linda as sweet as a rose.
She sang and she sang and she sang so sweet
Along came her boyfriend and kissed her on the cheek.

The peer group teaches social skills and transmits the culture of childhood through humor, magic-making words, secrets, codes, and distinctive ways of communicating. Children risk using swear words—words that wouldn't be sanctioned by their families—in order to feel part of a special group separate from the world of adults. Matters of taste, style, and behavior are strongly influenced by peer preferences because children want to be popular with the peer group. Because different peer groups have different values, influenced by such factors as socioeconomic class, race, gender, and age, a child's acceptance and popularity in any group depend on a match between what the child values and what the peer group values: a swimming club requires its members to have agility, coordination, and determination; a chess club rewards the child who has patience and the ability to analyze and strategize; a street gang values toughness and skill in fighting.

It is during the school years that a child's sense of self, sense of group, and sense of belonging are most affected by society's institutionalized responses to race, gender, and social class. The values held by lower-class children may conflict sharply with the teacher's middle-class expectations. Bias is keenly felt by children, especially minority children, who are rejected on the basis of their color or socioeconomic status. This bias has negative effects on a child's developing perceptions of fairness and justice and on the child's relationships with peers.

Every child needs at least one good friend: someone to share his or her innermost thoughts and feelings, someone who will provide warmth and affection, and someone to give feedback that validates the child's sense of competence and self-worth. Some children have only one or two close friends, usually of the same sex, whereas others have many friends. Some children have no friends at all and are socially isolated from their peers. Without peer acceptance, these children feel lonely and rejected and have no one to validate their sense of worth other than their parents. Isolation by peers has a decidedly negative impact on a child's developing self-concept.

Children who are good communicators and who are friendly and outgoing are usually popular with their peers. Aggressive, "in your face" type of behavior usually leads to rejection. Group leaders tend to have superior physical and mental abilities, to be physically attractive, and to have good social skills. Although boys and girls tend to stay with their own groups, they accept each other more as they grow older; by age 12, they entertain thoughts of partnerships and boyfriend/girlfriend friendships.

Erik Erikson's (1950) stage of *industry versus inferiority* (ages 6–12) is a time to get the job finished, instead of just started, and to achieve a sense of accomplishment. It is a time to learn the skills and technology of the culture. It is a time to learn rules, develop social skills, and make friends. It is a time to create, accomplish, and feel adequate and to incorporate these positive feelings into a developing sense of self. Whether the child develops a sense of industry or inferiority depends on whether he or she has lived up to the expectations of significant others. If the child fails to develop a sense of competence or if the feelings of inadequacy are too overwhelming, he or she will develop feelings of inferiority. These feelings will seriously diminish the child's self-esteem and sense of competence.

In summary, rapidly developing physical, cognitive, language, emotional, and social skills, combined with imagination and play, form the unique culture that is middle childhood. Children now have all of the necessary building blocks for school achievement. Their increased abilities to communicate, to think and reason logically, and to perceive a situation from another vantage point are all important to learning and mastery. As children mature socially and emotionally and intellectually, they are learning more and more about how people think and feel and are becoming capable of empathy. Socially, children are busy finding their place in a peer group, clarifying their values, and making friends. They are now able to distinguish between right and wrong and can make moral judgments based on increasing emotional and cognitive capabilities. School-age children are acutely aware of biases, and a child's self-concept is diminished by the prejudices of others, especially peers and teachers. During middle childhood, children confront the social issues of acceptance and rejection, fairness and injustice, right and wrong. They strive to conform to the values set by their family, school, peer, and community group. Sometimes these values conflict, making it particularly difficult for some children, especially those who represent a minority, in the school setting. As children strive to meet academic and physical challenges and to solve problems successfully, they hopefully will achieve a sense of competence rather than inferiority and be well prepared for the demands of adolescence.

The following section is devoted to special developmental problems children confront as they grow up. Although most of these developmental concerns disappear as children mature, some form the basis of more serious difficulties that require intervention.

COMMON DEVELOPMENTAL PROBLEMS

The normal course of development is not a smooth one, and children often step back, pause long enough to replay old problems, and then continue on the path to healthy development. Glitches in the development of trust and autonomy, initiative and industry, may show up as common growth problems that demand both attention and solutions along the way to maturity. Even with a firm sense of trust, children may feel insecure and frightened when a parent is absent too long or when a stranger appears suddenly. Even with a strong sense of autonomy, children sometimes indulge themselves in a temper tantrum or two or have an "accident" because they were too "busy" or too obstinate to go to the toilet. Just as fighting and jealousy between siblings are a normal part of development, so is feeling anger when provoked or blushing when embarrassed. Just as different fears are common at different ages, anxiety in small amounts helps get the job done, whereas too much anxiety slows things down. Occasionally, on the way to developing a sense of initiative, the child attempts to explore and master the world a bit too aggressively, plowing over anyone who gets in the way. Even with a healthy sense of initiative, the child can resort to physical violence to deal with his or her problems. As children mature, they define themselves in terms of the family, peer group, and the larger society. And as children slowly build their self-esteem, they need to know that they are doing well and that they are viewed as competent and are accepted by the important people in their lives. Even with a healthy sense of accomplishment, the sharp sting of criticism from parents, teachers, and peers may rekindle feelings of inferiority that result in a temporary loss of self-confidence.

Dependency and attachment, anger and aggression, jealousy and rivalry, and fear and anxiety are discussed in this section in terms of their positive as well as negative influences on development. Too much of a good thing can be problematic. Time and increasing maturity, coupled with the support and positive feedback and encouragement from parents, teachers, and counselors, usually help children get back on track and prevent developmental regressions from becoming serious behavioral disturbances. Most developmental problems are not severe enough to warrant remedial counseling, but a list of referral criteria is given at the end of this section, so that parents, teachers, and counselors can ascertain whether a particular situation is serious enough to warrant a referral .

Dependency and Attachment

Attachment is an active, affectionate, reciprocal, enduring relationship between two people—known in unscientific circles as love.
—PAPALIA & OLDS (1996)

Perhaps the most dramatic and important milestone in an infant's life is the creation of the bond between a nurturing caregiver and the newborn. Although mothers are usually the primary caregivers, fathers, grandparents, older siblings, or a loving mother substitute can promote healthy personality development in infants. This intense caregiver-child relationship characterizes secure attachment and is believed to be the basic building block for future socialization. Erikson (1950) concluded that the parent-child bond facilitates trust and sets the stage for the child's expectations that the world will be a good and pleasant place to be. In addition to establishing trust, a close relationship with a nurturing caregiver facilitates moral development and the proper expression of aggression. "The fact that children...value the presence, attention, and approval of significant others, and fear their loss, has been considered a most powerful motive for conformity to the expectations of others, for imitation and identification, for the acquisition of values, for the internalization of behavior controls, for academic achievement, and for many other aspects of socialization" (Ferguson, as cited in Clarizio & McCoy, 1983 p. 43).

As children grow and develop, they exhibit both instrumental and emotional dependency. In *instrumental* or *task-oriented dependency*, the child asks for help in doing things and in accomplishing tasks. *Emotional* or *person-oriented dependency* usually develops later as the child seeks recognition and approval from parents, teachers, and peers. Young children show their attachment to others by seeking closeness to their parents and by crying when they are separated. Preschoolers seek help to accomplish tasks such as tying their shoes and putting on their clothes, and school-age children ask for help with homework and science projects. As children mature, their dependency needs center more on striving for the recognition and approval of significant others, although some children continue to exhibit instrumental dependency to some extent.

In moderation, these are all healthy signs of dependency, essential not only to socialization but also to the development of autonomy, independence, and competence. Having been allowed to be dependent, the securely attached child can now grow increasingly independent in both thinking and behavior. However, as with all development, certain stresses and situational factors may cause the child to regress and exhibit behaviors that were more characteristic of earlier stages of development. For example, the 3-year-old who considers himself a big boy may want to climb on his mother's lap and pretend he is the baby when a new sister arrives. Similarly, the 5-year-old who has been going to preschool for 2 years without a hitch may refuse to let go of his mother's skirt on the first day of kindergarten.

Too Much Dependency

Problems arise when a child's excessively dependent behavior interferes with the development of autonomy and independence. Very dependent young children may cling excessively to parents and have difficulty leaving home. Some cry and scream when faced with the possibility of going to nursery school or preschool; others insist on sitting on mom's lap during card club. School-age children show their exaggerated dependency needs by wanting to be near the teacher's desk or by holding the teacher's hand as the class goes to recess or lunch. Other signs of overdependency include excessive attention-seeking behaviors such as constant demands to "watch me," "help me," "look at this."

According to Papalia and Olds (1996), the school-age child's overdependence on adults may be the result of insecure attachment. Some children have such strong approval needs that they are constantly asking for reassurance, preferring to ask the opinion of others rather than rely on their own judgment. Sometimes children depreciate themselves in conversations in the hope that significant others will validate them as persons. For example, children may say how awfully they perform at a sport or in a particular subject in the hope that others in their social group will contradict their negative self-assessment. The emotionally dependent child continually seeks support and approval from parents, teachers, and peers. Because peers are less likely to tolerate such dependency, the overly dependent child may withdraw into passivity, refusing to play children's games and preferring the company of adults. Continual overdependence on adults for the completion of tasks and for emotional support may be a sign of a child's lack of confidence in his or her own abilities, which may adversely affect the child's decision making.

Too Little Dependency

A secure and healthy bond is established when an infant comes to expect that the mother or primary caregiver will respond to its cooing or crying and that it will be fed, held, and cuddled. Infant behaviors such as smiling, approaching, embracing, and calling elicit responses in primary caregivers that increase secure attachment (Bowlby, 1969, 1989). This attachment makes children feel safe as they mature and permits them to explore and interact gradually with an ever-widening world. Some children, as a result of a variety of circumstances, do not have their expectations met and therefore fail to develop a secure attachment with their primary caregiver. Ainsworth (1979) found that securely attached infants were able to move away from their primary caregiver to play, whereas insecurely attached infants feared strangers, were upset by separations, and either avoided or resisted their caregivers' attention. She concluded that children need this secure relationship as a basis for the development of competence in the physical and social environment.

According to Clarizio and McCoy (1983), youngsters who fail to learn dependency are frequently difficult to socialize because they have not learned to desire approval from others. Consequently, there is a greater likelihood that these children will be at risk for social and behavioral problems.

Recent research, cited by Vasta, Haith, and Miller (1995), indicates that infants who are maltreated in the first year of life tend to lag in both cognitive and social development and that these problems persist into childhood and adolescence. Children are more at risk for social and emotional problems if they have experienced both *separation* and *deprivation* for an extended period of time. They are also more adversely affected if the separation is the result of a parent's chronic child abuse, alcoholism or drug addiction, or serious mental or physical illness. In some home situations, children do not develop a secure attachment because they are abused and neglected or because an inordinate amount of stress prevents the caregiver from responding to the child's needs. Infants are at special risk if their parents have mental retardation, a mental disturbance, or an addiction; are ill, poor, single, very young, or uneducated; or are burdened by such stresses as unemployment, poor housing, and family and neighborhood violence (these stresses were discussed in more detail in Chapter 1).

Papalia and Olds (1996) note that most children develop normally despite adverse environments. Whether or not a child suffers negative consequences by being separated from its primary caregiver depends on a number of factors including the age of the child, the duration of the separation, and the quality of care given by an alternative caregiver. Also factored in are the strength of the parent-child bond and the amount of support available to help the parent nurture the child. A warm and responsive alternative caregiver can do a great deal to minimize the damaging effects of separation and deprivation, especially if the child is still an infant. Since "babies do not build bonds of attachment solely on the basis of family relationships, but give their affection to those who win it" (Smart & Smart, 1977, p. 153), it is possible for a child to bond with an alternative caregiver.

At-risk families need the support and encouragement of human services professionals who can provide opportunities for parents to learn about children and their needs, to observe good parenting models, and to share their concerns with other parents. By helping parents feel confident in their abilities and giving them opportunities to share their burdens and alleviate stress, counselors can bolster parents' self-esteem, which will have a positive effect on the developing child. Clearly, many child development specialists (Papalia & Olds, 1996) would argue that children are much better off in the care of their families, and with the support and assistance of concerned professionals, there is much that parents can do to improve their capacity to nurture.

Fear and Its Related Responses

My dad scares me sometimes. My sister got punished the other day and he says, "You better be prepared for it too!" (The child illustrates by slamming his fist into his hand.)
—DAVID, age 11

In childhood, fear-related responses include shyness, embarrassment, worry, and anxiety. The subtle differences among these different reactions to fear are not easily distinguishable in children. Because each is an individualized response to a particular experience, it is often difficult for adults to ascertain whether the child's expressions represent fear, worry, or anxiety. The same holds true in trying to determine whether a child's behavior indicates shyness or embarrassment. Although all the various responses to fear are defined and explained, the terms *fear, worry,* and *anxiety* are often used interchangeably when applying the research to counseling strategies for helping children minimize their exaggerated responses to fear.

Fear has been described as an emotional response to an anticipated threat that is focused on a specific object or situation. Fear can be expressed as *shyness* when it is aroused by strange and unfamiliar people and by *embarrassment* when children fear how other people will judge them or their behavior. As children develop imaginative capabilities, they express a less intense fear, known as *worry*, about things that might or might not happen in the future. *Anxiety* is fear that is widespread, generalized, and unfocused (Hurlock, 1978; Spielberger, 1972).

Fear is a reaction to threat in the child's environment that is focused on a specific object, person, or situation. In infancy, innate fear responses are self-protective. As children mature, their perceptions become enriched through experience and they learn, in direct and indirect ways, to be afraid in certain situations (Jersild, 1960; Jersild & Holmes, 1935). As a result of being exposed to a painful experience, being startled, or being overwhelmed, children learn to be afraid of things that did not disturb them at earlier stages of development. For example, if Kim is burned on a hot stove, he may later fear a flame and may come to regard the stove itself as threatening and come to fear it. His fear might even generalize to the kitchen because he associates the setting with a painful experience.

The process by which fear is acquired may also involve indirect and intermediate steps. For example, after falling from a tree, Jasmine gets upset, has a nightmare, and is afraid to go to her bedroom in the dark. Dreaming has placed the accident and its upsetting emotional effects in a setting of darkness. The result is that Jasmine is afraid not of falling from trees, but of the dark; her fear has been generalized to other things and conditions.

Changing susceptibility to fear is interwoven with many other aspects of a child's development. Infants are more likely to express fear reactions to loud noises, unexpected events and strangers, pain and conditions associated with pain, and falling and loss of support. Two- and 3-year-olds express fear of the dark; 4- and 5-year-olds are more afraid of animals, especially snakes and dogs. With the development of imaginative abilities, the child's fears become increasingly focused on imaginary dangers such as monsters and being alone or abandoned. As competitiveness and awareness of status become important to children, children fear ridicule and loss of prestige (Jersild & Holmes, 1935; Morris & Kratochwill, as cited in Papalia & Olds, 1996).

As children develop a wider range of understanding, they are able to recognize the possibilities of danger and fit these apprehensions into images and thoughts. This awareness does not necessarily mean that the child becomes more and more fearful; with a gain in strength and understanding, children are better able to handle some of the situations that once frightened them.

Shyness

Shyness is a fear reaction to people, rather than to objects or situations. In the second half of the first year, children show their fear of strangers by frowning, crying, withdrawing, and clinging to a familiar person for protection. As children mature intellectually and realize that unfamiliar people do not pose a threat to them, their fear of strangers becomes less intense and of shorter duration. Some children, however, experience such intense fear that their shyness gives way to a timidity that persists beyond infancy.

As they get older, shy children may express their discomfort by talking as little as possible, blushing , stuttering, and displaying nervous mannerisms, such as tugging at ears or clothing and shifting from one foot to another. Some children show their shyness by using the *coy response*, which involves bending the head nearly to the shoulder and then raising it slowly to glance or smile at another person. Shy children try to avoid calling attention to themselves and generally speak only when spoken to or to answer a direct question. Although acceptable and even charming in toddlers, shyness can cause problems for school-age children when it affects their ability to establish meaningful social relationships with peers. (Hurlock, 1978).

Embarrassment

Our feelings get hurt in front of other people. Teachers think that just because they are teachers, they can do anything to the kids and I don't think that's fair. We're people too.
—GEORGIA, age 10

Unlike shyness, which is a fear reaction to strangers, embarrassment is a state of self-conscious distress that results from a fear of being judged unfavorably by others. Embarrassment develops at around age 5 or 6 when children have the cognitive ability to understand what others expect of them and to determine whether or not they can meet these expectations. As children grow older, memories of past humiliations may heighten their fear of how others will view them. Having previously suffered painful humiliation, children may develop awkward social behaviors that may provoke more negative feedback from others, thereby incurring additional embarrassment. Like shy children, embarrassed youngsters may blush, show nervousness, stutter, and avoid certain situations that cause discomfort. Unlike shy children, who speak very little, embarrassed children usually speak out and try to explain and justify their behavior in the hope of being viewed in a more favorable light (Hurlock, 1978).

Worry

Suppose you beat up a kid in school and then you hear that the teacher wants to see you. Then you worry!
—TOM, age 10

Worry is a specific, less intense form of fear that involves imaginary dangers, forebodings of what the future may have in store, and apprehensions about what the child has done or might do (Jersild, 1960). As children mature, the nature and intensity of their worries change. Early fears of monsters and other scary creatures are replaced by worries about family, school, and social adequacy as children grow into middle and late childhood.

Family worries center on the health and well-being of parents and siblings, being punished by parents, parents' quarreling, and losing a parent through death or divorce. School-age children are concerned about having a poor report card, finishing homework, and being scolded or punished by the teacher. Failing a test in school continues to be the number-one worry of elementary school children, as it has been for decades (Orton, 1982). As children mature, they are increasingly concerned about social and personal adequacy and worry about doing or saying the wrong thing, being ridiculed by others, and losing friends. As children approach puberty, their worries become associated with the developmental concerns of adolescence.

The content, frequency, and intensity of children's worries are influenced not only by the child's age, but also by the significant experiences in the child's life. Apparently, the societal and family concerns identified and discussed in Chapter 1 have had considerable impact on the worries of children in the 1990s. *Violence* was the top worry of 758 urban, suburban, and rural 10- to 17-year-olds who participated in a 1993 *Newsweek*/CDF poll. More than half of the youngsters worried that a loved one would become a victim of a violent crime. Although inner-city and minority children were the most threatened by violence, only one-third of the rural and small-town children felt "very safe" walking alone in their neighborhoods after dark. Other worries expressed by the children included an adult losing a job, being able to afford the necessities of life, a family member having a drug problem, and a breakup in the family (CDF, 1994).

> *"Lots of kids worry that their dad's going to beat them up when they get home."*
> *"I'm afraid that I'm going to do something wrong...a lot."*
> *"Fail a test and people think you're dumb."*
> *"Kids worry about their dad drinking...and beating up on their mom and them."*
> *"Kids worry about who likes them."*
> *"Mom and dad getting a divorce...you love them and can't choose."*
> —Quotes from children, expressing their worries

Anxiety

Anxiety is a vague, generalized fear response to an anticipated rather than an existing threat in the environment. Unlike worry, which is related to a specific event, anxiety usually has no readily identifiable source. An anxious child feels apprehensive and uneasy and may have a sense of foreboding about some future event over which he or she has no control. Sometimes anxiety is accompanied by feelings of helplessness as the child is unable to find a solution to the problem.

Because anxiety depends on the ability to imagine situations, it occurs later than fear. Children experience anxiety during the early school years, especially from the fourth to the sixth grade, and it usually becomes more intense during puberty (Hurlock, 1978). Whether children continue to experience anxiety as adolescents depends a great deal on how much pressure is placed on them to achieve, whether the expectations of parents and teachers are realistic, and their individual predisposition to anxiety. Although too much anxiety can be debilitating, a moderate amount can motivate children to achieve and can facilitate a child's social adjustment and promote problem-solving skills.

Intense worry about living up to the expectations of parents, teachers, and peers promotes self-doubt and predisposes children to generalized feelings of inadequacy, thus setting the stage for anxiety. Certain parent-child interactions may also contribute to anxiety in children: having an anxious parent or sibling as a model, growing up in an overpermissive atmosphere with few rules or opportunities to cope with stress, experiencing excessive punishment for not meeting expectations, and being used as a confidant by parents. When adults make unrealistic demands for perfectionism, exert unreasonable pressure to perform, and present children with problems that are beyond their ability to comprehend and to solve, they contribute to anxiety in children.

Anxious children are often lonely and unhappy. They are especially sensitive to criticism and are very concerned about what others think of them. For this reason, they may prefer the company of adults and be overly compliant to authority. Children may express anxiety as depression, nervousness, irritability, and mood swings, which include anger. Anxious children may experience restlessness, which interferes with sleeping and contributes to constant snacking. Some children mask anxiety by acting out or showing off, complaining of boredom, and withdrawing into fantasy as a means of coping or escaping from stressful situations.

Anger and Its Related Responses

Anger, like fear, is a primary emotion in childhood; but, unlike fear, anger involves lashing out rather than withdrawing. *Anger* is a universal emotional response to a frustrating situation, and it can be expressed as aggression, jealousy, and rivalry. Situations that give rise to anger in children include interfering with their movements and activities, thwarting their wishes or plans, and a variety of other irritations. Toddlers usually express anger against any form of restraint that interferes with their desire for autonomy by crying, yelling, throwing things, and wiggling away from the parent. As children balance the need for independence with the restraints of conformity, their anger is expressed as aggression. *Aggression* is defined as a more controlled and productive expression of anger, which can help children solve problems and contributes to the development of a sense of initiative. As children grow and develop, healthy expressions of aggression contribute to assertiveness, competitiveness, and self-confidence.

Goodenough's classic study *Anger in Young Children* (1931) indicated that anger outbursts are commonly triggered by physical discomfort and needs for attention in infancy, by toilet training during the second and third years of life, and by conflicts with peers in the years immediately following toddlerhood. The frequency and intensity with which children experience anger vary considerably from child to child. Much depends on individual differences in ability to tolerate frustration, the physical and emotional state of the child at the time, and the nature of the anger-provoking event. Children's reactions to anger vary also. One child may show nothing more than a mild annoyance; another may react by biting, kicking, or punching; and a third may withdraw and pout.

Aggression

There are basically two types of aggression—hostile and instrumental—and both can be expressed physically or verbally. *Hostile aggression* is an attack on another person with the motive to inflict injury or destruction. *Instrumental aggression* is an attack used to acquire or retrieve an object, territory, or privilege. Children utilize hostile aggression in a purposeful attempt to hurt another person when they beat another child as a response to being teased. Instrumental aggression is used when a child shoves another child in order to be first in line. Hartup (1974) maintains that it is not always easy to distinguish between the two types of aggression because one behavior may serve both goals.

APPLICATIONS TO COUNSELING

The following suggestions may help parents and professionals who work with children to reduce fear-related responses in children.

• *Have realistic expectations of children.* Consider not only their age and developmental level but also their abilities, needs, and interests. The parent or teacher who is never satisfied with the child's performance and continually raises the standard produces a child who is vulnerable to feelings of guilt, anxiety, and inadequacy.

• *Structure activities and set limits* for children so that they can feel secure. Overpermissiveness on the part of both parents and teachers contributes to anxiety in children because they are unsure about what is expected of them.

• *Provide firm discipline* rather than physical punishment, sarcasm, or verbal tongue-lashings that promote generalized feelings of inadequacy. Frequent and intense punishment is commonly associated with anxiety, and children learn that not measuring up to expectations can bring verbal and physical punishment, ridicule, and humiliation from parents, teachers, and peers.

• *Be a good role model.* Children learn to be anxious when they interact daily with overanxious adults or siblings. Parents and teachers should avoid pointing out every conceivable danger to children. Constantly admonishing children "Don't play near the flowers, you'll get stung by bees!" "Don't jump off that step, you'll break something!" or "Don't go to the playground, you'll get kidnapped!" may increase some children's anxiety and encourage others to prove you wrong.

• *Give appropriate responsibilities.* Some children are asked to perform tasks that grossly overestimate their capabilities. This is especially evident when parents place adult burdens on children by using them as confidants or when they expect children to fulfill the role of a parent in the household. Children become overwhelmed and anxious when confronted with problems they do not understand, cannot cope with, and cannot solve. The same holds true when children are given tasks that are impossible for them to complete.

• *Use praise sparingly* and only when it is well deserved. Shy children are often embarrassed by praise because they don't feel worthy of it.

• *Respect children's fears.* Never use a child's fear to discipline or control the child's behavior. Try to help children manage their fears and do what is necessary to diminish fear-provoking situations.

• *Encourage children to share their worries* and help them ward off anxiety with effective coping skills.

Preschoolers show more aggressive behavior than first- and second-graders, indicating that aggression declines as children get older and respond to effective outer controls on their behavior. Between the ages of 2 and 6 years, children conflict over toys and space and show more instrumental aggression. First- and second-graders use more hostile aggression, attacking each other's self-esteem with verbal aggression (Papalia & Olds, 1996). School-age children generally resort to name calling instead of overt physical attacks, and older children are more inclined to hold grudges longer and to sulk (Hartup, 1974).

A review of the research by Wicks-Nelson and Israel (1991) suggests that children model aggressive behavior that they see in their homes, in their schools, and in the mass media. Children who grow up in families that encourage fighting as a way to settle arguments are more likely to show physical aggression in interactions with their peers. Both boys and girls who are permitted to show more anger in social situations generally express more aggression. Similarly, children whose aggression is rewarded are more likely to use aggression as a way to get what they want.

Parental and peer approval serve as sources of positive reinforcement for aggressive actions. In the same way, children who are successful in keeping others from teasing, taunting, or hurting them because they strike the first blow are being reinforced also; thus the child's tendency to physically attack or shout is strengthened and continues as a pattern for settling conflicts (Clarizio & McCoy, 1983; Wicks-Nelson & Israel, 1991).

Aggression does has positive effects on the development of children, for without it, they would be at a serious disadvantage in coping with the demands of modern life. In healthy doses, aggression contributes to assertiveness, competitiveness, and self-confidence, which are important to achievement and socialization. Children who are considered either violent and uncontrolled, exceptionally passive or timid, or passive-aggressive are more likely to concern parents and teachers.

Uncontrolled hostile aggression   Although all people experience anger, some children express it as violence or *uncontrolled aggression*. A highly active child who does not receive outside control in the form of limits but is consistently exposed to situations that promote hostile feelings may come to enjoy being destructive when other forms of satisfaction are not available. At the other extreme, if outside controls are so strict that they even thwart efforts at exploration, inner controls may be stifled or never develop. Either situation can lead to violent expressions of anger. When a baby is treated cruelly, he or she is likely to make these forms of behavior part of his or her own (refer to the section on child abuse in Chapter 3). When given appropriate choices within the framework of firm limits and treated with love and respect by family members, even the highly active, aggressive infant can gradually develop his or her own internal controls (Lourie, as cited in Smart & Smart, 1977).

Passive aggression   Some children cope with their anger through veiled maneuvers such as stubbornness, sullenness, and pouting. In contrast to the child whose behavior is characterized by openly aggressive behaviors such as breaking things and hurting people, the *passive-aggressive* child chooses to obstruct and resist. Passive-aggressive children resist productive accomplishment by dawdling, procrastinating, forgetting, and performing tasks that are sloppy and incomplete. The credo of passive-aggressive children and adults is to sabotage all efforts at accomplishment, including their own. Such children want freedom and resent being told what to do or having demands made of them, yet they cling to dependency. They appear irresponsible and lazy to parents and teachers. They are very critical of others, most likely as a result of poor self-esteem, yet they are often overly sensitive to criticism by others (Clarizio & McCoy, 1983).

Submissiveness Because healthy amounts of aggression are needed to make decisions, solve problems, and get things done, children who overconform to rules and regulations may not be assertive enough to deal with the problems of life. Aggression expressed as assertive behavior implies a sense of initiative more than anger (Smart & Smart, 1977). Children who are encouraged in the preschool years to actively explore their environment and who are not too restricted by punishing guilt learn to manipulate and control their environment and to cope with frustration. Children who are more passive have a tendency to acquiesce to or withdraw from frustrating situations, rather than confronting them. During the elementary school years, this passivity may lead to avoidance of sports, retreat and withdrawal from peers, and timidity in social situations (Clarizio & McCoy, 1983).

Passive children may also be overly dependent on adults for attention and affection, further distancing themselves from the peer group. Submissive children, through their behavior, seem to invite others to take advantage of them, and they may be rejected, victimized, or exploited by peers. They allow others to "walk all over them," which further diminishes their self-esteem and heightens their resentment. Hidden resentment may be expressed as fear, embarrassment, and self-deprecation. Passive children are often poor decision makers, lack self-confidence in their own abilities, and are very concerned about what others think of them. If allowed to continue, a lack of assertiveness could predispose the growing child to abuse as an adult.

In summary, healthy amounts of aggression are needed for assertiveness, competitiveness, and self-confidence. Research indicates that children who are continually exposed to anger-producing situations and do not have any outer limits placed on their hostility are likely to grow up with uncontrollable aggression. Conversely, children who are punished at every turn do not develop internal control of their behavior either. Both methods of childrearing encourage the development of uncontrolled aggression. The expression of unbridled aggression is not socially acceptable and will likely cause problems for the child as he or she struggles to relate to others. Although uncontrolled aggression gets the most attention, passive-aggressive behavior and passivity can have important consequences to the child's overall development. Children who are too passive often lack self-esteem and may unwittingly invite rejection and victimization.

Jealousy and Rivalry

> "Sisters are different from brothers. All sisters are rotten."
> "In sharing, a brother flunks out. It is better not to have one."
> "A sister is a pest."
> —A child's view of sibling relationships, from McGrath & Scobey (1970a, 1970b)

Jealousy is a fear of being thwarted in the attempt to be loved best, and *rivalry* implies that a person is in competition with others to be first—to win or to possess what only one can obtain. *Sibling rivalry* is the classic struggle between brothers and sisters for the affection of their parents and a position of favor within the family. It is deeply rooted in human nature, is present in varying degrees in almost every culture on earth, and may continue into adulthood. Certain family interactions foster rivalry and jealousy among siblings. Comparing siblings unfavorably with one another, showing favoritism for one child or rejection of another, or emphasizing competition over cooperation can intensify sibling rivalry and resentment, sometimes with hurtful consequences for both parents and children.

Sibling rivalry is not a recent phenomenon, and some of today's sibling struggles pale when compared with those told in the Bible. In the Book of Genesis, stories of jealousy, resentment, and competition are tragically played out. Cain lost his special place to his brother Abel and rose up against him; Jacob secured his twin brother Esau's birthright by trickery, beginning a family feud that lasts for generations; and Joseph's coat of many colors, a sign of his father's love, provokes Joseph's brothers into faking his death and selling him into slavery.

Children want to be first in the affections of their parents, and they seek to gain power over siblings in order to place first. The firstborn, who knows what it was like to receive all the attention and affection of parents, wants very much to retain the spotlight. Jealousy is likely to occur when something disrupts the amount of attention and affection the child receives from parents. One event in family life likely to precipitate jealousy is the birth of a new baby. The firstborn, even though he or she has been prepared for the event, may view the newborn as an interloper who has come to steal the parents' affection and attention. A study by Dunn and Kendrick (1982) indicated that mothers were more negative to their firstborns following the birth of a second child, restraining them more and playing with them less. The older child often reacts to this change by suggesting ways to get rid of the newborn or by acting out aggression with toys, rough play, attacking the mother, whining, or withdrawing.

When Mrs. S. brought her newborn son home two days before Christmas, 5-year-old Allison wanted to hold him. She had been carefully prepared for the new baby and was allowed to hold him and give him kisses. After the Christmas vacation, Allison had to go to kindergarten while her mother, on a leave from her job, stayed home with the baby. One day Allison said, "Mom, I know he's nice and everything, but could we take him back now?"

Jeb's mom had just brought his new brother home from the hospital. Because Jeb was only 1 year old, his mother thought that he wouldn't feel any jealousy toward the baby. One day she discovered that Jeb had filled the baby's bassinet with toys while the infant was still in it. The baby had narrowly escaped injury as trucks, cars, and other toys were dumped in on top of him.

Later, as siblings get older and are able to defend themselves, jealousy may take the forms of bickering, fighting, teasing, and "stealing" toys (Dunn & Munn, 1985). As second-born children grow up, they are often the offenders. They knock down blocks, bite and kick, or otherwise wreak havoc on the firstborn's play time. Older siblings are expected to care for and protect younger siblings, and when they don't, parents may become more protective of the younger child.. Older children often complain about caring for younger ones, and younger siblings complain about being bossed around by older brothers and sisters.

APPLICATIONS TO COUNSELING

The following suggestions are offered as ways to help parents, teachers, and counselors deal with anger and the various aspects of aggression.

- *Show your love.* Most parents, teachers, and counselors genuinely love and appreciate children. Sometimes, however, it is difficult for adults to express their caring for children, particularly when they feel overwhelmingly stressed. Express interest and concern in concrete ways by taking the time to focus on the positive things children do. For example, you could say, "You have told a beautiful story" or "That was a kind thing that you did today."
- A *sensible, flexible approach* to child behavior works best. When controls are too rigid, children can develop extreme behavior. Sometimes humor can diffuse a situation that could otherwise be troublesome. For example, one mother who caught her children painting each other's faces took their picture instead of scolding them.
- *Don't set children up.* We often provoke children to anger and defiance. In other words, it is best not to use the "don't put beans in your ears!" approach. Constantly admonishing children not to do certain things is a virtual guarantee that some will try them.
- *Learn to handle your own anger.* Children who watch adults kick tires, slam doors, break things, or hurt other people learn firsthand how to express their anger. Coaches who scream at their players for fighting on the field are sending the wrong message about self-control. The father who tells his son to quit hitting the other children but beats his wife is showing his son how to express anger. The old axiom "Actions speak louder than words" certainly applies when one wants to help a child achieve self-control.
- *Avoid physical punishment.* When aggressive behavior is modeled for children, it teaches them that it is all right to be aggressive and hurt people as long as you are an adult. Aggression against the child produces more frustration, which in turn provokes more anger, which leads to more aggression.
- *Disapprove of hostile aggression* and put a stop to it in a firm manner. The tactics used will depend on the situation and the child. Sometimes it is necessary to hold a child until he or she is able to regain control.
- *Divert the child's attention.* Rather than get into a confrontation that is going to escalate into an aggressive act, many parents and teachers are able to divert the child's attention and diffuse the anger-provoking situation. .
- *Promote decision making.* Allow the child to make limited choices appropriate for his or her age (such as, Do you want peas or beans for dinner?). Avoid asking "Do you want peas for dinner?" because the child may say "No," leaving the caregiver stuck with a decision that is not in the child's best interest.

Jealousy and rivalry are often accentuated when children are blended into new family configurations such as stepfamilies. The following is an example of feelings of jealousy that a child might express toward a new family member.

Natalie, age 9, lived with her mother and stepfather in Florida. She spent Christmas at her paternal grandmother's Pennsylvania home, along with her father, stepmother, stepsister, and half-brother. During the visit, Natalie became

Applications to Counseling

Parenting is a very difficult job, especially given the changes in family and in society discussed in Chapter 1. Some of these changes leave less time to attend to children and less involvement by both parents. The following suggestions are designed to help counselors help parents alter certain types of family interactions that may trigger exaggerated feelings of sibling rivalry and jealousy.

• *Accept and appreciate each child in the family* as a unique individual. Look for strengths and remind the child of these often. Favoring one child over another intensifies jealousy and rivalry and often has negative effects on the favored child as well.

• *Avoid comparing siblings.* Children who can't measure up to more capable siblings may develop resentment and hostility, or they may retreat into hopelessness.

• *Promote a spirit of cooperation rather than competition in the family.* This goes for parents as well as siblings. Some children feel they can never live up to what other members of their family have achieved.

• *Allow the child to talk out his or her feelings* of jealousy, frustration, and anger regarding the actions of brothers and sisters. Set limits on how the child can act out these feelings.

• *Prepare siblings for the birth of a new baby.* Encourage parents to assure siblings that they are loved and to set aside quality time to be with them.

more and more irritated as her 4-year-old stepsister used the term *grandma* to refer to Natalie's biological grandmother. Finally, she couldn't tolerate the competition for her grandmother's attention any longer and admonished the preschooler with, "Can't you say Linda? Don't say *grandma*, say *Linda*—L-I-N-D-A."

Despite the fact that competition, jealousy, and resentment are often present in sibling interactions, a study by Abramovitch, Corter, Pepler, and Stanhope (1986) supported the notion that siblings care for and look out for one another, do nice things for each other, and are generally more affectionate than rivalrous and hateful. Lending credence to the old axiom that "blood is thicker than water," Furman and Buhrmester (1985) reported that children viewed their relationships with their siblings as more reliable and more important than their relationships with their friends.

> "Outside I do not like my sister at all. But deep inside I like her a little."
> "A brother is nice some of the time and a rat the other some of the time."
> "A brother is lovebul."
> —A child's view of the sibling bond, from McGrath & Scobey (1970a, 1970b).

Guidelines for Referral

Because most parents, teachers, and clinicians have their own set of internalized criteria for evaluating the appropriateness of child behavior, it is often difficult to know when to refer a child for help. Parents—who are subjected to the conflicting advice of the professional "baby raisers," often lack knowledge about child development, and have few opportunities for peer group comparisons—are understandably confused about when to seek counseling. With the latest round of self-help books and "how to" manuals, it would appear that every child is at risk for something. Teachers, who are sensitized to the needs of children, are often the first to refer children and their families for help. The child who is disrupting the classroom environment is usually at the top of the list. Such referrals are usually made to the elementary school counselor, school psychologist, home-school visitor, or school social worker, whose task it is to evaluate the seriousness of the child's problem. Members of the helping team in schools often refer the more serious cases to clinicians in private practice or in clinic settings. Evaluating whether a behavior is appropriate or not depends a great deal on the judgment and experience of the person making the determination. Beginning clinicians, who are fresh out of classes in child psychopathology, may see more deviance in a child's behavior than would a seasoned veteran, who has worked with many children and knows that nearly every child experiences some problems in the normal course of growing up. Parents, teachers, counselors, clinicians, and all those who work with children might consider the following questions in deciding whether a child is experiencing a normal behavior problem or one that requires some type of counseling help.

The following questions adhere to established assessment criteria related to appropriateness, frequency, duration, course, intensity, and impairment.

1. *Is the child's behavior appropriate for his or her age and developmental level?* Allowing for individual differences and for developmental lags, consider whether the child is able to manage the appropriate developmental tasks for his or her particular age range (early, middle, and later childhood).

> Masha, a healthy 4-year-old, is playing in a sandbox and wets her pants because she is too busy to go in the house. Is that behavior normal or abnormal given her age and developmental level? What if Sergio, at age 7, is engrossed in building model airplanes and wets his pants? Is that appropriate behavior for his age?

2. *Is the child's behavior appropriate considering the circumstances?* Is the child's behavior an expected reaction to the situation? For example, what if a child, embarrassed by the peer group, blushes? What if a provoked child fights back? Are these normal responses? What about the unexpected reactions? Sometimes a child overreacts, underreacts, or doesn't react at all. These unexpected reactions give clues to the child's stability.

> When Phuong's father committed suicide, he never talked about it. He did not seem sad; he did not cry. He did not react in any way. He continued to talk about his father as though he were still alive and even volunteered information about him in conversations with his teacher. Is Phuong's response appropriate for a child who has just lost his father?

3. *How frequently does the child display the problem behavior?* Development is not a smooth progression, and children often regress or slip back to behaviors that were characteristic of a previous level. Counselors, parents, and teachers need to be aware of how often the child has this problem.

Masha, our healthy 4-year-old, has wet her pants on three different occasions in the last year. On each occasion, Masha has been engrossed in play and explains to her mother, "I forgot." Sergio, at age 7, wets himself when he gets engrossed in an activity, when he is anxious or excited about something, or when he is around other children. Does either child need to be referred? If so, which one and why?

4. *What is the duration of the problem?* Determining how long the problem has lasted will help the parent, teacher, or counselor decide whether a referral is necessary. Many developmental problems seem to disappear as quickly as they came. Specific fears are a good example of a normal developmental problem.

Sara, age 4, is afraid of the dark and refuses to go to sleep without a night light. She says, "There's a monster under my bed." Her parents spend time reading to her and talking about her feelings. They even shine a flashlight under her bed to show her that there are no monsters. Now that Sara is almost 6, she knows that there are no monsters under her bed but she still wants the night light on. Should Sara be referred because of her fears?

5. *Has there been a sudden change in the child's behavior?* It is important to determine whether the behavior of concern is a sudden departure from the child's normal pattern of behavior. If so, the counselor or therapist must look to the child's immediate environment to see what might be causing this sudden change. Sometimes sudden changes of behavior are indicative of abuse or family disruptions caused by death, divorce, or domestic violence.

Josh successfully went through toilet training and was one of the lucky toddlers who remained dry during the day and at night. However, when Josh was 6, his father committed suicide, and now Josh lives alone with his mother. Ever since his dad died, Josh has had problems with diurnal and nocturnal enuresis. He dreams that he is arguing with his dad and then his dad shoots himself. In Josh's dreams, his father is angry with him for wetting the bed. Does Josh's sudden change in behavior following his father's suicide warrant a referral? If so, what should be the focus of the intervention?

6. *Is the behavior interfering with the child's overall functioning?* Is the child suffering somehow as a result of the problem? If so, to what degree is the child's functioning affected? Is the behavior causing the child to be rejected by agemates, preventing the child from benefiting from school instruction, blocking the healthy expression of emotion, or interfering with the child's happiness? Perhaps the behavior is affecting only one area of the child's development; perhaps it is affecting all areas.

Sergio, at age 7, has wet himself on numerous occasions during the day and at night. He doesn't play with other children because he is afraid he will have "an accident." His parents will not allow him to sleep over at anyone's house because they fear he will wet the bed. Is Sergio's problem interfering enough in his life to necessitate a referral? If so, why?

In conclusion, parents, teachers, and counselors need to know when a child's behavior signals a serious inability to master a particular developmental task. Because all children will pause temporarily to address unresolved problems or even retreat to the previous developmental task, it is not easy to decide when intervention is needed. Hopefully these guidelines will assist practitioners and parents alike in deciding when children need some extra support in their journey to healthy growth and development.

INSIGHTS AND IMPLICATIONS

To understand child development is to comprehend the interaction between the child and the environmental forces that shape his or her growth. Each child possesses a unique set of innate abilities; the characteristics of gender, race, and ethnicity; and the potential to establish effective and long-lasting relationships with other people. Significant others, such as family, teachers, and friends, exert a powerful influence on the child and are influenced by the child as well. In addition to family and significant others, both positive and negative social, cultural, political, moral, and economic forces shape a particular child's life at any given moment in time.

At each stage in the life cycle, children face predictable and particular issues that represent the coming together of the forces that influence their development. At each stage of development, children are constantly moving forward, gaining new readiness and acquiring new skills. Some do it quite rapidly, others more slowly. As children develop, they achieve a sense of self—a sense of who they are and what they can do. Whether this sense of self is positive or negative will depend a great deal on how well the child has mastered the physical, intellectual, emotional, and social milestones of development. Children who successfully master the psychosocial tasks of childhood (Erikson, 1950) will grow up with the capacity to love and be loved and to trust in others. They will balance their need to explore with their need to conform, achieve a healthy sense of initiative without too much punishing guilt, and develop a sense of competence to achieve and to produce.

Some children master the developmental tasks with ease, others with difficulty. As children travel the developmental road, which is not smooth under the best of circumstances, they often pause to rework old problems before they can continue. These regressions are common in the face of many of life's stresses. Some children are diminished by the failure to master a particular developmental task and need a little extra help to get back on the road to healthy development. All children have the capacity for healthy growth and development, but some need additional supports from their families and other significant adults. Human services professionals can help children and their parents ensure that each makes a positive contribution to the other's development as a person. Children leave their mark on the world, and the world, with all its power and influence, leaves its mark on children and on the future.

WISDOM ACCORDING TO ORTON

- *All children are different. Delight in their differences and dwell on their strengths.*
- *As children travel the developmental road, they meet and surmount obstacles. Be there to cheer them on.*

- *Respect the thoughts and feelings of children and their parents.*
- *Listen to the emotions that children express. They are telling you something.*
- *Nobody is perfect. If you have any doubts about this, take out your old report cards.*
- *Try to be the kind of person you wanted to talk to when you were a child.*
- *Approach your work with a sense of humor.*

ORTON'S PICKS

Elkind, D. (1988). *The hurried child: Growing up too fast too soon.* (Rev. ed.). Reading, MA: Addison-Wesley.

Elkind tells us how the push for "competence" has burdened children with pressures to "achieve." This "too much, too soon" philosophy has fourth-graders dieting to fit into designer jeans and children taking on the role of confidants to their troubled parents. The author warns that forcing kids to grow up too soon robs them of the joy and freedom of childhood.

Lauter-Klatell, N. (Ed.). (1991). *Readings in child development.* Mountain View, CA: Mayfield.

This collection of journal articles presents a variety of viewpoints about topics in child development. Contemporary issues related to the development of infants and toddlers, preschoolers, school-age children, and adolescents are discussed. Titles of special interest include: "The Day-Care Generation," "Disclosing Sexual Abuse," "Why Big Bird Can't Teach Calculus," "A Society That Promotes Drug Abuse," "Race, Class, Gender and School," and "Bicultural Conflict."

Santrock, J. W. (1994). *Child development* (6th ed.). Dubuque, IA: William C. Brown.

In this well-written and interesting text, John Santrock covers the development of children from birth through adolescence. Special chapters on self and identity, gender, families, and the importance of friends and play offer the reader a broad view of child development. Each chapter offers "Sociocultural Worlds of Children" and includes "Perspectives on Parenting and Education."

CHAPTER 3   *The Vulnerable Child*

> *Children are the most fragile members of a culture, the ones*
> *most affected by trouble in the family or upheavals in society.*
> —Naomi Feigelson Chase

As we approach the 21st century, an increasing number of children and families must cope with problems relating to the family's changing roles, structures and lifestyles and to the increasingly violent nature of life in the United States. Many problems that today's children face, such as living apart from a divorced parent, being homeless, being born addicted to cocaine, being threatened with a gun at school, and getting AIDS were either relatively uncommon or unknown just three decades ago. Other problems, such as child abuse, incest, parental alcoholism, and death of a parent, have affected children's lives for centuries. Because it is not possible to cover all the crises that affect children and their parents, discussion in this chapter is limited to child abuse and neglect, alcoholism, divorce, illness, and death, problems that seriously affect the growth and well-being of the developing child.

The vulnerable child in this chapter has been diverted from the road leading to healthy development by such forces as child abuse and neglect, parental divorce and separation, alcoholism, illness, and death. What impact these crises have on individual children's development will depend on their perception of events, their individual personality characteristics, and the strength of their coping skills. Children who have been weakened by many other crises and whose development has been slowed or halted in the past will need more time and more support to get back on track. How quickly and to what extent children recover and begin their journey anew depends on the guidance and support provided by their parents, family members, teachers, and members of the helping professions. An important part of the child's support system is a warm, caring, and effective counselor.

CHILD ABUSE AND NEGLECT

> *Child abuse is a serious social problem that goes back to the beginnings of history*
> —Chase (1975–1976)

Infanticide and abandonment have long been ways to deal with children whom societies could not care for or feed. Children, the most helpless among us, have always been vulnerable in times of social upheaval and political crisis. When civil disorder erupted in Europe in the 1500s, children were the chief victims. Massive unemployment was followed by rioting, begging, and looting. Bands of child robbers roamed the streets, stealing to survive. In an effort to stop this "crime in the streets," private charity for the poor was eliminated and a thinly disguised punishment of the indigent known as "work relief" was initiated. This program was the forerunner of modern welfare and the beginning of forced labor for children (Chase, 1975–1976).

The new work relief forced impoverished children to labor first at home, then in the public workhouses, and finally under conditions of semi-slavery in the 19th-century English textile mills. In England in the late 1770s and early 1780s, relief work at home or in the public workhouse gave way to factory labor, especially in the textile industry, where children were preferred because they were more manageable and had a lighter touch at the loom. The employment and apprenticing of children to work in factories led to new kinds of abuses. Poor children as young as 4 and 5, who lived in the public workhouses and had no parents to protect them were forced to work as many as 16 hours a day; some were chained to prevent their escape. "They were starved and beaten; many died from occupational diseases; and some committed suicide. Few who worked in that environment lived very long" (Chase, 1975–1976, p. 56).

The first child-labor reform movement started in England and resulted in the First Factory Act in 1802, which broke up the pauper apprentice system. The law reduced the number of hours a child could work from 16 to 12 hours a day, and employment of children under the age of 9 was forbidden (Watson & Lindgren, 1979). Interestingly, the law did not protect children whose parents were living because the government did not want to interfere with traditional parental rights. Therefore, "children whose parents allowed them or sent them to work in the mills still worked long hours, were beaten—often brutally—and sometimes dipped headfirst into barrels of cold water to keep them awake" (Chase, 1975–1976, p. 56).

Shocking cases of child abuse and cruelty went largely unnoticed and unpunished, and parents could treat their children any way they wanted. Lefrancois (1990) cited an example of a case brought before the British courts in 1761. Ann Martin was sentenced to two years in Newgate Prison for habitually poking out the eyes of the children she took begging. Her case is unusual in the fact that the children whose eyes she removed were someone else's children; if they had been hers, she wouldn't have been punished!

During the same period, poor urban children in England were often bound out as chimney sweepers who worked night and day and were exposed to all kinds of brutality. Many home dwellers did not let their chimneys cool first, so children were burned as they climbed inside. Supervisors often built fires under the children to force them up a chimney faster. These children frequently died early from cancer of the scrotum and from pulmonary consumption, which was so common it became known as the "chimney sweep's disease" (Chase, 1975–1976; Radbill, 1980).

The situation was no better in the United States. Except for infants, slave children labored in the fields and homes of their masters. Their mothers had no time off to nurse or nurture them. "Frederick Douglass could not remember seeing his mother until he was seven" (Coontz, 1992, p. 11). The early colonists, who sanctioned the beating and whipping of children as a legitimate form of punishment, had mixed feelings about the orphaned poor. Their feelings of obligation took second place to a stronger wish to spare themselves the costs of their keep. Orphans were often auctioned off to whomever would care for them at the least expense to the town treasury (Chase, 1975–1976; Coontz, 1992).

Many immigrant children on poor relief were thought to have deviant qualities that were un-American and so were taken from their parents on the pretext that they *might* become delinquent. By 1870, child-welfare organizations in New York sent 48,000 neglected paupers, whom they viewed as predelinquent criminals, to foster placement in the western states where they could learn "rural values" (Chase, 1975–1976). The "child savers" of Boston sent children to work on Midwest farms for the same reasons. Many of these children were actually auctioned off to farmers who exploited and abused them (Holloran, as cited in Coontz, 1992).

In the United States, a significant increase in child labor occurred during the last third of the 19th century. Some children worked at home in crowded tenement sweatshops producing cigars, dresses, and artificial flowers for Victorian "ladies." As the 1800s were drawing to a close, child labor and the abuse of children in industry and in tenement sweatshops came to the attention of middle-class reformers through newspaper accounts by muckraking journalists. Eventually, legislation to end child labor was enacted. Concern for the plight of a badly abused young girl in the 1870s led to the formation of the New York Society for the Prevention of Cruelty to Children (Coontz, 1992; Walker, Bonner, & Kaufman, 1988).

At about the same time, the inhumane conditions under which children lived and worked shocked the 19th-century reformers and provided the impetus for the child-welfare movement and the juvenile court system. The "child savers," as Anthony Platt (1969) called them, were mostly rich, well-educated, well-traveled women who believed that social evils such as poverty, exploitation, and crime could be corrected by treating the victim. Part of the treatment was to remove neglected and destitute children from their "deviant" and "depraved" families and place them in institutions where they could be either saved from a life of crime or "rehabilitated."

It is difficult to ignore the element of punitiveness and hypocrisy that existed behind these early efforts of intervention and prevention. Just as the children in the 1500s were victimized, abused, and exploited by work relief programs under the guise of preventing them from becoming lazy rogues, children in the 18th century were forced to labor for capitalism under the guise of making work for idle hands (Chase, 1975–1976). Later, the religious zeal of the reformers, in their efforts to "save" children from a life of crime, diminished the civil liberties and privacy of youth through forced institutionalization (Platt, 1969). Much of the same motivation for reform continues as we near the 21st century.

In 1995, children are still pawns in a political chess game. New legislation before Congress, if enacted, would cut nutritional programs for infants and children, replace welfare with "workfare," and ask that private charities once again take care of poor and indigent women and children. Once again we are faced with "crime in the streets," and once again there is a move to legislate morality. Once again we are trying to prevent children from growing up lazy by putting their idle parents to work; and once again there is a move by modern-day "child savers" to remove destitute and neglected children from their "unfit" mothers and place them in orphanages, where they will be "saved" from the bad influences that surround them. And, once again, it is difficult to ignore the punitiveness and hypocrisy of it all.

Definition and Scope

In 1962, Dr. C. Henry Kempe and his associates first identified the *battered child syndrome* as a frequent and often unsuspected cause of serious injury or death in children (Kempe, Silverman, Steele, Droegemueller & Silver, 1962). Today, *child maltreatment* is defined as "behavior towards another person, which (a) is outside the norms of conduct, and (b) entails a substantial risk of causing physical or emotional harm" (National Research Council, [NRC] 1993, p. 59). This definition encompasses a broad spectrum of acts of abuse and neglect by parents and caregivers. These actions and omissions can be intentional or unintentional. Physical abuse includes inflicting injuries such as burns, lacerations, fractures, and any other form of physical harm that lasts more than 48 hours (Walker et al., 1988). It can also include extreme physical punishment, close confinement, and Munchausen by proxy, a rare form of abuse wherein an adult feigns or induces illness in a healthy child to get attention and support from the medical community (NRC, 1993). Unlike physical abuse, which can sometimes be rationalized as deserved or at least as serving a need for attention (Wilbur, 1984), emotional or psychological abuse attacks the child's self-worth and cannot be rationalized. Emotional abuse consists of demeaning, denigrating, or ridiculing a child at any time, but especially when attention is focused on something the child has created or accomplished (Kluft, 1984). It also encompasses acts that place the child in situations of continual threat, fear, or terror. The broad term *neglect* encompasses acts of omission, which Fontana (1984) described as "emotional neglect or maternal deprivation, physical neglect, including malnutrition, inappropriate clothing, lack of supervision, medical neglect, educational neglect and abandonment" (p. 736).

According to data from *The State of America's Children* (CDF, 1994), the number of reported incidents of child abuse and neglect tripled between 1980 and 1992. More than 2.9 million cases of suspected child abuse were reported to child protection agencies in 1992, and half of the reports involved neglect. Many child abuse experts believe that numerous incidents, particularly of sexual abuse and psychological maltreatment, go largely unreported and that nearly 3 million abuse reports are only the "tip of the iceberg."

Whether the increases in child abuse reports are a result of the public's growing sensitivity to the problem of child maltreatment, practitioners' increased familiarity with reporting mandates, increasing stress on families, or a combination of all these factors is difficult to determine. The Children's Defense Fund cites increasing economic stress on parents and crises caused by drugs and violence as primary factors in the current epidemic of child abuse and neglect. Experts point to mothers' increasing use of crack cocaine as a factor in the large number of reports of abandoned and neglected infants (CDF, 1994).

Who Is Mistreated?

A 1991 study by the National Center for Child Abuse and Neglect (Pennsylvania Dept. of Public Welfare, 1993) found that 46% of all mistreatment reports involved boys. Girls represented 53% of all abuse cases, partly because of increasing incidents of sexual abuse. Although 7 is the average age of child victims, the most severe physical injuries are inflicted on children younger than 6. Seventy-nine percent of all *fatalities* involved children under age 5. Between 10 and 15% of all injuries caused by physical abuse occurred in infancy (Pennsylvania Dept., 1993).

Given infants' helplessness and dependence on adults, it is not surprising that infants suffer from all types of abuse and neglect, especially "failure to thrive." Some contributing factors to abuse and neglect might include prematurity, complicated births, and postnatal complications resulting in hospitalization after birth, which may interfere with the development of a strong parent-infant bond. Infants who are extremely irritable, have feeding problems, are colicky, cry excessively, or in other ways annoy and stress parents may be more vulnerable to abuse (Korner, 1974; Lefrancois, 1990).

Most child abuse experts concur that there is a pecking order in abusive families and that certain children in a family are more likely to be abused than others are. Children who are viewed as difficult, bad, selfish, or hard to manage are often targeted for abuse. Infants and children with specific physical, mental, or emotional disabilities are vulnerable as well (Fontana, 1984). Children who exhibit attitudes and behaviors parents don't want to recognize in themselves, or that once evoked the wrath of their own parents, are abused more frequently and more severely than are other siblings. If a child displays mannerisms or behaviors that remind parents of a hated ex-spouse or lover, that child may be singled out for abuse. It is also not uncommon for one child to be the scapegoat and be abused by the entire family.

When a severely abused child is removed from a family, often the child next in the pecking order becomes the new target of the family's frustrations, and the cycle of violence within the family continues. Sometimes removing children from large, abusive families diminishes the stress level enough so that parents do not abuse the few children remaining in the home. Careful monitoring, help, and support must be offered in these instances.

Who Are the Abusers?

A 1991 study by the National Center for Child Abuse and Neglect (Pennsylvania Dept., 1993) paints child abuse and neglect as a family affair. Nearly 91% of reported abusers were either parents or relatives of the child. Eighty percent of the abusers were parents, stepparents, or the mother's paramour, and nearly 11% were siblings, grandparents, and other relatives. These abusive families lived in large cities and small towns; were rich, middle class, and poor; and were members of every racial, ethnic, religious, and socioeconomic group (Pennsylvania Dept., 1993).

Some evidence suggests that economic stress, material deprivation, social isolation and lack of knowledge about child development—factors that are all closely associated with poverty—increase the chances that a person will mistreat a child. In addition, sole responsibility for the child, limited opportunities to interact with other adults, lack of support from family members and friends, and financial stresses such as unemployment increase the risk that a person will abuse a child. Personal stresses such as divorce, separation, and drug and alcohol addiction are all possible factors in child abuse, irrespective of social class.

Occasionally, severe and systematic child abuse, as well as chronic neglect, is the result of the parent's recurring mental illness, severe mental retardation, or pathology resulting from drug addiction. Although it is generally accepted that seriously disturbed parents represent only about 10% of cases of abused children, a much larger number of cases involve parental/family problems that necessitate removing the child from the home. In many such cases, the children will never be able to return safely to their parents (Walker et al., 1988).

Although it is generally agreed that child abuse is not caused by the same factors or combination of factors in every case, a review of the research provides an understanding of how abuse can occur. According to Kempe and Kempe (1978), the combination of a potentially abusive parent with poor coping skills, unrealistic expectations, a child who is seen as "different" or "difficult," a personal or financial crisis (even a minor crisis can be the trigger), and a nonsupportive environment that offers nothing to "stay the unkind hand" sets the stage for child abuse (refer to Figure 3-1). A current review of the literature reaffirms that these factors continue to have relevance in assessing the risk of physical abuse (Walker et al., 1988).

Nonfamily abusers   In 1991, nearly 10% of all reported abuse occurred when the child was in alternate care and not parental care. At least 22 states have now responded by enacting laws requiring applicants for employment in child care services to be screened by a statewide central register or the police to determine whether they pose a threat to children's safety. This action is in response to a growing number of allegations of abuse lodged against child care workers, day care workers, foster parents, teachers, and others—but not parents or relatives—who work directly with children. Unfortunately, no such screening yet exists for baby-sitters, the employees responsible for the highest number of injuries to children. For example, in Pennsylvania in 1993, nearly 90% of the reported abuse by baby-sitters was sexual, a figure higher than for stepfathers or mothers' paramours (Pennsylvania Dept., 1993).

The Kaleidoscope of Abuse

I was beat by my mom since I was little. Last August she put me in the hospital because she took a double cable cord and hit me all over the place. I was bleeding on the floor. My brother called the cops and they took me and him away. They put me in the hospital and the next day they put me right back with her. No matter how bad my mom hurts me, I will always love her.
—A 14-year-old girl

Physical Abuse

There is general agreement that abuse represents acts of commission and that physical abuse can involve both physical harm and endangerment. According to the National Research Council (1993), an example of demonstrable harm is when a child incurs injuries such as bruises, lacerations, burns, and fractures as a result of parental actions. Endangerment involves physical assault by the parent or temporary caregiver that may or may not cause injury to the child. Physical abuse can be mild or severe, and acts of similar severity can result in different injuries. For example, shaking may cause an infant's death but may not cause significant injuries to a 5-year-old. Examples of mild forms of physical attack on children include slapping, shoving, and spanking with the hand. Severe forms include hitting with a hard object, scalding, burning, poisoning, stabbing, suffocating, and drowning. The following vignettes are composite examples of physical abuse incidents that human services professionals have encountered.

Beatings

The young boy was beaten by his mother with a cast-iron frying pan until he would pass out. She wanted to teach him to be a "good boy." This went on for as long as he could remember, and finally stopped when he grew larger than his mother.

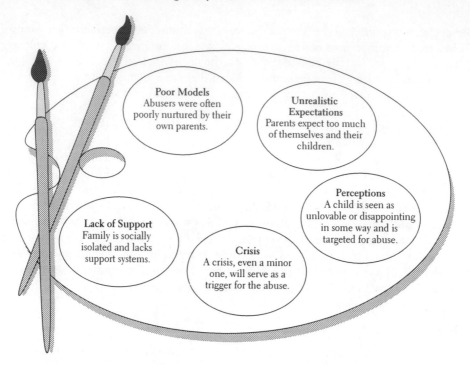

FIGURE 3-1 *Five Factors That May Precipitate Child Abuse*
SOURCE: Kempe & Kempe (1978, pp. 2–24).

She was whipped with a lamp cord from the base of her neck to the heels. Her mother "punished" her because she was "ornery." The 9-year-old, beaten so often, was finally put in a foster home.

Flesh Wounds

The toddler was only 2 when his mother began biting his hands so that he would not touch the knick-knacks in the house. She later bit his legs because he would wet his pants.

Burns

A 3-year-old had weeping sores on his body that wouldn't heal. The puzzled young visiting nurse, who came to care for a disabled family member, continued to put a healing salve on the child. The mother claimed she had no idea what caused the sores. One day, the nurse identified the outline of a nickel on the child's skin. The mother's boyfriend would heat coins and press them on his arms and legs.

The child was only 3 when her mother gave birth to her half-brother. At 4, she would sit and "play with herself." Her mother was afraid she would grow up to be "a sex maniac like her uncle," so she held the child's hand over an open flame.

The mother cried as she later related this story. Even though it stopped the behavior, she knew she had done the wrong thing.

Fractures

A third-grader came to school with his shoulder hanging and tears in his eyes from the pain. He said he fell out of a tree. His father was called and when he finally came, he grabbed the boy by his wounded arm and the child winced. He had a broken collar bone and his teacher wondered how he really got it. This was in the early 1960s when teachers didn't report suspected abuse.

Food Deprivation

Jane and Jill lost their mother when they were toddlers, and their father's new wife didn't like the siblings. She began to deny them food and often made them eat a can of cold sauerkraut and sleep under their trailer home, even on cold nights. Their father did nothing to stop this abuse. On weekends, the children had nothing to eat at all. Their last meal was lunch on Friday, and they didn't eat again until the cafeteria personnel fixed breakfast especially for them on Monday.

Prescription Drugs, Alcohol, and Illicit Drugs

A group of young people would form a ring and place a 2-year-old child in the center. Then they would blow marijuana smoke in the child's face as she tried to get out of the circle. They continued this until the child became disoriented and began to stumble and fall down. They thought it was funny.

Scotty was a colicky baby and kept his parents up at night. To keep him quiet, they started putting a little scotch mixed with water in his bottle each evening.

Sybil's mother was taking a sedative prescribed for insomnia. One night when Sybil was 6 and would not fall asleep, her mother gave her a tablet. Later, it became easier and easier to give Sybil the medicine to "calm her nerves."

Emotional Abuse

Before she was quite a year old, we began to correct her for crying. This has been a severe but wholesome discipline. It has taught her a command over her feelings, which we trust may be of great service to her in her subsequent life. Now, when she is grieved or displeased, unless she is in a bad humor from bodily suffering, she will suppress the disposition to cry, often with very perceptible struggle and effort. But even when she is unwell and bursts into a loud cry, we generally correct her, until she suppresses it....In this discipline, we sometimes use the rod; but more frequently shut her in a room alone, til she became quiet.
—"Extract from a Mother's Journal," *Mother's Magazine*, 1834

Some writers (NRC, 1993) argue that all children who are physically abused and neglected are emotionally maltreated to some extent. However, because emotional or psychological abuse leaves no physical marks, its presence is often undetected. And because most forms are subtle, emotional maltreatment can easily be overlooked in children who are not otherwise abused. Examples of emotional maltreatment include verbal abuse such as ridiculing, demeaning, and denigrating the child and placing the child in situations of continual threat, fear, or terror. Specific examples of emotional or psychological abuse are portrayed in the following vignettes.

Punishing with Fear

Andy, age 4, was a very hyperactive child and was terrified of the dark. He also had nightmares and would wet the bed. His mother could not control him because she said he was such a willful child. One day, when he was being especially obstinate, she put him in a dark closet to see if he would calm down. He screamed in fear until, exhausted, he fell asleep. Later, when the closet didn't seem to be as effective, his mother would lock him in the dark basement as punishment. In the first grade, Andy was placed in a class for the socially-emotionally disturbed.

Ridiculing, Demeaning, Denigrating

She was the one who most resembled her mother, Missy, in both looks and temperament. When her parents divorced and she went to live with her father and his new wife, she was constantly being compared unfavorably to her mother. Whenever she would show any temper, her stepmother would say: "Go ahead—throw a Missy-fit." Everything she did brought criticism. She couldn't comb her hair because it was coarse and wild like her mother's; she had poor table manners "like her mother," and she was "dumb as a box of rocks, like her mother." She was good at art but her drawings were never praised; she tried to help around the house but was called "lazy." Her stepsiblings joined in and she often took the blame for things they did. Sometimes even her dad would say, "You'll never amount to anything." When she was 14, she ran away.

Threatening with Abandonment

Hyperactive and mischievous, Todd was always the troublesome one. His alcoholic father, who could not control him with ever escalating physical punishment, threatened to send him to a nearby home for children and youth. One day, when Todd was about 6, his father stopped the car in front of the facility and forced the screaming youngster out. Later, he drove by and picked him up. This behavior was repeated several more times, each time with less and less effect. After a while, Todd did not cry. As a teen, Todd was placed at the facility for setting fire to his family's home.

Sexual Abuse

Kohn (1987) suggests that one in six Americans—about 40 million people—may have been sexually abused as children. Sexual abuse is defined as "the involvement of dependent, developmentally immature children and adolescents in sexual activities they do not fully comprehend, are unable to give informed consent to and that violate the social taboos of family roles" (Kempe, 1980, p. 198). Sexually abusive acts can include non-touching incidents, sexual contact, humiliation, and sexual torture (Herman-Giddens, 1984; Wilbur, 1984).

Specific examples of *non-touching sexual abuse* include: removing bathroom and bedroom doors so adults can observe the child bathing and toileting and the child can observe the sexual activity of parents, disrobing in front of the child, having the child sleep with adults, and bathing the child well past the age when the child could bathe him- or herself. *Contact abuse* includes oral-genital contact, attempted or actual intercourse, sodomy, and attempted or actual rape. Examples of *sexual humiliation* include putting clothespins on the penis, making an older child parade around the house in a diaper, pulling a young woman's pants down and spanking her in front of her first date, and forcing a child to disrobe for adults. Extreme cases of *sexual torture*, such as being raped by the entire family, being violated with foreign objects placed in the penis or vagina and rectum, or being subjected to extreme pain and terror, have been reported with disturbing frequency and are known to contribute to severe mental illness and multiple personality disorders. Wilbur (1984) maintains that severe systematic abuse, especially sexual abuse, was a precursor of multiple personality disorder in all the cases she has studied.

Incest, which was once described as a "one in a million occurrence," is widespread and underreported. No reliable data exist on the number of actual cases, but reports of sexual abuse have increased dramatically in the last decade. And whereas men are identified as the perpetrators in the majority of the cases, a disturbing increase in reports involving women has been noted. Incestuous behavior is often part of a pattern of disturbed relationships within the family and in extrafamilial relationships. According to the National Research Council (1993, p. 126), "49 percent of incestuous fathers and stepfathers abuse children outside the family at the same time they are abusing their own children."

Kempe (1980) found that fathers who are incestuously involved with their daughters tend to be socially isolated introverted personalities whose spouses often know of and encourage the incestuous behavior. Such spouses may arrange times for father and daughter to be alone, telling the daughter to "take care of Dad" or to "settle him down" (p. 205). In these instances, the mother's collusion in the abuse may represent her attempt to deny her disturbed relationship with her husband and with her daughter. Despite the fact that some spouses tacitly encourage the incestuous contacts, there are situations in which the noninvolved spouse is genuinely unaware of the abuse (Jones & Alexander, 1987).

Many perpetrators and coconspirators are adults who were themselves victims as children and who view sex between children and adults as a normal part of life. Steele (1980) quoted one father as saying, "My father had sex with all my sisters, so why should I not sleep with my daughters?" (p. 73). Steele also noted that the common denominator in sexually abusive families is the "absence of warm, loving, sexual relationships as a model for the child to emulate, the lack of appropriate sexual education and, most importantly for all, lack of empathic, sensitive care during the early impressionable, developmental years" (1980, p. 74).

Children who are forced into sexual relationships with a parent are robbed of developmentally appropriate sexuality and are deprived of normal interactions with peers. Their abusers often punish any signs of budding sexuality and maintain strict control of any dating relationships. The following is an example of a young woman who was sexually molested by her stepfather, yet humiliated when she tried to date young men of her own age.

Sally lived with her mother and stepfather. Her stepfather began abusing her sexually shortly after he came to live with the family. Sally remembers that she was about 5 years old. As the years progressed, so did the abuse; and by the time Sally was a teen, her stepfather was having sex with her on a regular basis. When any young man showed any interest in Sally, her stepfather reacted with extreme jealousy. When Sally's first date came to pick her up, her angry stepfather decided she needed to be punished for not doing the dishes. He pulled down her pants and spanked her in front of the young man. She was 16 years old. Sally never forgot this incident and did not tell anyone of her abuse until she was an adult.

Because incest is such a well-kept secret, its discovery may precipitate a crisis for the child. Discovery is, in fact, an extremely critical time because the child is usually bereft of all supports and must depend on the kindness of strangers. A caring and competent counselor is often the child's only hope. Sometimes, the abuse itself does not become known until years later, when other crises in the victim's life bring it to light.

One of the most disturbing consequences of child sexual abuse is that boys who are abused are far more likely to turn into offenders, molesting the next generation of children, and girls who are abused are more likely to produce children who are later sexually abused (Kohn, 1987). This phenomena holds such terror for children and for parents that it has prompted Terry (1991) to predict that "children molesting children" may be the next national crisis.

Understanding the Abusive Parent

I didn't mean to hurt her. I just wanted her to turn out good…like me.
—Mother whose child was placed in foster care

It is difficult to write about child abuse without evoking negative feelings about the parents who have done these terrible things to their children. However, most abusive parents love their children and wish to be "good" parents. "Ironic as it may seem, the parents are making a real effort to do what is right by their child" (Alexander, 1972, p. 40). It is usually not the parents' conscious intention to hurt their children or to damage them emotionally. Neglectful parents may have difficulty seeing past their own needs and are often so immersed in themselves that they have difficulty seeing the wanting child. Practitioners need to approach parents as fragile human beings who are emotionally vulnerable. Because of their vulnerability, parents should be treated with the same nonjudgmental, compassionate understanding that is recommended and usually reserved for the child in these situations.

Many parents do not understand child development and often have grossly distorted perceptions of a child's capabilities. This leads to unrealistic expectations that cannot possibly be met and produces frustration. Abusive parents usually have poor impulse control and displace their anger and frustration onto their children. Although the vast majority of parents are nonabusive, it is fair to say that some parents might become physically abusive under the right circumstances. For example, if punishing a child leads to desirable behavior, attempts to control the child's behavior in the future may involve increasingly higher levels of punishment (Mulhern & Passman, as cited in Lefrancois, 1990).

Parents who lacked nurturing, love, and a sense of belonging in their own child-hood often expect their children to fulfill their needs in a form of role reversal described by Helfer (Kempe & Helfer, 1980). This reversal of roles involves treating the child as an adult who is expected to meet the parent's desire to be loved. At the same time, the child's feelings, needs, and wants are disregarded. What parents don't realize is that children have to receive love before they can return it. Thus, an impossible set of circumstances is set in motion. The following story told by a judge after a placement hearing exemplifies this situation.

> One day a handsome little boy of 3 appeared before me in court and he was smil-ing. I was surprised because so few children come to court smiling. Puzzled, I asked his mother why she wanted to give him up. She said that in the last year, the child had begun to say "no" to nearly all of her requests and she was con-vinced he didn't love her anymore. (personal communication)

The same set of circumstances that produce child abuse and result in loss of self-esteem are often repeated later in life and in the next generation. Children who have nonresponsive, demanding, critical, rejecting, or cruel parents may grow up to think of themselves as "bad," unloved, or unlovable. As adults, they may select partners who are sadistic, exploitative, and uncaring, thereby confirming their assumption that they are unlovable and somehow deserving of abuse. This partially explains why so many abused children grow up to be battered. When abused children become mothers or fathers, their children's demands for care may intensify their own feelings of inade-quacy and may serve as painful reminders of the "bad" children they once were. Parents who have a variety of unmet dependency needs may expect their children to nurture them. When this doesn't happen, parents may see their own critical and demanding parent in their child's behavior and thus subject the child to the same abuse they experienced in childhood (Miller, 1980–1990).

Abusive parents who themselves were subjected to painful, recurrent beatings within the first 2 years of their life have not had a chance to rationalize this abuse. Consequently, they later act as both aggressor and victim (Miller, 1980–1990). They have forgotten (or repressed) all the pain and humiliation of their own childhood treat-ment. Parents often justify physical abuse against children as "good upbringing," "cor-recting," or "for their own good." Miller explained the true effect of abuse this way: "The knowledge that you were beaten and that this, as your parents tell you, was for your own good may well be retained (although not always), but the suffering caused by the way you were mistreated will remain unconscious and will later prevent you from empathizing with others" (p. 115).

The inability to empathize with the child is a factor in neglect as well as in abuse. Parents who neglect their children, sometimes seriously, are often emotionally imma-ture and needy and are unable to put their children's wants and needs ahead of their own (Kempe & Kempe, 1978). Their lack of ability to empathize with the child is often interpreted as self-centeredness, as though the parent is thinking "me first" because his or her needs for love, attention, and physical care were not given top priority in the family of origin. Examples of this "me first" attitude can be seen in a parent who takes something for his or her own comfort, such as a hat on a cold day, while the child goes bareheaded. Another example is the parent who goes to meet a friend while a child lies for hours with a broken arm.

Although studies of abusive parents indicate that many have experienced some significant degree of early life neglect or abuse (Steele, 1987), it is important to emphasize that not all abused children become abusive parents. According to Kaufman and Ziegler, about one-third of maltreated children will abuse their own children, and two-thirds will not: " Being maltreated as a child puts one at risk for becoming abusive but the path between these two points is far from direct or inevitable" (cited in NRC, 1993, p. 223).

In many abusive families, one parent is the abuser and the other passively accepts the maltreatment of the child. In case studies cited by Miller (1980–1990) in *For Your Own Good*, often a child is being beaten by the father while the mother stands in the doorway weeping. In many such cases, "the wife of a child-beating father shares his attitude toward child-rearing or is herself his victim—in either case, she is rarely the child's advocate" (p. 116). Sadly, some parents are coperpetrators in the abuse of their own children or are "silent co-conspirators" (Wilbur, 1984) and let abuse, especially sexual abuse, "just happen" without intervening. According to Jones and Alexander (1987), this failure to protect occurs when a patriarchal family structure robs the mother and children of the ability to protest; or when the family is so chaotic that it lacks the controls necessary to care for and protect its members. In some families, however, a nonabusive parent or sibling can offer enough emotional support to offset some of the devastating effects of abuse.

In a very real sense, abusive parents are victims as much as their abused children are. Many have had poor parenting models, a history of abuse, or experienced the incredible stresses associated with poverty, unemployment, and lack of educational opportunities to learn about child development. They know very little about children and about solving the problems associated with their care. They are not adept at negotiating the system on behalf of their children or themselves. Only a small percentage of abusive parents have extreme pathology and are beyond the reach of the average practitioner. This being the case, human services professionals need to recognize and help those parents who can benefit from counseling and support services.

Recognizing Child Abuse and Neglect

Some types of child abuse and neglect are so obvious they hit you in the face, but others are veiled and disguised in ways that make it extremely difficult for practitioners to detect. Physical abuse, with its accompanying bruises, lacerations, burns and other injuries, is the easiest type to identify; sexual abuse the least. Sexual abuse is usually not accompanied by any physical signs (Herman-Giddens, 1984), so the practitioner must look for sudden changes in behavior, emotional responses and sexual knowledge or behavior that is not consistent with the child's developmental level. Emotional abuse, heaped on the child in the form of ridicule, derogatory threats, and demeaning comments, is even more difficult to see because the bruises are on the child's self-esteem rather than on the child's body.

Neglect can be as insidious and damaging as abuse. *Physical neglect* is often confirmed by observing the state of the child's health and hygiene. Parents may delay medical treatment for the seriously ill child, may fail to seek preventative treatment that they can afford, or may give inappropriate home treatment for serious ailments (Fontana, 1984). In addition to medical neglect, children may be deprived of adequate food, clothing, and shelter and may be left alone and unsupervised for long periods of time. Children who suffer from educational neglect are often kept home from school until their bruises heal or are prevented from going to school in order to take care of parents or younger siblings when parents can't or won't provide care. Occasionally, children are kept home to perform forced labor. Frequent absences from school and the overall physical condition of the child are good indicators of educational neglect.

Emotional neglect is very difficult to discern, and the practitioner must rely on behavioral and emotional indicators (such as acting-out behavior, withdrawal, affect hunger,) except in the case of abandonment and maternal deprivation, where there are physical indicators as well. Abandoning a child totally or sporadically during infancy and early childhood can lead to insecure attachment and lack of trust, which have serious effects on a child's social, emotional, and physical development. "Failure to thrive" is a severe form of emotional neglect caused by maternal deprivation (Fontana, 1984). This type of impaired mother-child relationship has serious consequences for the child's physical and emotional development. It can lead to death during infancy and can result in a variety of psychological disorders during early childhood. Fontana (1984) believes that the only way to establish whether the child's condition is the result of maternal deprivation is to demonstrate significant recovery by hospitalizing the child or altering the mother-child interaction.

Various forms of abuse and neglect often overlap. For instance, the sexually abused child is both physically and emotionally abused by the experience. Children who are physically abused are often neglected as well. For example, they may not be comforted by parents, often get no medical attention for their injuries, and frequently are kept home from school until their bruises heal. Child abuse is not always obvious, nor is a single indicator evidence of abuse. Therefore, professionals who work with children must put together a number of pieces of information gleaned from behavioral observation, child and family histories, physical evidence, and interviews with parent and child to determine whether child abuse might be occurring.

APPLICATIONS TO COUNSELING

Counseling the abused and neglected child requires involving the abusive parents in the treatment because the child cannot be returned to the home unless something has changed. Communicating with abused or neglected children and their parents requires special sensitivity and skill. Members of the helping professions need to be warm and accepting of both parent and child and must refrain from making judgments. It is especially important that members of the helping professions work together in a coordinated effort to bring support and assistance to troubled families and their children. Some counseling strategies that can be effective in working with abused children follow:

• *Listen carefully to verbal and nonverbal clues.* Abused and neglected children need extra support and encouragement in order to be able to tell their stories. Counselors should allow children many opportunities to disclose their secrets through art, play or bibliotherapy. Children rarely tell anyone directly that they have been abused; instead they give direct and indirect verbal and behavioral clues. These clues can be detected through careful observation of behavior and by listening intently to what the child says and does not say.

• *Report suspected child abuse immediately.* In addition, make arrangements to protect and comfort the child until child protection workers arrive. Counselors who have direct evidence in the form of bruises or the child's statements about abuse must report it immediately. Even in cases where the abuse is just suspected and not confirmed, the counselor is obligated to report it. (Specific procedures for reporting child abuse can be found in Chapter 10.)

• *Let children know that they are not to blame.* Because most research indicates that children often blame themselves, particularly if they are sexually abused, it is important for counselors to help children release the feelings of guilt that surround the abuse. Helping children to understand that it is their parents who made these choices will help children rebuild their self-esteem. It is important not to condemn the parent but rather to let the child know that the parent will be receiving help also.

• *Remember that child abuse and neglect are symptoms of a breakdown in the family's interactions.* Helping abused and neglected children involves examining the interactions of family members, understanding the abusive parents' perception of the child or children, and being sensitive to the parents' needs and emotional reactions to stressful childrearing situations. Parent education, training and support programs, family counseling, and home-based programs are all effective ways to involve parents and families in treatment.

• *Make home visits.* One of the ways counselors can help abused children is to interact with their families in a warm, accepting, and supportive way. Some counselors do this by making home visits, where they can observe the interactions of family members and discover ways to improve the family environment. Engaging the family in counseling, games, and drawing are all productive ways to observe and may also help to mend. Supporting the family in this way may relieve some of the stresses associated with physical and emotional abuse.

• *Put the family in touch with support services.* It is often necessary to put parents in touch with services that will provide additional support (such as parent support groups, mother-to-mother programs, homemaker services) and to initiate referrals to social service agencies for additional help with food, housing, employment, and other stressors. Government programs such as Head Start, the Women with Infants and Children (WIC) food supplement program, and school breakfast and lunch programs are among the many services available to children.

In summary, physical, emotional, and sexual abuse have profound debilitating effects on children. A child's spirit can be mutilated by parents who do not know how to help the child grow and develop in healthy ways. Unfortunately, nearly 3 million children each year suffer in ways similar to those described in these pages. Although abused and neglected children provide practitioners with an extraordinary counseling challenge, counselors must remind themselves that they can make a difference. The kaleidoscope continues to project yet more profiles of the vulnerable child. The next section of this chapter discusses the plight of the vulnerable child in the alcoholic family.

CHILDREN OF ALCOHOLICS

Sometimes my dad lets us have a pillow fight and other times he hits us when we do. With him, you can't be sure of anything.

I worry that my mom will get drunk and embarrass me.

One day my dad got so mad he kicked the truck and broke his toe. I laughed...he deserved it.

—Children's reports about when a parent drinks.

According to the Children's Defense Fund (1994), at least 10 million children are affected by their parents' substance abuse, and Brake (1988) estimated that the lives of 8 million children are affected by the abuse of alcohol. This means that in every elementary school class, at least four and as many as six children live in a family where at least one parent is an alcoholic. Because of the prevailing view that little can be done to help the child unless the alcoholic parent receives treatment, children of alcoholics often do not get the help and support they need and deserve.

Portraying the Alcoholic Family

Alcoholism strains the financial, emotional, physical, and social resources of the entire family, and drinking becomes a preoccupation from which there is little diversion. Without enough money for both alcohol and food, the alcoholic may resort to selling the family's possessions. So compelling was the addiction that one child's father sold the toaster, prompting the child to say, "It doesn't matter; there's no bread anyway." Alcoholics have difficulty meeting the developmental needs of their children because they have often been inadequately nurtured themselves.

Like abusive parents, alcoholic parents are often emotionally immature and narcissistic and are unable to put their child's emotional and physical needs ahead of their own. Most alcoholics also do not have the physical energy to do all of the tasks that keep a home running smoothly and efficiently. As a consequence, children in alcoholic homes often are badly neglected, have inadequate food and clothing and live in homes that may be in disarray. Similarly, alcoholic parents often have neither the inclination nor the energy to be actively involved in their children's lives, to play with them, and to be involved in their school activities. The family is often socially isolated from extended family and friends. Children may not bring other children home to play because they are embarrassed or fear their parent's unpredictable behavior. The parent may become intoxicated at family gatherings and holiday celebrations, embarrassing family members and engaging in conflict with extended family members. Children are warned not to betray their family secret; Black (1984) found that 53% of children of alcoholics never tell anyone about a parent's drinking. Like abusive families, alcoholic families often bear their burdens in silence.

For the children of alcoholics, life is a series of empty and broken promises. Promises to go places, promises to buy things, and promises to stop drinking are made and broken. Some promises the parent intends to keep and can't; others are intended to control and to punish. For example, a parent might say, "Well, now that you got that F we're not going to the movies." In this way the parent, who would not have taken the child to the movies if the grade had been an A, can blame the child. As a result, the child may begin to feel responsible for the parent's behavior: "If I were a better child, my father would take us places."

Because alcoholics are subject to mood swings, it is difficult for children to anticipate how they will be treated at any given time. One adult child of an alcoholic recalled her father's behavior extremes: "One day my dad treated all of us to ice cream; the next day he threw spaghetti against the wall during dinner." Discipline, instead of being a fair and flexible response to a child's misdeeds, is often administered as punishment and applied arbitrarily and inconsistently, depending on the alcoholic's mood. Sometimes misbehavior carries no consequence; sometimes a very severe one. A child may be beaten for throwing a ball in the house one day and not another; or may be hit across the face at the dinner table and have no idea why. As a result, children of alcoholics are always waiting for "the other shoe to drop," which creates an abundance of anxiety. When exposed to violence, some children experience fear that translates into anxiety; others experience an abundance of anger that translates into aggression. As discussed in Chapter 2, children may develop uncontrolled hostile aggression when continually subjected to situations that provoke anger without the protection and security of well-defined outer controls on their behavior. The lack of firm and consistent limits, coupled with continual exposure to the uncontrolled anger and violence of an alcoholic parent, contributes to aggressive behavior in children.

Because alcoholics generally have no impulse control, experience disturbances in judgment, and lack skill in parenting and nurturing children, they are more likely to abuse and neglect their children than are nonalcoholics. A general lessening of inhibitions that accompany alcohol and drug abuse has been associated with child sexual abuse as well; Naiditch and Lerner (cited in Wilson & Blocher, 1990) claimed that alcoholism is involved in as many as 90% of all child abuse cases.

Recognizing the Child of an Alcoholic

Children of alcoholics experience a series of losses as they are growing up. In a sense, alcohol robs them of a warm, consistent, nurturing environment where they can enjoy structure, security, and positive attention. Their lives are characterized instead by conflict and the constant threat presented by their parent's volatile emotions and inconsistent behaviors. Many of the emotional and behavioral characteristics these children express are similar to those of children who are experiencing losses in families troubled by abuse, divorce, death, or illness.

Most research reviews indicate that life with an alcoholic parent produces many stresses in a child's life. In fact, Schall views alcoholism in the family as "the most widespread cause of severe stress for school age children in the United States today" (cited in Wilson & Blocher, 1990, pp. 98–99). Although children have different ways of coping with stress, Cork (1969), in a classic study of 112 children, found that children of alcoholics approached life with less self-confidence and more anxiety. They were more easily upset, had more school difficulties, and experienced more physical problems as a result of the stress. Possible physical problems might include ulcers, obesity, chronic stomachaches, and asthma (Black, 1986). The continual conflict, disharmony, and dissension experienced in the home environment contaminates interactions with siblings and peers alike. Children avoid inviting age-mates to their homes and refuse to play after school for fear of arriving home late and provoking parental anger. Some, more aggressive, children engage in physical fights or other misbehavior that brings rejection from peers.

Some of the most common emotional reactions of children of alcoholics include fear and worry, which turn into anxiety, and anger, which is expressed as aggression — either passive or hostile and uncontrolled. Some children who have had their attempts to express anger squelched, become passive and timid. Feelings of loneliness, rejection, and insecurity and lack of appropriate attention at home may lead to lowered self-esteem and a lack of confidence to cope with the stresses of life. Many children of alcoholics also succumb to depression, a feeling of deep sadness and helplessness. Children express depression in different ways: some withdraw and isolate themselves from stress, trying to hide and avoid confrontations; others compensate by acting out and misbehaving in school or otherwise calling attention to themselves.

Common school problems are fights with peers, poor academic performance, and disruptive classroom behavior. Because of the chaos that exists in their family life, children are often unable to complete homework assignments, are frequently late for school, and may skip school entirely. More serious school and behavior problems are truancy, delinquency, drug or alcohol abuse, and suicidal tendencies (Buwick, Martin, & Martin, 1988).

Research indicates that there is a genetic factor in alcoholism that may predispose children of alcoholics to the addiction. This predisposition, coupled with the modeling factor, results in a higher-than-average risk of alcoholism for the children of addicted parents. Black (1987) found this risk to be five times greater for boys and three times greater for girls of alcoholics when compared to children of nonalcoholics. Equally alarming is the age at which children experiment with alcohol. In a survey of the nation's adolescents in the 1987–1988 school year, almost 60% of eighth-graders said they had their first experience with alcohol in grades 5 through 8, and 14% said they first tried alcohol in the fourth grade (American School Health Association, 1992). The fact that children of alcoholics are overrepresented in juvenile justice and mental health facilities, are more likely to drop out of school, and have a higher rate of attempted and completed suicides (Wilson & Blocher, 1990) indicates that they do indeed need our help in the early years of their lives.

> When I was about 6, I thought I was the only kid that had a father that drank. I never wanted to go home from school so I took my time. One day, I told an older kid that I didn't want to go home and he asked "Why?" I didn't want to tell him but I finally said, "My dad drinks," and he replied, "That's okay, mine does too." Immediately, I felt like a big weight had been lifted off of me.
> — Parent who had an alcoholic father

Although individual children react differently to living in a home where one or both parents drink, all such children have certain behaviors in common (see Figure 3-2). Most children believe that because they have been told to keep their parent's

FIGURE 3-2   *Common Counseling Issues for Children of Alcoholics*

alcoholism a secret, they live in the only family that has this problem. One of the primary goals of therapy is to assure children that they are not alone and that many others have successfully overcome some of the problems they are now facing. Following are some of the areas of concern (Black, 1984, 1986, 1987) that should be addressed in counseling children of alcoholics.

Children of alcoholics usually protect their parents   Much like child abuse, alcoholism is something that children learn to keep secret. Part of the reason is that, for most alcoholics, denial makes a great wall of protection. As part of this conspiracy of denial, children are taught very early not to tell anyone about their parent's drinking problem, and they are forced to live the family lie. This makes it difficult for the child suffering in an alcoholic home to confide his or her problems to a teacher, counselor, or peer. Shame and embarrassment also are factors in the child's reluctance to disclose the real problem at home. This inability to tell anyone constitutes a great burden for the child, because to get relief, the child must risk losing whatever love and support is available from the family. As counselors, we have to help the child *and* the family.

Children blame themselves for their parents' drinking   Children may feel responsible for their parents' alcoholism. Because parents often say, "You are driving me to drink" and seek to blame others, children tend to think that they have caused the problem. They think that if they behave better, are nicer to the parent, or get better grades, then the parent will stop drinking. Counseling is important in helping the children understand that alcoholism is an addiction and that the child did not cause it and is powerless to stop it.

Children love their parents but are ashamed of their parents' behavior   Children often feel guilty and disloyal when they feel this way. Although children want and need emotional support and nurturance from their parents, it is often not forthcoming. When children realize that their parents are seldom there when they need them, they feel abandoned, rejected and unloved. Counseling can help children understand that they can still love their parents without liking or enabling their behavior.

Children take on the role and the responsibilities of the parent   In an odd form of role reversal, children become the physical and emotional supports of parents. This is especially true when parents burden their children with adult problems and responsibilities. When children are presented with problems for which there are no solutions, they worry. Children worry, not only about the immediate needs of the family, such as food and rent, but about the health, safety, and feelings of the alcoholic parent. Specifically, they worry about the alcoholic parent getting sick, hurt, fired, or arrested. In addition, older children often become substitute parents for younger brothers and sisters, cleaning the house, doing the laundry, and performing other chores usually assumed by a parent. So common is this role reversal, that many adult children of alcoholics later confide that they lost their childhood to their parent's alcoholism.

Children are caught in the middle of family violence   In many alcoholic families, fighting and arguing are everyday activities. For some inexplicable reason, mealtime is often turned into a battleground of such proportions that children are terrorized as parents verbally assault each other and food is thrown about. Many children are unable to eat, some actually lose their appetite, and others develop ulcers because of their parents' fighting. In some cases verbal abuse escalates to physical violence, which may be directed toward the spouse (usually the mother) and/or the children. In some instances, the nonalcoholic parent will form an alliance with the children for support, forcing them to take sides in the conflict. This action almost always produces guilt and anxiety in the children.

Children seek to avoid the arguing and violence   Children, as do all of us, seek peace and relief from conflict and stress and often withdraw physically and emotionally. Children sometimes retreat to the solitude of their room or find a special place to be alone. Older children spend less and less time at home and may seek refuge in after-school activities or in the homes of friends and relatives. Some children contemplate running away, whereas others escape by daydreaming about a better family and home life. It is the counselor's job to help children find constructive ways of coping with the stress of their home life.

APPLICATIONS TO COUNSELING

Following are some counseling strategies that have proven helpful in working with children of alcoholics. A great many strategies listed in other chapters of this book could be used with both children of alcoholics and their parents.

• *Form a relationship that will help the child trust.* This is not easy. From living with the broken promises, disappointments, and secrets of alcoholism, the child has learned not to trust. Even more painful, many children mistrust their own perceptions and have learned to rely solely on the approval or disapproval of a sometimes irrational alcoholic parent. They have also learned to deny their own thoughts and feelings.

• *Give the child important information about alcoholism that will help diminish self-blame.* Such information can be provided in a general way in large- and small-group discussions or in individual sessions. Obtaining the facts about alcoholism and having opportunities to ask questions can provide some relief to children who may or may not want to reveal the family secret.

• *In individual counseling, children can share their innermost thoughts and feelings with a warm, caring person who will help them discover healthy ways of coping.* Play therapy, bibliotherapy, and art therapy are all fun and nonthreatening techniques that are invaluable for helping children get by the barrier of "family secrets." If children don't want to talk about their family problems, they can simply draw them or play them out.

• *Small group sessions with children who have similar problems can be effective in letting children know that they are not alone and that others have similar problems.* It is best to use this technique only after a great deal of rapport has been established in individual sessions. The techniques of play therapy, art therapy, and bibliotherapy can be used in small-group sessions also.

• *Establish rapport with the family and, if possible, make home visits.* Parents may be reluctant to go to school because they fear they will be told how poorly their children are doing and be reminded again of their own past school failures.

• *Offer help to the family through referrals to self-help groups such as Alcoholics Anonymous and to support groups such as Alanon and Alateen for spouses and teens.* If other needs arise, put the family in touch with the necessary social service agencies that can help.

• *Invite the parents to participate in parent groups offered by the elementary school guidance counselor.* If the alcoholic parent doesn't want to come, see whether you can get the nonalcoholic parent to come.

• *Promote alternate after-school and summer activities for children.* Encourage parents to consider letting the children attend community recreation programs at the YMCA and YWCA, as well as programs with the Boys and Girls Club of America. For single-parent families, Big Brothers and Big Sisters match a child with a person who spends quality time with him or her. This might be just what the child needs in addition to a warm and supportive counselor.

• *Encourage teachers to give the child extra help at school.* This will help develop competency and instill feelings of confidence and self-worth. Nothing builds success and feelings of confidence like genuine mastery of academic tasks.

> • *Accept the child and his or her family, and focus on their strengths as a family.* Continue to accept both child and parent unconditionally and encourage their growth toward harmony, understanding, and happiness as a family.
> • *Recognize when the family is not the best place for the child.* Consider alternate placement if the child is being abused and there is no hope that the preceding interventions will succeed.

Once my mom was drunk and started to fight with me because I didn't do the dishes. I was angry and went to my room crying. After a while my dad came in and asked me to apologize. He said, "You have to be a grown-up about this. I was 11 years old. I thought to myself, "Why can't my mother be a grown-up?"
—Parent who had an alcoholic mother

In conclusion, it should be noted that not all children suffer serious negative effects from being raised in an alcoholic family. There are certain differences in families and in individuals that help lessen the negative impact of living with an alcoholic, just as there are for other family situations that make children vulnerable to adjustment problems. Whether or not children have long- or short-term emotional or behavioral problems depends on a number of factors, including: how abusive the alcoholic parent is; what the relationship is between parent and child when the parent isn't drinking; how much support the child receives from the nonalcoholic parent; how much support the child receives from significant others, such as extended family, teachers, and friends; how the child perceives and interprets what is happening in the family; and the child's temperament and personality characteristics. Some children survive alcoholism and grow up motivated to achieve, able to nurture their children and balance their concern for others with their own goals for happiness. Others have trouble making decisions, trusting their own judgment, and being open and honest. Many remain "super-responsible" and hypersensitive to criticism throughout their adult lives. A few are devastated by the alcoholism in their families and, perhaps because of abuse, become involved in delinquency and drug abuse. Many grow up to marry alcoholics or become addicted themselves.

CHILDREN OF DIVORCE

> *Children do not perceive divorce as a second chance, and this is part of their suffering. They feel that their childhood has been lost forever....But children of divorce do have second chances in the very futures they are worried about.*
> —Wallerstein & Blakeslee (1989, p. 14)

Separation and Divorce

The family represents the child's first support system, and the bond of attachment the child forms with parents fosters the development of trust. This bond contributes to the child's ability to love and be loved and is central to healthy personality development. Even with this secure attachment, the road to healthy growth and development is neither smooth nor continuous. There is always some backing up to rework old conflicts or pausing to consider new ones. These regressions are normal reactions for children, who retreat to safer ground when stressed. As children continue to grow and interact with the larger social group, the quality of their relationships with family members and their parents' relationship with one another are important and continuing influences on children's development. Children need the support of family and significant others to overcome temporary developmental setbacks and to return to a healthy developmental route.

Separation and divorce represents a situational conflict in the family that exacerbates any developmental conflicts the child may already be experiencing. When the family unit is fractured, children usually suffer a lack of support for their healthy growth and development and experience a profound sense of loss. The loss attached to divorce, like that associated with death, involves lasting changes in the rhythm of daily life and in the parent-child relationship. Loss is as central a theme in divorce as it is in death: loss of daily contact with one or both parents; loss of old friends, familiar schools, and neighborhoods; and loss of contact with the extended family. Unlike death, however, divorce involves choice and "comprises a special category of life crisis in that it simultaneously engenders new solutions and new problems" (Wallerstein & Blakeslee, 1989, p. 6).

Common Emotional Reactions to Divorce

How children react to divorce depends a great deal on their age, their developmental level, and their personality characteristics. Individual reactions will vary considerably from child to child because each has a different set of family circumstances, different personality strengths and weaknesses, and different ways of coping with stress. Perceptions of loss of the intact family not only vary from child to child but are viewed differently by the *same* child as he or she grows and develops. How a child reacts at a given moment may be far different from how he or she adjusts over the course of many months or years. Wallerstein & Blakeslee (1989) concluded that *"One cannot predict long-term effects of divorce on children from how they react at the onset"* (p. 15). This conclusion has important implications for mental health professionals, who have often focused their work on the crisis of divorce rather than on long-term adjustments. Wallerstein and Blakeslee were surprised to learn that children who were the most troubled, upset, and depressed at the time of the divorce were well adjusted 10 years later.

A review of the literature (Gately & Schwebel, 1992; Strangeland, Pellegreno, & Lundholm, 1989; Wallerstein, 1983; Wallerstein & Blakeslee, 1989; Wallerstein & Kelly, 1980) indicates that children express certain common reactions to divorce (see Figure 3-3). An understanding of these reactions is useful in helping children through the immediate crisis of divorce and in easing their long-term adjustment to it.

Grief for the loss of family   Wallerstein (1983) postulated that, for the child, parental separation and divorce is emotionally comparable to the death of a parent. Children not only mourn the loss of daily contact with one parent and diminished contact with

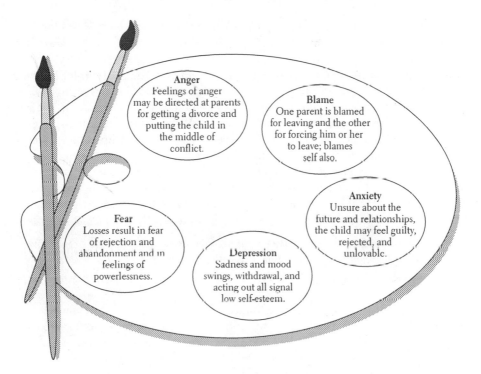

FIGURE 3-3 *Children's Common Emotional Reactions to Parental Divorce*
SOURCE: Wallerstein (1983); Wallerstein & Blakeslee (1989).

the other but they also mourn the loss of the security and sense of well-being the intact family provided. Changes in circumstances following the divorce might also mean that children will see less and less of grandparents and extended family members and will experience the loss of familiar neighborhoods, schools, friends, and lifestyle. Mourning responses may include confusion, anger, denial, depression, and feelings of hopelessness and powerlessness.

> *When my parents first got divorced, I missed my dad most when we sat at the dinner table. I would look over and see his empty chair at the end of the table. I knew then that we weren't a family anymore.*
> —Man whose father left when he was 10 years old

Fear of rejection, abandonment, and powerlessness Intense feelings of rejection, usually accompanied by self-blame, follow a divorce. Children interpret the parent's leaving as a rejection of them rather than of the marital relationship. This feeling also extends to visitation after the divorce. If noncustodial parents don't come as promised, children feel rejected and attribute this rejection to the fact that they are somehow unlovable. Children may have intense fears that the custodial parent will desert them too. They feel powerless to make things better, to prevent the divorce, or to "fix" their hurting parent.

When my dad left, I thought to myself, "What will I do if my mom leaves too?"
—8-year-old boy

Anger Children caught in the divorce process get angry at their parents for thinking only of themselves and for putting the children in the middle of their conflict. Many children experience loyalty conflicts when they are forced to choose sides in the battle. Children often despair over what they see as a betrayal of one of their parents. Some children keep their anger hidden because they don't want to upset their parents. Each child will have different emotional reactions to anger, including temper tantrums, aggressive behavior toward others, or a sense of powerlessness about the situation. Strangeland and associates, (1989) found that children with divorced parents reported being angry at their fathers, having trouble with school, and having difficulty sleeping.

> *I think my parents are acting like a couple of spoiled brats. They are acting like babies....They don't care about how I feel, I'm just the kid.*
> —8-year-old boy's reaction to his parents' divorce

Resentment and intense loneliness Children commonly feel resentment when they are not told about the impending divorce and do not have opportunities to discuss it. This lack of communication often translates into loneliness because of the loss of support from family, extended family, and peers. Wallerstein & Blakeslee (1989) reported that nearly 50% of the families they counsel wait until the day of the separation or later to tell their children of their decision. Fewer than 10% of the children in their study had any adult communicate empathy for them as the divorce process unfolded. Surprisingly, even grandparents offered little support to children during this critical time.

> *One day I came home from school and my mom was gone! My dad said that they had decided to divorce about two months before, but they had a big fight and my mom left before we got home from school. I started screaming and crying. I was so angry that they never told us. I still resent them for it.*
> —12-year-old girl

Guilt and self-blame Children often believe that if they had never been born or if they had been better children, their parent would not have left. Children also blame their parents; they blame the noncustodial parent for leaving and the custodial parent for forcing him or her out of the house. Because children love their parents and fear their loss, these angry feelings often generate guilt. Guilt and the accompanying anxiety can cause a number of emotional reactions in children.

> *Mom told me it wasn't true, but I still feel they were fighting 'cause of me.*
> —9-year-old boy

Anxiety and betrayal Because children fear that their lives will be forever disrupted by their parents' divorce, children may feel insecure about the future and about relationships. Adolescents in particular have difficulty trusting in others not to hurt them and may feel betrayed by their parents. Some children shy away from opportunities to give and receive love; others fear rejection and have decided that they are unworthy and unlovable.

> When my dad left, my mom cried all the time and never went out. Then she met a guy and wanted to go on a date. She wanted my dad to take us kids to the hunting camp for the weekend. He said he was too busy.
> —12-year-old boy

Psychological Tasks Associated with Divorce

Children who experience divorce encounter a set of divorce-related tasks in addition to the normal developmental tasks of childhood. The "psychological tasks" (Wallerstein, 1983; Wallerstein & Blakeslee, 1989) children must confront during the last days of their parents' marriage, through the separation and divorce, and in the post-divorce years are summarized below.

Understanding the divorce and its consequences Children who feel threatened with the loss of the departing parent and are angry with the remaining parent may have frightening and vivid fantasies of abandonment or of never seeing the departing parent again. Young children who have not yet developed the cognitive ability necessary to separate fact from fantasy have more difficulty adjusting to the reality of the divorce than do children who are able to think and reason logically. As children grow and develop, they realize that there is no basis for such fears and begin to assess the divorce in terms of how it affects their lives. As children get older, they come to understand why their parents divorced and can slowly repair relationships with both parents. Children need their parents' continual honesty and support in order to understand the divorce and its consequences to the family.

Disengaging from the crisis and resuming normal activities To successfully cope with the psychological task of disengaging, children need to acknowledge their concern for their parents and siblings, while at the same time striving to get on with the developmental tasks of growing up. Younger children who are preoccupied with worry about the divorce often show a decline in academic achievement, and older children may forego social activities because of the extra responsibilities divorce often places on them. For their own healthy development, youngsters need to place their own needs and priorities ahead of those that surround the divorce experience. Parents can help children achieve this task by encouraging children to remain children.

Coping with loss As was made clear earlier, children who experience divorce suffer the loss of security and protection and the loss of the presence of one parent. In reaction to this loss, children blame themselves and thus suffer a loss of self-esteem. As a result, children try to "undo" the divorce, win back the affection of the absent parent, and rebuild their self-esteem. The futility of these thoughts and feelings are often lessened when children can establish good relationships with the noncustodial parent during visitation or through joint custody arrangements.

Dealing with anger Although parents may view the divorce as a necessary relief from an unfulfilling and often unhappy relationship, children may experience it as a crisis that seriously threatens their stability. Consequently, children get very angry at their parents for being selfish and uncaring. Children love their parents and want to protect them, but at the same time they see their parents as responsible for their current unhappiness. A major task for children is to work through this anger and to recognize their parents as human and fallible. The task of forgiveness is important to healing: forgiving themselves for feeling anger and guilt and for being unable to repair the marriage; forgiving their parents for getting divorced.

Resolving guilt and self-blame   When parents divorce, children may somehow feel responsible for the breakup. Depending on their ages, children may fear that their hidden wishes have come true; they have succeeded in getting rid of one parent so they could be closer to the other. This same horrible guilt is present in children when a parent dies, especially if the child is going through what Freud called the Oedipal period. During this stage (ages 4 to 5 years), the child has feelings of jealousy for the parent of the same gender and wants to "marry" the parent of the opposite gender. Should the divorce occur at this time, the child may become terrified that he or she caused it.

Wallerstein and Blakeslee (1989) pointed to other instances where divorce follows the birth of a child, and children surmise correctly that they were indeed the cause of the breakup. Other children are aware that they play one parent against the other and that their behavior may cause a wedge between parents. In addition, children may blame one parent or the other for the loss of the intact family. It seems that blame and guilt are common after the marital split. The authors recommend that children be taught the skills to separate from the guilt that binds them too closely to a troubled parent and to move on with their lives.

Acceptance of the permanence of divorce   For children to accept divorce, they have to go through a series of grief and mourning responses similar to those that follow a death in the family. The first step in this process is usually denial, and children often cope with divorce by denying its finality. Wallerstein and Blakeslee (1989) noted that even after 5 or 10 years, children have not accepted the divorce as irreversible. They continue to hope, consciously or unconsciously, that the marriage will be restored, and they interpret every positive gesture as a hopeful sign of reconciliation.

This is apparently a desire that is difficult to outgrow. College students, whose parents divorced long ago and have since remarried, confide a deep longing for their family to be together again. They are tired of splitting holidays between parents and stepparents and of spending only a limited time with one parent. And when they talk of their families, the tears flow. If only their parents had stuck it out, they say, then everything would be different. Although less common, in some instances children have prayed for and benefited from their parents' divorce.

> I remember…asking Mom when Dad was going to come home. That's when she told me, "Dad isn't going to live here anymore. Now if you want to cry, go ahead." But I didn't want to cry. I was so happy at the idea of not having to live with the fear I had when he was around.
> —20-year-old woman (quoted in Rachel V., 1987)

Sometimes, as a reaction to profound feelings of rejection, children make repeated and vain attempts to bring their parents back together; in effect, they try to rebuild their own damaged self-esteem. Children who face their parents' divorce have more difficulty accepting it than do children who must cope with parental death. Death cannot be reversed; divorce can. Thus, children may continue to live with the hope that their parents will reconcile, and children seem to need their parents to be happy together. This is one of the most difficult tasks to address, and many children do not accept their parents' divorce until they are adults.

Achieving realistic hope regarding relationships   This last task is perhaps the most important of all, and it is dependent on accomplishing all the previous tasks. To achieve realistic hope, adolescents must put the model of their parents' failed marriage behind them and remain open to the possibility of relationships that involve love and commitment. Because children experience fear, anguish, and betrayal when their intact family splinters, they are understandably reluctant to get involved in relationships they fear might fail. Nevertheless, children who learn to risk themselves in relationships and who realize they can both love and be loved will achieve a certain "psychological freedom" from the effects of their parents' divorce. The resolution of this task is "the essence of second chances for children of divorce" (Wallerstein & Blakeslee, 1989, p. 294).

Recent studies reviewed by Gately and Schwebel (1992) suggest that children may escape long-term negative outcomes if the crisis of divorce is not complicated by multiple stressors and continued adversity. Positive outcomes may include increased maturity, self-esteem, and empathy for others. Single-parent families foster maturity when they involve children in appropriate decision making and in a healthy range of other responsibilities. In addition to maturity, increased self-esteem and empathy appear to be a function of successful coping with divorce-related changes. Gains in self-esteem are more likely when children are given moderate levels of responsibility and tasks that can be accomplished successfully. If older children are encouraged to provide age-appropriate emotional and practical support to family members, they may be able to gain an empathic understanding of others' feelings. This may result in increased compassion and warmth toward one or both parents. Children are more likely to experience increased maturity, self-esteem, and empathy if family members hold a positive view of divorce-related changes.

In summary, divorce is a stressful experience for children and their parents, and it precipitates many changes that can be distressing. Some of these changes might involve reduced contact with one or both parents, fewer opportunities to interact with grandparents and extended family, a move to another community, or a change of schools. How individual children react to these changes will depend on their overall adjustment as well as on their positive and negative experiences before, during, and after the breakdown of the marriage. Much will depend on the attitudes and behaviors of the child's parents and the child's ability to accomplish the "psychological tasks" associated with divorce. To make a successful adjustment, children must cope with their individual emotional reactions to the loss of the intact family. Once children grieve and accept the finality of the divorce, they are better able to put their parents' failed marriage behind them and move on.

Children need the support of both parents at this critical time. If the conflicts are severe and persistent and seem to be negatively affecting the child's social and emotional development or are interfering with the child's ability to enjoy life, parents may want to seek counseling for the child and for themselves. Counseling strategies applicable to children of divorced parents and to children who live with stepparents are included at the conclusion of the next section on blended families.

Blended Families

Unfortunately, the genuine love and tenderness between adults in a second marriage is not always shared with the children who come from a previous marriage.
—Wallenstein & Blakeslee (1989, p. 11.)

Most men and women who divorce eventually remarry. According to U. S. Census Bureau data presented in Chapter 1, at least 10 million children live in "blended" families with either a stepsibling, a stepparent, or both. One of the obvious problems of the blended family is its complex role structure. In decades past, when stepfamilies were created after a parent died and the other remarried, the stepparent assumed the role of the parent and did not have to compete with a living parent for the affections of children. In modern-day remarriages, the role of the stepparent is much more difficult and may be viewed in many different ways by children, depending on the circumstances of the divorce and remarriage.

In a longitudinal study of 113 children, Wallerstein & Blakeslee (1989) found that 55 lived with stepfathers during the decade following the divorce; and although 68 children had stepmothers, few lived with them. Stepmothers play a limited role in the emotional lives of children and are not considered serious rivals for the mother's love. The following discussion is centered on both parents, but the reader should bear in mind that the majority of children in blended families live with their biological mother and a stepfather. Examples of reactions to living with stepparents are from the author's own counseling experience with children.

Children fear the loss of the parent's time and affection   Most children of divorce have a great need for love and affection and a fear of being rejected. They worry that their parent will be less available to them when he or she remarries. Because parents are usually very physically and emotionally involved with one another during courtship and marriage, children often feel as if they are on the outside looking in. Although children love their parents and want them to be happy, some may feel that they are sacrificing their own happiness once again. It has come down to a choice of who should be happy: their parent or themselves.

I was just getting used to living without a father when my mom got married again. Now, my mom says, "Honey, would you like this? Honey would you like that?" She never asks me what I would like.
—9-year-old boy

Stepparents are not substitutes for biological parents   Even when stepparents have earned the love and respect of their stepchildren, they never replace the biological parent in the child's view. In a sense, children make room for additional people in their lives without eliminating their relationship to the absent parent. Children hold on to the thoughts, feelings, and memories that characterized their relationship with their biological parents and consider this relationship distinct from the one they have with the stepparent.

Children are aware of parents' sexuality in a new marriage Children who grow up in intact families have a tendency to view their parents' relationship as asexual. However, when the divorced parent gets a new boyfriend or girlfriend or remarries, children suddenly become aware of their parents' sexuality. Young children may model these expressions of sexuality as a way to get affection and attention. However, when this awareness coincides with adolescent development, it may add to the tensions between a stepdaughter and a stepfather. Even though most sexual feelings are not acted on, the second marriage may be threatened by these feelings and by the new parent's attempts to control them (Beer, 1989; Wallerstein & Blakeslee, 1989).

Loyalty conflicts are greater for older children Wallerstein & Blakeslee (1989) reported that two-thirds of the younger children in their sample were able to love their stepfathers and their fathers at the same time. However, more than 50% of the older children in the study resented their stepfathers, and 90% said that their lives were not enhanced by having a stepfather. Few children age 9 or older reported a good relationship with their stepfather; the major difficulty for adolescents was accepting stepfathers as authority figures.

> *Ray is a great guy and does things with us but it just isn't the same. Ray is a different person....He dresses fancy and looks good...but he can't even change a tire. My dad is tough and he can fix anything. My dad is who I want to be like.*
> —12-year-old boy whose mother remarried

Good relationships don't happen overnight Because healthy parent-child relationships are built on mutual affection, respect, and trust, they take time to develop. Children need time to adjust to the changes in routine, discipline, and lifestyle that a new stepparent brings to the family. If this new relationship is forced on them, children may rebel or withdraw. The same is true of relationships with children the stepparent may bring to the new marriage. In these situations, children often do not have time to either anticipate the arrival of stepsiblings or to adjust to the idea of living with these "perfect strangers."

Your children, my children, and our children In blended families, children from the original family must make a great many adjustments as they struggle to interact with a blended family. In addition to accepting the children born in the current marriage, the child may have to learn to get along with the stepparent's children. In some blended families, the stepparent's children live with their father; in other situations they live with their mother and visit their father on weekends, holidays, and summers. Regardless of the arrangements, there are bound to be conflicts when children are required to relate to children they barely know and to treat them as brothers and sisters. Intense competition is a frequent problem among stepsiblings (Artlip, Artlip, & Saltzman, 1993).

My dad said he didn't have money for the plane ride so I couldn't visit at Christmas. I found out later that he took his girlfriend's kids to Disney World. He never took me there.
—11-year-old girl

Wicked stepmothers are mostly in fairy tales   In the Wallerstein & Blakeslee (1989) study, stepmothers were generally viewed as contributing to the fathers' happiness. Children expressed fewer expectations of stepmothers and thus had fewer disappointments to report. Anger at stepmothers usually occurred if the children were not welcome to visit or if the stepmother was upset over child support payments and took it out on the children. Children generally do not view the stepmother as a replacement for their biological mother. However, adolescent girls sometimes establish relationships with younger stepmothers who treat them more as sisters.

My dad's girlfriend tries to be extra nice to us kids. She treats me like I'm her little sister and we talk about lots of stuff...girl stuff mostly. I kinda like her but I wouldn't want my mother to know.
—12-year-old girl

Stepparent-stepchild relationships can be successful   When trust develops gradually and respect is earned, some children develop genuine love and affection for their stepparents. Rather than establishing themselves as harsh and inflexible disciplinarians, successful stepfathers seem to establish better relationships with stepchildren if they mix patience and humor with love and commitment. Successful relationships with stepmothers are possible if both child and stepmother work at it. Stepparents can become important role models for children without replacing their biological parent.

APPLICATIONS TO COUNSELING

The following counseling strategies have been used successfully with children dealing with their parents' divorce and with new, blended families.

• *Encourage parents to talk to children about the divorce and how it will affect their lives.* With the counselor present, parents and children will have an opportunity to talk about their fears, anger, and resentment. Hopefully they can find ways to adjust to the many changes that are occurring in their lives. Use the family drawing as an ice breaker and to find out how each family member perceives the divorce.

• *Reassure children that they did not cause the divorce.* Help children understand that even though the parents are divorcing each other, they are not divorcing the children. Parents need to take time to be with children during this time and to give them opportunities to express their concerns. Counselors can help both parent and child by promoting a dialogue between them.

• *Recognize that children grieve.* Children mourn the loss of their intact family and their departed parent. Through counseling techniques such as play therapy, art therapy and bibliotherapy, children can be encouraged to express and cope with their grief. This process may take a long time.

- *Provide small-group guidance activities.* Several children who are at the same developmental level can be included in small-group discussions that focus on their feelings about divorce. Topics related to divorce in general such as fear, anxiety, and resentment can be introduced, which hopefully will help the participants talk about their own conflicts and experiences.
- *Recognize that children must adapt to changes.* Children who experience both divorce and remarriage have a lot of adjusting to do. Allow children to express their anger and frustration over some of the difficulties they have in getting along with stepsiblings and stepparents. Encourage children to talk to their parents about their perceived role in the new family constellation.
- *Include stepparents and biological parents in counseling.* Children seem to fare better if the divorce is amicable. It also helps if the biological parent and the stepparent get along. Children fear that their noncustodial parent will react angrily to the remarriage and take it out on them by seeing less of them or by battling with their remarried parent.
- *Help parents support their children through this difficult time.* Sometimes there is so much conflict between the parents that children get lost in the shuffle. Their needs are often overlooked and they believe their feelings don't count. It is important for counselors to develop a good relationship with parents, allow them to talk about their feelings, and encourage them to recognize their children's needs during this critical time.
- *Involve parents in groups.* Inviting parents to participate in groups offered through the school guidance program will give them an opportunity to talk with other parents. This group interaction will help parents express their own feelings and frustrations, learn more about what their children are thinking and feeling, understand more about child development, and find new ways of communicating with their children. All of these steps are important to finding solutions to the many problems divorce creates.
- *Help parents avoid burdening children with too much responsibility.* Use this as a topic for discussion in parent group. Many single parents are not aware that the responsibilities they have assigned to grade school children may be beyond the children's developmental level.

CHILDREN AND AIDS

AIDS (Acquired Immune Deficiency Syndrome) is a disease caused by the human immunodeficiency virus (HIV), and it is striking the nation's most vulnerable population—children. Dr. Lori Wiener of the National Cancer Institute notes that there were 4710 children with AIDS in the United States as of June 1993; thousands more have been infected with HIV but have not yet developed AIDS (Wiener, Best, & Pizzo, 1994). Even though the number of children who have active cases of AIDS is still quite small compared to the millions of children who live in abusive or alcoholic families, the HIV virus is spreading rapidly. Cohen (1993), citing 1992 data from the Center for Disease Control (CDC), noted that approximately 85% of children diagnosed with HIV or AIDS are infected by their mothers before or immediately after birth. Most children are infected in utero or through their mother's breast milk (Landau-Stanton & Clements, 1993).

Children in single-parent families struggling with poverty and drug abuse are most at risk. According to CDC data, nearly 60% of all pediatric AIDS cases result from the mother's use of intravenous drugs or from the mother's sexual activities with a known HIV-infected intravenous drug user. The second most common form of transmission (7.7%) is through transfusions of contaminated blood to the newborn (Cohen, 1993). Of course, not all children born to mothers with HIV will contract the virus. And because HIV can be a chronic disease, some children can go for months or years without symptoms (Weiner et al., 1994).

It is often difficult for pediatricians to determine whether an infant is suffering from the effects of HIV, because the symptoms of developmental delay, failure to thrive, and neurological impairment are also characteristic of babies who are born addicted to the drugs their mothers used during pregnancy. In addition, some of the earliest physical symptoms such as chronic diarrhea, failure to thrive, and upper respiratory and middle-ear infections are characteristic of many other childhood illnesses.

Diagnosis is further complicated by the fact that many children get poor or inconsistent care and may see a doctor only infrequently during infancy. Because many parents fear the possibility that their child might be diagnosed with AIDS, they may refuse to give consent for the testing. Some mothers are unaware that they carry the HIV virus; others may resist or deny the possibility of having the disease and refuse testing for themselves and their children (Reid, 1991).

The Impact of AIDS on Families

Many children with AIDS come from disadvantaged families headed by a single mother with more than one child. These families are among those with the least resources to cope with and support a child with AIDS. Sometimes mothers or fathers are sick themselves and may be dying. Some mothers are still addicted to drugs and are unable to provide the kind of nurturance and support their children need at this crucial time. Many do not have the financial or emotional resources to cope with the child's illness. The following are some concerns that families have when confronted with the overwhelming problems presented by this disease.

Parents may feel guilt and self-blame Because HIV is often the result of parents' drug abuse or high-risk sexual behavior, many parents must cope with the knowledge that their behavior directly resulted in the child's illness. Even in cases where children contracted HIV from blood transfusions needed to treat complications of birth, RH factor, or hemophilia, parents feel tremendous remorse over the child's affliction and may feel guilty about what they should and should not have done. Because guilt is an unproductive emotion that can further damage an already fragile, distraught parent and impact negatively on the parent-child relationship, counselors need to approach parents in an affectionate, caring, and nonjudgmental way.

Keeping secrets becomes a way of coping Some families choose to keep HIV a secret because they worry how such a disclosure would effect their child's friendships, education, and relationships. For other families, denial is the only method of coping; if family members don't acknowledge that the child is ill, they won't have to face the prospect of losing the child. Some parents avoid conversations about the child's diagnosis that would lead to painful questions about their own high-risk behavior. However, especially if a parent is already ill, some children suspect that something is wrong, and many wish to be told the truth. Keeping secrets places additional stress on other family members and does not provide an opportunity for the child and the family to share the burdens of the illness. It is difficult for children to talk about their illness if no one is supposed to know they have it. Thus, keeping AIDS a secret may diminish family support at a time when the child needs it most.

Some families cannot cope   Family members who live with HIV often must cope with the child's illness while also facing the illness and death of one or both parents. Many parents whose ability to cope is diminished by illness are unable to meet the physical, emotional, and financial challenges caring for a child with AIDS requires. Therefore, in some instances, children are placed with extended family members or are put into foster care. Depending on the child's age, this displacement may increase the sense of loss felt by children with HIV and may create anxiety among siblings who are still in the home. If a parent dies of the disease, the sick child often experiences a crisis of a series of losses.

The Impact of AIDS on Children

Because AIDS is still a much feared, misunderstood, and currently incurable illness, children with AIDS experience a series of losses that are unique to their condition. Children feel the loss of friendships with other children who avoid them or make fun of them. In addition to the loss of friendships that would provide comfort and support at this crucial time, AIDS involves the loss of energy to play and to be involved in activities children love. It also involves painful medical treatments, which involve restrictions the child often interprets as losses. However, the most profound loss children with AIDS experience is the loss of one or both parents through separation, abandonment, or death. As discussed in Chapter 2, children need a secure attachment to their caregiver during infancy. When a child is separated from the attachment figure, which in most cases is a parent, the child goes through three stages, which Bowlby (1973) described as protest, despair, and detachment. Children express these emotions as they mourn the loss of attachment to the parent, and these feelings need to be addressed in counseling children with AIDS.

Elizabeth Kubler-Ross (1983) suggested that children who face the possibility of their own death go through the same grief stages adults do. They may experience denial, anger, bargaining, depression, and acceptance. These stages can occur in any order, and the child does not necessarily have to go through each one. Some children do not live long enough to reach the stage of acceptance, but many do and they worry about the impact their death will have on their parents and siblings.

Children fear they will be rejected by friends   Because there is so much misinformation about how the HIV virus is transmitted, parents and children alike often fear the child with AIDS. Parents mistakenly believe that their children can contract the virus by sharing toys and school supplies or by touching a child who has AIDS (Walker & Hulecki, 1989). This unfounded fear has caused many heated protests by parents when a child identified as having AIDS tries to attend school. Consequently, children with AIDS fear the loss of friendships at a time when they have the greatest need for understanding and acceptance. In a book written by children with HIV entitled *Be a Friend*, a young girl wrote: "We just want to be accepted and loved like everyone else" (Wiener et al., 1994, p. 38).

Children with AIDS suffer in silence   Children who are not told that they have HIV because their parents want to protect them suffer in silence. But as the children get older and their illness progresses, they begin to suspect the truth. Reid (1991) concluded that children as young as 6 years may suspect that they have AIDS, particularly if either one or both parents also has the disease. Keeping the diagnosis a secret only intensifies fear and worry and deprives children of the opportunity to discuss their concerns with a caring adult. Even when children are told the truth about their illness, they may keep it a secret from their peers. Although children tire of the lie and want to be accepted as they are, they are aware of the attitudes and fears others have regarding HIV, and they usually remain silent about their condition. As a result, children with AIDS often feel lonely and isolated.

Children are confronted with sickness and death   Part of living with HIV is being sick, enduring painful medical treatments, hoping to get better, and knowing that you might not. Children with AIDS must deal with death—their own, that of their parents, and that of siblings and friends who also have the disease. Young children may view the loss of a parent as abandonment and may be concerned about who will take care of them when the parent is gone. Older children may react with confusion, anger, and desperation, which are mourning responses connected to the loss (Webb, 1991). For other children, denial may give way to outbursts of recognizable grief, only to be followed by depression (Halperin, 1993). Children who must face the possibility of their own death will grieve this loss in different ways, depending on their age. Some children worry about their declining energy to fight HIV and wonder if death will bring them relief; others worry about what their dying will do to their families. Many express the hope that their loved ones won't mourn them too long and will go on with their lives. The book *Be a Friend* chronicles how children face their fears about their own deaths with courage and insight, helping readers understand their struggle (Wiener et al., 1994).

APPLICATIONS TO COUNSELING

It is clear that children who have AIDS or are coping with the death of their parents and friends from the disease need a great deal of love and support, as well as opportunities to express their feelings. Some of the most important fears expressed by children with AIDS are highlighted in Figure 3-4. Children need to know that they can confide these fears to a concerned adult who will listen and understand, whether they are in school, at home or in the hospital.

Following is a list of types of treatment that have been shown to be effective in a variety of settings in helping children and their families cope with AIDS.

• *Use play and art as therapeutic techniques.* Play therapy techniques allow children to express hidden fears and anxieties and act out traumatic events. Because play and art do not rely on verbalization, children benefit from these therapies before they are able to articulate specific fears about death. The death of a parent

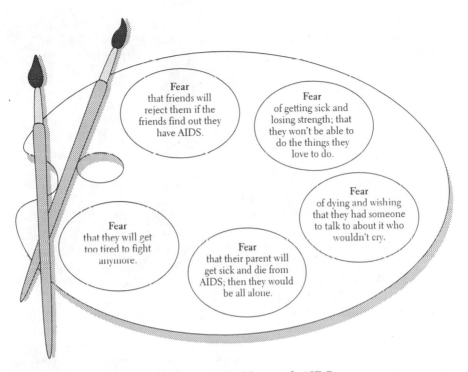

FIGURE 3-4 *The Special Fears of Children with AIDS*
SOURCE: Weiner, Best, & Pizzo (1994).

often produces a crisis situation for the child, and play therapy is an especially effective *crisis intervention technique* (see Webb, 1991).

• *In school settings provide education to dispel common myths about AIDS.* Correct information about HIV/AIDS needs to be communicated to children and their parents by school personnel. Kindness and understanding should be modeled by teachers and counselors, who often unintentionally wound children with offhand remarks about AIDS and the people who get it.

• *Help the child cope with the many difficulties that the school situation presents.* Schools need to make the same opportunities for individual counseling available to children with AIDS that are available to children with a variety of other troubled family situations. School counselors should be aware of referral sources so that children will get the full range of services that they and their families are entitled to.

• *Make in-home counseling available to terminally ill children and their families.* In some school guidance programs, the elementary school counselor can provide in-home counseling to terminally ill children and can help their families cope with the devastation of losing a child. Bertoia & Allan (1988) used spontaneous drawings as a technique to help a home-bound child cope with terminal illness. Such programs would certainly be beneficial for children who are too fatigued to attend school but are not yet in need of hospitalization.

• *Comprehensive treatment services should be available to children and their families in hospital settings.* Terminally ill children can receive medical care in

(continued)

addition to family counseling, therapeutic recreational services, opportunities for free play and educational programs.Counseling provides opportunities for children, parents, and siblings to share their feelings and offer each other emotional support. All children, not just children with AIDS, have a strong need to see their family as loving and caring.

• *Family-oriented, multidisciplinary treatment programs are needed.* Some programs are being designed to offer comprehensive treatment that includes support for the parents' recovery from addiction, home-based early intervention for identifying and enhancing children's developmental needs, and a referral network that helps families find and use support services in their community. Such programs often utilize a multidisciplinary approach to dealing with the many problems families face when drug abuse is involved. For example, a case manager with a background in counseling, social work, or education may lead a team of two or more professionals in either family counseling, speech therapy, or physical therapy; these teams may provide services for a caseload of 8 to 10 families. Case managers may visit families in their homes and coordinate a variety of services to ensure that children and families receive the necessary support and treatment.

In summary, AIDS is a devastating illness for children and families to cope with. Because there is currently no cure, children with active cases of AIDS often receive a death sentence before they have an opportunity to live. And because the disease is likely to be transmitted to children by mothers who engage in high-risk behavior, parents often also suffer from guilt and self-blame. Denial prevents many parents from seeking help for their children because they do not want to face the possibility that they have HIV and have given it to their child. Although different children with AIDS have different reactions to pain and loss, they express similar emotions: anger, fear, anxiety, and depression are the most common. Denial also helps protect children as they face the deaths of parents, friends, and loved ones. Children mourn and grieve, not only for their own illness but for their parents and their friends who have died. It is important for children to be able to express their anger, fear, and hurt. Although counseling can take place in a variety of settings, most is done in conjunction with hospital programs that provide medical treatment in addition to a variety of inpatient and outpatient services for children and their families. Play therapy, offered in many hospitals, clinics, and school settings, is an excellent therapeutic technique for children. The role of the schools is primarily to educate children, parents, and educators about AIDS and to provide a safe and comfortable environment for children. Finally, broad-based early intervention programs that help drug-addicted parents recover and provide for the needs of the developing child offer the best hope for children with AIDS.

CHILDREN IN MOURNING

My mother died when I was 7...she jumped or something. I don't know but I think it was my fault. My grandfather told me that she was sick...I dunno, I guess she was sick.

—8-year-old boy whose mother committed suicide

The death of a parent is one of the most profound losses in the human experience because of the nature of the bond between parent and child. This tie represents an emotional lifeline that nourishes healthy personality development and sets the stage for meaningful interpersonal relationships in the future. The love and stability the parent provides protects and nurtures the developing child and is essential to the child's development of trust. When children develop a secure attachment or bond with the parent (see Chapter 2) and that bond is severed by death or separation, the child reacts with anxious protest, despair, and detachment (see Bowlby, 1973, 1980). Although there is some disagreement over whether these responses represent grieving in the true sense of the word, Bowlby (1980) and others believe that the capacity to mourn begins once the child is able to form an internalized image of the mother through object constancy; thus even young children are capable of mourning responses.

These mourning responses are normal and appropriate following the death of a parent and might include: confusion as to why the parent had to die, anger at the parent for dying, anxiety about what will happen now that the parent is no longer there to take care of the child; guilt about their previous thoughts, wishes, or bad behavior toward the loved one; and despondency over the death. Even though the child has loving memories of the parent or the sibling—which survivors encourage them to express—the child suffers the loss of daily contact and interaction with the family member who has died. Similar grieving responses occur when a sibling dies, but an added fear of surviving children is that they might die also (Kubler-Ross, 1983). This additional stress may precipitate a crisis if the child or another sibling subsequently gets sick (Webb, 1991).

The Child's View of Death

The ability to understand the mysteries of life and death depends a great deal on a child's intellectual maturity. As children develop the ability to think and reason logically, their fears and perceptions about death change. As children grow older, they no longer believe that dead creatures can come back to life or that the boogie man will come and take them away as they sleep. Slowly children come to understand that those who die are not coming back, and they begin to understand some of the reasons people die. As children mature intellectually and they move toward abstract reasoning, their concepts about death change considerably. Therefore, how a particular child will be affected by the death of a family member depends a great deal on the child's age and intellectual capacity.

In a study of children ranging in age from 6 to 15, Koocher (1973) found that concepts of death corresponded to Piaget's preoperational, concrete operational, and formal thought stages (see Chapter 2). Fantasy, magical thinking, and egocentric reasoning were characteristic of younger children at the preoperational level; at this level, 40% of the children thought that dead creatures could be brought back to life. Children at the concrete operations level were able to articulate how death occurred by naming weapons and describing the nature of assaults. Children in the formal operations stage were able to give broader and more abstract reasons for dying, such as old age, illness, and accidents.

Preschoolers view death as temporary and reversible. When children see the Road Runner cartoon character flatten Wily Coyote with a steam roller, they are not at all surprised to see Wily alive in the next frame. In a form of magical thinking, children are able to bring the "dead" cartoon characters back to life. Because the preschooler's thinking is still centered very much on the self, young children may view the loss of a parent in terms of their own needs: "Who is going to take care of me?"

An extension of this egocentric reasoning is the child's perception that he or she is somehow responsible for the loved one's death. Preschoolers may blame themselves for misbehaving, fighting with siblings, having angry feelings toward their parents, or wishing that one parent would go away so that they could "marry" the other. According to Smart & Smart (1977), nearly every little boy at least once declares an intention to marry his mother when he grows up; girls have similar thoughts about their fathers. When the parent of the same gender dies during this period of the child's development, the child may reason that his or her angry feelings caused the parent to go away. These perceptions may leave the child vulnerable to feelings of guilt.

In most cases, the child feels a great deal of anxiety when the death is sudden and the child remembers having had angry feelings toward the deceased. Feelings of anger and jealousy toward siblings are common, and preschoolers may believe that these feelings caused the sibling to die. Even if they do not feel directly responsible for the death, children may feel guilty for having fought with a sibling or for not having an opportunity to say that they were sorry. In one case referred to in Chapter 6, two young brothers blamed themselves for every unkind word that they ever spoke to their sister, who died suddenly at age 8.

In the early elementary grades, children regard death as a vague and threatening concept, represented by skeletons, monsters, and other scary things. As children get older and see living things such as pets die, they see death as a cessation of bodily functions (Matter & Matter, as cited in Bertoia & Allan, 1988). Children understand that when people die they are buried, and at age 6 and 7, child survivors may have concerns about how the deceased person's needs will be met after the body is buried. One 6-year-old's concern following his sister's death was how a person (meaning himself) could get out of a grave without having anything to dig with. He made repeated requests to have his sister's grave reopened so that he could see her and say good-bye one last time (see Chapter 6).

As children move toward preadolescence, they begin to realize that death is final and inevitable and that one day they too will die. Although children may understand this concept intellectually, they still have difficulty accepting the possibility of their own mortality. As children develop increasing ability to think and reason logically, they give up the scary ghosts and monsters that frightened them when they were younger and replace them with a more realistic view of what causes death. However, just because youngsters are able to give broader and more logical reasons for dying, such as illness, accidents, and old age, does not mean that they fear it any less.

Coping with a Parent's Death

How a child copes with any crisis event, including the death of a parent, depends to a large extent on the interactions among the child's unique personality characteristics, the strength of the parent-child relationship, the child's daily experiences with the family and other social systems, and the child's perceptions of these experiences

(Webb, 1991). Children whose growth needs were met by the parents before their death will obviously make a better adjustment than will those who suffer from developmental deficits associated with maternal deprivation, father absence, or child abuse. Therefore, a child's adjustment to the death of a parent is dependent not only on individual differences in temperament and style of coping but also on the child's perception of the quality of the relationship with both the deceased and the surviving parent. In addition, the child's responses will also be affected by the reaction of the surviving parent and the lifestyle changes that occur following the death. Finally, the quality of the child's relationships with siblings, extended family members, and peers and the amount of support available from them—as well as from broader support systems such as the school and community—is important to the child's recovery from the trauma of parental death (Saravay, 1991).

Individual Reactions and Coping Styles

Two siblings can react in totally different ways to the death of a parent, just as they react differently to other events that transpire in families. Different responses should not be interpreted to mean that one child is mourning and the other is not. Children express grief in different ways, some have stronger defense mechanisms, and some adjust to traumatic situations faster than others. Children commonly use denial and regression to defend against the pain of separation from the parent. These are normal reactions and should not be of concern unless they are too rigid and are used too frequently over an extended period of time. As described earlier, children may show a variety of emotional reactions to the loss of a parent figure: confusion, anger, anxiety, guilt, fear, and despondency. Reactions may be mild or intense, depending on how the child perceives the magnitude of the loss. Which emotions are expressed and the method for their expression varies from child to child. Some children prefer to withdraw from others and suffer in silence. These children, who are grieving intensely, are often lonely and isolated and feel helpless and despondent. Others act out their anger in the form of aggressive behavior toward others. Some children express their anxiety through hyperactivity, which includes impulsivity, poor attention span, and inability to concentrate.

> My (younger) sister and I reacted to my mother's death in totally different ways. She cried all the time and was constantly clinging to my father. She had to sleep with him at night. I was just the opposite. I blocked it out of my head. I didn't want to think about it. I wanted to get on with my life.
> —KREMENTZ (1980, p. 63)

Individual reactions to the rituals surrounding death   Children have different reactions to the rituals surrounding death. Some want to attend the funeral home and go to the gravesite. Others prefer not to go at all or to wait until a year or so has passed. Some parents, in an effort to protect the child, do not permit the children to go to the funeral; but many children later relate that they wish they had gone because the death would be more believable if they had seen their parent in death. If the child chooses not to go to the funeral, he or she must be provided with other opportunities to say good-bye, and to confront the finality of death in other ways.

Individual reactions to support systems   Some children do not want everyone in their class to know about the death, particularly if it is a suicide. They may feel embarrassed and angry when the death is announced at school without their knowledge or permission. They don't want others feeling sorry for them. Other children are willing to discuss the death with their friends, if their friends bring it up. A few children seek out members of their extended family, such as a grandmother or an aunt to help them grieve.

Family Factors That Affect Coping

Quality of the child's relationship with the deceased parent   Children who enjoyed a healthy parent-child relationship characterized by mutual love and acceptance make the best adjustment to a parent's death, particularly if they have a supportive surviving parent who also had a good relationship with the deceased. When children have had a disturbed relationship with a parent and feel rejected and unloved as a result, they are more likely to experience problems adjusting to the parent's death.

Children who believed they could never measure up to parental expectations may feel that they lost their last chance to prove their worthiness when the parent died. This explains why children who have had the most troubled relationship with the parent are sometimes the ones who express the greatest sadness when the parent dies. To make matters worse, very young children may be under the impression that the deceased parent can still see and hear and is aware of their misbehavior (Gardner, as cited in Bertoia & Allan, 1988). This perception puts extra pressure on a child who has never been able to meet the parent's standards. Of course, the same feeling can work in a positive direction and can help children maintain the positive behaviors the deceased parent encouraged when he or she was alive.

Children often rely on memories of happy times to help them cope with the loss of a parent. Children are comforted by the sights, sounds, and smells in everyday life that serve as reminders of a parent whom they loved and who loved them. The smell of sawdust, the sound of a buzzsaw, a favorite story, or a look at a Halloween costume from long ago may flood the child with memories of a parent who has passed away. Good times that are remembered over bad help children cope. Because children depend a great deal on happy memories to sustain them in their grief, children who have not had a great many happy moments with the deceased parent may have fewer sources of comfort. Children who were beaten and abused by a parent may have disturbing memories, which are frequently played out in dreams and nightmares about the deceased parent. Furthermore, abused children may feel a sense of relief after the parent's death yet feel guilty for feeling that way. Sometimes, when the deceased parent either abused the child or allowed someone else to abuse them, the child both loves and hates the parent.

Quality of the surviving parent's relationship with the child   The reaction of the surviving parent is imitated by the children in the family. If the surviving parent adjusts to the loss in a healthy way, he or she can provide a good example for the children. Children who have open and honest relationships with the surviving parent feel free to talk over their worries about the parent's death. In some cases, a period of adjustment must be made, requiring the family to get along on less money or to celebrate birthdays and other holidays on the days that a parent isn't working. Some of the routines of daily life will be different, and children and parents will have to adjust.

A normal period of grieving should not interfere with the parent's ability to function as a parent. However, if the parent is incapacitated by grief and is unable to cope with the day-to-day routine established before the death, this situation may feed into a child's fears of not being cared for and may precipitate feelings of anxiety and insecurity. Furthermore, because depression is "contagious," children whose parents are depressed and unhappy may feel the same sense of hopelessness. Conversely, children may believe that they have to "take care" of the parent who cannot cope by assuming responsibilities beyond their developmental level. In this case, the child is burdened by both grief for the deceased parent and overwhelming responsibility for the surviving parent.

Additional problems may arise when the surviving parent would like to remarry. This may precipitate another crisis for the child for many feel that the parent is being unfaithful to the deceased parent. Children may also worry that if they are happy with the new stepparent, they are being disloyal to the deceased parent. .

Quality of the parents relationship with each other   The surviving parent's attitude toward the deceased parent is crucial to the child's future development. Very young children who do not have distinct memories of their absent parents have to rely on the surviving parent's perception. Because some parents did not have good relationships with one another, the surviving parent may present a distorted view of the deceased parent. The child lacks daily experience with the absent parent that might contradict this view, and so the child usually adopts the surviving parent's perspective (Grossberg & Crandall, as cited in Saravay, 1991). It is important, especially to young children, that the parent paint a realistic portrait of the deceased parent which neither idealizes nor vilifies the parent. This is true not only for death but also when divorced fathers do not see their children enough to contradict the negative image painted by the embittered ex-spouse. Parents who vilify the deceased parent, who is not there to defend himself or herself, run the risk that children will turn their anger on the surviving parent.

Dealing with a Sibling's Death

Many of the same factors that influence the child's response to the death of a parent also influence the child's response to a sibling's death. However, one of the main differences is that the children have a unique relationship with their siblings that is not shared in the same way with the parent. This sibling bond is characterized by love and affection as well as jealousy and rivalry. Sibling rivalry is the classic struggle among brothers and sisters to be first in the affection of their parents and to gain a position of favor within the family (see Chapter 2). It is normal for children to express both jealousy and anger through arguing and physical aggression. However, when a sibling dies suddenly, the survivors may be filled with remorse about this sibling conflict. Survivors may feel guilty about all the times they expressed jealousy and rivalrous feelings toward the deceased sibling.

When a child is terminally ill with AIDS or cancer and the possibility of death is always present, siblings have more time to adjust to and avoid the types of conflicts that they may later regret. However, when a child is terminally ill, siblings' feelings of jealousy may surface because the family is preoccupied with the sick child and may not have the time nor the energy to attend to the healthy child's feelings. Children with a terminally ill sibling are torn between two conflicting emotions: love and resentment. They love their brother or sister and do not want them to die, yet they resent all the attention and gifts the sick child receives.

> My brother is HIV, and he bugs me. He gets lots of attention, especially when he almost died. Sometimes when he gets lots of attention, I feel left out. When he gets new toys and Nintendo tapes, I often get nothing. I really want my brother to know that I love him even if I don't always show it.
> —WIENER, BEST, & PIZZO (1994)

When death is sudden and unexpected, children—and adults—are caught totally off-guard and do not have an opportunity to grieve in advance. As a result, the death of a sibling often precipitates a crises in the lives of the surviving children, who may feel intense survivor's guilt (Kubler-Ross, 1983) and regret every harsh word or act of aggression they ever directed toward the deceased sibling. They may react in ways that interfere with their ability to cope and may have serious adjustment problems following the death. They may also fear that they will soon die too.

Losing a child is one of the most devastating losses a parent can sustain. When a sibling dies, parents are usually so consumed with grief that they may not have the ability to attend to the emotional needs of the grieving siblings. This inattention may increase children's feelings of isolation and loneliness, which often accompany a sibling's death. In addition, the surviving children may not find a good model for adjusting to the death if the parent is unable to cope with the loss. Children who experience such a death in their families may need more love, support, and attention than their grieving parents are able to provide.

As with the death of a parent, the most common reactions to a siblings death are fear, anxiety, jealousy, guilt, resentment, and abandonment, and children may react to these emotions by withdrawing or by acting out. The extreme anxiety that often accompanies the death of a sibling and the fear the surviving children have about their own futures may also be evidenced in hyperactive, disorganized behavior, which renders the child unable to concentrate and be productive in play and in school.

APPLICATIONS TO COUNSELING

Following are some strategies that can be used in counseling children who are coping with a death in the family.

• *Counsel the children as part of the family group.* When a parent or sibling is dying or has died, the entire family is grieving simultaneously and each individual family member's grief responses have an effect on the family as a functioning unit. When a parent dies, the surviving parent is confronted with many additional responsibilities that he or she may be ill-equipped to deal with. Grieving children and parents need help to adjust not only to their grief for their loss but also to their individual adjustment to the many changes that are precipitated by the death. Counselors can be a source of support for such families, encouraging members to communicate with each other and helping them find outside sources of help and support for a variety of needs that arise.

• *Utilize play therapy to offer children a way to "play out" their grief.* Sand play, puppet play, and doll play are all techniques that have been used successfully with children who have suffered the death of a parent or sibling. (A demonstration of how sand play is used in play therapy with a young boy who lost his younger sister is illustrated in Chapter 6.) Because the death of a family member may precipitate a crisis, especially when it comes on the heels of other problems, play therapy has been shown to be an effective crisis intervention technique (see Webb, 1991).

• *Provide opportunities for children to express their grief through art.* This kind of expression has been shown to promote healing. The family drawing technique (see Chapter 7) would be an excellent technique for helping family members focus on warm memories of the deceased and would promote communication among family members who may or may not be sharing their feelings. Because children often cannot articulate their fears about death and the feelings that surround the loss of a loved one, counselors can garner important clues from their artwork. Such perceptions are essential in determining counseling goals that will help children cope with their grief and make a healthy adjustment to this traumatic loss. Art therapy can also be incorporated into individual counseling sessions with the children in school guidance programs.

• *Counsel children through bibliotherapy.* There are many excellent books (see Chapter 8) designed to help children of all ages understand death, and many that help them grieve. Because some children have difficulty articulating their feelings about a death in the family, counseling with books may help them talk about their grief. Even if children are unable to express themselves verbally, they are often able to identify with the grieving child in the book and are comforted.

• *Encourage children to write letters to the deceased.* When a parent or sibling dies suddenly, children have not had an opportunity to say good-bye. Writing letters to the deceased is a way children can resolve this dilemma. Encourage children to write a collection of happy and sad memories about the deceased, to tell stories about their families that include the deceased member, and to draw pictures to illustrate these stories. All these techniques will help the child cope with the loss while remembering the person as real.

In summary, how children react to the death of a parent or sibling depends on a number of individual factors such as age, intellectual development, individual styles of coping, and the quality of the relationship between the child and the deceased. Children who have healthy relationships with parents and siblings before the death adjust better than do those who have disturbed family relationships. The surviving parent's reaction provides a model for children following the death of a parent. If the surviving parent's ability to cope is impaired by overwhelming grief, extraordinary responsibility, or excessive guilt, the child will have a more difficult time adjusting to the loss. When a sibling dies, surviving children must cope with their grief in the midst of a grieving family. In some instances, children may not get the kind of time and attention necessary for them to work out their fears, guilt, and grief responses. If some of these issues are not successfully resolved, the child may experience problems in interpersonal relationships and school performance. Children who have the additional support of extended family, community resources, church or temple, and school make a better adjustment to the loss of a parent or a sibling. Members of the helping professions as well as teachers and other school professionals are often in the best position to offer help to the grieving family.

SUPPORT SERVICES FOR CHILDREN AND PARENTS

The following services are important resources for counselors and for referrals.

Help for Abused and Neglected Children

The C. Henry Kempe National Center for the Prevention of Child Abuse and Neglect, begun in 1972, is committed to multidisciplinary approaches to improve the recognition, treatment, and prevention of all forms of child abuse and neglect. The center provides a clinically based resource for training, consultation, program development and evaluation, and research. Many programs developed at the center, such as the Crisis Nursery and Home Visitor Programs, have been successfully replicated throughout the United States. To access the services provided to children, families, and professionals, contact:

> Kempe Center Programs
> University of Colorado Health Services Center
> 1205 Oneida Street
> Denver, Colorado 80220-2944
> Ph: (303)-321-3963
> Fax: 303-329-3523

Mentoring Programs for Children

Big Brothers/Big Sisters of America is a federation of more than 500 independent groups across the country that reaches out to youngsters who need a mentor. Volunteers are asked to make at least a 1-year commitment to meet with the child once a week for 3 or 4 hours. Currently, the organization is able to meet the needs of only 100,000 of the nearly 15 million children in need. To fill the gap, the national organization is currently working toward partnerships with the AFL-CIO, the National Guard, and the American Association of Retired Persons. For more information about how to become a Big Brother or Big Sister, contact your nearest agency or write to:

> Big Brothers/Big Sisters of America
> 230 N. 13th Street
> Philadelphia, PA 19107
> Ph: (215) 567-7000

Activity and Enrichment Programs for Children

The *Boys and Girls Clubs of America* is a nonprofit organization that helps young people, ages 7 to 18, to become productive members of their community. Each year, local clubs serve from 2,500 to 3,000 young people. Programming addresses the special concerns of at-risk youngsters as well as those with limited resources. Low dues of $1 per year per child enable all children to attend. A wide range of programs include health and physical education, cultural enrichment, education and guidance, social development and recreation, and citizenship and leadership. For more information, contact the local club in your area or contact:

Boys and Girls Clubs of America
1230 W. Peachtree Street, NW
Atlanta, GA 30309
Ph: (404) 815-5700

Support Groups for Children of Alcoholics

Al-Anon and *Alateen* are two support groups available to the families of alcoholics. These groups are especially designed to help family members share their experiences, strengths and hopes in order to solve their common problems. In closed discussion groups, children and adults can vent their feelings and receive empathy and support from others in the group. To locate a chapter, check the local telephone directory for a listing under Al-Anon or Alateen.

Self-Help Group for Bereaved Parents and Siblings

The Compassionate Friends is an organization dedicated to the promotion of the positive resolution of grief and the fostering of emotional and physical health of bereaved parents and siblings throughout the United States. The national headquarters generates a monthly newsletter which keeps the local groups informed and becomes a link among grieving parents across the country. The Compassionate Friends provides information, empathy and support at a time when it is needed the most. For information about local support groups, contact:

The Compassionate Friends, Inc.
P. O. Box 3696
Oak Brook, IL 60522-3696
Ph: (708) 990-0010
Fax: (708) 990-0246

Support Organization for Parents of Murdered Children

Parents of Murdered Children is a support group for survivors of murdered persons. In local chapters, families meet for mutual support, guidance, and direction. Help is available to newly bereaved parents and other family members in meetings, by letter, and by phone. This service is free and non-denominational. Contact:

Parents of Murdered Children
100 E. Eighth Street, Suite B-14
Cincinnati, OH 45202
Ph: (513) 721-5683

Support for Seriously Ill Children and Their Families

The Ronald McDonald House is a home-away-from-home for children with cancer and other serious illnesses. It provides temporary lodging for children and their families near local hospitals where the children receive outpatient treatment. If the nominal fee presents a hardship to families, it can be lowered or waived. The house provides an opportunity for families to lend and receive support, understanding, warmth, and love. Contact:

The Ronald McDonald House
405 East 73rd Street
New York, NY 10021
Ph: (212) 639-0100

INSIGHTS AND IMPLICATIONS

This chapter tells the story of vulnerable children who live in fragile families. It is a story of both violence and loss: violence in the form of child abuse and neglect and wife battering; loss caused by divorce, illness and death. Children who are abused and neglected experience violence firsthand because they are both victims and observers of family violence. Children of alcoholics often get a triple dose; they may be victims of abuse, witness domestic violence, and experience the profound loss of a parent who is consistently unavailable to meet their needs.

Children experience a similar sense of loss when the safety and security provided by the intact family is shattered by divorce, illness, or death. Children mourn the loss of daily contact with a parent when the parent is separated from the child and the family, whether through hospitalization, death, or divorce. Children of divorce rarely give up the hope that their parents will get back together again and that they can have their family back. Therefore, in some respects it is easier to accept death because it is clearly final. The child with AIDS faces a double specter of death: his or her own and that of his or her parents. Even, if the child is not faced with immediate death, having a serious illness involves many losses—the loss of freedom to play, to go to school, and to interact with friends.

How a child copes depends a great deal on the individual child and on the family situation. Because children have different personality characteristics, different coping styles, and different perceptions of the events that surround them, it is difficult to predict what any child's long-term adjustment will be. Much depends on the strengths and weaknesses of the child and the family and on the number of crises the child has experienced. Multiple crisis situations tend to weaken children emotionally, making them more vulnerable to serious long-term problems with adjustment. A great deal depends on the support the vulnerable child receives from parents and significant others, members of the helping professions, and agencies concerned with the health and happiness of children and their families.

WISDOM ACCORDING TO ORTON

- *Focus on the child's strengths and on those of the family.*
- *Show caring and compassion to parents. They need to be heard and understood.*
- *Avoid telling a parent who has lost a child that you know how he or she feels. You really don't.*

- *Most parents love their children and do not consciously intend to hurt them.*
- *To report child abuse, you need only suspect it, you don't have to prove it.*
- *Just when you think it is hopeless, you are probably making progress.*
- *Recognize when counseling is not enough.*

ORTON'S PICKS

Artlip, M. A., Artlip, J. A., & Saltzman, E. S. (1993). *The new American family.* Lancaster, PA: Starburst.

This entertaining book provides tools for strengthening stepfamilies. A sampling of the topics covered include: New Brothers; New Sisters; The "Other" Parent; Two Homes for the Holidays; and In-Laws, Ex-Laws, and Out-Laws. Written with candor and humor, this helpful guide provides insight into the special challenges presented by the "blended" family.

Kubler-Ross, E. (1983). *On children and death.* New York: Macmillan.

Elizabeth Kubler-Ross uses stories of children and their families to illustrate how coping with death is a natural way of preparing children for life. Loss becomes a catalyst for growth and understanding when parents allow children to share in the death of a loved one. This poignant book provides practical advice for helping parents and children through the grieving process.

Miller, A. (1990). *For your own good: Hidden cruelty in child-rearing and the roots of violence.* New York: Noonday Press.

In *For Your Own Good*, Alice Miller examines the root causes of violence. Using clear and powerful language, the author links violence against self and others to harmful and cruel child-rearing practices. This illuminating, and sometimes frightening, study of the consequences of child abuse is recommended reading for all who are troubled by what is happening to our world and to our children.

Wallerstein, J. S., & Blakeslee, S. (1989). *Second chances: Men, women and children a decade after divorce.* New York: Ticknor & Fields.

This engrossing book embodies the results of a 10-year longitudinal study of families that have experienced divorce. It addresses the psychological tasks that children and adolescents must accomplish in order to put the model of their parents' failed marriage behind them. The authors note that the resolution of these tasks results in "second chances" for the children of divorce.

Wiener, L. S., Best, A., & Pizzo, P. A. (Eds). (1994). *Be a friend: Children who live with HIV speak.* Morton Grove, IL: Albert Whitman.

This book is a poignant collection of art and writing by children hospitalized with AIDS. In their own words, the children express what they wonder about and wish for and their longing to be "normal." Siblings worry about their brothers' and sisters' illness and feel the strain of keeping the family's secret. The important message from these children is "Please do not be scared of us—we need you to be our friends."

PART 2

Counseling and Therapy with Children

QUIET REBIRTH

She heard the anger
in his eyes
and felt herself the target,
a counselor spurned

Cautiously, not wanting
to destroy their
legacy of trust,
she asked . . .
What's wrong?

No scream, only silence
until she turned her head
and almost missed the whispered
"no one cares"

And in her care she waited
and shared the silence of pain
until one hand touched another
in bondage.

Leading the way,
she found his self-esteem
wrapped in tomorrow
waiting for release.

Together they tempered
the hurts . . .
the obscenities . . .
the classroom capers. . . .

With childlike vision,
he relinquished
the rejections of the day
and found himself
worthy.
—BONNIE EDDY (1988)

WE ARE POISED ON THE BRINK OF A NEW ERA IN COUNSELING and therapy. With so many children needing so much from so few, practitioners are no longer subscribing to the "one theory fits all" philosophy. In assessing current trends in child therapy, Schaefer (1988) noted that more and more practitioners are adopting an *eclectic* or *integrated* approach to counseling and psychotherapy, rather than a narrow focus. There is a new flexibility in the application of knowledge and skills from different theoretical orientations and a growing recognition that no one therapeutic approach is equally effective with all children and adolescents. Combining techniques that complement each other adds power to the therapeutic process, and there is a new commitment to what works in practice, rather than just in theory.

In the following seven chapters, I present a number of strategies and techniques that can be used within a flexible, integrative framework. A variety of techniques, such as play therapy, art therapy, and bibliotherapy can be used by the well-trained professional of any theoretical orientation. This flexibility allows the counselor to use more than one strategy and to employ those techniques that are most helpful in addressing the child's concerns.

Chapter 4 addresses assessment and treatment planning. Essential to this process is the creation of a therapeutic environment in which children and their families feel comfortable enough to express their concerns. A number of examples of therapeutic settings are given and the conditions for the therapeutic relationship are explained. A complete assessment of all aspects of the child's development is obtained through a series of interviews, observations, and other formal and informal assessment techniques. These techniques are explained and illustrated using a case study. Goal planning is discussed and treatment options that address long- and short-term goals are explored. A sample developmental assessment and treatment plan can also be found in this chapter.

Chapter 5 presents an integrated approach to counseling that involves helping the child identify and explore concerns, gain new self-understanding and competence, discover alternative ways of thinking and behaving, and implement these changes in his or her everyday life through individual and group counseling. Goals can be achieved through a series of skills or strategies designed to facilitate change. An integration of process and skills is demonstrated through the case of Sterling S. Developmental counseling groups are explained and suggestions are given for forming and conducting groups. A variety of group techniques are also offered, including sociodramatic play, role playing, puppetry, games, unfinished stories, and other small- and large-group activities.

Chapter 6 is about play as a therapeutic technique. Play is a way for children to communicate their experiences, problems, needs, and strengths. This communication is enhanced by toys and play materials the child uses to "play out" his or her thoughts and feelings. A number of techniques used by play therapists are explained in this chapter, including doll and puppet play, storytelling, games, and sand play. An integrated play therapy approach is explained and illustrated with dialogue, and case presentation demonstrates how sand play and sociodramatic play can be used in the practice of play therapy.

Chapter 7 traces the importance of art in the child's development and in the therapeutic process. Art can be useful, especially when combined with other therapeutic activities, as a way to: (1) establish a relationship with children; (2) help children express and resolve their conflicts in therapy; and (3) promote growth in self-expression, problem solving ability, and confidence. Interpretation of art in child therapy is explained and illustrated with human figure and family drawings. Art as an assessment tool is explained and illustrated using a case study presentation. The chapter concludes with suggestions for individual, group, and family art activities.

Chapter 8 features bibliotherapy as another technique practitioners can use in a variety of settings. Steps in the process as well as factors to consider in selecting books are addressed. Practical applications of the technique are demonstrated in individual and group sessions using illustrative dialogue. Children's books that focus on common developmental concerns, understanding parents and families, coping with childhood crises, and dealing with disabilities are reviewed. More than 100 book reviews are included that may be of help to counselors who wish to use books as a part of child therapy.

Chapter 9 focuses on the behavioral approaches to child counseling. Principles of behavioral therapy, including positive and negative reinforcement, punishment, and response cost, are defined and explained. Included is a section on cognitive-behavioral therapy that discusses modeling, behavior rehearsal, response prevention, and self-monitoring. Assessing behavior, developing treatment goals, and identifying specific intervention strategies are part of treatment planning. Aspects of treatment evaluation are also included in this presentation, and a case study on sibling rivalry is used to illustrate the application of behavioral approaches to child therapy.

Chapter 10 focuses on safeguarding children's rights in therapy. Although most young children cannot legally consent to treatment, they should be included in treatment decisions and be given information on their progress that is easily understood. Children have the right to confidentiality except in those rare instances when they threaten harm to self or others. The counselor's task is to protect the child's rights while at the same time fulfilling his or her responsibilities to the child's parents. In addition, the counselor has a duty to protect from harm and must breach confidentiality when the child threatens harm to self or others or when child abuse is suspected. Common signs of abuse and neglect are included at the end of the chapter to aid practitioners in deciding when to report. A case study illustrates the need for follow-up care once abuse has been detected and reported.

CHAPTER 4   *Assessment and Treatment Plan*

> *Assessment includes...resources, strengths, motivations, functional components, and other positive factors that can be used in resolving difficulties, in enhancing functioning, and in promoting growth.*
> —CHARLES ZASTROW

Counseling is defined as "a process concerned with an individual's optimum development and well-being, both personally and in relation to the larger society" (Hansen, Rossberg, & Cramer, 1994, p. 6). When this global definition is applied to child counseling, the focus becomes helping the child overcome the obstacles that interfere with healthy growth and development. This therapeutic process maximizes strengths, improves weaknesses, and focuses on self-growth, self-awareness, and self-acceptance. It is not limited to crisis situations or child psychopathology but also serves to help children cope with ordinary developmental concerns, and it has a special place in prevention.

To help children overcome obstacles that interfere with their development, it is first necessary to know what these obstacles are. This knowledge is obtained through an assessment process that involves gathering, analyzing, and organizing information about the child and his or her family. A complete and accurate preliminary assessment is of critical importance in defining the child's specific needs, making tentative hypotheses, developing goals, and designing a treatment plan. Because assessment is an intricate part of the ongoing counseling process, the hypotheses formed in the assessment phase are continually revised as new information is revealed.

FACILITATING SELF-EXPRESSION

To facilitate the child's verbal and nonverbal expression of thoughts, feelings, and behaviors, it is necessary to create an environment in which the child feels secure and parents or guardians feel welcome. A second, equally important, aspect of assessment and counseling is the establishment of a therapeutic relationship that will encourage children and their parents to express their concerns. In this relationship, confidences are kept, decisions are respected, and children and parents enjoy nonjudgmental acceptance.

Creating a Therapeutic Environment

Before beginning therapy with children, it is necessary to create a physical environment that will help the child and family feel comfortable. Creating an inviting physical environment for child therapy can be accomplished by providing a room with furnishings, toys, and activities that let children know that this is their special place. The room itself should be bright and cheerful and have a variety of furnishings that accommodate children of various sizes and ages. If the counseling and play therapy area are housed in one room, it should be arranged to accommodate parents, family members, and, in some situations, small groups of peers who meet and talk about common concerns. In addition, parents need a place to interact with their children, the therapist, and other parents.

The furnishings in the child therapy room should accommodate small children as well as preadolescents, adolescents, and adults. This means that in addition to small chairs and tables, there should be at least one adult-size table for family drawing activities, parent group meetings, and for older children to play board games and engage in other age-appropriate activities. Preferably, the therapy room should have a private entrance so that families can come and go without going through the main building. It is also advantageous to have a sink in the therapy room so that children can have access to water they can play in, paint with, clean up with, and use in the sand.

The toys and materials should be sturdy enough to withstand repeated use, should be operated by imagination rather than batteries, and should be appropriate for the age and developmental level of the children who may choose to use them. Landreth (1991) suggested selecting toys and materials that facilitate the therapeutic relationship, promote a wide range of creative and emotional expression, stimulate nonverbal exploration and expression, and address the child's interests through nonstructured play activity.

Having a variety of toys and materials available allows children to choose activities that will serve as their own mode of communication. Suggested play activities that can be used during the assessment and therapeutic process include art, puppetry, storytelling, role playing, dramatic play, board games, and tree play. (The therapeutic value of these activities is well established and is explored further in the chapters on play and art therapy.) These play activities can also be used as informal assessment techniques.

Because counselors and therapists will have different needs, based on the setting where they practice, three separate child therapy rooms will be used as examples. The first room is designed for use by elementary school counselors who will need an area to conduct individual and small group sessions with children and their parents. Part of the elementary school counselor's space will be needed to conduct parent groups of about 10 to 12 persons. The second design is for a suite of rooms used by the private practitioner for play therapy, family counseling, and small group therapy. The third design is for a child therapy clinic in a university setting that provides training for students in individual and group child therapy and involves the children's parents in a play therapy group.

Children's Rooms at Schools

Some elementary school counselors are lucky enough to have their own private space within the school system. With a little creativity, some imagination, and a lot of enthusiasm, the elementary school counselor can turn even the dullest room into a haven for children. In this example, a double-wide trailer was provided for the guidance program and the counselor decorated it with donations and yard sale finds. This children's room has drapes on the windows, which are along one wall. A couch, two upholstered chairs, and a floor lamp are in one corner of the large room, and a fluffy rug makes the area warm and cozy. In this small "living room," the counselor can read and talk to children individually and meet with parents. At the other end of the room is a standard library table surrounded by ten chairs that can be used for small-group work with children in the upper grades and for parent groups. In the center of the room, 12 carpet squares in different colors (actually, donated carpet samples) are placed for children to sit on. These carpet squares give the tile floor a warm, inviting look, and children immediately gravitate to them in preparation for small-group discussions. Large-group guidance activities, usually held in the individual classrooms, can be held in this room, and children consider it a treat to come to this special place. It is good to have all the children here occasionally, because *elementary guidance is for all children.*

School bookcases house the collection of toys and other supplies that are used in play therapy and art therapy. A wide assortment of puppets find a home in a large wicker laundry basket and are used with all children—individually, in small groups, and for large-group guidance activities that involve entire classes. Two sets of large, cardboard cut-out puppets are available for large-group work with entire classes and are carried, along with other puppets, to the classrooms. Another large cabinet (built by one child's father) houses those toys that are not universally available to all children. A large rack, donated by a library, holds carefully selected books from the school library, which are exchanged for new ones every 2 weeks.

This particular area has many advantages. It is large enough to meet the needs of all the children and their parents, yet small enough to be cozy and homelike. Classroom activities are not disrupted by the noise of children delighting in small- and large-group activities. It is adjacent yet separate from the main school building so that parents can come and go without going through the main school area. In this way, privacy for parents who attend day or evening groups can be respected. A coffee pot, small refrigerator, and a popcorn machine make it possible to serve refreshments during evening group sessions. The absence of a sink in the children's room is compensated for by maintaining a small bucket of water with a lid on it. This water can be used for painting, cleanup, wetting the sand, or any other imaginative use.

Not all school districts will be able to allocate a special room for the elementary school guidance program. However, even in districts without sufficient resources, the school counselor can find ways to bring small- and large-group guidance activities to children. Classrooms can be utilized for art activities, puppetry, unfinished stories, bibliotherapy, and a variety of other activities that provide developmental guidance to all elementary school children. In addition, if no permanent play therapy room can be arranged, counselors can take toys and puppets in a small bag and meet with children in a number of different settings. Enthused counselors can turn their offices into safe havens for children and parents to discuss their concerns and can utilize other rooms in the building for parent groups.

Child Therapy Rooms in Private Practice Settings

The play therapy room can be included in a suite used for child therapy in private practice settings. The suite should be welcoming to children as well as adults. The waiting room should be equipped with child-size furniture and activities such as crayons and coloring books to keep young children entertained while they wait. Providing toys and activities helps make the experience more comfortable for parents who don't want to deal with a fussy or mischievous child. The suite consists of a fully equipped play room and two therapy or office rooms furnished with attractive couches and chairs upholstered in soft colors. All the rooms have large windows with shades for letting in various amounts of light and are wallpapered in soft colors. Soft lighting from table lamps provides a relaxing and comforting atmosphere, much like a living room in a private home. The practitioner's diplomas and other certifying credentials hang in the hall rather than on the office walls. There is an entrance through the waiting room and a separate exit that allows parents and children to leave unobserved.

Intake interviews with families and sessions with parents and adolescents are frequently held in the two therapy rooms. One of the therapy rooms doubles as an observation area, where activity in the play room can be observed and recorded. Play therapy activities take place in the play room, which is lined with cupboards that contain an assortment of toys, games, puppets, dolls and dollhouses, art supplies, and other expressive materials. (The types of toys and the rationale for their use are discussed in detail in the chapter on play therapy.) The play materials are within easy reach of children, who are encouraged to select whatever they wish.

Play room furnishings consist of a set of child-size table and chairs that allows younger children to engage in "pretend" play with dolls, teddy bears, and toy dish sets. A sandbox stands in the corner, inviting children to use it to tell a story through elaborate "sand pictures." A sink is provided to splash in, play in, or "drown" baby dolls in. Older children are accommodated with a drop-leaf table that can be used for board games and art activities. Folding chairs are easily stored and can be taken out as needed. A pool table attracts children who delight in "beating" the therapist. The types of furnishings and play therapy materials selected vary considerably, depending on the individual child therapist, the needs of the child clients, and the amount of resources the practitioner wishes to put into the private practice suite.

Child Therapy Rooms in University Clinics

This room design includes a fully equipped play room with adjacent observation room where the supervisor can observe student therapists as they engage in play therapy with individual children. Equipment for video- and audiotaping is available and is used only with permission of the child and his or her family. Each student is assigned a child for the semester and various rooms in the psychology suite are used for individual evening sessions. An adjacent classroom doubles as a therapy room where children and their parents engage in group play activities with student therapists.

The play therapy room includes a sink and a sand tray. The sand tray is on wheels and can be rolled from room to room. Bookcases line the walls and toys are arranged on the shelves within easy reach of the children. Cupboards in the large classroom contain more toys. (These are kept locked to prevent the college students from playing with them during the week!)

Establishing a Therapeutic Relationship

A therapeutic relationship is characterized by warmth and the *acceptance* of children as fully participating persons in their own right. To create this relationship, the counselor must have a genuine caring for the child that allows open and honest communication. This openness pervades the relationship, in which the child and the counselor are free to be themselves. According to Carl Rogers (1957, 1961), *genuineness* or *congruence* occurs when the therapist's verbal and nonverbal responses are consistent with his or her feelings. It is a "what you see is what you get" kind of feeling that relies heavily on respect or unconditional positive regard for the child. *Respect* takes the form of a nonjudgmental acceptance of the child's feelings, thoughts, and behaviors. Nonjudgmental acceptance implies that children are entitled to their feelings and that they can risk expressing them in therapy without fear of rejection or humiliation.

Underlying respect and nonjudgmental acceptance is empathy. *Empathy* is the ability to understand a particular thought, feeling, or behavior by seeing it through the child's eyes. Counselors are therefore able to respond to the child on a deeper level, to explore the child's problem, and to help the child develop insight and understanding. This empathic understanding will be communicated verbally and nonverbally to the child in the process of the therapeutic relationship. Acceptance, genuineness, respect, and empathic understanding engender feelings of *trust* in the relationship and are essential to both counseling and assessment (see Figure 4-1).

Counselors who interact with children from other cultural backgrounds can adopt several attitudes that will help the clients and enhance the therapeutic relationship. Intensified focus on communication and greater understanding of the child's particular culture creates trust and reduces defensiveness (Westwood & Ishiyama, 1990). Clients who believe their experiences have been heard, understood, and validated are more able to benefit from therapeutic intervention. Counselors may need to work more diligently and openly to establish honest communication, even acknowledging their lack of information about the child's culture or ethnicity. The resulting sharing process can create other inroads for the therapist and client to both relate to and interact with each other.

ASSESSING SPECIFIC COUNSELING NEEDS

Important Factors for Assessment

To understand the child's needs and establish goals for meeting those needs, the counselor will need to obtain an accurate picture of five important areas in the child's life (see Figure 4-2). A complete developmental assessment should include: (1) the special concerns that prompted the child and the family to seek help; (2) a thorough knowledge of the child's motor, cognitive, emotional, and social development; (3) an understanding of the child's relationships with parents, siblings, peers, and significant others; (4) a profile of the child's school life, including academics, activities, attendance, and attitude toward school; and (5) knowledge of the child's special strengths, including abilities, talents, interests, and supports available to the child to overcome his or her difficulties.

Concerns Precipitating Therapy

Usually a child comes into therapy because of one or more special concerns expressed by either the child, the parent, a teacher, or a significant other. The counselor must

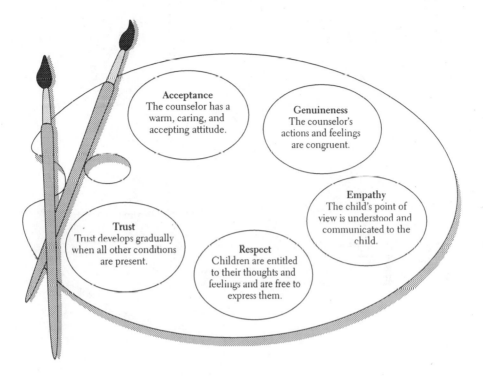

FIGURE 4-1   *Characteristics of a Therapeutic Relationship*
SOURCE: Rogers (1957, 1961).

understand these concerns within the context of the child's overall development and current psychological adjustment. This understanding is basic to the counseling process, and through it the counselor is able to establish therapeutic goals and an individualized treatment plan. It is especially important to understand the *child's* view of the presenting problem as well as the *parent's* view and to get a complete picture of the child's behavior in terms of appropriateness, frequency, duration, intensity, and degree of impairment.

As part of the assessment process, the practitioner will seek answers to some important questions about the child's behavior. First, is the child's behavior appropriate for the child's age and developmental level? An answer to this question requires both a general knowledge about healthy growth and development and the ability to recognize significant lags or deficits. In addition, specific knowledge of *this* child's development is needed before making a judgment about appropriateness. Because development is not a smooth progression and some children may stop or go back to an earlier, more comfortable stage, it is often necessary to ask, how frequently does the behavior occur? It is equally important to ask, what is the duration of the problem? Because some developmental conflicts appear and disappear in a relatively short time, it is important to know how long this problem has been noticed. Has it been present for a long time, has it just appeared recently? Also, has there been a sudden change in

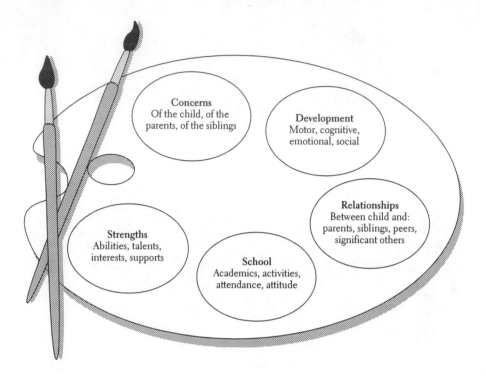

FIGURE 4-2 *Factors to be Included in the Assessment*

the child's behavior? Sometimes sudden changes in behavior are indicative of abuse or family disruptions caused by divorce, death, alcoholism, or domestic violence. A child's behavior can also be affected by a variety of factors, ranging from physical illness to conflicts with peers.

Finally, is the behavior interfering with the child's functioning? To what degree has this problem affected the child's healthy development? Is the behavior preventing the child from achieving in school, is it causing rejection by peers, is it blocking the healthy expression of emotion, or is it interfering with the child's happiness? Hopefully, many of these questions will be answered as the assessment process unfolds.

The Child's Growth and Development

An understanding of the child's motor, cognitive, emotional, and social development is essential to making a complete assessment. Part of this understanding comes from knowing as much as possible about the factors in the child's family, school, and sociocultural environment that influence his or her health and growth.

Health and early development   The child's general health influences other areas of his or her development. Therefore, information about serious illness, accidents, or injuries and about difficulties with vision, hearing, speech, and coordination are important to the assessment. For example, a child labeled "inattentive" may actually have a hearing loss. It is also important to ascertain whether other family members have health problems that could affect the total functioning of the family unit. Sometimes when the family is coping with a seriously ill family member, the identified child client may cope by misbehaving. Equally significant is an illness, accident, or emotional stressor that occurred during the pregnancy with the child client. For example, in one family the father left while the mother was pregnant, and this had a direct impact on the mother's feelings toward the child. Finally, the ages at which the child mastered motor and language milestones provide important clues about the child's early development. When serious developmental deficits are noted, the counselor should involve the family in counseling to see what steps can be taken to meet the child's physical and emotional needs.

Cognitive development Problems associated with learning frequently bring a child to the attention of the school counselor, school psychologist, or private practitioner. Therefore, it is important to get some measure of cognitive functioning and to rule out perceptual disabilities. Other professionals on the treatment team can supply these data. For example, the school psychologist may provide the results of an individual intelligence test, and the reading specialist may contribute pertinent information regarding the child's reading level and the results of any visual or auditory perception tests administered. Parents are knowledgeable about the child's early learning development and can provide their view of the child's current academic strengths and weaknesses. Generally, parents know how the child feels about school and which subjects he or she likes and dislikes.

Emotional development How emotion is expressed and regulated is very important to the child's overall psychological adjustment. Therefore, it is helpful to ask parents and teachers to characterize the child's mood and affect, for example, by asking them to use as many adjectives as possible to describe the child's emotional reactions (happy, depressed, quick to anger). The child's specific emotional reactions to stress and the nature, number, and intensity of his or her fears and worries are key concerns. Other important questions center on the way individual children express emotion and the degree of control they have over their emotional reactions. For example, when a child's outbursts of anger result in physical assaults on others, he or she is likely to come to the counselor's attention. Similarly, a child who cries constantly exhibits an inability to regulate emotion.

Social development Part of social development is learning how to behave as a member of particular social groups: racial/ethnic group, social class, family, and peer group. Because the importance of family and the peer group is discussed in a separate section, this section will deal specifically with *socioeconomic* and *sociocultural* factors that influence the child's development.

Education, income, occupation, and place of residence are factors that relate to a family's social and economic position. Parental teaching, family interaction, and attitudes toward counseling may vary according to the child's socioeconomic status, so it is important for counselors to be sensitive to the basic values held by families of social classes. Counselors can show respect for families with limited financial resources by recognizing some of the stressors that affect their daily lives. When parents want to be involved in their child's treatment but do not have reliable transportation or available baby-sitters, the school counselor might consider making home visits or putting the family in touch with community agencies that can help. When the child's problems cannot be addressed through the school, the counselor can refer the family to agencies that charge on a sliding scale. In addition, a number of community services are available to support children and their families at little or no cost (see the section on support services at the end of Chapter 3).

As minority and immigrant populations grow, practitioners are counseling children from increasingly diverse racial and ethnic backgrounds (Hardy & Laszloffy, 1992). Although these young clients may present a variety of needs, their ability to benefit from services can be linked to the counselor's understanding of their uniqueness. Although there is no magic formula for providing culturally sensitive counseling, much can be accommodated by the counselor's approach.

Historically, each ethnic and racial group has had one or more unique obstacles to overcome in American culture. African Americans endured the history of slavery and segregation and still battle the racial prejudice that adversely affects family development (Wilson & Stith, 1991). Asian American, Hispanic, Native American and other groups bring with them their own heritage of immigration or contact with other cultures, discrimination, acculturation, and adaptation. Children from these families bear both their individual needs and concerns and a unique cultural context that may conflict with standard therapeutic practices. For example, the Lakota view silence as an indication of respect, whereas European-American culture may view it as an indication of anger, inattention, or disinterest (Broken Nose, 1992). In the therapeutic relationship, that same silence may be interpreted differently by the counselor, which can directly impact both process and outcome.

Categorizing and stereotyping are common tools used to quickly learn about the unknown. When relating across cultures, these same tools can limit access to knowledge about the unique individual in treatment. A conscious commitment by the counselor to both understand the culture and maintain respect for the individual can provide a balanced approach in treatment (Niles, 1993).

When dealing with a child whose race or culture differs from the counselor's, it is still important to consider how many commonalities may actually be shared. The issues, complaints, and needs of a child, regardless of cultural and other differences, may be like those of any child. Therefore, it is imperative that the counselor be aware of both the similarities and the differences and integrate them into his or her approach. Ultimately, the counselor's role is to bridge the differences and enable the child to benefit from treatment (Solomon, 1992).

The Child's Relationships With Others

Because family structures are changing, children may be involved in many complicated parent-child relationships. Therefore, it is helpful to know the *quality* of the child's relationship with each parent or parental figure (such as a noncustodial parent, a stepparent, or a parent's significant other). It is important to understand how different family members view the child and how the child perceives his or her place in the family. Central to this understanding is information about the child's living arrangements, home responsibilities, parental methods of discipline, and the child's response to the discipline. Knowing what activities the parent(s) enjoy doing with the child and what the family does for fun is also helpful in treatment planning. Of course, much of this information will become evident as therapy progresses, especially as the therapist works with the child client and the family.

Sibling relationships are usually characterized by both conflict and caring (see Chapter 2). However, when families emphasize competition over cooperation, sibling rivalries often intensify. Therefore, the counselor needs to (1) determine how all the siblings in the family relate to one another and (2) assess the degree of conflict. Special alliances within the family structure make sibling conflict more likely and more intense. Sometimes the child client has been made the family "scapegoat," by parents and siblings alike, and is constantly being blamed for anything that goes wrong within the family. For example, children who are identified as "hyperactive" are frequently blamed for everything that gets broken, whether they broke it or not.

Peer relationships are important to children. Every child should have at least one best friend, someone to laugh and play with and to tell secrets to. Without at least one friend, the child is likely to feel lonely and rejected. Children, who lack friends their own age are often forced to play with much younger children or to associate mainly with adults. Assessing friendship patterns will help the counselor determine whether the child's relationships with peers are sufficient to satisfy the child's needs.

Often, if family ties are weak, children will gravitate to peers sooner than they would if the family bond was strong. Early adoption of peer values may lead to more antisocial behavior because the child wants so desperately to fit into the peer group. This is especially true of the school-age child who is approaching puberty. Information about the child's friendships or lack of them is often revealed in therapy sessions as time goes on.

Finally, because significant others often have a profound influence on how well children recover from various assaults on their development, it is important to find out what support children receive from significant others in their lives. Some children have strong ties to extended family members, such as a grandparent or a favorite aunt. Children who have extended family members support and encourage them are fortunate indeed. Some of these family members may be involved in therapy, depending on how great their influence is in helping the child overcome obstacles to their healthy growth and development.

The Child's School Life

Most children spend the majority of their day at school, so their academic and social successes are a very important part of their overall development. Children who experience repeated failures in school suffer from poor self-esteem, and they often engage in problem behaviors as a way of compensating. Failing grades should be an immediate warning sign that either the child is not appropriately placed in classes where learning is possible or the child has some physical, learning, or emotional disadvantage. Some clues about the child's ability to profit from his or her learning environment can be obtained through the formal testing procedures of the school's reading specialists and the school psychologist.

Many children are chronically discouraged, and this attitude affects their academic progress as well as their social relationships with peers and with teachers. Often this attitude of discouragement translates into a negative attitude toward school and may be reflected in the child's attendance. Children who don't feel accepted by their peers or who find school work difficult may take the easy way out and skip school. No matter what the reason, skipping school is usually an indication that something is wrong in the child's life that warrants a closer look.

Acceptance by the peer group is very important to the school-age child. Sometimes this acceptance is not forthcoming and has negative consequences on a child's self-acceptance. The child who is perceived as different in some way may be the object of cruel and insensitive remarks by other children. If the child is isolated or rejected by the peer group and has no one to confide in, he or she is likely to develop a negative self-concept.

The Child's Abilities, Talents, and Supports

To capitalize on the child's strengths, the practitioner needs to be aware of the child's special abilities and talents that can be incorporated in the treatment plan. For example, a child with a special music talent can build up his or her sense of competence through the arts. Special successes in one area can help to balance difficulties or failures in another. A child's special interests and activities can also encourage increased parental support. Sometimes parents and children find common ground for interaction and discussion when they enjoy doing things together. Children might enjoy team games, chess, stamp collecting, or any number of activities that can be integrated into a plan to strengthen the parent-child relationship.

The Techniques of Assessment

Before undertaking the counseling process, the counselor must know a great deal about all areas of the child's life. Information about the child can be gathered in several different ways: (1) the child information form, which is filled out by the child's parents; (2) intake interviews with the child and the family; (3) observations by parents, teachers, and the counselor; (4) supplemental assessment measures, such as behavior rating scales; and (5) informal information gathering techniques, such as art, unfinished stories, puppetry, games, and free-play activities (see Figure 4-3).

The Child Information Form

The child information form can be a valuable assessment tool if used in conjunction with the intake interview and other assessment measures. How the form is used is a matter of individual preference and depends on a great deal on the setting (school, hospital, clinic, or private practice). Some private practitioners ask parents to complete an intake form on the first visit. Others mail the form and ask that it be returned when the parents bring the child for the first session. Some counselors, particularly school counselors, use an abbreviated version as part of an informal get-acquainted session with the parent. Clinicians, especially in hospital settings, use a lengthy form that is usually filled out during the intake interview with the child and the parents. This form often includes a mental status examination and a detailed medical history.

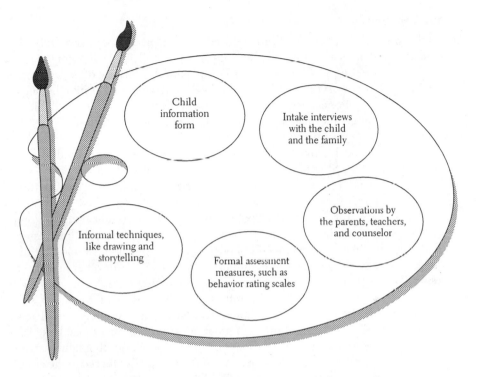

Child
information
form

Intake interviews
with the child
and the family

Observations by
the parents, teachers,
and counselor

Informal techniques,
like drawing and
storytelling

Formal assessment
measures, such as
behavior rating scales

FIGURE 4-3 *Strategies for Assessing Children's Counseling Needs*

The importance to be attached to the intake form depends on a variety of factors, including the practitioner's theoretical orientation. Counselors who rely less on written data and records may choose not to use an intake form, preferring instead to learn about the child and the family through observations and interviews. Other practitioners, particularly those using the medical model who need to make a psychiatric diagnosis, prefer to gather as much data as possible from formal assessment measures. A good rule of thumb is to make it as easy as possible for the parents. Whether this involves allowing time in the waiting room, sending the form home, or filling it out as part of an informal get-acquainted session is a matter for the individual practitioner to decide.

The sample child information form provided in Appendix A may be shortened or adapted to the individual counselor's needs. This form asks for important information related to the presenting problem and previous treatment, medical history of pregnancy and delivery, developmental milestones, learning development and school issues, social development and peer relationships, emotional development, special concerns, and family relationships and history. The practitioner may wish to include information not listed on this form or to address some information in the interview. The information given on the intake form is confidential and cannot be released without the parent's written consent. This restriction applies to the release of information to clinicians in other therapeutic settings as well. When referrals are made, a release is always required for this child information form.

The Intake Interview

The intake interview is an essential part of the counseling process because it helps the counselor establish a relationship with the child and the family that will form the basis for all future counseling and therapy. A successful intake interview offers a glimpse into the interpersonal world of the child and provides valuable insight into the family dynamics. Most practitioners, regardless of their theoretical orientation, use the interview process to gather information that will help them conceptualize the case and design an appropriate treatment plan.

Interviews can be highly structured, semi-structured, or unstructured (Wicks-Nelson & Israel, 1991). Structured interviews utilize a set of rules regarding how the interview will be conducted and how the data will be recorded. The highly structured interview usually addresses a list of problem behaviors and events and yields more objective data that can be used to facilitate formal diagnosis. Semi-structured interviews allow some flexibility in regard to how questions are asked and how data is recorded. Unstructured or open-ended interviews are usually conducted as part of a therapeutic process and are used in conjunction with a variety of other assessment measures. The unstructured interview, according to Greenspan (1981, p. 110), "follows the basic concept that the less you intrude, the more the child will tell you." Interviews with children need to be tailored to their age and developmental level (Barker, 1990). If play, art, storytelling, and other activities are used to facilitate self-expression, even preschoolers can provide valuable information about themselves. The interview format described in these pages is unstructured, is tailored to the child's developmental level, and utilizes a number of informal assessment techniques.

The number of interviews, the family members involved, and the order in which the interviews occur vary according to the practitioner's orientation and the opportunities for contact with the child's family. Some practitioners recommend a series of four intake interviews, one that includes the entire family followed by separate interviews with parents, siblings, and the child, in that order (Brems, 1993). Others suggest a single intake interview with the parents and child together (Gumaer, 1984). Generally, if the child is younger than 7, I interview the parents first so I can learn as much as possible about their concerns for the child. Family interviews may come later in the process as more rapport is established with the parents. Of course, the format, number, and order of the interviews is a very individual decision, and practitioners will have to decide what is practical for them.

Ideally the first interview should be with the entire family, but in practice the interviews can occur in any order. Sometimes the family interview occurs after the others are completed and takes place when all family members can participate. In other cases, the parent who brought the child to therapy is the one who participates in the first interview with the child. Sometimes, when both parents accompany the child, the parents may ask to see the therapist separately. This request is more common when the parents are divorced and each parent wants to give his or her individual perspective of the problem. In school counseling, the initial assessment may involve the child first, followed by interviews with one or both parents. Later, during home visits, the entire family is often involved. The intake interview, like everything else in counseling, has to be individualized to fit each family situation. No matter what the order or who participates in the intake interview, the focus should be on developing a relationship with the family, for this will be the foundation of the therapeutic relationship.

The family interview   The family intake interview is critical to the success of the therapy. It is during this process that the counselor helps set the tone for future sessions and conveys a sincere interest in helping the child and the family. The decision to enter into therapy is never an easy one, and the counselor must do everything possible to help parents understand how valuable they are to the therapy's success.

Family members who have lived together a long time (since birth, in the case of the child client and his or her siblings) develop their own interactional patterns and establish an interlinked system of defenses (Kwiatkowska, 1977). Family subgroups are formed (such as parents, parent and child, siblings) and transitional alliances are forged between members to enable the family unit to operate smoothly and efficiently as it changes and grows. When some family members form alliances or coalitions *against* other family members, the family's stability may be threatened (Goldenberg & Goldenberg, 1990). For example, when a grandmother forms a coalition with her granddaughter against her daughter-in-law, she is not only overstepping her authority and being intrusive, she is also damaging family boundaries. In this case, the grandmother is creating an alliance that may ultimately threaten the mother-child relationship and her son's marriage.

According to Goldenberg and Goldenberg (1990), all members of a family participate in several subgroups at the same time, both influencing and being influenced by the other subgroups. These subgroups are defined by boundaries that create invisible lines around the family as a whole, around each subgroup, and around individual family members. Healthy boundaries between parents and children are firm but flexible, and they allow for closeness when necessary while at the same time ensuring that autonomy is encouraged and individuality is protected. Both enmeshment and disengagement tend to contribute to unhealthy boundaries in families (Goldenberg & Goldenberg, 1990). *Enmeshment* occurs when boundaries are too weak and family members become overinvolved with one another. Examples of overinvolved parents are those who dote on a particular child, protecting and favoring him or her. *Disengagement* occurs when boundaries are too rigid and there is little interaction between family members. In homes where family members are uninvolved with each other, there is little support, concern, or mutual sharing of thoughts and feelings. For example, underinvolved fathers and mothers may work two jobs, ostensibly to provide the family with material goods but also to avoid being involved in their children's day-to-day lives.

The interactions among siblings is an important area of the family assessment. Goldenberg and Goldenberg (1990) maintained that "siblings represent a child's first peer group" (p. 47), and children develop patterns of cooperation, competition, and mutual support in the sibling subgroup that help them develop interpersonal skills. Interactions with siblings have an impact on the child's future attachment to friends at school and in the workplace. How much the sibling subgroup influences each child, and whether this influence is positive or negative, depends a great deal on how well the other subgroups are functioning. If the overall family is functioning effectively, able to maintain stability while accommodating change, this will be reflected in the various subgroups.

During the family interview, the therapist will learn more about the degree of closeness or distance, the types of alliances that exist, and the degree of involvement parents have with their children. Careful observation of the family in any setting will help the therapist determine which family members are closest and which are the most distant. Observing body language and listening to the family's discussion will also give clues as to which children are included in the conversation, which are listened to, and which are continually interrupted. The therapist will note whether a particular child "clings" to the parent or sits on his or her lap. All of these clues yield important information about family alliances, degrees of involvement, and boundaries. This is not to suggest that holding a child on one's lap means anything unhealthy is occurring in the parent-child relationship; rather, it suggests that the parent may be very involved with this particular child, perhaps too much so.

During this interview, it is important not only to find out what concerns the child but also to ascertain how the family views the child. An excellent technique for assessing the family dynamic from each member's perspective is to use a projective technique like the family drawing (Rubin, 1984; Tavantzis, 1984). The family drawing technique is a fun activity that builds rapport, gets the entire family involved, and facilitates interaction and communication. It requires only a large sheet of paper and some crayons, magic markers, and colored pencils. By asking family members to "draw your place in the family," the therapist can learn a great deal about the individual family members' perceptions of one another and of themselves. The family drawing provides important clues about how family members like to spend their time, how they view their relationships with each other, and which family members they identify with and feel closest to. The family interview provides important insight into the parents' relationship with each other, each parent's relationship with each child in the family, and each family member's interaction with the identified child client.

Various art techniques have been used to facilitate meaningful communication and interaction among family members for the purposes of assessment and therapy. During the initial assessment meeting with the family, it is especially important to find ways to elicit diagnostic information without relying on the usual verbal history-taking interview. Chapter 7 contains numerous family group art activities that can be used in conjunction with the family interview. These techniques are helpful in determining whether the family is a stable, cohesive, close-knit unit or whether members are divided and distant. The verbal and nonverbal behavior of family members give important clues to the interaction among members and between the family and the environment.

The parent interview   The intake interview with parents provides information about the child and the parent-child relationship that is important to future counseling sessions with children and parents. Because parents know their children better than anyone else does, they are a valuable source of information about the child. For parents to confide their unique insight into their child's problems, they have to feel comfortable with the counselor. Therefore, it is extremely important that the counselor relate to the parent as an equal in this first interview and as a partner in the therapeutic process. Counselors will want to keep their demeanor warm and friendly and to communicate with parents in a way that contributes to understanding and builds rapport. This involves some judgment on the part of the practitioner, who will want to use language that is neither confusing nor condescending.

To make parents feel comfortable, the therapist needs to establish a relationship of acceptance centered on the premise that most parents love their children and want to do what is best for them. The counselor who starts with this premise will be able to accept individual differences in interests, beliefs, values, and lifestyles and to help parents help their children. Even though the counselor may hold beliefs, attitudes and values that are very different from many parents of their child clients, the counselor can find ways to appreciate individual differences and convey this respect through verbal and nonverbal interactions with the family.

The counselor needs to learn as much about the child as possible, and in this case the parent is the expert. Parents are usually accurate in their perception of their child's troublesome behavior and often possess considerable insight into what may be contributing to the child's problems. They are seeking counseling not because they don't understand the problems but because they are at a loss to find solutions that work. Because they are so close to their child's "problem," they are unable to take an objective view. The counselor can help the parent put the problem into perspective and discover ways to improve the parent-child interaction.

Many human services professionals are employed by agencies that encourage home visits. The home can be an ideal setting for the interview because the atmosphere is less formal than a therapist's office. Generally, it is easier to develop rapport with parents when they are in the comfort of their own homes and believe they have a measure of control over the interview. Counselors who are fortunate enough to be able to make home visits must be careful to convey a nonjudgmental attitude through their actions, speech, and dress.

It is best to relate to parents using clear, easy-to-understand language. Technical language does not impress parents and may instead serve as a barrier between the counselor and the parent. Also, it is better to leave the clipboard and briefcase at the office. Writing a lot of notes during the interview might be a distraction, so it is best to either write things down immediately after the visit or tape the session (being taped is usually not as threatening to parents as it is to beginning counselors). Finally, the counselor should be a gracious guest in the parents' home and exhibit the same respect he or she displays at the home of family and friends.

Seeking help is a difficult step for parents, who see their children as an extension of themselves. Parent's often convey this insight by saying, "I was just like that when I was a kid" or "He's got my temper." Sometimes the child's problems bring back painful memories of the parent's own childhood experiences in school. Consequently, some parents are reluctant to go to the schools for help because they fear they will be "scolded" once more by "professionals" at school who have evaluated them and found them lacking. The same holds true for parents who are reluctant to seek help from private practitioners and clinics, fearing that their family will be viewed as "dysfunctional." During the intake interview and subsequent sessions, the practitioner needs to be sensitive to the fact that seeking help is difficult for some parents, and the practitioner should do everything possible to allay their fears.

Many parents feel a profound sense of guilt about their children's problems. The notion that they are somehow to blame is reinforced by today's popular literature, which uses catch words like "toxic" and "dysfunctional" to describe parents and families. Parents who have experienced problems such as alcoholism, drug abuse, or divorce are especially vulnerable to feelings of self-blame and remorse. It is important for counselors to help parents deal with these feelings and then help them to move on, underscoring that now is the time to focus on improving the parent-child relationship and setting blame and self-recrimination aside.

The child interview Unlike the family interview, this time belongs to the child alone. The therapist is there to provide warmth and understanding but follows the child's lead. In an atmosphere of permissiveness, the therapist creates an environment that allows the child to decide how he or she would like to spend this special time. The practitioner does not hurry the interview process, but rather lets the child reveal significant material when he or she is ready to do so. This means that the interviewer's approach is generally nondirective, does not include a lot of prying questions, and relies instead on open-ended questions that help clarify the child's responses. The therapist's responses are limited to what the child wishes to communicate; if the child chooses to use symbols to express his or her concerns, the therapist accepts this form of communication.

In the interview, the therapist allows the child to express every thought and feeling openly and does not judge the child or the child's parents. The therapist treats the child's verbal and nonverbal expressions with respect and safeguards the child's confidences. This acceptance of the child's right to feel as he or she does will help the child be open and honest about his or her particular worries and fears. Because younger children generally like to "play out" their concerns rather than talk them out, a variety of fun activities can be used in the assessment interview. Informal assessment techniques such as art activities (see Chapter 7), doll and puppet play, storytelling, board games, and other play therapy techniques (Chapter 6) can be used to establish rapport, learn more about the child's behavior, and catch a glimpse of conscious and unconscious conflicts that even the child may be unaware of. The therapist will need to interpret the symbolism of the child's play in light of all the other information gathered about the child during the assessment process.

Observation

Teacher and counselor observations are especially helpful in forming hypotheses about the nature of special problems the child may be having. To get a complete picture of the child's behavior and interactions with peers, it is necessary to make observations of the child in several different settings. Observations make it possible to learn more about the child's learning style, attention span, mood and affect, expression of emotions, and interactions with parents, teachers, and peers. It is ideal if the counselor is able to get observations of the child's behavior in the classroom, on the playground, and in the child's home. These observations can be made by parents, teachers, and counselors working as a team.

Observations are usually recorded within a specific time frame so that the practitioner can make some inferences about the child's activity level and attention span. Time frames are especially helpful when trying to determine whether a child might be suffering from attention deficit hyperactivity disorder or other learning disabilities. When a more structured type of observation is needed, behavior checklists are often used. In this type of observation, the teacher is asked to check whether specific behaviors are noted and, if so, how frequently they are seen. A follow-up form is usually given to teachers and to parents if the child is put on any medication. The purpose of these observations is to note any changes that have occurred as a result of the medication. In this respect, behavioral observations are an important tool for evaluating progress as well as for identifying problems.

Observation of classroom behavior The following is an observation of Kisha, a kindergartner who was referred by her teacher for impulsive and hyperactive behavior. This observation was done during rest time and provides a record of Kisha's behavior during a 10-minute period. Some children fall asleep during this naptime, whereas many just rest; Kisha does neither. This is a record of her activities from 2:55 P.M. to 3:05 P.M.

2:55 "I hasta go pee pee."
Pulls at Shelly's dress.
Pushes doll carriage.
Puts shoes on VCR cart and can't find them.
Gets coat and hat and goes to the door.
Hangs head down over edge of cot and chortles at the upside down view.
Comes and hugs (teacher): "I love you." "Can I kiss you?"
"I'm gonna tell mom somethin'—to feed Tip—he's hungry."
"I'm gonna give him some water."
3:02 Rattles crazy-car—almost climbs in it.
3:05 Has toy car on cot.
Up again—"Now can I go pee?"
Toy monkey clacking on cot.
"I'm gonna get a sleepy badge—I want this one—now give that to me!"
"I'm gonna pee my pants!"
"Can I put these (shoes) on my chair?"

Observation of parent-child interaction The following observation is of Holly, a first-grader who was referred because she is sullen and pouty and is constantly hitting and slapping her classmates, especially her best friend Jean. Teachers report mood fluctuations; anger and aggression followed by sullen withdrawal. The following observations were made on two separate home visits while the counselor was attempting to talk with Holly's mother. In subsequent sessions, Holly's mother was able to talk about her anxiety and frustration and to find more constructive ways of interacting with Holly. Without the valuable insight gained from these two observations, the counselor would have not been able to assess the parent-child interaction and formulate a plan to help both Holly and her mother.

First Observation

3:30 Holly is playing ball with a neighbor child.
3:40 Begins to cry—wants to play something else, friend doesn't.
Mother yells at the child to stop crying: "Knock it off, you big baby."
Again the children begin playing.
Holly pushes the other child and takes the ball.
Holly strikes the other child.
Mother hits Holly and says: "You can't go around smacking kids when you don't get your way."
Holly cries and screams.
Her mother yells at her, "Stop that screaming."

Second Observation

4:00   Holly is playing with her dolls.
4:05   Discussion between the counselor and the mother is interrupted with
          "Don't do that!" when Holly breaks crayons that she is coloring with.
4:10   "Sit still!" (Holly's mother admonishes her to stop running around.)
4:15   "I'm going to smack you!" is the response when Holly tries to get her
          mother's attention by dumping out the toy box.
4:20   Holly's mother is nervous and impatient. (Holly has changed activities for
          the fourth time.)

The purpose of observing the parent-child interaction is *not* to "find fault" with parents or to "blame" them for the child's behavior, but rather to help the parent discover ways of interacting with the child that will focus on the child's strengths rather than on the child's weaknesses. Once a child's behavior becomes an irritant to the parent, the parent-child relationship becomes tainted by "the problem," and it becomes the focal point of their interaction. Observations of the parent and child interacting together are helpful in discovering how "the problem" has affected the relationship and are essential in establishing treatment goals that will improve the parent-child relationship. Although this observation was made at the parent's home, similar observations could be obtained during play therapy when parents and children are involved in group, during family interviews, or in the counselor's office.

Formal Assessment Techniques

Some practitioners, depending on their theoretical orientation, may wish to obtain additional information through behavior rating scales, forms, or behavior checklists. The advantage of these techniques is that they provide a somewhat more objective view of the child's behavior than might be obtained in intake interviews or through observation. Most behavior rating forms focus on child behavior and rely on the judgments of parents, teachers and counselors about that behavior. Because teachers are in the best position to rate the child's classroom behavior and because they know their children quite well, they are often called on to make judgments regarding the severity of particular problem behaviors. Asking a number of teachers to evaluate the child's behavior will give a balanced perspective of the child's behavior in different classroom settings (such as regular classroom, reading resource room, music room).

Behavior observation forms   Occasionally, clinicians ask for an assessment of a child's behavior in the classroom in order to make a definitive diagnosis of a particular childhood disorder. In these instances, psychiatrists and clinical psychologists may provide their own forms, which usually contain a list of the behaviors typically associated with a particular disorder, such as attention deficit hyperactivity disorder (ADHD). Teachers and others are asked to determine how frequently certain behaviors are seen in the child's daily activities: for example, is the child "restless and fidgety" *seldom, sometimes, often,* or *always*? A sample observation form is included in Appendix A.

The data gathered on these behavior observation forms add to what is already known about the child and help complete the assessment picture. These data are useful to counselors who must help the child and the family deal with some of the troublesome behaviors that may accompany a particular disorder. In the case of ADHD, this information provides a baseline for monitoring the effects of any medication that may be given to the child after a diagnosis is made.

Behavior rating scales Designed for children in grades K–3, the *Child Behavior Rating Scale* (CBRS) (Cassel, 1962) consists of 78 items related to the child's self, home, social, school, and physical adjustment and provides a score to indicate total adjustment. Raters include parents, teachers, counselors, and other adults who have observed or know the child well. The CBRS assists school personnel and clinicians by providing a picture of the child as seen at home and at school. By studying different ratings of the same child, it is possible to: (1) pinpoint areas that need to be explored (for example, the child may be rated as making excellent home adjustments but poor school adjustments); (2) gain an understanding of the interpersonal relationship between the raters and the child (such as parent-child, teacher-child); and (3) understand the dynamics of the home (for example, father perceives the child as well-adjusted; mother does not) (Cassel, 1962).

The *Child Behavior Checklist* (CBCL) is another behavior rating form appropriate for children and adolescents (Achenbach & Edelbrock, 1983). This checklist, developed by Thomas Achenbach, was designed to assess the behavioral problems and social competencies of children age 4 to 16. In addition to the Child Behavior Checklist, which is completed by the child's parents, three other formats are available.[1] The *Teacher's Report Form* asks the teacher to rate the child on 112 questions related to 9 areas of problem behavior and 3 areas of social competence. The teacher's ratings can be used for comparison with parental ratings. The *Youth Self Report* is designed for older children and asks them to rate themselves. Finally, the *Direct Observation Form* allows an independent observer (such as counselor) to rate the child on 96 problem behaviors.

Because most rating scales identify problems rather than the factors that influence them, they are not helpful in assessing the child's personality characteristics, strengths, coping skills, intelligence, and abilities. Therefore, their usefulness is limited to providing additional information, rather than as a primary assessment strategy. This limitation can be overcome to some extent by using supplemental assessment measures such as the Bender-Gestalt Test (see Canter, 1996). This measure can provide a quick assessment of intelligence, help rule out serious perceptional problems, and offer insight into the dynamics of the child's emotional development.

The *Bender-Gestalt Test* (BGT), also known as the Bender Visual-Motor Gestalt Test, was originally designed by Lauretta Bender (1946)[2] to measure the visual motor perception of children age 3 to 11. Koppitz (1963) expanded its use as a perceptual and projective test for all children, age 5 to 10 years, by developing a standardized scoring system. Today, this test has multiple uses as a tool to assess emotional

---

[1] Manual and forms are available from Thomas M. Achenbach, Center for Children, Youth and Families, University of Vermont, 1 South Prospect St., Burlington, VT 05401.

[2] The Bender Test consists of nine cards, each with a design or pattern. The first card is identified with the letter A, and the others are numbered 1 through 8. These cards are currently available through various psychological test suppliers.

adjustment as well as intellectual and neurological functioning. "The Bender Test not only gives the examiner a rough measure of the youngsters' intellectual ability, but also serves as a nonthreatening introduction to the interview. Children tend to enjoy copying the Bender designs, and in some cases the Bender figures evoke associations and spontaneous comments which can lead to further discussions" (Koppitz, 1963, p. 51). In the following example, the examiner took note of Kent W.'s behavior, facial expressions and verbal comments as he drew the 9 Bender designs. These observations provide additional data for Kent's preliminary assessment (see the subsequent section, "Developmental Assessment: Kent W.").

Activity: Bender Cards		Analysis/Interpretation
Card A		
(Wants to turn the paper; erases)		Seems nervous; wants the drawing to be perfect
Card 1		
KENT:	Do I have to draw the dots *exactly* as they are?	Concerned about doing it right
COUNSELOR:	Do the best you can *(Draws big dots; strains to see them)*	
COUNSELOR:	You did fine.	
KENT:	Yeah, except they're crooked!	Self-deprecating comment
Card 3		
(Erases three times)		Shows anxiety and frustration
Card 4		
KENT:	Does it have to be the same angle?	
COUNSELOR:	Do the best you can.	
KENT:	This one is kind of hard! *(Erases)*	
Card 6		
(Erases several times and tries to turn the paper; shrugs shoulders, sighs, erases again)		Appears confused; strained; increasingly frustrated and discouraged
Card 8		
KENT:	Does it have to be *exactly* the same length here?	
COUNSELOR:	Do the best you can. *(Sighs, erases)*	
KENT:	Went too far on that one. *(Sighs, erases)*	Seems tense and unhappy with what he considers an imperfect drawing

Informal Assessment Techniques

Young children may not know exactly what is bothering them, or they may lack the words to express their problems. Play activities such as stories, poems, art, and games help children convey these conflicts, often symbolically, to the therapist. A variety of informal assessment techniques can be used in conjunction with the intake interview with families, parents, and children, including art activities, puppets, storytelling, board games, and free play.

Art Art activities are widely used as informal assessment techniques with individuals, groups, and families. Some art assessment techniques use assigned topics, some combine assigned topics with free choice, and others utilize free choice exclusively. Rubin (1984) found that when allowed a free choice of topics in the art interview, children structured the time in such revealing ways that structure seemed an unnecessary interference. Through art, children are able to express both positive and negative feelings about themselves, their families, and their world. By using art as an assessment tool, the therapist may be able to catch a glimpse of the child's unconscious thoughts and feelings that might not be available to them in any other therapeutic mode. An entire section of Chapter 7 is devoted to art activities that can be used in the assessment of children and their families.

Puppets Puppetry is an ideal way to capture the rich symbolism that is part of a child's spontaneous play. For children who wish to play with puppets as part of the initial interview, a basketful of puppets representing animals, human figures, and fantasy figures should be available to them to choose from. Puppet interviews can be both structured or unstructured. In *unstructured puppet play*, the child chooses the activity and decides which puppets to use, what story to tell, and how to tell it. The therapist follows the child's lead and can participate in the play if asked. In the unstructured interview, the therapist can reflect feeling and clarify responses while at the same time noting the symbolism in the child's play. In a *structured puppet interview*, the therapist asks the child to use the puppets to make up a "pretend" story. Then the therapist "interviews" the puppets or the puppeteer. In this way, the child is encouraged to talk through the puppets, and the therapist can clarify the child's responses and validate clinical hunches. Afterward, the therapist talks with the child about the story and its significance to the child's real-life situation (Irwin, 1993; Irwin & Malloy, 1975).

Storytelling Storytelling (Gardner, 1971) is another indirect technique that can be helpful in assessing the child's needs in therapy. Storytelling may be an ideal way to uncover the inner world of a child who has difficulty playing out his or her feelings. The child's story, told in the therapist's presence, can be lengthened by the skillful counselor's request for elaboration. Sometimes the therapist can encourage the child to elaborate by telling the child a story that ties into what the child is trying to express. Through storytelling, children are able to reveal their problems symbolically. This type of symbolic communication can be helpful in formulating and validating hypotheses about areas of conflict in the child's life. For instance, Karla continually told stories about a princess who wanted to move from a big castle (which resembled the big house that the family lived in now) to a very small cottage with a fireplace and a flower garden outside. The second house resembled her grandparents' house, where she had spent time following her parents' separation and divorce.

Board games   When given a choice of what they would like to play with, school-age children often choose board games (see Chapter 7). Playing a board game is a fun way to establish rapport and facilitate communication with the child client. While playing board games, the therapist has an opportunity to discover the child's level of intellectual functioning, emotional maturity, and socialization skills. By observing and listening to the child, the therapist can determine whether the child is happy or sad, cooperative or defiant, active or lethargic. Game playing also helps the therapist learn more about the child's personality strengths and weaknesses, ability to cope, and level of self-esteem (Frey, 1986).

Some children have difficulty staying seated or paying attention, even to the point of forgetting that it is their turn. Children who are easily distracted cannot complete the game and continuously move from one activity to another. Some children chatter incessantly as they play, hardly stopping to catch their breath. All these behaviors have diagnostic significance, especially if attention deficit hyperactivity disorder or anxiety are suspected. It is important for the therapist to pay attention to the child's verbal and affective expression. Some children are talkative; others are silent. Some children are animated and smiling; others are sullen and unhappy. There is much to be learned by staying in tune with not only what children are saying but how they are saying it. Finally, it is especially revealing to note how children react to the competitive games they choose. Children with low self-esteem have difficulty "losing," and some will do anything to win, including cheating. All these factors contribute to an understanding of the total child and his or her development and are helpful in assessing the particular conflict that brought the child to therapy.

Free play   Free play techniques are also valuable assessment tools. When the therapist utilizes a nondirective approach and allows the child to choose from a variety of toys in the playroom, the child will often select a toy and engage in an activity that does not fit into any of the above categories. In general, children will structure their own hour, providing the therapist with valuable insight into their thoughts, feelings, and behavior. The children will undoubtedly think of many creative and imaginative ways to tell the therapist about themselves.

"My Story"   "My Story" is a nonthreatening activity that combines writing and art to assess the child's perceptions of self, family, and school. These perceptions may include interactions with family members, significant others, and peers. As you can see in Figure 4-4, questions are designed to gather information about the child's interests, friends, and wishes, providing the counselor with a sense of the child's needs and desires and what the child likes to do when alone or with family and friends. Even though these questions are addressed in other ways during the assessment, "My Story" provides the counselor with the child's viewpoint. In addition to written commentary, this activity includes a self-portrait, a drawing of the child's family, and a picture of the child's perception of him- or herself at school. (Clues to interpreting these drawings can be found in Chapter 7.)

MY STORY

My name is _____

I am from _____

Things I like to do _____

People I like to be with _____

_____

If I had three wishes, I would want _____

_____

This is me!

THIS IS MY FAMILY

These are the members of my family _____

_____

My family likes to do these things _____

_____

My family is special because _____

_____

_____

My family

ME AT SCHOOL

The best things about school are _____

_____

What I don't like is _____

_____

The best teacher at school is _____

because _____

At school, I like to be with _____

At school

_____

FIGURE 4-4 *The "My Story" Activity*

DEVELOPMENTAL ASSESSMENT IN PRACTICE

• • • *The Case of Kent W.*

Information for the developmental assessment of Kent W. was gathered from (1) the child information form, (2) one interview with both parents and three interviews with Kent's mother, (3) an informal interview with Kent, (4) behavioral observations in the classroom conducted by four of Kent's teachers, (5) observations of Kent's behavior in various settings by the counselor and school psychologist, and (6) the results of specific tests administered by members of the treatment team, including tests of intelligence, achievement, visual and auditory perception, and specific skills in reading and math.

A case conference was held to discuss the results of these measures and to share them with the entire treatment team. The team, headed by the counselor, included four of Kent's teachers (reading, math, physical education, and classroom teacher), the school nurse, the reading specialist, and the school psychologist. The information gathered by members of the treatment team is included in the following preliminary developmental assessment.

Identifying Information

Name: Kent W.   DOB: 6-16-82
Age: 9.5   Grade: 5
Birth Order: Fourth and youngest child
Child lives with: Biological mother and father
Father: Age 58   Skilled factory worker
Mother: Age 52   Homemaker
Siblings: Paul: Age 32   Rose: Age 30   Betty: Age 26

Reason for Initial Referral

Punches and pokes other children for attention
Cries violently when others punch him back
Can't sit in his seat
Doesn't pay attention and is easily distracted
Speaks out in class; says things that are irrelevant

Medical History

Treated for allergies since age 6
Wears glasses
History of poor appetite
Below average height and weight

Birth History/Early Development

Mother was 42 when Kent was born
Pregnancy and delivery were normal
Child described as "difficult" since birth
Irritable and colicky infant
Constantly chewed on crib and furniture

Walked and talked early
Used words in sentences at earlier age than siblings
Difficulty with toilet training
"Wiggly," nervous toddler who said "no" to everything
Mother recalls: "He tried my patience at every turn"
Had few opportunities to play with other children
Fought with cousins so parents stopped inviting them to the house
Did not have to share with siblings because of age difference

Learning Development

Strengths

Has an IQ of 130 on the Stanford-Binet Intelligence Scale-Revised (SBIS-R)
    (Thorndike, Hagan, & Sattler, 1986)
Results of reading tests indicate steady improvement since first grade
Tests results and grades indicate math is Kent's strongest academic skill
Reading, math, and language are at or slightly above grade level according to
    standardized achievement tests
Rarely absent from school
Never repeated a grade
Attended the same school since kindergarten

Weaknesses

Achievement does not reflect true potential
Inability to concentrate on schoolwork
Cannot do independent seatwork
Has difficulty participating in class discussions
Loses interest in activities that are not highly motivating
Does not appear to benefit from large-group instruction

Social Development/Peer Relationships

In school

Is barely tolerated by other children in class
Has no best friend
Seeks attention from peers by shoving, pinching, insulting, and teasing
Unable to temper judgment with tact (e.g., "You stink" or "Boy, are you dumb!")
Cries or runs when classmates retaliate in kind
Overreacts when others respond to his aggression (e.g., falls completely to the
    floor to emphasize the "injustice")
Is unaware of how his behavior affects others

In the neighborhood

Doesn't get along with neighborhood children
Got into fights on the walk home from school in grades 1 and 2
Older cousins now walk him home from school to protect him
Recently fought with a younger female cousin

Emotional Development

Emotionally immature for age
Lacks empathy for others

Cries easily when tired or frustrated
Frank to the point of hurting others' feelings
Rejects praise even when it is earned
Shows kindness and concern for some teachers
Has difficulty making decisions
Is verbally and physically aggressive toward other children

Family Relationships

Parent-Child Relationship

Mother is very protective and overinvolved with Kent
Father is rarely involved in Kent's activities
Kent is seldom disciplined and is overindulged by both parents
Grandparent-child relationship exists due to age of parents
Mother performs tasks for the child because it is "easier" and "faster"
Kent displays excessive emotional and task-oriented dependency on parents,
   particularly his mother

Sibling Relationships

Siblings describe Kent as "spoiled"
Age differences between Kent and his siblings precluded a close relationship
Betty, who lived at home until Kent was 6 years old, was his "second mother"

A Team Approach to Assessment

In a case conference initiated by the counselor, seven members of the treatment team
met to give their individual perspectives on Kent's problems. (Sample case conference
forms are provided in Appendix A.) The team agreed on the following areas of
concern:

- Exhibits a pattern of inattentiveness, impulsivity and hyperactivity suggestive
  of Attention Deficit Hyperactivity Disorder
- Is unaware of the impact of his behavior on his peers
- Is unable to control his behavior or regulate his emotions
- Is isolated and rejected by peers
- Has low self-esteem
- Is easily frustrated
- Feels inadequate and lacks confidence
- Shows poor judgment and lacks decision-making skills

The treatment team agrees that Kent's behaviors are consistent with attention
deficit hyperactivity disorder (ADHD) and that many of his behavior problems are
interrelated. For example, his inability to control his impulsivity appears to precipitate
assaults on other children, which contributes to peer rejection. The team recommends referral but also recognizes that Kent will need continual teaching and counseling support to help him overcome problems related to ADHD.

As a result of the team's recommendations, Kent and his parents are referred to
a neuropsychiatrist for further evaluation. The psychiatrist requests additional
behavioral observations from Kent's classroom teachers and supplies a form for this

purpose. Armed with these additional observations, the physician makes a preliminary diagnosis of ADHD, and Kent is placed on psychostimulant medication for a 1-month trial period. Additional observations are then made by the counselor, teachers, and parents to determine whether any behavioral changes have occurred. After receiving feedback that some positive changes have occurred at home and at school, a diagnosis of ADHD is confirmed.

DSM-IV classification system Some mental health professionals, especially clinicians who seek third-party reimbursement for their services, need to organize data around the multiaxial system set forth in the fourth edition of the Diagnostic and Statistical Manual of Mental Disorders (DSM-IV) (APA, 1994). The DSM-IV provides five axes that facilitate a comprehensive and systematic evaluation of: Clinical Disorders (Axis I); Personality Disorders, Mental Retardation (Axis II); General Medical Conditions (Axis III); Psychosocial and Environmental Problems (Axis IV); and Global Assessment of Functioning (Axis V). A complete discussion of the DSM-IV (APA, 1994) diagnostic classifications is beyond the scope of this book. However, the reader is encouraged to become familiar with the DSM-IV multiaxial system of assessment because is provides a standardized and objective format for organizing and communicating clinical information (see APA, 1994, pp. 25–35).

Kent is given a DSM-IV diagnosis of Attention Deficit Hyperactivity Disorder-Combined Type (APA, 1994, pp. 83–85) because he has 6 symptoms of inattention and 6 symptoms of hyperactivity/impulsivity that have lasted more than 6 months. In addition, Kent's developmental history indicates that some symptoms were noted before the age of 7 and that there is significant impairment of functioning at home and at school. The Global Assessment of Functioning (GAF) scale ranges from 0 (no basis for a rating) to 100 (superior) and reflects an individual's level of psychological, social, and vocational/academic functioning (APA, 1994). Kent's pretreatment GAF score of 60 indicates moderate difficulties in social and school functioning. Kent's diagnostic evaluation is presented in Figure 4-5. ●

FIGURE 4-5 *DSM-IV Diagnosis: Kent W.*

Axis I: **Clinical Disorders**
Attention Deficit Hyperactivity Disorder—Combined Type   314.01

Inattentiveness:
- Doesn't pay attention in class
- Doesn't seem to listen
- Is easily distracted
- Written work is carelessly done
- Cannot spontaneously complete a task
- Forgets homework, loses pencils, etc.

Hyperactivity/impulsivity:
- Can't stay seated
- Is restless and fidgety
- Speaks out in class
- Interrupts others
- Has difficulty playing with classmates
- Talks nonstop

(continued)

FIGURE 4–5 (*continued*)

Axis II: **Personality Disorders**
            Deferred   799.9
            There is not enough information to make a judgment at this time.

Axis III: **General Medical Conditions**
            None

Axis IV: **Psychosocial and Environmental Problems**

- Overprotected by parents
- Lacks adequate and consistent discipline
- Is verbally and physically abusive to classmates
- Has not established a close friendship with an agemate
- Achievement does not approximate potential

Axis V: **Global Assessment of Functioning (GAF = 60 current)**
            Indicates moderate difficulties in social and school functioning

DESIGNING THE TREATMENT PLAN

Treatment planning bridges the gap between assessment and treatment. Once the pre-liminary assessment is completed, it is time to begin to make sense of all of the data that have been gathered. The interpretation and meaning of the data depend on the counselor's particular philosophy of counseling (such as behavioral, Adlerian, client-centered). Each counselor has developed a particular view about the nature of people, what motivates behavior, how the personality develops, and how maladaptive behavior can be explained. Therefore, the individual counselor will conceptualize the case according to his or her beliefs about what factors have influenced each client.

I will use an Adlerian approach to conceptualize the case of Kent W. This approach has often been identified as " very close to an eclectic position" (Hansen et al., 1994, p. 182). This holistic approach focuses on the whole person and includes "one's physical, emotional-interpersonal, intellectual, and spiritual aspects as they interact within the unity of the self" (Garfinkle, Massey, & Mendell, as cited in Hansen et al., 1994, p. 40). The Adlerian counselor (and those using other approaches as well) looks for both *assets* and *liabilities* in each facet of the child's personality and family life. In both assessment and treatment, the counselor gives equal weight to thoughts, feelings, and actions.

Adlerian counselors are among those who include parents and other family members in both the assessment and the treatment process. In addition to being valuable sources of information about the child, parents can support any changes that the child makes during therapy. The counselor helps family members learn new ways of communicating and interacting with the child (see Chapters 11 and 12) and parents also take on an important role in helping the child build cooperative relationships with others including siblings, relatives, peers, and teachers.

Making Tentative Hypotheses

In this phase of the treatment planning, the counselor makes some tentative interpretations of the information he or she has received through the assessment process. These hypotheses will be based on the counselor's educated guesses about what may be causing the child's problems. Again, how individual counselors interpret these causes will depend on their theoretical orientation. My tentative hypotheses are as follows.

Kent has been behaving in ways that reinforce others' beliefs that he cannot do anything for himself. Because he has not been encouraged to make decisions and has been pampered and overindulged by all members of his family, he is convinced that he is not capable of doing many of the things his age-mates can do. He blames others for his problems and refuses to take responsibility for any of his actions. He complains that he is being treated unfairly and has dramatized the "injustice of it all" for the entire class. He sees himself as a victim: a person who does not have the ability to effectively deal with the tasks that are required of him. Therefore, his behavior is designed to convince others that he is indeed an inadequate person.

Kent seems to have the following misperceptions of himself and his world:

I am unable to make decisions on my own. I need to depend on my mother and my teachers to help me.
If I show people that I can't do something, they will do it for me.
Others don't like me. There must be something wrong with them.
The only way I can get attention is to fight with other kids.
My dad doesn't care about me or he would help me more.

In essence, Kent has developed a style of life that involves minimal effort on his part. He gets adults to do things for him and thereby gains a measure of control. However, the downside to this behavior is that Kent lacks a sense of accomplishment at being able to do things for himself. This contributes to his feelings of inferiority and diminishes his self-esteem. He is unable to relate to his peers because they are not as eager to attend to his every need as some adults are. Therefore, he tries to control his peers by physically and verbally assaulting them. When this doesn't work, he again portrays himself as the victim and seeks comfort and support from adults.

The counselor needs to remember that hypotheses are just educated guesses based on what is known at any given moment in time. As therapy progresses, the counselor will develop more insight into the problems the child is currently experiencing. The therapist will continue to learn more about the child's relationships with his or her family, teachers, and peers and about the impact of family, social, and environmental factors on the child's development. Interactions with the child's parents will give some clues about the family dynamics and help the counselor understand how the behaviors and attitudes of parents and significant others, as well as the parent-child interaction, is influencing the child's personal adjustment. As additional information becomes available, the counselor may amend or change some of the tentative hypotheses and adjust treatment goals accordingly.

Setting Goals

Some of the goals addressed in the treatment plan will be those of the child or parents, and others will be developed by the counselor after he or she has reviewed and interpreted the data from the assessment phase of counseling. All counseling orientations have as their goal the resolution of the presenting problem and the child's return to a healthy developmental trajectory. Treatment plans usually include specific goals for the child; Adlerian counselors also include goals for work with parents. The following goals are based on my conceptualization of Kent's case.

Goals for Kent are to help him:

Strengthen his ability to make choices by involving him in making decisions in the counseling process.

Develop alternative ways of responding to peers in order to get his needs for acceptance and belonging met.

Diminish his fear of being wrong and see that he is capable of doing more for himself.

Verbalize his feelings to his father and invite him to get involved in his life.

Acquire a sensitivity for the feelings of others by using role-plays and other activities.

Goals with Kent's parents are to:

Encourage them to provide opportunities for Kent to assume more responsibility for completing tasks at home.

Help both parents to be more consistent and effective in disciplining Kent by allowing him to experience the consequences of his behavior.

Help Kent's parents to define those tasks that Kent can complete by himself.

Encourage parents to join a support group where they can share their concerns with other parents who are experiencing similar problems. In this way, parents can give as well as receive support.

CHOOSING TREATMENT STRATEGIES

The following list contains some suggestions for strategies and activities that counselors might want to consider including in the treatment plan. This list is by no means exhaustive and reflects only general categories that might be included.

Strategies/Activities

Play therapy techniques
Art activities
Board games
Bibliotherapy
Drama
Puppetry
Roleplaying
Storytelling

Group guidance activities
Affective education
Confidence building
Cultural awareness
Problem resolution
Social skills development
Values clarification

Group activities for parents
Parent support groups
Parent-child groups
Play therapy groups

Consultation
Teachers
Other professionals

Counseling
Children
Parents
Families

Identifying and capitalizing on strengths An important aspect of the treatment process is the focus on strengths. Even children who are experiencing serious problems have an abundance of strength that will aid in their recovery. Some of these strengths are immediately apparent, whereas others need to be discovered and nurtured. Sources of strength and potential strength can be found in the individual personality characteristics of the child, the family unit, and the supports that surround the family. Additional sources of strength can come from the child's social support network consisting of friends, church, school, health care facilities, and other institutions.

Illustrative Treatment Plan: Kent W.

Strengths and Potential Strengths

Child's strengths
IQ is in the above-average range
Reading is slightly above grade level
Math skills are above grade level
Has the ability to reason logically and to see relationships
Occasionally, he is able to accept responsibility for his actions
Handwriting has become more legible in the last year

Strengths related to family/background
Family is intact and supportive
Parents are willing to have child evaluated for ADHD
Family has the resources to pay for medical care
Parents cooperated in the assessment process
Mother is willing to attend the parent group

Positive impact of significant others
Extended family live nearby and provide support
Kent interacts with numerous cousins of various ages

Positive impact of school and community
Teachers are interested in helping Kent
A teacher's aide is available to work with him individually

Negative Factors/Potential Negative Factors

Potential consequences of the child's negative behavior
Widening gap between academic achievement and potential
Inability to form relationships with peers that meet his needs
Overdependence on parents to fulfill his needs
Low self-esteem

Family behavior/background liabilities
Parental discipline ineffective and inconsistent
Parents' denial of the problem delayed treatment
Overprotected and overindulged by mother
Father remains uninvolved
Father will not participate in parent group

Goals	Strategy/Activity	Participants
SELF-DEVELOPMENT		
Develop Competence		
Increase self-confidence	Allow child to make choices	Counselor parents/ teachers
Self-Esteem	Encourage structure and consistent discipline	Parents/teachers
	Increase chances for success	Parents/teachers/counselor
	Require mastery at appropriate level	Parents/teachers/counselor
Encourage Independence		
Increase responsibilities	Help parents let Kent do more for himself	Parents/counselor
Facilitate decision making	Allow limited choices	Parents/counselor
Strengthen Coping Skills	Play therapy	Child/counselor
	Teacher consultation	Counselor/teachers
	Parent support group	Parents/counselor
MOTOR DEVELOPMENT		
Diminish ADHD symptoms	Medication	Neuropsychiatrist
Decrease impulsivity	Structured classroom activities	teachers/child
Decrease activity level	Task-oriented activities	Teacher/parents/counselor
Increase physical exercise	Play activities/games	Teachers/parents/child
COGNITIVE DEVELOPMENT		
Increase attention span	Board games/ tutoring	Counselor/child/tutor
Improve concentration	Storytelling/ board games	Counselor/child
Integrate cognitive and social skills	Teach game of chess	Teachers/counselor/child
Improve academic skills	Specialized tutoring	Tutor/child
SOCIAL DEVELOPMENT		
Demonstrate empathy for others	Group guidance activities: story telling, puppetry, play	Counselor/child
Decrease social isolation	Invite another child to share activity session	Counselor/child/guest
	Invite children to home	Parents/child
Learn consideration of others, sharing, and playing by the rules	Chess tournament	Teacher /children
	Large-group guidance activities	Teachers/counselor
EMOTIONAL DEVELOPMENT		
Decrease anxiety	Games with rules	Counselor/child
	Consistent discipline	Parents
	Provide structure	Teachers/parents
Diminish verbal aggression	Role playing	
	Play therapy	
	Group guidance activities	Child/counselor

(continued)

Goals	Strategy/Activity	Participants
EMOTIONAL DEVELOPMENT		
(continued)		
Develop tact	Bibliotherapy	Child/counselor
	Puppetry	Teachers
	Storytelling	
Encourage empathy	Group guidance activities	Child/counselor
	Role playing	Teachers
	Play therapy	
	Bibliotherapy	

Anticipating Obstacles in Treatment Planning

Because child counseling involves people other than the child, progress may be thwarted when significant others in the child's life do not cooperate in the process. Sometimes this lack of cooperation is related to parent's fears that their parenting is somehow not good enough. Therefore, counselors need to approach parents as partners and let them know how important they are to the process. Most parents want to help their children, and their inability to meet with the counselor may have more to do with practical matters than with a lack of concern for the child. In some cases, there is no one to baby-sit the other children, the car doesn't run very well, or the parents have to work two jobs.

Occasionally, teachers may refuse to be involved in the child's individual treatment plan, perhaps because they perceive it as either additional work or because they think their teaching is somehow being criticized. Counselors in the school system must be careful not to threaten teachers by acting as an authority about the child. It is best to *ask* teachers to suggest strategies that will help the child and to involve them as part of the treatment team. Generally, teachers are more willing to implement a treatment plan that they have helped to design.

Finally, children themselves may resist therapy out of fear that what they have to say may bring some sanction against their parents. For example, the abused child fears that if he or she discloses the abuse, the offending parent will go to jail—or worse, that the child will be forced into placement in a foster home. Such fears are usually diminished when the counselor and the child form a bond of mutual trust.

Evaluating Progress

Measuring progress is often difficult because some of the evaluation process is subjective. However, goals that are stated in behavioral terms are much easier to measure. A number of inventories can be used to measure gains in self-esteem, and behavior rating scales, filled out by teachers and parents can help to identify areas of improvement. In addition, improvement in grades in both academic areas and in conduct are positive indicators of progress.

Reports from parents' observations about the progress their children have made toward healthy growth and development are especially helpful. For example, if the child is able to sleep without having disturbing nightmares, this improvement would be noted by the parents and reported to the counselor. Another example might be a child who has begun to take more responsibility for completing tasks that are assigned at home; being able to complete tasks brings a sense of accomplishment that is crucial to developing a sense of competence. Similar improvements in the child's attitude and behavior are often noted first by parents and then by teachers. When all this feedback is charted, the therapist is able to monitor the effectiveness of the particular counseling strategies being used. •

INSIGHTS AND IMPLICATIONS

The creation of a therapeutic environment in which the child (and family) will feel comfortable enough to express his or her concerns is essential to the assessment and treatment plan. Along with creating a special place for children and parents to feel welcome, it is imperative that the counselor establish a therapeutic relationship characterized by unconditional acceptance, genuineness, respect, and empathy. These facilitating conditions are essential not only to the therapeutic process but also to the establishment of rapport in the intake interview. Specific counseling needs can be assessed through interviews, observations, and other formal and informal assessment techniques that can be used to help the counselor understand all areas of the child's development. This understanding is essential for formulating appropriate treatment goals. After the assessment process is complete, the child, parents, and counselor can develop short- and long-term goals. Then the counselor can identify treatment options and design a treatment plan that includes the child and significant others in the child's life.

WISDOM ACCORDING TO ORTON

- *The "children's room" where child therapy takes place should communicate warmth and security.*
- *When children don't let you into their world immediately, respect their feelings. Slowly, by communicating this respect, you will win their trust.*
- *In observing children's behavior, it is important to know what to look for and how to make sense of what is seen. This is not easy, and it takes practice.*
- *Because some problems are not known to anyone—even to the child—the counselor must slowly and meticulously gather clues, form hypotheses, and painstakingly put the puzzle together, piece by piece.*
- *When choosing treatment options for meeting specific goals, focus on the strengths of the child and his or her family. Sometimes these strengths must be discovered and nurtured.*

ORTON'S PICKS

Barker, P. (1990). *Clinical interviews with children and adolescents*. New York: Norton.
In a clear style that is easy to read, the author describes the basic principles of interviewing children in the office, at school, at home, or during a walk in the park. Suggestions are included for establishing rapport and exploring the child's fantasy life through games and activities. The second half of the book focuses on interviewing physically and mentally challenged children, observing infants, and detailing the skills necessary for interviewing the abused child.

Broken Nose, M. A. (1992, June). Working with the Oglala Lakota: An outsider's perspective. *Families in Society: The Journal of Contemporary Human Services.* 380–384.
The author explores basic differences between the Lakota and the dominant culture in communication, religious beliefs, customs, and traditions. She encourages non-Indian practitioners to be aware of these differences, acknowledge their own biases, and ask clients respectively to help educate them. In this way, counselors can help clients explore options and resources in their own culture.

Greenspan, S. I., with Greenspan, N. T. (1991). *The clinical interview of the child* (2nd ed.). New York: American Psychiatric Press.
This book explains how to create an unstructured interview setting that will encourage communication. Special strategies geared to the child's developmental capacities are included, and examples of successful interviews with children illustrate key concepts. A special chapter deals with interviewing parents, assessing the family, taking a history, and providing feedback.

CHAPTER 5

Individual and Group Counseling with Children

> *Children awaken your own sense of self when*
> *you see them hurting, struggling, testing;*
> *when you watch their eyes and listen to their*
> *hearts. Children are gifts if we accept them.*
> —KATHLEEN TIERNEY CRILLY (Blau, 1996)

COUNSELING THE DEVELOPING CHILD

Once the assessment process is completed and goals are established to help the child overcome the problems that are interfering with his or her healthy growth and development, a counseling plan can be implemented. Although specific goals for helping the child achieve a healthy adjustment depend on how the counselor conceptualizes the case, most counseling orientations have as their common goal the facilitation of change in the child's behavior and the child's return to a healthy developmental course.

In designing and implementing a counseling plan, it is necessary to consider the child's developmental level, personality strengths and weaknesses, current style of coping, and cultural background as well as related cultural perspectives of the role of counseling in the family, and the child's (and family's) perception of the presenting problem. The counselor also should take into account the strengths and weaknesses of the child's relationship with parents, siblings, peers, teachers, and significant others and should assess the impact of these interactions on the developing child. The strength of the child's support systems is critical to the success of the therapy and is helpful in deciding who should be involved in the counseling process.

A number of individual and group approaches involve not only the child client but also his or her parents, siblings, peers, and significant others. Because improving the interaction between the child and his or her parents is central to developmental counseling, no treatment plan would be complete without including approaches designed to help and support parents in their efforts to help their children (see Chapters 11 and 12). In addition, securing the cooperation and support of teachers and other human services professionals makes it more likely that the counseling intervention will succeed.

As mentioned before, some of the individual and group techniques available to the child counselor are play therapy, art therapy, and bibliotherapy. These therapeutic approaches are designed especially for children, and they use a combination of talking and playing. Because play is the child's natural form of expression, many play activities such as puppetry, doll play, games, music, drama, and storytelling can help children express their concerns in a nonthreatening way. Play therapy techniques can help children resolve developmental and situational concerns or cope with crisis events (see the case of traumatic grief in Chapter 6). Role playing, puppetry, unfinished stories, and sociodrama can be used in developmental counseling groups to help children explore and clarify their personal values, beliefs, attitudes, and decisions.

Similar techniques can also be used in small groups designed to address the common concerns of a few children, such as children of alcoholics or children of divorced parents.

A Bit of Background

Our survey has suggested that much, if not all, of the effectiveness of different forms of psychotherapy may be due to those features that all have in common rather than to those that distinguish them from each other.
—Frank (1961)

Three primary theoretical viewpoints—psychoanalytic, humanistic, and behavioral—are represented in the counseling approaches currently being practiced. The psychoanalytic orientation is reflected in traditional Freudian psychoanalysis, Adlerian individual psychology, and contemporary psychodynamic approaches. The humanistic point of view is represented by Carl Rogers' client-centered therapy, the existential viewpoint, and the Gestalt approach. Within the behavioral context, representatives are the classical behavioral approach of B. F. Skinner and others, the cognitive-behavioral theories of Beck and Meichenbaum, and the rational-emotive concepts of Albert Ellis (see Hansen, Rossberg, & Cramer, 1994).

Because a review of all these counseling approaches is beyond the scope and purpose of this text, I recommend that the reader consult texts that review each theoretical orientation (see Hansen et al., 1994; Thompson & Rudolph, 1996) or consult the original works cited in these and other counseling texts.

Hansen and his colleagues (1994) cited research (Frey, 1972) summarizing the relationship among various theoretical orientations, and they examined some of the commonalties of the major counseling approaches. These common themes are relevant to counselors who are striving to develop a personal integrative approach to counseling, and they are summarized as follows. Virtually all counseling approaches:

- Acknowledge that human behavior has the capacity to change.
- Recognize the importance of early childhood experiences.
- Believe that the process of personality development is a function of a person's needs being met.
- Agree on the importance of the environment in shaping personality. Most practitioners take a centralist position, believing that people have rational control but are also subject to internal and external forces beyond their control.
- Acknowledge that during early childhood a person can have experiences that lead to maladjustment or maladaptive behavior later in life.
- Have the common goal of facilitating changes in behavior. These goals can be global, specific, or a combination of the two.
- Involve therapeutic relationships that consist of the working alliance, real relationship, and the transference relationship, although the emphasis and importance of each will vary according to the theoretical approach of the counselor.
- Have at least a medium of transference and countertransference as originally defined by Freud.

- Share the belief in the necessity for a good relationship. All stress the need for the client to feel accepted and understood in the relationship; for the client to feel that the counselor is concerned and able to help; and for the counselor to be genuine and honest with the client. (from Hansen et al., 1994, pp. 176–180)

The Therapeutic Process

All developing children have a number of specific needs that relate to the counseling process. Therefore, the counselor needs to provide the kind of environment that will allow the child to (1) mature in self-understanding and self-acceptance; (2) gain an awareness of strengths and weaknesses; (3) develop a more realistic self-evaluation; (4) develop and mature in social relationships; (5) develop independence; and (6) take on responsibility, make choices, and be responsible for these choices (from Dinkmeyer, 1966, p. 263).

Most child counselors, regardless of their theoretical orientation, are concerned with helping children to identify and explore their concerns; gain a new understanding of self and others; and discover and experiment with alternative ways of thinking, feeling, and behaving. Although all forms of child therapy focus on thought, affect and overt behavior, the emphasis on each area is not the same in all theoretical orientations. For example, the psychodynamic therapist, who focuses on the cognitive and emotional aspects of treatment, expects changes in behavior to follow. Conversely, the behavioral therapist believes that changes in behavior will influence the child's attitudes and feelings. Despite the differences in emphasis, all child counselors have the common goal of facilitating changes in behavior.

Also common to all counseling approaches is a process that utilizes various skills and strategies to facilitate change. The Group for the Advancement of Psychiatry (1982, p. 48) have identified the following five stages in the therapeutic process: (1) establishment of the working relationship, (2) analysis of the problem and its cause, (3) an explanation of the problem, (4) establishment and implementation of the formula for change, and (5) termination.

Establishment of the working relationship This working relationship enables the therapist to understand and respond to the child, the family, and the child's conscious and unconscious needs. This phase is usually more prolonged in child therapy, than in adult therapy because children may need more time to accept the therapist as a person who can help. This first stage of relationship development provides the basis for a corrective emotional experience which is believed to play an important role in child therapy (Group for the Advancement of Psychiatry, 1982). This stage is described further in the section "Explanation of the problem."

It is during this stage that some therapists begin to build a partnership with the child's parents. Parents' intimate knowledge of the child puts them in a unique position to help the counselor understand the child's strengths and weaknesses. Parents are often accurate in their assessment of their child's problems but may feel frustrated or overwhelmed by the child's behavior. In these instances, the counselor needs to validate the parents' feelings and help them to discover and strengthen the positive aspects of the parent-child relationship.

Analysis of the problem and its cause   This stage involves identifying problem areas and selecting goals. Problem analysis always relates to the child's life experience and involves some self-exploration by the child. In the course of therapy, the child reveals thoughts, feelings, and actions that relate to his or her current functioning and past behavior. Depending on the counselor's conceptual framework, the investigation of the youngster's life experience can be broad and unstructured or narrowly focused (Group for the Advancement of Psychiatry, 1982). Some techniques therapists use involve recreating the event through play or reinterpreting past events (early recollections).

Explanation of the problem   The explanation or interpretation of the problem may be a brief or lengthy process, depending on the counselor's orientation (for example, behavior therapists pass briefly through this stage). Often the child's family is involved so that parents and siblings can make important changes in their interaction with the child. Some therapists use play, stories, and art activities together with the child's verbalizations to enhance the interpretation. Insight, which is critical to this phase, can be experienced as self-understanding. The child's new self-understanding can be arrived at either directly or symbolically or can be conveyed through the therapist's interpretations to the child.

This new understanding may lead to a *corrective emotional experience* (Group for the Advancement of Psychiatry, 1982). A corrective emotional experience occurs when a child reexperiences "an event or relationship in a different way and with a more positive outcome than that of the original event" (O'Connor, 1991, p. 100). These experiences often result from reenacting experiences through play, but they can also occur through verbal reenactments.

Establishment and implementation of the formula for change   In this phase, changes in the child's life occur. This process involves working to achieve change and translating insight into action. To help the child in this process, the "therapy must also provide experiences, either in reality or in fantasy, that allow the client to sense the value of making choices and instituting change. If at all possible, the therapy should also provide those experiences that allow the child to experiment with new behaviors in her relationship with the therapist" (O'Connor, 1991, p. 101). Through a process of internalization, the child modifies his or her behavior in harmony with new insights and a new set of relationships.

Although this therapeutic work can be done directly and exclusively with the child, it frequently involves the child's family and other significant persons in the child's ecosphere. "Sometimes the therapist makes it clear that the process of change is largely in the hands of those who surround the child and that they must carry the main burden of the treatment" (Group for the Advancement of Psychiatry, 1982, p. 57).

Termination   By this final phase, the child has hopefully improved so much that he or she can now function without the therapist's help. In some forms of brief therapy, the work toward independence from the therapist begins at the start of the therapy. Treatment often results in mastery over certain problems, adjustment to some, and acceptance of others. When this balance is acceptable to the child and to his or her family, termination is in order (Group for the Advancement of Psychiatry, 1982).

The Helping Skills

All counseling approaches acknowledge the need for a relationship in which the client will feel accepted, respected, and understood. All stress the need for the client to feel that the counselor is concerned and able to help and that he or she is genuine and honest in the relationship (Hansen et al., 1994). In essence, the therapeutic conditions of congruence, unconditional positive regard, and empathy, first described by Carl Rogers (1957, 1961), are essential to all counseling relationships. Carkhuff (1969) described a practical model for helping based on Rogers' original conditions. This model includes the four counseling skills of attending, responding, personalizing, and initiating and is used by counselors to help clients achieve the goals of self-exploration, self-understanding, and action. Recent models (see Egan, 1994) extend Rogers' core counseling dimensions to include advanced levels of empathy, concreteness, immediacy, and confrontation. Egan (1994) identified a number of counseling skills that help clients: (1) identify, explore, and clarify their problem situations and unused opportunities; (2) identify what they want in terms of goals and objectives, based on an understanding of the problem situations and opportunities; and (3) develop action strategies for accomplishing goals (pp. 22–23).

Outlining the step-by-step development of all the skills necessary to bring about behavioral change is beyond the scope of this text. Readers should consult *The Skilled Helper* (Egan, 1994) and *Theory and Practice of Group Counseling* (Corey, 1995) for a more in-depth presentation of individual and group counseling skills. These texts will provide students the opportunity to learn and practice the skills necessary to facilitate change.

Key Factors in the Therapeutic Process

Transference and countertransference *Transference* refers to those needs, feelings, and desires derived from past experiences that are reflected in the therapeutic relationship. The key issue of transference is the distortion that prior relationships impose on the therapeutic relationship. For example, because of past experiences with an abusive parent, a child may have difficulty placing his or her trust in the therapist. In child therapy, the transference relationship also contains elements of the child's present-day reality (Group for the Advancement of Psychiatry, 1982). For example, a child who is angry at his or her parents may transfer this hostility to the counselor. And children who have unmet approval needs may bring their report cards or school papers to show the counselor how "good" they are. The major difference between the counseling situation and the actual childhood experience is the absence in therapy of a positive or negative evaluation of what the child is expressing or experiencing. As the child projects anxiety-related feelings onto the counselor, the counselor accepts these and reflects them back to the client in an attempt to aid the child's understanding of them.

In a form of transference that is commonly labeled *countertransference*, the therapist contributes characteristics that may hinder the child's expression of his or her feelings, wishes, fantasies, and behavior. An example of countertransference might involve a counselor who has unresolved anger about being placed in a foster home and who transfers these feelings to a child who is about to be removed from his or her abusive parents. This transference may hinder the child's progress in coping with the placement. Therapists should be alert to their own unresolved issues and take steps to resolve them before undertaking work with children who are experiencing similar conflicts.

Self-protective behaviors   Generally, *resistance* refers to the child's attempts at self-protection through the use of defensive behavior. Resistance is a natural part of the therapeutic relationship, and it can aid as well as impede the therapeutic process (Brems, 1993). A child's resistance can take many forms and can result from a variety of perceived internal and external threats. When children are threatened, they protect themselves by withdrawing, acting out, regressing, or evidencing other problem behaviors. Rather than challenging a child's resistance to treatment, the therapist should explore the reasons for the resistance. Children may refuse to participate because they fear reprisals from parents for revealing "family secrets," they have not been adequately prepared about what to expect, their previous experiences with adults have been hurtful and disappointing, or they have a strong belief that they are (as one youngster put it) "a hopeless case."

During therapy when the child is facing painful issues he or she may divert attention from what has been disclosed by either chattering constantly or falling silent, leaving the therapist to guess what the child is thinking. Although silence is often considered resistance, for some children it is a time for "working through" solutions to problems presented. When children refuse to allow any access to their private thoughts and feelings, the therapist should accept this refusal and not challenge the child's resistance. In this way, the therapist communicates an underlying respect for the child. The child's perception of this respect builds trust and helps the child use the relationship to reduce anxiety. Thus, resistances are not only allowed, they are also understood and overcome.

Symbolic forms of communication   Because children have not yet developed the sophisticated language necessary for more traditional forms of verbal therapy, they sometimes use an indirect form of communication known as the *metaphor*. A metaphor is a form of symbolic communication, that uses stories, myths, parables, and fairy tales to convey meaning. It is defined as "a pattern of images, symbols, words, emotions and actions which synthesizes, conserves and represents experiences" (Santostefano, as cited in Kottman & Stiles, 1990, p. 149). This nonliteral form of communication is used in the mutual storytelling technique (Gardner, 1971) as a way to help children identify and explore problems in a nonthreatening way. In this technique, the child first tells a story. Then the counselor, being careful to remain in the child's frame of reference, tells a story with a more positive ending, illustrating for the child alternative problem-solving skills.

Children, especially young children, "play" out their concerns rather than "talk" them out. Because children use play as a way to communicate conscious as well as unconscious concerns, the child counselor must understand the child's symbolic meaning. In much the same way that the counselor interprets the child's metaphor, he or she will need to understand the child's play communications. To make interpretations about the meaning of the child's nonverbal communication, the counselor needs to understand the child's worldview and the factors (familial, cultural, environmental) that have influenced the child's life experiences.

An Integration of Process and Skills

Establishing the Working Relationship

Hope, the expectation of help and belief in a helping person, is a key to this phase. Independent of the type of therapy, this ingredient itself is responsible for rapidly relieving symptoms.
—Group for the Advancement of Psychiatry (1982)

In this stage, the counselor creates and maintains a relationship with the child based on cooperation and mutual respect. The child participates fully in this relationship by helping to decide on counseling goals, choosing which activities to participate in, and determining how much to reveal of self. For many children, this relationship is unique.

In an atmosphere of warmth and acceptance, children feel safe enough to share painful thoughts and feelings about past and present events. *Listening* and *attending* to the child's verbal and nonverbal communication helps the child express and identify feelings. *Responding* to the child's feelings, as well as to the experiences and behaviors that underlie those feelings, is an important part of empathic communication (Egan, 1994).

In responding to the child's feelings in this phase of the counseling process, the counselor helps the child clarify exactly what he or she wishes to communicate, which heightens rapport and encourages the child's further involvement. When feelings are accurately reflected, the child feels understood and is able to get a clearer sense of what he or she is feeling. This understanding leads to greater self-awareness as counseling progresses.

The counselor relates to the child in a way that implies an understanding of the child's point of view. This understanding is arrived at by seeing the world through the child's looking glass and becoming sensitive to the child's feelings as if they were one's own. The counselor communicates this empathy either verbally or symbolically, and it helps children feel accepted and understood.

Sometimes, *silence* can be an effective way for a therapist to respond. Being silent communicates that the therapist is listening and allows children the necessary time to put their thoughts into words. Gumaer (1984) believes that silence can sometimes create a mild anxiety, which "may motivate the child to change courses and often moves the child to deeper levels of thinking, feeling and self-disclosure" (p.41).

Analyzing the Problem

In this second phase of the therapeutic process, children are encouraged to explore troublesome events, thoughts, and feelings. Through this process, the counselor learns about the child's concerns and then assesses how these concerns are affecting the child's current adjustment. The child may share early recollections or memories that are relevant to his or her current concerns, which provide the counselor with an understanding of how the child views self, others, and the world (Kottman & Johnson, 1993). Younger children are more likely to share their problems symbolically through play or art, whereas older children may share them verbally or write them down. To gain an understanding of the child's worldview and his or her behaviors, some counselors provide opportunities for the child to re-create the problem situation through play.

Counselors use their skills to listen to the child, to try to understand the child's concerns, and to communicate this understanding back to the child. In addition to listening and attending skills, the counselor can use *empathy* as a communication skill (Egan, 1994). Empathy used in this way is more than a sentimental expression of caring; it is a useful skill for the development of insight. To facilitate self-disclosure, the counselor may wish to ask *open- ended questions* to help the child put the problem in more concrete terms. Open-ended questions encourage children to elaborate on their stories. When children have difficulty expressing themselves, the counselor may want to encourage, prompt, or help them to say what it is that they wish to say. In this way, the counselor uses a combination of *probes* and empathy to help children clarify and identify their concerns (Egan, 1994).

Clarification is a skill used in response to confusing and conflicting aspects of a child's disclosure by focusing on the underlying message and helping to sort out ambivalent feelings. Clarifying statements let the child know that he or she is understood and that the troublesome event, thought, or feeling has been correctly identified. When using clarification as a technique, the counselor stays within the child's frame of reference, thus forming the basis for empathic understanding. Once the therapist has communicated this empathic understanding to the child, the therapist can help the child identify and understand his or her own feelings. This process of self-understanding is an important beginning of therapeutic change. As the child becomes aware of his or her own feelings, and knows that these feelings are accepted and understood, he or she can grow in self-acceptance. This in turn enhances the child's self-confidence and boosts his or her self-esteem.

Summarizing combines the communication skills of attending, listening, empathy, and probing in a way that provides focus and challenge (Egan, 1994). Summarizing captures the essence of the content and feelings expressed in the session and relates it back to the child. Children who are developmentally ready, can summarize the important aspects of the session themselves, which encourages their involvement in and ownership of the problem and can be a useful skill in any phase of therapy. Summary statements are especially valuable in helping children focus their attention on a particular issue and explore their concerns in more depth. The most effective summary statements are brief, focus on important points, communicate understanding, help the child develop insight, and encourage the child to consider changes in his or her thoughts and behavior.

Explaining the Problem

During this phase, the counselor helps the child understand and reduce troublesome thoughts, feelings, and behaviors; compare conflicting ideas; work through defenses and resistance; and link understanding to action. Sometimes children need to keep painful material hidden, even from themselves. As a result, they may ask questions or make comments that do not seem to have any logical connection to the presenting problem. Helping children identify and understand these hidden meanings requires interpreting the child's verbal and nonverbal symbolic communication.

When labeling the child's feelings directly would be too threatening, the counselor can use the "as-if" scenario (O'Connor, 1991). Rather than requiring that the child own a feeling or need he or she has expressed, the therapist may make a statement that attributes the feeling or need to children in general. For example, the therapist might say "Some children might feel angry if something like this happened to them." Another version is for the therapist to own the feeling: "When I was your age, I used to worry if other kids liked me. Do you think that kids today worry about those things?"

Helping children understand the hidden meaning behind their messages can sometimes be accomplished by identifying and exploring themes or patterns in their communication (Egan, 1994). These themes can include the child's mood and affect, needs, desires, or behaviors and can be expressed directly or indirectly through words or symbols. Some children consistently express the same feelings, behaviors, or experiences during play or through their artistic expression. Interpretation of the symbolism in the child's communication requires an in-depth knowledge of the child and his or her world. Recognizing these themes and sharing them with the child is a way of helping the child develop insight.

Insight is described as "understanding translated into constructive action (Mosak, as quoted in Corey, 1995, p.196). Through interpretation, the counselor attempts to put what the child discloses into a more understandable framework so the child can see the reasons for his or her feelings or behavior. These open-ended exchanges should be in the form of tentative hypotheses ("Could it be...") and should be geared to the child's needs and capacity for abstract thought (see Chapter 2). Interpretative responses require a level of cognitive reasoning and insight that is usually not found in younger children. Therefore, offering clarifying responses, using "as-if" scenarios, and identifying and exploring themes in the child's expressions may be more appropriate ways of helping children identify, label, and understand their feelings. Although interpretative statements help children make connections between past events and feelings and their current thoughts and behaviors, they are not absolutely essential to the process. Sometimes this connection is made through nonverbal or symbolic communication as the child plays rather than verbalizes unconscious thoughts and feelings.

Once this connection is made, the counselor can point out how the child's behavior affects the lives of important people in his or her world. As the counselor and the child search for and explore the feelings and behaviors of other participants in the problem, the counselor links these associations to the child's own world and helps the child understand the impact of his or her feelings and actions on other people. Sharing these associations helps the child personalize (Carkhuff, 1969, 1987) his or her role in the problem. Once the child understands what that role is, he or she can gain control over the problem.

Establishing and Implementing the Formula for Change

During this phase of therapy, the child translates new understanding and learning into action through the process of internalization. *Internalization* enables the child to use the strength of the therapeutic alliance to form a realistic self-appraisal, to enhance self-esteem, to define values, and to strengthen coping skills. "This dynamic is similar to an ordinary developmental process in which children begin to make their first internal judgments about their worth (their essential "goodness" or "badness") and about the dependability and trustworthiness of their caretakers" (Hansen et al., 1994, p. 195).

Internalization is a powerful catalyst for change that is present throughout the therapeutic process. It involves the same modeling, imitating, and internalizing that is present in the child's early interactions with parents and significant others. As children grow and develop, they use imagination to try on the roles of the important people in their world. The most vital roles are those of their parents, which children imitate first and most often. The child imitates some of the parents' behavior and thinking, including his or her standards and goals. As children identify with and model after their parents, they define their worth by internalizing the responses of their parents and caregivers. If the parents believe that the child is basically good, capable, and lovable, the child will believe this also. However, if the parent sees the child as bad, incapable, and unlovable, these perceptions are internalized and thus lower the child's self-esteem.

Just as the young child masters the developmental stages of childhood by asking questions, imitating, and experimenting, the child can use the therapeutic relationship to explore his or her capabilities, increase understanding, internalize new learning, and try out new behaviors. Through the internalization process, the positive aspects of the child's interaction with the counselor become part of the child's perceptions. This relationship with the therapist can alter the child's evolving self-portrait and offers a positive experience that enhances self-esteem.

When children lack acceptance and respect from the significant people in their lives, they often expect to be rejected by everyone, including the counselor. Convinced of their unworthiness, children who lack self-esteem often behave in ways that invite the rejection of others, and they may test the therapist by demonstrating their worst behavior. Once the therapist has passed the test, his or her unconditional acceptance of the child provides a *corrective emotional experience* that enables the child to internalize the positive aspects of the relationship. Such total acceptance allows the child to bring both the accepted and rejected aspects of his or her personality out into the open, which reduces defensiveness, encourages self acceptance, and builds self-esteem.

Enhanced self-esteem and the corrective emotional experience are reciprocal processes (Horwitz, 1974). As children are accepted and understood in the relationship, they are able to explore those aspects of self that may have been rejected previously by others in their lives. They can bring out their true feelings, no matter how antisocial, when they feel safe enough to do so. In the warmth and security of a therapeutic relationship that is free of positive or negative evaluation, children are encouraged to test alternate ways of thinking and behaving and to internalize solutions to problems.

Initially, the child may identify with some of the attitudes and feelings that the counselor demonstrates toward him or her (Horwitz, 1974). During the counseling process, when children's thoughts and feelings are understood and respected, the child may begin to modify his or her self-portrait. By identifying with the therapist's genuine caring and concern, the child gradually accepts himself as a person worthy of respect. This *identification* process occurs naturally in the course of healthy development when children model after, imitate, and internalize their parents' responses, values, standards, and goals. However, in situations where children fail to identify with their parents because of a conflict in the parent-child relationship or because parents represent an inappropriate model, the child is able to use the therapeutic relationship to modify and strengthen his or her self-representation. In the therapeutic relationship, the counselor does not impose his or her values on the child. Instead, the therapist reflects the child's positive, negative and ambivalent feelings and does not value any specific content or attitude above the rest. "As neither praise nor blame is forthcoming, the child's expressions are determined by his needs, rather than by the therapist's persuasion" (Dorfman, 1951, p. 254). Identification, which is central to the internalization process, can occur verbally or nonverbally (such as through play) and does not require sophisticated insight.

Transference, in this context, implies that the child will endow the relationship with the therapist with a special significance that stems from what the child has learned and experienced over the years. Both the child and the therapist contribute to this transference. The therapist contributes by providing an environment in which the child's thoughts, feelings, and experiences can be expressed and understood. The child contributes experiences from his or her own interpersonal relationships and family environment. Therefore, the child's self-expressions can be understood in the context of his or her unique history and family environment (Brems, 1993).

Transference takes on a special significance during this phase as the child begins to internalize the favorable aspects of the relationship and makes changes in his or her behavior as a result. This process of internalization is seen in the child's effort to please the counselor by engaging in more adaptive behavior. Strong and positive internalization contributes to transference improvement and behavioral change. "When a client has a positive reaction to the counselor and tries new appropriate behaviors in an attempt to please the counselor, the client can receive sufficient internal and external reinforcement to stabilize the new behavior. Thus, the transference improvement that develops in the context of a trusting relationship can be expected to persist" (Hansen et al., 1994, p. 196).

Encouragement is an important aspect of all phases in the therapeutic process, but it is especially valuable as children begin to experience the power of their own inner resources. To hold on to the gains made in therapy, the child needs encouragement and support. Encouragement can instill feelings of worth, power, and control in children.

Terminating Therapy

At this, the final stage of therapy, the child has made important changes in his or her thoughts, feelings, and behavior. These changes are a result of the child's ability to translate new understanding and learning into action. Through the process of internalization, the child gains sufficient strength and understanding to resolve certain problems, cope with some, and accept others. When the child, the parents, and the counselor agree that a balance between mastery, adjustment, and acceptance has been achieved, termination is often in order. Hopefully, the child will be able to integrate the healthy changes that were made during counseling into his or her everyday life.

INDIVIDUAL COUNSELING IN PRACTICE

The Case of Sterling S.

Background information   Sterling S., age 10, is the middle child in an intact family of five children. He has two older sisters and two younger brothers. Both parents are employed and are active in church and community affairs. Mrs. S. characterizes herself as an authoritarian disciplinarian who believes in being "strict" with her children. Mr. S. is a very tense person who has some difficulty relating to others. Although both parents are interested in helping their children, they have difficulty relating to them as children and prefer to treat them as miniature adults.

All the children have some problems in their interpersonal relationships. The oldest child in the family has been experiencing some emotional problems and is currently in treatment. The parents report that the children fight continually with a ferocity that is beyond normal sibling rivalry. Their punishment usually involves being isolated from each other emotionally. The parents tend to be harsh, inflexible, and emotionally detached when disciplining the children.

Presenting problem   Sterling S. was referred for counseling because he has been walking stiff-legged, using robotlike speech and gestures, and telling his classmates that he is an alien from outer space. His behavior has made him the object of ridicule in his peer group. Sterling is a very quiet and withdrawn youngster who, according to a recent sociogram, has no friends in his fifth-grade class. His teacher wrote: "Today, Sterling hid behind my curtain for 40 minutes instead of going to math class. No explanation—just cries!"

According to his teacher, Sterling chooses not to associate with the other children and withdraws from all social opportunities. His "best friends" are movie and television superheros. Most of Sterling's conversations center around his exploits with creatures from outer space and his extraordinary powers. He seems preoccupied with a fantasy life that serves to protect him from close associations with peers and others whom he perceives as a threat to his innerself.

Phase I: Establishment of the Relationship

Initial session with Sterling   During the initial session, Sterling appeared frail, nervous, and very pale. He used robotlike speech to detail his life on other planets. He said he had been having dreams lately and that he will write them down and bring them in to the counselor. He likes to draw and enjoys activities that he can do alone. When asked if he would like to draw something for the counselor, he responded with "I'll draw my family." He then drew a family of stiff, robotlike figures who did not touch each other. He drew a witch with an ugly distorted face which he identified as Joleen (the eldest child in the family).

STERLING:	I hate Joleen!
COUNSELOR:	Sounds like you dislike her a lot. (*Responding to the child's feelings.*)
STERLING:	You bet. She's just plain mean.
COUNSELOR:	Tell me how she treats you. (*Clarifying response. Encourages the child to elaborate.*)

STERLING: She's always hitting me and punching me. She scratches and bites and no one can stand her, especially me.

COUNSELOR: You think that other members of your family dislike Joleen almost as much as you do? (*Exploring the child's perceptions of family interactions.*)

STERLING: Not my dad. He likes her. It's always "Joleen this" and "Joleen that."

In this initial session, Sterling reveals his feelings toward his sister Joleen. In Sterling's view, Joleen is his father's favorite and he envies her special place in the family. The fact that so much attention has been focused on Joleen because of her recent illness compounds Sterling's feelings of jealousy and may be at the root of the sibling rivalry the parents describe. Sterling feels lonely and unsure of where he belongs in the family group.

The counselor uses the initial session to begin building a partnership with the child's parents. In addition to building rapport and establishing a working relationship with the child, the initial session provides parents with an opportunity to express their concerns and to feel valued and understood. When parents feel valued for the positive contributions they make to their child's development, they are more likely to make the necessary changes to improve the parent-child relationship. The initial session provides the counselor with insight into the parenting style and the parents' interaction with the child. In exploring the parent-child relationship, the counselor needs to search for strengths, which can be found even in the most disturbed parent-child relationships.

Initial session with Sterling's parents Mr. and Mrs. S. believe that Sterling's older sister has consumed most of the family's attention, and they think that Sterling's problems are minor by comparison. However, they are somewhat concerned that Sterling has headaches and has been throwing up for the last three days. They blame his emotional upset on his sister's aggressive behavior toward him. They report that "she is always beating him up!" Sterling's parents are only mildly concerned about Sterling's lack of friends and the fact that he consciously avoids interacting with other children. They acknowledge that he prefers to isolate himself even from his brothers and sisters. His parents are aware that he spends a great deal of time fantasizing about life in outer space and about possessing special magical powers. Mr. and Mrs. S. are not too concerned about this behavior and think that it indicates an overly active imagination that Sterling will "outgrow."

The parents emphasize how much kinder Sterling is than his older sister Joleen who is always kicking, biting, and hurting others. The following story, told to illustrate Sterling's kindness to his sister, reveals a style of discipline that is inflexible and severe. Joleen was instructed to open the front door so the family could bring in some of the Christmas presents they had purchased. When she didn't do it immediately, her younger brother was sent to help. They began fighting and Joleen hit her brother. To punish Joleen, her parents would not allow her to open any presents during that Christmas season. As she begged to open her presents, Sterling was the first to offer her one of his, even though he confesses "I hate Joleen." The parents pride themselves in being consistent and not excusing the slightest infraction of their "rules."

The family appears to have ganged up on Joleen, who is their scapegoat for everything that goes wrong. However, Mr. S. states that despite all of Joleen's problems, he feels closest to Joleen. It appears that Sterling is his mother's favorite and his father's least favorite child. Both parents have difficulty relating to their children emotionally. Mr. S. tends to intellectualize and seeks logical rather than emotional responses from others, whereas Mrs. S. is emotionally cold toward the children. This enables them both to have a strict style of discipline that is harsh and unrelenting. Both parents need help in their interactions with their children.

Phase II: Analysis of the Problem

First session with Sterling   In the first counseling session, Sterling drew the picture shown in Figure 5-1 to explain his dual role as a fifth-grade boy and an alien from outer space. The boy on the left is smiling and saying, "Hello Everybody," whereas the alien on the right is saying "Crush, Kill, Destroy." This picture illustrates Sterling and his alter ego KOTU; "KOTU" is Sterling's name for himself, which means King of the Universe.

Sterling drew the first figure with a rigid body and legs that come directly out of his midsection. Like Sterling, this boy has no muscles and appears weak and ineffective. He refers to himself as "friendly but friendless." KOTU, by contrast, is muscular in build and menacing in words. He appears to have the power and strength that Sterling lacks. He has a sturdy body and is properly proportioned. Interestingly, he has eyes in the front and back of his head and openings for his mouth and nose.

When asked about the drawing, Sterling told the counselor about his desire to escape back to Saturn, where he is a king. He said he was born on Saturn and "flew into my mother's body." Sterling's active fantasy life seems to be a way to compensate for what he perceives as a lack of warmth and affection in his family life. As the king of the universe, he is all powerful and does not have to struggle for significance.

After this session, the counselor identified certain strengths that will help Sterling accomplish his goals in counseling. Additional strengths will likely be uncovered as counseling progresses:

Assessment of Sterling's Strengths

Is bright and capable of insight
Is verbal and open with his feelings
Expresses his ideas well in both written and spoken language
Is talented in art and does well academically
Has supportive parents
Physical, medical, and educational needs are being met

Specific Counseling Goals for Sterling

To feel safe and secure within the counseling setting
To express his fears through his drawings and stories
To feel more powerful by allowing him to make decisions about what he
     wants to change
To realize that he can get support from others and that he is not all alone

FIGURE 5-1 *Sterling's Depiction of Himself and His Alter Ego KOTU*

First session with Sterling's parents In the first session with Mr. and Mrs. S., the counselor was able to learn a great deal about the family dynamics and style of discipline. During this session, the counselor learned more about Mrs. S.'s family of origin and how her early experiences with her stepsister are influencing her interaction with her own children. Sterling's mother recalled that after her mother died she went to live with an older stepsister who treated her as a live-in maid and baby-sitter. In the years that followed, Mrs. S. came to view herself as "Cinderella" without Prince Charming. Sterling's mother could not recall any closeness or warmth from her own alcoholic and mentally ill mother and saw her father only infrequently after she moved in with her stepsister. She reported that on one occasion her sister surprised her with a beautifully wrapped Christmas present, which turned out to be coal and ashes. She felt that she had absolutely "nothing" during those bleak years—"No mother, no father, and a sister who hated me!" Mrs. S. was careful to add that she has gotten her revenge in a way. Today, her sister's children regard her as their mother and are closer to her than to her stepsister.

Mrs. S. says that she lacked confidence as a youngster and felt lonely and rejected. She had a speech problem that made it difficult to pronounce some letters. Other children made fun of her speech and she reacted by withdrawing more and more into herself. She admits that she is especially impatient with her daughter's speech problems and wishes that she had more patience. In this session, the counselor gently used Mrs. S.'s experiences as a child to help her develop empathy for her own children, who seem to be having the same feelings of loneliness and rejection.

After several sessions, a number of family strengths were identified that would help Sterling meet his needs in a more adaptive way. In addition, the counselor developed a number of goals for helping the parents to improve their relationship with Sterling and to find ways to help him find his place in the family.

Assessment of Family Strengths

Parents share a common goal of wanting to help their children.
Parents have the financial resources to seek outside help for Joleen.
Mother and father are both involved in a partnership with the counselor to help Sterling accomplish his goals.
Both parents are willing to be involved in a parent support group.
Both parents take excellent care of their children's physical and medical needs.
Parents recognize the need to be more emotionally responsive to their children and want help in achieving this.

Goals for the Parents

To find ways to demonstrate their affection for Sterling
To be more flexible and forgiving in their interactions with their children
To find ways to have fun together as a family

Phase III: Explanation of the Problem

The goal of this phase of counseling is to help children understand and reduce troublesome feelings, compare conflicting ideas, work through defenses and resistances, and link this understanding to action. In this case, Sterling described to the counselor a series of frightening dreams that involved a monster. His drawing of the monster is depicted in Figure 5-2. These dreams, combined with Sterling's artwork, were used to help him gain a better understanding of his troublesome thoughts, feelings and behaviors. Most of the dreams were recounted verbally; the first one was written down, and Sterling titled the dream "Electric Monster":

(*Dream 1*)

ELECTRIC MONSTER

One day electric monster hit the magic science building. Suddenly the creature came. It screamed: "ra-ta-rat-ta." It destroyed many buildings. It blinded people. It used its tongue to spray poison. This is what the monster looked like (Figure 5-2).

Suddenly, Ultraman appears. He uses his vapor capsil (sic) to destroy the deadly creature. Just then I woke up.

(*Dream 2*)

STERLING: I was flying…flying in a helicopter. I couldn't get down. We fell…most of us were not injured, except one. We went to find

FIGURE 5-2   *Sterling's Electric Monster*

help but…back at the plane, the ground began to rumble. Up came the monster! Edo ran for help. I was with the Safety Patrol. I wasn't injured. We tried to shoot at the monster…but even with our super powers, we couldn't kill it.

COUNSELOR: You were trying to get away, but you couldn't. (*Clarifying statement.*)

STERLING: No, I was up in the helicopter when it came in. I was with the Safety Patrol. (*Sterling corrects the counselor's interpretation that he was trying to get away.*)

COUNSELOR: The Safety Patrol…you were safe? (*Clarifying question; used to determine the meaning of Sterling's role in the Safety Patrol.*)

STERLING: No! We're supposed to keep other people safe…but he (monster) got someone this time. (*The emphatic no indicates that the counselor was way off base. The Safety Patrol is supposed to guard others. Sterling doesn't want the counselor to think he was safe while others were killed.*)

COUNSELOR: The monster killed someone. (*Restating to see whether the child could identify who was killed.*)

STERLING: Yeah…but I didn't see who.

COUNSELOR: This time the monster killed someone and you and the others, even with your superpowers, weren't able to kill the monster. (*Summarizing; a way of encouraging the child to explore further.*)

STERLING: Right. We couldn't do anything.

COUNSELOR: You must have felt frustrated that you couldn't kill the monster. That wouldn't be a good feeling.

STERLING: It was awful. I felt bad that someone got killed. It was like I let them down, but I couldn't help it. The monster was just too big.

(Dream 3)

STERLING: I was invited with the Safety Patrol and we were having a feast. When we were having dessert, the ground began to rumble and a monster with horns and sharp teeth came out. Safety Patrol said to me, "Hurry hide…too late now!" I ran and I ran and I ran and when I reached the city, the monster was still chasing me. The monster was so big…the monster destroyed my house. No one was in it at the time. The monster was heading for Japan. When I saw that the creature had destroyed my house, I cried and cried and cried. But when I saw what the monster had done, I was more sad. He had destroyed the Safety Patrol Building!

COUNSELOR: You cried when your house was destroyed but you felt even sadder when the Safety Patrol building got destroyed. (*Gently challenges the child to compare his reaction to the destruction of his house with that of the Safety Patrol building. The counselor didn't believe that the child was ready to deal with the fact that the patrol building is imaginary whereas his house is a real part of his life.*)

STERLING: Yeah, no one got hurt at my house but I worried about my friends at the patrol.

COUNSELOR: You must really like the patrol. (*Reflecting the child's feelings about his "imaginary friends."*)

STERLING: I really do. We have superpowers but they didn't work this time.

COUNSELOR: You felt bad that you couldn't protect your friends. (*Communicating empathy for the child's inability to protect anybody, including himself.*)

STERLING: I tried…but the monster was too powerful.

COUNSELOR: Sometimes, people in our lives are just too powerful and we feel weak. Is that how you felt? (*Interpreting the child's feelings of powerlessness.*)

STERLING: Exactly.

In this instance, Sterling has made the connection between his feelings of powerlessness and his needs for safety and security. Interestingly, he has named this space group "The Safety Patrol." He is still searching for a way to fulfill his needs as a person rather than as an alien. He seems unable to get the warmth and affection that he needs from his family. He is lonely and, in his own words, is "friendly but friendless."

(Dream 4)

STERLING: I didn't have a family. The Safety Patrol had to take care of me. My mother was still alive but all the rest were destroyed.

COUNSELOR: The monster destroyed your whole family. (*Clarifying statement to let the child know he is heard and understood.*)

STERLING: My mother is still alive...but the Safety Patrol takes care of me. (*Probably the child wishes that he didn't have to live with his family and has "killed" them symbolically; however, he would feel too guilty if something happened to his mother.*)

COUNSELOR: Your mother survived but the rest of your family died? (*Earlier it was noted that he is closest to his mother but feels his father favors Joleen.*)

STERLING: Yeah, I felt very sorry for them. I hope God sends them to heaven.

COUNSELOR: You must feel very sad. (*Response to feelings combined with a gentle probe.*)

STERLING: Well, I do but the Safety Patrol takes care of me. We don't cry when we get together.

COUNSELOR: You don't...(*Clarifying.*)

STERLING: No, we have superpowers, so we can shut our tears off.

COUNSELOR: Is it easy to shut your tears off, or do you still feel like crying? (*Open-ended question that allows the child to explore his feelings more fully.*)

STERLING: It's easy sometimes, but sometimes it isn't.

COUNSELOR: If I said, "It is easy to cry"...how would you answer that? (*Open-ended question designed to learn more about the child's thoughts, feelings, and behaviors.*)

STERLING: It is easy to cry if I think of something happening to the Safety Patrol. My mother is still alive...but the Safety Patrol takes care of me.

COUNSELOR: You would rather live with the Safety Patrol. (*Gently confronting the child about his feelings for his family.*)

STERLING: Yeah, they like me.

It is evident that Sterling feels rejected by his family. He has "killed off" everyone except his mother. At this point, the family needs to be more responsive to his needs for affection and security within the family. During this phase, Sterling's parents are encouraged to attend a parent group where they can (1) share common concerns with other parents, (2) receive support and encouragement in their efforts to improve their interaction with their children, (3) discover ways to meet their children's emotional needs, and (4) have more "fun" with all their children.

Phase IV: Implementation of the Formula for Change

Sterling has developed a rich fantasy life to compensate for his loneliness. He is rejected by the other children in his peer group and has made little effort to get involved with them. He is struggling to find his place in his family but is unable to connect with parents who have difficulty meeting their children's emotional needs. He perceives his family as cold and uncaring and cannot get the warmth and attention he needs. To compensate, he has simply invented a "family." He feels safe with his new family and calls them the "Safety Patrol."

Fantasizing about life with the Safety Patrol helps Sterling feel safer and more powerful. Sterling's fantasy life has brought him some comfort from his incredible loneliness, but it has also caused him to be taunted and rejected by his peers. The counselor's task in this case is to help Sterling to find a degree of comfort in being a fifth-grade boy rather than "King of the Universe."

In this phase of counseling, Sterling needs help to gain the skills to effect those changes he has decided to make in his thoughts, feelings, and actions. Sterling needs to be provided opportunities to learn and practice effective ways of relating to others. In addition, his parents need continual help and encouragement to strengthen the parent-child relationship. In the course of this session, it is evident that Sterling's father is taking a more active role in meeting Sterling's emotional needs.

COUNSELOR: Last time you said that the Safety Patrol likes you. Are there any times when your family shows you that they like you? (*Helping Sterling focus on some of the positive aspects of his family life.*)

STERLING: Well…yeah. My dad has been playing ball with me. He never did that before.

COUNSELOR: Sounds like you had a great time. (*Responding to Sterling's obvious delight.*)

STERLING: I did! We had fun!

COUNSELOR: Could it be that this was your dad's way of telling you that he loves you and wants to spend time with you? (*Interpreting.*)

STERLING: Yeah, I guess. I just thought that he liked Joleen better than me. I still think that he likes her a lot, but I'm starting to think that he likes me a little.

COUNSELOR: You seemed to enjoy playing with your dad. Could it be that you will have to "invite" him to play with you some of the time? (*Gently challenging Sterling to become more assertive in expressing his needs.*)

Phase V: Termination

Slowly Sterling began to discard his rigid, robotlike stance and staccato speech. He had fewer dreams of death and destruction. He stopped being sick and cried less often. Eventually, he was accepted by another youngster in his class, and they began to play chess together. At the culmination of his treatment, Sterling found that it was more comfortable to be a boy than to remain an alien.

COUNSELOR: You haven't mentioned any bad dreams lately. Does that mean they are gone?

STERLING: Yeah, I don't dream like I used to.

COUNSELOR:	That's great news. Guess we don't need to talk about monsters anymore.
STERLING:	No. I don't think so. You know…(*pauses*) I don't know…
COUNSELOR:	It's okay…go ahead.
STERLING:	Well, I don't think I need to talk about things like I used to. (*In this case, Sterling decides he doesn't need to come to counseling anymore. He has met his goals.*)

COUNSELING CHILDREN IN GROUPS

Group counseling strategies seem to offer a number of advantages for counselors as they struggle to meet the needs of children growing up in the 21st century. Now more than ever counselors need effective strategies to help countless children overcome a variety of developmental and situational problems. Although individual techniques work best for some children, group strategies seem to hold the most promise for helping large numbers of children to return to a healthy developmental course. In addition to obvious cost and time savings, groups have certain advantages over individual sessions. In groups, children have an opportunity to share their problems and benefit from feedback from their peers. Another important advantage to group work is that children learn that they are not the only ones struggling with a particular problem, and they are encouraged and supported by the other children as they practice solutions to problems and learn new coping skills.

Group counseling is an increasingly popular form of therapeutic intervention for children in a variety of settings, including schools, child guidance clinics, hospitals, residential treatment centers, and other human services agency settings. Practitioners working in clinical settings use group therapy to help children cope with a variety of emotional and behavioral problems, and elementary school counselors are now facilitating therapy as well as educational groups (Corey, 1995; O'Rourke, 1990). Counseling groups and large-group guidance activities in the schools help children address a variety of educational, vocational, social, and personal concerns; make effective use of counselor time; and bring the elementary school guidance program into the lives of all children.

Developmental Group Counseling

Group counseling is defined as a dynamic, interpersonal process that focuses on conscious thoughts, feelings and behavior (Corey, 1995; Gazda, Duncan, & Meadows 1967). The group creates and nurtures a climate of mutual trust, caring, understanding, acceptance, and support that enables children to share their personal concerns with their peers and the counselor. Although some groups are problem-oriented, the developmental growth groups discussed in this section focus primarily on children who don't require extensive personality change and whose concerns center on the developmental tasks of childhood. "Group counseling tends to be growth oriented in that its focus is on discovering internal resources of strength" (Corey, 1995, p. 7). Members may use the group to "increase understanding and acceptance of values and goals and to learn or unlearn certain attitudes and behaviors (Gazda, et al., 1967, p. 306).

Developmental group counseling is growth-oriented but has a preventive and remedial function as well. Group counseling provides children with an opportunity to explore and examine their values, beliefs, and decisions as they strive to accomplish the developmental tasks of childhood. In groups, essentially healthy children build on their decision-making skills, strengthen their coping skills, and learn new problem-solving strategies. In this way, developmental problems are both prevented and overcome. Growth-oriented groups can help children resolve situational or personal conflicts or alter self-defeating behavior. They can be designed to help children learn a specific skill, such as how to settle disagreements by negotiation rather than violence, or address a particular problem, such as parents' divorce. Developmental groups help children utilize inner resources to cope more effectively with life events and to gain a greater awareness, understanding, and acceptance of self and others.

The Value of Developmental Groups

As a microcosm of society, the group provides a simulated reality where children are able to test their ideas and behavior in safety. In much the same way as a well-functioning family operates, the group provides the child with a sense of belonging and security. As children interact in the group, they explore their personal values, beliefs, attitudes, and decisions and receive feedback from their peers. In this sharing process, children learn effective social skills and acquire a greater concern and empathy for the needs and feelings of others. They see themselves in the mirror of the other children's perceptions—catching a glimpse of who they are and who they want to become. In this supportive environment, children can experiment with new ways of behaving, discarding some and keeping others. They can learn alternate ways of coping with normal developmental issues or situational conflicts. The children can then decide what changes, if any, they wish to make (Corey, 1995; Gumaer, 1984).

Another unique value of group counseling is that it gives children a chance to be a force in their own and in each other's growth (Corey, 1995). In expressing their concerns and in being heard and understood, children can achieve a greater awareness and understanding of themselves and others. This greater self-understanding helps children gain a measure of control over their everyday lives and become masters of their own destiny, so to speak. With mastery, the child can achieve more successes than failures. Success inspires self-confidence, which can be seen in increased self-direction, autonomy, and a sense of responsibility toward self and others. A set of circumstances is thus set in motion that has the potential to influence the child's positive growth and development throughout the life span. The benefits of developmental group counseling for children are outlined in Figure 5-3.

Stages in the Group Process

A number of authors have proposed dividing the development of the group process into either four or five stages. Mahler (1969) detailed five stages: formation, involvement, transition, working, and ending. Gumaer's (1984) four stages are identified as establishment, exploration, work, and termination. Hansen, Warner, and Smith (1980) described five stages: initiation of the group, conflict and confrontation, development

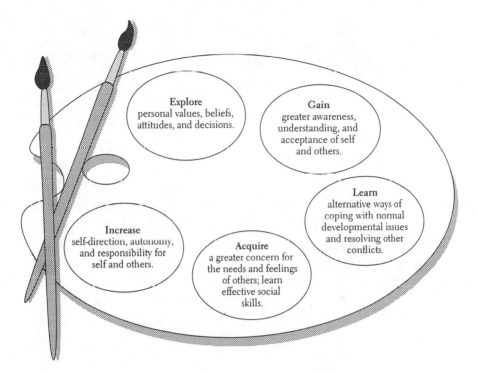

FIGURE 5-3 *The Value of Developmental Group Counseling for Children*
SOURCE: Based on Corey (1995, pp. 7–8).

of cohesiveness, productivity, and termination. Finally, Corey (1995) outlined an initial stage of orientation and exploration, a transition stage of dealing with resistance, a working stage of cohesion and productivity, and a final stage characterized by consolidation and termination.

For the purposes of understanding the group process, I will describe the five stages featured in Figure 5-4: formation, exploration, transition, working, and ending. These five stages of group counseling utilize the same skills necessary for facilitating the therapeutic process in individual sessions. Because the skills are applied somewhat differently to groups, readers are advised to consult those texts that deal specifically with the group leadership skills needed for each stage of the process (see Corey, 1995; Corey & Corey, 1992).

Stage I: Formation

Preplanning is an important first step in forming a successful group. In agency settings, it is well to get the professional staff involved in planning the group and to ask for their input about which children might benefit most from group therapy. This promotes a coordinated treatment team effort that will benefit the children who are served by the agency.

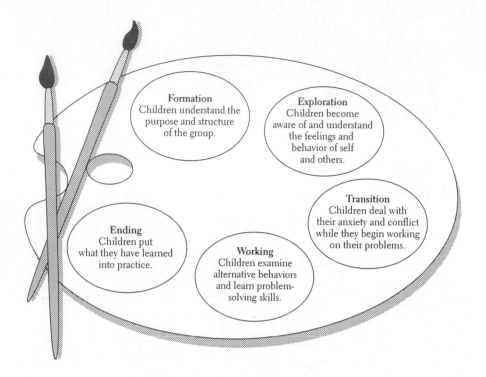

FIGURE 5-4   *Stages in the Development of a Group*
SOURCE: Based on Corey (1994); Gumaer (1984); Hansen, Warner, & Smith (1980); Mahler (1969).

In school settings, teachers and other school professionals can help the counselor identify children who have specific situational problems that need to be addressed. Teachers usually have many creative ideas for activities that will help teach children specific coping skills. Involving teachers in planning will help interest them in conducting group activities themselves as a way to supplement the counselor's group work.

Parents and children should also be involved in preplanning. Parents are especially helpful in judging whether or not their child will profit from the group experience. Also, parents who are involved in planning a group are more likely to give their permission for the child to attend. Children can make their wants and needs known to the counselor, who in turn can decide whether there is a need for a specialized group.

What are the needs of the children to be served? The first step in organizing the group is to assess the needs of the children to be served. Teachers, parents, and children can help in this process. Parents can give the counselor important clues about the problems their children are encountering as a result of situational and crisis events, whereas teachers are especially helpful in identifying the common developmental concerns of the children in their classes. For instance, one teacher reported that a large percentage of the children in her class were trying to solve their problems through aggression and that their arguments had taken a decidedly violent turn. The counselor then designed group activities related to dealing with feelings of anger. Conversations with children will yield many ideas that can be used as a basis for group activities in the classroom. Children who are asked for their ideas for topics and activities often respond with creative ideas that can be developed into large-group activities.

Who's in a group? Group guidance activities, conducted as a part of the guidance program, should include *all* children and should focus on helping them master age-appropriate developmental tasks. The children then come to recognize the counselor as a person who is willing to interact with them on a regular basis. This relationship and familiarity with the counselor is important because it reduces the threat to both children and their parents if the counselor later chooses to form a group designed to help some children address a specific problem.

In selecting members for small, growth-oriented groups, the question of voluntary versus involuntary membership may arise. In my view, it is best to include children who want to be part of the group rather than to force children to participate. It has been my experience in school settings that there are usually many more children who wish to be in the group than there are spaces available. However, in some agency settings in which participation in groups is compulsory, counselors can help children change their negative attitudes by carefully preparing them for the group (Corey, 1995).

Many group leaders conduct individual interviews or conferences with children before forming the group to determine what each child's needs are and to assess his or her developmental readiness for group work. It is certainly true that some children, especially those with severe behavior problems, are not yet ready for group work. These children and those who have experienced traumatic events that they do not wish to share in the group are better served in individual sessions.

Heterogeneous, culturally diverse groups are recommended for helping children address most developmental concerns. Because groups are a microcosm of the larger society, they should represent the culturally diverse population of children being served. This means that children of all races and both sexes who are shy and outgoing, boisterous and quiet, liked and disliked, well-adjusted and poorly-adjusted, happy and sad, humorous and humorless should be included in a well-balanced group. This balance is not easy to come by and requires a great deal of effort by the counselor. Even if groups cannot include the kind of balance that the counselor would like, steps can be taken to prevent the group from being lopsided. For example, including just one black child in a group of seven white children or putting one boy in a group of four girls (or visa-versa) makes the group lopsided. It is especially important not to put a lone abused child into a group of well-cared-for children who might reject him or her. Putting children together who are very dissimilar may impair communication and interfere with group functioning (Gumaer, 1984). Therefore, the counselor should learn as much about the children as possible by interacting with them in pregroup interviews, individual counseling sessions, or group guidance activities. Teachers are an excellent source of help in selecting children for inclusion in the group.

A heterogeneous grouping provides peer models and peer reinforcement for children who are trying to learn more effective ways of coping. For example, if the group's goal is to find alternatives to violent behavior, then there must be children in the group who do not use violence as a way to solve their problems. These children can suggest alternate ways of reacting during the group and can be good role models for group members who have difficulty controlling their temper.

Homogeneous groups are needed for certain situational problems that children encounter as they grow. In these groups, children who have had similar experiences are needed to help the group accomplish its goals. For example, when the group goal is to develop more effective ways of coping with parental divorce, then group participants have to be selected from a pool of children who are worried about their parents' impeding or actual separation or divorce. However, homogeneous groups can be counterproductive in some instances. For example, it is not a good idea to have a group exclusively for children with attention deficit hyperactivity disorder because there is no one to model calm, productive behavior. A group made up exclusively of children who can't sit still or focus their attention will likely disintegrate into chaos and nothing will be accomplished.

How large should a group be?   The size of the group will depend on the participants' age and developmental level. Younger children (grades 1 through 3) will need a smaller group of perhaps three to five members. In this way, the children can get more individualized attention from the counselor, and it will be easier to keep them focused on the group discussion. Children in the upper elementary grades can function in a somewhat larger group of from six to eight members. In some instances, the nature of the problem to be discussed may affect the size of the group. For example, children who have difficulty controlling their impulses and cannot seem to focus their attention may need to be in a group of only three or four members. However, children who are older and want to discuss their worries about their parents' divorce might do well in a larger group. Thus, the size of the group will depend on such variables as the children's age and developmental level, the nature and purpose of the group, and the time and space available.

In addition to deciding on the size of the group, the counselor must decide whether to have an open or a closed group. Adding new children after the group has established trust causes group members to regress as they struggle to accommodate the new members. Conversely, new members may be threatened by the level of trust and cohesion that already exists in the group. Although closed groups are preferred, they are not always possible; in some agency settings, open groups are more common because the children might be at the agency for only a short time and the population is continually changing.

When does the group begin and end?   Because structure is an important element in counseling with children, there should be a set time to begin and end the group. The counselor will have to decide the length and frequency of the sessions as well as the duration of the group. These decisions are usually based on the children's age, the group's goals, and the time available in the particular setting. In schools, groups generally run the length of the class time, which varies depending on the children's ages. Kindergartners may have as few as 20 to 25 minutes in a class period, whereas older children may have 40 minutes. In agency settings, there is more flexibility in terms of length and frequency of sessions. However, it is still wise to consider that the average attention span of kindergarten children is relatively short. Therefore, play therapy, art therapy, or bibliotherapy may be needed to focus very young children for even a short time. As children get older, their attention span lengthens and discussion groups can extend for longer periods of time.

Most writers (for example, Gumaer, 1984; Thompson & Rudoph, 1996) agree that as age and maturity levels increase, the counselor can work with more children for longer periods of time. For example, a small group of 4- and 5-year-olds may have to meet two or three times a week for 20 minutes, whereas a larger group of 11- and 12-year-olds could meet for 40 to 60 minutes only once a week. In some agencies, practitioners conduct groups much more frequently. It is not unusual for children in some residential and partial treatment programs to be involved in groups each day for a specified period of time.

In my view, more children can be served by conducting developmental large-group guidance activities in each grade every week or two. The school counselor can interact with an entire class of children for 20 to 40 minutes and identify those children with special concerns who need to meet in smaller groups. In this way, special growth-oriented groups can be planned for youngsters who have specific concerns that cannot be addressed in the larger group.

In closed growth groups, the number of sessions is usually determined before the group begins so that the children know that there will be a beginning and an ending. It is best to be flexible from group to group and determine the number of sessions needed to accomplish the goals of each particular group. Generally, counseling groups should be long enough for cohesion to develop and for the children to explore alternative ways of thinking, feeling, and behaving. This may take 10 weeks or longer. Some growth groups that are formed for specific reasons may take fewer sessions. In these groups, specific but limited topics are discussed in from four to six sessions. According to Gumaer (1984), these brief growth-centered groups require homogeneity of membership and topic. In other words, children with similar characteristics meet to discuss similar concerns. For example, children who will be going to the middle school might meet to discuss the transition.

Stage II: Exploration

Children become aware of and understand the feelings and behavior of self and others.   Trust is essential at this stage of the therapeutic process, when children need to feel safe enough to explore their thoughts and feelings beyond a superficial level. The counselor plays a key role in establishing trust and supports the therapeutic atmosphere of openness in the group. As children test the atmosphere and get acquainted, they may be uncertain about what is expected of them. Counselors can diminish the children's anxiety by providing structure within the group. Structure provides children with security and encourages them to self-disclose. Initially, the counselor may want to use an unfinished story, a book, or an art activity as a way to get the discussion going. As the children begin to apply the activity to their own lives, self-disclosure becomes easier.

The main task of the leader at this stage is to help the children identify, clarify, and develop meaningful goals. According to Corey (1995), there are *general group goals*, which vary from group to group, and there are *group-process goals*, which apply to most groups. These group-process goals include helping the children to stay in the here and now, discuss their feelings and behavior, listen and respond to others, take risks, give and receive feedback, deal with feelings and conflicts, and apply new behavior in and out of the group. Gradually, as trust and cohesion develop, the children become more willing to express what they are thinking and feeling. As the group discussion unfolds, the counselor uses the same skills that were identified in the exploration phase of the therapeutic process described earlier. Counselors reflect the children's feelings, clarify their thoughts and feelings, encourage sharing through the use of open-ended questions, and summarize the important points of the group discussion as a way to (1) heighten self-disclosure and (2) begin and end each session.

Stage III: Transition

Children deal with their anxiety and conflict while they begin working on their problems. It is during this stage that children experience some anxiety as they increase their self-awareness. Children may resist disclosing their innermost thoughts and feelings because they fear that they will be misunderstood or misjudged by others. As the children reveal themselves to the group, they worry whether the others in the group will accept or reject them. Some children may even have difficulty accepting themselves. During this stage of the group process, when children are not yet secure in their acceptance in the group, they may find ways to divert the group's attention. Diversionary tactics may include storytelling, nonstop talking, withdrawing, or acting-out behaviors that take the focus away from the child and his or her self-disclosure.

As trust and cohesion continue to develop, children receive more acceptance, support, and encouragement from the group. Children soon learn that others have the same problems and the same fears. And when children feel safe enough to take risks, a deeper level of self-disclosure is possible (Gumaer, 1984).

Positive feedback serves to strengthen group cohesion and to help children overcome their anxiety and resistance. Feedback can involve both self-disclosure and confrontation. It can be either positive or negative, and it helps the child develop self-awareness. Children generally are not used to giving and receiving feedback, and the counselor will have to explain and model the process. In addition to utilizing the group counseling skills discussed previously, counselors are encouraged to use *linking* to connect themes that emerge during the group. Linking promotes member-to-member interaction and increases the level of group cohesion (Corey, 1995).

Stage IV: Working

Children examine alternative behaviors and learn problem-solving skills. In the working stage, children begin to share their innermost thoughts and feelings with the group. The anxiety and resistance of the previous stage has been replaced by a sense of warmth and security within the group. Although children continue to regard themselves as individuals, they now feel they are also an integral part of the group. A feeling of security and a sense of belonging help the children identify their goals and concerns and take responsibility for them. "The group has almost become an orchestra, in that individuals listen to one another and do productive work together" (Corey, 1995, p. 113). Productive work is possible at this stage because the level of trust and cohesion is high and children are able to self-disclose at a deeper level than in the previous stages. Feedback from the counselor and other children offers both challenge and support for change. Lacking the defensiveness that characterized the early stages of the group, children are now able to examine new ways of thinking and behaving. As children relate to one another, they learn to identify effective and ineffective social skills. After experimenting in the group and selecting those behaviors that are most effective, children are ready to try these behaviors out in their everyday life and share the results with the group. Finally, children learn effective decision-making and problem-solving skills in the group, which they can apply to their everyday lives when the group ends.

Some of the functions of the group leader in the working stage (Corey, 1995, pp. 122–123) are summarized as follows:

- *Reinforce* desired group behaviors that foster cohesion and productive work.
- *Look* for common themes.
- *Model* appropriate behavior, especially caring confrontation.
- *Support* members in their willingness to take risks and assist them in carrying this behavior into their daily living.
- *Interpret* the meaning of behavior patterns at appropriate times so that children can reach deeper levels of self-exploration and consider alternative behaviors.
- *Focus* on translating insight into action; encourage members to practice new skills.

Stage V: Ending

Children put what they have learned into practice. The final stage of ending, or termination, is initiated when children begin to practice new learning in their everyday lives. At this point, children experience greater self-awareness, become more goal-directed, and actively work toward making behavior changes that can impact their lives in a positive direction. In this stage of the group, children can practice alternative ways of thinking and behaving through play activities, sociodrama, and role playing.

During this final stage of the group counseling process, consolidation of learning takes place. It is a time to use the skills of summarizing, integrating, and interpreting the group experience. It is in this final phase that children internalize what they have learned about themselves in the group and translate this new understanding into action.

In the final phase of the group, it is important to allow children to put into words what they have learned about themselves during the group experience. Gumaer (1984) calls this a *self-evaluation* and it involves having the children identify and write down two strengths and two weaknesses. If children have difficulty with this activity, they can be paired off and the partners can help one another. Once the strengths and weaknesses are identified, the children read them aloud to the group. The group members can then give feedback indicating their agreement or disagreement with the child's self-evaluation. This feedback period is followed by asking the children to complete two sentences indicating how they can use their strengths and overcome their weaknesses.

Just as the children were encouraged to express their fears about beginning the group, they should now be encouraged to share their feelings about ending it. As children prepare for the group to end, their feelings about the separation may involve denial, anger, and anxiety, as well as a deep sadness. Children should be allowed to talk about these feelings and to understand that they are common to beginnings and endings. Children who have been caring and supportive of one another and who have made a commitment to work together will feel a sadness when the group ends. The counselor can help the group accept the inevitability of ending by sharing his or her own feelings about it. Through positive feedback, the counselor can help the children understand that the same successful combination of choices and commitment that they made in the group can be extended to the other relationships in their lives.

GROUP GUIDANCE ACTIVITIES

Group guidance focuses on helping large numbers of children address common developmental concerns and has a special place in prevention. Large-group activities can address a variety of social, interpersonal, and academic concerns and are designed to help children develop competencies that contribute to increased self-understanding, self-acceptance, and ultimately enhance self-esteem and self-confidence.

In large-group activities, children can discuss situations that involve moral decisions and values. These activities don't force values on children but rather help them clarify their own. Unfinished sentences that pertain to the moral dilemmas present in everyday life can be used to stimulate class discussions: for example, "What would you do if you found a ring on the sink in the bathroom?" or " What would you do if your best friend told you she had AIDS and asked you to keep it a secret?"

Puppetry, games, unfinished stories, art activities, music, storytelling, books, writing, and sociodrama are just a few of the activities available to counselors for use in developmental groups. Although it is impossible to present all the countless activities that can be used in group work with children, a few examples are provided here that are not included in other chapters of this text. The reader is invited to use and expand on the activities presented in the chapters on art, play and bibliotherapy. Many specific books, and activities can be modified and adapted for group work with children. The possibilities are endless, and creative and innovative practitioners will continue to add to the ever-growing list.

Unfinished Stories

The counselor may want to divide a large class into groups of 4 to 5 children and present the unfinished story as a written situation to be discussed in the smaller groups.

The group's conclusions can be recorded and shared with the larger group at the end of the session. This strategy works especially well for fourth-, fifth-, and sixth-graders who are able to read and discuss solutions to problems. For younger children, the unfinished stories can be read aloud or acted out with puppets.

The unfinished stories should reflect real-life dilemmas and should be based on the input of teachers and children. The stories should be appropriate for the age and developmental level of the children in the group and should accurately reflect the children's concerns. It is very important that the situations portrayed in the unfinished stories do not embarrass or threaten a particular child in the group, and specific problems of a personal nature should be reserved for individual or small group sessions.

"SHOULD I CHEAT?"

I am 9 years old and in the fourth grade. I do well in all my studies. One day I am taking a spelling test and I can't remember a word. I see a paper with the spelling words sticking out of my desk a little. I pull it out and peek at the word I need. I do the same thing each time we have a spelling test. One week the teacher tells us not to look at each other's papers. I start to wonder if I am cheating. I like getting 100's on my papers. What should I do?

"I'M HOME ALONE!"

Everyday I am home alone after school until my mom gets home. This is usually about an hour. It is OK because I have a snack, watch TV, and play with my toys. Today I heard a knock at the door. I didn't know what to do. What would you have done if you were me?

"DON'T CALL ME A FATSO!"

I am in the fifth grade. Today, before lunch I hit a kid in the stomach for calling me fatso. I got sent to the principal's office because no one heard the remark. The other kids said I got mad and hit this kid for no reason. I wouldn't say I was sorry. My parents punished me for fighting. I have to stay in my room all night. My mom baked my favorite cookies. I can smell them. I'm not supposed to go downstairs. I didn't get lunch. My mom just left to visit my Gramma…maybe just one…

"TRY IT. IT MAKES YOU FEEL GROWN UP!"

This is my first week in a new school. It's miserable because none of the popular kids will talk to me. In my other school, I was very popular. At home, my mother is always telling me that I should "be a friend to have a friend." Today, one of the popular kids invited me to "have fun" after school. This is my big chance to be friends with the popular kids. We all went to a store and I noticed that these kids were putting store items in their book bags. They said, "Try it. It makes you feel grown up." What should I do? What if these kids never speak to me again?

Role Plays

A favorite large-group counseling activity involves using a set of family puppets to play out family situations that involve some sort of resolution. The family puppets are cardboard cutouts that children "wear," and they can be used with children in grades K–4. The puppets are about 3 feet tall, and children place their head and arms through the openings, instantly becoming a mother, father, brother, sister, or baby. With a second set of puppets, a family can have two sisters, two brothers, a mother and grandmother, or twin babies. In this way, more children can participate in each role play, and all of the many types of family constellations can be represented. Generally, all children want a turn, and every effort is made to include as many children as possible in the time allotted. The children who did not get to participate will be sure to remind the counselor when they are due for a turn!

The following are sample situations that can be used in role-play situations with the cardboard puppets. Because the children need a certain amount of structure, the counselor can explain the scenario, and then the children can act out their various roles in any way they wish. Some of these role plays require two sets of puppets so that families with more than three children can be depicted. Also, the adult puppets can double as teachers, grandparents, and significant others in a child's life. A discussion follows each role play, and the children give suggestions for solutions to the problems discussed.

"I'M TELLING…"

The children in the Jones' family are always fighting. There are two boys and two girls in the family and the youngest girl is always "tattling" on her older brothers and sisters. When they are in the back of the car, she screams, "Tom is touching me!" or "Linda hit me!" The older children are always getting punished. Play this scene out.

NOTE: This role play takes two sets of puppets because there are two brothers and two sisters. The children can even pretend they are in a car by arranging the chairs in the front of the room to simulate a two-door model.

"HE'S ONLY A BABY!"

Every time the other children in the family have anything—a toy, an ice cream cone, or a favorite chair—the baby comes in and screams until he gets what one of the other children have. The baby is always screaming to get his way. The parents are tired from working all day so they always say, "He's only a baby!" The parents make the older kids give in to the baby again and again and they are sick of it. Play out what you think will happen.

NOTE: The counselor can get involved in the role play by taking on the role of the baby. The children are amused and delighted when the counselor cries and carries on like a baby. The brothers and sisters show their frustration as they struggle to deal with this problem. This is a fun way to get the children involved in finding solutions.

"WHAT IF I FAIL?"

Janet got an F on her report card and now she has to go home and tell her family. Her mother and older brother, who is home from college, are waiting for her when she comes home from school. Play out what you think will happen.

NOTE: Do not give the role of the child with an F on his or her report card to anyone who is getting poor grades. This would be too threatening for the child. This role play provides a glimpse of how pressured children feel about grades. The counselor can vary this scenario by having one child play the teacher and others play parents, grandparents, and others.

Games and Activities

Activity:	Dealing with Feelings
Objective:	Help children express their thoughts and feelings
Materials:	The cards from "The Talking, Feeling, and Doing Game" and the "Ungame" (see Chapter 6 for order information)
Technique:	Divide children into small groups of 5 or 6. Children can sit on carpeted floor or arrange their desks in a circle. Give each group a stack of cards and ask them to take turns discussing each question. The counselor can screen the cards ahead of time.

Activity:	What's in a Word?
Objective:	Stimulate a discussion on thoughts, feelings, or relevant issues
Materials:	Index cards that have one word printed on them: examples might include love, hate, fun, lonely, etc.
Technique:	Divide children into groups of 4 to 6 and allow them to find a place on the floor (if carpeted) or arrange their desks in a circle. Then give out the cards and ask the children to choose which feelings they would like to discuss.

Activity:	Name that Strength
Objective:	Enhance self- concept
Materials:	Large index card or piece of paper and pencil
Technique:	Have children select partners and list all of each other's personality strengths on a card. Next, ask children to discuss each other's strengths. The counselor may have to explain what personality "strengths" are and give examples first.

Activity:	Group Logo
Objective:	Promote small-group cohesiveness, cooperation, and group identity
Materials:	Pencil, eraser, crayons, and tag board or bulletin board paper
Technique:	Divide students into small groups of 4 to 6. Give one piece of tag board to each group. Ask first group member to make a large, closed shape without lifting the pencil from the board. Next, each group member makes a similar shape so that they overlap each other. Afte

the last member completes a shape, the group tries to make a familiar object, animal, or face from the picture. When the group agrees, they color the picture and add details as needed. They then choose a name for their picture and share it with the class (Bergin, 1989).

Activity: Ice-breaker

Objective: Promote small-group cohesiveness, cooperation, and group identity

Materials: Index cards, adhesive tape, scissors, stapler, colored paper, boxes, and so on.

Technique: Divide large group into smaller groups of 4 to 6 children. Have children arranged in groups on a carpeted floor or on individual mats. Place materials between groups so children have to share. Instruct groups to build a free-standing tower with the cards and other materials. The group that builds the tallest, free-standing structure wins.

SPECIAL ISSUES IN COUNSELING

The following are just a few of the challenges presented by children in the course of individual and group counseling. Counselors need to be aware of ways of handling these sensitive issues so that they don't interfere with the child's ability to obtain needed help.

Do I have to be bad to come to see you? It is especially important for school counselors to develop strong developmental and preventive counseling programs, in addition to providing services to children who are struggling with long- and short-term adjustment problems. In my view, it is a serious mistake to limit the services of the elementary school counselor to severely troubled children or to those who present the greatest challenge to teachers and administrators. Although there is no question that these children need help for chronic problems, the guidance program will gather more support from the school and the community if it is available to all children. Furthermore, parents will be much more willing to come to parent groups that are for all parents and not just for "troubled parents of troubled children." The same holds true for children. By attending small and large developmental and preventive guidance groups that involve everyone, children will encounter less stigma when they wish to confide in the counselor individually.

I hate you and I mean it! Genuine warmth and caring from an adult may be a totally new experience for some children. Children who have been abused and rejected have internalized an image of themselves as unworthy of acceptance and respect. Constant criticism and rejection can engender feelings of inferiority in children that lower their self-esteem and make self-acceptance difficult, if not impossible. These children cannot believe that anyone could like them; therefore, they seek to test the counselor in countless ways. This often results in misbehavior that tries the patience of even the most caring counselor.

This "trial by fire" is a critical time in therapy. Therefore, counselors must continue to be patient, accepting, and caring in order to convince the child that he or

she is a worthy person. It is at this point, when the child seems to be rejecting the counselor, that the child is actually beginning to internalize acceptance of the counselor. The next logical step is for the child to grow in self-acceptance by repairing her or his tattered self-esteem.

Consider the note Hector sent to his counselor, which is reproduced in Figure 5-5, complete with his misspellings. He enclosed a picture of his counselor on the telephone. The logical conclusion is that Hector thinks that his counselor is too busy talking on the telephone to really care for him. After all, how could the counselor care for Hector when he considers himself so unlovable?

Can I go home with you?　The therapeutic relationship has helped shape and change the child's internal landscape and has forever altered his or her self-portrait. Through the counselor's mirror, the child has come to see him- or herself as a person of worth—someone who is listened to and respected. Therefore, it is understandably difficult for the child to break this bond, and it is equally difficult for the therapist. The counselor, who has shared the child's laughter and tears through good times and bad and who has passed the child's many tests, now feels a sadness in ending the relationship. This sadness is a normal part of saying good-bye and is not to be confused with countertransference (the counselor's overdependence on the child).

Good-byes are a necessary and inevitable part of therapy. *Natural* termination occurs when the child, the family, and the therapist agree that counseling has accomplished its purpose. When termination occurs naturally, it is often signaled by both the child's and the therapist's acquisition of new feelings, attitudes, and behaviors, indicating that therapy is no longer needed. When the child is ready to leave, he or she may begin to talk about issues related more to his or her plans for the future and may dwell less on the problems of the present. As the child grows stronger and immediate problems are resolved, the counselor will have less need to continually support the child.

When the termination is *premature* or when therapists must change midway through therapy, parting may be especially difficult for the child and the counselor. When therapy is terminated by the child's parents, it is still important that the therapist have a few sessions to say good-bye to the child and to deal with the child's feelings of sadness, anger, and helplessness. If the counselor must end the sessions, he or she should gradually and gently prepare the child. Termination is always complicated if the therapist must end therapy abruptly because of illness or some other compelling reason.

Another form of termination occurs when children must change counselors midway through therapy. This occurs most often in clinic settings with counselors-in-training. Children become very attached to their student-therapists, whose task is to focus solely on one child for an entire semester. Leaving is especially difficult for children who have not experienced such warmth and affection in other relationships. This transition, although difficult for children, is equally difficult for the student therapist, who may believe that she or he is the only person capable of helping this particular child. Supervisors need to help students bring the therapeutic relationship to a close and prepare the child for the transition. In these instances, the child may grieve for the therapist, and this grieving may take the form of tears, depression, acting-out behavior, or entreaties to go home with the therapist. These situations are always

FIGURE 5-5 *A Child's Note to His Counselor, Illustrating His Feelings of Unworthiness*

difficult for the child and his or her student therapist and both must be helped to make a smooth transition before sessions end for the semester.

When therapy comes to a natural termination, the counselor may have opportunities to stay in touch with the child and follow-up on his or her progress. In schools, counselors have an opportunity to interact with the children during large- and small-group work. The counselor can thus maintain a relationship with the child, albeit not the intense relationship of individual counseling, and can continue to reinforce the positive changes that occurred in therapy without encouraging dependence on the counselor. In private practice, it is not unusual for parents to call three or four months after therapy has ended and ask the therapist to meet with the child. In my view, children should be allowed to return to share their triumphs and trials in a few follow-up sessions. These sessions are a way to keep in touch with the child's life and to reinforce the good things that are happening. Because the goal of counseling is to prepare children to make transitions in their everyday lives and to begin and end relationships, good-byes should be thought of as transitions. These successful transitions help children continue to change and grow in their relationships outside of therapy.

INSIGHTS AND IIMPLICATIONS

This chapter presents an integrated approach to counseling that involves forming a working relationship with the child to help him or her identify and explore concerns, gain new self-understanding and competence, discover alternative ways of thinking and behaving, and implement these changes in his or her everyday life. Goals can be achieved through a series of skills or strategies designed to facilitate change. An integration of process and skills is demonstrated in the case of Sterling.

This chapter gives examples of both individual and group techniques that can be used to bring about behavioral change in children. Group techniques are given that can be applied and adapted for use in numerous settings by beginning counselors as well as by seasoned veterans. A number of individual and group techniques are available to counselors, including sociodramatic play, roleplaying, puppetry, games, unfinished stories, and other small- and large-group activities. Some of these have been discussed and illustrated in this chapter; others will be discussed in subsequent chapters.

WISDOM ACCORDING TO ORTON

- *Every child wants to be treasured and respected as a person.*
- *Sometimes the positive attention and caring of a concerned adult is therapeutic, in and of itself.*
- *A child may "test" the counselor to see whether his or her acceptance of the child is unconditional.*
- *Each child adds something new to the counselor's understanding of children.*
- *Much like the developing child, a developing counselor is continually learning new ways of helping children, keeping what works for them and discarding what doesn't.*

ORTON'S PICKS

Corey, G. (1995). *Theory and practice of group counseling* (4th ed.). Pacific Grove, CA: Brooks/Cole.
    In a thoroughly readable text, Corey describes the stages in the group process and the skills that the group leader uses to facilitate change. Excellent examples help the reader understand how the group process works.
Egan, G. (1994). *The skilled helper: A problem-management approach to helping* (5th ed.). Pacific Grove, CA: Brooks/Cole.
    Egan presents an overview of the counseling model, along with all the basic communication skills for helping. Excellent examples guide the reader in understanding each step of the process.
Hansen, J. C., Rossberg, R. H., & Cramer, S. H. (1994). *Counseling: theory and process* (5th ed.). Boston, MA: Allyn & Bacon.
    Excellent explanations are offered for all the major counseling approaches. Chapters 12 and 13 are especially helpful for readers who want to know more about counseling as a relationship.

Thompson, C. L., & Rudolph, L. B. (1996). *Counseling children* (4th ed.). Pacific Grove, CA: Brooks/Cole.

This comprehensive text offers a view of child counseling from all the major theoretical perspectives. Excerpts from counseling transcripts illustrate how each is applied in practice. Relevant research in the field of child counseling is also included.

CHAPTER 6 *Play Therapy*

> *Play is the royal road to the child's conscious and unconscious inner world; if we want to understand his inner world and help him with it, we must learn to walk this road.*
> —BRUNO BETTELHEIM (1987)

Play is pleasurable and fun. Play, with imagination and fantasy as its partners, enables children to explore their world—first through their senses and then by thinking and reasoning. Because play is "the child's natural medium of self-expression" (Axline, 1947, p. 9), it affords children an opportunity to express their innermost thoughts and feelings. Play is a safe, fun way for children to experiment with different behaviors and to find out what works and what doesn't. By setting and achieving their own goals, children gain a sense of competence and control over their actions. Social play promotes understanding of other people's behavior and feelings and helps children develop an appreciation of another person's point of view.

In play, children can "try out" the roles of adult model figures, attribute their human frailties to puppets and stuffed animals, and act out socially unacceptable behavior through "make believe." Children can play alone, with another person, or with a group. They can dream of great things and create strategies for making their dreams come true. They can fantasize about having superpowers to ward off imaginary danger, while thinking and acting out ways to solve problems with their own human powers.

Certain activities allow children to challenge themselves both physically and mentally by overcoming obstacles that test their strength, ability and daring. Sometimes, the challenge is competing with oneself through a solitary game or activity; other times, the task is competing with others. Imaginative play can also help the child achieve self-mastery. In the process of expressing fears, hostility, or fantasies through dramatic play and by distinguishing between imagination and reality, the child gains a sense of control.

Almost every adult has at least a fleeting memory of the wondrous nature of play. Even though most are not conscious of the growth potential of play, it is critical to problem solving, initiative, and creativity. Even after objectivity has been attained, children who solved their problems through imagination will have "a resource of initiative remain, to enliven, sparkle, inspire, and push throughout the rest of life" (Smart & Smart, 1977, p. 243).

A BIT OF BACKGROUND

During the Middle Ages, children had virtually no childhood and therefore, special nurseries, playgrounds and special children's toys were unknown. After a few short years of dependency, children entered the world of adults and took part in adult games (Aries, 1960–1962). Future kings were allowed to play with dolls and other crude toys

SOURCE: Reprinted with special permission of King Features Syndicate.

such as windmills on sticks but, like other children of the wealthy, leisured classes, they were involved in many adult-type activities such as dancing, fencing, singing, and watching "farces." Things that we consider an integral part of childhood, such as fairy tales, nursery rhymes, puzzles, and board games, were unknown 400 years ago (Aries, 1960–1962). Books for children written in language they could understand and about topics of special interest to them did not appear until the 19th century.

In the 1700s, life for most children involved heavy labor and exhausting 12- to 14-hour shifts, and no time for play. For children who had leisure time, entertainment included participating in games and festivals, which were also enjoyed by adults (Aries, 1960–1962). Separate activities were reserved for privileged children, who were given riding and dance lessons and were taught the avocations of the leisure class.

In colonial America, puritanical parents were suspicious of play and games and discouraged anything that prompted laughter and enjoyment. Instead of playing games, young children learned the vocations of their parents; girls played house and learned to cook, and boys learned to hunt and fish. Children were allowed to play sports but only for physical exercise and to maintain good health. Colonial children did have a few toys, which included dolls for girls and marbles for boys, but most children's play consisted of copying adult activities and learning something useful in the world of work (Gibson, 1978).

In the Victorian period, which began in the mid-1800s, a "time to play" was reserved for the privileged children of the era. Young "ladies" of the period played with beautiful tea sets made of sterling silver and fine china dishes, toddlers rode toy horses covered with real horse hide, and young "gentleman" played with a variety of iron toys, particularly train engines. In sharp contrast, were the lives of poor and slave children, whose work involved ensuring that members of the privileged classes enjoyed a prolonged childhood.

Rooted in the American work ethic, the prevailing view until the turn of the 20th century was that, although child's play is fun, it was also a waste of time and that children should spend their time doing something more worthwhile. Because preschool children could not make any meaningful contribution through work or school, it was acceptable for them to play. However, when children grew old enough to go to school, they were expected to learn to do something useful, and play activities were confined to the end of the day and holidays (Hurlock, 1978).

In societies where children have to assume work responsibilities at a very early age, there is far less childhood play—this is also often true of children who are economically and socially disadvantaged (Schwartzman, as cited in Lefrancois, 1990). Much of the disparity in childhood opportunities for play noted throughout history can be applied to children today. Whereas many middle- and upper-class children enjoy a wide variety of toys, games, and fun-filled childhood experiences, many poor children cannot afford stimulating toys, children's books, or school supplies; and safe playgrounds or trips to amusement parks are often beyond their reach.

Regardless of economic background, today's children are not often encouraged to be creative and imaginative in play. Instead, from an early age, they are pushed toward computers and battery-operated toys, television, and a multitude of "how-to" lessons. Therefore, many children are developmentally deprived and preprogrammed for an adulthood void of creative problem-solving abilities. Play experiences, as the following discussion reveals, are essential to healthy development.

A DEVELOPMENTAL PERSPECTIVE OF CHILD'S PLAY

Play is a synthesis of cognitive, imaginative, and motor activities that facilitates the child's growth and development. This growth occurs in a series of stages in which the child's sense of self is developed and defined. Through play, children can express their thoughts and feelings, their likes and dislikes, and their hopes and fears. Decisions can be made and unmade without fear of failure, humiliation, or sanctions. Positive and negative feelings can be expressed and pent-up emotions can be released by playing rather than talking. In play, children can try out new solutions to old problems and integrate these into their experience. In this way, children are able to achieve control over their thoughts, feelings, and actions. This control contributes to a sense of mastery and builds up the child's self-confidence. An accumulation of positive experiences helps children achieve a sense of competence.

As children grow and develop, symbolic play is gradually replaced with social play. Through social play, children can practice the skills necessary to build relationships with others and to model socially acceptable behavior; children learn to get along with other children, to share, and to cooperate. The peer recognition that comes with playing by the rules and performing well helps children achieve a sense of mastery over their social and physical environment. Such experiences, developed in early childhood, form the basis for future satisfying interpersonal relationships, which are essential for the health and happiness of children and adults.

Developmental Stages in Child's Play

Sensorimotor play   All the information that the infant needs for thinking, imagination, and language is available through the senses. Shortly after birth, the young baby gathers sensory information by manipulating objects and performing certain motor activities. "Looking and touching have become coordinated and the child learns that to push the toy hanging from its cot will make it swing or rattle. Once learned the action will be repeated again and again. This is play" (Millar, as cited in Jernberg, 1983, p. 127).

Until babies are about 3 months old, their play consists mainly of looking at people and objects and making random attempts to grab objects in front of them. From 3 months on, infants are able to grasp, hold, and examine small objects. They examine everything they can reach by sucking, banging, or pulling on it. Everything they can't reach, they merely look at. After children learn to creep, crawl, or walk, their hands are free to touch, explore, and examine everything that was formerly off limits. During the first year, toddlers begin to play with toys. They experiment with sounds by using their voices to make engine noises when trucks are stuck in the mud or roaring noises when lions are present; they push buttons or pull strings to hear toys talk and pound on toy drums and xylophones. Activities such as rocking, swinging, riding piggyback, being bounced on a parent's knee, being twirled around as a human airplane, or being tossed (and caught) by a parent or other strong adult are exciting forms of sensorimotor stimulation.

As children approach age 2, pretense is already noticeable in their play. When children sputter like airplanes as they "fly" from room to room, they are preparing for imaginative play. Sensorimotor play sets the stage for "later symbolizing, make believe, fantasy and pretense" (Jernberg, 1983, p. 128).

Imaginative play   The ability to symbolize, so central to imaginative play, signifies major advances in both intellectual and language development (Piaget, 1962). Imaginative play commonly occurs between ages 2 and 6 when children learn to "make believe." Imaginative play can include pretending, in the form of dramatic and sociodramatic play, and fantasizing, in the form of daydreaming or the creation of an imaginary friend.

The child's first steps toward make-believe scenarios are played out in dramatic play (Smilansky, 1968). In dramatic play, the child tries on the roles of the important people in his or her world. He or she "pretends" to be another person, and adopts that person's speech, gestures, and activities. During pretend play, make-believe objects are used to represent other things, and there is a certain informal plot that includes real or imagined experiences (Smilansky, 1968). As preschoolers continue to develop their cognitive skills, the complexity, duration, and frequency of their play increases and solitary pretending gives way to sociodramatic play involving other children.

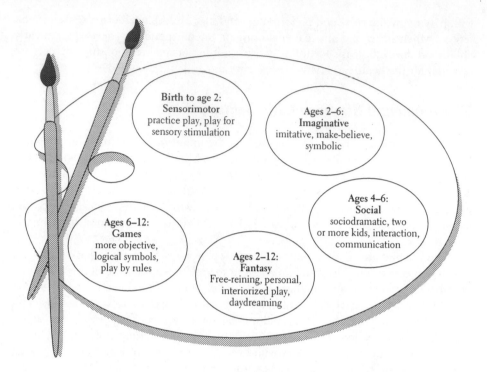

FIGURE 6-1   *Types of Developmental Child's Play*
Source: Piaget (1962); Smilansky (1968).

Sociodramatic play   Sociodramatic play, as defined by Smilansky (1968), is based on the premise that individuals *react* to each other and also *interact* with each other in a form of social play. This play form incorporates all the elements of dramatic play but adds shared pretend play and verbal interaction between two or more children. In this type of play, children need other children in order to imitate both actions and reactions and to reproduce the world as they see it. Through interactive play, children can practice their language skills, express their emotions, and work out their own interpretations of their social world. In this make-believe world, children can develop skills for coping with real-life situations.

Fantasy   Imaginative play can take the form of fantasy, which includes pretending, daydreaming, and creating imaginary playmates. Fantasy has been described as a "free-reining, personal, inner method of symbolic play" that is the child's "natural medium of action" (Smart & Smart, 1977, p. 245). Not only is fantasy a pleasurable activity of childhood, but it allows children to retreat from reality long enough to process new experiences and solve problems.

Young children often do not know what is troubling them, and, even if they do, many are unable to express their concerns directly. Therefore, they use a form of symbolic communication to express thinly disguised emotions in stories and other forms of play. This expression may help children vent their feelings and work through their problems. The following story, retold by Smart and Smart (1977) illustrates how hostility can be conveyed through symbols.

> I'll push you out the window and you'll make a mess on the pavement and my Daddy will scrape you up with a knife and spread you on bread and eat you. Then he'll vomit you up. (p. 246)

Although fantasy has not always been encouraged, it performs a valuable function in childhood (Lefrancois, 1990). This type of imaginative play enables the child to apply inner solutions to the outer world of reality. (This concept will be explained more fully in the section on play as therapy.)

Games   As children grow and develop, they move from spontaneous, unstructured "pretend" play to more structured, formal, and organized games with rules (Schaefer & Reid, 1986). By the time children are 4 or 5 years old, they play games to test their skills rather than just for fun. For young children, game play is individual and competition is with their own past achievements. The rules are few and are often modified or even violated. The traditional games of early childhood, such as cards, guessing games, and puzzles, are played first with parents and siblings and only later with peers. As children grow older, rules become stricter and competition keener.

Between the ages of 7 and 11, games with rules begin to take precedence over imaginative or pretend play because children have the increased cognitive ability to think and to reason logically (Piaget, 1962). Game playing requires more of children in terms of exercising impulse control, tolerating frustration, accepting the limits placed on their behavior, and following the rigid rules of the game. Many games played by children in the upper grades involve the intellectual capacity to strategize, plan, organize, think logically, and solve problems (Schaefer & Reid, 1986). Games are important to the child's physical, cognitive, and social development and because games generally involve interaction with two or more players, they are important to the child's social development as well.

PLAY AS THERAPY

> *In all likelihood there would be general agreement among all therapists that a "successful" therapeutic experience for a child would bring about marked and noticeable changes in the child's behavior—physically as well as psychologically.*
> —AXLINE (1950, p. 53)

Theoretical Perspectives

Play therapy evolved from early efforts to adapt psychoanalysis to the treatment of children. After discovering that children were unable to use free association to describe their anxieties, Melanie Klein (1932) and Anna Freud (1926–1946) incorporated play activities into the therapeutic process. Klein used play as a form of analysis for children under 6 years of age, whereas Anna Freud used play as a preliminary activity to the real work of analysis. Klein saw unconscious meanings and sexual symbolism in most play activities and interpreted these to the child. In contrast, Freud did not believe that all play had symbolic meaning, and therefore she did not use it as a basis for interpretation.

Melanie Klein (1932) felt that most children lacked the necessary verbal skills to express their fantasies, fears, and anxieties. Therefore, she utilized play as a substitute for verbalizations that would ordinarily be obtained by adult-style free association. Exploration of unconscious motivation and analysis of the child's transference relationship with the therapist was the focus of Klein's "play analysis." This analysis involved in-depth interpretations of the child's play behavior and accompanying verbalizations. These interpretations, which focused on the symbolism of the child's play, were then interpreted to the child. This process was intended to help diminish the child's anxieties and to supply the child with a motive for continuing with therapy. Because the emphasis was placed exclusively on the relationship between child and therapist, there was minimal contact with parents or teachers.

Anna Freud, on the other hand, employed games and toys as a way to get acquainted with her child patients and to interest them in therapy. She essentially used play to create a therapeutic alliance with the child and to obtain clues about the child's inner life. After forming a relationship, Freud slowly shifted the emphasis from play to more verbal interactions. To encourage verbal communication, she would ask her child patients to create visual images of their fantasies or daydreams. This technique, which was a modified version of dream analysis, was intended to help the children verbalize and understand their thoughts and feelings. Freud's version of analysis concentrated on bringing unconscious thoughts into conscious awareness. It was an educative process that, in some cases, involved significant others in the child's life.

Alfred Adler was the first theorist to break with traditional psychoanalytic thought. His split with Freud centered on Adler's belief that individuals were not driven solely by aggressive and sexual drives. Instead, Adler placed more importance on social and interpersonal dynamics in the development of personality. Adlerian therapy is developmental and growth-oriented, focuses less on unconscious processes, and is more concerned with the here and now than is Freudian psychoanalysis. "The Freudian approach looks for what has gone wrong in the hopes of making a correction, while the Adlerian approach looks for what is right to make it stronger." (Hansen, et al., 1994, p. 36).

Although Adler's theories were adapted for use with children and their families, no model for play therapy existed until recently. Kottman (Kottman & Johnson, 1993; Kottman & Schaefer, 1993) adapted Adlerian theory, processes and techniques for use with children in play therapy to construct a developmental approach that can be used in a variety of settings. Some of the techniques used in Adlerian play therapy, such as tracking, restatement of content, reflection of feeling, and encouragement, can be used in play therapy, regardless of the therapist's orientation.

In the late 1930s, two distinctly different approaches to play therapy emerged: *active* play therapy, in which children were given freedom within a certain structure; and *passive* play therapy, in which therapists allowed the child to engage in unrestricted play. In the active or structured therapies, as they were later called, the therapist used a more direct, goal-oriented approach within the traditional psychoanalytic model. Although the therapists relied on catharsis as a technique, they were more active in determining the direction and focus of the therapy.

David Levy (1939, 1979) developed a technique called release therapy that helped the child recreate a traumatic event through a structured play format. Although the child was not forced into a set play pattern, Levy provided the child with only the toys and materials most likely needed to reconstruct the traumatic event. Hambridge (1955, 1979) used an even more directive approach by recreating the anxiety-producing situation or traumatizing event for the child to play out. This technique was used after the therapeutic relationship was well-established and the therapist was sure that the child was sufficiently strong to manage such a direct approach.

The passive play therapy techniques first introduced in the 1930s were modified and used as a basis for the development of relationship therapy. The original basis for relationship therapy came from the work of Otto Rank, who "deemphasized the importance of past history and the unconscious and stressed the development of the therapist-client relationship as crucial with a consistent focus on the present, the here and now" (Landreth, 1991, p. 31). Rank's philosophy was adapted by Allen (1942) and Moustakas (1959) for use in play therapy with children. Relationship therapy emphasizes a strong positive relationship between the child and the therapist and encourages children to play out their current interpersonal situations in the safety and security of the playroom. In relationship therapy, children have complete freedom in play; the therapist can participate in play only at the invitation of the child; and both therapist and child can discuss the experiences encountered in play.

According to Dorfman (1951) client-centered therapy owes much to the work of both Sigmund Freud and Otto Rank. From the Freudians, client-centered play therapy "retained the concepts of the meaningfulness of apparently unmotivated behavior, of permissiveness and catharsis, of repression and of play as the natural language of the child" (p. 237). Dorfman further explained that from the Rankians (relationship therapy) came "the lessening of the authoritative position of the therapist, the emphasis on response to expressed feelings rather than to a particular content, and the permitting of the child to use the hour as he chooses" (p. 237).

In the 1940s, Carl Rogers developed a nondirective client-centered therapy with adults that was modified by Virginia Axline (1947) for use in play therapy with children. The child-centered therapist follows the child's lead, focuses on the child's strengths, reflects the child's feelings, believes in the child's potential for growth and change, and recognizes the therapeutic power of a warm, accepting and empathic relationship. Axline's (Axline, 1947, pp. 73–74) eight basic principles of the nondirective play therapy approach are as follows:

1. The therapist must develop a warm, friendly relationship with the child in which good rapport is established as soon as possible.
2. The therapist accepts the child exactly as he or she is.
3. The therapist establishes a feeling of permissiveness in the relationship so that the child feels free to express his or her feelings completely.
4. The therapist is alert to recognize the feelings the child is expressing and reflects those feelings back in such a manner that the child gains insight into his or her behavior.

5. The therapist maintains a deep respect for the child's ability to solve his or her own problems if given an opportunity to do so. The responsibility to make choices and to institute change is the child's.
6. The therapist does not attempt to direct the child's actions or conversation in any way. The child leads, and the therapist follows.
7. The therapist does not attempt to hurry the therapy along. It is a gradual process and the therapist must recognize it as such.
8. The therapist establishes only those limitations necessary to anchor the therapy to reality and to make the child aware of his or her responsibility in the relationship.

In the 1960s, Bernard and Louise Guerney developed an innovative technique known as filial therapy (Guerney, 1964). This client-centered play therapy approach involves training parents to conduct weekly play sessions with their children at home. In these parent-child play sessions, children are encouraged to communicate their needs, thoughts, and feelings to their parents through play. During the process, both parents and children alter their perceptions of one another. As parents become more tolerant and accepting, children grow in self-confidence and in their feelings of self-worth.

The behavior therapies, based on the principles of conditioning and social learning theory, emerged during the late 1950s. The goal of behavior therapies is to modify or eliminate maladaptive behavior and replace it with more adaptive and constructive behavior. To achieve this goal, the therapist utilizes the concepts of reinforcement and modeling. The behavioral therapist is concerned only with the problem behavior; no attempts are made to help the child express his or her feelings or to understand the child's conflicts. Instead, inappropriate behaviors are reduced or extinguished by withdrawing the reinforcers that maintain or strengthen them. Behavioral approaches such as reinforcement and punishment, modeling, relaxation training, and systematic desensitization are used with children in the play setting and may be taught to parents and teachers. Behavioral therapists do not see play as valuable or curative in and of itself; for them, play provides a way to establish rapport and implement treatment that will result in positive changes in the child's behavior.

In 1947, Slavson experimented with art activities and games as a way to help latency-age children release their feelings and in 1950, Schiffer developed what became known as "therapeutic play groups" (Gil, 1991). Today, group play therapy continues to be popular with practitioners because of its perceived effectiveness in helping children in all areas of their development. O'Connor (1991) developed a group format that incorporates cognitive, motor, behavioral, social, and emotional modalities in a way that is fun for participants. Each 1-hour session includes relaxation time, discussion time, structured activity, and free-play time.

Recent changes in play therapy have included strategies for combining family and group therapy approaches with individual play therapy strategies. Gumaer (1984) outlined a play process that focuses on providing children with intensive one-on-one contact with a caring adult and includes individual and group developmental play with children and their parents, teachers, or other caring adults.

Play therapy techniques such as the Family Puppet Interview (Irwin & Malloy, 1975), Family Sculpture (Simon, 1972) and the Family Drawing (Rubin, 1984) are all examples of creative ways to involve families in a play situation during some part of the session. Griff (1983) combined elements from play and family therapies with adult education methods, and Ziegler (1980) incorporated play into family sessions in order to include young children.

In summary, play therapy has its roots in the traditional psychoanalytic model. Early pioneers like Melanie Klein and Anna Freud interpreted play as symbolic of the child's conflict. Play therapists who use this approach rely heavily on insight, interpretation, and the transference relationship between child and therapist. The release and structure therapies, as developed by Levy and Hambridge, introduce or recreate anxiety-producing life situations in play. In these models, there is less emphasis on the relationship, as the therapist prepares and directs structured play scenes that encourage emotional release through catharsis. Client-centered play therapy is based on the therapist's belief in the child's natural striving toward health and growth. Virginia Axline modified Carl Rogers' client-centered approach into a play therapy technique. This growth model depends on the creation of a warm and caring therapeutic environment and a belief in the child's ability to solve his or her own problems. In contrast to the other theories, behavior therapy focuses on the problem behavior itself and not on interpreting and understanding conflicts or on helping children express their feelings. Behavioral therapists utilize reinforcement, relaxation, and desensitization approaches within the play setting. Their goal is to replace maladaptive behavior with more appropriate and constructive behaviors.

Current Trends

One of the most dramatic trends in the last decade has been the application of the healing powers of play by therapists from other theoretical orientations, including cognitive-behaviorists, family therapists, and Adlerians (Kottman & Schaefer, 1993). Current practitioners "have broadened the focus of play therapy from the traditional psychodynamic focus on the child's unconscious to include the child's cognitions, observable behavior, family system, and peer or social system" (Schaefer & O'Connor, 1983, p. 2).

An integration of theories and techniques defines the work of many play therapists today (see O'Connor, 1991). An integrative approach allows play therapists to use a variety of techniques such as doll and puppet play, sand play, storytelling techniques, dramatic play, and other creative art forms in their treatment of children. These techniques can be used in nondirective and directive therapy and have broad application across a variety of theoretical orientations. Many practitioners are now using play techniques as an integral part of counseling in elementary school settings (Kottman & Johnson, 1993; Landreth, 1987), and it continues to be an effective form of child therapy in a variety of settings.

The Value of Play Therapy

Play helps establish the therapeutic relationship, assists children in communicating their concerns, aids in assessment, and promotes healing and growth (see Figure 6-2). Play, which is free from evaluation and judgment by adults, affords children an opportunity to communicate thoughts and feelings directly or symbolically. Play is central to the assessment process because it enables the therapist to understand the child's needs, emotions, conflicts, and fears, while at the same time identifying the strengths the child brings to therapy. Play heals because it allows children to release pent-up emotions and recreate traumatic events and experiences. Through play, children are often able to act out problems and seek resolutions by experimenting with new behaviors. In an environment where they are protected from failure or criticism, children have an opportunity to try out solutions to their problems. This experience helps children gain a sense of competence, which promotes growth in self-confidence and self-acceptance.

Relationship building   To be invited to participate in children's play is to be privileged indeed, for few adults ever get the opportunity to interact with children in this special way. Even if the therapist is directed to "Sit there!" or "Answer that phone!" he or she has been granted admission to a special place in the child's world where only a few trusted adults are allowed to enter. The entire climate of the "children's room" is conducive to creating a therapeutic atmosphere that facilitates the child's self-expression. As the therapist observes and interacts with the child through play, he or she is building a relationship with the child in which they can communicate with one another through the manipulation of play materials and toys.

Communication   Play is a natural way for children to convey their conscious and unconscious thoughts and feelings, both verbally and symbolically. Children who are not capable of the sophisticated language required to explain their conflict or trauma may "play it out" instead. In addition, children can use play to reveal information that is too painful or too difficult to talk about. Children can reveal their hidden wishes, their pain, and their loneliness. They can express hostility and aggression, not only toward others but toward themselves. In the safety of the play therapy setting, children can act out traumatic life experiences that they may be only vaguely aware of, thus affording the therapist a glimpse of the children's unconscious thoughts and feelings.

Assessment   When the child's verbal and symbolic communication is heard and understood, it provides important clues about every aspect of the child's development. During play, children tell us about who they are and who they are not. Through the symbolism of play, children share their experiences, their problems, their needs, and their strengths. Because children modify their play reenactments to suit their own unique perspective, observers are able to learn about their values, interests, beliefs, and special interests. In addition, children often reveal their fears and worries as they play out their interactions with family, peers, and teachers, which affords counselors the opportunity to assess the strength of the children's coping skills. All this information helps the counselor paint a portrait of the developing child that assists in treatment planning; but more important, it provides children with an outlet to express thoughts, emotions, and behaviors related to past events, present situations, and future activities.

> For children to "play out" their experiences and feelings is the most natural and self-healing process in which children can engage.
> —LANDRETH (1991, p.10)

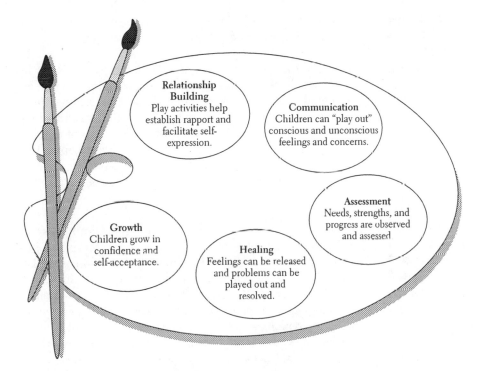

FIGURE 6-2   *The Value of Play Therapy*

Healing   Play therapy is not dependent on highly developed communication skills; therefore, it is especially helpful to the withdrawn, nonverbal, or emotionally wounded child who is unable to express his or her feelings in words. Through play, the reluctant, hurt, or hostile child can find joy and release by symbolically expressing forbidden wishes and conflicts, acting out fears, and safely venting hostile and aggressive feelings. When a caring therapist encourages this catharsis and provides empathic responses, this encouragement alone may provide relief for the child.

Children can release pent-up feelings while at the same time learning to regulate the expression of emotion. For example, Harry, a hostile child who often fights with other children and torments cats, can express his anger by tearing the heads off all of his clay figures and "beating up" the puppets. In this way, he can vent his anger and rage in the safety of the play room. In addition to this catharsis, Harry can learn to control the expression of his anger and practice more appropriate ways of managing his rage that spares both children and cats.

Through play, children can express and explore conflicts, work through defenses, and assimilate and integrate painful experiences. In the security of the therapeutic relationship, a child may feel safe enough to relax his or her defenses long enough to see how it feels to operate without them. By accepting the child exactly as he or she is and communicating this underlying respect to the child, the therapist helps reduce the child's anxiety. This encourages the child to bring the rejected as well as the accepted aspects of self out into the open and to form some kind of integration among them (Dorfman, 1951).

The play therapy setting provides children with an opportunity to bring their real feelings, no matter how antisocial, out into the open, which allows children to recognize and gain insight into hidden thoughts and feelings. The next logical step in the process of healing is to find new solutions to old problems. Through play, children are able to explore alternative ways of thinking and behaving without fear of criticism, humiliation, or rejection. Children can practice new behaviors in play, keeping those that work and discarding those that do not. The final step in the healing process is the child's ability to transfer their practice behaviors to situations outside of the play therapy environment.

Growth Play enhances self-development and facilitates and integrates motor, cognitive, imaginative, creative, and social behaviors and abilities. In essence, play is practice for life and so facilitates adaptive behavior. Through play, the child consolidates developing cognitive skills, language skills and motor skills and explores the boundaries of his or her emerging competencies (Smart & Smart, 1977). As children try all sorts of actions and combinations through play, they find out what they can and cannot do. They improve their problem-solving abilities as they try out solutions to problems and learn what works and what doesn't work. As children experiment with different ways of thinking and behaving, they are strengthening their coping skills. Combining these competencies into new organizations, children grow in self-confidence and self-acceptance, and these competencies contribute to the child's overall development.

GETTING READY FOR PLAY THERAPY

Some therapists have a special room for play therapy, and others carry their play materials with them in a suitcase. The fortunate therapist who has an opportunity to plan or redecorate a special place for child therapy may get some ideas from the three sample rooms described at the beginning of Chapter 4. These rooms, complete with furnishings, are offered as examples of ways to meet the needs of children and their therapists in a variety of settings. The elementary school counselor using play activities with children individually and in groups, the clinician in private practice, and the supervisor of therapists-in-training all have different needs. However, they have the common goal of establishing an atmosphere in which therapeutic change can take place. Part of this atmosphere depends on the kinds of toys and materials selected.

Selecting Toys and Play Materials

Selecting toys that promote clear understanding for the therapist and allow the child to play out themes of real life, aggression, and creative expression help to establish clear communication.
—LANDRETH (1991, p. 117)

As the therapist gets ready to begin play therapy, he or she will need to select some toys and materials that will facilitate the child's communication. Play materials should be selected for their therapeutic value to the child. Toys should be simple, of sturdy construction, easy for children to manipulate, and powered by the child's imagination rather than by batteries.

Although different therapists choose toys depending on their particular therapeutic objectives, some general guidelines can be found in the literature. Ginott (1960), one of the first clinicians to develop a rationale for selecting toys, believed that toys should: "(1) facilitate the establishment of contact with the child; (2) evoke and encourage catharsis; (3) aid in developing insight; (4) furnish opportunities for reality testing; and (5) provide media for sublimation" (p. 243). Landreth (1991) presented the most comprehensive rationale for toy selection, maintaining that play materials should facilitate creative and emotional expression, stimulate the child's interests, and allow for exploration and self-expression in unstructured activities.

Most play therapists (Axline, 1947; Ginott, 1960; Landreth, 1991) agree that toys and play materials should facilitate expression, encourage creativity, help children release emotion, and provide an outlet for the expression of aggression. Toys and play materials in these categories may serve different therapeutic purposes depending on how the child chooses to use them. For example, whereas one child may use clay to make a cookie to be shared, another may create a human figure that quickly loses its head and other important body parts.

Toys to Facilitate Expression

"Toys are children's words and play is their language" (Landreth, 1991, p. 116). Therefore, counselors should provide toys that facilitate the expression of a wide range of thoughts and feelings. For example, a child may want to act out real-life situations with a family of dolls and a dollhouse. The child can further elaborate on this nonverbal communication by adding a car, truck, or school bus. In some instances, animal puppets may help the child express strong emotions that he or she does not want to attribute to humanlike dolls. According to Ginott (1960), it is a good idea to provide toys that the child would not ordinarily be allowed to play with at home. The presence of these toys conveys an attitude of permissiveness and helps the therapist understand the child's inner world.

Toys to Encourage Creativity

Some toys, by their very nature, encourage creativity. Different kinds of hats, dress-up clothes, and jewelry allow a child to be magically transformed into someone else. An old box in the corner can become an instant dollhouse if a fancier one is not available. Some toys discourage creativity, whereas other play materials seem to invite it. When selecting toys, the counselor will want to keep in mind that simple things can sometimes spark the imagination.

Toys to Release Emotion

Children can use sand, water, paint, and clay to release strong feelings that they do not dare communicate more openly. The reversibility of these media allows children to change the identity of their creations to suit their evolving emotional needs. For example, sand can be transformed into "snow" or "water" or it can be a burial ground for dolls and other toys (Axline, 1947). Clay, sand, and paint provide children with opportunities "to conceal what they do not want to reveal, and to do and undo acts without detection or embarrassment" (Ginnot, 1960, p. 245). In addition to providing a safe way to explore and release feelings, sand and water play can also soothe, relax, and quiet some children.

Toys to Express Aggression

Toy guns, rubber knives, plastic swords (some light up or glow in the dark), wooden shields, and hammer and nails offer children a means of expressing hostility and aggression. Shooting, stabbing, hitting, and pounding are symbolic expressions of anger, and permitting their release through play may provide therapeutic catharsis and opportunities to rechannel energy. Using a plastic sword to "attack," pounding pegboards, shooting guns, driving nails, and building things are activities that require concentration and coordination. In Ginott's (1960) view, such activities help children "focus [their] energies on projects and goals, both in and out of the playroom" (p. 245).

The following is a list of toys and play materials that will help you get started in using play therapy.

Suggested Toys and Play Materials

Doll family (bendable, anatomically correct)
Baby doll with bottle
Pots, pans, dishes, and pretend food
Dollhouse with furniture and dolls
Stuffed animals
Puppets (animals, people, nondescript)
Puppet theater (can be homemade)
Sand tray and digging utensils
Sand tray miniatures
Toy guns, knives, and swords
Dress-up clothes, hats, and accessories
Building blocks and Legos
Toy cars, trucks, and boats
2 plastic telephones
Crayons, markers, paints, and fingerpaints
Newsprint, paper, child scissors, and glue
Play dough

Suggestions for Counselors on a Budget

Children and their therapists can make puppets out of socks and use fabric paint to color in facial features and hair. Buttons and yarn can also be used to give the puppet eyes, a nose, and some hair.

It may not be necessary to spend a lot of money to outfit a play room. Puppets and dolls can be handmade, toys and games can be found at yard sales and thrift shops, and play dough and finger paint can be made from scratch (see Chapter 7 for recipes). In addition, many individuals, stores and toy companies are willing to donate toys and play equipment.

Therapists and children may be able to make puppets out of cloth, socks, and or pipe cleaners. In addition, resourceful practitioners are often able to find people in the community who are willing to make family and animal puppets and anatomically correct dolls.

Suitable toys, games and playroom furnishings in good condition can often be found at yard sales and thrift shops. Child-size table and chairs, dolls, and board games are among the many "finds" in such places. Always check to make sure that toys are in relatively good condition and that all the pieces are included in board games. Occasionally, department stores will have stuffed animals or animal puppets at reduced prices. Large and small companies as well as children and parents are often willing to donate toys and materials for play therapy.

> Large end-rolls of newsprint are available at most newspaper companies free of charge.

PLAY THERAPY TECHNIQUES

Directive and nondirective therapists, regardless of their counseling orientation, can utilize the following techniques and materials to facilitate communication with children in play therapy. These techniques can be used to meet the needs and goals of individual children in schools, mental health clinics, child guidance centers, agencies, hospitals, and private practice settings. Common play therapy techniques include doll and puppet play, storytelling and bibliotherapy, board games, sand play and various other activities involving the graphic and performing arts. However, because Chapter 7 is devoted to art activities and Chapter 8 offers various strategies for using books in therapy, the techniques discussed here are limited to doll play, puppet play, storytelling, board games, and sand play. This list represents only the most common techniques and does not take into account the infinite number of creative and therapeutic techniques used by imaginative and innovative children and therapists.

The lists of materials given for each technique in Figure 6-3 are by no means exhaustive nor absolutely essential. Many therapists, especially those getting started or those on a limited budget, can get by with just a few toys for each technique. Actually, there is something to be said for simplicity. Sometimes, as the old axiom goes, "Necessity is the mother of invention," and what isn't in the toy room can be made by the children or the therapist. This is especially true of puppets and props that add to sand play, storytelling, and other play activities. Often when commercial toys are not available, children are able to use their imagination and creativity with wonderful results. One 5-year-old expressed his feelings about his family with a set of finger puppets that he and his therapist made from paper. Their facial features reflected each family member's mood and affect.

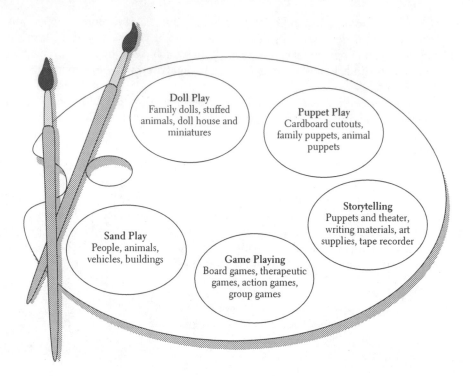

FIGURE 6-3 *Play Therapy Techniques and Materials*

Doll Play

Dolls provide a nonthreatening way for children to play out their thoughts and feelings. During doll play, "the child (1) identifies with the doll or puppet, (2) projects his or her own feelings onto the play figure, and (3) displaces his or her conflicts onto the doll or puppet" (Webb, 1991, p. 33). In this process, doll play often provides the therapist with a view of thoughts, feelings, and behaviors that the child may not know or fully understand.

Dolls for play therapy can include life-size baby dolls, anatomically correct dolls, family dolls, dollhouse dolls, stuffed animals, and other humanlike dolls. Whenever possible, the dolls used in play therapy should represent all the various racial groups, not only in color but in features as well. Therefore, African American dolls, Hispanic dolls, Asian American dolls, and Native American dolls, as well as Caucasian dolls should be available to the children.

A set of anatomically correct dolls includes an adult male and an adult female doll, a child male and a child female doll, and a baby doll. Boat and Everson (1993) suggested that these dolls can be used to: (1) gently help the child focus on topics that he or she is reluctant to discuss; (2) assess the child's knowledge of sexuality, including the child's names for and understanding of the function of various body parts; (3) enable the child to show what happened and to clarify alleged abusive acts; and

(4) provide opportunities for children to interact with the dolls in ways that might differentiate them from children who are not sexually abused. However, there is "little evidence thus far that abused and nonabused children can be reliably differentiated on the basis of their *behavior* with the dolls alone, to the exclusion of their verbal statements" (Boat & Everson, 1993, p. 63). Therefore, their use must be supplemented with verbal responses that encourage the child to verbalize as well as to demonstrate.

Because their detailed anatomical features may be too closely related to the trauma the child has experienced, these large sized dolls are usually presented fully clothed, and the child can decide whether or not to undress them. Some children choose not to use the dolls, and this refusal should be respected. Interpretations should be made cautiously because the "preponderance of research supports the use of anatomical dolls as an interview tool but not as a litmus test for sexual abuse" (Boat & Everson, 1993, p. 65). Readers who want to know more about using anatomically correct dolls with sexually abused children should consult Boat and Everson (1993) and Shamroy (1987).

Family dolls serve an important function in play therapy. Brems (1993) suggested that the anatomically correct dolls can double as just another human doll set, and when fully clothed, they are no different from any other large dolls. The therapist may also want a set of miniature bendable family dolls. These sets include a mother, father, girl, boy, baby, grandmother, grandfather, teenager, woman, and man and come in skin colors that correspond to the various racial groups. In reporting on her work using bendable dolls with traumatized children, Webb (1991) noted that youngsters often match the dolls they select to the characteristics of their own family, and preschoolers may even give the dolls the names, voices, and actions of real family members. In using family dolls, children often reenact exchanges they have witnessed in their own families. By watching and observing these exchanges, the therapist is able to learn a great deal about the child's interaction with other family members and about the child's perception of his or her place in the family.

Dolls and dollhouses serve as symbolic expressions of the child's experiences within the family. Using two houses with dolls, Kuhli (1979) was able to help a traumatized child work through unresolved conflicts resulting from separation and placement. "Feelings of rejection, anger, fear, and guilt were reexperienced in the 'old' house, while the second house provided a more positive alternative" (p. 431). Kuhli (1993) also suggested that the two-house approach could be used to help children mourn the loss of day-to-day contact with loved ones that results from divorce, prolonged hospitalization, or death. This technique also helps children adjust to stresses that are introduced into family life by the birth of a new sibling or by the addition of stepparents and stepsiblings. The second house provides children with a safe way to discharge feelings, to experiment with different ways of relating to family members, and to discover the support that is available to them from other caring people in their world.

Children who find humanlike dolls too threatening may prefer using stuffed animals. Because stuffed animals are somewhat distant from the actual object of the child's distress, it is often easier for children to project their feelings onto them and to displace conflict. Often, as with animal puppets, children are able to endow stuffed animals with human characteristics. For example, a child who cannot bear to say "I hate you" to a parent doll can do so to a stuffed lion. Cuddly animals such as teddy bears and monkeys seem to bring out soothing, loving behaviors, whereas animals like snakes, lions, and tigers can be used to displace feelings of fear and anger.

Suggested Materials for Doll Play

Lifelike baby dolls: Many have skin color and features that correspond to different racial groups and come with baby bottles.

Teach-A-Bodies (anatomically correct dolls): 2544 Boyd, Fort Worth, TX 76109.

Dollhouse complete with furniture.

Family dollhouse figures: Mother, father, boy, and girl.

Bendable 6-inch family doll set: Includes mother, father, girl, boy, baby, grandmother, grandfather, teenager, woman, and man. Doll sets are available with skin color to correspond to various racial groups.

Stuffed animals: Might include a teddy bear, monkey, turtle, snake, lion, tiger, or any other animal that children can use to express feelings.

Puppet Play

Puppetry enables children to tell stories rich in symbolism and to "play out" their fantasies. Puppetry can be structured or unstructured and has gained popularity as a technique with children, groups, and families (Irwin, 1983; Irwin & Malloy, 1975). Through puppetry, children can act out and deal with thoughts and feelings that are difficult for them to acknowledge as their own. Using puppets, the child can create a separate person that reveals those things that the child cannot express directly. In this way, the child is not only identifying with the personality that the puppet represents, but is also projecting his or her thoughts onto the puppet. Puppetry serves yet another important function in allowing children to displace strong emotions (such as anger) onto the puppets without causing harm to others and creating guilt for themselves (Woltman, as cited in Webb, 1991). Children are thus able to vent their feelings in a safe and healthy way. Although children as young as 3 have benefited from using puppets in therapy, some writers (Jenkins & Beckh, 1993) suggest that puppetry is most suitable for children from ages 5 to 11.

The therapist will want to provide a variety of puppets for the children to choose from. The selection should include several sets of family puppets that include a mother, father, sister, brother, baby, grandmother, and grandfather. Other adult and child figures should be provided to represent stepparents and stepbrothers and sisters. Like dolls, these puppets should represent various racial groups in complexion and facial features.

Family puppets can be made out of a variety of materials. Some therapists make their own hand or mitten puppets, whereas others purchase commercially available sets. Jenkins and Beckh (1993) suggest making a family of finger puppets using rubber balls for heads; these finger puppets can be made by the children with the help of the therapist. Various accessories such as spoons, pencils, and handmade paper creations add to the puppet presentation. For example, folded paper serves as a boat for the family to ride in and a small spoon doubles as an oar.

Animal puppets have a special place in child therapy because they provide a non-threatening way for children to explore their unacceptable thoughts, feelings, and behaviors. It is especially important to have a variety of animals, because the children can and do attribute human characteristics to the puppets. These characteristics can include emotions such as anger, sadness, shyness, fear, anxiety, or jealously and behaviors such as aggression, withdrawal, crying, or laziness. Animals like alligators, sharks, or dragons might be used to represent aggression, whereas the rabbit, mouse, or lamb might represent timidity. In the hands of the aggressive child, a dragon puppet suddenly comes alive, breathing fire and bringing death and destruction on "pretend" enemies. By attributing aggressive characteristics to the dragon, the child is venting his or her anger in a way that doesn't bring negative consequences or excessive guilt. Similarly, the mouse puppet is often timid and afraid, the snake is treacherous and evokes fear, and the shark almost always lies in wait to bite someone. In identifying with the shark, the child is able to displace aggression safely instead of attacking his or her real-life tormentors. It is also helpful to have a few neutral puppets such as puppies, pigs, and chicks that don't evoke any particular emotion or need. Because neutral puppets are essentially free of symbolism, children can attribute to them any emotion or need they choose.

Puppet play is an excellent group activity and can be used with large and small groups of children, particularly in school settings. Life-size cardboard cutouts of a mother, father, brother, sister, and baby are especially useful puppets and are excellent ways to facilitate group discussion and get all children involved. (It is advisable to have more than one set in order to do group work with large groups of children.) Because these puppets are designed to be worn, the puppet takes on the ethnicity of the child. Puppet play, especially in groups, provides children with an appreciation of another's point of view and contributes to increased problem-solving and social skills.

Suggested Materials for Puppet Play

Family hand puppets: These are available in all racial groups and include mother, father, boy, girl, and baby. Additional puppets can represent step-parents, step-siblings, grandparents, and other extended family members.

Finger puppets: These can be made from a variety of materials including paper and cloth. The child's fingers, painted with facial features, serve as heads. If the child and the therapist prefer, heads can also be made from rubber or Styrofoam balls. Puppet accessories can include spoons, straws, cloth, and paper hats.

Cardboard cutouts of the family: Cutout puppets include the mother, father, boy, girl, and baby. Several sets are needed for group work with children.

Animal hand puppets: A wide variety of animal puppets are available. Turtles with heads that retreat into their shells; possums with babies that attach to their backs; and alligators with mouths that zip shut, trapping a hapless fish puppet inside, are just a few examples. Additional suggestions that can be bought or made include pig, rabbit, monkey, teddy bear, chicken, shark, dragon, snake, and dinosaur. Therapists may want to have more than one set for group work.

Storytelling

There is a special place in play therapy for the mutual storytelling technique first developed by Gardner (1971). This technique uses the child's self-created stories in a play therapy approach that helps the child (5 years or older) explore alternate solutions to existing problems. First, the child tells his or her story, and then the therapist creates a responding story that introduces healthier resolutions of the conflicts evident in the child's story. This technique can be supplemented with audio- and video-tape recordings, which allow children to see and hear themselves telling the stories (Gardner, 1993).

Gardner's structured approach has been adapted for use in both nondirective and directive play therapy. Creative variations of the storytelling technique, tailored to meet the needs of individual children, are limited only by the imagination and creativity of the child and the therapist. Suggested creative variations include writing down the child's stories and putting them into book form or having the child write the stories instead of telling them. One 9-year-old girl dictated her "story" in a series of segments while her student-therapist typed it. These stories were later bound into a book that included the child's illustrations. Storytelling can also be combined with doll or puppet play (see Webb, 1991, pp. 52–66). This variation on the technique enables children to act out their stories rather than write them down.

Storytelling provides an enjoyable way to establish rapport and learn more about the child. As children tell their stories, they communicate important information about themselves and their families while learning to express and master their feelings. By listening to the child's story, the therapist is able to better understand the child's defenses, the child's conflicts, and the family dynamics (Gardner, 1983). In analyzing the child's stories, the therapist will want to look for repeated themes that give important clues about the child's feelings and struggles. As with any interpretation, the general themes in the child's stories must be interpreted in light of everything else that is known about the child. Because each situation is unique, interpretations of children's stories are just one indication of what might be troubling a particular child. Consideration must also be given to the child's capacity for imagination as well as the child's age and developmental level. In addition, the therapist must be familiar with and skilled in interpreting the nature of symbolic communication. Interpretation of the child's stories depends a great deal on the therapist's skill and judgment.

Suggested Materials for Storytelling

Writing materials, such as paper and pencils

Art materials, such as construction paper, crayons, colored pencils, and so on for illustrating stories

Puppets and dolls for children to reenact their stories, and a puppet theater for putting on puppet plays (the puppet theater can be made from a large appliance box and can be decorated by the children)

Tape recorder and video equipment (if available)

Game Playing

As children grow and develop, their play moves away from fantasy and toward reality. Increased use of reason and logic prepares the developing child for the "games with rules" stage. At first, games are played for fun and have rather loosely defined rules, which children often modify or even violate. But as children get older, the rules become stricter and competition is keener. Individual and group games help children learn how to share, wait their turn, and play by the rules. Games teach children self-discipline, cooperation, and competition and are, in essence, training grounds for life.

Games applicable to play therapy can be played alone, with two people, or with two or more. Most board games are designed to be played by four to six persons, and they include parlor board games as well as "therapeutic" games, or games designed with therapy in mind. Board games help children focus their attention, internalize self-discipline, and learn to win and lose gracefully. Games also build trust; help children develop cognitive, motor, and social skills; and enhance self-esteem and self-confidence. The so-called therapeutic games have an additional benefit in that they provide the therapist with a glimpse into the child's private world of thoughts, feelings, attitudes, and behaviors. These games are designed to provide information about the child's interests, attitudes, beliefs, values, defenses, and family dynamics.

When given a choice of play materials, school-age children often choose board games. Parlor games such as checkers, chess, "Scrabble for Juniors," "Life," and "Sorry" are frequent choices. Popular therapeutic games are "The Talking, Feeling and Doing Game" and "The Ungame." In addition to board games, action games such as "Hot Shot Basketball" are favorites among both boys and girls who seem to delight in racking up points against a less able therapist. Other games in this action category but that require only two players include "Battleship," "Rock 'em Sock 'em Robots," and "Mouse Trap."

Group Games and Activities

Group games, stories, and discussions provide children with an opportunity to talk about their thoughts and feelings, try out new behaviors in the group, and receive feedback from their peers. Group discussions can be initiated by using the cards from the "Ungame" or "The Talking, Feeling, and Doing Game" and through carefully chosen stories. Reading stories to children is an excellent way to initiate group discussion on sensitive issues (see Chapter 8).

Group games such as "Gossip, I've Got a Secret" and "Hot Potato" are excellent ways to help children develop such important social skills as playing by the rules, having consideration for others, cooperating and taking turns. In addition, games can help children communicate their concerns directly and indirectly through their behaviors and their verbalizations. Icebreakers like "Duck, Duck, Goose" and "Musical Chairs" help children learn each other's names, build group cohesion, and have fun.

Extra benefits are realized when parents are involved in play groups with children and therapists. Including parents, at least for part of the session, encourages parent-child communication, helps parents understand child development, and provides opportunities for children and parents to have fun together.

Suggested Games for Use in Play Therapy

Therapeutic games
The Talking, Feeling, and Doing Game
Creative Therapeutics, 155 County Road
Cresskill, NJ 07626

Parlor games
Sorry (Parker Bros.)
Scrabble for Juniors (Milton Bradley)

(continued)

Therapeutic games (continued)
The Ungame (five versions)
The Ungame P.O. Box 63882
Anaheim, CA 92806

Parlor games (continued)
Life (Milton Bradley)
Chess
Checkers

Action games (two players only)
Battleship (Milton Bradley)
Rock 'em Sock 'em Robots (TYCO)
Hot Shot Basketball (Milton Bradley)
Mouse Trap (TYCO)

Action games (one player at a time)
Perfection (Milton Bradley)
Rebound (TYCO)

Games to use in groups
I've Got a Secret
Gossip
Simon Says

Duck, Duck, Goose
Hot Potato
Mother, May I?

Sand Play

Children love to play in the sand, whether at the beach, in the backyard, or in the play room. Before they realize it, youngsters are shoveling, digging, tunneling, and sculpting to create castles, tunnels, mountains, runways, and riverbeds. By moving sand and adding water, they create rivers and ponds. When miniature toys are added, fantasies and dreams come alive, and the onlooker gets a special glimpse into the child's inner world. When the sandbox is transported to the play therapy room, children are provided with a fun, relaxing, and therapeutic medium.

In a review by Allan & Berry (1987), sand play was first described as a therapetic technique by Margaret Lowenfeld, who called her method "The World Technique" because children kept their toys in a box dubbed "the world." Later, Dora Kalff's work helped gain acceptance for sand play as a psychoanalytic technique that gave disturbed children an opportunity to resolve traumas by expressing their fantasies and developing a sense of mastery and control over inner impulses (Allan & Berry, 1987).

Sand play, conducted within a relationship characterized by genuine warmth and acceptance, helps the child play out inner problems and allows for therapeutic progress and growth. This technique can be used by nondirective counselors, who allow the child to lead the way, as well as by more directive counselors, who wish to structure the sand play experience. How the counselor chooses to incorporate sand play into the play therapy process is a matter of individual style and counseling orientation. Vinturella and James (1987) reported that sand play is used by practitioners of all orientations to accomplish certain therapeutic goals: for example, behaviorists use it as a diagnostic tool whereas client-centered counselors use it to create a climate of acceptance.

Sand play as an option during play therapy is often an irresistible draw, and many children choose it over and over again. Vinturella and James (1987) believe that sand play has a distinct advantage over other therapeutic approaches because it requires no particular skill unlike art and drama. Therefore, children seldom say "I can't" as they create something in the sandbox. No matter what children create as they shovel, dig, tunnel, and sculpt, it is a masterpiece! As children play in the sand, they are able to create scenes, reenact trauma, and play out their innermost thoughts and feelings. By having complete control, the child is able to work through pent-up feelings and to ask the kinds of questions that have been troubling him or her. Gil (1991) suggested that abused children feel soothed and nurtured during sand play.

During the time in the play room, the child is free to play in the sand and to use as many of the available miniatures as desired. During the sand play process, the child decides what to construct, which figures to use, and how to use them. The child is free to build a scene, make a landscape or simply play in the sand. (See the illustration of sand play given in the section "Play Therapy in Practice" later in this chapter.) Whereas some children choose a sort of random sand play experience, others use sand pictures as a way to depict experiences they cannot tell us about in words.

Sand play is not only a way for the child to work out feelings, conflicts, and worries that occur in the real world; it is also a valuable tool to assess the child's concerns as well as his or her progress in therapy. By observing the child at play and listening carefully to the child's verbalizations, the counselor is able to tell a great deal about the child's thoughts, feelings, and behaviors. As with any form of art, the therapist will want to pay special attention to reoccurring themes in the child's sand play. It is also worthwhile to note the particular toys the child uses and to pay special attention to the child's verbalizations as he or she acts out a particular problem or makes a "sand picture." What the child says during the process of making a sand picture or acting out a scene, as well as the child's verbalizations about the finished product, is very important to assessment and to the interpretation of the child's sand play.

Like other forms of play and art therapy, sand play often involves symbolism that has a special meaning for individual children. Therefore, it is important for the counselor to identify and clarify the meaning of the sand picture as the child perceives it rather than as the therapist perceives it. Because children can act out their concerns both literally and symbolically, it is important that the therapist remember that there is no single interpretation for a given symbol. Interpretation depends on knowing as much about the child as possible and then making tentative hypotheses about what this sand picture means to this particular child. Symbols are arbitrary and cannot be viewed in isolation, so it is important that the counselor interpret the symbols of sand play in light of everything else known about the child. Sand play is just one more piece of a complicated puzzle and, as such, cannot be used as a sole determinant of a child's social conflict.

To offer sand play as a therapeutic option, the therapist needs some basic materials, including a sand tray, a sink, and some miniature toys and figurines. A large metal tray measuring 24" × 30" × 4" only partially filled will reduce the amount of sand that excited children spill onto the floor. The tray can be placed on a cart with wheels so it can be moved from room to room if necessary. Although not absolutely essential, a sink is a desirable piece of equipment for a play room where sand play is used, giving children ready access to water for soaking the sand and for cleaning up. In my experience, sand that is somewhat damp is preferable to dry or soaked sand; however, it is up to the child to decide how wet or dry the sand should be. Some children just love to flood the sandbox, and occasionally limits must be placed on how much water is allowed in the box. It is wise not to allow children to put a lot of sand in the sink because it might clog the drain.

Some practitioners place a variety of miniature toys on shelves so that children can choose which ones they want to use in their sand play. Certain toys can be grouped together, such as a group of toy soldiers together with tanks, or a family grouping of dolls. Sometimes, this system is difficult to maintain because children may want to throw everything into one big box. How the miniature toys are grouped and organized will be decided by such factors as space, time, and temperament. Some practitioners do not have endless shelf space, nor do they have the time to help children organize materials on shelves during cleanup. Others think it is more fun for children to "find" miniatures in a big box, and using a box may make cleanup easier also.

Suggested Miniatures for Sand Play

People: Includes family, military, or fantasy figures

Animals: Includes wild, domestic, and prehistoric animals

Vehicles: Cars, trucks, bulldozers, tanks, and rockets; small helicopters, airplanes, and tiny boats are also appropriate

Buildings: Houses, schools, and so on can be provided, but children love to build their own caves and castles

Miscellaneous items: Optional items might include plastic trees and shrubs, straws, popsicle sticks, large nails, large spoons, and paper cups

THE THERAPEUTIC PLAY PROCESS

Play is also a vehicle for the creation of the child's corrective experience. Either the therapist or child may set up play interactions that allow the child to reexperience an event or relationship in a different way and with a more positive outcome than that of the original event.

—O'CONNOR (1991, p. 101)

Most writers agree that the therapist must do more than play with the child if the therapy is to be successful. Gumaer (1984) stressed that "without purposeful counselor interaction, the use of play media is hardly more than random play" (p. 65) The focus of this interaction is the communication between the child and the therapist. When the child's symbolic and verbal communications are heard and understood, and the therapist communicates this understanding to the child, the child is free to explore troublesome thoughts, feelings, and behavior. In the security of the play room, children can re-create situations that might be too threatening in "real life." These re-creations, which can be set up either by the child or by the therapist, provide children with opportunities to play out conscious and unconscious feelings and to reexperience events and relationships (O'Connor, 1991). This process allows uncomfortable feelings to be worked through and mastered. Through this corrective experience, the child discovers alternate ways of thinking and behaving. As a final step, children need opportunities to practice their new behaviors in the therapeutic relationship so they can resolve the problem or develop more effective coping strategies to deal with those problems that cannot be resolved.

An Integrated Approach

The five stages in the play therapy process are depicted in Figure 6-4 and include the five R's of play therapy: *relating* to the therapist; *releasing* feelings; *re-creating* events,

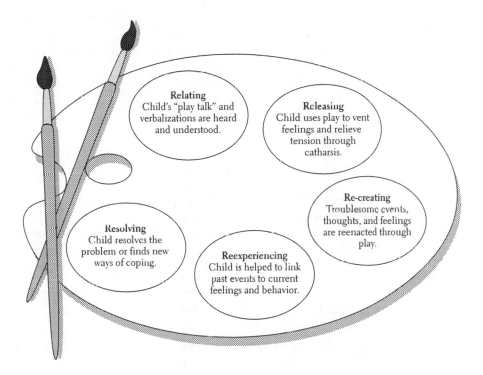

FIGURE 6-4   *The Play Therapy Process: An Integrated Approach*

experiences, or relationships; *reexperiencing* troublesome thoughts and feelings in a way that facilitates new understanding; and *resolving* problems and conflicts by practicing new behaviors in play. This integrative approach is based on the well-established psychodynamic, relationship, and developmental approaches to play therapy. Because children are unique individuals, some may not go through each phase in an orderly fashion. Rather, they may combine several stages, skip one, or stop at a particular stage in the therapeutic process. For example, as a child is releasing feelings, he or she may already be working out ways to resolve the problem. The child's relationship with the therapist changes and deepens as play therapy progresses, and the interaction between the two acts as a catalyst for change. The therapist can be directive or nondirective in this relationship and generally uses a variety of counseling skills such as listening, responding, clarifying, challenging, and interpreting to help children resolve problems and develop better coping strategies.

Relating

> A *therapeutic relationship can be established and maintained only if the therapist understands the child's communications.*
> —GINOTT (1960, p. 243)

Most therapists recognize the need to establish a warm and accepting relationship with the child in which children are free to be themselves. They can express their feelings, no matter how negative, and their right to these feelings will be respected (Axline, 1947). As children feel accepted and understood, they usually reveal more of themselves, and these self-expressions help the therapist view the world from the child's unique perspective. As the relationship develops and the therapist learns more about the child and his or her unique life experiences, the therapist begins to develop empathy for the child. This empathy is an understanding of how the particular child is feeling, given his or her unique life experiences. When this empathic understanding is communicated to the child, it facilitates insight (Egan, 1994).

Many practitioners believe that the creation and maintenance of a relationship is a necessary but not sufficient condition for change (see O'Connor, 1991). O'Connor suggested that, in addition to creating a warm and permissive atmosphere, play therapists must be able to create corrective experiences that help the child link his or her thoughts and feelings to current behavior. Therefore, therapists may need to consider using the therapeutic setting to establish limits that structure the therapy, help the child assume responsibility for his or her behavior, and teach the child better ways of fulfilling those needs.

Releasing Feelings

In the safety and security of the play room, the child is free to express the thoughts and emotions that have been kept hidden. Some children furiously pound clay, forming people and then ripping them apart; some bury figures in the sand and then quickly put straws in so they can "breathe"; others give the baby a bath by holding its head underwater. These activities provide children with a way to release their emotions and express their feelings through play. Because this catharsis enables children to relieve tension, it can be therapeutic in and of itself. In most cases, however, the therapist needs to help the child deal with the feelings expressed.

Clay, age 4, is venting his anger over the recent death of his sister. (The case of Clay and his brother Clinton is presented later in the chapter in "The Case of Traumatic Grief.") In the following scene, Clay seems to be expressing anger at his mother (the therapist) for her failure to bring his sister back to life (the mother had tried in vain to resuscitate the child).

> For the first 5 minutes, Clay kicks everything in the room. He dumps over boxes and hits toys. He tells the therapist what she can and cannot do. Shouting orders, he begins to rummage through the toys, making a huge mess. He finally focuses on the large cardboard family cutouts. He assigns the therapist the role of the mother and he takes the role of the baby. In his play, he speaks in a very angry tone to the therapist (representing the mother). He keeps asking the therapist (mother) to do things for him. "Get me a bottle!" "Give me that spoon." As the therapist hands him the things he requests, he pretends to break each one. The therapist responds: "You seem angry at me." "I am!" replies the child. Clay then lines up the cutouts of the other family members and begins punching them. He instructs the therapist to punch the sister in the face. "She doesn't have a face," the therapist replies. (The cardboard puppets require the child to provide the face.) Clay replies, "She's dead. You killed her." He then begins to kick at all the family cutouts.

At this stage, children express their emotions and relieve tension through play, but they have not yet connected these troublesome feelings with their current problem or conflict. This understanding will come much later in therapy. For now, the therapist needs to focus on attending to the child's verbal and symbolic communication and on responding to the feelings the child is expressing. In an effort to understand the child's expression of feeling, the therapist may ask open-ended questions when necessary and appropriate. If the child chooses to remain silent or to communicate only through play, the therapist respects that choice.

Re-creating Significant Events

As the relationship between the child and the therapist matures, the child feels secure enough to explore the significant events in his or her life that generate troublesome feelings and emotions. In this stage of therapy, the child re-creates both past and present events in play and experiences the uncomfortable feelings that so often accompany them. Although the child knows that certain events in his or her life trigger uncomfortable thoughts and feelings, the child has not yet made the link between these feelings and the current problem or conflict. It is appropriate to respond by restating what the child has expressed, to show that the child's message has been heard and understood. Clarifying responses can also help both the child and the counselor focus on the underlying message of the child's play.

In the following example, Clay pretends to be Santa and "buries" presents for the therapist to find. Then he pretends to be "buried" in the snow and wants the therapist to use the flashlight to find him.

> Clay selects several toys and accompanies the therapist to a small office room. Upon entering the room, he discards all toys but the flashlight. He will not let the therapist touch it but gives her "permission" to play with the other toys. He turns the lights off and walks around the room, shining the light in every corner. Finally, Clay decides to pretend to be Santa Claus. He uses the flashlight to find presents "buried in the snow." Surprisingly, Clay allows the therapist to hold the flashlight to find them. Clay pretends to be covered with snow and instructs the therapist to "find me." He turns the lights off again so that the therapist would use the flashlight to find him.

Clay recreated scenes that help him face his fears of death and darkness. He seemed to be testing his fear of the darkness, proving to himself that he could turn off the lights and still be okay. When he turned the lights back on, the look of fear appeared on his face for an instant, and then his smile lit up his face!

Reexperiencing Events

At this stage, children begin to establish an understanding of past events and to link that understanding to their current thoughts, feelings, and behaviors. Adults usually communicate this insight verbally, but for children this recognition often comes as they "play out" situations in which they can reexperience the event and assimilate it into their current understanding.

The therapist who communicates empathy helps the child understand and assimilate painful experiences. Once the therapist understands the symbolic meaning of the child's play responses and links this understanding to the child's past experience, this understanding can be communicated in the form of an interpretation. If this interpretation is within the child's frame of reference, it helps the child feel understood. An example of this kind of interaction is presented in the section on the case of traumatic grief, under the heading "Summary of first three sessions with Clay."

It is in this stage of the child-therapist relationship that the child may transfer the actions of the parents and significant others onto the therapist. For example, some of the positive as well as the negative qualities that the child attributes to the mother or father may be transferred to the therapist as they work through the problem together. As part of this relationship, the therapist enables the child to express thoughts, feelings, and behaviors associated with the child's unique perception of past life experiences and to gain a better understanding of them.

Resolving

At this final stage in the therapy process, the child is able to act on the understanding that he or she has of the problem and to experiment with various solutions. Because some problems will have no solutions, the child can develop the skills necessary to cope with the problem. Trusting in the relationship with the therapist, the child may feel secure enough to relax his or her defenses and see how it feels to be without them. With less anxiety, the child is able to experiment with alternative ways of thinking and behaving. The child can experiment with a number of different solutions and keep only those that work. This process provides an interim step between the play therapy process and the application of these solutions to the child's everyday life.

Special Issues in Play Therapy

Various issues that may present challenges to practitioners have been identified in the literature (Brems, 1993; Landreth, 1991; O'Connor, 1991). Some of these challenges relate to the child's (1) curiosity about the play situation; (2) fears, anxieties, and ambivalence; (3) interest in the counselor; (4) relationship with the counselor; (5) exploration of the limits of the play room, and (6) expression of aggression. These issues are discussed here in a effort to acquaint the reader with some of the common reactions children have to play therapy. Some of the children's questions and statements relate to underlying issues of trust and are relevant to rapport building, others represent the many and varied ways that children seek assurance or defend themselves against anxiety. Some practical suggestions are also given that may help counselors recognize and deal with problems as they arise.

Curiosity about the Play Situation

"Why am I here?"
"Does someone pay you to play with me?"
"Are these toys yours?"
"Anyone else been here?"

Children, unlike adults, rarely come to therapy on their own. Instead, they are referred because they have worried or annoyed their parents, teachers, or some other significant adult. Therefore, it is not unusual for children to express curiosity about why they are there and to ask whether anyone else has visited the play room. Newcomers also generally have a lot of questions about the play materials and furnishings. For example, they may ask who owns all the toys and whether they can play with them.

Many children accept the play situation, enjoy it, and benefit from it without ever knowing the exact reason for their visits. However, occasionally a child arrives and asks, either directly or indirectly, why he or she is there. The therapist, who has a general idea of the concerns about the child's behavior, should answer the child's questions as truthfully as possible. A frank explanation is a gesture of respect for the child's feelings and should be given when the child asks for it (Dorfman, 1951). When the child asks, "Why am I here?" the therapist could simply say, "Your grandmother knows that you have had a hard time since your mom died and she thought that you might like someone to talk to about it."

Fear, Anxiety, and Ambivalence

"Can my Mom come in with me?"
"Don't shut that door!"
"I'm scared in here, but I like it."
"Can I go home now?"

Occasionally, children express fear, anxiety, or ambivalence about coming to play therapy. Fear of separating from the parent, uncertainty about trying new and unfamiliar tasks, and a wish to avoid anxiety-producing situations can result in a reluctance to participate fully in play or a desire for early termination. In these instances, the therapist needs to acknowledge and understand the child's feelings and communicate this understanding to the child. In addition, several positive steps need to be taken that will diminish the child's apprehensions.

To minimize separation anxiety, it is sometimes necessary to involve parents in the transition from waiting room to play room (Brems, 1993; O'Connor, 1991). An effective way to do this is to invite the parent to join the child in the initial session. When 5-year-old Carlos arrived for play therapy, he was crying and clinging to his mother. His student-therapist quickly invited him and his mother to join her in a game of hide-and-seek. All three enjoyed the game and Carlos stopped crying and began to laugh with the others. After this initial session, Carlos was able to leave his mother and play alone with the therapist.

Whereas Carlos was afraid to enter the play room, Tasha was afraid to stay there. Six-year-old Tasha had been locked in a dark closet by an abusive parent. Consequently, Tasha insisted that the play room door remain open at all times. She would scream and cry if the door accidentally closed. Keeping the door open during therapy reassured Tasha that her feelings were understood and respected. Gradually, after many weeks, she was able to close the door herself.

Although Tasha was able to stay in the play room, some children have so much anxiety that they do not wish to stay. What does the therapist do when the child wants to terminate early or refuses to participate? Some practitioners advocate making an attempt to find out why a child wants to shorten or terminate the therapy but advise against letting the child leave (Brems, 1993). Others maintain that the child's right to refuse to participate should be respected. Dorfman (1951) stated that, although not permitted to leave, children should be free to spend the therapy hour in any way they want to. Another approach is to ask the child to participate, agreeing that after giving it a fair trial the child can leave if he or she wishes. Using this second approach, children often discover that play therapy is so much fun they want to stay.

Interest in the Counselor

"How old are you?"
"Do you have kids?"
"I think I went by your house before."

Children are curious about the counselor and want to know things about his or her personal life. These questions often pop up in the early stages of therapy as the child's way to establish a relationship with the counselor. Generally, a truthful answer helps establish rapport and builds trust. It is seldom wise or necessary to embark on a lengthy self-disclosure. Children frequently ask whether the therapist has children, what their ages are, and other questions about the therapist's home and family life. Sometimes, personal questions of this nature are a child's way of determining whether the therapist has room in his or her life for one more child. It is well for therapists to assure children that they there is plenty of love to go around.

The Child's Relationship with the Counselor

"You be the baby, and I'll be the Daddy."
"Help me. I can't do this."
"Bet you can't guess what I'm going to do?"
"Is this okay?"
"Should I draw my ugly sister too?"
"What do you want to do now?"

When children come into therapy, they begin to explore the parameters of their relationship with the counselor. Through questions and statements, they establish what role they will play in the therapeutic relationship. Some children will immediately assume a leadership role and direct the counselor's activities ("You be the baby and I'll be the Daddy"), whereas others depend on the counselor to lead the way ("Help me. I can't do this"). Sometimes, in an effort to include the therapist in the activity, children may ask the counselor to "guess" about their activities or actions ("Bet you can't guess what I'm going to do").

Children commonly ask the therapist to make a guess or give an opinion about certain projects and activities. These questions are often not intended as stated and should not be taken literally (Brems, 1993). Instead, they can be viewed as the child's way of seeking approval ("Is this okay?") or of requesting permission to share his or her thoughts and feelings ("Should I draw my ugly sister, too?"). When the therapist answers the child's questions directly, he or she runs the risk of disappointing the child or discouraging his or her attempts at self-exploration. Instead, the therapist should ask the child for his or her own opinion, thus returning the responsibility to the child.

Some of the children's questions ("What do you want to do now?") may represent attempts to avoid making decisions and to place the responsibility on the therapist. If the therapist makes the decision for the child, he or she is fostering the child's dependency and increasing his or her feelings of inadequacy. Therefore, it is best to allow children to search for their own answers to the questions they frequently ask. In this way, the therapist returns the responsibility for action and direction to the child and encourages self-discovery (Landreth, 1991).

Exploring the Limits of the Play Room

"Can I stay? Please, pretty please?"
"Just five more minutes."
"Can I take this puzzle home?"
"Let's go get a Coke."

Time limits   Children usually enjoy play therapy and are reluctant to see it end. Nevertheless, all therapy must end and some children need to be gently reminded that the time is up. If approached in a friendly and honest manner, most children cooperate by beginning to clean up a few minutes before the end of the session. If a child occasionally dawdles or has something very important to work out, the therapist can be flexible in meeting the child's needs. If dawdling becomes a habit or is used to extend the hour every time, then the therapist must be gentle but firm in reminding the child of the time limit. In settings where group play therapy follows the individual session, children have an extra incentive to end on time. They are usually eager to get to group, where they will have an opportunity to interact with peers and therapists in group games, have a snack, and socialize before making the trip home.

Taking toys from the play room   Occasionally, children beg to take a particular toy home with them. When this situation arises, it is usually not possible to *give* the toys to the children, but occasionally the therapist can *lend* them if there is a compelling reason to do so. For example, a family can be allowed to borrow a board game they don't have at home. Although it is not recommended that clients borrow therapeutic games (they may be too threatening), other games are fun to play and encourage family togetherness.

Although toys and games usually stay in the play room, children should be allowed to take their artistic creations with them. A Polaroid photo allows the child to keep an image of his or her sand tray scene. Pictures of children with their therapists can be framed for special occasions and presented as gifts. In this way, children have a tangible reminder of their play therapy experiences that they can take home with them.

Eating and drinking   Occasionally a child will ask for food or drink during the play therapy session, and there is often a good reason for such a request. Some children get thirsty during a particularly active play session, or if they have not eaten prior to the session, they may be hungry. Therefore, it makes good sense to satisfy the child's basic physiological needs for food and drink before attempting to satisfy his or her psychological needs through therapy. A small snack of juice and crackers usually pacifies the child, and children will make fewer requests for food if a snack is provided at the end of each session.

Sometimes a child's requests are not related to thirst or hunger but have more to do with anxiety about something that is occurring in therapy. If the child makes repeated requests to get a drink or to go to the soda machine, he or she may be trying to avoid the session. If this is the case, the child's continual requests to leave the room should not be granted. Rather, the therapist needs to help the child address his or her anxiety within the therapeutic setting.

PLAY THERAPY IN PRACTICE
The Case of Traumatic Grief

Background information   Clinton, age 6 years, is the third of four children and the firstborn son of Mr. and Mrs. Street. Clay is 4, and he is the youngest child in the family. The boys have an older sister, Farrah, who is 12-years-old. The second daughter, Angel, died from a rare heart disorder when she was 10 years old. Mr. Street and all the children have the potential to develop the heart condition, and they are aware of this fact. The heart malfunction has a rapid onset and can strike virtually without warning. Since Angel's death, the family has made numerous trips to hospitals for heart studies. .

Presenting problem   Clinton and Clay were brought to play therapy by their parents after the sudden and traumatic death of their sister Angel. The Street children were frolicking in the family swimming pool when Angel was suddenly stricken with a massive heart attack. All three children were present when efforts were made to resuscitate Angel, and they were traumatized by the events that followed. It was the boys' grief over Angel's death and the fear that they too would die that prompted Mr. and Mrs.

Street to seek help for their sons. The parents are especially concerned about the boys' fears, which have become exaggerated since the tragedy. Consistent themes have been fear of the dark, of the water, and of dying before they have a chance to grow up.

Interview with parents   Because the children were so young, the therapist decided to interview the parents first to get their unique perspective on the children's thoughts, feelings, and behaviors. In the interview, Mr. and Mrs. Street expressed their grief over the loss of Angel and their concern about helping their surviving children deal with their fear, anger, and loss. The parents are worried about the very real possibility that this heart condition could strike any or all of the surviving children without warning.

Mr. Street will soon have a pacemaker implanted and fears that his children may need to have the same procedure done. He is visibly worried about the current threat to his children's health and to his own. He has been dealing with his grief over Angel's death by learning as much as possible about the heart condition. Arrangements have been made for the family to take part in a study that may help other families detect the problem in time to take preventive measures.

Mrs. Street says she feels she is surrounded by death and thoughts of death. She worries about her children's future and about their current adjustment to the trauma they have endured. She notices that the boys have many fears that they didn't have before the tragedy. They are afraid of the dark, of water, and of dying. In addition to expressing similar fears, each son is handling the stress differently. Clay seems to be overly active, talks nonstop, and can't focus his attention; Clint reacts by keeping things inside, and worrying, and he is having nightmares. The oldest child, Farrah, is considered to be coping with her sister's death and is not going to come to play therapy at this time.

Initial sessions with Clinton and Clay   Because the boys are so young, the initial interviews consisted of play sessions to allow the therapist to observe such things as activity level, ability to concentrate, mood and affect, and verbalizations about self and family. It has already been determined that the children are experiencing a number of fears related to their sister's death and are in the process of grieving. An effort was made to determine what strengths the children have that will help them to cope with their loss and put them back on the road to healthy growth and development.

Assessment

Assessment of family's strengths   Mr. and Mrs. Street appear to have a healthy relationship with each other and with their children. Both parents are professionals, are of the same religious faith, and have a broad network of support from the extended family. A large extended family helps care for the children and provides support and assistance to the parents.

Mrs. Street is a warm, nurturing person who has a good relationship with all of her children. Her warmth and caring are extended to her husband as he struggles with his current health problems. Mr. Street is determined to prevent any future health problems and to seek help for his family in dealing with their current fear, anger, and loss. He faithfully brings the children to therapy each week or picks them up.

Assessment of Clinton's strengths   Clinton is genuinely friendly and easy to relate to. Generally bright, he smiles often and maintains direct eye contact easily. His affect is appropriate and he appears oriented to time and place. Clint displays a vivid but age-appropriate imagination. He is able to move back and forth between imaginative play and reality with clear demarcation and without blending the two.

Clinton is able to attend to task and focus on the activity he is engaged in at the time. He is also able to play games to completion. His energy level is age-appropriate when he plays alone, but his activity level increases noticeably when he is playing with his younger brother. He is able to bring his activity level within reasonable bounds when redirected by the therapist. His brother's high activity level was somewhat more difficult to redirect.

Clinton is decisive in choosing what activity he and the therapist should participate in. While playing a game with the therapist, Clint is energetic, verbal, imaginative, and intense. He clearly enjoys winning table games but displays a sense of fairness and sympathy toward the loser. He expects the therapist to display these traits as well. He particularly enjoys playing moderately violent versions of "cops and robbers" in a good versus evil context, consistently identifying himself with the "good guys."

Assessment of Clay's strengths   Clay is a delightful youngster who is very affectionate. He will crawl up on the therapist's lap and talk incessantly. He is animated and lively. There is some concern that he is overly active, and he has difficulty focusing his attention. His mother believes that his activity level is the result of his intense anxiety and that it is somewhat exaggerated since his sister's death. Although his activity level is high, he can focus on what he finds interesting and he says that play therapy is "fun." He showed no separation anxiety when leaving his mother and relates well to his student therapist, who provides him with a great deal of positive attention. He appears to be a very healthy, well-cared-for little boy who is reportedly doing well in preschool. His family and his preschool teacher do not consider him overly active. Perhaps the permissive atmosphere of the playroom heightens his activity level.

Treatment Goals

After the initial interview and assessment, the therapist established the following specific treatment goals for Clinton and Clay.

1. Provide opportunities for the boys to express their fears about death and dying.
2. Reassure the boys that nothing that they said or did caused this tragedy.
3. Help them to talk about Angel and to remember the good times they enjoyed.
4. Focus on helping the children to rediscover ways to enjoy school, sports, and other activities that will speed their recovery from this trauma.

In addition, the parents were encouraged to consider the following goals for themselves.

1. Join a support group for parents who have lost a child.
2. Talk about Angel and encourage the children to talk about her too.
3. Focus on "life" rather than "death" issues in their communication and activities with all the children.
4. Enjoy some activities as a couple and get some relief from constant child care responsibilities.

Treatment Strategies Using Play Activities

Session using sand play Initially, when the boys were still trying to understand death and its finality, they often preferred to play in the sand. Clinton, who had some limited understanding of the concept of death, constantly chose the sandbox to act out his concerns about his sister's being buried in the ground and to plan ways to help her escape. In one of his sessions, he stuck straws in the sand where he had buried the soldiers "so they could breathe." Later, as it became more apparent to him that his own health was in jeopardy, he began to express a great deal of anxiety about dying. He mentioned several times to his brother that they wouldn't live long enough to go to college.

The brothers attended play therapy for a total of 24 sessions. The majority of time the children attended individual sessions with separate therapists. In these individual sessions, Clinton often chose the sandbox and seemed preoccupied with burying figures and then unearthing them or providing ways for them to survive under the sand. He seemed to be working through his sister's death and subsequent burial. The following is an excerpt from a joint session with Clinton and his brother, Clay. For this particular session, the brothers chose to work together, which was unusual because they usually fought with each other.

(*Clint and his younger brother are playing in the sand with a student therapist-in-training. Four-year-old Clay is busy building a sand castle.*)

CLAY: Are you having fun?
THERAPIST: Yes.
CLAY: Me too! I'm going to make a castle. Here's the castle. (*Clay puts his handprint in the sand. His older brother Clint is on the other side, quietly making holes in the sand.*)

(*Clint takes several of the army figures and buries them deep in the sand.*)

CLINT: I'm putting in a trap door.
THERAPIST: You are?
CLINT: Yes. He's trapped...so I built a trap door so he can get back out.
THERAPIST: You left a door....
CLINT: Yeah. He has to get out somehow. (*At this point, Clint takes all the soldiers and buries them deep in the pile of sand.*)
THERAPIST: You buried them all.
CLINT: Would you like to be there? (*Clint points to the tomb he has made for the soldiers.*)
THERAPIST: No. Would you?
CLINT: What if you had a flashlight? (*The thought of a flashlight seems to comfort Clint. Perhaps it helps him ward off his fears.*)
THERAPIST: Well, it would have to be a big flashlight.
CLINT: No, it has to be a little flashlight to fit in the hole.
THERAPIST: Oh, then I don't think I'd go in. It would be too scary. (*Using the word* scary *gives Clint an opening to discuss his fears, but he doesn't take it.*)
CLINT: I mean, it has 12,000 batteries, so it shines. It really shines.

THERAPIST: Ah, Okay.

CLINT: What if you were *buried* there?

THERAPIST: I'd start digging. (*The student therapist is responding to the child's question literally. She hasn't related this interaction with the child's concept of death or his fears about it. Nevertheless, her genuine warmth toward the child and her forthright answers keep Clint asking questions he apparently needs to ask.*)

CLINT: What if you didn't have a shovel?

THERAPIST: I'd use my hands.

CLINT: What if it was real hard?

THERAPIST: I'd take off my shoe, I guess.

CLINT: What if it was real hard. I mean *real* hard.

THERAPIST: How hard? (*Knocks on her head.*) Harder than my head?

CLINT: I mean…hard as a brick…hard as a brick.

THERAPIST: That hard.

CLINT: What if I came with a big machine that would go burr…ooom…burr…ooom…burr...ooom. Then we would get out, right?

THERAPIST: Right! (*The student therapist points to the figures still buried in the sand.*) Is he still buried in there?

CLINT: Yeah, I can't get her out. (*Notice how the child refers to the figure as "her" instead of "him." This is a reference to his inability to get his sister out of her grave.*)

In a subsequent individual session with Clint's mother, it was learned that after his sister died, the family took the surviving children to the grave so the children could see where Angel was buried. Clint had asked his mother if they could "dig up" the grave so he could say good-bye to his sister and see her one more time. His mother explained that this was not possible and that the casket was put into a cement box so that it could not be opened again. This session illustrates how Clint is working through the concept of death and the fact that he still thinks that it is reversible. If he could only get a big enough machine, one that would go "burr…ooom, burr…ooom," he could help his sister escape from her grave. In subsequent sessions, Clint always chose the sandbox and always buried the figures. Sometimes, he would put straws in the sand so that the figures could "breathe." Because he is only 6, he still has concerns for his sister's well-being while she is buried in the ground, and he has fears that he too will die at a young age.

Summary of play therapy sessions with Clinton   Clint demonstrated his affection for the therapist by giving hugs and sharing his Halloween candy. In response to a general discussion about Halloween, Clint talked about his sister's death: "There used to be six of us….My sister died…some people live to be a hundred….I want to go to heaven." Clint appeared embarrassed by these revelations. In the following session, Clint talked about his sister's death and his emotional responses to it: "I'm still sad…at night." Spontaneously, he stopped playing our game of table basketball and talked about his sister's death: "She didn't drown…her heart stopped. I think about her every night….The sad part isn't as bad as before….I'd like to go visit her in heaven"; but he indicated he is not ready to die yet. After making these statements, he stopped speaking and started playing again.

Clint's verbalizations regarding his sister's death indicate that he is making progress toward resolving his feelings of fear, anger, and loss at Angel's death. He has a structured spiritual belief system that is helping him in this process. However, he still has concerns about his own vulnerability to heart failure, as evidenced by the following exchange with his brother.

CLAY:	When I grow up, I'm gonna be a ballplayer.
THERAPIST:	You mean a pro?
CLAY:	Yeah.
CLINTON:	You can't do that.
CLAY:	Can too.
CLINTON:	You have to be 19.
CLAY:	I know.
CLINTON:	Clay, you know we aren't going to live to be 19.

Summary of first three sessions with Clay In the first therapy session, Clay was very active and was kicking everything in the play room. He dumped over boxes and began hitting toys. After a while, he focused on the sandbox. He seemed intent on burying the army men. At one point he said, "I'm going to bury Clinton." Although he thinks a lot of his brother, he says that they "fight" and that he is "mad" at him. Part of this is just normal sibling rivalry; however, some of his aggression may be due to the anger and frustration that he feels at this time in his life, and Clint is a good target.

The following is the fifth session with Clay following the death of his sister. Although a fear of the dark is common for 4-year-olds, Clay's fears have been exacerbated by his sister's death. He also has developed a fear of the water, which he did not have before. Developmentally, Clay is not able to understand death as irreversible. He still believes that when you die, you can come back to life. Consequently, he views death as something temporary and fun. Pretend play is a way for Clay to work through his fears about death.

(Clay is pretending that the playroom floor is "water that you can drown in" and that the only safe places are the couch, the table, and the base of the coat rack.)

CLAY:	Watch out! This is water that you can drown in. *(Recall that Clay's sister died while in the swimming pool.)* We have zero lives, so we can never die.
THERAPIST:	We do?
CLAY:	Yep. *(At this point Clay goes totally limp and does not respond to the therapist as she speaks to him and lifts his limp arms.)*
THERAPIST:	*(Pretends to cry.)* Boo-Hoo.
CLAY:	*(Suddenly "comes alive." Smiles. He believes that when you die, you can come back to life, just as cartoon characters do.)* You're dead. You lay on the couch! *(Assumes control of the session; is truly "the boss.")*

(Clay places a large piece of cardboard over the therapist and crawls underneath the cardboard with the therapist.)

CLAY: It's dark in here. We have to get out.

THERAPIST: Yes.

CLAY: You can't talk; you're dead. (*Pauses.*) This is very heavy. We have to get out. (*Reference is to the cardboard that Clint put over them. Here, Clay is reenacting his conception of Angel's death and burial. He is trying to see it in concrete terms, but he still sees it as reversible: "We have to get out."*)

(*Clay then begins to put the cardboard on the two of them and lifts it back up. He repeats this several times. When the cardboard is on, it is night; when it is off, it is morning.*)

CLAY: It's not bad being dead. It's fun.

Evaluation and Follow-up

As therapy progressed, the children and their parents were encouraged to focus on "life" issues, and the emphasis on death began to diminish. In the weeks following their last session, the boys took swimming lessons in the hope that they could conquer their fear of the water. This strategy succeeded. Gradually the boys came to accept the death of their sister, and their fears about their own health issues lessened with time. As of this writing, the family is doing well and the boys are thriving.

INSIGHTS AND IMPLICATIONS

Play is: infants reaching for mobiles; toddlers molding wet sand into castles; preschoolers taking their dogs, dressed and protesting, for a stroll in the baby carriage; and school-age children making wishes on fireflies that they catch in a jar. Play helps children grow physically, intellectually, emotionally, and socially, whether it occurs at home, at the playground, in the classroom, or in the therapy room. Play is a natural way for children to express their thoughts and feelings, explore relationships, and take on different roles. In this way, children develop empathy toward others. Play is important to a child's social development, and when children perform well, play by the rules, and cooperate with others, they achieve a recognition by their peers that gives them a sense of mastery over their physical and social environment. Play is also a way to describe experiences, regulate the expression of emotion, and experiment with new ways of thinking and behaving. As children try out new behaviors in play, they find out what they can and cannot do. Combining these skills helps the child achieve a sense of competence that promotes self-confidence and self-acceptance.

Through the rich symbolism of play in therapy, children reveal their experiences, their problems, their needs and their strengths. When the therapist hears and understands the child's verbal and symbolic communication, important information about every aspect of the child's development is revealed. This understanding, communicated to the child as empathy, helps the child feel accepted. Wrapped in the warmth and acceptance of the therapeutic relationship, children can release their pent-up emotions, recreate situations that might be too threatening to deal with in "real life," recognize and master uncomfortable feelings, and explore alternative ways of thinking and behaving without fear of rejection. Children can practice new behaviors through play, keeping those that work and abandoning those that do not. The final step in the healing process is the child's ability to transfer these newly learned methods of coping and newly discovered solutions to situations in everyday life.

WISDOM ACCORDING TO ORTON

- *Appreciate and respect the child's invitation into his or her world. Few adults are granted such a privilege.*
- *Divert an aggressive child's attention before a major incident develops, and involve shy and reluctant children in a fun activity before they have time to cry or fuss.*
- *Keep your voice soft and calm so that aggressive children can be reassured and reluctant children won't be frightened.*
- *Model the kind of behavior that you want from the children. Modeling also includes starting to clean up so that they can follow your lead.*
- *Don't worry about your ability to make interpretations. You will be surprised how easy it all fits together when you know the child.*
- *Play is fun and relaxing for adults as well as children. Enjoy it!*

ORTON'S PICKS

Gil, E. (1991). *The healing power of play: Working with abused children.* New York: Guilford Press.
   This highly readable text offers valuable insight and practical approaches for mental health professionals who work with abused children. Gil offers step-by-step guidelines for assessment and intervention in six vignettes of trauma from different types of abuse. Her caring, concern, and competence are evident on every page.

Kottman, T. & Schaefer, C. (1993). *Play therapy in action: A casebook for practitioners.* Northvale, NJ: Aronson.
   This casebook offers concrete applications of play therapy by experienced clinicians from various theoretical perspectives. It offers step-by-step treatment guidelines for a number of childhood problems. A broad range of psychotherapeutic approaches are represented, and each is explained with illustrative dialogue.

Landreth, G. L. (1991). Play therapy: *The art of the relationship.* Muncie, IN: Accelerated Development, Inc.
   Written in a style that is clear and understandable, this text details the client-centered approach to play therapy. Landreth gives the beginning play therapist many helpful tips on the selection of toy and play materials and offers practical advice on "what to do if " certain situations occur during therapy. The last half of the book is dedicated to case illustrations of the play therapy process.

O'Connor, K. J. (1991). *The play therapy primer: An integration of theories and techniques.* New York: Wiley.
   This primer describes play therapy as a balance between cognitive and verbal work. Using cognitive developmental theory as an organizing framework,

O'Connor offers a description of play therapy that integrates elements from several existing theories and techniques. This book offers a combination of theory and practice that will foster the therapist's ability to identify and interpret the multiple systems of which the child is a part.

O'Connor, K. J., & Schaefer, C. E. (1994). *Handbook of play therapy. Volume 2: Advances and innovations.* New York: Wiley.

This latest volume on play therapy updates readers on significant advances in sand play diagnosis, theraplay, group play, and other well-known approaches. Comprehensive in coverage, this volume includes a variety of theoretical approaches (such as Adlerian, cognitive, behavioral, and family) as well as methods and techniques. Case studies highlight how each theory or technique can be applied to adults as well as to children.

CHAPTER 7   Art Therapy

Since prehistoric humans first carved pictures on the walls of caves, people have used art to express what they wish to say. Today, when children draw boats they've never sailed and sculpt creatures they've never seen, "they are building upon the creative impulse which is the heritage of all mankind" (Kellogg, 1967 p. 77). This creative impulse is a basic human need that can be expressed in many art forms including writing, drawing, sculpting, painting, poetry, dance, and music.

Art is a relaxing and fun way for children to express their individuality, their creativity, and their uniqueness. It provides children with an outlet for the expression of both positive and negative thoughts and feelings about themselves, their families, and their world. When their creative images are valued by adults, children develop a sense of self-worth. Even the reluctant, hurt or hostile child can find joy and release through art.

Art provides the counselor with a means to relate to all children and is an especially important way to establish a relationship with the withdrawn, nonverbal or wounded child. Counselors can catch a glimpse of the child's unconscious thoughts and feelings, which might not be observable in any other therapeutic mode. Children's art can reveal hidden wishes, pain, and loneliness; it can portray hostility and aggression, not only toward others but also toward self. Art, like play, is a spontaneous expression of a child's imagination that serves as a temporary sanctuary from reality. It provides the child with an opportunity to release feelings and resolve conflicts safely.

A BIT OF BACKGROUND

Art therapy can be used in a developmental, preventive, and remedial context by well-trained professionals of all persuasions. Art is currently used in individual and group therapy with children and with families by counselors, therapists, and psychotherapists in school, hospital, clinic, and private practice settings. Art therapy is used to quell children's fears about being hospitalized, to comfort children coping with the death of a parent or sibling, to help children confront all manner of fears, and to heal children in the aftermath of abuse. It can be a release valve for the hostile, explosive child, a haven for the hurt and wounded child, and a liberator of the shy, withdrawn child.

Art therapy combines the creative impulse with the need for self-expression. *Art* focuses on artistic creation, whereas *therapy* generally involves communication and insight. When the two are blended in the therapeutic setting, the practitioner focuses

Once upon a time. There was a rich prince, who lived in a shining castle. One night a mugly wicked witch came to the castle and asked if he would marry her.

not only on the process used to create the art but also on the symbolism of the finished product. Art therapy is goal-directed and involves the creation of a symbolic object as a means of communication. Painful and frightening conflicts that may have been passively endured in the past can be actively reexperienced through art, and the finished product can be understood by others (Kramer, 1971).

Two early theorists, Margaret Naumburg (1966) and Edith Kramer (1958, 1971, 1979), are responsible for the development of art therapy. Both agree that free artistic expression is central to the art therapy process and that interpretation plays a key role. They differ, however, on the importance of the role of unconscious material to the therapeutic process. Naumburg's traditional psychoanalytic view stresses that (1) art is yet another window to the unconscious, (2) insight is central to the process, and (3) treatment depends on obtaining the client's own interpretations of his or her symbolic art images. Naumburg is responsible for the *therapy* in art therapy.

Kramer's work centers on the *art* in art therapy, and, unlike Naumburg's focus on individual therapy, she advocates a group setting for therapeutic art activities. Kramer focuses on the healing powers of the creative act and the artistic product itself. She believes that expressive art media can bring about therapeutic change in and of itself, even without the uncovering and interpretation of unconscious meaning. Believing that art therapy supplements psychotherapy, Kramer views the artistic process and product as a way to release conflict, reexperience it, rechannel it through sublimation, and resolve it.

For example, using clay as a medium of artistic expression, a child sculpts a figure symbolizing the school bully. After the figure is complete, the child punches it, cuts it into pieces, and throws it against the wall, thereby rendering it helpless to hurt anyone again. In this way, the child is able to release, reexperience, and rechannel the conflict within the safety of the therapeutic setting and without damaging self or others. Finally, in a subsequent discussion with the therapist, the child is able to find ways to resolve the conflict and apply it to his or her own real-life situation.

Therapists can be nondirective, very directive, or somewhat in between. Although Naumburg (1966) and Kramer (1971, 1979) use free art and generally do not prescribe specific projects, Landgarten (1981), suggests giving topics for children to address in their artwork. Such topics may include general or specific themes such as emotions, wishes, dreams, fantasies, plans, self-images, family constellations, and situations. In response to Landgarten's directive to *"make something which shows what you wish you could change,"* an enuretic child made a clay figure, which she placed on a toy toilet. She described her creation as "a little girl who goes on the toilet, not in her pants," indicating both her desire and commitment to stay dry (Landgarten, 1981, p. 112).

A pioneer in the use of art therapy as a psychotherapeutic technique for the family group, Hanna Kwiatkowska (1977; 1978) found that the unique aspects of family art therapy differentiate it from group art therapy. Unlike groups that are linked only by a common maladjustment, families maintain subgroups and may form alliances against each other. Each member of the family develops a pattern of thinking that contributes to the special culture or climate of a given family. Kwiatkowska uses three types of family art techniques to help therapists understand the interactions between and among family members: (1) family art therapy as an adjunct to conjoint verbal family therapy, (2) family art therapy as a primary mode of treatment (both types of family art therapy could be short or long term), and (3) the family art evaluation (1978, p. 8).

Janie Rhyne (1973, 1987), challenges clients toward growth and the development of their innate potential using individual and group Gestalt approaches. Her use of art activities to encourage self-expression and self-perception in groups of persons without adjustment problems has obvious implications for work with children. Using this approach, children and adolescents can be encouraged to express their feelings with art media or through role playing, storytelling, creative dramatics, and other kinds of expression. By making art activities available to developmental groups, all children—not just those with severe problems—can take advantage of art as a way to assist healthy changes in lifestyle.

A DEVELOPMENTAL PERSPECTIVE OF CHILDREN'S ART

Rhonda Kellogg (1967), in a delightful book entitled *The Psychology of Children's Art*, tells us that artistic expression in children is universal and that all children, no matter where they live, draw the same things in the same way at the same ages. "So strong is the creative impulse among the young that this universality holds true for thirty houses drawn by thirty different children in thirty different countries" (pp. 11–13). As their art-work progresses from scribbles to pictures, all children pass through the same developmental stages. However, as with all development, these stages may vary from child to child and may overlap.

Most art experts (Kellogg, 1967; Lowenfeld & Brittain, 1987; Rubin, 1984) agree that children go through various stages in their artistic development. Kellogg (1967) identified the stages of art development for children from 2 to 7 years old; Lowenfeld (1957; Lowenfeld & Brittain, 1987) proposed five stages including scribbling, preschematic, schematic, gang, and pseudo-naturalistic; and Rubin (1984) outlined nine phases that children must pass through in learning a new art form. For the purpose of simplifying the discussion, I'll use five stages to describe the primary art product of most children at each level of development. These stages—the (1) scribbling stage, (2) picture stage, (3) human figure stage, (4) realistic representation stage, and (5) the naturalistic stage—include many of the elements of developmental theory described by the leading art development experts but do not necessarily bear the name of a particular theorist.

Developmental Stages in Art Expression

Scribbling Stage

At about the age of 2, children begin to scribble. They scribble with pencils on paper if they are available, and with crayons on walls if they are not. Children scribble with sticks in the mud, toes in the sand, and chalk on the sidewalk. From the ages of 2 to 4, the child's random scribbling begins to form shapes, and by the age of 3, the child has entered the stage of outline shapes. It is at this stage that children draw circles, squares, rectangles, triangles, crosses and big fat Xs. The mandalas (magic circles) that children draw from ages 3 to 5 are an important beginning for suns, radials, and eventually human figures. The human face drawn by a 3-year-old can look pretty inhuman (Kellogg, 1967).

The role of the counselor is to admire, encourage, and accept the child's work. It is best to let children tell you about what they have drawn. The child may display a mass of scribbles and proudly announce, "This is my grandma's car." Of course, it is the child's interpretation of grandma's car and does not resemble a car at all to the adult. A truly helpful counselor, teacher, or parent will admire the work, comment on it truthfully, and accept it as the child's artistic impression of a car. A therapeutic relationship, characterized by warmth, trust, support, and encouragement will enable the counselor to focus on some of the activities and emotions reflected in the child's artwork.

Picture Stage

At about the age of 4 and 5, having mastered scribbling, patterns, shapes, and designs, children begin to make pictures. This stage is divided into two parts: "almost pictures" at ages 4 to 6 and more refined pictures at ages 5 to 7 (Kellogg, 1967). The early drawings simply suggest human figures, animals, trees, and so on, whereas the later drawings are clearly defined and easily recognized by adults as familiar objects. The child's first drawings of the human figure often look strange, with round bodies and arms that come out of the figure's head. Distortions and omissions of body parts are common and are to be expected (Lowenfeld & Brittain, 1987).

In their early pictorial work, children may draw houses and people but they are still designs. It is not until children are 5 or 6 that their pictures begin to tell their own story. At these ages children can put trees, houses, sun, sky, and children all in one picture. At ages 5 and 6, children bring new physical strength and coordination to their artwork. They are able to handle almost all art media, even paintbrushes, well. Their artwork seems more advanced at this age, partly because children have greater dexterity. They are able to control the crayon better, can bear down harder or draw lighter, and can color within boundaries (Kellogg, 1967).

Although most people think of children's art in terms of stick figures, "the stick figure is not a spontaneous product of child art. It is a figure that children learn after the age of five from adults or from other children whose parents or teachers already have shown them this particular formula for a person" (Kellogg, 1967, p. 87). If not influenced by adults, the child's human figure symbol is flexible and constantly changing (Lowenfeld & Brittain, 1987).

The counselor's role is to support and encourage children in their efforts at self-expression and communication. Each child's creative sense and developing autonomy need to be carefully nurtured. Adult disapproval can stifle creativity, "ruin" art as a medium of expression, and contribute to a lack of confidence for the developing child. At this stage, children are capable of expressing their perceptions of themselves and their world.

Human Figure Stage

Between the ages of 7 and 9, children represent their perceptions of the environment in their artwork. During this phase, which Lowenfeld (1957), described as the "schematic stage," the child's art centers on the human figure and reflects the child's psychosocial growth. By age 7, the child's human figure should contain a head, complete with distinct features such as a mouth, nose, eyes, and some hair. This human symbol should have a body with a hint of a neck, arms with hands attached, and legs with feet. Some children draw clothes in place of the body. Drawings of family members are now developmentally possible, and the depictions help counselors understand the child in relation to the family group.

At this stage, figure and ground are emerging in landscape representations and objects are drawn in relation to one another. This relationship is frequently expressed with the use of a baseline. Occasionally, a skyline is also used, and the space in between indicates "air." Color has a definite relationship to what is drawn, and the child assigns a color to each object in the environment. Although there are common colors assigned to objects (yellow to suns, green to grass), the child's first meaningful relationship with an object can determine the color selected. For example, if playing in the mud was the child's first impression of the back yard, then the ground will be brown, even if it is covered with grass (Lowenfeld & Brittain, 1987).

The counselor's role is to provide a warm and permissive atmosphere in which the child can create. Because art is the child's product, it should be self-initiated and self-controlled. A truly helpful counselor will not try to "correct" the child's interpretation or his or her artistic effort. Too often children lose interest in art at about the age of 7 because they feel the disapproval of adults who try to prod them into neat and conventional art molds (Kellogg, 1967). By accepting and valuing what children have to say about themselves, their families, and their environment, the counselor is learning to understand and interpret "child talk" through art.

Realistic Representation Stage

Between the ages of 9 and 11, the child's increasing self-awareness is reflected in a more realistic representation of the environment. The high priority given to peer relationships at this stage prompted Lowenfeld (1957) to name it the "gang stage." Children at this stage are able to draw their world in two dimensions and to overlap objects. Human figures are drawn in more detail and a greater emphasis is placed on clothes and sexual differences. The use of color is often based on the emotional significance of the object to the artist (Lowenfeld & Brittain, 1987).

Children may experience anxiety and frustration as they attempt to represent things as they are. Children who are too self-critical may become discouraged and may abandon art in favor of more verbal forms of expression (Rubin, 1984). How children view themselves in relation to their peers and family members is often reflected in their artwork. The counselor's task is to help children focus on their own strengths, values, interests, and beliefs and on maintaining a sense of individualism while striving for peer acceptance.

Naturalistic Stage

At ages 11 to 13, children's artwork reflects the expression of preadolescent reasoning, realism, and emotionality (Lowenfeld & Brittain, 1987). With increasingly refined visual perception and spatial relations, youngsters are now capable of two- and three-dimensional drawing. Human figures are drawn in greater detail, body movement can be captured and interpreted, and body parts are in proportion. Color is used to express visual impressions as well as emotional experiences. At this stage, young people are concerned with their own emerging identity. They have increased intellectual capacity, are verbally oriented, and are capable of empathy for others. Counselors can encourage young people to understand and deal with the conflicting emotions that often accompany this stage of development and help them develop confidence in who they are.

GETTING READY FOR ART THERAPY

Selecting Art Materials

Ideally, art therapy should be conducted in a room equipped with a sink, aprons, easels, and easy-to-clean tables. Therapists who do not have a play room can conduct art therapy by carrying materials with them and setting up in any quiet room or office. Therapists who do not have access to soap and water for cleanup may not be able to use finger paints. All other mediums for artistic expression—including painting, which requires only a cup of water and needs little cleanup—are possible and should be available to children.

It is important for children to select the medium of expression for their own artwork, and a wide assortment of art materials should be made available. Many colors and sizes of crayons (remember that 3- to 5-year olds will need the big crayons), all colors of finger paint (green, blue, and yellow are very popular, but purple, black, and brown will be needed to capture those depressing moments), magic markers in all sizes and colors (children love the kind that smell like fruit and are nontoxic), and paints (including tempura paints in all colors) should be within easy reach of the smallest child.

Because art therapy is not limited to drawing and painting, clay and play dough will be needed. It is important to have brown-colored clay or play dough so that children of color do not have to make their faces white. A wide assortment of paper, including special paper to finger paint, construction paper in many colors, and drawing paper should be available. Scissors, paste, glue, glitter, and any other materials that the child "needs" to tell his or her story should be made available as needs arise.

Individual children have individual preferences in their art media. Many children, especially younger children, love to finger paint. An old shirt turned around will protect a child's clothes and keep them from getting too wet when they clean up in the sink. Incidentally, the cleanup is half of the fun and doesn't need to be a big chore. Some children loathe finger painting because they are afraid to get dirty or they don't like the feel of it on their hands (some college students have the same reaction). Other children love to finger paint but are afraid to try it for fear they might be scolded if they get some paint on their clothes. Some children love to work with clay and play dough; it can be thrown, pounded, cut, and shaped. If the child is angry with siblings, he or she can just crumble them into a ball and make a dog instead. Children can demonstrate activity with clay that is more difficult for them to execute with two-dimensional surfaces. Older children may wish to express their creativity and their feelings in a variety of media and may elect to do a picture with paint and brushes, pen and ink, or paper and pencil. The need for more sophisticated methods of artistic expression will evolve as the therapist gets to know the child better through ongoing art therapy.

Art Materials for Counselors on a Budget

The first year that we outfitted our play room, I bought a $10 sink at a yard sale that the school maintenance men graciously plumbed. We made play dough from scratch

RECIPE FOR PLAY DOUGH

Put in a saucepan:
1 cup flour   1/2 cup salt
2 tbsp. cream of tartar
1 tbsp. oil   1 cup cool water
Food coloring

Directions:
Mix ingredients together. Stir over medium heat until sticky. Turn onto waxed paper and knead. Store in tightly closed container.

and "borrowed" regular paper, glue sticks, scotch tape, pencils, and scissors from the school's office supplies for the children to use. We had a box of broken crayons donated by a parent, we purchased large crayons and colored pencils with personal funds, and we had to get special permission to buy our first set of finger paints, in primary colors only. None of our children were "depressed" that year—or at least they had no colors to express it with!

This personal account illustrates that it doesn't take a lot of money nor an expensive play room to offer art as a therapeutic option. Many items can be donated, and the therapist can involve both parents and children in making as many of the supplies as possible. An added benefit for all concerned is a sense of having been a part of the creation of a program that can be a source of pleasure and enjoyment for all involved.

The accompanying recipe for finger paint (from Kellogg, 1967) will enable art therapists to make finger paint in all colors at a fraction of the cost of the ready-made variety.

RECIPE FOR FINGER PAINT

In a saucepan, mix 2 cups of flour and 5 cups of cold water; dissolve the flour in the water by whipping it with a fork until all the lumps are gone. Cook until smooth. Add some salt and let cool. Then add bakers food dye and the paint is ready.

THE VALUE OF ART AS A THERAPEUTIC PROCESS

Art in therapy helps children better understand themselves and how they function as part of a family (Landgarten, 1981). Through art, children can express their thoughts and feelings about past, present, and future events. They can recognize problems, feelings, and needs that they may not want to acknowledge openly or that are buried in their unconscious. In this way, children are often able to release their feelings, recognize their needs, work through their conflicts, and resolve them safely. Art is also a means of fostering a sense of identity and promoting maturation (Kramer, 1979).

Through the artistic process, both the art media and the finished product provide a means of (1) building a relationship with the child, (2) assessing the child's needs, (3) soliciting diagnostic information, (4) releasing emotion through catharsis, and (5) facilitating growth (refer to Figure 7-1).

Building a Relationship

Whether art is therapeutic for children depends, to a large extent, on the strength of the bond that is forged between therapist and child. This therapeutic relationship, like all counseling relationships, is characterized by the same facilitative conditions discussed in Chapter 4 (see Figure 4-1). The discussion here centers on those aspects of trust, communication, understanding, acceptance, and support as they apply to art therapy.

Generally, trust is developed when the child feels safe and secure within the relationship and knows that the therapist can be depended on to be there for him or her. According to Rubin (1984), consistency and structure are especially important in building trust in art therapy. She recommends that children meet at the same time and place, have the same supplies available in the same locations, and handle routine transactions in a predictable way. Once trust is earned, growth is possible for both the child and the therapist.

Acceptance implies a genuine respect for the child as a unique individual and as a partner in therapy. Nonjudgmental acceptance frees children to express their innermost thoughts and feeling through their artwork. They are able to risk revealing those aspects of self that have previously been perceived as negative without fear of being diminished in the relationship. The ability to risk disclosing aspects of the self is an important step toward facing and eventually coping with what has been revealed.

As children draw, paint, or sculpt, they are communicating their thoughts and feelings in a form of "art talk" that the counselor can listen to and understand. Many children, especially those who are verbal and outgoing, will converse as they create; others, especially those who are shy or withdrawn, may not say a word. It is with these children that art becomes an especially important tool for establishing rapport. "It may take time, and even some trial and error, to discover the words and images and frames of reference which 'make sense' to a particular child" (Rubin, 1984, p. 81).

To achieve understanding, the therapist must be able to relate to the child's conflict and to perceive it in terms of the child's overall development. Clues to a child's perceptions are often hidden in his or her artwork. For example, Julio drew violent pictures of a knife dripping with blood and would repeatedly say, "I'm going to kill my brother!" He went on to say that Carlos was his "real" brother and the rest of the children belonged to his current father, whom he hated. When the counselor responded, "You're very angry with your brother and you want to hurt him," Julio responded, "NO, I don't want to kill my real brother!" Later, it was learned that the boys' mother favored Carlos and allowed him to lock Julio in a closet when he was "bad." Carlos was the younger of the two, yet he had been given a special power over his older brother. This special insult fueled Julio's rage against his mother and his brother. Yet, Julio could not bring himself to admit that he had murderous thoughts about his real brother; a brother who was bonded to him by blood and love.

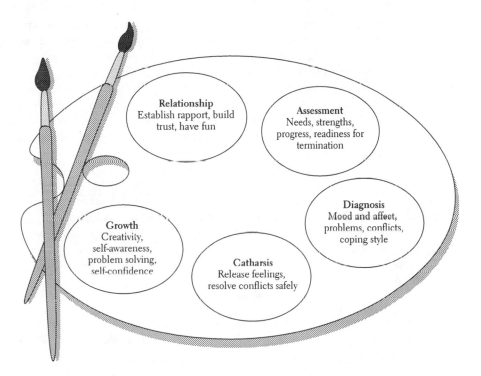

FIGURE 7-1 *The Value of Art as a Therapeutic Technique*

One of the vital functions of the counseling relationship is to provide the necessary support and encouragement for change. Ensuring a warm, safe, and protective environment that will promote growth and encourage change is part of this support. However, change is difficult for children, and they often regress as they attempt to modify their behavior, sliding back to familiar behaviors that feel more comfortable. Children may be at the highest risk for regression when they have revealed some inner secret in their art and must now acknowledge its existence. It is at this point that counselors need to provide extra support and assurance for the child. Therapists are patient supporters of change, encouraging growth, acknowledging setbacks, and never giving up.

Assessing the Child's Needs

Children are telling the therapist a story about themselves with the particular *art medium* they select, the *process* by which they produce the art, and the final *product* itself. Through their art, children are able to express both positive and negative thoughts and feelings. They can tell a story of past events that thrilled or terrified them, describe current events that make them happy or trouble them deeply, or depict future events that they look forward to with anticipation or worry. These unique, personal expressions of inner experiences, when used appropriately, can offer clues that are helpful in therapy and in assessment (Oster & Gould, 1987). As part of the assessment process, the counselor needs to "listen" to the colors, messages, and themes in the child's artwork, observe the child's affect as he or she is producing the art, and pay close attention to the child's verbal and nonverbal communication about it. Only then can the therapist put together a tentative diagnostic picture of the child's conflicts, needs, and affects. Of course, each child's art represents an individual effort and needs to be viewed in relation to everything else that is known about the child. In this chapter, the case of Ivan illustrates how art can be a valuable assessment tool that supplements other assessment strategies.

By carefully listening to children, observing them in the creative process, and interpreting their art, the therapist will be able to determine whether the child has made any progress toward a resolution of the problems the child is experiencing. For instance, if the child is less hostile, pounds the clay less vigorously, or uses a color other than black, the therapist may conclude that the child is making progress toward healing. Continued progress will indicate a readiness for termination.

Soliciting Diagnostic Information

Drawings have also become an excellent source for measuring current functioning and for expressing present concerns and conflicts during an evaluation.
—OSTER & GOULD (1987, p. 8)

Up to this point, the discussion has centered on the use of the child's spontaneous, unstructured artwork produced for the purposes of assessment. This unstructured approach can be used in a variety of settings to get to know the child, find out what the child's concerns are, and determine how he or she is dealing with those concerns internally (Rubin, 1984). However, some therapists, particularly in clinical settings, prefer to use more formal procedures of assessment, often in conjunction with free art.

Some of the formal assessment tools include the Draw-A-Person Test (Machover, 1949), the House-Tree-Person Drawing (Buck, 1948), the Kinetic House-Tree-Person Drawing (Burns, 1987) and the Kinetic Family Drawing (Burns & Kaufman, 1970). **Note that these procedures require special training for therapists to learn how to administer and interpret them.**

Draw-A-Person (D-A-P) This procedure is based on Karen Machover's (1949) experiences with the Goodenough technique for assessing children's intellectual capacities. She expanded on the use of human figure drawings as a technique to explore aspects of personality and self-concept. The child is provided with a sheet of paper and a pencil and is asked to "draw a person." These directions are intentionally simple and unstructured so that the child can contribute his or her interpretations, feelings, and needs to the drawing. The D-A-P is widely used as a projective test and is a valuable tool in the hands of an experienced clinician. It is considered to be a useful and non-threatening way to gain access to information about the child's conflicts, wishes, fantasies, defenses, and personal adjustment. This drawing technique can also be used to begin discussion and to assess treatment progress and outcomes.

There is consensus in the research regarding the interpretation of some features expressed in human figure drawings. Generally accepted hypotheses are based on the overall quality of the drawing (line quality, integration, proportion, shading); specific features typically not seen in human figure drawings (large or small head or teeth, cut-off hands or arms); and expected emotional indicators such as nose, feet, and neck, which are significant if omitted. Meaningful diagnosis can be made only after considering the total drawing as well as combinations of indicators (Oster & Gould, 1987).

Kinetic House-Tree-Person Drawing Test (K-H-T-P)   In this test, (Burns, 1987), the house-tree-person concept of the original H-T-P test (Buck, 1948) is merged with the concept of movement borrowed from the Kinetic Family Drawing (K-F-D) test designed by Burns and Kaufman (1970, 1972). The child is given one piece of $8\frac{1}{2}$" x 11" paper and is instructed to "Draw a house, a tree and a whole person on this piece of paper with some kind of action" (Burns, 1987, p. 5).

In addition to the commonly accepted interpretations for the D-A-P, this test is helpful in exploring the interpersonal dimensions of a child's life. The Kinetic-House-Tree-Person drawing provides additional information about how children view themselves in relation to their environment and to other people. (For more information on interpreting this test, see Burns, 1987.)

Kinetic Family Drawing (K-F-D)   This technique introduces the concept of movement into family drawings. The child is given a sheet of $8\frac{1}{2}$ x 11 paper and a pencil with an eraser and is asked to "draw everyone in your family, *including* you, doing something" (see Burns, 1982; Burns & Kaufman, 1970, 1972). The K-F-D provides practitioners with a clearer picture of the family dynamics, interpersonal interactions, and emotional relationships among family members. This technique is useful in determining how the child views his or her place in the family and is helpful in understanding and communicating with the child about family problems and issues (Handler, 1996).

These projective techniques offer different ways to solicit additional information from children's artwork. Because they are more structured, formal, and directive, they can be used to gather specific information that may be needed for a complete diagnostic workup.

Finding Joy and Release Through Catharsis

Art therapy is a great release. It is an opportunity to dump negative feelings and start over. Children who might otherwise fight with another child, set a fire, or steal a toy may instead be able to express their anger, rage, hostility, depression, or rejection through art. And they can do it in a way that doesn't harm anyone physically or emotionally. Children can vent their emotions in the safety of the play room and they can talk about their rage, humiliation, and frustration. Through art, children have an opportunity to re-create past events, enact present conflicts, and create scenarios of future worries. In the process of this creation, children are able to express both positive and negative feelings about past, present, and future events and to master their feelings. The therapist facilitates the child's spontaneous expression of both emotion and conflict and encourages conflict resolution.

Facilitating Growth

The medium, the process, and the finished art product provide children with a means to foster creativity, explore alternative approaches to problem solving, and work through conflicts. Because art is something the child can both initiate and control and because the product belongs solely to the child, art can be a tremendous source of self-esteem. Art is, in a very real sense, a way to discover a sense of self. At first, the spontaneous use of art materials enables children to express their limitless, natural creativity. Children can combine their thoughts, feelings, perceptions, and aesthetic sense together with various art media to create a scribble, a painting, a picture, or a sculpture. The result is often a sense of personal satisfaction and accomplishment. Children may spend an hour creating something and two hours admiring it, thus increasing their self-confidence. Second, children can explore alternative solutions in the unhurried creativity of art. They can try different solutions "on for size" without the consequences of real-life acts. Finally, children are able to express conflicts through the medium they choose, the process they go through to create the art, and the final art product itself. Through art, children can try alternative solutions and work toward the resolution of conflict.

Sometimes, a child's creation, like play, can be done just for the joy of it, and the simple act of creation can be healing for the child. Of course, the interpretation of the child's art is important to the therapist, although not necessarily to the child, and all beginning therapists should learn all they can about the meaning that is expressed in children's art. Kellogg (1967) maintains that children's artwork is usually not fully understood and that adults tend to perceive it from their point of view. "The hidden message, when fully deciphered, will enable the viewer to recapture the un-*adult*-erated vision of the child" (Kellogg, 1967, p. 95).

INTERPRETATION OF ART IN CHILD THERAPY

In order to utilize the unstructured art interview effectively, it is important to know how to look, what to look at, what to look for, and how to make sense out of what has been observed.
—RUBIN (1984, p. 66)

Techniques

Much of what the child communicates to the therapist is symbolic, told in the child's working process as well as in the form and content of the final art product. In all three areas, hidden messages are communicated to the therapist either verbally or nonverbally that provide valuable clues to the child's conflicts (Rubin, 1984). The essence of interpreting children's art lies in the ability to listen to their "art talk," carefully observe their verbal and nonverbal behavior, and make intuitive guesses regarding what their artwork means.

Listening to the child's "art talk" Art provides the counselor with a window into the child's world that may not be available in any other therapeutic setting. Through this window, the therapist can often gain access to unconscious material without having to disturb the child's fragile and necessary defense mechanisms (Kramer, 1958). Thus, the counselor may have an opportunity to learn about the child's conflicts, defenses, coping style, and interaction with family friends, and peers. To comprehend what is seen during this glimpse into the child's world, the counselor must "listen" to the child's communication. The *way* something is being said, is as important as *what* is being said.

It is important to listen to the overall "flavor" of the child's communication: the form and quality of speech as well as its tempo and intensity, stress, articulation, and quality (Rubin, 1984). It is necessary to listen to *what* the child is saying and *when* the child is saying it. For example, a boy who draws hearts around a "mother" figure and subsequently stabs holes in the hearts while talking about a visit with her may be commenting verbally and symbolically about his feelings for his mother.

> *She loves me, she hates me, she loves me, she hates me, and then she loves me again.*
> —5-year-old boy, drawing a woman described as "mother"

Observing Observation is one of the key strategies used in interpretation. Because the creation of art is largely a nonverbal activity, the therapist needs to focus his or her powers of observation on the process as well as on the form and content of the child's artwork. In interpreting process, methods of nonverbal communication such as posturing, facial expressions, gestures, and proximity to the therapist tell the practitioner a great deal about the child and his or her conflict. The therapist should observe how children respond to the art materials, which medium they select, how individual children manipulate a particular art medium, and how they combine the various art materials. Furthermore, the child's approach to the creative process should be observed carefully, noting "individual rhythms, tempos, and energy levels" (Rubin, 1984, p. 68). Such observations also provide important clues about the child's current functioning and are particularly helpful in forming hypotheses about mood and affect, preferred defenses, and coping styles.

Intuitive Guessing The child's artwork is only a sampling of what the child is thinking, perceiving, and feeling at a given moment. It is "a moment of truth" captured on paper that is often disguised in symbolism. This symbolism is subject to many and varied interpretations which are, in effect, hypotheses. Information about the child gleaned from other interactions such as play therapy, doll and puppet play, bibliotherapy, and individual counseling can be used to strengthen these hypotheses. The therapist's role in this process is complicated indeed, for to make a fairly accurate guess, he or she must know the child and understand the child's point of view. To accomplish this, it is important to get on the same wavelength as the child and to understand the child's vocabulary, motor, intellectual, emotional, and social development as well as his or her interests, relationships, and conflicts. Only after the therapist has been able to get a glimpse of the child's world and has gathered data from a variety of other sources will the therapist be able to put forth a hypothesis or informed guess. Even then, the therapist must always be open to other possibilities and new information that contradict or reaffirm the original guess. It is often difficult to form educated guesses about what children are trying to say because so much depends on their age and developmental level, their past experiences, and their perception of events.

Interpretation of Process, Form, and Content

Most art therapists agree (Kramer & Schehr, 1983; Rubin, 1984) that the interpretation of children's art involves the art medium the child chooses, the creative process by which the art is produced, and the form and content of the final product. For the purposes of evaluation, these areas should be considered together with everything else that is known about the child. The following guidelines provide only generalized suggestions for interpretations, which must be individualized for each child.

Interpreting Process

During art therapy, a 9-year-old girl and her therapist-in-training were finger painting when the child decided to use her feet instead of her hands!

Some of the initial decisions a child makes before beginning the art process are very important to the therapist in determining the meaning inherent in the process. The therapist needs to observe how the child approaches and interacts with the therapist, how the child deals with the unstructured art activity, and how the child makes use of the art materials. It is helpful to the overall interpretation for the therapist not only to observe the child's overall manner and style of working with the art materials but also to determine whether the child's approach to either the therapist or the artwork changes over time (Rubin, 1984).

According to Edith Kramer (1958, 1971, 1979), five art activities are important to the art therapy process: precursory activities, chaotic discharge, art in the service of defense, pictographs, and formed expression. These categories are not rigidly separated, and children may go from precursory playful experimentation to formed expression. They may regress to chaotic discharge, retreat into compulsive defensive work, and then move back again to formed, creative work.

Precursory activities are things that children do to prepare for the creation of art. Children get ready by scribbling, smearing, and otherwise exploring the nature and the uses of art materials such as clay, paint, crayons, and finger paint. Children test the art materials to see how they feel and to create what is pleasing to them. Because scribbles are the building blocks of art, this is an important, necessary, and positive process.

Chaotic discharge refers to spilling or splashing paint and pounding, throwing, and ripping clay, which might indicate the release of pent-up emotions or signal the loss of control. These types of activities should be interpreted as a way to release emotion within the safety of the therapeutic setting.

Art in the service of defense is what children do when they are unable to express their feelings freely in their artwork. Children who wish to defend against their conflicts and negative emotions may engage in copying, tracing, or stereotypically repeating commonplace patterns or themes. The following description of a painting entitled "Flag" illustrates the concept of art in the service of defense.

Remo placed his flagpole into a meticulously painted brick base. He brushed in the main features of a flag, added three dark-gray clouds and an outburst of red flamelike brush strokes. His therapists noted feelings of depression and anger, and elements that could conceivably come together to convey a message. However, "as long as Remo hid behind the empty symbol of the American flag, he had no theme around which an evocative painting could crystallize." (Kramer, 1979, p. 18)

Pictographs are a special form of communication that uses pictures or models to replace or supplement words. Pictographs represent a specific communication between client and therapist that is not readily understood by others and that develops as the therapeutic relationship grows.

Finally, *formed expression* is art in the truest sense of the word. It is the final product that serves as a means of self-expression and communication. It is a symbolic representation of what the child is thinking, feeling, and perceiving. The following example illustrates how Eduardo restores his internal image of his absent mother and "heals" her through his sculpture.

Eduardo is a blind, eight-year-old whose previous art efforts involved making shapeless lumps of clay into "chickens." After his mother had surgery, however, his concern and longing for her motivated him to make her image in clay. He worked diligently to form all of his mother's most important parts. Her face included a large mouth, ears, nostrils and two cheeks. He made his mother's long hair, her body, arms and fingers, legs and toes. Finally he placed two clay bandages over her belly. After he was finished, he stroked the figure tenderly. He had healed his mother (with the bandages), restored her image and revealed his worries. (Kramer, 1979)

The type of materials children choose and the way in which they handle the materials tells a great deal about their individual personalities, styles of coping, and type and intensity of emotion that they are feeling. Some children like to get as messy as possible, putting finger paint all over their clothes; others want to stay neat and so avoid using paints or finger paints. Some children love to touch everything, exploring each medium and what it can do and in general making a big mess. Others draw with the same materials week after week, carefully choosing a few crayons, colored pencils, or only pen and ink.

Children react in a variety of ways. Some scoop up all the materials for themselves, refusing to share with anyone; others choose one or two crayons or a pencil and do not require more. Some children work well individually; others work well in groups. Some children have boundless energy and flit from one art activity to another, never fully completing any; others are slow and methodical, often spending the entire session on just one portion of the face (see Figure 7-13 in "The Case of Ivan").

As children experience different emotions in the art therapy, some may react by becoming more restrictive and inflexible in their artwork. Some may draw finer lines, or depict smaller and smaller images. Others may try to hide their work by painting or scribbling over it. Others may respond by what Rubin (1984) terms emotional "flooding," which is what she interpreted as regression. In this instance, the child's artwork "explodes" with feeling and causes the child to lose control, perhaps spilling and splashing paint or pounding clay in a form of "chaotic discharge" (Kramer, 1971).

Each child has a different relationship with the therapist. Initially, some children are timid and wait to see what the therapist is going to instruct them to do. When no instructions are forthcoming, the child usually begins to draw, paint, or sculpt and may look to the therapist for some sign of approval. Other children want the therapist to create something so they can model it. Others plunge themselves into the activity without giving much thought to the therapist's involvement or to his or her approval. As rapport is established and children feel comfortable in the setting, they have a tendency to become more relaxed and to be more verbal. This happens in most therapeutic environments once trust has been firmly established.

Interpreting Form

During the art interview, the therapist has an opportunity to listen to the child's communications and make observations about the form of the final art product. In interpreting form, the practitioner might answer the following questions about the child's art: Is it neat or messy? Is it finished or left undone? Is it done in black or has the child used blues, greens, and yellows? Is all of the drawing placed in the lower margin or does it fill the page? Are some areas shaded or scribbled over? Are there figures in the drawing and, if so, are they large or tiny? Answers to these questions provide the art therapist with important clues about how the child is thinking and feeling. The organization of the drawing is shown by its placement on the page, its completeness, and how well it is balanced (see Figure 7-2). In addition, the line, shading, and color of the child's artwork provide important clues about the child's motor, intellectual , emotional, and social development.

Size and placement   Anxious children may draw very small figures that occupy only a portion of the available space. Such drawings may feature a small figure standing on feet that are too tiny to support it, which may be placed at the lower margin of the page. This arrangement may suggest that the child has great feelings of inadequacy and insecurity (Burns & Kaufman, 1972; Di Leo, 1973, 1983). Conversely, secure, well-adjusted children will create a figure "that expresses, by its size, sweep, and conspicuous placement on the page, freedom from inhibiting anxiety" (Di Leo, 1973, p. 36).

Shading   Some experts in the field of art therapy have associated excessive shading with anxiety (Di Leo, 1973; Machover, 1949). Children might shade the face of the figures in their drawings or they might shade the lower half of the body. Machover found that children who used excessive shading in the genital area were anxious about the onset of puberty. Di Leo believes that black children do not shade the faces of their drawings unless they too are anxious. Shading the sun, which is normally colored yellow and has rays emanating from it, or darkening clouds is thought to indicate unhappiness. When interpreting shading, it is especially important to consider it as one piece of a very large puzzle.

Color   Color has been used to identify emotions and personality traits for centuries. We have all heard the phrase "She was positively green with envy," "He is a yellow-bellied coward," or "She's in a blue funk." Colors populate our vocabulary and our

FIGURE 7-2 *A Well-Proportioned Drawing* This picture was drawn by a bright, well-adjusted 7-year-old girl. Her older brother is on the left and her baby brother is beside the swing. Notice how well-proportioned the drawing is and how it takes up the entire paper. The tree is larger than the swing set and the ladder is an appropriate height. The original drawing was done with colored markers. There are red apples on a tree of green leaves; the ladder is red; the sun is yellow with a smiling face. All of the children's clothing is in color: the boys' trousers are in blues; the girl's dress is pink. All are appropriately represented according to their ages.

culture. Entire studies have been done to see what colors attract a person's attention and how color affects everything from blood pressure to product choices. Although most practitioners recognize that color is an important variable to consider in analyzing the form of a child's artwork, there is far from universal agreement on what various colors and combinations of colors mean. According to Lüscher (1969), dark blue signals peace and tranquility, yellow tells of warmth and exhilaration, and black symbolizes feelings of nothingness. Excessive use of red is associated with anger, but red is also the color of vitality and warmth (Kramer, 1979). Continued use of dark colors is often associated with depression (Oster & Gould, 1987). Black can also represent night, which invites rest (Kramer, 1979), or it can express pride when used by a black child (Axline as cited in Rubin, 1984). Here again, it depends on the child. A child may simply choose a particular color because it is the only one available. (This situation occurred in our first year when we had only enough money to buy the four basic colors of finger paint.)

Interpreting Content

Because children often represent themselves and their problems in disguised ways, it is necessary to use three basic methods to interpret the content of the child's artwork. Rubin (1984) sees content as something that must be viewed on three levels: (1) the manifest content, which refers to the surface topic or subject matter and includes abstractions; (2) the associative content, which refers to the projected images and stories that are related to the product both during and after its completion; and (3) the latent or symbolic content, which refers to those distortions, including exaggerations and omissions, that the child does not verbalize and that are not part of the child's conscious awareness.

Surface content   Surface content, sometimes called manifest content, refers to what is obvious in the child's drawing. For example, if the child draws happy scenes punctuated with hearts or weaves "I love you" into a drawing and gives it to the therapist, it should be interpreted literally. An example of surface content can be seen in Figure 7-3. Surface content is not always this easy to discern, and other types of interpretation may be helpful in ascertaining what a child's artwork means. Surface content can also include abstractions.

Associative content   Associative content is expressed in the child's verbal or nonverbal communication about his or her artwork. The therapist must be a good listener and a good observer and be tuned into the child as the art is progressing. Associative content is best understood by what the child titles the artwork or what stories he or she tells about it. For example, a 5-year-old's scribbles revealed very little about his feelings of rejection or his mother's inconsistent warmth and affection for him until he explained his picture by saying, "She loves me, she hates me, she loves me, she hates me and then she loves me again." The child's communications about his or her artwork helps the therapist make hypotheses concerning the symbolism in the work. This type of content is especially important when the therapist is unable to decipher the meaning of the child's art.

Symbolic content   Often referred to as latent content in the literature, symbolic content is evident in the distortions or symbols the child selects; it is not necessarily alluded to in the child's verbalizations. This symbolic content is often disguised, even to the child. To form hypotheses regarding the symbolism in the child's artwork, the therapist needs to consider everything that is known about the child, including the child's verbal and nonverbal behavior during the art therapy process. Hypotheses should be based on all of the available information and therapists are cautioned not make sweeping generalizations based on one drawing. A drawing is just one indication among many and needs to be viewed in the context of the child's overall development and life experiences.

There is general agreement that there exist a number of formal or universal symbols that are significant in children's art (see Burns, 1982, 1987). It is generally accepted that the sun is likely to represent the father's influence in the child's life and that a house represents the mother and family life in general (Di Leo, 1983; Rubin,

FIGURE 7-3 *An Example of Surface Content* This drawing was done by a 10-year-old girl who was part of a small-group therapy session for children of recently divorced parents. When asked to draw her feelings about the divorce, this child portrayed her broken heart and her failing grades. Her drawing also tells how divorce has blocked out the happiness in her life. She conveniently labeled the content for the therapist. Her drawing also hints at the love-hate relationship that she has with her parents, an area that needs to be explored further.

1984). A darkened sun, a moon, and rain may be associated with depression (Burns, 1987). Hammers, knives, and other dangerous objects are thought to indicate anger or passive aggression (Burns, 1982). Scars or knotholes in a tree trunk may indicate a particular trauma in the child's life, and their placement may indicate the point in the child's life when the trauma occurred (Di Leo, 1983; Oster & Gould, 1987). In understanding the symbolism of children's art, the therapist needs to be a good listener and observer and be genuinely open to the child's interpretation of the hidden meanings in his or her artwork. "A symbol may be universal, but its meaning is individual. Drawings may provide new insights; they may confirm what we already know. Taken out of context, they may mislead" (Di Leo, 1983, p. 207).

According to Rubin (1984), central themes in children's art include aggression and the need for love and affection. The child's need for nurturance may be disguised in an oral theme, and phallic symbols may appear as sharp piercing objects that render enemies helpless. If the child's art always relates to the same theme, it may be an indication that the child feels conflicted in this area. Special attention needs to be directed toward patterns that will help the therapist make intuitive guesses about what might be important to the inner life of the child.

Symbolic Content in Human Figure Drawings

The human figure is a consistent and favorite subject in children's art, and its depiction is a nearly universal phenomenon (Kellogg, 1967). Just as children go through certain stages in their physical, emotional, and social development, the way they draw the human figure changes and grows with them. Because human beings are social by nature, other people have an important role in the lives of young children. This interaction with other human beings is also a frequent theme in children's art.

Proponents of the human figure drawing agree that "no one-to-one relationship exists between any specific sign or emotional indicator and a definite personality or trait" (Oster & Gould, 1987, p. 23). Therefore, the authors emphasized that inter-pretations should not be made from a single sign. Instead, combinations of indicators in the context of the total drawing should be considered. In addition, such factors as age, maturation, emotional status, social and cultural background, and other relevant history play an important role in understanding the child's human figure.

Omissions in children's drawings are usually significant and tell us something about how children view themselves and their relationships with others. A number of researchers (Burns & Kaufman, 1972; Di Leo, 1973, 1983; Machover, 1949) offer some suggestions for interpreting omissions. Vague or missing arms or hands may indicate a lack of confidence in social interactions, whereas hands hidden behind the child's back might be explained as avoidance or evasiveness. Handicapped children who are unable to walk often omit legs or draw seated figures. Children who deliberately omit facial features while defining other body parts in a drawing may be indicating difficulty with interpersonal relationships. These correlations, however, are only hypotheses that may or may not be confirmed by the child's gestural, physical, and verbal associations (Rubin, 1984).

Exaggerated or *diminished features* often have special significance. According to Oster and Gould (1987), theoreticians and researchers concur on the interpretations of some features. There is general agreement that tiny figures may indicate feelings of insecurity, withdrawal, and inadequacy, whereas big figures might suggest expan-siveness and poor inner controls. Short arms suggest a tendency to withdraw, whereas long arms may be seen as a reaching out toward others. Excessively large hands and arms may symbolize aggressive tendencies in a self-portrait. Small hands may indicate that the child feels ineffectual and lacks confidence. Small feet symbolically suggest that a basic feeling of security is lacking and that the child feels unsupported and anx-ious (Burns & Kaufman, 1972; Di Leo, 1973, 1983). The mouth drawn in a straight line might indicate tension, whereas a short heavy line may suggest aggression. Eyes can create an image of hostility or paranoia if they are large, rounded, and menacing (Di Leo, 1973, 1983; Machover, 1949). Hostility may be projected onto drawings by creating glaring eyes and bared teeth (Hammer, as cited in Oster & Gould, 1987).

Efforts to *conceal* or *minimize* certain portions of the body may also suggest something about the child's current conflicts. Drawing hands inside the pockets might indicate that the child feels ineffective in controlling his or her world. Children who are experiencing conflicts related to sex may draw themselves only from the waist up or may draw their legs coming out of the chest with no lower torso at all (Di Leo, 1973).

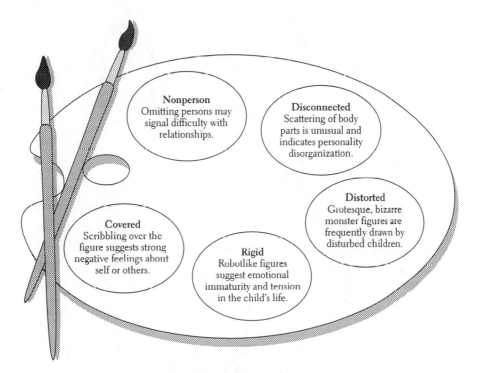

FIGURE 7-4 *Signs of Emotional Disturbance in Draw-A-Person Activity*
SOURCE: Based on data from Di Leo (1973, 1983).

Content Symbolic of Emotional Disturbance

In analyzing the drawings of hundreds of children, Di Leo (1973, 1983) suggested that certain symbolic content appears more frequently in the drawings of disturbed children than in the drawings of healthy children. Five factors based on Di Leo's (1973, 1983) work are presented in Figure 7-4 along with examples that illustrate symbolic content.

Drawing without human figures   Human figures are usually present in drawings that may also include pets, a house, flowers, a tree, and the radiant sun. Therefore, it is unusual for children to omit persons from their drawings (see Figure 7-5) and even more unusual to draw human faces on other creatures, such as dogs (Di Leo, 1973, 1983).

Disconnected figures   Disconnected figures could include disjointed figures, figures that don't resemble human beings, or drawings that represent bits and pieces of a person. Drawings that consist of scattered body parts are considered unusual and deviant, because most children will draw an integrated human figure. Even when the person is only a head, the child usually places features in the circle that represents the head and does not have features scattered all over the page. Clearly, a human figure

FIGURE 7-5 *Drawing without Human Figures* This drawing was done by a 9-year-old who is very withdrawn and socially isolated from peers. The house and tree are outlined in blue-colored pencil; the sun and flowers are done in red marker. In the doorway to the house there appear to be two arms (without hands), and they do not touch. The tree is barren and lifeless. Even though the presence of the sun and the flowers promise the hope of some warmth, the entire picture projects the emotional coldness and lack of meaningful relationships in the child's life.

drawing in which the body parts are disconnected from each other is a deviation from the norm. This inability to produce an integrated figure has been noted in seriously disturbed children and is indicative of their own disorganized personality (Di Leo, 1973, 1983).

In Figure 7-6, a 6-year-old represented human figures in a disorganized and abstract way. The body parts, although not scattered across the page, are not discernible as such. The primitive figures are featureless and facial features that are evident are scattered. A big heart is placed in a face and is surrounded by lines, which the child describes as "veins." The "faces" on the figures, which the child identified as the therapist and the child, are not recognizable as human. The bodies are just stems with no arms, legs, or human features. The only recognizable faces are on the dogs, which have been given faces with smiles. Affection for the therapist is expressed by using three hearts that bind the therapist and the child together.

FIGURE 7-6 *Disconnected Body Parts* This picture was drawn by an emotion-ally-disturbed child, age 6. The figure on the left represents the therapist, and the middle figure represents the child. The two figures with the smiling faces represent the therapist's two dogs. Three circles containing hearts build a bridge between the therapist and the child.

This artwork reflects the child's poor self-image and strong need for affection. A disturbed mother-child relationship is suspected, which might be compounded by abuse or neglect. Although the child is physically well cared for, there is evidence of emotional deprivation and affect hunger. There is every reason to believe that this child is very bright but is unable to function at the appropriate developmental level because of overwhelming emotional problems. Play therapy and art therapy would be appropriate therapeutic interventions.

Distortions When children portray themselves and others, they use varying degrees of disguise. Rubin (1984) suggested that therapists consider both the nature and degree of distortion or disguise in the child's self-representation. Some children represent themselves by using a figure of the same age and sex. Other children use a greater degree of disguise and depict themselves as an animal, a fantasy creature, or an inanimate object. Others may use some form of abstraction. Di Leo (1970, 1973) noted that grotesque, monster-like figures are often drawn by children who are experiencing some degree of emotional disturbance. Children who wish to disguise their thoughts and feelings may draw pictures of creatures that appear in their nightmares or their imaginations. Many of these images represent frightening aspects of their thoughts that are ordinarily concealed even from them. Interpreting these distortions presents the greatest challenges to therapists.

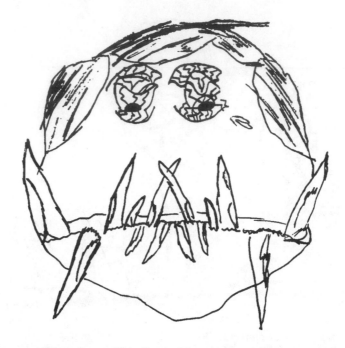

FIGURE 7-7 *Distortions* This distorted human figure with monstrous teeth and blood-shot eyes is the work of a very bright 9-year-old boy. His mother reportedly took him to places where rituals were performed to "get the devil out of him." He related stories of monsters, vampires, witches, and other creatures that claw and devour him and said these are stories that "I make up." In these stories, he gives himself magical powers, such as the ability to fly.

Figure 7-7 represents one of the monsterlike figures consistently drawn by one 9-year-old boy. He suffered a great deal of trauma in his life, including his mother's recent suicide. In his words, "she was sick." His mother was an alcoholic who may have been suffering from some form of mental illness. While the child lived with his mother, he was exposed to bizarre religious rituals designed to "get the devil out of him."

Stiff figures Rigid robotlike figures are another way that children express their anxiety. Although Di Leo (1973) and others have not been able to associate a specific disorder with these types of figures, emotional immaturity and an atmosphere of tension in the home seems to prevail in children who represent themselves and their families in such rigid fashion. These children are often inflexible in their behavior, indicating excessive use of defense mechanisms as a way of protecting themselves. The drawing in Figure 7-8 is of a person with rigid posture as well as extra long legs that come out of the torso.

Expressions of sexuality When drawing human figures or self-portraits, children tend to draw members of their own sex. Di Leo (1973, 1983) speculated that a

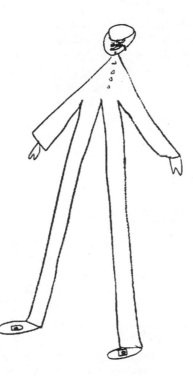

FIGURE 7-8 *Stiff and Rigid Figures* This is a self-portrait of a 9-year-old boy who was referred to counseling because he would dissolve into tears for no apparent reason. His teachers reported that he is quiet and withdrawn in class and has no friends. He avoids contact with peers, shuns group games and activities, and prefers to fantasize about extraordinary adventures. His stiff figure and straight-line mouth might be an indication of the tension that fills his relationships with his family and peer group.

tendency to draw members of the opposite sex may suggest the possibility of gender confusion or failure to assume the same-sex identity. This confusion may stem from the child's interaction with a parent whom the child sees as most dominant or aggressive. Unlike younger children, who may be expressing gender confusion, adolescent girls usually draw male figures because they are becoming interested in the opposite sex.

When drawing figures of the same or opposite gender, most children indicate sex differences through the figure's hair, eyelashes, ornaments, or clothing. Most children do not draw explicit genitalia on their representations of human figures. In analyzing thousands of drawings, Di Leo (1973) collected only half a dozen in which the penis or vulva were clearly portrayed. "It is so unusual to see the genitalia that their presence may be highly significant" (p. 54). Child sexual abuse may be one of the reasons for this portrayal. If children do include explicit genitalia in their human figure drawings, the therapist should be alert to possible sexual abuse and take steps to either confirm or deny this hypothesis.

Scribbling over the drawn figure Rubin (1984) stated that the child's attitude toward the final product is important. Is the child's attitude one of shame, pride, disgust, pleasure, hostility, or ambivalence? When children draw a human figure and then scribble all over it, they may be expressing shame, disgust, or hostility. In an attempt to hide or block out the artwork, the child is expressing strong negative feelings about himself or herself. Perhaps the child is saying, "I don't want you to see this because then you will know what I am all about." Perhaps the child is expressing feelings of depreciation: "I hate this, I look dumb!" or "This is so-o-o-o ugly." In any event, children who try to obliterate their artwork may need help to overcome their negative feelings about themselves.

Children's Family Drawings

Children's family drawings are especially significant indices of how children view themselves in relation to their family and social environment. Given the central role of the family in the child's development, the family drawing gives important clues as to how the parents care for and nurture the child, what characterizes the child's interactions with family members, and how secure the child feels about his or her place in the family. As the child grows older, people outside the family circle become increasingly influential in shaping attitudes and behavior, but the family continues to exert the most enduring influence on the child. It is within the family that the child learns how to deal with his or her own feelings and develops empathy for others. Thus, the family drawing can be a significant expression of the child's emotional life (Di Leo, 1973).

On the basis of his studies, Di Leo (1973, 1983) developed some broad guidelines for interpreting family drawings by observing the relative size, position, and similarity of family members to one another, as well as taking note of omissions, interactions, and isolations (see Figure 7-9). Interpretations of the following representative drawings should always be viewed as hypotheses that may be reinforced by additional information gathered from counseling sessions, observations, and other therapeutic activities.

Relative size Sometimes when children portray their families, they use size as a way to express how important a person is to them. A child may exaggerate the size of a person that is especially dominant in his or her life, which is why some parental figures are portrayed as larger and taller than their more submissive and ineffectual partners. The child may even say, "That's my mom; she's the boss." Sometimes, in addition to being portrayed as a taller or more imposing figure, an abusive parent may be drawn with especially large hands. This exaggeration may indicate that the child views this person as being hostile and threatening.

Position In some family drawings, children place themselves next to a favorite parent or sibling. In order to do this, some children draw two separate families on the same paper. Other children arrange all of the family members in chronological order, usually starting with the oldest parent and featuring the youngest child last. In the

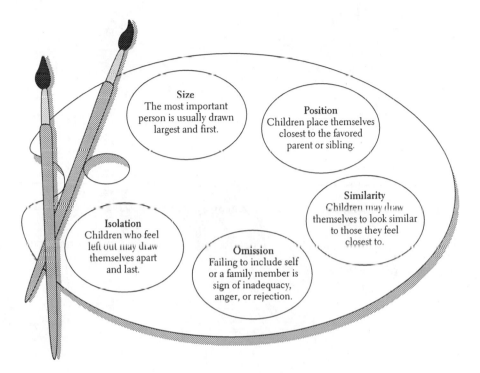

FIGURE 7-9 *Factors in Interpreting the Draw-a-Family Activity*
SOURCE: Based on data from Di Leo (1973, 1983).

family group illustrated in Figure 7-10, the child is the "queen" of the family and her favorite brother is her "king." The other two sisters are depicted as witches and are placed in "jail" in their home. The mother and father are conspicuously absent. It is evident that this is not a close family and that sibling rivalry is intense. The client wants very much to be favored, and perhaps she is; but the problems of the siblings are diverting much-needed attention from her. The lack of nurturance and support from the parents is noted by their absence. The intensity of negative feelings about her two sisters is seen in the way that they are depicted: as ugly witches that she wants to keep locked up. When the counselor said, "You really dislike your sisters, don't you?" She replied, "I hate them."

Similarity Similarity in dress or other features often links the child with a favored parent or sibling. In one drawing of a child's "blended" family, she depicted herself as the only child of this marriage and the only one dressed in a skirt like her mother. She also placed herself in the middle of her mother and father.

Omissions Di Leo (1973, 1983) believes that "forgetting" to include a family member indicates a rejection or a symbolic elimination of that family member. It is unusual for a child to draw the family and not include all the members. To omit

FIGURE 7-10 *Position in the Family*   This family drawing is set in the child's house and features the 9-year-old client as queen. She is holding hands with her favorite sibling, a younger brother who doubles as her king. Her two older sisters, drawn as witches, are in the rooms of the house, which she describes as "jails." The sisters are given ugly features and have bars on their windows. The mother and father, who live with the family, are conspicuously absent from the picture.

oneself is especially significant and may indicate that the child lacks a sense of belonging to the family or may not feel valued by its members (see Figure 7-11). Some reasons for this feeling may be that parents are excessively critical or compare siblings unfavorably. Other omissions in family drawings are similar to those covered under the section on human figure drawings. These include omitting hands, feet, facial features, torsos, or other body parts. I have found that hands are the most commonly omitted features in family drawings. Missing hands to touch and hold each other may be an indication of a lack of warmth and affection among members. A lack of communication is evident if family members lack smiles or if they have no faces with which to communicate. Lacking a mouth, the family members cannot say kind words or give verbal affirmations of self-worth. If they have no eyes, they can not see each other's happiness or pain. In any family drawing where there are significant omissions, the child and the family should be part of the counseling or therapy so that the

FIGURE 7-11 *Omissions in the Family Drawing* This family grouping is unique because the facial features and the arms and hands are missing. All the family members are dressed similarly, and the mom is distinguished by her hair. The child is female but gives no real definition to her figure. The omissions portray a lack of communication and interaction among family members. The child has given them no mouths to speak kind or harsh words, no eyes to see each other's happiness or pain, and no arms to comfort one another. In this case, the therapist would want to see the family as a group and assess the interaction among the members.

practitioner can help family members interact more positively and work toward fulfilling one another's needs for love and affection.

Isolation When children are separated from parents by some type of physical or psychological barrier, they often represent this isolation in their family drawings. As more and more families break up and children have half-siblings and stepsiblings in their lives, these conflicts and adjustments are increasingly evident in their artwork. Some children draw lines that separate two families: the original family and the parent's "other" family. Other children show rejected family members walled off by lines or surrounded by electric waves. Sometimes rejected family members are given ugly features, which distinguish them from other siblings. These types of family groupings

FIGURE 7-12 *Isolation and Separation*   This is a drawing of the client's siblings and her half-siblings. The children of her father's current wife are shown to the left of the barrier. The client's perception of them is that they are "smart" and "spoiled." To the right of the barrier is the client and her two brothers. Her older brother, who loves to play basketball, is described as a "black sheep" and is isolated from the others. Her other brother is good at building things. It is interesting that the client places herself next to the barrier that shields the stepsiblings and close to her isolated older brother.

are becoming more frequent as the divorce and subsequent remarriage rates increase dramatically. In Figure 7-12, the child's half-siblings are shown behind a barrier. It is clear that they are the favored ones, as evidenced by their good grades and the ice cream cone. The client is portrayed on the right side of the barrier with her two brothers, one of whom she describes as a "black sheep."

In summary, interpreting a child's art is a multilevel process that involves listening, observing, and forming hypotheses about the child's inner conflicts. To do this effectively, the therapist must pay attention to the process by which the art is made as well as the form and content of the final product. The three types of content include the surface content; the associative content, which involves the child's communications about the art; and the symbolic content, which reveals what children are thinking and feeling. Children are not always aware of the symbolism in their artwork, because much of it may be on the unconscious level. Examples of children's drawings were presented here to assist the reader in identifying some common symbols. Most of the drawings were done by children who are experiencing temporary family conflicts; a few are examples of more serious emotional disturbance. The following case study of Ivan will illustrate how therapists formulate tentative hypotheses regarding the conflicts expressed in children's artwork.

ART THERAPY IN PRACTICE

Karen Machover (1949) found that there is an intimate connection between the figure drawn and the personality of the artist. Her hypotheses regarding the interpretation of the human figure have been validated by a number of other researchers (Burns & Kaufman, 1970, 1972; Di Leo, 1973, 1983; Hammer, 1971), and her analyses of the parts of the face are especially helpful in forming hypotheses about the monster face we will study in "The Case of Ivan." Again, the reader is cautioned that these are only *possibilities* and should be viewed in the context of the total assessment.

Parts of the Face

1. *The head.* The head is the most important organ relating to the emotional security of the child, and some children offer it as the completed person. The head may symbolize the smile, approval, the frown, or scolding of adults in the child's life. Young children who are experiencing emotional and social problems frequently draw a large head.

2. *The face.* The face is the center of communication. If facial features are missing and other parts of the body are carefully drawn, this may indicate difficulties in interpersonal relationships. Overemphasis and reinforcement of facial features may characterize fantasy as well as a compensation for inadequacy.

3. *The mouth.* Emphasis on the mouth may be expressed by omission, reinforcement, special size, special shape, erasure, shading, or displacement. Overemphasis may be tied to eating problems, profanity, or temper tantrums. A single line for a mouth may indicate tension and a mouth drawn with a heavy slash may communicate aggression. Teeth showing, in adult drawings, may suggest aggressive or sadistic tendencies.

4. *The eyes.* The eye is regarded as the "window of the soul" and, as such, is very important to the interpretation of the face. The eyes are the focal point of a child's emotional life and sense of security, because he or she experiences approval or rejection through the eyes of others. Large, dark, accentuated or menacing eyes that create an image of hostility and suspicion are projected by the paranoid child. Small, beady eyes may indicate suspicion.

5. *The ears.* It is less significant if the child omits the ears than if he or she omits a more active part of the face such as the mouth. An ear that is outstanding either by size, shape, placement, or erasures may indicate a range of things from a mild reaction to criticism or social opinion to active auditory hallucinations. Individuals who are guarded, suspicious, or distrustful may place special emphasis on the ears, and the child who is quick to take offense or is resistant to authority may show some moderate accentuation of the ear. (from Machover, 1949, pp. 40–58)

• • • *The Case of Ivan*

Family information　When fighting erupted in one of the breakaway republics of the former USSR Ivan's grandfather was killed in the fighting. According to his grandmother, Ivan was 5 years old when he witnessed a number of people "being murdered right in front of him." Ivan, his mother, grandmother, and great-grandmother fled with only one suitcase containing clothes and photographs. After a short stay in Russia, the three women and Ivan emigrated to the United States, leaving behind Ivan's only uncle, who died of an inoperable brain tumor before he was able to emigrate.

The family reports that Ivan's father was an alcoholic who abandoned him when he was a year old. His mother, who also had a long history of alcoholism, committed suicide. Surviving family members say that she was despondent because she was unable to find employment. According to relatives, Ivan's mother threatened suicide on numerous occasions and was preoccupied with strange religious rituals and bizarre thoughts about possession by the devil. The child is reported to have been subjected to religious rituals designed to "get the devil out of him." The nature and extent of his exposure to these rituals is unknown, but his grandmother believes that they began when his mother took him away to another city. She said that he has had nightmares ever since.

Throughout most of his childhood, 9-year-old Ivan has been cared for by his maternal grandmother, but his mother took him from his grandmother when she wanted to "punish" the grandmother. In the year prior to her death, Ivan's mother took him to California, where he changed schools three times. He returned to his grandmother's home only three weeks before his mother's suicide. Currently, he is being cared for by his maternal grandmother and great-grandmother. Ivan has been surrounded by women most of his life, and the only male influence is a great uncle who tries to spend time with him.

Interview with Ivan's grandmother   Ivan's grandmother does not speak any English, but she spoke through an interpreter at the initial interview and was able to give her perspective on all of the trauma and loss that has characterized Ivan's childhood. Through tears, a universal form of communication, the grandmother was able to tell of the unspeakable horror of witnessing murder and war, the terror of flight from their homeland, and the constant specter of death that has been part of Ivan's childhood. She spoke of the many losses in his life and in hers. She had lost a husband, a son, and now a daughter. He had lost a father, a grandfather, an uncle, and a mother. Having lost his mother years ago to alcoholism and mental illness, Ivan now suffered the final abandonment and was, according to his cousin, "emotionally numb."

His grandmother says that Ivan did not show very much emotion when he learned of his mother's death, but that he did cry. Her niece contradicted this account, saying that Ivan showed no emotion after his mother's death and did not cry. Both women agree that he has difficulty expressing emotion, particularly anger, and that he mourned his mother quietly. This lack of any outward expression of grief did not seem to concern his grandmother. She perceives his lack of tears as a strength that is characteristic of his cultural heritage. In her words, "strong men do not cry."

His grandmother describes Ivan as bright and clever. He does well in school, getting all As and Bs, and speaks English very well. She says that Ivan can be difficult and stubborn at home but that, for the most part, he is cooperative and is easy to discipline. She is somewhat concerned that he watches too much television and seems to prefer the most violent movies and television programs. He does play with the neighbor children on occasion, but he spends a great deal of time at home doing homework and playing video games. The grandmother describes their relationship as "close" and says that her grandson is a "good boy" who has had a lot of bad things happen to him.

Report from teachers   Outside help was first suggested by Ivan's classroom teacher because he did not have any reaction to his mother's recent suicide. He is described as an exceptionally bright child with a vivid imagination. He is not a problem in class. If anything, he seems to be extremely quiet and withdrawn. His teacher confirms that he has no friends and that other children tend to avoid him because he talks about aliens and outer space. He claims that he can see "energy rings" around people. His teachers referred him for counseling because of his lack of an emotional response to his mother's death.

Previous evaluation   In response to the crisis of his mother's suicide, Ivan was evaluated previously in a clinical setting where an intake interview, complete with a mental status evaluation, was conducted. No remarkable health or developmental concerns were noted. The child had no previous psychiatric history. The mother's previous psychiatric history included alcoholism and depression punctuated with numerous suicidal threats. Emotional abuse, in the form of bizarre rituals that Ivan was forced to endure, was detailed. A mental status evaluation noted that Ivan's thought process was organized and relevant. However, because of his stories about seeing aliens, flying saucers, and "lights" around people, there was some question about his thought content. The examiner suggested the possibility of both delusions and hallucinations.

Presenting problem   When asked to describe why they sought counseling, the family members identified a number of concerns. The major concern was that Ivan was emotionally unresponsive to his mother's suicide. He did not cry or show distress and, after three months, "he seems strangely unaffected by his mother's death." It was also noted that Ivan does not express anger overtly but instead disguises it by acting out in subtle ways, always being careful not to get caught. There is concern that he is preoccupied with violence and prefers horror shows to other television programming. He has a very active imagination and makes up stories about having superpowers and seeing strange creatures from outer space. His bizarre stories serve to isolate him from peers by making him appear strange. He tells fantastic stories about aliens and space creatures and speaks of wanting to have special powers, among them, the ability to fly.

Sessions with Ivan   The first meeting with the therapist was spent getting to know Ivan and playing a game with him. Ivan is a very bright and verbal young man who likes to draw. He says he does well in school and that it is "too easy." As Ivan was telling about his desire to be big and strong and to have superpowers, he began to draw a monster, depicted in Figure 7-13, that he says he sees in his dreams.

FIGURE 7-13 *Ivan's Monster*   Ivan's imposing, menacing picture fills the entire page. The head is large and the facial features are expressed with the kind of perfection, conviction, and over-detailing that suggests active fantasy.

Using an ink pen, Ivan drew the head of the monster, slowly and meticulously, commenting little as he worked. He bore down hard on the pen as he sharpened the features, working with special emphasis on the teeth. The teeth are numerous, threatening, and suggest aggression. (This is later reinforced in the dialogue.) Emphasis on the mouth could mean that Ivan has been subjected to verbal attacks or that he is himself verbally aggressive. (The former is more likely in this case.)

The monster's eyes are alert and drawn in great detail. The large, dark eyes create an image of hostility and suspicion. The thick eyebrows add emphasis and seem to give a look of wariness to the face. The ears are large and each is pierced by a knife. (Ivan mentions that he believes his mother's death was his fault.) Such exaggerated ears could mean that this child is sensitive to criticism or that he is experiencing active auditory hallucinations. (The former hypothesis is confirmed after talking with Ivan and his grandmother.)

Ivan draws thin wispy hair on the monster's head, along with what appear to be hornlike growths out of the back of the head, giving the creature the appearance of a devil. This could be his perception of "the devil" that his mother wanted to rid him of. The monster also lacks a neck, which is not unusual given that the rest of the body is not drawn.

The overall impression is that the monster represents Ivan's fears and his wariness of a menacing and threatening environment. All the threats to Ivan's healthy development are not immediately apparent, but it can be assumed that the emotionally abusive rituals designed to "get the devil out of him" have contributed heavily to his fears, guilt, and feelings of inadequacy.

The following perceptions of himself, others, and his environment seem to be influencing Ivan's thoughts, feelings, and behavior.

"The world is a scary and threatening place."
"I cannot trust others to protect me from harm, therefore I must depend on myself."
"The only way that I can feel protected is to endow myself with superpowers."
"My mother left me because I wasn't a good boy. It must be my fault."
"Other children do not like me because they don't understand me."

It is apparent, at least from the initial hypotheses, that Ivan is struggling with a number of problems. He is still grieving over the loss of his mother and is coping with the effects of severe emotional abuse. He feels guilty whenever he thinks that his mother may have been the cause of his abuse, so he creates monsters and other creatures to deal with his problems. He escapes into a fantasy life that offers him some relief from punishing thoughts. He even may have wished at times that his mother would not be there to torment him, and now he feels that his wishes have come true. Thus, he sees himself as the cause of his mother's suicide. ("I think it was my fault...My grandma told me she was sick...I guess she was sick.") This is a terrible burden for a little boy to carry.

To deal with his guilt, anger, and fear, Ivan has developed a rich fantasy life. He has not yet accepted his mother's death and views himself as strong because he didn't cry. He claims to have superpowers that include the ability to fly. This is how he escapes from his feelings of inadequacy. He shields himself from interaction with other children through his bizarre stories and sees himself as intellectually superior to them.

The following tentative diagnosis takes into account all the information that has been gathered during interviews with Ivan and his grandmother. It is organized according to the multiaxial system found in the *Diagnostic and Statistical Manual of Mental Disorders* (4th Edition)(APA, 1994).

Diagnostic Impression: DSM-IV

Axis I	Adjustment Disorder with Mixed Emotional Features (309.28)
	Rule out: Posttraumatic Stress Disorder
Axis II	Deferred
Axis III	No disorder
Axis IV	Loss of mother (Suicide)
	Loss of grandfather
	Victim of emotional abuse
	Exposure to war
Axis V	GAF = 65

Therapy needs to be directed toward helping Ivan understand that he is not to blame for his mother's suicide and that she was suffering from an illness. Information about alcoholism might be helpful in this regard. He needs opportunities to express his painful thoughts and feelings and to move away from the fantasy world he has constructed. Given Ivan's active imagination, art and play are the best therapeutic modes.

Ivan will participate in a play therapy clinic where he will be able to receive 12 weekly sessions at little or no cost to his family. Specifically, the therapist working with Ivan will (1) help him feel safe and secure in the therapeutic relationship, (2) encourage him to express his feelings through art or play, (3) help him make the link between his current feelings and his past experiences, and (4) help him discover healthier ways of thinking, feeling, and behaving. Part of Ivan's treatment will involve group play therapy sessions with other children. His grandmother will be involved as much as possible and will be encouraged to allow Ivan more opportunities to play with other children in the neighborhood. Ivan's attendance at school and community activities will also be encouraged. If significant progress is not noted at the end of the planned treatment period, Ivan will be able to continue at the clinic for another 12 sessions. •

Art Therapy Activities

Family Art Therapy

Family art therapy, pioneered by Hanna Kwiatkowska (1977, 1978), is unique in that it involves a group of people who have lived together for many years. Over time, the group members have developed their own interactional patterns and have established a system of interlinked defenses. They have formed subgroups within the family and alliances with and against each other and have developed their own patterns of thinking. All these factors produce the special climate of a given family and are important to art therapy and assessment.

Art is used as a family group technique to promote spontaneous self-expression and as an alternate way of observing family interactions (see Figure 7-14). Art activities, as a supplement to family therapy (see, for example, Tavantzis, 1984) or as the sole family treatment mode (for example, Landgarten, 1981; Rubin, 1984), help family members get involved in the therapeutic process. This informal approach helps lessen the participants use of emotional controls and defense mechanisms. Symbolic images can be communicated through the family's artwork, and each member is free to express conflicts that may be too intense for words. Hostility is more likely to be accepted when it is illustrated rather than spoken or acted on, and there is much less guilt associated with anger that is portrayed visually (Kwiatkowska, 1977). Art can also encourage flexibility in the way family members interact, and it can equalize age differences. Because children are generally more comfortable with concrete activities, art activities put them on a more equal footing with adults (Oster & Gould, 1987).

Family art evaluation   The family art evaluation is extremely useful to the clinician. Sometimes it provides material for further therapy sessions with the child and his or her family, even if no further use of art is made. Kwiatkowska (1977, 1978) developed a series of activities that can be used to learn more about children and their families. These techniques are helpful in getting to know family members and understanding how they relate to one another. Kwiatkowska uses six art activities in evaluating children and their families in a single session that lasts between 90 minutes and 2 hours. In this evaluation format, participants are asked to draw a free picture, a portrait of the family, an abstract family portrait, an individual picture from a scribble, and a joint scribble. The evaluation concludes with a final free drawing. In a variation of this evaluation format, Rubin (1984; Rubin & Magnussen, 1974) uses three activities, which include an individual picture from a scribble, family portraits, and a joint mural. If one family member finishes these activities before the others do, he or she is encouraged to create artwork using any medium and topic.

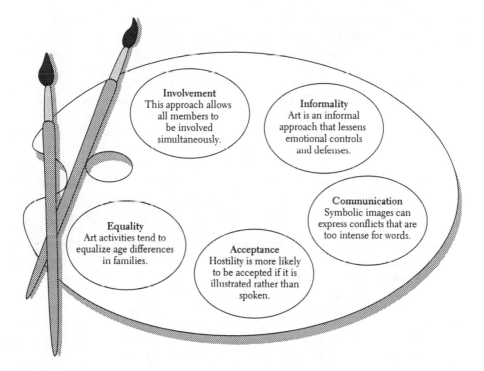

FIGURE 7-14 *The Value of Art as a Family Group Technique*
SOURCE: Based on data from Kwiatkowska (1977); Oster & Gould (1987).

Activities

A free picture For free pictures, there is no subject assigned and each family member is encouraged to draw whatever comes to mind. Often an individual member uses this drawing to introduce him- or herself or to reveal certain aspects of the family problem. Individuals are encouraged to explain and explore the meanings of what they have produced, and the evaluation is considered a learning experience for the family and the therapist. Members are usually asked to title, sign, and date their work. Often a title adds meaning to the picture and may provide additional symbolism. Other factors such as size and the placement of the signature may be indicative of the individual's self-perception (Kwiatkowska, 1977, 1978).

A portrait of the family As a second activity, Kwiatkowska asks participants to draw each member of the family, including themselves. They are not asked to draw a detailed resemblance but are requested to draw more than a stick figure. Kwiatkowska adds an "abstract family portrait" as the third activity in her family evaluation format. For families who do not understand the concept of abstraction, the therapist may ask members to use motion, shapes, lines, or color to represent each person. In one example of abstraction, a young girl encompassed her family within a huge eye and drew a line down the center to indicate her perception of a split family (Oster & Gould, 1987). In a variation of this technique, Rubin (1984; Rubin & Magnussen, 1974) asks each individual in the family group to create either an abstract or a realistic portrait of the family in two or three dimensions. Individuals are asked to create the family portrait in any medium they desire, such as realistic drawings, paintings, reliefs, or sculptures.

Individual picture from a scribble   All family members do arm-loosening exercises in preparation for making a scribble as the starting point of a picture. Each participant then draws a picture inspired by any line or lines in his or her own scribble. This activity provides a vehicle for association and also helps to lessen defenses and relax emotional controls (Kwiatkowska, 1977). In a variation of this technique (Rubin, 1984; Rubin & Magnussen, 1974), each participant is asked to draw a continuous line scribble with his or her eyes open or closed and then to pick out one (or more) image in the scribble, elaborate on it, and give it a title. Each family member does the same, and then they take turns describing their own work and responding to each other's.

Joint picture started from a scribble   Each family member does a scribble and then, among themselves, all decide which scribble they will use to start a joint picture in which all family members will collaborate. This procedure not only encourages families to work together but it also permits the family to express, recognize, and express feelings that are below the conscious level. It helps family members accept their real perceptions of themselves and of others in the family. Both the family and the therapist gain insight into the interactional pattern in the family and can observe each member's interaction with the identified client (Kwiatkowska, 1977).

Joint mural   Family members are given a choice of art media and are asked to create something together on a large piece of paper (3' x 6'), which has been taped on a wall. Family members must decide what they want to do and then work on the mural together. Individual characteristics, family interaction patterns, and problem-solving strategies emerge as the mural is planned and drawn. The finished mural reflects the family's ability to work as a unified whole, and some families may not be comfortable with the process. When completed, family members are encouraged to discuss the mural and their experiences in drawing it (Rubin, 1984; Rubin & Magnussen, 1974).

Life-space drawings   Rubin (1984) includes the life-space drawing as part of a format for mother-child art therapy groups. In initial group meetings with mothers (before the children are included), assigned tasks include making a family drawing and a picture of each participant's "life space." For the latter task, each mother is asked to choose the size and color of paper that seems "right" and to make a picture of her life space at the present time, including both positive and negative elements. Each participant's drawings (family drawing and life-space picture) are shared and discussed with the other mothers in the group. These activities are helpful in assessing how the child client is viewed in the mother's current perception of her family and herself. This format is useful for improving parent-child communication and can be used with groups that include both parents.

Family drawing technique   The family drawing technique (Tavantzis, 1984) can be used in any setting where there is adequate room for the family to gather around a table. This art technique is an informal and fun way to get the family involved in helping the child and in identifying family strengths as well as weaknesses. It gives the therapist an opportunity to observe the parents' relationship with one another, with the identified child client, and with the other family members. The family drawing involves taking a large sheet of paper (such as end rolls from the local newspaper), some colored pencils, magic markers, crayons, pens, and pencils. Simply ask family members to draw themselves on the paper, which has been placed on a table with the family seated around it. The counselor may wish to ask the participants to draw themselves and other family members in the household doing their favorite activities. After a few simple directions, the counselor can watch and listen to family members as they represent their interaction both verbally and nonverbally. The drawing is a lasting record of the family's thoughts, feelings, and interactions with and about each other. If the therapist wishes, he or she can tape record (with permission) what family members say to one another as they draw, as well as their subsequent discussion about the meaning of the drawing.

In summary, art activities can be used in combination with family therapy, as a primary mode of treatment, or in assessment. These activities can be used alone or in combination with other types of therapy and can be used in ways that correspond to the practitioner's theoretical orientation to therapy. They are informal, fun activities that involve all family members simultaneously and can be used for assessing the strengths that each family brings to therapy. During these activities, symbolic images can be expressed that may be too painful for words. There is more acceptance of hostility when it is illustrated rather than spoken, and there is less guilt associated with what is revealed on paper. These advantages make art a valuable tool for practitioners who work with families.

Individual and Group Art Therapy

The following individual and group art therapy techniques (Denny, 1977; Oster & Gould, 1987; Robbins & Sibley, 1976) are suggested for use with children and adolescents. Some of these techniques could also be used with parent-child groups, whereas others are ideal for group work with children in elementary school guidance programs. The therapist can use these techniques within his or her own theoretical framework (see Rubin, 1987) or as part of an integrated approach. It is best to consider each technique in the context of the therapist's skill and the client's needs. A flexible approach to counseling and therapy, coupled with a thorough awareness of the child and his or her developmental level, should guide the therapist in the selection of the best techniques.

Activities

Understanding Self
Technique: Automatic Drawing (Scribble Technique)[1]
Materials: Paper, felt-tipped pens, or pencils

---

[1] Denny, J. M. (1977). Techniques for individual and group art therapy. In E. Ulman & P. Dachinger (Eds.), *Art therapy: In theory and practice* (2nd ed.),(pp. 132–149). New York: Schocken Books.

Directions: The child is encouraged to relax, make free lines or scribbles on the paper, and stop when he or she decides each drawing is complete.

Purpose: This activity is a valuable tool for establishing rapport. It is an entertaining and nonthreatening way to release spontaneous images, and it allows preadolescents to express those aspects of their inner selves that they may be reluctant to share.

Technique: Free Drawing[1]
Materials: Paper, pencils, pens, crayons, paints, colored pencils, and markers
Directions: The child is encouraged to express himself or herself freely and not to "plan" the picture.
Purpose: The results often show the client's current problems, defenses, and strengths.

Technique: Drawing Completion[1]
Materials: Paper with a few simple lines or shapes drawn on it.
Directions: Child is invited to complete the drawing.
Purpose: This technique can be used in group work to stimulate conversation or as a way to encourage a child to express his or her thoughts and feelings in an individual session.

Technique: Affective Words[1]
Materials: Paper, pencils, pens, crayons, paints, markers, and colored pencils
Directions: The therapist states a "feeling" word (love, hate, anger), and the client depicts the word in a drawing. The child may volunteer words also.
Purpose: Shows the client's inner feelings and is an opening for discussion.

Technique: Masks of Affects [2]
Materials: Paper maché, paint, egg cartons, and miscellaneous "junk" materials
Directions: Choose an emotion and make a mask that expresses it.
Purpose: This technique provides opportunities for discussion and follow-up of important feelings. It also provides clues to the experiences in the child's life that evoke strong emotions.

Technique: Problems and Feelings[1]
Materials: Variety of drawing and painting materials
Directions: The child paints or draws a recent "problem" or "feeling."
Purpose: This technique is useful with older children. It helps the client to be aware of his or her feelings and to work them out through the drawing and/or the discussion.

Technique: Three Wishes[1]
Materials: Variety of drawing and painting materials
Directions: Ask the child to draw three (or five) wishes.

[2] Robbins, A., & Sibley, L. B. (1976). *Creative art therapy*. New York, Brunner/Mazel.

Purpose: These drawings can be used to discuss the strength of the wishes, whether they are obtainable, and what short-term goals would be needed to reach the long-term goal. This activity can be used in groups.

Technique: Immediate States[1]
Materials: Variety of art media for drawing, painting, or sculpting.
Directions: The child picks one or more of the following statements to illustrate and discuss: "I am"; "I feel"; "I have"; or "I do."
Purpose: This technique provides a way for children to express their feelings to others and to themselves.

Technique: Draw-A-Story Game [3]
Materials: Pen, pencils, crayons, markers, colored pencils
Directions: The therapist first draws a simple line on the paper and directs the child to elaborate on it to make a picture. Then the child is asked questions (i.e., "What is going on there?"). The process is then repeated until a sequence of pictures develops into a story.
Purpose: This technique increases the child's awareness of alternative feelings and actions and encourages more adaptive solutions to problems (Gabel, as cited in Oster & Gould, 1987).

Understanding Self in Relation to Others

Technique: Family in Clay [2]
Materials: Clay
Directions: The child is invited to sculpt his or her family, stepfamily, or extended family. This "family in clay" can be the one the child currently lives with or it can be the family that he or she wishes for.
Purpose: Because the figures can be moved about, information can be obtained concerning family dynamics and thought processes.

Technique: Family Tree [2]
Materials: Paper and markers
Directions: Ask the child to make a family tree and put the family members on it. Encourage the child to list age, relationship, and feelings toward each member represented.
Purpose: This technique is helpful in learning about the child's perceptions of his or her place in the family. Children may leave out a family member or draw themselves closest to the favorite parent.

Technique: House Plan [2]
Materials: Newsprint and crayons
Directions: The therapist draws a house plan and asks the child to indicate where family members would be and what they would be doing.

---

[3] Oster, G. D., & Gould, P. (1987). *Using drawings in assessment and therapy.* Brunner/Mazel.

Purpose: This activity provides insight into family roles and how the child relates to his or her interpersonal environment.

Technique: Theme Mural with Interchangeable Cutout Figures.[2]

Materials: Mural paper, drawing paper, scissors, crayons, pastels or markers, masking tape

Directions: The child places cutout figures onto a group mural depicting a fantasy theme. Counselor may start with: "We are in school. The teacher is absent and there is a substitute, How will the class behave?" or "We have traveled to a distant planet, What will we do? What will it be like?"

Purpose: Group members or the therapist can offer a wide variety of fantasy situations to address any issue that is relevant to the group. Possible themes might include separation, frustration, tolerance, cooperation, and peer relationships.

The techniques presented in this section are approaches that are useful only when the child's particular personality and needs have been considered. They are not intended to be used at random or in isolation; rather, they are suggestions for activities that might be integrated into a well-thought-out treatment plan. The choice and timing of any approach, as well as the selection of specific art activities, will depend on the needs of the particular child or group. Children, if given the freedom to lead, will signal the therapist when they are ready to benefit from a certain activity (Denny, 1977).

INSIGHTS AND IMPLICATIONS

Art is a technique that even beginning therapists can use to get to know children and their families better and to understand the problems they bring with them to therapy. Art can be useful, especially when combined with other therapeutic activities, as a way to (1) establish a relationship with children, (2) help children express and resolve their conflicts in therapy, and (3) promote growth in self-expression, problem-solving ability, and confidence. Art activities provide a fun and nonthreatening way to establish rapport, which is so essential to building trust. In this atmosphere of trust, children are able to express their innermost thoughts and feelings. Hidden conflicts, which may not even be known to the child, are often revealed to the therapist in the child's art products. Verbal and nonverbal clues, revealed while creating the artwork, are equally important to the interpretation. In addition, art provides a means to assess the strengths the child brings to therapy and to monitor the child's progress.

Children who choose art as their medium of expression will structure their time in a way that is meaningful to them and that will enable them to recognize and work through their problems. In addition to addressing current conflicts, the therapist may be able to assess the child's overall personality strengths and weaknesses and coping style. As a result, plans can be made for subsequent treatment that can maximize the child's overall growth and development. The process, form, and final art product provide the therapist with important clues about the child's mood and affect, conflicts, and coping styles.

In addition to free art, a number of formal assessment measures exist, but they require special training and skill to interpret. Interpretations regarding children's art, whether from structured tasks or free art, should be in the form of tentative hypotheses that may or may not be strengthened by other data. The child's artwork should be viewed not in isolation but in combination with everything else that is known about the child and his or her family.

Art therapy is recognized as a specialized discipline that requires special training and skill. However, even the novice therapist can incorporate art as a therapeutic medium in counseling. As children draw, paint, and sculpt, they express their creativity and build their confidence. They express themselves as unique individuals with their own unique perspective. This chapter presents art activities and techniques that can be incorporated into the work of the well-trained counselor or therapist who wishes to use art as another way to get to know children and their families better and to help them change and grow.

WISDOM ACCORDING TO ORTON

- *Art is a fun activity for children. Don't spoil it with questions or suggestions.*
- *Ask the child to explain the drawing to you if you don't know what it represents.*
- *Wait for the child to invite you to participate in any art activity. Once invited, participate with enthusiasm.*
- *Allow children to express their creativity as much as possible. If children want to make footprints with fingerpaint and it is possible to do it, allow them to do so.*
- *Even cleanup can be fun if it is shared.*

ORTON'S PICKS

Landgarten, H. B. (1981). *Clinical art therapy: A comprehensive guide.* New York: Brunner/Mazel.

This book, rich with examples, acquaints the reader with a structured, psychodynamic approach to art therapy. Of special interest are the chapters on family art therapy and group therapy with children. Family therapy features work with an intact family and with a group of single-parent families. These family art therapy groups help members clarify their communication, identify their own goals, and explore their concerns. A chapter on group therapy with children uses collages to facilitate self-expression and uses metaphors as catalysts for exploring feelings. Children are encouraged to make a commitment to change in these therapy groups.

Linesch, D. (Ed.). (1993). *Art therapy with families in crisis: Overcoming resistance through nonverbal expression.* New York: Brunner/Mazel.

This collection of works by various authors provides a family systems model that lends itself to the creative process. Individual chapters provide information on helping single-parent families, alcoholic families, and displaced families. A special chapter is devoted to using family art therapy with sexually abused children. This book is an excellent source of information for counselors who want to use art in conjunction with family therapy.

Oster, G. D., & Gould, P. (1987). *Using drawing in assessment and therapy: A guide for mental health professionals.* New York: Brunner/Mazel.

This handy manual is helpful for practitioners who want to understand more about using art in both assessment and therapy. In addition to giving the commonly accepted interpretations for human figure drawings, the authors offer some suggestions for interpreting other projective tests. An especially helpful chapter uses drawings as a group technique to help participants identify problems and goals, increase interaction, and build cohesiveness.

Rubin, J. A. (Ed.).(1987). *Approaches to art therapy: Theory and technique.* New York: Brunner/Mazel.

Each chapter, written by an expert in the field of art therapy, translates theory into technique. Psychodynamic, humanistic, behavioral, cognitive, and developmental approaches are all represented, and accompanying case examples clarify how each theory can be applied in practice. Although this book was written for art therapists, it is helpful to practitioners who want to use art techniques within their particular theoretical orientation.

CHAPTER 8   *Bibliotherapy*

> *For a story to work its magic in reaching a child's mind it must entertain, not through the front door of logic, but through the back door of intuition and feeling.*
> —SMITH (1989)

Books, poetry, plays, and other literary art forms have been used for centuries to make people think and wonder, laugh and cry, resolve and act. The fact that ancient civilizations valued books for their ability to add to the quality of life is best epitomized in an inscription over the library of Thebes that denoted it as "The Healing Place of the Soul" (Schrank & Engels, 1981). We have long used books and stories to create a love of reading, to quench the thirst for knowledge and to improve the quality of life, so the application of books to therapy is a logical one. The term *bibliotherapy* originates from the Greek words *biblion*, meaning "book" and *therapeio*, meaning "healing" (Moses & Zaccaria, 1978). This chapter describes bibliotherapy as a form of child therapy that can both teach and heal.

THE MEANING AND VALUE OF BIBLIOTHERAPY

What Is Bibliotherapy?

Bibliotherapy has been described in many ways by different writers. A broad definition was offered by Berry (1978), who described bibliotherapy as "a family of techniques for structuring an interaction between a facilitator and a participant...based on their mutual sharing of literature in the broadest sense possible" (p. 186). Berry went on to say that bibliotherapy utilizes all literary forms including, but not limited to, short stories, autobiographies, life histories, and personal diaries. The definition that best fits the art of using books in counseling with elementary school children is the one advanced by Morris-Vann (1979), who defined it as "guidance through reading" and described its usefulness as follows:

> Bibliotherapy is one technique which may help a child to face his (or her) feelings and reveal them, if not to others, possibly at least to (her- or) himself. It is the child who makes the most effort in a bibliotherapeutic program. He (or she) must read or listen, discuss, interpret and verbalize his (or her) insights and then integrate them into (her- or) himself. The facilitators (teacher and/or counselor) primarily function in a supplementary and supportive role. (p. 3)

Bibliotherapy can be used in a variety of settings including schools, clinics, and hospitals. In fact, bibliotherapy was first used as a therapeutic technique by psychotherapists and analysts who wanted to access their patient's innermost feelings, and it was used widely in psychiatric hospitals in the 1930s and 1940s (Gumaer, 1984). Summarizing the research in the field, Pardeck and Pardeck (1993) reported that - bibliotherapy is widely used by elementary school counselors, psychologists, psychiatrists, and medical doctors. They also found that the more experienced therapists are the ones most likely to use bibliotherapy as a technique in both counseling and therapy.

According to Berry (1978), there are three basic differences between the clinical and educational uses of bibliotherapy: the different roles and functions of the facilitator, the different characteristics of the participants, and the different goals of the therapeutic process. Clinicians usually assume the role of therapist to treat patients or clients who are experiencing a variety of problems and want to "get well." In educational uses, the facilitator is more likely to be a group leader who discusses various developmental problems with students who wish to attain an educational goal or to grow toward self-actualization. Bibliotherapy also has a special place in prevention. In school settings, it can be used to impart information, strengthen coping skills, and prevent some problems before they occur (Hollander, 1989).

In this chapter, bibliotherapy is presented as a technique that can be used by mental health practitioners to help children understand and cope with a variety of developmental *and* situational conflicts. Books are a valuable therapeutic tool that can be used in individual, small-group, or large-group sessions, depending on the type of conflict presented. Teachers and parents can also use books to help children gain knowledge, express feelings, and solve problems. Bibliotherapy implies the potential for both healing and growth in self-actualization.

The Value of Bibliotherapy

In a review of bibliotherapy, Gumaer (1984) summarized the work of four researchers and concluded that books promote children's socialization and help them gain insight into human behavior; examine and clarify their attitudes and values, focus on self-awareness, identify and solve problems, and relax and have fun. The following five values, summarized in Figure 8-1, highlight the major benefits of bibliotherapy.

Encourages free expression of problems and concerns that are sometimes hidden Psychoanalytically oriented therapists believe that children use repression and denial to deal with traumatic events; therefore, much of what is troubling them is often hidden from their conscious awareness. When a book is a perfect match to the child's problem, the child may be able to gain insight into a hidden conflict that has been causing anxiety. Especially valuable is the fact that some children may feel comfortable in talking about issues that they have kept secret in the past.

Helps children analyze their thoughts and behavior in relation to self and others When children are able to listen to and identify the thoughts and behaviors of the protagonist in a story, they are able to examine their own thoughts and behaviors as well. Some children conduct this self-examination silently and in the safety of their own thoughts, whereas others choose to share their insight with the counselor. In either case, the child benefits.

Teaches by providing information needed to solve problems and promotes positive thinking Children's literature now represents a broad range of topics that were formally taboo. Death, divorce, sex, drugs, and a variety of other concerns are

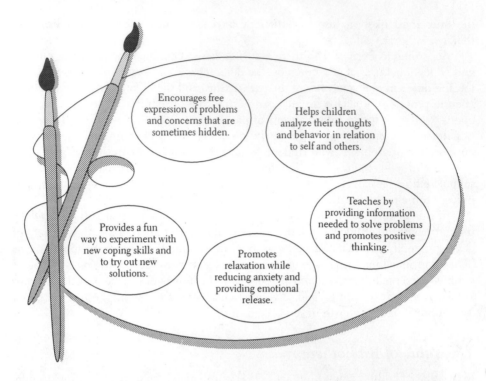

FIGURE 8-1 *The Value of Bibliotherapy as a Therapeutic Technique*

addressed in fiction and nonfiction books. Children who need information about the mysteries of life and death have access to it through books. Expectant mothers can read books about the unborn baby that will answer the dozens of questions that preschoolers have and that will address the child's concerns about his or her own relationship to mom once the sibling is born. Death, at the other end of the continuum, is discussed sensitively in numerous books for children, which provide insight into the feelings and reactions of other bereaved children. A thorough knowledge of the child's developmental level is needed to choose just the right book to use in discussing these topics and to choose the appropriate time.

Promotes relaxation while reducing anxiety and providing emotional release   One of the primary benefits of bibliotherapy is the emotional relief from anxiety children feel when they discover that other children have the same feelings and have lived through similar experiences. This knowledge reduces the loneliness and isolation troubled children typically feel and promotes a feeling of security and well-being.

Provides a fun way to experiment with new coping skills and to try out new solutions
Because children can read a variety of books on any topic that interests them, they can also try out new solutions to old problems by using their imagination. Often the mental rehearsal necessary to solve various problems is a solitary activity that the child does not share with anyone. Another added benefit for children is that not only is reading

informative, fun, and relaxing, but the child can carry this particular problem-solving technique into adulthood.

STEPS IN THE PROCESS OF HEALING WITH BOOKS

There are a number of steps in the healing process that occurs in bibliotherapy. Like all other therapeutic interventions, much depends on the relationship that exists between the child and the therapist. After establishing a warm and trusting relationship, the therapist needs to assess the child's conflict and decide whether individual or group counseling is most appropriate. Knowing the child well and previewing the literature will help the therapist match the book to the child, and a good match will help the child experience identification, catharsis, and insight. These experiences are necessary for problem resolution, growth, and change. (See Figure 8-2.)

Establish a Therapeutic Relationship

As with all other counseling endeavors, the counselor needs to establish an atmosphere of warmth and trust with the child. The same facilitating conditions of unconditional acceptance, genuineness, empathy, and trust discussed in Chapter 4 apply to bibliotherapy. To establish a therapeutic partnership with children, the therapist must be involved in the children's personal development and be aware of and understand the child's feelings, emotions, and behavior. This involvement means that the counselor genuinely cares about the children and their concerns. In addition to this awareness, the therapist must communicate this understanding and caring to the child. It is essential that the facilitator be an effective listener and become aware of the child's feelings, perceptions, values, and goals. By listening intently to both words and meanings, the therapist is able to get into the child's world and see the world through the child's eyes. This type of respect between child and counselor is something that takes time to develop and is hard won. It means that the counselor keeps the child's confidences and protects all members of the group as well.

Assess the Conflict and Choose the Counseling Method

The therapist must first determine whether the conflict is a common developmental concern of all children or whether it is a situational conflict experienced only by a few. It is important to determine whether or not the problem is one of crisis proportions that needs some sort of immediate resolution (see the case of Rayann later in this chapter) and to assess the severity of the problem as well as the impact that it is having on the child's overall functioning. The therapist decides whether the conflict warrants an individual session or a small-group session or whether it can be dealt with in a large-group activity. Intensely painful events that affect children should *always* be dealt with in individual sessions.

Small-group discussions can be used to talk about concerns that several children share. In small groups, it is advisable to include children who are close in age and developmental level and who are experiencing the same type of problem. Latency-age children may prefer to be in a same-sex group. Decisions can be made based on how

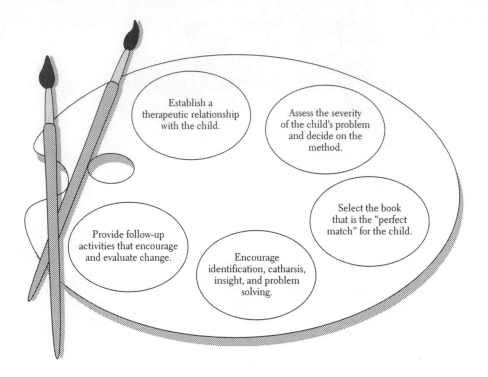

FIGURE 8-2   *Steps in the Process of Healing with Books*

well the counselor knows each child who might be included in the group. Large-group guidance activities with books should be reserved for children who can relate to common developmental concerns like feelings, friendships, or values clarification.

Select the Literature

Using the criteria for choosing books outlined in this section, select the book that is the "perfect match" for the child. Part of this match extends beyond the child's conflict to include the child's reading level, age, sex, and developmental level. Additional factors that need to be considered are the child's individual skills and talents as well as his or her coping skills. Counselors can capitalize on individual interests and special talents by planning additional activities such as art, drama, and other methods of artistic expression that will enhance the benefits of bibliotherapy.

Focus on the Child's Experiences

As children read or listen to the story, they experience identification, catharsis, and insight. Discussion about a particular book, combined with follow-up activities, can help children gain insight into their own thoughts, feelings, values, and behaviors. As a result of the insight gained through identifying with the characters in books, children often arrive at decisions that help them resolve conflicts and change their attitudes or behaviors (Morris-Vann, 1979; Pardeck & Pardeck, 1986, 1993; Schrank, 1982).

Identification   When the child and the book are a good match, the child can identify with the protagonist and may be able to identify family and friends among the book's characters. If the child and the protagonist share many of the same characteristics, such as, age, sex, race, feelings, and problems, the child will be able to imagine him- or herself as the character in the story. As a result of this identification, children will begin to experience vicariously the motivations and the conflicts of the story character. Some of the therapeutic purposes of identification through literature include the child's ability to recognize his or her own problems when reading about the problems of others and to mentally rehearse resolutions without interference.

As a result of identification, not only does the child begin to share the motivation and the conflicts of the story characters, but the story also becomes part of the child's personal experience. Children identify with the story's characters and through them, imagine experiencing the same emotions, ideas, decisions, and behaviors. This process is essential for the development of catharsis and insight, which eventually lead to problem solving and positive change. The child is able to think of alternatives, to solve problems, and to resolve conflicts just as the storybook character is able to do.

Catharsis   As children identify with the literature, they are able to experience catharsis. This psychological release often occurs when the characters in the story resolve their conflicts. When the character triumphs, the child's tensions are released as the child experiences the triumph vicariously. In addition, the child begins to develop insight into the character's experiences and recognizes that his or her own conflicts are understood. In a sense, the catharsis that literature encourages is a freeing experience that allows the child the opportunity to express, at least for a brief moment, tightly held emotions that might not find an outlet in any other setting. This release of the child's tensions paves the way for clarification and insight.

Insight   Through identification and catharsis, children develop an understanding into their own thoughts, feelings, and behaviors and are able to get a clearer picture of how others are behaving toward them. Children often develop this self-awareness in solitude, but they may use group discussion as an impetus (Morris-Vann, 1979; Schrank & Engels, 1981). Central to the development of insight is the child's ability to relive the experiences of the book character(s). Through books, children are able to analyze their own problems more objectively by identifying with the story and projecting emotions, thoughts, and actions onto the book's character(s). Through this process, the child is able to mentally step away from his or her own problems and focus on those portrayed in the book. This allows children to take an in-depth look at how the story character's problems relate to their own lives and to gain insight and understanding into their own conflicts. Such analysis often leads the way to greater awareness of self and a deeper understanding of self in relation to others. Insight enables children to alter their perceptions of events and contributes to more productive behavior.

Conflict resolution Bibliotherapy allows children "to see solutions to problems without the burden of in-depth verbalization, confrontation and interpretation, all strategies often critical to successful therapy" (Pardeck & Pardeck, 1993, p. 12). Children, with the help of the therapist, can first identify with the character in the book who is having similar problems, see how the character resolves the problem, and finally realize possible solutions to his or her own problems. Problem resolution and change in both attitude and behavior is a gradual process and depends on the development of insight. It is a process that cannot be hurried and requires the successful completion of all steps in the therapeutic process: developing rapport and a trusting relationship with the child, knowing the child and understanding the nature of the child's conflict, getting the "perfect match" between book and child, and allowing time for the child to vicariously experience the motivations and the conflicts of the characters in the books. Gradual changes in attitude or behavior are observed, often over a number of sessions, as children develop insight.

Follow-Up Activities

For some children, having the therapist read to them is enough for them to experience all the therapeutic benefits of bibliotherapy. In these instances, listening to the child's verbal responses and observing the child's behavior and facial expressions will give the therapist important clues about how the story has affected the child. Some children, however, need more help and encouragement in the form of follow-up activities that will evoke insight-producing discussions and help children toward conflict resolution. Activities that combine motor, cognitive, and verbal skills can enhance self-awareness and contribute to problem-solving skills (Pardeck & Pardeck, 1984, 1986).

Follow-up strategies that can be used in conjunction with bibliotherapy include art activities, story writing, drama, puppetry, and doll play. After reading or being read to, the child could dictate a story to the therapist, write a different ending to the story, compose a letter to one or more characters in the story, or role play certain story plots. Using various art materials, the child can produce collages, pictures, and sculptures that make the story characters relevant to their own lives. Puppet plays, complete with handmade puppets and scenery, have also been used as follow-up activities. The number and kinds of follow-up activities are limited only by the child's imagination and the therapist's willingness to try creative and innovative techniques.

SELECTING THE BOOKS

Most writers (Gumaer, 1984; Morris-Vann, 1979; Moses & Zaccaria, 1978; Pardeck & Pardeck, 1993) agree that three important keys to successful bibliotherapy are knowing the child, recognizing the child's conflict, and previewing the literature.

Knowing the Child

Bibliotherapy, like all other therapeutic interventions, relies on the therapist's knowledge of both the general developmental needs of children and the specific conflicts that can either enrich or impede their healthy growth. In addition to considering the child's age, sex, and developmental level, the bibliotherapist will want to assess the child's individual personality strengths and weaknesses. In making a "perfect match" between the child and the book, the bibliotherapist needs to consider the child's experience, feelings, interests, talents, and skills. Because children's reading interests are clearly related to their age and sex, it is best to choose a book in which the protagonist's characteristics are similar to the client's. An 8-year-old boy who has been molested by an uncle will find little in common with the story of a young girl who has been sexually abused by her father. This mismatch may embarrass the child and seriously diminish the story's therapeutic effect.

Knowing the child's reading interests, ability, and attention span helps the counselor choose just the right book. For example, *Dinosaurs Divorce: A guide for changing families* (Brown & Brown, 1986) appeals to young children through its humorous portrayal of a serious subject, whereas preadolescents will prefer a frank discussion about some of the problems that divorce creates for them. Finally, an understanding of the child's perception of the conflict and an assessment of his or her ability to cope can help the counselor choose the right books and the best therapeutic mode. Common developmental problems that most children encounter can be addressed in groups; intensely personal and private conflicts such as abuse or parental alcoholism call for individual sessions.

Recognizing the Child's Conflict

The course of normal development is not a smooth one, and even well-adjusted children slide back and reenact old problems. *Developmental conflicts* occur when children are thwarted in their attempts to master certain developmental tasks. Most conflicts are resolved without serious consequences to the child's development. Getting along with parents and siblings, understanding and controlling feelings, learning to play and share with peers, balancing the wish to be a free spirit with the need to conform, and eliminating behaviors that were more characteristic of an earlier stage of development, (such as temper tantrums, thumb sucking, and pouting) are common developmental problems young children experience. Older children often struggle with how to keep their individual identity intact while still being part of the peer group, learning to interact with peers of the opposite sex, clarifying personal values and attitudes, and becoming more independent. *Situational conflicts* such as child abuse and neglect, substance abuse, domestic violence, parent's divorcing or remarrying, and losing a parent or sibling to death may pose a more serious threat to the child's healthy growth and development. Counselors can help children gain insight into some of the problems associated with these conflicts and develop problem-solving skills by using bibliotherapy in conjunction with a wide variety of other techniques found in this text. Finally, books can be used to help children understand and cope with a range of physical, emotional, and learning disabilities. Stories and books that focus on how children cope with disabilities can help all participants develop empathy for and understanding of others.

Previewing the Literature

Bibliotherapists must have knowledge of children's literature. Counselors are expected to be familiar with the many children's books that relate to the developmental and situational conflicts of children and to take the time to read the book before either using it in bibliotherapy or recommending it to parents, teachers, or children. Pardeck & Pardeck (1993) concluded that therapists should select books that depict problems realistically, present a number of different solutions, and provide a well-balanced perspective. Morris-Vann (1979) suggested that counselors be aware of the conflicts that are expressed in the book; the characters' goals; and the opinions, moods, and ideas expressed. She pointed out that one should also be aware of the author's bias. Short stories are good choices because they are easy to read and to recall, and "the less time spent on the actual reading the better" (Morris-Vann, 1979, p. 6). Books with many large and colorful illustrations heighten reader interest and make excellent choices for bibliotherapy. Finally, it is important to choose books that match the child's reading level. Because independent reading level differs from instructional reading level, the beginning counselor should seek the help of the reading specialist or classroom teacher in determining the child's reading ability and ask the librarian about the reading level of various children's books. When a book is above the child's independent reading level, it is best to read the book aloud to the child.

Types of Books Used in Bibliotherapy

A variety of different types of books can be used in counseling, including works of fiction or nonfiction, fairy tales, picture books, and self-help books (Morris-Vann, 1979; Pardeck & Pardeck, 1993).

Short stories — fiction   Works of fiction that portray a specific conflict and the anxiety that often accompanies it are excellent choices for bibliotherapy. Children, either by reading or being read to, are able to identify with the fictional characters and develop empathy for their plight. At the same time, insight and self-understanding develops within the child, and a bond of trust is formed between the child and the therapist. By empathizing with the fictional character, the child is better able to understand and cope with his or her own conflict.

Biographies — nonfiction   Some nonfiction books are about children who are coping with problems as diverse as being adopted into a family and caring for a sibling with cerebral palsy. When nonfiction books are a good match to the child reader's characteristics and circumstances, he or she can identify with the child in the story who overcame conflicts, difficulties, or handicaps. Morris-Vann (1979) cautioned that child clients might have trouble identifying with central characters who are adults rather than children. In addition, nonfiction biographies might encourage the child to have unrealistic expectations of his or her own ability to deal with similar events.

Self-help books   Long a favorite of adult readers, the self-help concept is now appearing in children's literature. One such book is designed to help youngsters stop thumb sucking: *David Decides: No more thumb-sucking* (Heitler, 1985) has all the essential ingredients of a self-help book. It could be used in therapy with children who have a similar problem.

Fairy tales   Although fairy tales have been condemned of late because of their often violent and stereotypical content, Morris-Vann (1979) maintains that fairy tales continue to be a favorite way for children to learn about problem solving. Fairy tales offer simple portrayals of the universal problems and fears that concern children. They often offer a way for children to use their vivid imaginations as a tool for problem solving.

Picture books Children love picture books that have few words but many vivid and colorful images. These books, which often reflect the character's thoughts and feelings, can be interpreted by children in light of their own experiences. Children can project their inner feelings and perceptions onto the book characters, thereby making it easier for them to reveal their own conflicts in a nonthreatening way. These books provide a safe opportunity for children to tell their own stories in both individual and group therapy.

BIBLIOTHERAPY IN PRACTICE
Individual Session: Child Sexual Abuse

• • • The Case of Rayann

Family information Rayann T., age 9, is an only child who lives with her mother, age 28, and her mother's boyfriend, age 18. Rayann's father died about a year ago of a drug overdose. Rayann's mother reports that Rayann is very close to her maternal grandmother but sees her paternal grandmother only infrequently because Mrs. T. doesn't like her former mother-in-law. Mrs. T. says that Rayann does whatever she can to please and likes Mrs. T.'s new boyfriend so much that she calls him "Dad." She believes that Rayann is adjusting to her father's death and maintains that she is just a "little slow" and can't do any better in school.

Presenting problem Rayann was referred for counseling because the quality of her schoolwork has taken a sudden drop in the last six months. Reading has always been a struggle for Rayann, but now her fourth-grade teacher reports that Rayann has little interest in school and has stopped trying. Her teacher is also concerned because Rayann is always sad. Since her father died, Rayann has been quiet and withdrawn, clinging to teachers rather than interacting with classmates. Her teachers report that lately Rayann has been coming to school without bathing or changing clothes and that the other children shun her.

Counseling sessions On Rayann's first visit, it was difficult to ignore her poor hygiene and her very depressed affect. She didn't smile at first but seemed to enjoy the warmth and attention provided by the counselor as they played a board game and talked.

The following account is of the third session when Rayann decided that she would like the counselor to read to her.

> COUNSELOR: Rayann, I'm so glad to see you today. Is there something special that you would like to do with our time together? (*Gives the child a measure of control by letting her decide which medium of expression to use.*)

RAYANN: Would you read me one of these books?
COUNSELOR: I'd love to. Which book would you like to hear?

(Rayann chooses I Can't Talk About It, *by Doris Sanford. Perhaps it was the beautiful girl on the cover that caught her eye or the small print: A child's book about sexual abuse.)*

RAYANN: Can I sit beside you on the couch?
COUNSELOR: Yes, that's the best place to be when someone is reading.*(Counselor begins to read this beautifully written book as Rayann sits contentedly beside her. It is obvious that the child is enjoying the warmth and attention.)*

(The story continues to detail how Annie's father touches her private parts. Annie has tried to tell her mother three times and her mother ignores her or makes her feel guilty for not wanting to be with her father. Annie begins to tell a white dove at the beach how she feels.)

RAYANN: *(Sighs audibly but says nothing. At this point in the story, the counselor suspects that Rayann, like Annie, may be a victim of sexual abuse. She decides to give Rayann the choice of continuing or not).*
COUNSELOR: Do you want me to keep reading this story, Rayann?
RAYANN: Yes. *(Quietly.)* I want to see what Annie does.

(The counselor reads a passage where the mother in the story wishes that the father would get a job but cautions Annie not to repeat that because he might get angry and leave them. This gets a frightened reaction from Annie and she tells the reader again that her Dad does awful things to her and that she has started to wet the bed and have nightmares. At this point Rayann speaks.)

RAYANN: That's happening to me. *(This could mean several things. It could mean that she is wetting the bed, that she is having nightmares, or that her mother's boyfriend is sexually abusing her.)*
COUNSELOR: Some of these things are happening to you and you feel frightened like Annie does. *(Restates to clarify.)*
RAYANN: Yes, I get all scared cause my Mom always says that she hates it when Troy doesn't work and I *hate* it when he stays with me while Mom works. *(Rayann's response heightens the counselor's suspicions of sexual abuse and puts bedwetting and nightmares on the back burner for now. The focus should be on letting Rayann talk about the abuse.)*
COUNSELOR: You don't want to be alone with Troy because he is behaving like Annie's father in this book.
RAYANN: YES. *(Said very softly, almost inaudibly.)*
COUNSELOR: Troy hurts you and you are afraid to tell your mom.
RAYANN: Yes, yes, he hurts me real bad…I can't tell my mom cause he hits her and *she still likes him!*
COUNSELOR: Troy hurts your Mom and you, but in different ways. Let's talk first about how he hurts you.

RAYANN: He waits until my mom goes to work...and then he comes in to my room and says he has to tuck me in...he rubs my back...and then he pulls my nightgown up to my neck and touches me all over. (*Begins to sob.*)

COUNSELOR: (*The counselor holds the child until she is able to continue.*) You have been hurt for a long time now and it is good that you are telling someone.

RAYANN: And that's not all...(*Sobs.*) He...

COUNSELOR: He does other things that hurt you even more.

RAYANN: Yes, yes...sometimes he puts his wiener in me and I scream and cry. He says he'll kill me if I tell. (*Sobs.*)

COUNSELOR: (*Holds child, lets her vent her hurt and anger. It is best that the counselor let the child tell the whole horrifying story before the counselor will take the necessary steps to protect her and her Mom.*)

COUNSELOR: You've been keeping this a secret because you were afraid Troy would kill you or your mom.

RAYANN: (*Nods.*) Yes. (*Sobs.*) And one time...(*Hesitates.*) one time...I can't say it.

COUNSELOR: It is okay, no matter what it is. If you want to say it, maybe it needs to be said. (*The child raises another issue in the hopes that someone will let her explain it. Believing the child is essential to trust. Children don't usually make up lies about such serious matters as sexual abuse.*)

RAYANN: Well...one time Troy took...a movie.

COUNSELOR: He took a movie while he was hurting you?

RAYANN: (*Sobs.*) Yes...I didn't want to come to school...but Mom made me. Do you think she knows? (*A common concern of sexually abused children is that everyone at school will know about the abuse. They often feel dirty and purposely neglect their hygiene. Rayann has entered another area when she asks, "Do you think she knows?" Many abused children suspect that their parent knows and is failing to protect them or—worse yet—is siding with the abuser. The issue of how much her mother knows takes precedence for now.*)

COUNSELOR: Are you asking me if your mother knows about the movie? (*The counselor guesses that Rayann is deeply worried about how much her mother knows about the abuse and fears that her mother may have seen the movie.*)

RAYANN: Yes...

COUNSELOR: What do you think Rayann? Do you think your mother knows? (*Making an effort to find out what the child senses.*)

RAYANN: I dunno....One time I heard them fighting and Mom said, "I'll see your a— in jail if you touch her again."

COUNSELOR: So you think your Mom has some idea of what's been happening but doesn't make him leave.

RAYANN: Yeah, cause she's scared that he'll beat her up! He did lots of times. One time he said he'd kill her before he had to go to jail. (*The child is now in a terrible bind, for even if her abuser is punished, she fears he will make good on his threats.*)

COUNSELOR: So even though your Mom knows about what has been happening to you, at least a little bit, she is afraid to throw Troy out.

RAYANN: Yeah. I think she's as scared as I am. (*Often, children experience a lot of anger against the parent who knew about the abuse but didn't protect them. This anger is not dealt with in this session.*)

COUNSELOR: You're scared that if you tell and Troy has to leave, he'll hurt your Mom.

RAYANN: Yeah, and it will all be my fault. (*Sobs.*)

COUNSELOR: Rayann, none of this is your fault. You are just a little kid. This is something that a grown-up did and he is to blame, not you. (*To deflect the fact that abused children often find ways to blame themselves for what has happened to them.*)

RAYANN: I know…I guess.

COUNSELOR: Rayann, because Troy has hurt you in such a bad way I have to tell the people who protect children about this. Remember, when we first started our sessions, and I said I might have to tell someone if you were being hurt real bad?

RAYANN: Yes.

COUNSELOR: Well this is one of those times. Right now, I am going to tell the people who protect children so that you and your mom aren't hurt anymore. (*Counselors are mandated reporters in most states, and child protection and the police must be notified in this case. Counselors must learn the proper reporting procedures and must safeguard the child until child protection workers arrive. The authorities must be told all the facts of the session, including that a videotape was made.*)

RAYANN: (*Begins to cry softly again.*)

COUNSELOR: Something is worrying you Rayann, what is it?

RAYANN: Will I have to leave my Mom?

COUNSELOR: I can't say for sure, but usually when this happens, a child gets to stay with mom or with Grandma. (*Mention of her Grandma brings a faint smile to a tearful face.*) It is Troy that is going to have to leave your house. (*Answering all the child's questions as honestly as possible helps her know that she can trust some adults.*)

COUNSELOR: You don't have to keep your feelings a secret anymore. You can talk to me anytime about anything that bothers you. (*The child has not had an opportunity to express all the myriad details of her ordeal, nor has she had a chance to express all her hurt and angry feelings. It is good to let her know that she will still have lots of other opportunities to talk.*)

RAYANN:	Good, because even if I live with my Grandma, I'll still come and see you.
COUNSELOR:	I'll always be happy to see you. (*Giving a hug for comfort and support.*) Would you like to play a fun game while we wait for Mrs. W. to come from the place that protects children?
RAYANN:	Yes. ●

● ● ● *Small-Group Session: Coping with Divorce*

Small Group: Seven 6th-Grade Students

Small discussion groups that deal with particular childhood crises, such as divorce and separation of parents, can use books in a number of ways. Books can serve as an ice-breaker, a springboard to discussion, or as a way to focus on particular issues in a nonthreatening way. Before facilitating any small-group discussion on any crisis topic, it is essential to get permission to participate from both parents and children. Most parents are willing to help their children through this difficult time and want to have their child included in such a group. Groups can be found in school guidance programs, church groups, therapeutic groups as part of a private practice, or as part of special organizations designed to help kids cope with specific issues such as divorce (Parents Without Partners). Regardless of the setting, counselors and therapists can use books to stimulate discussion and get everyone involved.

For the small-group session on coping with divorce, two excellent books to help get the discussion started are *The Divorce Workbook: A Guide for Kids and Families* (Ives, Fassler, & Lash, 1985) and *Changing Families: A Guide for Kids and Grown-ups* (Fassler, Lash, & Ives, 1988). The first book deals with the process of divorce itself—the fighting, the separation, the legal issues, and the feelings associated with the break-up of the family. The second book deals with many of the same issues but adds the extra adjustments necessitated when divorced parents get a new boyfriend or girlfriend or when they remarry.

Small Group of Sixth-Graders

The following is an example of a small group discussion with 7 sixth-grade students, who have recently experienced a family breakup. The discussion focuses on the positive and negative aspects of divorce and separation. In *The Divorce Workbook* (Ives, Fassler, & Lash, 1985), the following lead is offered as a way to get the discussion started: "Sometimes a separation is a hard thing to talk about. It's not always easy to tell people that your mom and dad are not living together" (p. 28). The counselor can then ask, "What are some of the things that you remember about your parents' divorce or separation?"

CHILD 1:	It was hard. When my dad and mom split, I almost died. I never knew it was that bad. Maybe I didn't know everything.
CHILD 2:	My dad and mom were fighting all the time. I didn't like it when dad would come home drunk and fight with mom.

CHILD 3: Dad started staying away and I was scared something bad was going to happen. I thought he was mad at me 'cause I forgot to take out the garbage.

COUNSELOR: Some of you have mentioned that your parents fought a lot before they separated, and Tim worried that it was his fault. Does anyone else worry that you may have caused your parents' breakup?

CHILD 4: Yeah, once the dog made a mess, and I was busy and forgot to clean it up and my dad yelled at me about my dog. Me and mom were crying and he left and didn't come back.

COUNSELOR: And you thought it was your fault.

CHILD 4: Yeah, if I had done what I promised, he wouldn't have left.

COUNSELOR: A lot of kids feel that way. If only they had done this or that, the divorce would never have happened. This book says that kids can't cause a divorce and they can't keep their parents together either. Do you agree with that?

CHILD 1: I thought that I could keep them together, but I was wrong. One time, after the divorce, we all went to a wedding and my dad asked my mother to dance and my brother said, "Oh, boy! They're going to get back together" but it didn't happen.

CHILD 6: It's my fault that they got a divorce, I know cause my Grandma said so.

COUNSELOR: It must have hurt when your grandmother said that.

CHILD 6: Yeah, I felt bad 'cause they yelled a lot at each other about me....I guess I have done a lot of bad things.

COUNSELOR: Joe's grandmother didn't know what we know. Kids can't cause a divorce and they can't keep their parents together.

CHILD 5: Maybe it wasn't my fault; maybe dad will come back and we can live together again.

CHILD 7: I did that too. I hoped we would all be together again but when my mother brought Ralph home, it was over.

CHILD 4: When my dad married Sue, I didn't like her. She just wasn't like mom.

COUNSELOR: When parents remarry a lot of things change. We've talked a lot about some of the bad feelings that happen when parents get divorced. Are there any good things about divorce and remarriage?

CHILD 6: Well, there's no fighting anymore and my mom plays with us kids more now.

CHILD 3: Yeah, its not so bad now. I still have to clean my room and sometimes I forget but mom doesn't yell at me. I don't think I would like a stepdad.

CHILD 2: My new family is cool. I have two brothers and one sister and at Christmas I got a lot more presents.

CHILD 7: When I see my dad on Saturdays, we do a lot of neat stuff and he buys me anything I want.

COUNSELOR: It sounds like there are happy as well as sad times when parents get divorced. Next time we'll talk more about both these things. •

• • • *Large-Group Activity: Dealing with Feelings*

Books can be used in large-group activities to address developmental as well as preventive guidance issues. In this instance, *Every Kid's Guide to Handling Feelings* by Joy Berry (1987) was used to talk about both comfortable and uncomfortable feelings. The purpose of this particular large-group guidance activity is to get children involved in talking about the emotions they experience everyday that help them to cope. The counselor starts the group by asking the children to talk about some of the times when they feel love, pride, joy, and contentment. With comfortable emotions as a cushion, the counselor can then direct the group in a discussion about some of the more unpleasant emotions such as fear, anger, frustration, failure, jealousy, and humiliation.

Large Group of 25 Second-Graders

The following is an example of the discussion of feelings in a second-grade class. Each counselor will have his or her own unique way of facilitating the discussion and can use the book in a number of creative ways. Because children can identify with this book and because it is delightfully illustrated, some facilitators may want to use it in its entirety. Others may want to use it as a starting point, let the children determine where the discussion will go, and then go back to the book after the children explore ways to cope with various emotions.

COUNSELOR: Today we're going to talk about two kinds of feelings—good feelings and bad feelings. Good feelings are love, happiness, pride, and feeling safe. These are feelings that make us feel comfortable and good. Close your eyes and think of ways to end this sentence: I feel good when…

CHILD: I get a hug from my mom.

COUNSELOR: That's a great feeling. You might say that is *love.* (*The counselor might write L-O-V-E on the blackboard and put lots of hearts around it.*) Can anyone else tell me when they feel loved?

CHILD: When my puppy licks my face.

COUNSELOR: Yes, that's a great example. Anyone else?

CHILD: When Grandma makes cookies.

COUNSELOR: These are all great examples of love. Can anyone think of a time when you feel proud of yourself, like when you say, "Wow, I did a good job at that!"

CHILD: When I get an A in spelling.

COUNSELOR: That's a great example. Anyone else?

CHILD: When I do dishes and don't break any.

COUNSELOR: Good.

CHILD: When I get good papers.

Counselor:	Okay. Now what happens to your feelings when you get a D or an F?
Child:	That's bad...my brother gets those.
Counselor:	What do you think you should do if you get an F?
Child:	Get a spanking. That's what my brother got.
Counselor:	What might be something else that you could do.
Child:	Do your work better.
Child:	Get help from your Mom.
Counselor:	Those are all good ideas. The book says that it is best if you work harder, practice more, and keep trying. These ideas could be used if you lose at a game as well as if you get a bad grade. The important thing is not to give up on yourself. You can do it!
Counselor:	We have just talked about feelings of failure. Sometimes we have other feelings like when we get real angry with someone. Can you give me some examples of when you get angry?
Child:	When my brother picks on me, I get mad.
Counselor:	What are some things that kids do when they get mad?
Child:	They cry and yell...
Child:	They hit things...like brothers.
Child:	They break toys and stuff...
Counselor:	Sometimes kids get so angry that they hurt themselves and other people. Do you think this is a good idea?
Child:	Yes, if your brother bugs you, hit him!
Child:	No...you might hurt somebody.
Counselor:	What might be some other ways to get your anger out but not hurt anyone.
Child:	Tell your teacher...
Child:	Tell your mom if someone makes you mad.
Counselor:	It is good to tell someone that you are angry. What else can you do?
Child:	You could talk to your sister if she makes you mad. That's what my mom says.
Counselor:	Good idea! Talking is better than fighting because you won't get hurt that way.
Child:	Yeah, but my brother hits me first.
Counselor:	Sometimes kids don't know how to handle their feelings. This book, *Every Kid's Guide to Handling Feelings,* suggests that there are four steps to handling uncomfortable feelings. Let's talk about these. *Step 1* is to face it: Ask yourself, "What do I feel?" *Step 2* is to accept it: Try to understand why you feel this way. *Step 3* is decide what to do: Decide what action you need to take to feel better. *Step 4* is do it: Do what you have decided to do.
Counselor:	Let's suppose that you were feeling very lonely and you didn't have anyone at home to play with. What could you do to feel better?
Child:	You could go to your Aunt's house to play.
Child:	You could call someone.

CHILD: Play with your sister or brother.
COUNSELOR: These are all good ideas. It is better to do something than to sit and cry or feel all alone. Our time is up today, but you have had some very good ideas about dealing with feelings. Remember the four steps. We will talk about some of our other feelings next time. •

SUGGESTED BOOKS FOR COUNSELING AND THERAPY

Every book recommended here has been carefully read and selected for use in this section on bibliotherapy. These outstanding works can be used in counseling children individually, and many are excellent choices for counselors and teachers to use with groups of children as well. This list has been divided into five sections: "On Growing Up" includes books about situations and relationships that all children experience in the process of growing up. "Common Developmental Concerns" includes books about thoughts, feelings, and behaviors that may or may not become problems. Although these potential problem areas usually do not develop enough to need remediation, these books can be used in preventive and developmental counseling. "Understanding Parents and Families" includes books about all kinds of families and some of the difficulties children experience adjusting to them. Helping children understand and cope with changing family configurations and living arrangements is an important function for today's child therapist, and this list of books should help. "Childhood Crises" includes many excellent books in the areas of child abuse, drug abuse, violence, chronic illness and death. Some of the most current and troubling topics in this area are covered in children's books from 1990 to the present. Finally, selections in "Dealing with Disabilities" stress the "abilities" in disabilities and talk about a number of physical, mental, emotional, and learning disabilities that challenge many of our children.

On Growing Up

All children everywhere are concerned about the birth of a new baby, their relationships with their brothers and sisters, and being loved and protected by their families. Beyond their families, children are busy defining who they are and how they fit into the larger world. Like all of us, they want the friendship, love, and respect of others and want to be accepted for who they are. These are a few of the books that we found that address these general, very basic human concerns.

Banish, R. (1982). *I want to tell you about my baby*. Berkeley, CA: Wingbow Press. (46 pages)(Gr. K–3). A little boy explains his mother's pregnancy and childbirth, the care that the newborn needs, and his feelings about his baby brother. Excellent photographs help parents tell young children about the miracle of birth and allow children the opportunity to express the feelings they have about having a new baby.

Hamanaka, S. (1994). *All the colors of the earth*. New York: Morrow Junior Books. (unpaged)(Gr. K–6). The book jacket says it all: "With soaring text and majestic art, Sheila Hamanaka celebrates the dazzling diversity of children laughing, loving, and glowing with life. Multiethnic heritage is presented in a way that helps children take pride in their differences and to see humanity reflected in many colors."

Kurtz, J. (1990). *I'm calling Molly*. (Pictures by I. Trivas.) Niles, IL: Albert Whitman. (unpaged)(Preschool–Gr. 2). Preschoolers Christopher and Molly are best friends and neighbors. Having just learned to use the telephone, Christopher calls Molly and uses various ploys to get her to play with him. She refuses because she is engaged in dress-up play with another friend. Later she calls. Great story for small children.

Miles, B. (1975). *Around and around love*. New York: Alfred A. Knopf. (unpaged)(Gr. K–6). Magnificent photographs coupled with Betty Miles' powerful words about *love* give this book a memorable place in everyone's heart. A must read for everyone who knows about the many meanings of love or wants to.

Rosenberg, M. B. (1991). *Brothers and sisters*. (Photographs by G. Ancona.) New York: Clarion Books. (32 pages)(Gr. K–3). This book follows the ever-changing and growing relationships between brothers and sisters in three different families. Jessica is the oldest of three sisters, Justin is the youngest of two boys, and Joseph is in the middle of two sisters. All three describe their feelings about each other from their unique perspective. Good book to use in developmental guidance groups.

Senisi, E. B. (1993). *Brothers and sisters*. New York: Scholastic. (unpaged)(Gr. K–3). This pictorial essay of brothers and sisters examines the interaction between siblings of all races and ages, including those yet to be born. Siblings—created by birth or adoption, toddlers or teens, agreeing or disagreeing—have a special bond. Use with young children.

Simon, N. (1981). *Nobody's perfect, not even my mother*. (Pictures by D. Leder.) Niles, IL: Albert Whitman. (unpaged)(Gr. K–3). A warm, well-illustrated story that highlights the fact that we are all human and that no one is perfect. It points out that we are all good at some things, but no one is perfect at everything.

Stanton, E. & Stanton, H. (1978). *Sometimes I like to cry*. (Illus. by R. Leyden.) Chicago: Albert Whitman. (unpaged)(Preschool–Gr. 2). This book gives a number of occasions when children cry and when tears are appropriate. Joey tells us that he cried when he cut his finger, when he was not invited to a party, and when the cat ate his hamster. Mothers cry sometimes too. Use when talking about the emotions that we all have.

Common Developmental Concerns

As children grow and develop, they learn to cooperate with others and to operate within the framework of socially acceptable behavior set by their family, school, and the broader community. Some of the difficulties that children have accomplishing these goals are addressed, sometimes lovingly and with humor, in the books in this section. Many of the thoughts, feelings, and behaviors that parents and teachers are concerned about may or may not develop into problems that require remediation. However, parents, teachers, and counselors need to help children cope with developmental difficulties and help them to continue to grow and develop in healthy ways.

Berry, J. (1987). *Every kid's guide to handling disagreements*. Chicago: Children's Press. (48 pages)(Gr. 3–6). Differences of opinion and the disputes they cause are carefully examined and explained. Delightful cartoons illustrate each point with humor as they lead the reader through the preadolescent group's experience of planning a club party. Steps to conflict resolution are presented.

Berry, J. (1987). *Every kid's guide to handling feelings*. Chicago: Children's Press. (48 pages)(Gr. K–6). This delightfully illustrated book deals with feelings that everyone has. It teaches children about common comfortable and uncomfortable feelings and how to handle the uncomfortable ones. Great book to use in developmental counseling.

Berry, J.(1987). *Every kid's guide to understanding nightmares*. Chicago: Children's Press. (48 pages)(Gr. K–3). This guide to the common nightmares of childhood helps children understand why they have nightmares and how they can both understand and handle them. Delightful cartoons illustrate the emotions that are played out in nightmares and how circumstances in everyday life can be the basis for bad dreams. Ways to prevent nightmares are an important part of the book.

Berry, J. (1984). *Let's talk about disobeying*. (Illus. by J. Costanza.) Chicago: Children's Press. (30 pages)(Gr. K–3). This delightfully illustrated book talks about a clashing of wills between a little girl and her parents. A major weakness is that the parent is always saying, "I told you" and the child's viewpoint is not given. However, it would still be a good book to start a discussion with children, especially in groups.

Clifton, L. (1975). *My brother fine with me*. (Illus. by M. Barnett.) New York: Holt, Rinehart & Winston. (unpaged)(Gr. 1–3). This tale of sibling rivalry is told with humor, warmth, and tenderness through Lucille Clifton's vibrant prose. Johnetta's brother Baggy plans to run away, and Johnetta is more than pleased until she realizes that there will be no one around to make motor sounds at night or to play with.

Crary, E. (1992). *Dealing with feelings: I'm frustrated*. Seattle, WA: Parenting Press. (30 pages)(Preschool–Gr. 3). Alex wants to roller skate like his brother and sister, but he falls down whenever he tries to stand up. This book models recommended behavior for helping a child learn to cope with frustration and move on to achievement.

Heitler, S. (1985). *David decides: No more thumb-sucking*. (Pictures by Paula Singer.) Denver, CO: Reading Matters.(unpaged)(Gr. K and up). This is a story of David's thumb sucking and his search for ways to quit. First he consults his brothers and sisters and then decides to quit sucking his thumb so he won't get crooked teeth, be made fun of at school, or have socks put on his hands! *David Decides* is a self-help book for children who want to stop thumb sucking that includes an informative 25 page guide for parents.

Palmer, P. (1977). *Liking myself*. (Illus. by Betty L. Shondeck.) San Luis Obispo, CA: Impact Publishers. (80 pages)(Gr. K–4). *Liking Myself* is an introduction to feelings, self-esteem, and assertiveness for children from ages 5 to 9. Charmingly illustrated, this book provides blank pages for the young reader to write or draw a response.

Palmer, P. (1977). *The mouse, the monster, and me.* (Illus. by Betty L. Shondeck.) San Luis Obispo, CA: Impact Publishers. (78 pages)(Gr. 3–6). Assertiveness concepts for youngsters age 8 and up are explained using nonassertive "mice" and aggressive "monsters." This book offers young readers an opportunity to develop a sense of personal rights and responsibilities, to become appropriately assertive, and to gain a greater sense of self worth. A teacher's guide is available.

Powell, R. (1992). *How to deal with parents.* Mahwah, NJ: Troll Associates. (unpaged)(Gr. K–3). This delightful book is a practical guide to dealing with parents in such areas as mealtime, riding in the car, watching television, and bedtime. Behaviors are modeled that will help everyone get along and be considerate of others. Could be used in play therapy or as a group technique for younger children.

Simon, N. (1974). *I was so mad!* Niles, IL: Albert Whitman. (40 pages)(Gr. K–2). Everyone can relate to the anger-producing scenarios described by the children in this book. Here anger is recognized and validated as an emotion that most of us might share in many situations.

Simon, N. (1976). *Why am I different?* Niles, IL: Albert Whitman. (31 pages)(Gr. K–2). Everyday individual and family differences are accepted joyfully in this straightforward, nonjudgmental book. Presented to evoke discussion, the common experiences represented are geared to build a sense of self-respect and respect for others.

Wilhelm, H. (1986). *Let's be friends again.* New York: Crown Publishers. (unpaged) (Preschool–Gr. 3). It all starts when a younger sister sets her brother's pet turtle free, causing him to get so angry that he imagines many ways to punish her for his loss. How the boy learns to handle his terrible anger and forgive his sister is a satisfying glimpse of his first steps toward maturity. Told with warmth and humor, this is a story that could be read to young children.

Understanding Parents and Families

As discussed in Chapter 1, many of today's children are growing up in families that bear scant resemblance to those represented on 1950s sitcoms like *Leave it to Beaver.* Even shows that depicted blended families, such as the *Brady Bunch,* or extended families like *The Waltons,* tended to gloss over some of the conflicts inherent in different family constellations. In reality, children live in a variety of family structures with adoptive parents, divorced parents, single parents, stepparents, grandparents, gay parents, or homeless parents. They need to know that other children live in similar situations and that there are advantages as well as disadvantages to living in any type of family group. The ups and downs of these different lifestyles are eloquently portrayed in the following books.

Adoptive Families and Foster Families

Anderson, D., & Finne, M. (1986). *Jason's story: Going to a foster home.* Minneapolis, MN: Dillion Press. (45 pages)(Gr. 1–4). When Jason was a baby, his teen mother neglected him so he was placed with a foster family that loved him as their own. At age 2, his birth mother took him to live with her but later became abusive, so Jason was placed again in a different home. He felt sad and lonely and believed he was a bad boy. After Jason and his mom get help, Jason returns to live with his mom.

Bannish, R., (with Jennifer Jordan-Wong)(1992). *A forever family*. New York: Harper Collins. (43 pages)(Gr. K–3). Eight-year-old Jennifer Jordan-Wong describes her adoption by a family after four years of living as a foster child with two different families. Told from a child's point of view, this story emphasizes the importance of belonging to a family forever. This is especially true for children in multiple foster homes.

Bunin, S. (1976). *Is that your sister?* New York: Random House. (35 pages)(Gr. 2–6). The Bunin family already had two adopted children when they adopted Catherine, who had been in a foster home for only a few months. This book gives a child's view of adoption in a transracial family and would be a good book to recommend to parents.

Girard, L.W. (1989). *We adopted you, Benjamin Koo*. (Illus. by L. Shute.) Niles, IL: Albert Whitman. (unpaged)(Gr. 2–6). Benjamin Koo, adopted as an infant from Korea, soon learns that even though he looks different, he is still his mother's child. Not everything runs smoothly, but he learns to cope with the few mean kids at school because he has a lot of people who love him. This is a heartwarming story about keeping your own culture while being loved and accepted into a different one.

Livingston, C. (1978). *Why was I adopted?* (Illus. by A. Robins.) Secaucus, NJ: Lyle Stuart, Inc. (unpaged)(Gr. 1 and up). A delightful book for young children that gives the facts of adoption with love and illustrations. Answers all of the most frequently asked questions about adoption and uses humor that appeals to everyone. Highly recommended for use by counselors and parents with young children.

London, J. (1993). *A koala for Katie: An adoption story*. (Illus. by C. Jabar.) Morton Grove, IL: Albert Whitman. (unpaged)(Gr. K–3). Katie asks countless questions about her birth mother. Katie's mother provides warm and honest explanations about how she grew inside her birth mother and that she was loved very much. Katie pretends that she has adopted a stuffed koala and provides mothering for her new "baby" when its mother is not able to.

Miller, K. A. (1994). *Did my first mother love me? A story for an adopted child*. (Illus. by Jami Moffett.) Buena Park, CA: Morning Glory Press. (unpaged) (Preschool–Gr. 3). Morgan's adoptive mother reassures her that she is loved by reading a letter written by her birth mother. In clear, understandable, and loving language, the letter reveals all of the good things that Morgan's birth mother wished for her but could not give her. The book includes a section: "Talking with your child about adoption."

Rosenberg, M. (1984). *Being adopted*. (Photographs by G. Ancona.) New York: Lothrop, Lee and Shepard Books. (unpaged)(Gr. 1–4). Seven-year-old Rebecca, 10-year-old Andrei, and 8-year-old Karin are adopted children in transracial or transcultural families. Photographed with their adopted parents and siblings, they each relate their personal stories, fears, and feelings about adoption.

Rosenberg, M. (1989). *Growing up adopted*. New York: Bradury Press. (95 pages)(Gr. 4 and up). This book features interviews with children and adults about the adoption experience. Each story is unique but the sense of family is the common theme. Excellent for older children.

Sobol, H. L. (1984). *We don't look like our Mom and Dad.* (Photographs by P. Agre.) New York: Coward-McCann. (32 pages)(Gr. 1–4). This moving study, in words and photographs, shows how the Levin family shares their love with their two Korean-born adopted sons, 10-year-old Eric and 11-year-old Joshua. Occasionally, the boys feel different from other kids and wonder about their birth mothers, but most of the time they don't think about being Korean. They are too busy being kids.

Stewart, G.(1989). *The facts about adoption.* New York: Crestwood House. (45 pages) (Gr. 5–6). This book discusses the process by which people adopt, who adopts, sources for adoptive children and other aspects of adoption as seen from both children's and parents' perspectives. Gives an interesting history about adoption and defines transracial as well as transcultural adoptions.

Homeless Families

Bunting, E. (1991). *Fly away home.* (Illus. by R. Himler.) New York: Clarion Books. (32 pages)(Gr. K–3). The airport is the only home that Andrew and his dad have. Although it's warmer and safer than the streets, Andew longs for the way life used to be before his mom died. He longs for a home of his own. This poignant story, told with hope but no happy ending, is beautifully illustrated and is a must read for all children. Could be used with groups to promote understanding of homelessness.

Single-Parent and Stepfamilies

Boyd, L. (1990). *Sam is my half-brother.* New York: Viking. (unpaged)(Preschool– Gr. 3). When Hessie's dad and stepmother have a new baby, Hessie is afraid the baby is going to get all of the attention. Slowly, Hessie sees that she isn't being replaced and she actually begins to like Sam. This is a delightful book about the relationships between stepchildren and stepmothers and helps children identify some of the common feelings that children have in stepfamilies. For ages 3 to 8.

Brown, L. & Brown, M. (1986). *Dinosaurs divorce: A guide for changing families.* Boston, MA: Little Brown. (unpaged)(Preschool–Gr. 3). *Dinosaurs Divorce* helps youngsters deal with the confusions, misconceptions, and anxieties that often arise when parents decide not to live together any more. Delightfully illustrated, the book makes it easy for children to project their own thoughts, fears, and feelings onto the dinosaurs and find new ways to cope with the many new situations and difficulties that divorce brings.

Fassler, D., Lash, M. & Ives, S. (1988). *Changing families: A guide for kids and grown-ups.* Burlington, VT: Waterfront Books. (179 pages)(Preschool–Gr. 6). This book uses a workbook format to help children deal with some of the difficult transitions they experience when parents separate, divorce, and remarry. It can be used by parents, teachers, and counselors. I recommend it as a therapeutic tool in individual and group sessions with children to help facilitate discussion about sensitive topics and to offer support and reassurance that the child's experiences are similar to those of other children. For ages 4 to 12.

Forrai, M. S. (1977). *A look at divorce.* (Text by M. Pursell.) Minneapolis, MI: Lerner Publications. (unpaged)(Gr. 1–3). Maria Forrai uses outstanding photographs accompanied by text to describe the problems parents and children face when a divorce occurs. It features excellent photographs that tap into the children's particular feelings about the changes that divorce has brought to their lives.

Hazen, B. S. (1983). *Two homes to live-in: A child's-eye view of divorce.* (Illus. by P. Luks.) New York: Human Sciences Press. (unpaged)(Preschool–Gr. 3). This book discusses divorce from a child's point of view. Nicely illustrated, it deals with feelings of fear when parents fight, loss when they leave, and anger when they date new people. It also deals with the little girl's wish that her parents will remarry and her realization that it won't come true.

Hodder, E. (1990). *Understanding social issues: Stepfamilies.* New York: Gloucester Press. (59 pages)(Gr.6 and up). This book is designed for older children and talks about all the issues that involve children when divorced parents remarry. Stepfamilies are confronted by many problems that intact families do not have to face. All these emotions and difficult situations are discussed. Excellent points could be used to stimulate group discussion.

Ives, S., Fassler, D., Lash, M. (1985). *The Divorce workbook: A guide for kids and families.* Burlington, VT: Waterford Books. (145 pages)(Preschool–Gr.7). An excellent workbook that covers the important points of divorce from a child's point of view. It could be used to facilitate discussion on all aspects of divorce in either individual or group sessions with children. In addition to use in bibliotherapy, themes in the book could be used in conjunction with other expressive techniques such as play, art, music, and drama.

Mazzenga, I. B. (1989). *Compromise or confrontation.* (Drawings by A.C. Green.) New York: Franklin Watts. (90 pages)(Gr. 6 and up). Good guide for dealing with difficult situations that may accompany divorce and remarriage. Helpful in understanding how to reach successful compromises with adults. Includes tips on how to listen, when to respond, and knowing when it's better not to respond. Excellent book for older kids as they approach puberty.

Rofes, E. E. (Ed.). (1981). *The kid's book of divorce: By, for and about kids,* by The Unit of Fayerweather Street School. Lexington, MA: The Lewis Publishing Co. (122 pages)(Gr. 2 and up). As only young people can tell it, this book portrays the intense feelings and lifestyle changes that usually accompany the breakup of a family and offers advice on coping. Legal issues, letting go of feelings, and not taking sides are some major highlights. This book ends by dispelling some of the common perceptions about children of divorced parents. Can be used in group counseling.

Stanek, M. (1985). *All alone after school.* (Illus. by R. Rosner.) Niles, Illinois: Albert Whitman. (unpaged)(Gr. 1–4). This story is about a young boy who becomes a latchkey kid when his single mom has to work and can't afford a babysitter. He is carefully drilled in all the right things to do, but he still feels lonely and sometimes a little afraid. Soon he develops confidence in his ability to handle his homework and chores on his own.

Stanek, M. (1981). *I won't go without a father.* (Illus. by E. Mill.) Chicago: Albert Whitman. (unpaged)(Gr. 1–3). Steve refuses to go to the school open house because he doesn't have a father. He feels cheated and thinks he is the only one with this problem. Warm and caring adults help Steve realize he is not alone. Great book for helping children in one-parent families realize that extended family members and friends can provide love and support.

Watson, J. W., Switzer, R., & Hirschberg, J.C. (1988). *Sometimes a family has to split up.* (Pictures by C.B. Smith.) New York: Crown Publishers. (Unpaged) (Preschool–Gr. 1). This very simple, nonjudgmental story allows children to understand that they are not alone with their feelings about their parents growing further apart, arguing, and perhaps even separating. It provides a springboard for discussion of these important issues.

Willhoite, M. (1990). *Daddy's roommate.* Boston, MA: Alyson Publications. (unpaged)(Preschool–Gr. 1). This is the story of a little boy whose parents get divorced and he finds out that his dad has a male roommate. The child, with the help of his mother, is able to maintain a loving relationship with his father while at the same time understanding that love can be expressed in many ways.

Childhood Crises

As discussed in Chapter 3, children in the 21st century face a variety of crisis situations. Many crises, like child abuse, are centuries old; others, like violence at school or AIDS, are relatively recent. Of all of the crises that affect children, one of the most devastating is child abuse, which is the root of many long-term problems that counselors and therapist see every day. Child abuse is directly linked to other crises, such as parental substance abuse and domestic violence. The violence occurring against children in their homes has spilled out into the schools, neighborhoods, and streets and affects everyone. This section lists books on the crises of violence as well as on the crises of loss manifested in death, suicide, and illness, including AIDS.

Child Abuse

Anderson, D., & Finne, M. (1986). *Liza's story.* Minneapolis, MN: Dillion Press. (45 pages)(Gr. 1–4). Liza, who is often dirty and hungry, causes big trouble one night and the police are called. This is how they discover that Liza is being neglected and left alone while her father works. A counselor helps Liza and her father get closer, and getting a housekeeper solves the neglect problem.

Anderson, D., & Finne, M. (1986). *Margaret's story.* Minneapolis, MN: Dillion Press. (45 pages)(Gr. 1–4). This is the story of a little girl who was sexually molested by a neighbor and had to go to court. It explains what happens after abuse is discovered and the police are involved. Margaret is helped through the court process by a friendly lawyer and supportive parents. Excellent for children who may need to go to court.

Anderson, D., & Finne, M. (1986). *Michael's story.* Minneapolis, MN: Dillion Press. (45 pages)(Gr. 1–4). Michael, emotionally abused by his parents, believes that he is stupid and unloved. A supportive counselor helps him and his parents work through some of the problems they are having. Michael's parents begin to see that their harsh words are hurting Michael, and they try to change.

Anderson, D., & Finne, M. (1986). *Robin's story.* Minneapolis, MN: Dillion Press. (45 pages)(Gr. 1–4). Robin is being physically abused by her mother and one day gets hurt. Although her mother made her promise not to tell, Robin tells, goes to the doctor and later sees the school social worker. Robin and her mother both get the help they need. This book provides children with information about what happens *after* they tell.

Girard, L.W. (1984). *My body is private*. (Pictures by R. Pate.) Niles, IL: Albert Whitman. (unpaged)(Preschool–Gr. 3). Julie and her mother have a heart-to-heart talk about touching. Her mother lets her know that she has a right to her body and can tell people when they are touching her in ways that she feels uncomfortable with. No abuse actually occurs in this book, but it is great for initiating conversation about it.

Girard, L.W. (1985) *Who is a stranger and what should I do?* (Illus. by H. Cogancherry.) Niles IL: Albert Whitman. (Gr. 2–6). Explains how to deal with strangers in public places, on the telephone, and in cars. The never-never rule is discussed, as well as when it is best to run and when to talk to another adult. Provides practice and discussion at the end. Good for group work.

Lowerey, L. (1994) *Laurie tells*. (Illus. by J. Karpinski.) Minneapolis, MN: The Lerner Group. (unpaged)(Gr. 4 and up). Every child who has been sexually abused will be able to understand the pain and anguish in Laurie's cries. This poignant story reveals how Laurie was abused by her father from the age of 9 until she poured out the whole story to her aunt. In the safety of her aunt's home, she can begin to heal. A *must read* for all counselors to understand a child's feelings about sexual abuse.

Newman, S. (1985). *Never say yes to a stranger: What every child should know to stay safe*. (Photographs by G. Tiboni.) New York: Putnam/Perigee. (128 pages)(Gr. K–6). This book teaches children about the dangers of contact with strangers and what to do when they find themselves in trouble. It is an excellent book to use in large groups for apprising children of the various ploys that strangers use to catch them off guard. Could be adapted for use in K–6.

Patterson, S. (1986) *No-No the seal*. (Songs by J. Feldman.) New York: Random House. (unpaged)(Preschool–K). No-No the seal is sexually abused by an uncle that he admires while his parents are on a trip. No-No seeks advice from a friendly whale and decides to tell his parents. Like real children, No-No is molested by someone he knows, is told to keep it secret, and is afraid to tell. With accompanying tape, this book is excellent for both individual and group prevention efforts.

Satullo, J., Russell, R., & Bradway, P. (1987). *It happens to boys too...* Pittsfield, MA: Berkshire Press. (35 pages)(Preschool–Gr. 6). This magnificent book deals with the myths and realities of the sexual abuse of boys. It encourages children to express their feelings and to tell someone. Parents are given some of the behavioral changes that might occur in children that are being abused and are encouraged to get help in dealing with their own feelings about the abuse. This book provides excellent, practical knowledge in an easy-to-understand format. It is helpful in counseling young children who have been abused.

Sanford, D. (1986). *I can't talk about it*. (Pictures by Graci Evans.) Portland, OR: Multnamah Press. (unpaged)(Gr. K–6). At her grandmother's beach cottage, Annie reveals her father's sexual abuse of her to a dove who helps her heal and learn to trust again. This book is an extraordinarily sensitive portrayal of the feelings associated with sexual abuse and is a *must* for any child counselor dealing with sexual abuse.

Wachter, O. (1984) *No more secrets for me*. (Illus. by J. Aaron.) Boston: Little, Brown & Co. (46 pages)(Gr. 1–4). Four different scenarios were presented that involved inappropriate touching or undressing, and each was resolved when the child told someone he or she trusted. In each case, the child was frightened and confused, knew the touching was inappropriate, and didn't want to participate.

Death and Dying

Breebaart, J., & Breebaart, P. (1993). *When I die, will I get better?* New York: Peter Bedrick Books. (25 pages)(Gr. K–4). Seeking to understand the sudden death of his younger brother, 5-year-old Joeri dictated this true story to his father. Childlike illustrations of a rabbit family and their animal friends detail the events as Joeri saw them and reflect his emotions as he works through grief to acceptance.

Douglas, E. (1990). *Rachel and the upside down heart: A true story.* Los Angeles: Price Stern Sloan. (32 pages)(Gr. K–3). Rachel was 4 years old when her father died. This true story tells how a very young child grieves the loss of her daddy and slowly adjusts to a whole new life.

Jordon, M. (1989). *Losing Uncle Tim.* Niles, IL: Albert Whitman. (28 pages)(Gr. 2–6). Daniel loved his uncle and was devastated when he learned Tim had AIDS. This story describes Daniel's heartbreaking struggle to understand the progression of Uncle Tim's illness, and eventual death.

Krementz, J. (1988). *How it feels when a parent dies.* New York: Alfred A. Knopf. (110 pages)(Gr. 5–9). This book, accompanied by photographs, is based on interviews with 20 children who have suffered the loss of a parent through suicide, illness, or accident. The individual stories are poignant reminders of the resiliency of the human spirit and are designed to help other children cope with the emotional upheaval that follows the death of a parent, regardless of the circumstances.

LeShan, E. (1986). *When a parent is very sick.* Boston: Joy Street Books. (132 pages) (Gr. 4–7). Writing to children in the middle to upper elementary grades, Edna LeShan describes the confusing feelings of many children who experienced the trauma of a very ill parent. She assures her readers that all these feelings are normal and understandable, both in themselves and in others; shows them how they can ask for information; and explains ways to become strong enough to help themselves and their families.

McLendon, G.H. (1982). *My brother Joey died.* New York: Julian Messner. (Gr. 6 and up.) This story follows a preteen through her personal struggle with the death of her brother. It describes her sorrow, guilt, and fears, and the grieving process of Joey's family until they reach understanding and acceptance.

Maple, M. (1992). *On the wings of a butterfly.* Seattle, WA: Parenting Press. (Gr. 1–6). A beautifully written and illustrated account of a real little girl who confronted terminal illness with the help of Sonya—a caterpillar preparing for transformation into a monarch butterfly.

Powell, E. (1990). *Geranium morning.* Minneapolis, MN: Carolrhoda Books. (Gr. 1–4). Tim's dad dies suddenly in a car accident; Frannie loses her mother slowly to cancer. These two grade-school children meet in school, learn to share their experiences and feelings together, and become close friends.

Rogers, F. (1988). *When a pet dies.* New York: G.P. Putnam's Sons. (unpaged)(preschool–Gr. 1). Mr. Rogers' provides poignant color photographs and simple, sensitive text to help children talk about the death of a pet.

Simon, N. (1986). *The saddest time*. (Illus. by Jacqueline Rogers.) Niles, IL: Albert Whitman & Co. (unpaged)(Gr. 1–4). This story explains death as an inevitable end of life and provides three situations in which children experience powerful emotions when someone close dies. The first is when Michael has to deal with the loss of his Uncle and finds ways to help his aunt and cousins. The second is when Teddy Baker, age 8, gets hit by a car and is remembered and mourned by his classmates. And finally, when Emily's grandma dies, she remembers good things and comforts Grandpa.

Wilhelm, H. (1985). *I'll always love you*. New York: Crown Publishers, Inc. (unpaged) (Preschool and up). This warm, fully illustrated book portrays the close relationship between a boy and his dog, Elfie. When Elfie dies in her sleep, the boy takes comfort in the fact that he told the dog "I'll always love you" each night. A moving story that imparts a gentle philosophy of telling loved ones how you feel while you still can.

Illness

Aiello, B., & Shulman, J. (1988). *Friends for life: Featuring Amy Wilson*. Frederick, MD: Twenty-First Century Books. (48 pages)(Gr. 3–6). A book in "The Kids on the Block" series, *Friends for Life* describes the shock and fear that rocks an elementary school when a well respected Video Club sponsor is discovered to have AIDS. Fifth-grader Amy Wilson not only learns a great deal about AIDS, but also how to speak up for what she believes in.

Coerr, E. (1993). *Sadako and the thousand paper cranes*. (Illus. by E. Young.) New York: G. P. Putnam. (unpaged). (Gr. 2–5). A Japanese legend holds that if a person who is ill makes a thousand paper cranes, the gods will grant that person's wish to be well again. This moving account of Sadako's struggle with leukemia is portrayed in beautiful pastel drawings, which capture her strength and courage.

Kisher, T. (1992). *Kathy's hats: A story of hope*. (Illus. by N. Westcott.) Morton Grove, IL: Albert Whitman. (unpaged)(Gr. 1–5). Kathy's love of hats comes in handy when the chemotherapy treatments that she receives for her cancer make her hair fall out. Based on the true story of a child's courage and optimism as she fights cancer, *Kathy's Hats* has a happy ending.

Vigna, J. (1993). *When Eric's mom fought cancer*. Morton, Grove, IL: Albert Whitman. (unpaged)(Preschool–Gr. 3). Eric is often frightened, lonely, and sad when his mother must be hospitalized for long periods of time. But he also becomes understandably frustrated and angry after she comes home and is still very sick and unable to play with him. Eric and his Dad spend a day skiing together and Eric takes the opportunity to ask his father the questions about cancer that have worried him.

Wiener, L. S., Best, A., & Pizzo, P. A. (1994). *Be a friend: Children who live with HIV speak*. Morton Grove, IL: Albert Whitman. (40 pages)(Gr. 2–6). This book is a poignant collection of art and writing by children who are hospitalized with AIDS. In their own words, the children express what they wonder about and wish for and their longing to be "normal." Siblings worry about their brothers' and sisters' illness and feel the strain of keeping the family's secret. The important message from these children is, "Please do not be scared of us...We need you to be our friends."

Substance Abuse

Berger, G. (1992). *Meg's story: Get real! Straight talk about drugs.* Brookfield, CN: The Millbrook Press. (62 pages)(Gr. 7 and up). This is a first-person account of a young girl who undergoes a personality change as a result of an accident at age 12. It describes how she became addicted to drugs, her experiences as an addict, and her struggles to recover and take charge of her life. It also deals with the impact of her behavior on her parents. Recommended for older children only.

DeStefano, S. (1991). *Drugs and the family.* (Illus. by L. Raymond.) Frederick, MD: Twenty-First Century Books. (85 pages)(Gr. 5–8). This book examines some of the thoughts and feelings that children in addicted families have. Abuse and neglect are talked about, as is hope and recovery. Excellent for older children.

Garner, A. (1987). *It's O.K. to say no to drugs.* (Illus. by R. Detorie.) New York: Tom Doherty Assoc. (115 pages)(Gr. 4 and up). This parent-child manual makes the reader aware of the reasons children might experiment with drugs and in what situations they might be tempted. Cartoons add to the appeal as children are invited to discuss their choices. This book could be used as a guide for group discussion.

O'Neill, C. (1990). *Focus on alcohol.* Frederick, MD: Twenty-First Century Books. (55 pages)(Gr. 4 and up). This is a drug alert book designed to educate young people about the use and abuse of alcohol. Pressures to drink are examined from a number of different viewpoints. Could be adapted for group work with young people in middle school on such topics as self-esteem building.

Pownall, M. (1987). *Understanding drugs: Inhalants.* New York: Franklin Watts. (61 pages)(Gr. 6 and up). Designed for older kids, this book tells you everything you need to know about inhalants. It makes readers aware of the risks and of ways to seek help.

Seixas, J. S. (1979). *Living with a parent who drinks too much.* New York: Greenwillow Books. (Gr. 5 and up). This insightful book offers youngsters ways to cope with an alcoholic parent. Special emphasis is placed on how to seek help for the parent and counseling help for the child. Knowing that you are not alone and not to blame is the central message.

Seixas, J. S. (1989). *Living with a parent who takes drugs.* New York: Greenwillow Books. (101 pages)(Gr. 5 and up). Jason's moving story offers insight into common behavior patterns of addicts and suggests ways to cope. It offers sound advice on where and how to go for help and offers valuable information on the rights and responsibilities of children and how the law relates to drug abuse.

Shuker-Haines, F. (1994). *Everything you need to know about a drug abusing parent.* New York: Rosen Publishing Group. (57 pages)(Gr. 7 and up). This wonderful book helps older children learn how to cope with their parents' substance abuse. The messages are: You are not alone; your parent has a disease; it's not your fault, and you can lead a drug-free life. Discussion involves all types of drugs and their effects on the parent and on the children. Could be used in groups.

Talmadge, K. (1991). *Drugs and sports.* (Illus. by L. Raymond.) Frederick, MD: Twenty-First Century Books. (87 pages)(Gr. 5–8). This book, written for middle-school children, discusses what happens when athletic performance is boosted by drugs. Athletes share their stories about their own drug addiction and the pain that was associated with it.

Taylor, C. (1992). *The house that crack built*. (Illus. by J. Dicks.) San Francisco, CA: Chronicle Books. (All ages). Using rap music as an inspiration, Clark Taylor, has transformed a well-known nursery rhyme into a powerful poem about destruction. From the harvesting of the coca plants to the dealers and gangs on the streets to the innocent crack babies born everyday, cocaine's journey is traced from beginning to end. Appealing to all ages from children to adults, this powerful book can be used by counselors in group therapy.

Vigna, J. (1990). *My big sister takes drugs*. Niles, IL: Albert Whitman. (unpaged) (Gr. K–3). When Paul's sister Tina was found taking drugs in the park, a nightmare begins for the family, and Paul's new friendship with Jose and his plans for soccer camp both seem lost. Tina's drug problem is treated realistically and so is the effects of sibling drug use on younger children. Excellent for even young children.

Zeller, P. K. (1990). *Focus on marijuana*. Frederick, MD: Twenty-First Century Books (55 pages)(Gr. 2–4). This drug-alert book describes the history, effects, social aspects, and physical dangers of using marijuana. Using statements from young people, (ages 12 to 16) about their drug use, the book attempts to give some of the facts about marijuana and some of the reasons young people smoke it. Easy to read, it could be adapted for group work with middle-school children.

Suicide

Kunz, R. B., & Swenson, J. H. (1986). *Feeling down: The way back up*. Minneapolis, MN: Dillion Press. (45 pages)(Gr. 5 and up). This story is told through the eyes of a boy whose older sister has recently tried to take her own life. It sensitively portrays the family's involvement in psychotherapy and the young boy's feelings, stressing more communication and effective coping skills. Ideas for discussion are included.

Violence

Bernstein, S. C. (1991). *A family that fights*. Morton Grove, IL: Albert Whitman. (32 pages)(Gr. K–4). Henry's dad has a very bad temper. Often angry, Dad frightens Henry and his younger brother and sister when he yells and hits their mom. This sadly realistic story describes behavior that frequently develops in children who witness chronic domestic violence and suggests things they can do to help themselves.

Cohn, J. (1994). *Why did it happen?* New York: Morrow Junior Books. (unpaged) (Preschool and up). After a robbery at a nearby store, 6-year-old Daniel struggles to understand his anger and fears. Clearly written text and charming color drawings depict a multicultural neighborhood, supportive parents, and sensitive adults who show Eric how to express his needs.

Palmer, J. (1994). *Everything you need to know when you are the victim of a violent crime*. New York: Rosen Publishing Group. (61 pages)(Gr. 6 and up). With our increasingly violent society, more and more young people are victims of violent crime. This book helps young people cope with both the physical and the psychological damage that crime causes and encourages them to seek help through professional counseling, legal advice, and a support group.

Dealing with Disabilities

The following books emphasize the *abilities* in childhood disabilities. A variety of stories featuring children with visual and hearing impairment, cerebral palsy, spina bifida, Down's syndrome, and mental retardation are included. Although often invisible, attention deficit hyperactivity disorder (ADHD) is one of the most common disabling conditions of childhood. A number of books on this important topic, as well as some on other learning disabilities, are included in this list. Books on understanding various types of mental illness are also a part of this section. These books enable children to obtain information about different types of disabilities and to discover ways to get help and to cope.

Aiello, B., & Shulman, J. (1988). *It's your turn at bat: Featuring Mark Riley*. Frederick, MD: Twenty-First Century Books. (48 pages)(Gr. 3–6). Mark Riley is all boy, he just happens to have cerebral palsy and rides in "The Cruiser," his wheelchair. Although an epilogue contains questions and answers about CP, the thrust of the story centers on Mark's struggle to accept new challenges and responsibilities. A happy ending results when he does.

Aseltine, L., Mueller, E. & Tait, N. (1986). *I'm deaf and it's okay*. (Pictures by H. Cogancherry.) Niles, IL: Albert Whitman. (unpaged)(Gr. 1–4). In this story, a young boy tells about his frustrations and fears caused by his deafness. Brian, a deaf teenager, helps by being a friend and showing that deaf people can do most things that hearing people do. Excellent section on common words in sign language that children and adults can learn.

Bergman, T. (1989). *Seeing in special ways: Children living with blindness*. Milwaukee, WI: Gareth Stevens. (unpaged)(Gr. 4–5). Interviews with a group of blind and partially sighted children in Sweden reveal their feelings about their disability and the ways they use their other senses to help them "see."

Bergman, T. (1989). *We laugh, we love, we cry: Children living with mental retardation*. Milwaukee, WI: Gareth Stevens. (unpaged)(Gr. 4–5). Beautiful photographs tell the remarkable story of two sisters with mental retardation. Their home life, physiotherapy, and schooling are chronicled, but it is their spirit and courage to meet the challenges of this disability that remains with the reader. Epilogue answers questions and gives activities that help others learn about mental retardation.

Dunn, K. B., & Dunn, A. B. (1993). *Trouble with school: A family story about learning disabilities*. (Illus. by Rick Stromoski.) Rockville, MD: Woodbine House. (unpaged)(Gr. 1–5). Allison tells the story of her feelings about her learning disability; her mother gives an adult perspective. This commonsense, helpful little book, illustrated to add humor, provides information and insight into the effects of learning disabilities on the child and the family. Includes a guide for parents.

Dinner, S. H. (1989). *Nothing to be ashamed of: Growing up with mental illness in your family*. New York: Lothrop, Lee & Shepard. (197 pages)(Gr. 5 and up). In what amounts to a textbook on various types of mental illness, Dr. Dinner carefully describes both symptoms and treatment in terms that young people can understand. She shares with the reader the common experiences that children have when they are living with a mentally ill family member and gives techniques for relieving worry and stress.

Dwight, L. (1992). *We can do it*. New York: Checkerboard Press. (unpaged) (Preschool–Gr. 4). Accompanied by photographs that capture the essence of childhood, this delightful book deals with disabilities such as spina bifida, Down's syndrome, cerebral palsy, and blindness. The reader is treated to all the things that the child can do.

Emmert, M. (1989). *I'm the big sister now*. (Illus. by G. Owens.) Niles IL: Albert Whitman. (unpaged). (Gr. 2–6). This is Michele's story about her life as the older sister of Amy, who is severely handicapped by cerebral palsy. With love, the story tells the reader about CP and about a big sister who is loved and cared for by her family and friends. An epilogue explains about cerebral palsy.

Exley, H. (Ed). (1984). *What it's like to be me*. New York: Friendship Press. (125 pages)(Gr. 4–11). Written and illustrated entirely by disabled children, this book chronicles their laughter and tears; their hopes and fears. In their own words, the kids tell us how it is to have a variety of disabilities. Great for promoting discussion in groups for ages 9 to 14.

Filsom, B. (1986). *There's a monster in your closet! Understanding phobias*. (Illus.by T. Enik.) New York: Julian Messner. (71 pages)(Gr. 1–4). This delightfully illustrated book is about common and uncommon phobias and their causes. Some of the ways to overcome these mysterious afflictions are discussed in terms that children can understand. This is an excellent book for children with exaggerated fears.

Calvin, M. (1988). *Otto learns about his medicine: A story about medication for hyperactive children*. New York: Magination Press. (32 pages)(Preschool–Gr. 6). Otto, a fidgety young car, has trouble paying attention in school, has trouble remembering important information, and is unable to listen long enough to learn how to drive. Otto and his parents visit a special mechanic who explains about a "car medicine" that can help him control his behavior. Written to be read to and by young children with ADHD, this delightful story is meant to assist children in understanding their behavior and the role of psychostimulants.

Geared, M. A. (1991). *Eagle eyes: A child's guide to paying attention*. Fairport, NY: Verbal Images Press. (36 pages)(Gr. 1–5). Developed to help children understand and manage behavior frequently associated with attention deficit disorder, this book describes a young boy's failure to feel good about himself and how he is able to change.

Gehret, M. A. (1992). *I'm somebody too*. Fairport, NY: Verbal Images Press. (159 pages). (Gr. 4–7). What is it like to be the big sister to a brother with ADD? Not Easy! Emily describes the pressure she puts on herself to be perfect, her resentment at being caught in the chaos produced by Ben's behavior, and the loneliness she feels as her parents, focused on Ben, fail to see her needs. However, with the help of ritalin for Ben and professional counseling for everyone in the family, life becomes more satisfying. An epilogue offers suggestions for managing strong emotions.

Gehret, J. (1990). *The don't-give-up kid and learning differences*. Fairport, NY: Verbal Images Press. (159 pages)(Gr. 1–5). What's a kid to do when reading problems get him in trouble and make him the target of teasing? As Alex becomes aware of his different learning style, he realizes that his hero, Thomas Edison, faced similar problems. Inspired, he learns to try new solutions until he can succeed at his dreams. This edition contains an expanded parent resource guide.

Gordon, M. (1991). *Jumping Johnny get back to work!: A child's guide to ADHD/ hyperactivity.* DeWitt, NY: GSI Publications. (24 pages)(Gr. 1–4). This book is told by a youngster who truly struggles to achieve but doesn't always meet with success or acceptance. Although he moves through the day experiencing frustration and embarrassment, he still maintains his sense of humor and spirit of determination. Along with his family and teacher, he finds that he has ADHD and learns to cope with his disability.

Gordon, M. (1992). *My brother's a world class pain: A sibling's guide to ADHD/hyperactivity.* DeWitt, NY: GSI Publications. (34 pages)(Gr. 4 and up). The sister of a boy with ADHD describes her frustrations and resentments at having to frequently bear the brunt of her siblings impulsiveness and distractibility. Children who read this story are introduced to many of the basic concepts involved in understanding ADHD and the demands that a child with special needs places on all family members.

Holcomb, N. (1987). *Andy finds a turtle.* Exton, PA: Jason and Nordic. (unpaged) (Preschool–Gr. 2). Called a "turtle" by his physical therapist when he doesn't cooperate in exercises, Andy wonders what a "turtle" is. His imagination runs wild until, on a picnic with his family, he meets a turtle and learns what he and a turtle have in common.

Holcomb, N. (1984). *Danny and the merry-go-round.* Exton, PA: Jason and Nordic. (unpaged)(Preschool–Gr. 2). Born with cerebral palsy, Danny sits in a wheelchair while other children play. One day, however, a little red-haired girl brings her father to meet Danny and to help him sit with his mother on the merry-go-round.

Holcomb, N. (1989). *Patrick and Emma Lou.* Exton, PA. Jason and Nordic. (unpaged)(Preschool–Gr. 2). Three-year-old Patrick has cerebral palsy. He wishes he could walk easily like other children, but has a problem just learning to use a walker. With the help and encouragement of his therapist and his friend Emmy Lou, Patrick perseveres, improves, and eventually is very pleased with himself.

Johnson, J. T. (1989). *Understanding mental illness.* Minneapolis, MN: Lerner Publications. (68 pages)(Gr. 6 and up). This book is written for teens who care about someone with mental illness. It not only explains many types of mental illness but also offers assistance to those children who are living with someone who is mentally ill. Designed for older children, it gives the child's point of view through stories.

Landau, E. (1991). *Dyslexia.* New York: Franklin Watts. (51 pages)(Gr. 5–8). This is the story of Mark's battle with dyslexia and how it affects his schoolwork, especially in reading and writing. He talks about his feelings of embarrassment when he couldn't read cards or menus and his frustrations at being different. With the help of supportive teachers, he makes the best of things. For use with children age 9 to 12.

Litchfield, A. B. (1976). *A button in her ear.* (Illus. by E. Mill.) Chicago, IL: Albert Whitman. (unpaged)(Gr. 2–4). Angela discovers that she has trouble hearing and is fitted with a button in her ear. Her teacher encourages her to tell her classmates about the button, and she finds that she can "tune out" her friend Buzzie when she wants to. Great story for helping children accept a hearing loss.

Muldoon, K. (1989). *Princess Pooh.* (Illus. by L. Shute.) Niles, IL: Albert Whitman. (unpaged)(Gr. 2–5). This delightful story puts a new twist on sibling rivalry. Jealous of her invalid sister's royal treatment as she sits in her wheelchair, Patty Jean tries it out and discovers that life in a wheelchair is no fun at all. Written with humor, this is a great book for helping children see that the grass is not always greener on the other side of the fence.

Quinn, P., & Stern, J. (1991). *Putting on the brakes: Young people's guide to understanding attention deficit hyperactivity disorder (ADHD).* New York: Magination Press. (64 pages)(Gr. 4–7). An honest, accessible overview of ADHD for children age 8 to 12, this book focuses on the feeling and emotions of young people with ADHD and suggests specific techniques for gaining control of the situation, becoming better organized, and functioning better at home, at school, and with friends.

Lasker, J. (1974). *He's my brother.* Chicago, IL: Albert Whitman. (40 pages)(Gr. 1–3). A young boy describes his brother James, a child who suffers from "the invisible handicap"—a combination of behavior and social skills that make him different from his siblings and peers and hard to diagnose. This easy-to-read, non-judgmental narrative records James' relationship with others and records his strengths as well as his problems.

Moss, D. (1989). *Shelley the hyperactive turtle.* Rockville, MD. Woodbine House. (20 pages)(Gr. K and up). Specifically intended to increase an understanding of ADHD and encourage ADHD children to pursue their dreams, the imaginative story of Shelley offers a realistic yet positive look at hyperactivity. Shelly's behavior problems, diagnosis, and treatment are described in easy-to-read text and delightful color illustrations.

Rabe, B. (1988). *Where's chimpy?* (Photographs by D. Schmidt). Niles, IL: Albert Whitman. (unpaged)(Preschool–Gr. 2). Misty, a little girl with Down's syndrome, stars in this book with her Daddy. A delightful portrayal of the everyday play activities of Misty, beautifully photographed, provide a story that other children with Down's can identify with. Great for counselors to use with children.

Sanford, D. (1986). *Don't look at me: A child's book about feeling different.* Portland, OR: Multnomah, Press. (28 pages)(Gr. K–6). Patrick doesn't feel good about himself. He struggles with his schoolwork, his classmates are mean to him, and even his father gets angry when Pat makes mistakes. Lucky for Patrick, his pet lamb Fluffy speaks up to explain to him how he can begin to make changes and to show him how he is loved.

Counseling

This last book is the only one available that tells children what to expect when they visit a psychotherapist. Private-practice offices and clinics might want to consider this type of children's book for their waiting room.

Galving, M. (1987). *Ignatius finds help: A story about psychotherapy for children.* (Illus. by S. Ferraro.) New York: Magination Press. (unpaged)(Preschool–Gr. 6). Ignatius the bear has trouble getting along with the others at home and in school—he is too "hugnatious." Ignatius and his parents are referred to Dr. Pelican, a psychotherapist, and Ignatius learns how to solve his own problems. This book is a delightful and nonthreatening way for children to learn about psychotherapy and should be a fixture in private-practice settings for parents and children to read together.

INSIGHTS AND IMPLICATIONS

Healing through books is an ancient art that is still practiced today in the form of bibliotherapy. Because reading is natural and fun, it is an excellent way for children to get in touch with their own emotions, thoughts, and actions. Bibliotherapy can help a child achieve a renewed awareness and understanding of self and others, provide a release for pent-up emotions, and contribute to conflict resolution. Problem-solving abilities are strengthened when the child vicariously experiences the situation in the story. As the child explores alternatives, he or she tries each solution on for size, rejecting some while accepting others. In this way, the child is thinking through the problem and applying problem-solving skills to finding a solution. Of course, some problems cannot be solved by the child alone. In these instances, bibliotherapy can help the child cope with things that cannot be changed, such as the death of a parent.

In practice, books can be used to help children tell stories that may be too painful for them to talk about. Because bibliotherapy can be used in conjunction with other therapeutic techniques, children often express their thoughts and feelings in a series of follow-up activities. Art activities, storytelling, writing, role playing, and other creative follow-up strategies encourage children to use their motor, cognitive, and verbal skills to increase their self-awareness and self-understanding. Insight-producing discussions are a normal part of bibliotherapy and help children achieve clarification and understanding of their feelings, thoughts, and behaviors.

Books can also be used as a springboard for group discussions in which children may relate the topic to events in their own lives. In this way, follow-up discussions become personalized and relevant to the individual children involved in the group. Through the process of identification and projection, children can relate to the story and find similarities to their own situations.

Bibliotherapy is another technique to add to the therapist's repertoire. It fits well in a developmental counseling framework and can be used to help children overcome common problems encountered in growing up. Bibliocounseling also plays a special role in prevention. Books can provide valuable information, suggest more adaptive ways of coping, and help prevent some problems from developing. Although as a therapeutic approach bibliotherapy promises no magical solutions, for some children it may open a window to self-understanding that would not be opened by any other therapeutic mode. Therefore, bibliocounseling and therapy have a special place among the many approaches available to practitioners and can be adapted to suit individual children and their counselors.

WISDOM ACCORDING TO ORTON

- *Sometimes a child can ponder an idea, an inspiration, a feeling or an action as a result of reading a book, and we may never know if or how it has affected his or her life.*
- *Books have a way of revealing information without the need for embarrassing questions.*
- *Books provide a safe haven for dreams and happy endings. They are refuges from reality when we need them.*
- *Through reading, children can solve problems that are too painful to talk about.*
- *Once children discover the power of books, they may come to rely on it .*

ORTON'S PICKS

Bernstein, S. C. (1991). *A family that fights.* Morton Grove, IL: Albert Whitman.
> Henry's dad frightens him and his younger siblings when he yells and hits their mom. This sadly realistic story describes behavior that frequently develops in children who witness chronic domestic violence and suggests things they can do to help themselves.

Bunting, E. (1991). *Fly away home.* New York: Clarion Books.
> With an airport for a home, Andrew longs for the way life used to be before his mom died. This poignant story, told with hope but no happy ending, is beautifully illustrated and could be used with groups to promote understanding of homelessness.

Gordon, M. (1992). *My brother's a world class pain: A sibling's guide to ADHD/hyperactivity.* DeWitt, NY: GSI Publications.
> A girl describes her frustrations and resentments at having to frequently bear the brunt of her brother's impulsiveness and distractibility. Children who read this story are introduced to many of the basic concepts involved in understanding ADHD and the demands that a child with special needs places on all family members.

Muldoon, K. (1989). *Princess pooh.* Niles, IL: Albert Whitman.
> Jealous of her sister's royal treatment, Patty Jean takes a turn in the wheelchair and discovers that it is no fun at all. This delightful book, written with humor, helps children appreciate the abilities that children with disabilities have.

Taylor, C. (1992). *The house that crack built.* San Francisco, CA: Chronicle Books.
> Using rap music as an inspiration, Clark Taylor, has transformed a well-known nursery rhyme into a powerful poem about cocaine's destruction. Appealing to all ages from children to adults, this powerful book can be used by counselors in group therapy.

CHAPTER 9   *Behavioral Approaches with Children*

LEADELLE PHELPS

> *Although many people associate behavior modification with a specific form of treatment, in fact the approach embraces a large number of quite different intervention techniques...clinical problems, populations, and conceptual views.*
> —KAZDIN (1994, p. 2).

Behavioral and cognitive-behavioral interventions are two major theoretical orientations in today's mental health services for children. A number of studies support the use of explicit and active treatment directed toward increasing adaptive prosocial behavior and reducing maladaptive behavior. Since the inception of behavior modification in the 1950s and 1960s, growth in the field has been phenomenal. Today, behavior therapy and cognitive-behavioral therapy (CBT) are effectively used to treat a wide range of childhood problems including anxiety, depression, oppositional-defiant behaviors, eating disorders, underachievement, enuresis, encopresis, obsessive-compulsive disorder, social skills deficits, attention deficit/hyperactivity disorder, phobias, and conduct disorder. As Kazdin stated, "it has brought about a major reconceptualization of psychological problems and their treatment" (1978, p. ix).

A BRIEF HISTORY

The use of rewards for positive behavior is as old as history itself. In ancient Greece and Rome, successful military performance was rewarded with gifts of property, privileges, and even freedom itself. Similarly, examples of punishment to reduce maladaptive behavior abound in the Old Testament of the Bible.

In recent times, dissatisfaction with the traditional psychoanalytic model led to the emergence of behavioral approaches to psychotherapy. Among the criticisms of intrapsychic approaches were their lack of empirical support or research base. In 1952, Hans Eysenck published a seminal work in which he reviewed the counseling outcome research and concluded that evidence did not support psychotherapy as an effective intervention. In fact, he noted that no treatment at all was as productive as psychotherapy. Eysenck further suggested that traditional approaches were ineffective because they lacked explicit learning or behavioral components.

These conclusions were hotly debated. Since the publication of Eysenck's work more than 40 years ago, a considerable amount of research into the efficacy of treatment modes has been accumulated. Although these data do not validate Eysenck's original claim that no treatment is equally effective, they do support his contention that techniques oriented toward behavioral change that emphasize learning and cognitive restructuring are superior to approaches that focus solely on insight or the expression of feelings.

Perhaps the most significant event that propelled behavioral interventions into the forefront was Bandura's 1969 book *Principles of Behavior Modification*. Up to that time, behaviorism had followed a rather unidirectional model, suggesting that people respond passively to whatever reinforcers or punishers the environment provides. An example of this paradigm was Skinner's (1971) statement that "A person does not act upon the world; the world acts upon him" (p. 211). Although many found it interesting that rats could be trained to engage in rather intricate behaviors through the use of reinforcement and punishment, therapists found little appeal in such approaches, especially when working with complex human interactions. Fortunately, Bandura (1969) was able to show that the person-environment relationship was highly reciprocal: "Persons, far from being ruled by an imposing environment, play an active role in constructing their own reinforcement contingencies through their characteristic modes of response" (p. 46). His research confirmed that children (and adults) develop many behaviors by watching others. He further documented that learning new behaviors did not always depend on the presence or absence of reinforcers and that children often covertly provided their own self-reinforcement. He concluded that many maladaptive behaviors were learned this way. Aggressive behaviors in children, for example, could be explained by the aggressive models that parents, the media, and peers provide, as well as by the frequent positive outcomes that result from such behavior: for example, children get their way on the playground by following the verbally aggressive models they have observed.

In 1977, Bandura published his classic text *Social Learning Theory*, in which he added a cognitive component to the person-environment reciprocity model. That is, Bandura concluded that how one *interprets* events has a significant impact on both consequences and behavior. For children, the belief or expectation that certain behaviors will have certain consequences has a notable effect. For example, Maya continues to whine because she believes it will get her what she wants. Behavioral outcomes are therefore not only a function of complex interdependencies between personal and environmental influences; they include a cognitive factor as well. Thus, cognitive-behavioral therapy was born.

EFFICACY RESEARCH

The recent development of a statistical procedure called meta-analysis has greatly enhanced our knowledge of how therapeutic interventions work with children. Through meta-analysis, the findings of numerous studies can be combined and systematically compared. The combined results are called an *effect size*, which is an estimate of the magnitude of the treatment effect on measures of psychological functioning. A positive effect size of 1.00 indicates that the treatment groups achieved better results at a magnitude of one standard deviation; a negative effect size of $-.50$ indicates that the control group fared one-half standard deviation better. Generally, effect sizes of around .20 are considered small, .50 are considered of medium strength, and .70 are considered large.

Three recent meta-analyses evaluated a wide variety of interventions with an assortment of childhood disorders and found significant support for the effectivenss of behavioral approaches. In the earliest meta-analysis, Casey and Berman (1985) reviewed 75 studies published between 1952 and 1983 that included some form of psychotherapy (behavioral, client-centered, cognitive-behavioral, psychodynamic) to treat children aged 3 through 15 for a wide range of clinical problems. When these various treatment approaches were compared to no treatment, the researchers reported an effect size of .96 for behavioral approaches, .81 for cognitive-behavioral approaces, .49 for client-centered approaches, and .21 for dynamic approaches.

One common complaint about data on behavioral therapy's efficacy is that outcome measures are frequently similar to the activities that occur during therapy. For example, treatment activities with an anorectic adolescent may be to eat balanced meals coupled with engaging in regular exercise; *treatment goals* would include gaining weight and discontinuing daily bingeing and purging. In this case, using the occurrences of daily meals and exercise as the outcome measures would be viewed as inappropriate because they are duplications of the treatment activities. However, outcome measures such as the number of pounds gained or the number of days in which bingeing and purging did not occur would be acceptable. When therapylike outcome measures were excluded in the Casey and Berman meta-analysis, the effect size was .55 for behavioral approaches and .34 for nonbehavioral approaches. (Note that both behavioral *and* nonbehavioral interventions were affected.)

The second meta-analysis included more studies (N = 108) with a larger age range (4 through 18) (Weisz, Weiss, Alicke, & Klotz, 1987). Weisz and associates found results similar to Casey and Berman's, reporting a mean effect size of .79 across different treatments, clinical problems, and patient samples. When unnecessary therapylike outcomes were omitted, effect sizes were larger for behavioral (.93) than for nonbehavioral (.45) approaches. Simiarly, effect sizes tended to be greater for children (age 4 to 12) than for adolescents (age 13 to 18), but there were no differences between females and males.

The final study (Weisz, Weiss, Han, Granger, & Morton, 1995) used an entirely new sample of 150 outcome studies and approaches, and effect sizes again supported behavioral (.54) over nonbehavioral (.30) approaches. The researchers concluded that

> The main effect of therapy type supports the hypothesis that behavioral treatments are more effective then non-behavioral treatments.... When we excluded outcome measures coded as unnecessarily similar, behavioral methods showed more pronounced superiority to nonbehavioral methods (mean effect sizes .52 vs. 25). (pp. 455–456)

Other studies indicate that treatment that is specific, well planned, and individualized to the client and the problem behavior is far more effective than diffuse, vague, and eclectic models. As Kazdin (1995) indicated, seeing a child once a week for 50 minutes—regardless of the reason for referral, diagnosis, chronicity, or severity of behavior—is simply not supportable.

PRINCIPLES OF BEHAVIOR THERAPY

Using the theoretical foundation of operant conditioning, behavioral therapy's treatment goal is to increase infrequent appropriate behaviors or eliminate excessive inappropriate ones. In many cases, the therapist seeks to both: replace excessive inappropriate actions with more instances of adaptive conduct. There are four general principles of operant conditioning: positive reinforcement, negative reinforcement, punishment, and response cost (see Figure 9-1). Although numerous techniques are used in behavioral therapy (such as shaping, time out, and overcorrection), these procedures are generally subsumed under the four general categories.

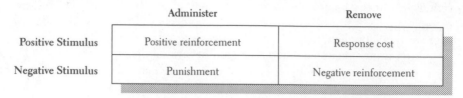

FIGURE 9-1 *The Four General Principles of Operant Conditioning*

Positive Reinforcement

Reinforcement refers to increasing a behavior by following it with a specific consequence. Conversely, a consequence that does *not* increase the behavior is not a reinforcer. A *positive reinforcer* is one that is viewed as a favorable event, but what may be significantly reinforcing to one child (shopping with Aunt Louise) may be a punishment to another. Similarly, what is often assumed to be punishment (being sent out into the hall for talking in class) may be viewed as a positive event by some children (a chance to avoid classroom instruction). Therefore, the defining characteristic of a positive reinforcer is an increase in the frequency of the behavior it precedes.

Negative Reinforcement

Negative reinforcement refers to increasing a behavior by the *removing* of an aversive event. Thus, an event is a negative reinforcer only if its *removal* after a response increases performance of that response. For example, nagging is a negative reinforcer if the child finally practices the piano in order to stop the parent's repeated requests. Other examples would be allowing students to skip a later assignment if they obtain 95% or better accuracy on an exam, or refunding a portion of a dental bill for patients whose flossing reduces dental plaque. Again, all these examples involve removing or reducing an aversive stimulus (parental badgering, schoolwork, and monetary fees).

Punishment

The corollary of positive reinforcement is punishment. *Punishment* refers to reducing a behavior by administering an aversive or unpleasant stimulus when the behavior occurs. As mentioned previously, because what appears to be aversive may in fact be positive to some children, only a close analysis of how a consequence affects behavior (increases or decreases its occurrence) will confirm whether the event is a reinforcer, a punishment, or neutral. For example, while grocery shopping, a parent repeatedly verbally reprimands a young child for grabbing objects off the shelves. The more the parent admonishes, the more unruly the child becomes. Finally, in desperation, the parent promises to let the child have one object if he or she *stops begging*. What is the interpretation of this transaction? Although the parent assumed that the scolding was punishing the child, the negative behavior actually *increased*. What was assumed to be a punishment turned out to be a reinforcer! No doubt the child learned that begging and grabbing eventually pay off, and the parent was unknowingly reinforcing unruly behavior.

Response Cost

The withdrawal or removal of a positive event when a behavior is emitted is called *response cost*. The effect of the removal is to suppress or *reduce* the likelihood that the preceding response will be repeated. To activate a response cost, one must first identify positive reinforcers by determining what increases a behavior, and then these positive reinforcers need to be made readily available to the child. Response cost then occurs when a positive reinforcer is taken away when a behavior one wishes to decrease occurs. Let's return to the example of grocery shopping with a young child. A far better alternative to reinforcing begging and grabbing behavior would be to first (1) specify the desired prosocial behavior before entering the store, (2) identify something that the child highly desires to be given as a reward when the *positive behavior* is emitted (an individualized positive reinforcer), (3) delineate the inappropriate behaviors that should not occur, and (4) specify what positive reinforcer will be lost if the child engages in the undesired behavior (the response cost). Thus, the parent may say to the child: "I expect you to walk quietly behind me and keep your hands to yourself. If you do so, you may pick one item at the end of our shopping. If you beg or grab, I will put you inside the shopping cart for the rest of our time in the store and you will not get to choose a purchase." Of course, it is imperative that the parent follow through with these specifications. If there are two children, their actions must be treated independently. For example, if Jessica does demonstrate appropriate behavior but Jeremy begs or grabs, Jeremy must immediately be placed inside the cart and lose his food selection privilege (response cost). However, Jessica would be able to continue to walk behind her parent and make a selection when the shopping is done (positive reinforcement). In this way, Jessica's appropriate behavior is reinforced and Jeremy will quickly learn what is expected of him by observation and modeling (social learning).

PRINCIPLES OF COGNITIVE-BEHAVIORAL THERAPY

Cognitive-behavioral therapy (CBT) is an expansion of the behavioral paradigm. By adding a cognitive component to the therapeutic approach, many complex behaviors that are maintained by the child's faulty beliefs can be successfully treated. A counselor need not choose *between* behavior therapy or CBT; Rather, because the two approaches complement one another, they are often used simultaneously. Although there is some evidence that CBT may result in longer-lasting behavior change, such data are far from conclusive. In addition, CBT is more intensive and time-consuming than is behavior therapy. When demonstrated, the superiority of CBT over a more behavioral approach must be weighed against the greater commitment in time, resources, effort, and efficiency. Instead of pitting one against the other, it is better to view the two approaches as working in harmony.

Although there are numerous techniques associated with CBT, most are highly dependent on the client's ability to engage in philosophical discourse, hypothetical-deductive reasoning, logical analyses, and abstract thinking. Given young children's stage of concrete reasoning, these techniques would not be developmentally appropriate. CBT procedures that are suitable with younger clients include modeling, behavioral rehearsal, response prevention, and self-monitoring.

Modeling

Modeling is frequently used to teach children more adaptive or prosocial behaviors. Whereas a strict behavioral approach would use gradual shaping, modeling provides an opportunity for children to master complex and novel responses rather quickly. Modeling provides not only new skill acquisition but also fear reduction. As Bandura (1969) stated:

> [Through modeling] one can acquire intricate response patterns merely by observing the performance of appropriate models; emotional responses can be conditioned observationally by witnessing the affective reaction of others undergoing painful or pleasurable experiences; fearful and avoidant behavior can be extinguished vicariously through observation of modeled approach behavior toward feared objects without any adverse consequences accruing to the performer…and, finally, the expression of well-learned responses can be enhanced and socially regulated through the actions of influential models. (p. 118)

The modeling procedure works best if it is provided by high-prestige models of the same age and gender. Live models are better than filmed models, and several models and situations are better than one-time exposures. Finally, client participation in the procedures, referred to as *participant modeling*, has been shown to produce long-term behavior change.

Modeling is very effective in treating fears, phobias, and anxieties. For example, Tara is a 6-year-old girl who is afraid of water. No doubt some experience, either personal or observational, has taught Tara that water is dangerous. Her fear is such that she will not run through a sprinkler hose on the family lawn, let alone go near a swimming pool. Cori, Tara's best same-age friend who is not afraid of water, is selected as a model. First, the therapist and Tara watch as Cori plays in the "kiddie pool" in Cori's backyard. Gradually, the therapist encourages Tara to approach the kiddie pool, offering such support as hand holding and positive attribution statements like "You are a brave girl." Cori is encouraged to model positive statements to Tara as well. Every movement Tara makes toward the kiddie pool should be accompanied by encouragement and support from the therapist, Tara's parents, and other significant family members.

An important part of this technique is to gradually increase the intensity of the model's approach behavior. As Tara overcomes her fears, Cori will steadily model more and more difficult behaviors, including sitting on the edge of a swimming pool, playing on the steps in the pool's shallow end, and gradually moving about freely in waist-high water. Tara is expected to participate with Cori in each successive increase in approach behavior (participant modeling). This modeling example incorporates not only the CBT principal of observational learning but also the well-known behavioral techniques of reinforcement and gradual systematic desensitization.

Behavioral Rehearsal

To master new behaviors, observational learning is often not enough. *Behavioral rehearsal* provides an opportunity for structured practice opportunities along with corrective feedback. Rehearsal works best if it is provided in a graduated format and is coupled with positive reinforcement. As with modeling, behavioral rehearsal is designed to increase appropriate behaviors.

For example, in the treatment of an elimination disorder, the procedure would be to have the child practice appropriate toileting behaviors. The child would be taught to attend to bodily cues in a timely fashion and to practice holding the bladder muscles to control urine flow. For an older student who suffers from test anxiety, simulated testing experiences, overpreparation, and several dress rehearsals—including walking to the testing room and seating at a desk—would constitute behavioral rehearsal. In all cases, the counselor is present during behavioral rehearsal, providing corrective feedback whenever difficulties arise and dispensing frequent reinforcement for positive attempts. Only after all the major components of the desired action have been taught and successfully practiced does the client attempt the genuine product.

Response Prevention

A key CBT component in treating excessive or maladaptive responses is the client's recognition of the need for change. In response prevention, maladaptive behaviors are not allowed. This CBT procedure can be conducted with or without the client's consent, but the technique works far better if the child (1) agrees that a specific behavior is not desirable and should be eliminated, and (2) gives permission to significant others to interfere with the maladaptive response. Therefore, the sole purpose of response prevention is to eliminate the dysfunctional behavior. Replacing the action with a more adaptive response is preferable to simply eliminating the behavior.

Darrell is a 10-year-old suffering from obsessive compulsive disorder who is plagued with recurrent and persistent thoughts about germs. In spite of his attempts to ignore or suppress such thoughts, they occur with such regularity that they have become problematic. To neutralize these thoughts, Darrell repeatedly washes his hands. He washes so frequently that sores and abrasions cover his skin. Although Darrell finds washing his hands painful and unpleasant, the behavior continues because it seems to temporarily neutralize his fears.

The therapist discusses the irrational nature of the germ obsession with Darrell, outlining the link between reducing anxiety and hand washing. Although this "insight" proves interesting, Darrell's anxiety and ritual behaviors do not abate. Therefore, the therapist recommends that Darrell has only limited and supervised use of washroom facilities; Darrell is allowed to use the restroom only when accompanied by an adult who monitors his hand washing. If Darrell unnecessarily or excessively washes his hands, the supervising adult turns off the faucet water and prevents him from doing so. In lieu of hand washing, Darrell is instructed to clasp his hands firmly together until his anxiety subsides. Thus, the maladaptive behavior is quickly eliminated through extinction and is replaced with a less obtrusive action.

Self-Monitoring

Older children may benefit from the cognitively oriented CBT procedure of *self-monitoring* or self-instruction, in which strategies are developed to assist the youngster in regulating her or his own behavioral responses. Self-monitoring may be successfully used to increase positive behaviors or eliminate maladaptive ones. In either case, the client takes an active role in assuming responsibility for self-control. Primary strategies in this approach include active problem solving and the development of a self-change plan. Specific techniques include logging the frequency and timing of behavior, using empowering self-statements, avoiding overattendance to unpleasant events, self-reinforcing successes, and dealing effectively with failures. The therapist assists in self-monitoring procedures by facilitating appropriate problem solving, promoting realistic self-change plans, modeling efficacious self-statements, and supervising behavior logs to ensure client compliance and honesty.

PLANNING THE TREATMENT

The goal of any therapeutic intervention is to accomplish change. Unlike approaches that seek change through insight, support, or personal validation, behavior therapy and CBT are designed to activate change by focusing primarily on behavior. Although feelings are important, primary attention is given to transforming overt behavior, which has been found to be most effective in modifying affect and cognition in youths (Kendall & Panichelli-Mindel, 1995).

It is important to note that not all behavior can be altered; nor do most advocates of behavioral approaches adhere to the view that all behavior is learned. Rather, actions are a reflection of diverse biological, social, and cultural factors. Human behavior is far too complex to simply pit nature against nurture. The key feature of behavioral approaches is the recognition that most behavior is amenable to change when systematic learning experiences are provided.

A-B-C Assessment

Part of the therapists' behavioral assessment and intervention plan is to complete an A-B-C (antecedents-behavior-consequences) analysis. *Antecedents (A)* refer to stimuli such as gestures and looks from others that cue the behavior in question; the *behavior (B)* refers to observable actions, and the *consequences (C)* represent the events that follow the behavior. An A-B-C analysis frequently identifies how the antecedent events and consequences maintain a maladaptive target behavior. The analysis can also identify why antecedents and consequences are not increasing desired behaviors. Thus, the analysis can lead to the identification of appropriate intervention strategies.

In this phase of treatment, emphasis is placed on altering the consequences so that the target behavior is either increased or decreased. For a consequence to modify behavior, it must be *dependent*, or *contingent*, on the occurrence of that behavior. Let's return to the grocery store incidence discussed earlier. First, the A-B-C analysis (A = shopping, B = grabbing and begging, C = food selection) indicates that grabbing and begging behaviors are rewarded. But what happens if the child is quiet and compliant? If the parent ignores such positive and appropriate behavior, it may quickly vanish. Similarly, if the child is reinforced (via a food selection) every time the family goes shopping *regardless of behavior*, the consequences are indiscriminate and the maladaptive behavior will be maintained.

Deficit Behavior

As illustrated in the examples given thus far, behavior therapy and CBT utilize numerous strategies designed to either increase deficit behaviors or decrease maladaptive actions. After conducting an A-B-C analysis, the therapist determines the target behavior and develops a systematic plan to alter that behavior. It is imperative that the behavior be observable and clearly defined. Another important decision is whether to target a behavior that seldom occurs (deficit) or to focus on an excessive behavior. Often behavioral deficits and excesses are on the opposite ends of the same behavior continuum (such as excessive talking without permission and not enough hand raising for permission to speak). Generally, it is better to teach, model, and reinforce a desired behavior than to try to eliminate an undesired behavior. Maladaptive behaviors are often replaced with other inappropriate actions if there is no active instruction regarding appropriate behaviors; this follows the common-sense edict of instructing a person what *to do* as opposed to what *not to do*. Similarly, trying to increase a deficit behavior is less intrusive and more positive than seeking to omit an action.

Procedures that increase deficit behaviors include those already discussed: positive reinforcement, negative reinforcement, modeling, behavioral rehearsal, and self-monitoring. Other procedures include shaping, in which successive approximations of the desired behavior are reinforced; contracting, in which the client and therapist agree on the behaviors to be performed and the reinforcers to be provided; and token economies, in which stars or points are earned and later cashed in for reinforcers.

Contracting, token economies, and self-monitoring strategies are useful if the behavior is clearly within the client's repertoire (clients can emit the behavior if they so choose). Shaping, modeling, and behavioral rehearsal are very helpful if the client has seldom or never emitted the behavior. For example, the "best practices" (treatment that has clear empirical support) approach for an enuretic child who has seldom demonstrated bladder control would be behavioral rehearsal: the child drinks large quantities of water and practices urinating on a potty chair on an hourly basis (referred to as *positive practice* in the research literature) coupled with a bell-and-pad device for nighttime training. An enuresis alarm (bell and pad) consists of sensor pads worn on the child's undergarments, which are attached to a small alarm box on the wrist or shoulder. When the child wets, the alarm sounds and the child awakens. In this way, appropriate urination is reinforced, whereas soiling requires only that the child change clothing. Note that the child is being taught correct behaviors, not simply being punished for incorrect behaviors.

Shaping breaks the desired behavior into smaller sequential components, the simplest of which is within the client's behavioral repertoire. Gradually, the therapist increases the behavioral requirements for reinforcement by requiring closer and closer approximations of the target behavior. If a child suffers from extreme separation anxiety, for example, the therapist would first reinforce the child for staying in the kitchen while the primary caretaker went into another room. The therapist would then gradually increase separation time within the parameters of the family home. Progressive shaping procedures would then reinforce the child for playing outside the house for longer and longer periods, always without the presence of the caretaker, and finally require the child to play at a schoolyard or community park under adult supervision but without the caretaker's presence (the terminal behavior).

Excess Behavior

As with the treatment of behavioral deficits, there are a series of procedures designed to eliminate excessive or undesired actions. The first, differential reinforcement of other behavior (DRO), is the least intrusive and best fits the model of teaching new desired behavior. Rather than focusing on a targeted maladaptive behavior, the therapist reinforces an *incompatible* positive behavior. Because the two behaviors are contradictory, the emission of the positive behavior results in the omission of the negative behavior. For example, suppose a therapist is working with an 8-year-old male (TJ) who is diagnosed as oppositional-defiant. The parents are angry with TJ because he frequently loses his temper, argues with adults, refuses to comply with requests, and deliberately annoys others. After consulting with the family, the therapist decides that the first behavior to be eliminated is arguing. An A-B-C analysis indicates that TJ's parents and teacher frequently reinforce his arguing by visually attending to him, verbally interacting with him, and often arguing back when he engages in this behavior. Further analysis indicates that TJ's father virtually never attends to his son when TJ is being quiet or compliant. Therefore, a DRO intervention is implemented wherein TJ's parents and teacher are told to visually and verbally attend to and reinforce TJ *only* when he *complies with requests* (incompatible behavior) and to ignore him when he argues. "Ignoring" means that the adults are to have no social interaction with TJ, avoid eye contact with him and, if necessary, leave the room when he persists in arguing. However, when he is compliant with requests, the adults are to provide positive reinforcers and actively attend to TJ, including making eye contact, smiling, nodding, and making positive comments such as "Thank you," "I like how cooperative you are being," or "You are one great kid!" Because this behavior may not be within the repertoire of TJ's father, he may need considerable training, prompting, modeling, and reinforcement by the therapist and TJ's mother!

Another procedure designed to reduce or eliminate inappropriate behavior is the time out—moving the child from a reinforcing setting to a nonreinforcing setting for a specified period of time. The "best practices" model of time out suggests the child be placed in another room or, if that is not feasible, seated in a chair facing the wall. The recommended length of time out is 1 minute per year of age, during which time the parent or teacher should avoid eye contact and all social interaction with the child. Finally, the youngster must be quiet for the *last 15 seconds* of time out. If this does not occur, the time out procedure should be continued until 15 seconds of quiet time is achieved (Jenson, Rhode, & Reavis, 1996).

Overcorrection is another strategy to modify maladaptive behavior. Overcorrection consists of restitution *and* positive practice of a related behavior. For example, if an adolescent is caught stealing, overcorrection would require that the stolen goods be returned *and*, an appropriate amount (say, $50) of the adolescent's allowance be donated to a charity of her or his choice.

Final options for dealing with undesired behaviors are punishment, response prevention, and extinction. Extinction occurs by completely eliminating reinforcers for the behavior. Unlike punishment, wherein negative actions are actively castigated, extinction simply means ignoring the behavior and removing *all* reinforcers that may occur as a result of the behavior. This is quite difficult to accomplish, because many reinforcers are beyond the therapist's control. Returning to the example of theft, if a child is caught 50% of the time (an unlikely scenario), the youngster is still actively reinforced the other half of the time. The child quickly learns that sometimes crime *does* pay. It would be very difficult to ensure that all reinforcement is unavailable in this case. Furthermore, extinction does not typically cause immediate response reduction. If the conduct is dangerous to others or to the child, waiting for it to slowly diminish is not an acceptable option. Finally, it is common for clients to experience an extinction burst—an increase in the behavior when it is no longer reinforced. For example, putting additional money in a vending machine that has failed to deliver the goods is a common example of extinction burst. The thinking behind the action is, "This has always worked before!" Because the extinction burst is very common, all parents and teachers should be forewarned.

Treatment Goals

It is evident from this discussion that behavior therapy and CBT require an active treatment plan with ending *goals* defined in broad behavioral terms. By comparison, treatment *activities or strategies* are specific interventions that use behavioral techniques (such as positive reinforcement, time out, behavioral rehearsal) directed toward increasing or decreasing designated actions. So although various treatment strategies can occur sequentially or concurrently, they are all directed toward achieving the treatment goals. For many dysfunctions, the associated behaviors are of such chronicity, severity, and breadth that a broad range of treatment strategies is required.

For example, with an adolescent who has a chronic eating disorder, the treatment goals (stated in broad behavioral terms) are (1) elimination of all bingeing and purging, (2) a decrease in body dissatisfaction, (3) an increase in personal efficacy or power, and (4) an increase in physical self-esteem. These goals can all be *measured* by administering the Eating Disorder Inventory-2 (EDI-2) (Garner, 1991) and the Multidimensional Self-Concept Scale (MSCS) (Bracken, 1992). Another measure is the analysis of the adolescent's daily self-monitoring log, which tracks meals eaten, time spent in exercise, number of bingeing episodes, and number of purgings. Comparisons of pretreatment and posttreatment results would verify the intervention's efficacy.

The treatment goals selected for the client with an eating disorder are based on the specific problem behaviors and are empirically driven (the best practices model). That is, previous research indicates that increasing the adolescent's sense of personal power, coupled with helping her recognize the positive attributes of her own physical appearance will reduce her acceptance of current sociocultural mores and significantly diminish her dissatisfaction with her body. This, in turn, will lead to a reduction in bingeing and purging (Phelps, Augustyniak, Nelson, & Nathanson, in press). To achieve these end goals, intermediate treatment *strategies* would include: (1) development of a self-change plan that encompasses a moderate daily exercise program and three regularly scheduled meals a day, (2) speedy elimination of all purging behavior, (3) active problem solving that incorporates identifying and recognizing the sociocultural exaltation of thinness, as well as objectively evaluating peer pressure regarding weight control, and (4) reducing bingeing behavior. As with the end goals, all intermediate treatment strategies should be measured to determine the treatment's effectiveness. Finally, specific techniques utilized with this client would include positive verbal reinforcement, differential reinforcement of other behavior (DRO), response prevention, logging the frequency and timing of behavior, and use of empowering self-statements.

TREATMENT EVALUATION

The effectiveness of a behavioral intervention should be reviewed frequently. If the treatment strategies are not achieving the desired changes in behavior, it is necessary to reassess the factors influencing the behavior (A-B-C analysis). Some programs fail because of a misunderstanding of the components that are maintaining the behavior. Often behaviors are influenced by a constellation of factors, and, by careful examination, the therapist may be able to identify particular conditions that continue to have an influence. For example, with clients like TJ (the 8-year-old who argues), strategies that require parents or teachers to reinforce certain behaviors while ignoring others are frequently misused. The adults may not follow the procedure, and must be retrained through modeling and reinforcement. With eating disordered clients, it is not unusual to find peers continuing to praise the adolescent for being thin. If this reinforcement overshadows the behavioral techniques, the bingeing and purging will persist. In this case, alternative strategies incorporating peer involvement need to be implemented.

It is important that the treatment goals and strategies be objectively and quantitatively evaluated. Although it is comforting to hear from clients, teachers, or parents that the interventions "seem" to be working, only an impartial assessment can verify those conclusions (or refute them) and can help identify the treatment strategies that need to be modified. In short, never rely on feelings or impressions; treatment will be far more successful if you conduct systematic and objective evaluations.

BEHAVIORAL APPROACHES IN PRACTICE

• • • *The Case of Sibling Rivalry*

Initial interview Keesha is a 4-year-old who has recently been having difficulty interacting with her 1-year-old brother Kyle. During the initial interview with Keesha's parents, they specified that Keesha did not willingly share toys or belongings with Kyle. When asked to share, Keesha would refuse, stage temper tantrums, and throw toys at Kyle. A number of times, Keesha actually hit Kyle with toys, slapped his face with her hand, and pushed him over. In addition, Keesha frequently asked her parents to do things only with her and to leave Kyle home during family outings. These were relatively new behaviors. Until approximately 6 months before, Keesha had bragged to others about her baby brother and had tried to help in his care by getting a bottle or diaper, changing his clothes, and attempting to sooth his crying. But as Kyle has become more independent in walking and talking, Keesha has responded in a negative manner.

The parents left the initial conference with instructions to keep a week-long daily diary of *both positive and negative interactions* between Keesha and Kyle, including time of day, what events occurred prior to the interactions, who was present, specific actions both Keesha and Kyle demonstrated, and how the parents responded. Because Keesha attended (without Kyle) preschool three times a week, the parents gave written permission to contact the preschool teacher who was asked to keep a similar diary of Keesha's interactions with her peers. In addition, the entire family was scheduled for a session and was asked to bring some of Keesha's favorite toys. This session was planned to allow independent confirmation of the problem behaviors.

Session with the family During the second session, Keesha was first invited to play with the therapist without the presence of mother, father, or Kyle. During this time, Keesha was talkative, friendly, and shared toys appropriately. No aggressive behaviors were evident. When Keesha was told that Kyle would be joining the play, Keesha asked that he not be allowed to join and started to pick up her toys. When the therapist brought Kyle in, Keesha placed all her toys behind her. The therapist then took additional toys out of the play box and proceeded to play with Kyle, ignoring Keesha. Within two minutes, Keesha approached, requesting that she and the therapist move to another room "without Kyle being around." When it was suggested that she join in the play instead, she started to cry and left the office. No attempt was made to dissuade her from leaving. After approximately 15 minutes, the therapist returned to the waiting room and invited the parents and Keesha to join in the play with Kyle. Keesha refused, and so the session ended with Kyle, mother, father, and therapist playing in the office while Keesha sat alone in the waiting room.

Assessment After one week, the daily diaries completed by the parents and preschool teacher were evaluated, and an A-B-C assessment indicated that the primary antecedent (A) to Keesha's negative behaviors was the presence of Kyle. That is, she engaged in appropriate behaviors when playing with neighborhood children, when working or playing with preschool peers, and when interacting with her parents while Kyle was sleeping. Keesha's negative *behaviors* (B) consisted of crying; arguing with her parents; and hitting, pushing, slapping, and throwing toys at Kyle. Consequences (C) for the negative behaviors consisted of the parents admonishing Keesha to be "nice," taking her into another room and spending "alone" time with her to "calm her down," and discussing with Keesha "why she did what she did." By comparison, when Keesha played appropriately with Kyle, the parents frequently did nothing.

The A-B-C results clearly indicated that treatment should be directed toward changing the parents' reactions to Keesha's behavior toward Kyle. At present, the consequences for Keesha's maladaptive behaviors were an *increase* in parental attention and verbal interaction, and, unfortunately, appropriate behaviors were being ignored. The therapist then met with the parents and discussed these observations with them, illustrating that they were actually reinforcing negative behaviors and overlooking positive actions. During the consultation, it became clear that the parents had considered their admonishments, discussions, and removal of Keesha to another room as "punishment." When asked, the parents stated that they did not actively reinforce Keesha for sharing with Kyle because "it was expected of her."

Treatment goals and implementation The parents were cooperative throughout this session and indicated a willingness to try different strategies with Keesha. Together with the therapist, they developed treatment goals for Keesha that consisted of increasing sharing behaviors with Kyle and eliminating all aggressive behaviors directed toward Kyle. To achieve these treatment goals, the following intermediate treatment strategies were implemented: (1) a star was placed on a chart kept on the refrigerator door every time Keesha *spontaneously* shared her toys and belongings with Kyle, (2) verbal reinforcement was given every time Keesha *immediately and without complaining* responded to a parental request to share with Kyle, (3) Keesha was visually and verbally ignored every time she cried or attempted to argue, and (4) time out was immediately imposed every time Keesha attempted or was successful in hitting, pushing, slapping, or throwing items at Kyle. Time out consisted of 4 minutes (Keesha's age) of isolation in her bedroom with the mandatory 15 seconds of quiet time at the end of the period. Finally, when Keesha had a total of ten stars on her chart, she would cash them in for 30 minutes of "special" time, which consisted of selecting an activity that she and one parent would engage in without Kyle's presence. Activities Keesha selected included such things as reading stories, watching videos, making popcorn, and playing in the backyard. Thus, the treatment techniques included token economy (stars), positive reinforcement (verbal), extinction (ignoring), and time out.

These strategies were monitored daily by use of a log the parents kept. The therapist reviewed the log on a weekly basis. The interventions worked well and at the end of two weeks had resulted in a 75% increase in spontaneous sharing, a 45% increase in immediate noncomplaining responses, and a 90% decrease in aggressive behaviors directed toward Kyle. However, Keesha's crying and attempts at arguing had not significantly decreased. The program was then altered; the behavioral technique directed toward reduction of crying and arguing behavior was changed from extinction to time out, a more active measure. Also, because spontaneous sharing behaviors and immediate responses to parental requests had improved significantly, it was time to increase the behavioral requirements for the token economy and verbal reinforcement. And finally, because aggressive behaviors were considered injurious and not to be tolerated, the time-out procedures were continued as in the original plan. Thus, the parents were instructed to: (1) use time out as instructed every time Keesha cried or attempted to argue, as well as for attempted aggressive behaviors; (2) continue posting a star every time Keesha engaged in spontaneous sharing, but the cash-in requirement for "special time" would now require 15 stars; and (3) give nonverbal reinforcement —nods, smiles, a thumbs-up sign—every time Keesha shared with prompting, but only on a random basis. These changes were carefully explained to Keesha, stressing how well she was behaving toward her brother.

Treatment outcome   These changes were successful in maintaining Keesha's adaptive behaviors as well as in decreasing her maladaptive actions. The program continued with the gradual elimination of continuous nonverbal reinforcement and the token economy system until the treatment goals were achieved; aggressive behaviors were completely eliminated and spontaneous sharing behaviors were significantly increased. At the end of treatment, the parents were randomly reinforcing Keesha for appropriate interactions and were utilizing time out for crying and argumentative behaviors only two or three times a month. ●

INSIGHTS AND IMPLICATIONS

As we have seen, behavioral approaches with children and adolescents rely on a focus on behavior, the use of clearly specified treatment procedures, and an objective assessment of treatment efficacy. The applications occur across a wide variety of settings and with a broad range of problem behaviors. The active involvement of significant others (parents, teachers, peers) in this process is imperative. People who interact frequently with the client can have a major impact on treatment success. Behavioral techniques seldom, if ever, are carried out solely in the therapist's office. Only by engaging the people who are responsible for the client's daily care and education can the therapist have a broad impact. In the case of deficit behaviors, these people can model, reinforce, and assist with behavioral rehearsals in the natural environment, thereby encouraging treatment generalization. These important people in the client's life can identify excess behaviors when they occur and immediately provide consequences intended to develop more adaptive behaviors. In short, involvement of key people in the client's life is essential to effective treatment.

KEY POINTS TO REMEMBER

- *Before starting behavior or cognitive-behavioral therapy, complete a careful analysis (A-B-C assessment) to determine how, where, and when behavior is being shaped.*
- *Always first determine whether you want to increase a behavioral deficit or decrease a behavioral excess.*
- *Focus on a few very specific behaviors.*
- *Remember that reinforcement always increases and punishment always decreases behavior.*
- *Expect and plan for an extinction burst when you are seeking to eliminate a behavior that has been frequently reinforced in the past.*
- *Utilize self-monitoring or self-instructional procedures whenever the client has the requisite cognitive skills.*
- *Employ the valuable strategies of modeling and behavioral rehearsal whenever appropriate.*
- *Recognize that behavior therapy and cognitive-behavioral therapy strategies coexist in harmony and can be implemented simultaneously.*

PHELPS' PICKS

Barkley, R. A. (1987). *Defiant children: A clinician's manual for parent training.* New York: Guilford Press.
> An outstanding handbook that outlines very effective interventions for parents to use with acting-out children. It includes a parent workbook. A must for every therapist's library!

Duriak, J. A. (1995). *School-based prevention programs for children and adolescents.* Thousand Oaks, CA: Sage.
> A very helpful text for teachers and mental health service providers who work with schools.

Kazdin, A. E. (1994). *Behavior modification in applied settings.* Pacific Grove, CA: Brooks/Cole.
> An excellent general reference for more clinical cases that includes special techniques to enhance client performance, numerous examples of behavioral applications, and a discussion of legal and ethical issues.

CHAPTER 10   *Safeguarding Children's Rights*

CHILDREN'S BILL OF RIGHTS
The right to privacy
The right to be protected from abuse and neglect
The right to be protected from exploitation
The right to help to recover from victimization
The right to live with or maintain contact with parents
The right to protection when placed in alternative care
The right of access to quality health care
The right to be educated and to enjoy one's own culture
The right to receive special help to achieve self-reliance
The right to express an opinion and be heard
The right to play
—UN Convention on the Rights of the Child,
Based on a summary by WILCOX & NAIMARK (1991)

THE EMERGING RIGHTS OF THE CHILD

Historically, children have been denied the most basic human rights. In the crowded slums of Europe before the 18th century, unwanted children were abandoned on streets and on the doorsteps of churches and orphanages, and dead babies were buried in backyards like animals. Children were maimed to make them better beggars, often hanged for small offenses, and forced to work long hours at young ages (Lefrancois, 1990). In both England and the United States, the courts granted all rights of control to parents, and children who disobeyed could be put to death (Hart, 1991). In fact, there were no laws to protect children and no provision for consequences if parents or caretakers abused, abandoned, exiled, maimed, or even murdered their children.

During the 18th century, children were highly prized for their economic value and were treated as chattel—sometimes literally bought and sold (Chase, 1975). In the mid-19th century, children in the United States were given special legal protection. At this time, child labor laws were enacted and school attendance became compulsory. However, it was not until the 20th century that children were regarded as persons, and not until the middle of the century that the courts recognized children as persons under the law. In 1959, the rights of the children of the world were unanimously proclaimed by the UN General Assembly in the Declaration of the Rights of Children (Gibson, 1978). It was from this status as persons that children finally gained the right to nurturance and protection.

The 1989 UN Convention on the Rights of the Child is a significant document for it balances nurturance and protection rights with the rights of self-determination and autonomy. It is important to note that in this document, the United Nations granted the rights of autonomy and self-determination to children for the first time. In addition, children were viewed as individuals, not as family members, and so the rights of the child were placed ahead of the rights of the family (Cohen & Naimark, 1991).

353

The years 1989 and 1990 may have been watershed years for the worldwide advancement of children's rights. In 1989, the 159 member states of the United Nations adopted the UN Convention on the Rights of the Child. The treaty, ratified by 20 member nations went into force on September of 1990. Since then, 54 other nations have ratified the treaty, although the United States is not one of them (Wilcox & Naimark, 1991).

Some of the rights addressed at the 1989 UN Convention on the Rights of the Child, summarized by Wilcox and Naimark (1991), include:

1. The right to privacy and legal protection
2. The right to be protected from all forms of abuse, neglect, and exploitation
3. The right to rehabilitative care to recover from victimization
4. The right to live with parents or to maintain contact with both parents
5. The right to protection when placed in alternative care
6. The right of access to quality health care
7. The right to be educated and to enjoy one's own culture
8. The right of children with disabilities to receive special care and training
9. The right to express an opinion and to be heard
10. The right to play, leisure, and recreation

The UN Convention recognized the dignity of the child and the child's right to protection and treatment, as well as the child's rights to self-determination. It also took into account the child's developmental level and advocated treatment that was developmentally relevant and appropriate. These rights and privileges have major implications on how mental health professionals will work with children in the future.

The (UN) Convention is the first official bill of rights for children with a coherent, comprehensive vision of children's policy. If ratified, it will provide the legal foundation for a reformation of children's status toward respect for their personhood.
—MELTON (1991, p. 70)

Melton (1991) summarized the major implications of the UN Convention into the following six principles that he suggests are relevant to future public policy regarding children's mental health.

High-Quality Services for Children

In his first principle, Melton (1991) suggests that "the provision of high-quality services for children should be a matter of the highest priority for public mental health authorities" (p. 68). The 1993 data from the Mental Health Services Program for Youth indicates that 87% of the available public resources were spent on just 2% of the children—those that compose the most severely disturbed group. In sharp contrast, only 0.2% of our mental health dollars were spent on the 75% of the children who are at risk. It is clear that we need community-based systems of care to promote earlier investments, primarily in prevention and treatment for children at risk (CDF, 1994).

Children as Active Partners in Treatment

Melton (1991) interprets the UN convention to mean that "children should be viewed as active partners in child mental health services with heavy weight placed on protection of their liberty and privacy" (p. 69). In a therapeutic partnership, children are regarded as persons in their own right who enjoy equal status in the relationship. Within the parameters of this partnership and taking into account the child's age and level of maturity, children can set goals, plan treatment, and assume responsibility for their actions. In this therapeutic relationship, the counselor communicates respect for the individual rights of children, meaning that confidences are kept, privacy is respected, and feedback is given. The child's right to refuse to participate in treatment is also respected, and children should have the option to end treatment and be permitted to do so, if they wish.

Child Counseling Should Support "Family Integrity"

The assertion that "mental health services for children should be respectful of parents and supportive of family integrity" (Melton, 1991, p. 69) implies that parent involvement is an essential ingredient in the child's treatment plan and emphasizes the importance of the family in the child's growth and development. Most parents love their children and want to do what is best for them. However, some parents simply do not know how to cope with the many stresses that currently plague families. Therefore, parents need a warm and caring person to listen to their problems and to support them in their efforts to help their children. Counseling strategies to be used to help parents improve the parent-child relationship and to support them as they struggle to meet the rigorous challenges of child-rearing are outlined in Part III of this text.

Provide Alternatives to Residential Placement

Melton's fourth principle deals with the need to find alternatives to residential placement and advocates that "states should apply a strong presumption against residential placement of children for the purpose of treatment, with due procedural care in decision making about treatment and with the provision of community-based alternatives. When out-of-home placement is necessary for the protection of the child, it should be in the most family-like setting consistent with those objectives" (1991, p. 69). States typically spend more on residential treatment of children with the most serious emotional disturbances than they invest in school guidance programs, early intervention, family preservation, parent training and support programs, or any other type of care that focuses on preventing children's problems from escalating (CDF, 1994).

The goal of the next century should be to develop strong family-centered and community-based systems of care that will focus on family preservation and provide "wrap-around" services to children who are at risk for out-of-home placement because of serious emotional problems. We need local systems of care that are family-focused, multidisciplinary, and multiagency in their approach; that provide flexibility; and that are individualized to meet the needs of each child and family. The good news is that some national programs such as the Child and Adolescent Services System Program (CASSP) sponsored by the National Institute of Mental Health, as well as some state programs, have already initiated these types of services (CDF, 1994).

Protect from Harm

Fifth, "when the state does undertake the care and custody of emotionally disturbed children, it also assumes an especially weighty obligation to protect them from harm" (Melton, 1991, p. 69). So often, children are further abused by the system that is designed to protect them. As they move farther away from their family and into foster care, group homes and residential treatment centers, the possibility of abuse increases (Chase, 1975). When deciding placement, the state bears the responsibility for the child's care and safety.

Prevention Is Central

Finally, "prevention should be the cornerstone of child mental health policy" (Melton, 1991, p. 69). Despite a lack of strong funding support, both public and private, prevention remains a central theme in elementary school guidance programs, government preschool programs such as Head Start, family preservation programs, and community sponsored programs to help children before they get into trouble. Although most human services professionals favor prevention over remediation, it is certainly fair to say that most investments in mental health services for children have been expensive reactions to problems that are already well developed and severe enough to attract our attention. A more proactive and sensible response would be to expend existing resources on supports and interventions that would prevent problems or lessen their severity before they take their toll in human and economic hardship.

In conclusion, each clinician will have to balance his or her child clients' rights to protection and nurturance with their rights for self-determination and autonomy. Although legal and ethical issues are sometimes difficult to apply in practice, having a genuine concern for the child and his or her family will help the practitioner determine the right course of action.

CHILDREN'S RIGHTS IN THERAPY

All that may come to my knowledge in the exercise of my profession or outside of my profession or in daily commerce with men, which ought not to be spread abroad, I will keep secret and will never reveal.
—Hippocratic Oath

Mental health professionals who work with children and their families have a moral, ethical, and legal responsibility to serve the best interests of the child. All clients, including children, have the right to informed consent, the right to feedback regarding therapeutic progress, the right to privacy, and the right to confidentiality. The mental health professional should fully understand the obligation to protect these rights before initiating a therapeutic relationship with a child and his or her family in any setting. This protection, along with its limitations and constraints, should be explained to all participants in a way that is easily understood by everyone, including the child.

Therapy with children presents a special challenge to mental health counselors for three important reasons. First, children generally do not have sufficient understanding and ability to make informed decisions on their own about whether to accept or refuse different therapeutic interventions; second, young children are not considered *legally competent* because they have not reached the statutory age; and third, children rarely come to therapy voluntarily.

Conflicts often arise when the child is identified as "the problem" and the parents seem to be pressuring the child into treatment. It is not unusual for the therapist to discover that the child's problem is a reflection of the difficulties the family is experiencing and that the entire family needs the counselor's help and support. In instances where the child's improvement presents a threat to the family (if the child is the family scapegoat), the therapist's attempts to be supportive and helpful to the child may be met with resistance.

The child therapist's primary responsibility is to protect the child's rights while maintaining his or her professional and legal obligations to the child's parents. This is not an easy task. Even when it is clear that the parent has the right to decide for the child, the child's goals may be at odds with the parents' goals for the child. The therapist's dilemma is further compounded if the goals of the parents and the means by which they prefer to reach those goals are in direct contrast with what the therapist believes to be in the best interest of the child. Occasionally, a therapist may encounter situations in which a parent insists on the most restrictive treatment or refuses any type of treatment for a child who is obviously in need.

Mental health professionals should help parents find ways to discuss the proposed therapy with their children. Careful explanations by the therapist and support from the parents during the course of therapy will help put children at ease and establish trust. If parents are contemplating placing their child in residential or group home settings, the therapist has an obligation to recommend treatment in accordance with the child's right to the least restrictive alternative. Ideally, this would mean that outpatient therapy would be the first choice, day care would take precedence over inpatient hospitalization, and positive interventions would be chosen over negative ones.

The Right to Consent

> Unless state laws specifically allow it a minor is incapable of giving binding legal consent to counseling treatment.
> —SWENSON (1993, p. 376)

Legally, consent requires that "an individual's permission be given knowingly, intelligently and voluntarily" (Grisso & Vierling, 1978, p. 415). *Informed* consent implies that a client has sufficient information about a particular therapeutic intervention and its possible consequences to make a rational decision for or against it. To give permission *knowingly*, the client must be given a fair and accurate description of the proposed intervention in language that is readily understood. This description would include information about the therapeutic process and the benefits and risks of therapy, as well as an explanation of the right of confidentiality and its limitations. To consent *intelligently* implies competence, which, in the United States, is defined by age.

The age at which a child is competent to give informed consent varies widely from state to state. Until the child is old enough to give informed consent, the child's parents or legal guardian usually make decisions regarding mental health care unless it can be proved that the parents are not acting in the child's best interest. On the basis of the *parens patriae* doctrine, the state can make decisions for the minor against the parents' wishes if the state decides that the parents are not providing adequate protection for the child's physical needs, psychosocial needs, or both (Swenson, 1993).

"Most jurisdictions allow minors to consent to treatment without parental knowledge in specific situations in which obtaining parental consent may jeopardize the likelihood that the minor will receive that treatment" (Gustafson & McNamara, 1987, p. 503). These specific situations apply mostly to adolescents and include counseling or medical care for substance abuse, sexual abuse, pregnancy, sexually transmitted diseases, and contraception. In addition, the law has recognized four general exceptions to the requirement for parental consent (Gustafson & McNamara, 1987; Swenson, 1993). The first is the "mature minor" exception that pertains to minors who are of "sufficient intelligence" to understand the nature and consequences of the treatment. The second exception is for "emancipated" minors who are entitled to the same rights and responsibilities as adults (such as a married adolescent). "Emergency treatment" is the third exception; in this instance parental consent is implied because of the urgency of the situation, and consent expires once the emergency ends. The final exception is when treatment is court ordered.

Because the states differ in their definitions of competence, each practitioner is responsible for knowing the laws and statutes of the state in which she or he is practicing. Grisso and Vierling (1978) point out that different states have different statutory ages for different treatments and that age limits vary even within the same state. "For example, various states allow minors to consent to treatment related to pregnancy without parental consent or knowledge; but in different states, the minimum age allowances are 12, 14, and 15. The ages at which minors may consent to treatment for drug dependency range from various early adolescent ages to no minimum age at all" (p. 415).

Some writers (Grisso & Vierling, 1978; Gustafson & McNamara, 1987) suggest that a developmental approach should be taken to the issue of consent. They agree that minors below age 11 generally do not have the intellectual capacity to give informed consent and that children from ages 11 to 14 may not have the ability to comprehend the complexity of treatment alternatives, risks, and benefits and to provide informed consent. Grisso and Vierling (1978) conclude, on the basis of their research, that minors age 15 and older are as competent to provide consent as adults are. Although many believe that the "mature" child should be given the right to make independent decisions regarding his or her own health care, the fact remains that states require parental consent unless either the minor meets one of the exceptions previously mentioned or the parent is not acting in the child's best interest.

Because most minor clients are unable to give legal consent, the practitioner must obtain the written informed consent of the child's parent(s) or other guardian(s) before beginning therapy. In obtaining informed consent, the practitioner needs to take special care to ensure that the child client and his or her parents understand the types of services that are offered as well as the risks and benefits of therapy. The practitioner needs to explain the right to confidentiality and to note instances when confidentiality cannot be maintained. It is important to stress that information will be released only to qualified professionals and only with the express written permission of the client or the client's parents. Written permission needs to be obtained from the parent (and in some cases from the child) if the mental health practitioner wants to consult with other professionals regarding the child. The child's family has to be informed if the therapist is being supervised for licensure or is a student-in-training and if audio- and videotaping are used in the supervision or therapeutic process. Similarly, written authorization is needed to use case materials in research, teaching, and publishing. If applicable, fees and billable services should also be discussed to prevent any misunderstanding.

This information is usually discussed with the child and his or her family prior to beginning therapy and is included in a written professional services agreement that is signed by the parents, the minor child, and the therapist (Swenson, 1993). Part of this agreement or contract is a consent to treatment form (sample copies in English and in Spanish, can be found in Appendix B). The consent form should be carefully explained to the parent(s) or guardian(s) who are signing on the child's behalf. In the event that the signers cannot read or cannot read English, the practitioner must provide someone to read and interpret the form for them. If the minor client is an adolescent, many practitioners invite the client to sign this form also. If the child will be included in the treatment process, the practitioner may want to use the child's version of the informed consent form (also in Appendix B). This form helps explain the therapeutic process and the limits of confidentiality in language that children can understand. It is written on a second-grade level and can be read independently by most children age 6 or 7. If the child is not able to read the form independently, the counselor can read it to the child to make sure that children younger than 6 understand its intent.

Although not legally binding, the child consent form helps the therapist determine whether the child understands the procedures and limitations of therapy, and it gives children an opportunity to ask questions about what they don't understand. Older children, particularly in states that have the legal right of informed consent, can sign the consent to treatment form with their parent or guardian. Of course, although these procedures satisfy legal and ethical considerations, nothing can replace the warm, personal interest that clinicians display in their efforts to help both children and parents understand their rights to privacy and the need to protect themselves and others from harm.

The Right to Feedback

If children are to be active participants in the therapeutic process, they should be apprised of their progress in ways they can comprehend and that can help them make positive changes in their attitude or behavior. Child clients have the right to understand the range and seriousness of their problems so they can work toward some type of resolution. Parents, too, have the right to be kept informed of their child's progress in an objective and caring way. Providing feedback to both parent and child heightens rapport and engenders trust. It is recommended that parents be told just enough to keep them informed and involved but not so much as to violate the child's right to privacy.

If children are to be tested for specific disabilities, children have the right to know the purpose of the testing and what the test discovered that might help them understand their school difficulties. For instance a child labeled "stupid" and "unmotivated" might be relieved to know that he or she has a learning disability that can be helped. When interpreting test results to the child, the practitioner will have to take into consideration the child's developmental level and how much the child is capable of understanding. In addition, responsible feedback to third parties who requested the testing (such as teachers and principals) will make those responsible for the child's education aware of the child's specific disability; this will help them design programs specifically for the child and will dispel common misconceptions that the child is "lazy" or "not trying."

Abuses are more likely to occur when psychological evaluations are done at the request of third parties and the mental health professional does not have complete control of how information from a particular assessment is being used. For example, a psychological assessment done in a school setting should give valuable feedback to increase the child's academic performance. However, Rinas and Clyne-Jackson (1988) warn that if such requests for assessments are "being used to channel students of lesser abilities into dead-end or poor-quality programs" (p. 7), then mental health professionals have a responsibility to point out the ethical concerns of such a practice and to educate the facility on the proper use of such testing information. "If the mental health worker is unsuccessful in changing how the information is used, however, he or she should consider discontinuing the service despite the personal risk it entails" (Rinas & Clyne Jackson, 1988, p. 7).

The Right to Privacy

Privacy differs somewhat from confidentiality because it involves the right of the individual to withhold information (Rinas & Clyne-Jackson, 1988), a right given to children with ratification of the UN Convention on the Rights of the Child in 1990. However, because the legal right of informed consent is dependent on chronological age and because the UN treaty was not ratified by the United States, a child's legal right to privacy in this country cannot be guaranteed. However, individual practitioners can help protect the child's right to privacy by: (1) not pressuring the child to divulge information that he or she does not wish to disclose, (2) discussing with the child the general progress reports that are to be shared with parents, and (3) letting the child know that it is not necessary to share information about the therapy sessions with parents if the child doesn't want to.

The Right to Confidentiality

> Establishing a trusting relationship may be more important than promises of confidentiality when one is dealing with minors...[and] verbal explanations of confidentiality, although necessary, may not be as important as real-life experiences with a therapist who maintains confidentiality.
> —GUSTAFSON & MCNAMARA (1987, p. 505)

Privileged Communication

Historically, our legal system has protected communication between doctor-patient, attorney-client, and priest-penitent. These relationships fall under the category of privileged communications, which protect professionals from being forced, or prevent them from volunteering, to testify in court about a client's statements that were originally made in confidence. Prior to the 1950s, no statutes dealt with the privilege of psychotherapeutic communications, and protection was available only under existing physician-patient privilege. In the 1950s and 1960s, several states extended privilege to psychologist-patient communications and in some cases provided much broader protection than existed for physician-patient communication (Fester, as cited in *In re Lifschutz*, 1970). By the mid-1970s, many states had extended privileged communication to include therapist-client relationships in psychology, nursing, and social work (Rinas & Clyne-Jackson, 1988). Because privileged communication does vary from one state to another, professionals need to be aware of their status with regard to court appearances.

In states that grant client-therapist privilege, "clients, not therapists, are protected under privilege statutes. Once a client waives his/her privilege, a therapist is legally obligated to testify" (Jagim, Wittman, & Noll, 1978, p. 462). Therapists who refuse to testify on ethical grounds risk possible penalties, including being held in contempt of court (*In re Lifschutz*, 1970). For children, privilege may also be claimed (and waived) by the child's parents or guardian.

There are certain situations in which the client's privilege may be waived by the court, such as when the client wishes to use his or her psychological status as part of a legal defense. An example would be a plea of guilty but mentally ill. Other situations in which confidentiality can be broken and client privilege can be waived are in cases of child abuse, threats of harm to self and others, involuntary commitment, and psychological examinations that have been court ordered (Corey, Corey & Callanan, 1993). Once unheard of, we now have examples of children as young as 11 and 12 who are murdering other children. Recently, a 14-year-old admitted killing a 4-year-old and his lawyers used mental illness as a defense. See the box titled Insanity Defense Fails—14-year-old Guilty of Murder, which illustrates an instance when privileged communication was waived so that expert witnesses could give testimony to the child's mental and emotional status.

Rinas and Clyne-Jackson (1988) advise practitioners who are not covered by therapist-client privilege to explain this to their clients at the beginning of therapy. If the practitioner is called to court to testify, he or she need only divulge information that is relevant to the particular problem being addressed. "Only formal notes need to be entered as evidence and the professional is not expected to reveal personal notes on the client, even if the client requests that this be done" (pp. 57–58). Counselors should write their notes in a clear and concise style, taking care to separate what the client says from their interpretations of it. Judgments or impressions that cannot be supported should not be included in the notes.

In some states, if a professional believes that revealing information will do irreparable harm to the therapeutic relationship, he or she may ask for a special private session with the judge to share these concerns *in camera*. The judge will then have an opportunity to review the case and decide how much of the privileged communication will remain confidential and how much will be available for use at trial.

Insanity Defense Fails—14-Year-Old Guilty of Murder

Privilege Communication Waived by the Court

John was 13 years old when he bludgeoned and strangled his 4-year-old neighbor. The eighth-grader, who had a history of violent and bizarre behavior, said that he saw the youngster walking along the sidewalk to a day camp they attended and lured him into the woods to take a "shortcut." Once in the woods, John said that he squeezed the child's neck, stuffed a plastic lunch bag in his mouth, and then crushed his skull with a very large rock.

The defense team contended that John suffered from "intermittent explosive disorder," a rare rage disorder characterized by episodes in which a person cannot control violent impulses. They also blamed his mother's use of an antiepilepsy drug during pregnancy. Because John used the insanity defense, privileged communication was waived by the court and expert medical witnesses were able to testify about his mother's medical condition and John's psychiatric diagnosis.

John was tried as an adult and prosecutors portrayed him as a methodical killer who lured his victim into a trap. The jury found him guilty of second-degree murder and he faces at least five years' incarceration and possibly life imprisonment.

This account was based on an actual case.

This procedure will protect the rights of the parties involved while granting the court access to information that is needed to maintain confidence in the outcome of the trial (*Reynolds v. State*, 1993).

Confidentiality

> When counseling clients who are minors or individuals who are unable to give voluntary, informed consent, parents or guardians may be included in the counseling process as appropriate. Counselors act in the best interests of clients and take measures to safeguard confidentiality.
>
> —Code of Ethics (American Counseling Association [ACA], 1995)

Most mental health professionals believe that, in addition to protecting the rights of clients, confidentiality helps practitioners build a warm and trusting relationship with the client, which is essential to the therapeutic process. Practitioners agree that strict confidentiality regarding release of information to other agencies and individuals should be maintained; however, conflicts arise when parents request information regarding the child's treatment. Ethically, the child has a right to confidentiality and the practitioner must determine what is in the child's best interest. Legally, however, a parent who provides consent has a right to information about his or her child's therapy (Swenson, 1993). To compound the problem further, some jurisdictions allow minors to obtain treatment without parental consent while at the same time allowing parental access to the child's records (Gustafson & McNamara, 1987).

Professionals are divided on how best to satisfy the parent's request for information and still maintain the child's right to confidentiality. Some limit the parents' access to the child's treatment records, whereas others share information freely with parents

(Gustafson & McNamara, 1987). Most, however, try to balance the child's right to confidentiality with the parent's legal right to know. Rather than show parents the actual records, many practitioners try to satisfy the parents' need for information in informal ways that will protect the child's right to privacy. Asking the child's consent, including the child in family sessions, and screening information that would adversely affect the child's position in the family are ways to protect the relationship and satisfy the parents' request for feedback.

If the child refuses consent, some therapists recommend talking to the parents about the importance of confidentiality in the hope that they won't press the issue (Swenson, 1993). However, because the consent is not legally binding, the child's refusal would not be sufficient to deny access if the parent insists on seeing the records (Brems, 1993).

There is a general consensus that children age 12 and older are competent to participate in some treatment decisions (Gustafson & McNamara, 1987). As a result, many states now recognize a minor's right to seek mental health services, and many states have set ages at which a child may consent to treatment. Therefore, in some states, additional permission from the child may be needed before information can be released to other agencies or individuals. In Illinois, for example, minors age 12 or older have the right to their confidential files and they must give written authorization for others, including parents, to access their file (Foster, as cited in Rinas & Clyne-Jackson, 1988). Because laws vary from one jurisdiction to another, practitioners need to consult their own state's statutes regarding the release of information to third parties, including parents and guardians.

In group work, counselors clearly define confidentiality and the parameters for the specific group being entered, explain its importance, and discuss the difficulties related to confidentiality involved in group work. The fact that confidentiality cannot be guaranteed is clearly communicated to group members.
—Code of Ethics (ACA, 1995)

Confidentiality in groups Rinas and Clyne-Jackson (1988) point out that many legal statutes regarding confidentiality apply only to individual contacts with clients. "In most states, protective guidelines have not been developed for clients seen in either group or family therapy" (p. 55). Therefore, in many states, information given to a therapist in a group or in the presence of a third party is not legally confidential.

Most counselors agree that confidentiality is very important to the development of trust in the group process, and many fear that when confidentiality is not assured, the level of self-disclosure might be significantly reduced. It is up to the counselor to advise group members of the limitations of confidentiality in groups and to protect them from disclosing information that could harm them if revealed to anyone outside the group. Of course, in the initial group session, the therapist should inform members that confidentiality cannot be maintained when a clear danger to self or others is communicated to the group.

When Can Confidentiality Be Breached?

Confidentiality can be breached in certain situations when the child's safety takes precedence over the client's (or the parents') right to confidentiality. Corey, Corey, and Callanan (1993), summarizing a number of sources, list the following circumstances under which the therapist *must* provide information obtained during therapy:

- when the therapist is acting in a court-appointed capacity—for example, to conduct a psychological examination or to serve as an expert witness in a child-custody case
- when the therapist makes an assessment of a foreseeable risk of suicide
- when the client initiates a lawsuit against the therapist, such as for malpractice
- in any civil action when the client introduces mental conditions as a claim or defense
- when the client is under the age of 16 and the therapist believes that the child is a victim of a crime—for example, incest, child molestation, rape, or child abuse
- when the therapist determines that the client is in need of hospitalization for a mental or psychological disorder
- when information is mandated by a court
- when clients reveal their intention to commit a crime or when they can be accurately assessed as dangerous to society or dangerous to themselves (p. 104)

POTENTIAL RISKS TO CHILDREN'S RIGHTS

Practitioners must do everything in their power to protect the child's rights to privacy by holding sacred the right to confidentiality, except in instances where it must be breached for the child's safety and protection. One of the commandments for mental health counselors should be "thou shalt do no harm." If a child's confidences are not respected, entering into a helping relationship with a mental health practitioner may put the child at risk for emotional harm and may further subject the child to the prejudicial attitudes of friends, family, the educational system, and society.

The most likely potential risk areas are cumulative records, tapes of client contacts, information stored in computer data banks, and disclosures to third parties (Rinas & Clyne-Jackson, 1988).

Cumulative Records

Professionals working in schools and in other settings where cumulative records are kept should be aware that notations in children's folders or notes about a child's social and emotional adjustment and family life pose a serious threat to a child's right to privacy. These data, even if judgmental and inaccurate, could remain as an unchallenged testimony to the child's emotional stability. Therefore, counselors and teachers should be particularly careful about what goes into permanent records. Confidential information about the child's family life, fears, emotional problems, and inappropriate behavior should be kept in a separate file with limited access.

Cumulative school records should note academic achievement and school behavior in an objective and nonjudgmental way. Using clichés and judgmental phrases, such as "an all-American boy" or "rotten to the core" (which were actually seen in cumulative records from the early 1970s) should be avoided entirely. Not only do these types of notations prejudice the next reader of the file, they also don't convey anything helpful about the child.

All notes by counselors, teachers, nurses, and others should be evaluated in terms of how they will enhance the child's progress and healthy development. Purely negative comments do little to help children or practitioners address weaknesses and may actually contribute to problem behavior. For example, in psychiatric hospitals, nurse's notations about a child's behavior may result in increased medication or in denial of privileges. Professional notations should be made carefully and accurately. They should be written with the thought in mind that they may someday be read by others (quite possibly by the student or client when he or she comes of age) or be subpoenaed in court.

The Federal Educational Rights and Privacy Act (1974) gives parents and students of legal age the right to inspect their records. In an effort to keep institutions accountable regarding the accuracy and relevance of information kept in cumulative files, Rinas and Clyne-Jackson (1988) suggest that individual records should be open for inspection by the client or guardian so that inaccuracies can be challenged and appropriate modifications made when justified. Because keeping records for lengthy periods of time increases the risk that confidentiality will be violated, it is recommended that the records should be properly destroyed after a reasonable time has passed and there are no further contacts with the client.

Taped Counseling Sessions

Counselors obtain permission from clients prior to electronically recording or observing sessions.
—Code of Ethics (ACA, 1995)

Another potential violation of a child's right to privacy may be present when counseling sessions with the child are taped. If sessions are either audio- or videotaped, which is often the case when counselors are still in training or are being supervised for licensure, the child's right of confidentiality might be compromised by those who are not yet bound by a professional code of ethics (Rinas & Clyne-Jackson, 1988). It is always necessary to get both the child and the parent's consent to be taped and to limit access to the taped session to the counselor and his or her supervisor. Playing tapes for the entire class increases the risk that the child might be identified, and the practice should be avoided.

Computerized Data Storage

Psychologists maintain appropriate confidentiality in creating, storing, accessing, transferring and disposing of records under their control, whether these are written, automated or in any other medium.
—Ethical Principles of Psychologists (American Psychological Association [APA], 1992)

The fact that such a vast amount of health-related data is stored in computer data banks heightens the risk that confidential information will be released to unauthorized persons and will be used in a way that was not intended by the mental health professional. Many government and health-related agencies, most notably insurance companies, have ready access to client information.

According to data cited by Rinas and Clyne-Jackson (1988), court decisions have supported the right of agencies to access client files in the interest of ensuring quality care. Because insurance companies are increasingly requesting audits to control costs, monitor care, and prevent abuse, many private practitioners are recommending that the content of their client records be withheld and the frequency of such contacts be reported instead. Practitioners should get informed consent and advise all clients that their files may be audited by insurance companies in the future.

The fact that such a vast amount of personal medical history finds its way into data banks that can be accessed by any number of people has serious implications for child clients. Unauthorized and inappropriate disclosure that a child required professional help for emotional problems has potentially far-reaching negative effects on the lives of children that may not be apparent until the child is an adult and is no longer in need of any treatment. For instance, treatment for drug abuse as a teen may influence future employment prospects, and a history of conduct disorder may label a person a security risk.

> In order to minimize intrusions on privacy, psychologists include in written and oral reports, consultations, and the like, only information germane to the purpose for which the communication is made.
> —Ethical Principles of Psychologists (APA, 1992)

Third-Party Disclosures

There are many circumstances under which confidential information about a client can be released to a secondary source, with or without explicit consent: for example, (1) cases of public safety such as the reasonable suspicion of child abuse or an explicit threat to bomb the school (2) involuntarily commitment proceedings when the client is a danger to self or others and (3) court proceedings where privilege either has been waived by the court or does not exist between the client and the therapist (Rinas & Clyne-Jackson, 1988). Informed consent by the client or the parent is required when information is released to governmental or private agencies such as insurance companies, when data is used in legitimate research (but the client's identity must be protected), and in direct care intervention when other health professionals need the data to assist in the client's treatment.

Rinas and Clyne-Jackson (1988) recommend that clients be informed about the nature and extent of what was disclosed, to whom it was disclosed, and for what purpose. Client's should also be advised of the risks involved in a review of their files by an external source such as an insurance company. Even with a written release, it is important for private practitioners to be careful what they communicate in summaries to third parties. This is particularly true when this information will be used to make some type of decision about the client. It is *not* advisable to send all the progress notes on a particular client unless those notes are subpoenaed.

If privileged communication does not exist between the client and therapist, confidential information must be released to the court if requested. In addition, "communication between a client and a professional is not privileged in situations where a professional's involvement with the client is at the request of a third party such as the court, an employer or a child protection agency" (Rinas & Clyne-Jackson, 1988, p. 63).

For example, if a child protection agency refers a parent for therapy as a necessary condition for keeping the children in the family, the agency has the right to information on the client's progress and mental state during therapy. Parents should be told, up front, that their communications may be revealed to the referring agency and that their progress in therapy or lack of it could have an impact on the agency's decision.

LEGAL AND ETHICAL ISSUES FOR PRACTITIONERS

Mental health professionals have a responsibility to promote and protect the rights, goodness, and growth of their clients, their colleagues, their profession, and their society. This is a weighty responsibility, given that the needs of the client, the laws of society, professional codes of ethics, and the practitioner's personal values and interpretations may sometimes conflict.

Professional Ethics

Professional ethical guidelines, such as Ethical Principles for Psychologists, American Psychological Association (APA, 1992), Code of Ethics and Standards of Practice, American Counseling Association (ACA, 1995) and the Code of Ethics of the National Association of Social Workers (NASW, 1990) provide standards for all areas of professional practice and assist members in meeting their responsibilities as well as provide penalties for failing to meet them. Although these ethical guidelines are not legally binding, they serve to monitor each professional group and the conduct of its members.

All codes of ethics for mental health providers have certain principles in common. These principles address professional responsibility, competence, and training and provide behavior codes that regulate the nature of the therapist-client relationship. Members of the helping professions are expected to provide services only within the realm of their competence. They are not to claim or imply professional qualifications they do not possess.

There is general agreement that counselors should understand their own value systems if they are to be effective in fulfilling their responsibilities to their clients, to their individual professions, and to the general welfare of society. Blocher (1987, p. 36) outlined a set of values that govern counseling practice:

1. Respect for human life.
2. Respect for truth.
3. Respect for privacy.
4. Respect for freedom and autonomy.
5. Respect for promises and commitments.
6. Concern for the weak, vulnerable, or helpless.
7. Concern for the growth and development of people.
8. Concern lest others be harmed.
9. Concern for human dignity and equality.
10. Concern for gratitude and reparation.
11. Concern for human freedom.

As individuals change and grow in the therapeutic relationship, their attitudes and values may change also. Therefore, some writers suggest that counselors should take an active role in promoting self-determination as a value for clients (see Corey, Corey, & Callanan, 1993). In the following passage, which is especially relevant to child counseling, Bergin (as quoted in Corey, Corey, & Callanan, 1993) compares effective therapy to good parenting:

> Trust is established; guided growth is stimulated; values are conveyed in a respectful way; the person being influenced becomes stronger, more assertive, and independent; the person learns ways of clarifying and testing value choices; the influencer deceases dependency nurturance and external advice; and the person experiments with new behaviors and ideas until he or she becomes more mature and autonomous. (p. 62)

It is important for counselors to communicate their values openly and honestly and in ways that will enhance the therapeutic relationship. Most writers agree that it is virtually impossible (and equally undesirable) for counselors to remain value neutral (Corey, Corey, & Callanan, 1993). Instead, "The counselor is better advised to recognize and accept his or her values, using them to promote a greater awareness in the counseling relationship and expressing them when it appears that doing so will improve or further the relationship" (Hansen, Rossberg, & Cramer, 1994, p. 379).

Occasionally, a value conflict interferes with a counselor's ability to provide adequate client care. Referrals are suggested when the therapist experiences any of the following: extreme discomfort with the client's values, inability to remain objective, fear of imposing his or her values on the client, or the boundaries of his or her competence have been reached (Corey, Corey, & Callanan, 1993).

In addition to providing standards of practice that govern the profession, the codes of ethics provide guidelines for safeguarding client's rights. These guidelines conform to existing mental health laws with regard to a therapist's duty to warn and protect and the duty to report. These duties, as they pertain to counseling with children, are discussed in the following pages.

Duty to Warn and Protect

In most states, a mental health practitioner is obligated to violate confidentiality if he or she has reason to believe that a client poses a clear and imminent danger to self or others. This is often difficult to determine because clients—including children—who are emotionally disturbed, often make vague threats to self or others that they have neither the intent nor the ability to carry out. Because there is a lack of adequate criteria for distinguishing a "clear and imminent danger," therapists will have to rely on their best clinical judgment.

If it is determined that the current situation does not present a clear and imminent danger, the therapist can continue to follow the child and the family in therapy and continue to evaluate the danger. If, however, it seems that a substantial danger to self or others exists or a *concrete* threat has been made, the therapist must take the threat seriously, discuss it fully, and take the necessary action to prevent the loss of either the life or the well-being of the intended victim or the client. Appropriate action might include warning the potential victim or others likely to apprise the victim of the danger, alerting parents to the child's suicidal ideation or plans or threats against others, notifying the appropriate authorities, and arranging hospitalization, if necessary.

The Duty to Warn

The duty to warn potential victims of the possibility of violent attack was established with the landmark ruling in *Tarasoff* v. *Regents of the University of California* (1976). In this case, a patient confided to his psychologist during therapy that he intended to kill a readily identifiable victim. The psychologist notified the police who detained the patient briefly but then released him because he appeared rational. Two months later, a young woman was killed and her parents sued the psychologist, psychiatrists, and the police officers on the grounds that they failed to warn the victim or others likely to apprise her of the danger. Despite the therapist's arguments that first, mental health professionals have an obligation to safeguard the confidentiality of psychotherapeutic communication and second, that therapists cannot accurately predict whether or not a patient will commit specific acts of violence, the judge held that the victim should have been warned and that "the protective privilege ends where the public peril begins" (*Tarasoff*, at 347).

The court held that when a therapist determines or should have determined that a patient poses a serious threat of violence toward another, the therapist incurs an obligation to use reasonable care to protect the intended victim against such danger. "The discharge of this duty may require the therapist to warn the intended victim or others likely to apprise the victim of the danger, notify the police or take whatever other steps are reasonably necessary under the circumstances" (*Tarasoff*, at 340).

This "duty-to-warn" law, as it was later called, has been expanded by various court decisions. In *Peck* v. *Counseling Services of Addison County, Inc.* (1985), a young man disclosed a threat to get even with his father by burning the barn down. After promising the therapist that he wouldn't carry out the threat, the young man nevertheless burned the barn and endangered the lives of his family. The Vermont Supreme Court "found that, on the facts of this case, the therapist's failure to warn the identified victims...constituted a breach of duty to take reasonable steps to protect them." (*Peck*, at 423). Since then, the Arizona Supreme Court in *Hamman* v. *County of Maricopa* (1989) held that the duty to warn be extended to include any general threat to a general group of people. The court ruled that "We hold that the duty (to warn) extends to third persons whose circumstances place them within the reasonably foreseeable area of danger where the violent conduct of the patient is a threat" (*Hamman*, at 1122).

The courts continue to interpret cases of psychotherapist-patient privilege based on the "dangerous patient" exception, first decided in *Tarasoff*. Recently, in *Menendez* v. *Superior Court* (1992), the Supreme Court of California ruled on four tape-recorded sessions in which details of two murders were discussed. The Menendez brothers claimed psychotherapist-patient privilege to prevent these taped sessions from being used as evidence against them. The court held that communications on the first two tapes, which contained threats to the psychotherapists and two associates, lost their "confidential" status when they were disclosed by the psychotherapist in separate warnings. The court further held that the two subsequent recordings were still subject to privileged-communication protection because the "dangerous patient" exception was not met (*Menendez*, at 788).

The "duty to warn" also applies to dangerousness to self. Therapists, particularly those who deal with individuals in crisis, have a responsibility to be sufficiently trained and to be able to make a thorough assessment of the risk of suicide. The therapist is liable if he or she fails to foresee the risk of suicide and does not respond adequately to an emergency situation. The failure to accurately evaluate and prevent suicide could result in a lawsuit against the mental health practitioner (Corey, Corey, & Callanan, 1993; Swenson, 1993). If the client discloses an intent or a plan of suicide during therapy, the mental health professional should warn either the parents or the police, and the client may need to be hospitalized or committed involuntarily.

Applying the Duty-to-Warn Law in Practice

The duty to warn, although not invoked often in child therapy, presents the practitioner with many difficult decisions. Schutz (1982) pointed out that breaking a client's confidence can deter clients from seeking therapy, destroy his or her trust in the therapist, inhibit frank and open discussion about violent impulses, and violate the client's right to privacy. Given these serious and adverse effects on the therapeutic process, practitioners must be fairly certain that their clients present a clear and imminent danger to self or others before breaking confidentiality. Some practical suggestions to protect both client and therapist include securing informed consent, allowing children to fully express any violent wishes, carefully documenting sessions, being knowledgeable about verbal and behavioral clues, being skilled in crisis management, and consulting with other professionals.

First, and most important, children and their parents should be informed at the start of the therapy that confidentiality cannot be maintained when anyone—including the client—is threatened with harm. These limitations can be explained informally in terms that are readily understood by both the child and his or her parents and should be included on the informed consent forms. Second, even vague threats of harm to self or others should be listened to and fully discussed. Child therapists should not respond with phrases like, "You don't mean that, do you?" or worse yet, "I know *you* would never do anything like that!" When therapists give responses that deny children an opportunity to disclose harmful intent, they are, in effect, saying, "Don't give me any bad news because I wouldn't know what to do about it!" Such denial does not prevent children from carrying out the threat, it only prevents them from talking about it. By encouraging children to discuss their intent to hurt themselves or others, the therapist may be able to distinguish wishful thinking or manipulation from a carefully thought-out plan to inflict harm. In this way, the clinician is able to assess the foreseeable danger, if any, to self and others.

Third, careful documentation is essential to all client-therapist interactions, but it is especially important in cases where the duty to warn involves breaching confidentiality. Special care should always be taken with all reports and progress notes, but it is especially important when a threat is made. In these instances, which are rare, the "exact nature of the threat must be recorded along with the procedure followed by the clinician either to rule out the threat and to maintain confidentiality or to validate the threat and warn" (Brems, 1993, p. 41).

Fourth, mental health professionals should be skilled at assessing the danger the child's behavior presents. However, studies introduced by the American Psychiatric Association (*Tarasoff*, at 438) indicate that practitioners tend to overpredict violence and that they are more often wrong than right. Ideally, the therapist should be sufficiently trained to deal with a child in crisis, able to assess the danger that the child's behavior presents, and able to weigh the need to hospitalize the child against the child's right to the least restrictive treatment.

Finally, it is always wise to consult other professionals, especially those who work in crisis settings, because they know the danger signs and can arrange hospitalization for the child if necessary. Beginning therapists should *always* consult their supervisor or a more experienced therapist; even seasoned veterans should consult colleagues just to verify their own opinions. Remember that in *Peck* the therapist did not disclose the fact that a young man threatened to burn down his father's barn and was later found negligent.

> *Courts expect professionals to foresee dangers and prevent harm. Therapists hearing children speak of suicide give this duty to prevent harm a higher value than the protection of the child's privacy.*
> —SWENSON (1993, p. 396)

Suicide and confidentiality   Should a child's parents be informed if a child threatens suicide during counseling? The answer is yes. If child clients reveal a desire to hurt themselves or talk about a plan to commit suicide, the therapist must take appropriate steps to save the child's life. Although it is much easier to assess the danger if the child actively announces an intent or details a plan to harm himself or herself, this is rarely the case.

When children do disclose a desire to hurt themselves, the disclosure is more likely to be disguised in some way—perhaps revealed in the child's artwork or in the course of play therapy. This makes it especially difficult to detect because an overt threat has not been disclosed. Therefore, mental health professionals must be especially observant and open to any behavioral or verbal signs indicating that a child may be having thoughts of suicide.

In conclusion, the child therapist may never have to invoke the duty to warn. If, however, the child makes a concrete threat to harm a parent or a sibling, it is advisable to notify the parents. Sometimes, this will be sufficient, especially if the parents are able to protect the child and the entire family. But if the therapist has any misgivings about the family's ability to provide the kind of supervision and protection that the child needs, then the police must be notified. In the case of a threat to another child or adult outside the family, the therapist must notify the potential victim (if known) or others who can apprise the victim of the danger. In addition, the child's parents and the police must be notified. If a vague victim or group of victims is specified (a child threatens to bring a gun to school to "settle things"), the police must be notified. When threats are made against self *or* others, the therapist should either arrange for the child's hospitalization or refer the child and the family for emergency mental health services immediately. It is always advisable to work closely with the child's parents at this particularly stressful time.

Duty to Report Child Abuse

> *Are we, collectively and individually, willing to take the bold steps necessary to create a future where children are protected? Millions of children throughout the world await our answer.*
> —HELFER (1987, p. 459)

Virtually every state has a child abuse reporting law requiring anyone who comes into contact with children in the course of their employment or in the practice of their profession to report child abuse and neglect. Recent changes in child protection laws have obligated professionals to report even suspected cases of child abuse. Mental health practitioners, school counselors, nurses, doctors, educators, human services workers, and other mandated reporters should have a clear understanding of what their particular state law does and does not require (see Appendix B for copy of Pennsylvania's reporting procedures). Students and practitioners are encouraged to get a copy of the reporting procedures for their particular state, as well as the child abuse statutes.

In the course of therapy, counselors can often discover physical and sexual abuse if the child is willing and able to communicate what has happened. It is much more difficult to establish the presence of emotional abuse or neglect, consequently fewer of these cases are reported and acted on. Once a professional becomes suspicious that child abuse or neglect may be occurring, such suspicions should be carefully documented and reported to the appropriate authorities. The "good faith" provision in child abuse statutes protects mandated reporters from legal prosecution if the report turns out to be unfounded. This provision protects all reporters except those with an ulterior motive, such as to punish or harass the parents in some way.

According to David Sandberg (Sandberg, Crabbs, & Crabbs, 1988), a noted attorney who specializes in children's issues, several conditions are *not* necessary for a child abuse report to be filed.

1. The reporter does not have to "prove" that child abuse has occurred but needs only "suspect" that it has occurred.
2. The child does not have to acknowledge that abuse is occurring as a precondition for reporting.
3. The child protective services bears the responsibility for determining whether there is enough evidence to warrant an investigation.

The need to be sensitive to potential abuse situations is a serious responsibility for the professional and has serious implications for the child and society. Failure to report may ruin the child's life and increase the likelihood that the abuse will continue in future generations. In addition, there is mounting evidence that today's victims, particularly victims of sexual abuse, will become tomorrow's perpetrators; thus, unreported crimes and untreated victims may contribute to an increase in these types of crimes against children in the future. To motivate the professional to notify the appropriate authorities of suspected abuse, many states have failure-to-report statutes in their child abuse law that include the risk of prosecution and the fines that can be levied.

Professionals have an obligation to assist children and their families in dealing with their feelings, family relationships, and other issues in the aftermath of abuse. In counseling with the parent, the therapist should avoid blame and condemnation and help the person to become a more effective parent, while at the same time safeguarding the child's well-being. Because children are most at risk immediately after abuse is reported, effective family intervention is crucial. In addition, because some abuse never stops regardless of how much help and support the family receives, it is absolutely essential that human services professionals recognize when a child is in continuing danger and take steps to protect the child.

Applying the Duty to Report to Practice

Some abused children appear to live normally, whereas others, feeling unloved and unwanted, are on the brink of suicide. Because children can be abused and neglected in a variety of ways and to varying degrees (see Chapter 3), it is especially important for counselors to be aware of some of the contradictions in the child's behavior. One such contradiction is that, in a family in which all of the children seem well cared for, one child may be singled out for abuse. It is equally puzzling to practitioners when they observe an abused child's loving behavior toward the abuser. Abused children do look to their parents for love, and because the abuse is their only form of attention, they accept their treatment as normal (Kempe & Kempe, 1978).

Children can be abused physically, emotionally, or sexually, and each kind of abuse is intertwined with the other, slowly destroying the child's spirit and self-esteem. Few clear-cut characteristics have emerged to differentiate neglect and abuse (Kempe & Kempe, 1978). Both interfere with a child's physical, emotional, social, and intellectual development and can cause developmental delays in motor, social, cognitive, and speech skills. Kempe and Kempe, (1978) believe that much of the retardation seen in abused children is related less to the physical abuse itself than to the emotional abuse and neglect that often accompany it.

Because it is often impossible to separate the signs of abuse and neglect, they are presented here as a group. The following list of behaviors is by no means exhaustive, and the reader is cautioned not to interpret the presence or absence of these behaviors as definite proof of abuse or neglect. Any one of these behaviors could have other explanations, such as a physical or neurological disorder. However, when combined with everything else that is known about the child, this list (Fontana, 1984; Goldstein, 1987; Helfer & Kempe, 1987; Herman-Giddens, 1984; Kempe & Kempe, 1978; National Research Council, 1993) will help the practitioner determine whether a report is warranted.

Common Signs of Abuse and Neglect

- *Injuries that cannot be explained as accidental.* A pattern of bruises, cuts, burns or other injuries: for example, the imprint of a steam iron on the upper leg, burns on the small of the back, or lacerations made by a lamp cord. Other signs are frequent and repeated injuries or injuries in various stages of healing. Genital or rectal tears, pain, bleeding, infection, or sexually transmitted diseases in the mouth, vagina, or anus are signs of sexual abuse. Denial of medical treatment or long delays in seeking help for the child are often a part of the pattern of abuse.
- *Lack of trust.* Often the victim of inconsistent parental punishment, deceit, and broken promises, the abused child learns that it is unwise to trust others.

- *Fearful, shy, and withdrawn behavior.* Hypervigilant and always alert to danger, the child avoids conflict (and punishment) by being compliant and submissive.
- *Aggressive, acting-out behavior.* The child moves constantly and is often unable to sit still or attend. He or she seems unaffected by disapproval and is more concerned with avoiding punishment than avoiding wrongdoing. This may lead to delinquent behavior.
- *Extreme difficulty in recognizing and verbalizing feelings.* The child needs encouragement to express both negative (fear, hurt, loneliness) and positive (joy, pleasure) emotions. Some children do not cry even when they are in pain; others cry easily.
- *Feelings of profound sadness.* Crying spells, sleep disturbances, changes in eating habits, and avoiding contact with others are common signs. The child may evidence self-destructive behavior such as head banging, scratching, cutting, or hair pulling. Some older abused children think about committing suicide.
- *Excessive fears, sleep disturbances, and regressive behavior.* The child may fear going to bed, have nightmares, want the light on, wake up in the middle of the night, and fear sleeping alone. These behaviors may be accompanied by renewed fears of the dark or of monsters in the closet. The child may regress and begin wetting the bed again or sucking the thumb. These responses are often associated with sexual molestation of children.
- *Poor self-esteem.* Abused children tend to see themselves as "stupid," "bad," or "unlovable." Some abused and neglected children are labeled as "lazy" by teachers because of their inability to concentrate and because they are underachievers. Sexually abused children may see themselves as "dirty."
- *Incapable of playing acceptably with other children.* Abused and neglected children have difficulty having fun. They may avoid activities with peers such as sports and gym class. Sexually abused children may avoid playing with peers for they fear that others can tell they are abused just by looking at them.
- *Persistent and inappropriate sexual play with self and peers.* This includes sexually aggressive behavior toward others, excessive masturbation, and excessive sexual curiosity, which are commonly seen in sexually abused children They have sexual knowledge that is beyond their developmental level: for example, a 3-year-old simulates intercourse during doll play.
- *Adultlike behavior.* Neglected children, who must care for their entire families at young ages, or children who are sexually abused often act "grown up." Adultlike in their speech and behavior, these children have little understanding of the meaning and consequences of adult behaviors. Older abused children model adult behavior and may abuse younger, weaker children or severely punish children left in their care.
- *School attendance.* Some abused children have few absences, arrive early, and find excuses not to go home. Others are frequently kept home to care for younger children, to wait for bruises to heal, or to be sexually available to a male caretaker while the mother is working.
- *Evidence of care.* Poor hygiene, lack of preventive health care (teeth decayed) undernourished (always asking for food) inappropriately dressed for the weather (no coat in winter), or lack of supervision after school and in the evening (home alone or roaming the streets at night) may be signs of abuse or

neglect. In addition, the child may wear long sleeves in summer to hide bruises. Sexually abused children may bath excessively or not at all, because some children hope that being dirty and unattractive will stop the abuse.

Reporting child abuse is a serious responsibility that cannot be taken lightly. The counselor must decide whether the child is being abused on the basis of his or her observation of the child's physical condition, mood, and affect, as well as the child's direct and indirect verbal and nonverbal cues. The counselor needs to know the child well enough to detect changes in the child's behavior. Teachers are especially helpful in pointing out patterns of suspicious behavior, although some abuse is never noticed at school. Sometimes an anxious parent will bring a child in for counseling because the parent suspects the child is being abused by an estranged spouse, neighbor, family member, or other adult. In these instances, the child-therapist relationship remains intact because the parent is not the one committing the abuse.

Reporting child abuse always puts the child at risk, and it has serious consequences for the therapeutic partnership. Children are the most vulnerable at the time of reporting because a terrible secret has been revealed. They may feel betrayed by the therapist, or the family may retaliate against the child if he or she remains in the home. This is why follow-up and careful monitoring of abusive situations is absolutely essential. Although it may not always be possible, it is important for the practitioner to try to maintain contact with the child and his or her family. In school systems where the counselor reports the abuse to a supervisor, rather than reporting it directly, the counseling relationship between the counselor and the child and his or her family may remain intact. If this is the case, the counselor can continue to give the family support and help to become better parents. The counselor will be assisted in this effort by child protection workers who will provide additional help to the family.

SAFEGUARDING CHILDREN IN PRACTICE

• • • When Counseling Is Not Enough: The Case of Kelsey

One of the greatest challenges to counselors and human services workers is to recognize when parents—as the result of such problems as drug and alcohol abuse, psychopathology, or child abuse in their family of origin—do not possess the strength, skill, motivation or ability to care for and nurture children. Despite the current emphasis on keeping children in their family of origin and focusing on family strengths, we must recognize that to safeguard the child's physical and emotional health and well-being, foster placement is often an appropriate and necessary alternative. The following is a composite case based on actual documentation of several cases involving children and their families. It illustrates how much harm can be done when human services professionals fail to recognize the signs of abuse, misjudge a parent's ability to care for a child, and do not follow up to make sure that the child is protected.

Kelsey (born 5-16-84; died 3-27-94)   In her short life, Kelsey was physically and emotionally abused and neglected by her mother and sexually abused by her mother's many boyfriends. Kelsey died of AIDS just short of her tenth birthday, a victim of the system as much as of the virus. The following is a fictionalized account of Kelsey's painful journey through the bureaucracy designed to protect her.

July 1987   Police respond to a report of domestic violence involving Kelsey's mother and her current boyfriend. A second man involved in the dispute told police, "The kid grabbed my penis and this guy (mother's boyfriend) taught her to do it!" A frightened Kelsey, age 3 years 2 months, denies the report. Case closed.

February 1988   Police respond to a report that a girl is being locked in a closet and denied food as punishment. Kelsey is not in the closet when police arrive, but she shows evidence of physical abuse and neglect. She was not examined for sexual abuse at this time. Placed in temporary shelter.

March 1988   During her stay in a temporary shelter, Kelsey, according to reports, "pulled her pants down in front of the other children" and was "frightened and withdrawn"...She "drew houses and people shaped like penises" during art therapy.

April 1988   A psychological evaluation of Kelsey's mother indicates that she is mildly mentally retarded and has "very poor parenting skills."

May 1988   Counseling is court ordered. Kelsey is returned to the custody of her mother with the recommendation that she "not be left in the care of her mother's male friends."

July 1988   A counseling session indicates "inappropriate sexual behavior and knowledge for her developmental level." Kelsey demonstrated sexual intercourse with anatomically correct dolls during the session. The counselor also noticed bruises around her mouth. Child placed with maternal grandmother; caseworker assigned.

July 1989   Kelsey is diagnosed with herpes and gonorrhea. Medical report states: "perforated hymen, inflammation, and damage to vagina." The child has been the victim of "chronic sexual abuse," according to medical report. Returned to custody of the grandmother, but it is known she spends most of the time with her mother.

August 1991   Kelsey is diagnosed with syphilis and venereal warts. Kelsey remains in the custody of her grandmother pending the outcome of charges against one of her mother's boyfriends. Kelsey's mother continues to deny that she left the little girl alone with her male friends, and Kelsey cannot identify any one perpetrator (it is alleged there were many).

December 1991   Court records indicate that just before Christmas (a holiday she never got to celebrate), one of her mother's boyfriends raped her. She was 7 years old.

February 1992   Kelsey's mother's boyfriend is finally brought to trial. The mother denies that anything happened to Kelsey and defends her boyfriend. He pleads guilty to a lesser charge and gets 10 years in prison. Medical tests reveal he does not have the AIDS virus.

February 1992	Caseworker finds Kelsey locked in closet in. her mother's home. Fevered and dehydrated, the child has not eaten for several days. The child is removed from her mother and grandmother's custody. Medical tests reveal Kelsey has AIDS, as does her mother.
March 1992	Timid and frightened, sometimes hiding in closets and hoarding food, Kelsey goes to live with her foster parents.
March 1992 to March 1994	Foster parents take Kelsey to Disneyland, to have breakfast with Santa, out to dinner, and to family events. They do all the things a little girl longs to do. Kelsey basks in the love of a real family
March 27, 1994	Kelsey, not quite 10, dies of AIDS, child abuse, and a system that failed her. •

INSIGHTS AND IMPLICATIONS

The 1989 UN Convention on the Rights of the Child balances children's rights to nurturance and protection with their rights to self-determination and autonomy. For the first time, the rights of the child were placed ahead of the rights of the family. In counseling relationships, children have the right to consent, the right to feedback, the right to privacy, and the right to confidentiality. Child counselors face some unique challenges as they struggle to protect the rights of children while at the same time fulfilling their professional responsibilities to their child client's parents. Although most young children cannot legally consent to treatment, they certainly should have the right to refuse to participate or to terminate if they wish. Children have the right to privacy and to have their communication kept confidential, except in those *rare* instances where the child threatens harm to self or others. The child also has the right to know how he or she is progressing and has the right to have this information communicated in a way that he or she can understand.

Basic to protecting the child's rights is an underlying respect for the child as a unique human being who deserves the same consideration as an adult. Whenever, confidentiality must be broken, the counselor should be available to the child, especially in the case of abuse, so that he or she can continue to support the child and his or her family. Reporting abuse and providing follow-up care is essential if we are to stem the tide of abuse and neglect that imperils the lives and futures of millions of our children. What will the reader's response be to Dr. Helfer's (Helfer & Kempe, 1987, p. 459) question, "Are we, collectively and individually, willing to take the bold steps necessary to create a future where children are protected?"

WISDOM ACCORDING TO ORTON

- *Remember that a secret told to just one person isn't a secret anymore. Guard clients' confidences except when they must be broken in cases involving danger to self and others.*

- *If something bothers you about a particular decision or course of action and if you sense that it isn't right, either legally, ethically or morally, don't do it!*
- *Listen to your inner voice when it comes to reporting suspected child abuse. Better to report and be wrong than fail to report and be right.*
- *Be careful what you commit to in writing about a child in the file or in personal notes. Ask yourself: Would I want someone to say this about me or about my child? Will this information harm the child (even as an adult) if it ever becomes public?*
- *Remember that a child's parents are partners in therapy, as is the child. Keep the parents and the child involved in therapy decisions and provide positive feedback to both.*
- *The best way to avoid the possibility of lawsuits is to develop a warm relationship with your clients, always have their best interest at heart, and* do no harm. *It is difficult to sue someone who acts in "good faith."*

ORTON'S PICKS

Corey, G., Corey, M. S. & Callanan, P. (1993). *Issues and ethics in the helping professions.* Pacific Grove, CA: Brooks/Cole.

This comprehensive text is packed with vignettes that are designed to encourage readers to think about complex ethical issues and arrive at their own solutions. User-friendly and helpful, this sourcebook is a "keeper" for students and practitioners alike.

Rinas, J. & Clyne-Jackson, S. (1988). *Professional conduct and legal concerns in mental health practice.* Norwalk, CT: Appleton & Lange.

Written in clear, easy- to-understand language, this excellent text is an indispensable guide for professional conduct. The authors make difficult concepts easy to understand and provide practical information on the ethical and legal issues of our time.

Swenson, L. C. (1993). *Psychology and law for the helping professions.* Pacific Grove, CA: Brooks/Cole.

Issues that are especially relevant to work with children are discussed in two separate chapters. Chapter 15 presents an in-depth discussion of children's rights, informed consent and the problems that arise for the therapist who treats minors with divorced parents. Child suicide, mandatory reporting of child abuse, and the child witness are additional topics of interest to those who counsel children.

PART 3   Counseling Parents and Families to Effect Behavioral Changes in Children

He cried, I cried, we all cried!

—Mother describing the impact of her child's behavior
on the family.

ALMOST ALL EXPERTS AGREE THAT PARENTS OF THE 21ST century face some formidable challenges. Unlike parents of previous generations, who shared the work and joys of parenting with both father and mother and with grandparents, aunts, and uncles, today's parents often go it alone. The traditional family is rapidly being replaced by the vulnerable family. Part of this vulnerability is due to rising divorce rates and an increase in the number of single-parent families. Gerler (1993) stated that as many as 80% of the children in some school districts come from broken homes. Pressures on all families, both traditional and nontraditional, are increasing, and the time and energy available to meet the emotional, social, and educational needs of children is diminishing. Now, more than at any time in our recent history, school counselors, psychologists, social workers, and others working with children in schools, agencies, hospitals, and private practice settings must give active consideration to involving parents in counseling activities—in individual and in group and family counseling—that will help parents encourage and support their children. Parents and families need some assistance to help children achieve happy, healthy, and fulfilling lives and to enable them to grow up better equipped to parent the children of tomorrow.

Chapter 11 details an innovative and practical model for involving parents as partners in the counseling process. This counseling approach is proactive, positive, and growth-oriented and builds on the strengths of the parent and the child. The focus is not on the child's problem or on the parent's complaints about the child's behavior; instead, it is on improving and strengthening the interaction between the parent and the child. The parent is helped to get a more objective view of the child and his or her interaction with the child. Part of the therapeutic process is helping the parent gain insight into what he or she may need to change and offering the encouragement and support necessary to achieve and maintain change. This step-by-step process is illustrated with a case study and accompanying dialogue. As the case example illustrates, strengthening the parent-child relationship often results in positive changes in the child's behavior. It also enhances parental confidence and self-esteem, which positively affects the interaction between parent and child.

Chapter 12 provides a structure for a parent support group. Counselors assess the need for the group, involve parents in planning it, and receive input about parental concerns. These concerns are then incorporated into hypothetical family situations that are used to stimulate group discussion. Parents have an opportunity to share their concerns with other parents and to give and receive information and support from the group. Group topics focus on improving the communication between parent and child, and parent-child groups are designed to help parents *practice* communicating with children. Opportunities to converse with other people's children often have a positive effect on the parents' communication with their own children. Chapter 12 also provides examples of open-ended situations that counselors can use with both parent and parent-child groups.

CHAPTER 11 *Parents as Partners in Child Counseling*

> *I never had anyone that I could talk to about it before.*
> —Mother describing how she waited for someone to come
> along who would listen to her and understand

If someone were to write a job description for parenting, there would undoubtedly be few takers; yet every year, millions take on the job without any prior training, education, or experience. Armed with little more than the model provided by their own parents or caregivers, they take on responsibilities that would present a Herculean challenge to a team of professionals. Parents are expected to be child development experts; great communicators of love, acceptance, morals, and values; strong disciplinarians who know when to be firm yet fair; nurturers who can dry a tear or kiss a hurt; nurses who know what to do about all manner of illness; teachers who can help with homework for any subject from reading to algebra; psychologists who soothe broken hearts and heighten self-esteem; and peacemakers who arbitrate family conflicts and disagreements. Is it any wonder, given all these tremendous expectations, that mistakes are made, promises are broken, dreams are shattered, resentments are harbored, and parents and families are stressed?.

It is the task of the child counselor to help parents, whether they be birth parents, stepparents, single parents, grandparents or anyone else who assumes a parenting role, understand that theirs is a difficult task and that no one—parent, professional, or expert—can do all the things that parenthood requires and do them perfectly with every child in every instance. All parents make mistakes because they are human. With this in mind, this chapter offers a unique and practical model for counseling with parents that focuses on the strengths of both parent and child and helps strengthen the special bond that exists between them.

An Adlerian Approach

One of the basic assumptions underlying Adlerian theory is that all behavior has a purpose or goal and the actions of individuals—including children—are determined by the *striving for significance* within the social group. This striving represents "movement toward the fulfillment of the goal to achieve unique identity and to belong" (Dinkmeyer, Dinkmeyer, & Sperry, 1987, p. 16). The attainment of a unique identity has been referred to variously by other theorists as self-actualization, self-expansion, and competence. It begins with the individual's attempts to overcome *feelings of inferiority* that are generated by the child's helplessness and dependency on adults. These feelings of inferiority, rather than being viewed as negative, are seen as motivating forces. Starting out in a basically inferior position, the individual engages in attempts to compensate by striving for mastery over his or her world. Problems arise when children develop overwhelming feelings of inferiority, which are reflected in a display of inadequacy (Dinkmeyer, Pew, & Dinkmeyer, 1979).

Adlerians take a holistic approach to understanding the individual's unique style of life. The *lifestyle* refers to the basic beliefs that children have developed to help them understand and cope with their world. These beliefs are influenced by the child's perception of events and interactions with others, especially family members. "The style of living is created in the course of an ongoing drama that takes place in the theater of the family, with parents and siblings all playing a part" (Dinkmeyer, Pew, & Dinkmeyer, 1979, p. 29).

According to Dreikurs and Grey (1968), if the parent doesn't recognize the child's desire to belong or is unable or unwilling to respond in ways that will allow the child to satisfy this basic goal through cooperation, collaboration, and good behavior, then the child may develop mistaken goals, which will result in varying degrees of misbehavior. Misbehaving children are discouraged children who are under the false impression that their behavior is the only way to achieve the acceptance they so desperately want and need.

Four Goals of Misbehavior

Adlerians believe that children behave the way they do for a purpose, and that purpose is compatible with their need for acceptance and approval. Children try to conform to socially acceptable behavior first, and then, when that doesn't work, they misbehave to reach their goal. In essence, the desire to belong and be accepted is so strong that children will do whatever works for them. Dreikurs and Soltz (1964) classified all child misbehavior into four categories, each corresponding to the appropriate goal: attention, power, revenge, and display of inadequacy. Although each goal increases in severity and reflects an increasing degree of discouragement, the child does not necessarily progress through all four goals.

Attention

All children want to be noticed, and attention-seeking behaviors are a normal part of childhood. Lynn Johnston, in her cartoon strip *For Better or for Worse*, captures the premier attention-seeking behavior—the temper tantrum. This cartoon will surely bring a smile to the millions of parents who have seen the same behavior in their own children. Children find many ways to get our attention—some of them delightful, and some very annoying.

All children (particularly in the preschool years), have a repertoire of attention-seeking behaviors. These attention-seeking behaviors are often present during the primary school years and then begin to diminish as the child finds a secure place within the family and the peer group. Children who have been unable to satisfy their exaggerated need for attention in positive ways will continue to misbehave in ways that keep parents and teachers providing the service and attention that they need. Children who cannot get attention through positive behavior will exhibit either active or passive behavior that can be either constructive or destructive (Dreikurs, 1958; Dreikurs & Soltz, 1964). The active constructive attention-seeker is often the successful student or "model child," whose goal is to secure attention for self rather than to cooperate with others. The purpose of the child's dependability and achievement is to secure attention, but this is accomplished in constructive ways that often go unrecognized as self-serving and so are not apt to get a negative response from parents, teachers, and

Copyright 1995 UNIVERSAL PRESS SYNDICATE. Reprinted with permission.
All rights reserved.

peers. The passive constructive child may be shy and lacking in self-confidence but seek attention in quiet ways. This child is often overly conscientious and charming and secures help from parents and teachers in a subtle manner.

The active destructive attention seeker is the most annoying child. This child may seek attention by showing off, getting into mischief, or asking endless nonsensical questions. This child is often labeled the "class clown" and is a source of irritation to nearly everyone. This is the child that makes you want to tear your hair out. The passive destructive attention seeker, on the other hand, may be lazy, demanding, and manipulative. These children are more covert about their actions and force others to do their work for them. Parents may fall victim to this trap and become virtual slaves to these children, constantly picking up after them, waiting on them, and doing their homework for them.

Parents often respond to both active and passive destructive demands for attention by nagging, reminding, coaxing, lecturing, punishing, and giving service. These actions satisfy the child's need for attention for a short time, but then the child soon renews his or her attempts to gain attention in negative ways. As a result, adults are often left feeling frustrated, fatigued, and resentful, and children are left feeling unhappy and ineffective in obtaining the acceptance they need. Parents of children who continue to seek excessive amounts of attention beyond the primary grades need help to examine their reaction to their child's behavior and give more focus and attention to positive behavior.

Power

At around age 2, children learn to say "no," and some children continue to challenge adults in either active or passive ways. Children who actively seek power do so by arguing, contradicting, constantly breaking rules, throwing temper tantrums, or being rebellious and defiant. Children who are more passive usually battle for power in more covert, obstructive ways that include being stubborn, lazy, and forgetful.

Often the child's efforts to gain a measure of acceptance by cooperation have not been successful, and so the child develops an exaggerated need for power and control. When adults engage children in a power struggle, it reaffirms the child's belief that power is important and worth seeking. If power were not so important, the child reasons, why would adults go to such lengths to try to attain it?

A good example of a power struggle is the "bedtime battle." As the bedtime battle rages, the parent becomes angrier, and the child more resistant. Parents often find themselves begging their children to go to bed. After a great many tears, some parents give in and allow the children to stay up as long as they want to or to sleep on the sofa until the parent goes to bed. In extreme cases, some parents adopt the child's bedtime as their own. In any case, by giving in to the child's tears and temper, the parent has told the child that he or she has won the bedtime battle.

Children who engage in power struggles with adults often win the battle but lose the war, so to speak. Children can think of very creative ways to defy both parents and teachers, and both authority figures are limited in the type and extent of their response. Few parents want to resort to behavior that would be considered physically abusive. In this sense, the child wins the battle. However, after engaging in frequent and severe power struggles with their parents, children often feel punished, defeated in their goal to find acceptance within the family, and helpless to control the situation through positive behavior. The child has, in effect, lost the war.

Parents need help to keep from slipping into a conflict with their power-seeking child. Parents need to examine the purpose for the child's misbehavior and find firm, fair, and consistent ways to deal with a situation and avoid either engaging in power struggles, arguing, or giving in to the child's demands. Rather, parents have to expect and recognize proper behavior and help the child achieve acceptance in the family through cooperation rather than defiance.

Revenge

Children who feel punished, hopeless, and powerless to do anything about their situation may exact revenge or retaliation for what they have interpreted as parental indifference or rejection. Some of the ways children actively retaliate against their parents or caretakers may include acts that harm property, such as coloring on walls, smashing mother's favorite antique treasure, breaking windows, and setting fires. Other examples of behaviors intended to harm others include stealing, striking a parent, and, in extreme cases, causing serious injury or even death. Children might engage in more passive retaliation, which includes moodiness, threats, sneaking, running away, and withdrawal.

Children's retaliatory behaviors range from mild to severe, and children are not always aware of the purposes for their misbehavior. Most young children retaliate in ways that are designed to bring grief to their parents or teachers; however, their misbehavior generally causes them considerable grief as well.

Display of Inadequacy

Withdrawal or a display of inadequacy is a severe form of discouragement. Children can use or develop inadequacy as a protection so that less is expected or required of them. Because these children don't participate or contribute, they do not have to risk failure (Dinkmeyer, Pew, & Dinkmeyer, 1979). The goal of this misbehavior can be likened to shooting yourself in the foot. Children who are intent on displaying their inadequacy are likely to be inattentive in school, fail to do homework, and refuse offers of help. In short, these youngsters try to become the failures that they are so convinced that they are. Even children who are earning good grades may fail to turn in assignments (many have the completed assignments in their desks) or fail to do any of their required homework. This is their way of forcing teachers to confirm their own perception that they are inadequate as learners and as human beings. Children who are labeled as troublemakers as a result of their acting-out behavior often continue to provide parents, teachers, and peers with plenty of examples of their inadequacies. At this stage, these children have simply given up and are misbehaving in a way that is consistent with their belief that they are "never good enough."

Adlerians believe that misbehaving children are discouraged children and that encouraging them implies having respect and faith in their inherent capacity to grow (Dinkmeyer, Dinkmeyer, & Sperry, 1987; Kottman & Johnson, 1993; Main, 1986). Believing that reward and punishment are detrimental to the developing child, Adlerian counselors favor encouragement over praise and natural and logical consequences over reward and punishment.

Natural and Logical Consequences

Based on the Adlerian belief that children are capable of developing in healthy and effective ways, natural and logical consequences allow children to experience the results of their behavior. These two techniques are favored over reward and punishment as ways to motivate children toward appropriate behavior (see Main, 1986). When Mei Ling leaves her bike in the driveway and her mother backs over it, Mei Ling has learned the *natural consequence* of her irresponsible behavior. As a result, she will be motivated toward more responsible behavior because she cannot ride a broken bicycle. Natural consequences occur without any planning or direction by parents, but some are so dangerous that they must be prevented. It follows that Mei Ling cannot be permitted to stick a fork in a light socket in order to experience the electric shock as a natural consequence. *Logical consequences* are established by family rules rather than by natural consequences, and they are the direct, consistent, and logical result of the child's behavior. For instance, children who come home late for dinner may find that they have to eat liver instead of the steak that was available earlier. This is usually enough to encourage children to be on time!

Children who are able to experience the consequences of their behavior grow in responsibility, decision making, and competence. Both natural and logical consequences help children internalize a sense of responsibility for self and others that cannot be achieved through punishment.

The Child's Place in the Family

The principles of individual psychology suggest that children follow a path toward growth and cooperation because they have a fundamental need to belong, to find acceptance, and to contribute to the overall benefit of the social group. The first social group that the child holds membership in is the family, which has a profound effect on the child's personality development. Although the child's social interest is innate, it is nurtured and developed first by the early dependency relationship established between the caregiver and the infant and later by the family environment.

Children are influenced by the style of coping with life that the family models, the quality of the parents' interaction with the child, and the child's place in the family constellation. In addition, the child's behavior is affected by his or her perceptions of his or her place in the family and by the responses the child receives from parents and siblings (Dinkmeyer, Dinkmeyer, & Sperry, 1987). If the family environment is healthy and the child's perceptions are accurate, he or she will continue on a positive path toward growth and will develop adaptive behaviors such as tolerance, respect, cooperation, and collaboration. However, if the child's picture of the family environment is faulty or if the family environment does not meet the child's needs for love, acceptance, and approval, the child may stray from the positive path and follow a more negative route that may result in misbehavior and maladaptive ways of coping.

The personality characteristics of each family member, the emotional bonds between family members, the sex of the siblings, their age differences, and the size of the family are all factors in the family constellation (Dinkmeyer, Pew, & Dinkmeyer, 1979; Sherman & Dinkmeyer, 1987). To understand the child's unique personality and lifestyle, it is necessary to be familiar with the family dynamic and the child's place in the family. According to Adler (Ansbacher & Ansbacher, 1956), where a child falls in the birth order is critical to the development of his or her lifestyle pattern. Particular goals and behaviors are attributed to the only child, the first- and second-born children, and the youngest child (see Main, 1986). For example, the firstborn child is likely to be characterized as more competitive and responsible than the youngest child. Although certain characteristics are associated with the child's ordinal position in the family, children tend to develop their own unique attitudes and behaviors based on their perceptions of what their place in the birth order means.

Siblings often have distinctly different perceptions of their family life because "no two children are ever born into the same family situation" (Pepper, as cited in Dinkmeyer, Dinkmeyer, & Sperry, 1987, p. 27). Children have different experiences in the family because family environments change. The parents may be more experienced and relaxed (or tired) as they grow older, the family's finances may have improved or worsened, or the family may be coping with the chronic illness or death of one of its members. In addition, new members may have been added (stepparents or grandparents), or the children may be living with a single-parent because of divorce or death. All these changes affect each child's perceptions of his or her role in the family.

According to Mosak and Dreikurs (as cited in Kern & Carlson, 1981), each child looks for his or her own "place in the sun" within the family constellation: "One child may fit in by being the best and another by being the worst. The child is not, however, a passive receptor of family influence. He actively and creatively is busy modifying his environment, training his siblings and 'raising' his parents" (p. 303).

Children can assume many roles in the family, depending on with whom they are interacting, and each child's perception of these roles is often quite different. The only girl in a family of boys might see herself as "Daddy's little girl," "Mommy's helper," and "My brothers' favorite punching bag." The child's interaction with family members, as well as the child's positive or negative perceptions of his or her place in the family, exert a powerful influence on the child's developing sense of self. The child's perceptions of the family environment, including the atmosphere and his or her place in the family, affect the child's patterns of behavior and attitudes.

Reprinted with special permission of King Features Syndicate.

The Family Atmosphere

In *Children: The Challenge*, Dreikurs and Soltz (1964) focused on the effects of the family atmosphere on the developing child. The attitudes and values that children in a particular family share are a reflection of this family atmosphere. Many family atmospheres provide adaptive models for coping, and even though parents aren't perfect models in every instance, the children grow up feeling accepted by their family, siblings, and peers and go on to live happy, productive lives. Many children have had negative family environments (alcoholic homes, foster homes, and orphanages) and have prospered either because they didn't view their family atmosphere as negative or because they were able to focus on the positive aspects of their interaction with their family. In these instances, children perceived themselves as loved and accepted, regardless of the parent's style of coping.

Dewey (as cited in Dinkmeyer, Dinkmeyer, & Sperry, 1987) identified 12 parenting styles thought to contribute to negative family atmospheres. However, because family attitudes and values vary considerably and children react to them with varying degrees of acceptance and rejection, a negative family atmosphere does not always affect children adversely. A great deal depends on the way the children view both the quality of their interaction with their family and their place in the family unit.

Each of the following 12 parenting styles are explained by using sample cases to illustrate some possible negative outcomes. However, because families are so unique and their day-to-day interactions often do not fit neatly into categories, there is a great deal of overlap in parenting styles in actual cases.

Authoritarian In an authoritarian family atmosphere, the parents have a "do as I say, not as I do" attitude, and they demand that the children obey them without question. Children in this type of home know that their parents usually present a united front, and these children often grow up well mannered and well behaved. They also tend to be very anxious and may harbor hidden resentments fostered by total obedience. The difficulty with this style of parenting is that the parent cannot tell the child how to behave forever, and the parent is not helping the child become self-disciplined. Often, when these children decide to rebel, they misbehave in serious ways.

> The D. family knows that what their father says, goes. He is the undisputed head of the house and is the one who decides the discipline. Mrs. D. acquiesces to her husband's wishes when it comes to controlling the children, and some would say that he controls her as well. When the D. children do something wrong, Mrs. D. says, "Wait until your father gets home!" This always makes the children afraid, although Mr. D. is not a cruel person. Robert, the middle child, always obeyed his father because he feared him. However, lately he is beginning to rebel by experimenting with drugs and has been arrested once for tearing out a stop sign with a group of teenage friends.

Suppressive A suppressive home is one in which children are not free to express their thoughts and feelings. For example, little boys are not allowed to cry and little girls aren't allowed to get into fights or show anger. The family maintains total control, similar to the authoritarian family, and the opinions expressed in the family have to be approved by the parents. The children learn very early to hide their emotions, which often makes it difficult to express their feelings in relationships outside the family. Children are often not allowed to express feelings that would project a less-than-perfect image of the family to the outside world.

> Mr. and Mrs. P. have three daughters and project the image of the perfect family. By outward appearances, they are living the American Dream. They live in their own home in a quiet small town, have a large backyard, pets, and a dual income from two careers. The parents never quarrel openly, attend all their children's school and community events, and attend church each Sunday as a family. However, their world was shattered when, just before her 13th birthday, their middle daughter Anika developed anorexia. Anika was determined to control the only thing in her life that she could and she refused to eat anything. Despite outward appearances, the family did not have a warm or close relationship with each other. Family members swept their feelings under the rug, rather than discussing them openly. One of the obstacles to Anika's treatment was her inability to share her feelings about herself and her family with her therapist.

Rejective Although most parents love their children, many have difficulty expressing this love in ways that children interpret as unconditional. In these families, parents often have difficulty expressing love and affection without attaching it to acceptable behavior. Many children who grow up in a rejective family atmosphere feel unloved and unwanted. In response to their perceptions of rejection, they may become discouraged and misbehave just to get some form of attention or power in the family. it is not uncommon for children to either retaliate or simply give up trying to win their parent's affection.

Sari had lived with her mother until her mother died of cancer last year. Suddenly she was told that she would be living with her birth father, a man she had never known, and his new wife. When Sari came to live in her new family, she had stepbrothers and stepsisters and half-brothers and half-sisters, and her father and his new wife had a child of their own. Suddenly, Sari went from living as an only child to living with five siblings. Sari has had a great deal of difficulty adjusting to her new situation and cannot seem to please her new family. She disappoints them with her grades and her unwillingness to do the household chores that are required of her. She is often compared unfavorably to her siblings, and her birth father claims that her stepmother "picks on her constantly." In family therapy, her father says he is having difficulty bonding with Sari because she reminds him so much of his ex-wife, Sari's mother.

Disparaging Most children who live with constant criticism learn to be failures. If children can never do anything right in their parents' view, they become cynical and distrusting. Statements like "You're stupid" or "You'll never amount to anything" often become self-fulfilling prophesies.

Mr. and Mrs. O. raised three sons, whom Mrs. O. characterized as a "handful." Mr. O. had a drinking problem and didn't spend a lot of time with the boys while they were growing up. Most of his interaction with them was to tell them how "bad" and "worthless" they were. On many occasions, the O's would take their sons for a drive past a home for troubled boys, located a short distance from their home. On these occasions, Mr. O. would warn his sons that they would end up at the Boys' Home if they didn't "straighten up." On at least one occasion, the father stopped the car and forced the youngest son (age 8) to get out. He then drove off, leaving the terrified child in front of the Boys' Home. He drove around and came back for the child about five minutes later. Several years later, when the child was about 12, he was a resident of that very home for troubled boys.

High standards Most parents want their children to have a better life than they had. They want them to be better educated, have a better job or career, and live in a bigger house. The difficulty is that the parent who has impossibly high standards is setting the child up for a great deal of stress and anxiety. A parent who has extremely high standards might say to the child who brings home a B +, "This is good, but you could have gotten an A if you had studied harder!" Always raising the requirements is very discouraging to children, and they feel as if they have failed even when they have succeeded.

> Mr. and Mrs. A. could be described as average parents. They are both high school graduates and wanted to go to college but couldn't afford it. They have worked their way up in their jobs and earn a good living between them. When they were in school, they earned good grades but were not A students. Now they have a family of four children and they want their children to have more than they do. They want them to get good grades, go on to college and graduate school, and have professional careers. There is constant pressure on the children to get all As and to take the hardest courses so they can get into the best schools and the best careers. Two of the children are very bright and can meet their parent's expectations most of the time, although they have little time to socialize and join in other school activities. The other two children are average students, and lately they have resorted to cheating but still cannot meet their parents' impossible standards. All four children are filled with the fear of failure and of the future.

Inharmonious   In an inharmonious setting, there is a great deal of quarreling and fighting, which sometimes escalates into violence. In this family atmosphere, children learn that power is important and that it is better to control than to be controlled. Often children are punished rather than disciplined, and sometimes the punishment doesn't fit the "crime". The punishment is apt to be erratic, punitive, and inconsistent and serves as a vehicle for the parents to displace anger. Children are sometimes punished simply for being in the wrong place at the wrong time, rather than for what they have done.

> Mr. and Mrs. V. grew up in violent homes. Mr. V. had an alcoholic father who physically abused his wife. As a boy, Mr. V. tried to protect his mother, often getting severe beatings in the process. He grew up feeling angry and unloved. Both of Mrs. V's parents were alcoholics, and she was taken to bars with them. When she was a preschooler, she danced on tables for the entertainment of bar patrons. She grew up knowing that she was pretty and smart, but felt lonely and insecure. When Mr. and Mrs. V. married, they continued the cycle of violence and alcohol abuse that they knew as children. Their home became an "armed camp," and they settled their differences by quarreling and fighting. Their 8-year-old son has now come to the attention of the school counselor for fighting, stealing his classmate's lunch money, and setting a fire in a wastebasket in the boys' lavatory.

Inconsistent   An inconsistent parenting style leaves children with a lot of anxiety and confusion as to how to behave in order to get their parents' approval. They are always "waiting for the other shoe to drop," wondering whether the latest transgression will bring some form of punishment or whether they will get away with it. Children who lack structure in their lives often grow up lacking in self-control, motivation, and concern for others. They have difficulty putting others' needs ahead of their own and are often so self-centered that they have difficulty with interpersonal relationships.

> Mrs. I. is a single mother of five children. She has two sons (age 10 and 12) from her first marriage, twin girls (age 7) from her second, and a 3-year-old son with her current live-in boyfriend. Mrs. I. works all day at a local restaurant, and her boyfriend's job allows him to come home only on weekends. Mrs. I. admits that the only child she is able to control is the baby. She says she disciplines the children when they misbehave, but sometimes she is just too tired to bother, so she lets them "fight it out." At other times, when her boyfriend is there, he punishes them severely for fighting and for not doing well in school. The children have no contact with their birth fathers. Teachers complain that all the children are anxious, hyperactive, and poorly motivated to do their school work. They seek attention constantly and cannot seem to concentrate. It seems that they can never get enough of anything—food, toys, attention, and so on. If a snack is offered at school for a party, they want to take as much as possible rather than thinking of the others in the class. Consequently, they have few friends.

Materialistic In materialistic homes, money is everything, and the children define their worth in terms of possessions. The family credo is "money does buy happiness," and children learn that material things are much more important than family and friendships. Parents often buy gifts as a way of showing love to their children. Instead of lavishing time, attention, and warmth on their children, they shower them with money, expensive clothes, or fast cars. The parents are showing affection in the only way they know how and are securing a secondary gain for themselves. In effect, they say to themselves, "I can buy my family expensive things because I am successful."

> Mr. M. is the president of a large company and has five children, a lovely wife, and a mansion. Mr. M., an only child, inherited the family business from his father. Whenever Mr. M. travels on business, he brings back many expensive gifts for his wife and children. He regrets that he can't spend more time with his children but says that he needs a lot of money to keep them "in the style to which they have become accustomed." Mr. M.'s oldest son, Denzel, is a sensitive young man who expresses pride in his father's success. He invites other boys his age to come to the mansion to play, but the children seldom go more than once. Denzel is experiencing difficulties in school and has been diagnosed as learning disabled. He fears that he won't be as successful or as rich as his father. He worries constantly.

Overprotective Overprotective parents, under the guise of helping their children, promote helplessness and dependency. By always doing things for children, parents tell the children that they are not capable of doing anything for themselves. This message has a very negative effect on self-esteem. The overprotective parent hampers the child's decision-making ability and encourages reliance on others for advice and approval. Often parents, particularly mothers, need to feel needed and therefore promote this cycle of dependency by doing things for their children. However, extreme dependency often foments resentment. Parents are not always going to be able to protect their children from the consequences of their behavior, and, therefore, the children may grow into adulthood looking for other people to direct their lives.

> Mr. and Mrs. S. had four children. Their youngest son, Harry, was born when Mrs. S. was 42. Harry is 8 now, and Mrs. S. is 50. Mr. S. died of a heart attack two years ago at age 55. All the other children are grown, and Mrs. S. dotes on "her baby." She waits on Harry "hand and foot," laying out his clothes each morning, fixing his breakfast, and taking it in the living room so he can eat it while he watches cartoons. She has to remind him a thousand times to get dressed as he dawdles and plays. His cousins come to the door to walk him to school and bring him back. Mrs. S. helps Harry with his homework, and sometimes she does it for him because she gets so tired of waiting for him to complete it. Mrs. S. says she would rather do Harry's chores herself because she can do them so much faster and easier. Mrs. S. feels both needed and resentful.

Pitying   Pitying is a negative parenting style in the sense that it is demeaning and robs children of the opportunity to do their best. People with disabilities recoil at a pitying tone or comment because they know that it implies that they can't do something; it also implies that the person doing the pitying is somehow superior to the one being pitied. Statements made by parents to the effect that they "feel sorry" for their children engender the same kind of negative feelings that the actions of overprotective parents do. Children may begin to feel sorry for themselves and give up in their efforts to accomplish something, thereby relinquishing the good feelings that come from accomplishment. All of this has a negative effect on the children's self-esteem, confidence, and self-reliance.

> Raoul was born with cerebral palsy, and Mr. and Mrs. X. always felt guilty that he had so much pain and discomfort. They felt sorry for him and expected the schools, the medical profession, and special agencies to make up for Raoul's pain and the family's heartbreak. At the same time, however, Mr. and Mrs. X resisted any suggestion that Raoul or his family could do more for themselves. When Mr. and Mrs. X. divorced several years ago, Mrs. X. became obsessed with Raoul and his disability. He applied for disability benefits and, after receiving them, he gave up trying to do some of the things he had learned to do for himself. He also dropped out of school and began to take drugs to fit into a peer group. Raoul's mother died last year, so he has no one to pity him now, except himself.

Hopeless   Many times grinding poverty, unemployment, and poor housing join forces to create an atmosphere of pessimism that is contagious. Children growing up in these conditions often see no way out, and so they follow the same path—not because they like the way they live, but because they have never known a different life. Often parents are so terminally discouraged both with their lives and with the system that they cannot inspire their children with thoughts of a better life.

Connie is a child of the streets. She has been homeless for as long as she can remember. She thinks it began when her father lost his job and the family shared one run down tenement after another with people they barely knew. One day, he disappeared, and the family went to a women's shelter where they had warm clothes, toys, and hot food. Now, for the first time in her ten years, Connie lives in an apartment with her mother and four brothers and sisters. This apartment is only temporary, but the family can live there for a year while Connie's mother gets a job and they save enough to get a place of their own. A nice lady from the women's shelter comes to help Connie and her siblings with their schoolwork, and Connie loves having her own bed and enough food to eat. She enjoys the attention and the comfort but she knows in her heart that this is too good to last. When her mother can't find a job or gets fired, they will be homeless again.

Martyr   In the martyr family atmosphere, the parent feels pessimistic and hopeless about the future, much as the parent in the hopeless family atmosphere does. However, the martyr parent's way of dealing with this pessimism is to make the child the object of all the parent's sacrifices. In addition to feeling hopeless and discouraged, the child may get caught in a dependency-resentment relationship with the parent. Eternal gratitude is a heavy price for any child to pay for a parent's sacrifices.

Trau showed a talent for skating at age 5, and his parents decided that if he took skating lessons, he could play pee-wee hockey. Mr. and Mrs. M. were just getting by on their paychecks, so paying for lessons and ice time for Trau was a consider-able sacrifice. His father would get up every morning at 6:00 to drive him to the ice rink for lessons. By the time Trau was playing youth hockey on the traveling team, his parents were traveling with him to every event and paying for admission fees, rooms, and meals. Hockey equipment was always needed, and the family took their only vacation each year to a neighboring state to buy what they could at a small savings. When Trau went to high school, he didn't make the hockey team and his parents' dreams of him being a pro-hockey player were shattered. From that day on, his parents have reminded him, in direct and indirect ways, of how much they sacrificed, only to have him fail them.

Recent changes in family life have contributed to a parenting style that is charac-terized by the loss of authority that the parent usually has over the child. Glenwick and Mowrey (1986) found that this authority, which usually exists in two-parent families, is often absent in one-parent families, perhaps because the single parent feels inadequate and overwhelmed. When boundaries between adult authority figures and children become less well defined, the parent begins to interact with the child as a peer rather than as a parent figure.

Parent-becomes-peer (PBP) family   According to Glenwick and Mowrey (1986), this family atmosphere is one that is seen most frequently in the divorced-produced, single-parent family in which intergenerational boundaries have blurred. In the PBP family, the single parent abdicates the parental role and instead becomes a peer to the latency age child (age 9 to 13). In their study, the authors discovered that the child is used as a confidant by a mother who often avoids making decisions and commitments and cannot face her own fears. She may seek the child's opinion on a variety of personal issues (such as which men to date) and confides adult problems and worries to a child who is helpless to do anything about them. This relationship sometimes results in a form of role reversal in which the child takes care of the parent by fulfilling her need for support and nurturance and assuming adult responsibilities. This situation often propels children into adulthood before they are ready and before they have had their own needs for affection and nurturance met. Consequently, problems such as truancy, sexual and aggressive acting out, withdrawal, running away, substance abuse, overcompliance with parental requests, and a decline or unevenness in academic performance may be noted (Glenwick & Mowrey, 1986).

> Sally, age 9, is the only child remaining with her mother after four failed marriages. Her half-brothers and sisters are being raised by their respective grandmothers. Ever since her father left when she was three, Sally has been her mom's best "buddy." Relating like sisters, Sally's mom lets her experiment with makeup, and the two of them talk about boys, clothes and sex. Sally is bright and verbal and gives the impression that she is much older than 9. Despite her intelligence, she nearly failed the fourth grade because her mom was unable to drive her to school until ten o'clock. Her mother cannot seem to hold a job for more than a few months because she has so much difficulty getting up in the morning. Sally thinks it is because her mom is "sick." She does take prescription pain medication that makes her very groggy in the mornings. Lately, Sally seems to be "sick" a lot also and takes aspirin for her headaches. She thinks she is "in love" with a boy of 13 who lives in the neighborhood.

In summary, it is important to remember that the child's perception of his or her place in the family and the family atmosphere help shape behavior patterns and attitudes. For example, children who are given adult responsibilities at early ages may not perceive themselves as overburdened. Instead, these extra duties may help them acquire a sense of accomplishment. Similarly, children are often able to find effective ways of coping with parental inconsistencies and foibles. If children perceive themselves as loved, they are often able to overcome negative circumstances and become responsible, caring, and successful adults.

COUNSELING WITH PARENTS

Parents want to discuss their children with someone who is going to relate to them on a person-to-person basis, accept them as they are, use commonplace language and talk to them in commonsense terms. They want an opportunity to communicate as equals, coupling their experience with the counselor's knowledge.
—ORTON

Parent counseling is a partnership between the parent and the counselor who interact as equals on behalf of the child. Counseling, as described in this chapter, is more than traditional parent consultation, but it is not intended to help parents with their personal problems (marital or adjustment problems). Instead, it is designed to enhance the child's overall growth and development, reduce problem behavior by strengthening the parent-child relationship, increase the positive communication between the parent and the child, and build parenting skill and confidence. The focus of this intervention is on improving and strengthening the relationship between the child and the parent and on promoting a greater understanding and acceptance of the child. In addition, the parent and the counselor together can help the child assume responsibility for his or her behavior and understand its consequences and impact on others, including the family.

Because children are often powerless to affect change, the parent needs some gentle assistance in understanding and improving the parent-child relationship. Parents may need help in gaining the skills of listening and communicating as well as in encouraging their children. In addition to providing assistance and encouragement, counseling can also be a growth process for the parent, which results in heightened self-esteem. Improvements in the parent's self-esteem and confidence can in turn contribute to a more positive interaction with the child, which can have beneficial effects on the child's behavior.

The Value of Counseling with Parents

Counseling that encourages parents to relate to their children with warmth and acceptance has positive effects on the behavior of all the children, not just the identified child client, and it contributes to the health and growth of the entire family. Helping one or both parents change the family environment is often more effective than trying to influence the child's behavior directly (Schaefer & Briesmeister, 1989). It eliminates the need for time-consuming individual sessions with each child in the family and is a more effective use of the practitioner's time.

Involving parents in the helping process enables them to (1) talk about their concerns with someone who listens and cares, (2) explore the strengths and weaknesses of their interaction with their child, (3) understand the parent-child relationship from the child's perspective, (4) strengthen the relationship by changing its negative aspects, and (5) grow in self-confidence and competence (see Figure 11-1).

Generally speaking, parents have few opportunities to share their hopes and fears regarding their children. Instead, parents are often judged and misjudged, labeled, or given "advice" by well-meaning professionals who do not fully comprehend their situation. Treating parents as equals and not inferiors is an important first step in helping them help their children. When parents feel respected and valued for their positive contributions to their child's development, they are better able to talk about and examine the negative aspects. Encouraging parents to take the child's perspective can help them develop insight into how to improve and strengthen the parent-child relationship. With this insight comes new, more positive behaviors, which are in turn reflected in positive changes in the child's behavior. As a result, the parent gains confidence in his or her ability to parent effectively, which contributes to greater competence. And, according to Schaefer and Briesmeister (1989), the impact of these changes in parental behavior continues and is maintained long after formal counseling has been concluded.

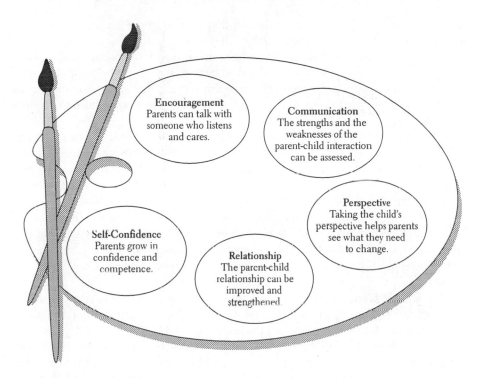

Encouragement
Parents can talk with
someone who listens
and cares.

Communication
The strengths and the
weaknesses of the
parent-child interaction
can be assessed.

Perspective
Taking the child's
perspective helps parents
see what they need
to change.

Self-Confidence
Parents grow in
confidence and
competence.

Relationship
The parent-child
relationship can be
improved and
strengthened.

FIGURE 11-1   *The Value of Counseling with Parents Individually*

THE COUNSELING PROCESS

The focus of the counseling intervention is not on the child's problem or the parent's complaints but rather on ways to improve and strengthen the parent-child relationship.
—ORTON

Stages in the Process

The Adlerian counseling process consists of four phases: (1) the relationship phase, (2) the investigation of behavior dynamics, (3) insight, and (4) reorientation (Dinkmeyer, Dinkmeyer, & Sperry, 1987). This process has been adapted for use in this chapter on counseling with parents to bring about behavioral changes in children.

In the *relationship phase*, a unique partnership is formed between the counselor and parent that makes it possible to identify mutually acceptable goals. In an atmosphere of warmth and caring, a special bond is forged that enables the counselor and the parent to work together to bring about changes in the child's behavior. Within the relationship, the counselor listens attentively as the parent discusses his or her innermost thoughts, feelings, and actions as they pertain to the parent-child interaction. The counselor then tries to identify with the parent as a person who, like all of us, experiences joys as well as frustrations in everyday personal relationships. Communicating this empathic understanding back to the parent helps the parent to feel valued and respected. In communicating this respect, the counselor supports the parent in his or her exploration of the parent-child relationship and efforts to improve and strengthen it.

The *assessment of behavior dynamics* involves the exploration of the strengths and weaknesses of the parent-child relationship. The counselor discovers the parent's view of the child as well as the child's interaction with the family unit. The counselor gently encourages the parent to view the child in a more objective way and to examine the parent's relationship with the identified child client and the other children in the family. The counselor and the parent embark on this investigation together, for they are both in the process of learning about the interaction between parent and child. This is often the first time that the parent has thought about this interaction, so both counselor and parent may be exploring the parent-child relationship for the first time.

The *insight phase* of the counseling process involves helping the parent understand how his or her relationship with the child may be affecting the child's current behavior. A helpful way to promote this insight is to take parents back to their own childhood and ask them to explore their relationship with their own parents. Often, when parents examine their own feelings as children, they are better able to understand and empathize with the identified child client. In this way, they are able to see how the parent-child interaction may be encouraging the child's misbehavior.

The *reorientation phase* is the time in which the parent examines the relationship and focuses on the child's strengths rather than on the behavior problem. The counselor provides encouragement to the parent to develop insight and implement alternative behaviors and attitudes. The counselor must have an abiding faith that the situation can be changed and then should gently encourage the parent in that direction. The reorientation phase cannot be hurried. The process of change is a slow one, and the parent needs continual encouragement to see it to its completion. In addition, when one child in a family changes in response to improved interaction with a parent, negative changes may occur in the behavior of other children in the family. This may be a source of discouragement to the parent(s) and needs to be addressed in family counseling. Of course, the reverse may also be true, and all the children can benefit from a more confident and competent parent.

Counseling Techniques

The counseling techniques presented in this chapter, particularly those involved in the relationship phase, are adapted from the work of Carl Rogers. In the early 1940s, Rogers proposed a counseling relationship based on warmth and responsiveness that would enable clients to freely express their thoughts and feelings. His model is a key part of the counseling process, regardless of one's theoretical orientation, and it is actually a guide for all interpersonal relationships. The interpersonal dimensions of the helping relationship identified by Rogers (1957) as congruence (genuineness), unconditional positive regard (respect), and empathy were later expanded by Carkhuff

(1969) to include the helping skills of attending, responding, personalizing, and initiating.

Person-centered techniques used in this chapter include listening and attending, reflecting feelings, empathic understanding, clarification, summarization, and confrontation, as well as open-ended leads that facilitate client self-exploration. In addition, the Adlerian techniques of intuitive guessing, interpretation, and encouragement are discussed and illustrated. Interpreting can be seen as a form of clarifying; rather than searching to find some hidden secret, the counselor tries to determine what the parent is trying to say and to understand its significance to the parent-child relationship. Intuitive guessing is essential to this skill and can be likened to a hunch (Egan, 1994). Intuitive guessing is a tentative hypothesis by the counselor about what the client is expressing or implying and helps the parent talk about things that he or she may be only alluding to. Encouragement is used in each phase of the counseling process to illuminate strengths (Dinkmeyer, Dinkmeyer, & Sperry, 1987).

Listening to the Entire Person

True *listening* involves much more than hearing. It involves understanding the content, the feelings, and the intentions of another person. Coming into contact with someone who really listens is a powerful encouragement for parents to express their thoughts and feelings about their children. Counselors who know how to listen are so engrossed in what the parent is saying that they are not distracted by background noise or by worries about what they will say next. They have the ability to be responsive to the parent's communication and to clearly communicate this attentiveness. Listening and attending will help counselors understand what the parent is expressing both verbally and nonverbally. This understanding is essential to intuitive guessing and interpretation; if the counselor does not understand what has been said, he or she cannot interpret what it means.

Responding to Feeling and Communicating Empathy

Helping others begins with listening to them, helping them understand their concerns, and sharing this understanding with them. This *empathic understanding* involves capturing the essence of someone's feelings and formulating a response that communicates an understanding of the experiences and behaviors that accompany these feelings (Egan, 1994). Responding to feelings is a skill involved in communicating empathic understanding, which lets the client know that he or she has been heard and understood. In counseling parents, this responding skill involves helping parents identify and understand those issues that influence their interaction with their children. In addition, it is a way to check the accuracy of the counselor's perceptions of what has been said, parents may need to correct the counselor if his or her feelings have been inaccurately reflected. Empathy, as a communication skill, increases the parent's awareness and self-understanding and makes it possible to facilitate change.

PARENT: This man called me from the alternative school and complained that my son was fighting again. Then he said, "Do you want me to handcuff him and bring him to the phone?" I couldn't even find the words to answer him.

HELPER: It sounds like you felt afraid and helpless.

PARENT: Exactly—I was terrified to think that they were going to handcuff him. I didn't even know what he had done and I didn't know what to say or do.

Intuitive Guessing

As part of the process of exploration and discovery, the counselor has to be somewhat of a detective. The parent may have certain thoughts and feelings about the child that the parent is unable or unwilling to put into words. Often parents feel too much guilt or deny—even to themselves—how they feel about the child. Perhaps they don't like a particular child and wish the problem that the child represents would just go away. Sometimes parents see traits and behaviors that they don't like about themselves in their children, or they see traits and behaviors in the child that remind them of an ex-spouse or ex-lover whom they dislike. The parents are, in effect, rejecting the child because of these traits but can't admit it to themselves. Parents often disguise their true feelings, and it is up to the counselor to use what is called *intuitive guessing* to uncover what the parent is trying to say. This counseling technique is an especially valuable aid to interpretation. If the counselor is able to guess and interpret back to the parent what the parent is unable to admit even to themselves, it often opens the way to insight.

PARENT: Sometimes, I wonder what life would be like without any kids.
HELPER: You are wondering what it would be like not to have to deal with some of the problems you are having with your son.

Clarifying What Has Been Said

Again, listening skills come into play when the counselor attempts to understand what parents are saying about their children, themselves, and their situation. Counselors need to listen beyond what is said and respond in a way that indicates that they understand the parents' situation. *Clarification* is not merely restating content or mechanical "parroting" but is, instead, a reworking of what has been said. This reworked version is presented back to the parent in order to simplify and reach an understanding of what was meant. Clarification is a skill that can help the parent continue to self-explore and one that can deepen the level of involvement between parent and counselor.

PARENT: Juan is constantly getting into fights at the alternative school. The school officials call me every day and threaten to throw him out. This is his last chance, and I don't know what will happen if he gets expelled.
HELPER: You worry about what will happen to Juan if he can't control his fighting.

Challenging

If parents are to grow and better understand their interaction with their children, the counselor cannot agree totally with the parents' interpretation of events. The counselor will have to challenge the discrepancies between what the parent says and what the parent actually does when he or she is with the child. If the counselor has built a good relationship with the parent, gentle confrontation will encourage the parents to continue to gain insight into their behavior. Summarizing the important points in the session is a form of *challenging* that helps clients focus and then move on (Egan, 1994).

PARENT: I want to have a better relationship with my son, but we don't seem to have anything to talk about. He answers my questions, but he doesn't talk to me.

HELPER: You seem disappointed that your son won't share his thoughts and feelings with you. Could it be that you aren't sharing your thoughts and feelings with him?

Interpreting

Interpretation is a skill that is invaluable to counseling and is essential to the development of insight. Through interpretation, the counselor attempts to perceive accurately what the parent is trying to say and interprets it back to the parent. This is a process that must be done slowly and only after a great deal of rapport and trust have been established in the counseling relationship. The accuracy of interpretation often depends on the counselor's skill. The more skilled the counselor is at intuitive guessing, the more accurate the interpretation. Counselors-in-training should not be afraid to interpret; the client will tell you when your interpretations are inaccurate. Skill at interpretation is developed over time and it is a process that cannot be hurried. If the counselor is a good listener and has been mentally gathering information and observing client behavior, interpretation becomes easier.

PARENT: Every time the school calls, I panic. I think that they are going to put my son in a detention center because they can't handle him. What am I supposed to do? I can't go to school with him.

HELPER: You're fearful of what might happen and feel helpless to prevent it.

Encouragement

Encouragement helps individuals recognize and capitalize on their strengths and assets and recognize their power to make decisions and choices (Dinkmeyer, Dinkmeyer, & Sperry, 1987). When applied to parent counseling, encouragement capitalizes on the strengths of the parent-child relationship and empowers the parent to utilize these strengths to improve weaknesses. When parents feel discouraged and inadequate, as they often do, this feeling is reflected in ineffective parenting. Therefore, encouragement helps counteract the parents' negative perceptions and sets the stage for change.

According to Dinkmeyer, Dinkmeyer, & Sperry (1987), encouragement can be used in many phases of the counseling process. In the relationship phase, it can be used to let parents know that they are valued as full and equal participants in the process. In later stages, it is designed to illuminate strengths and promote change by stimulating the individual's awareness of his or her own worth. Encouragement permeates and contributes to every aspect of the counseling process.

PARENT: Juan is constantly fighting at school, but at home he is kind and considerate.

HELPER: Let's explore some of the positive ways that your interaction with Juan contributes to his kindness and consideration at home.

Special Issues

"I didn't know what you would think of me"   Kay M. revealed years after the fact that one of the most difficult things she had ever done was to tell "the whole story" in an effort to help her son. She explained that she had always had the feeling that school personnel thought of themselves as a level above ordinary mothers and, intentionally or otherwise, this was the image that they projected.

Kay had distinct feelings of inferiority before her initial contact with the counselor. She expressed her feelings this way: "I didn't know what you would think of me. I thought you had made it and I had not and now I had to come in and admit I'd been a rotten mother."

Parental apprehensions about consulting with teachers, counselors, psychologists, and other school personnel are very real and appear to fall into several general categories.

- Parents think that school personnel regard them as second-class citizens who are inferior socially and intellectually.
- Parents resent being summoned to school to hear primarily negative reports about their children. They perceive these reports as negative evaluations of themselves.
- Going to school on behalf of their children often brings back unpleasant memories of the parents' own school experiences.
- School personnel who use professional jargon reinforce the parents' feelings of inferiority. This language, which is often unintelligible to a layperson, confuses and frustrates parents and convinces them that "the psychologist needs a psychiatrist!"
- A list of do's and don'ts recited by someone who never had children makes parents wonder why they bothered to come in the first place. The advice they receive, however well meaning, is often impractical.
- Parents lament the fact that they are rarely asked what they know about their children. Often they are subjected to a long discourse of what the teacher or other professional has discovered in just six weeks!

Essentially, parents want to discuss their children with someone who is going to relate to them on a person-to-person basis, accept them as they are, use commonplace language, and talk to them in commonsense terms. Parents want an opportunity to contribute to the professional's knowledge of their child, and they want to hear a little bit about what they are doing right. Basically, parents want and need to feel that the counselor likes them and their children. Parents want to communicate as equals, coupling their experience with the counselor's knowledge. All these considerations will have a profound influence on the success of both the counselor's work with parents and the total school guidance program.

"So this is what counselors do"   The first contact that many parents have with a counselor frequently occurs in the school setting. Therefore, a positive or negative

experience with the school counselor often influences the parents' perceptions regarding the value of counseling. When parents have a warm and trusting relationship with the school counselor, they are more likely to accept referrals for services that are not offered by the school. Because the referral process can confuse and frighten some parents ("I thought people go to psychiatrists because they are crazy"), the counselor's attitude can make a difference. A positive association with the counselor will help dispel misconceptions about the purpose of the referral, will ease parental apprehensions, and, will make follow-up more likely.

Helpful intervention by the school counselor can provide parents with a positive view of the counseling program and the school. With the knowledge that there is a warm and empathic supporter within the school system, the parent will hopefully view the school as a help and reflect this positive attitude about the school to the child (and to other children in the family who are not yet of school age).

Finally, a positive experience with a school counselor has a ripple effect in the community, particularly if the school is small. Parents who receive a warm welcome are likely to communicate this positive feeling to their friends. In this way, other parents will be more willing to seek help from the school counselor and the counseling program will have the support of the community. This support is essential if programs designed to meet the needs of children and their parents are to be successful (see Chapter 12).

"I'm in over my head" Counselors and therapists who work with children have, as their first obligation, the health and welfare of the child. Their primary interest in parents and other adult caretakers is to help them modify the child's home environment so that the child can overcome the presenting problem and get back on the road to healthy growth and development.

Part of maintaining high levels of professionalism involves knowing one's limitations. This means knowing when to decline service and refer the client elsewhere (Dougherty, 1992). Therefore, counselors who lack the training and expertise to help parents improve their interaction with their children need to seek assistance from other professionals. Similarly, when the child counselor recognizes that a parent needs help for personal adjustment or marital problems or when it is impossible to maintain the focus on the parent-child interaction, the counselor needs to refer the parent to a practitioner who specializes in counseling with adults.

In addition to a lack of knowledge and skill, some counselors have value conflicts that interfere with their ability to work effectively with some children and their parents. According to Dougherty (1992), value conflicts are common and need to be dealt with in a straightforward, professional, and nondefensive manner. Counselors need to be aware of their values and needs and avoid imposing their values on others.

If, for reasons of training, experience or value conflicts, a counselor is unable to work with some or all parents on behalf of their children, he or she should recognize these limitations and refer parents to other professionals who can help them.

"Do you make house calls?" Increasingly, a wide range of professionals, including social workers, nurses, teachers, counselors and psychologists, are providing family support in the home in an effort to meet children's social, psychological, educational, and health needs. (Crutcher, 1991; Roberts, Wasik, Casto, & Ramey,

1991). Currently, home visiting programs serve families and children from birth to age 18, and most programs involve psychological support and information about child development and parenting (Roberts et al., 1991). Family-focused services in the home have been guided by several assumptions: (1) parents are usually the most caring people in their children's lives; (2) parents can respond more positively and effectively to their children if they are provided with knowledge, skills, and support; and (3) the parents' own emotional and physical needs must be met if they are to be more responsive to their children's needs (Wasik et al., as cited in Roberts et al., 1991).

Although, some families worry about the appearance of the house or the children (Crutcher, 1991), most welcome home visits from a warm and accepting counselor. Home visiting eliminates many of the problems that families face in getting to counseling appointments (such as work schedules, baby-sitting, and transportation problems), and it gives parents a measure of control over the session. In the comfort of their own homes, parents often feel relaxed enough to talk about their concerns. In addition, the counselor can observe the family dynamic and help the parents gain insight into the behaviors and attitudes they may wish to change.

Being invited to someone's home is a privilege; therefore, the same courteous behavior extended to parents in other settings should be observed during home visits. The counselor should always keep the appointment, should be on time, and should write or phone if the appointment must be cancelled.

Roberts and associates (1991) predict that, over the next decade, there is likely to be a considerable increase in home visiting services. Some of this increase will be due to an increased emphasis on early intervention and on providing services for children. with disabilities. However, many of the social problems discussed in Chapter 1 (high incidence of births to teenage mothers, increasing reports of child abuse and neglect) will necessitate more home-based services to children and families.

COUNSELING WITH PARENTS IN PRACTICE

In many instances, the most effective and enduring changes in caregiving attunement and responsiveness come from insight into the sources of faulty family interaction in the caregiver's own developmental experience a generation earlier, rather than from teaching, advice or suggestion.
—LEVIN (1985)

This section presents a model for counseling that provides an opportunity for parents to assess their interaction with their children, gain insight into what they would like to change, and decide on a course of action. This model is carefully explained using sample dialogue from a counseling session with the mother of Jai, a young boy who has developed encopresis. In this case, it was decided that bringing about changes in Jai's family environment would be more effective than trying to modify the child's behavior directly.

Parent counseling is the strategy used to help Jai overcome his encopresis because he is unable to alter his home environment or to improve his interaction with his mother without her help. The counseling session focuses on the parent-child relationship and not on Jai's problem. Each step in the counseling process illustrates how Jai's mother expresses her thoughts and feelings about Jai and his siblings and examines her day-to-day interactions with him, identifies with and develops empathy for him, searches for his strengths, and formulates ways to change their relationship.

• • • *The Case of Jai*

Jai is a pleasant 9-year-old who is clean and neat in his personal dress. Because he is small for his age, he appears younger than 9. In the first session, he seemed a bit nervous but quickly got over it and began talking about his family and the things he liked best about school. He was pleasant and cheerful and rapport was quickly established. Jai did not mention his bowel control problem (encopresis) nor the fact that he had difficulty with his schoolwork, and the counselor made no mention of it either. Jai talked about reading and arithmetic being his favorite subjects. He talked of flying a kite with his father over vacation and playing with his brother and sisters. He said that sometimes his brother gets into his things but not too often. He said that "yelling" sometimes made him nervous. When the counselor encouraged Jai to say what kind of yelling, he quickly said the "yelling of the kids in school." He did not mention his mother.

Background Information

Family   Jai lives with his mother, two sisters (age 7 and 5), and one brother, (age 8). Jai's parents divorced shortly after his youngest sister was born, and the children visit their father on weekends and school holidays. The parents are congenial to one another, and Jai has a close relationship with his father. Jai's mother does not work outside the home and the family is on public assistance.

Physical development and health record   Jai's health record indicates that he is below the norm for both height and weight. He wears glasses to correct severe nearsightedness. His hearing is within the normal range, and the school's medical examination record indicates no overt physical defects. The school nurse recommended a physical examination for Jai, and no organic reason for encopresis was discovered.

School development   Jai's reading is below grade level. He is now reading at the first-grade level and is in the third grade. Report card grades indicate that Jai does unsatisfactory work when compared with children in his age group but does satisfactory work when rated as an individual. His report card grades reflect the difficulty that he is experiencing in school. On the Wechsler Intelligence Test for Children (WISC), Jai's performance score is much higher than his verbal score and helps explain some of his difficulties in reading.

Teachers' comments on the permanent record indicate that Jai's strengths are his pleasant, cheerful disposition and his ability to get along with his classmates. Areas of concern include his short attention span, his preference for play instead of work, and his poor school performance.

Presenting problem   Jai was referred to the school counselor by the third-grade teacher because of his inability to control his bowel functions (encopresis) over the last two months. A physical exam has ruled out any organic cause. The teacher states that Jai defecates while at his desk and does not report the problem until the situation is such that other students and the teacher have detected the problem. She notes that this is causing him a great deal of embarrassment despite the fact that she tries to get him to the nurse's office in a quiet, routine manner. The school nurse reported that the first time Jai phoned his mother, she scolded him over the telephone and refused to come to get him. The nurse also noted that Jai did not have any accidents during his mother's recent hospitalization, but he did have them when his mother came home from the hospital.

Jai's teacher further noted that Jai has a tendency to exaggerate in the classroom situation. She calls on him first because he will outdo what anyone else volunteers. He will always have more pets, more experiences, and so on than anyone else has mentioned. The teacher says that Jai describes pets that do not actually exist.

Counseling strategy   The counselor met with Jai's mother for two sessions to talk about some of her concerns about her son. During the initial session, Mrs. J. poured out her feelings as though they had been bottled up for a long time. After many of Mrs. J.'s frustrations had been vented, the counselor focused on her perception of Jai's strengths. However, the "problem" had overshadowed the positive aspects of their relationship, and Jay's mother had difficulty articulating his strengths during this session.

It was during the second session that the mother explored her relationship with Jai in depth and confided thoughts and feelings that she had kept hidden, even from herself. During this session, Mrs. J. was asked to describe Jai as a person, and not as her son. This was difficult for her to do because, like most parents, she had never thought of him as a person with strengths and weakness. She had only thought about him as a son, an extension of herself. This approach helped Jai's mother explore her interaction with her son, which was very negative and focused on "his problem."

Although parents generally love their children deeply, this love is often not without conditions. In this case, there were many things that Mrs. J. did not like about her son's behavior, and she was having difficulty separating the doer from the deeds. In an effort to help Jai's mother identify and empathize with her son, the counselor focused on Mrs. J.'s own unpleasant childhood experiences. The next step involved helping Mrs. J. find something positive about Jai that could be used to build a bridge of good feelings between them. In this way, Jai's mother was helped to formulate some ways that she could change her relationship with her son.

In this case, only two sessions with Mrs. J. were required before Jai's encopresis diminished and then ceased. It was six weeks before Jai was symptom free. One follow-up session was held with Mrs. J. to encourage her to continue building a positive relationship with her son. •

Illustrating the Model: A Session with Jai's Mother

Most parents truly love their children and want to do whatever is necessary to have a harmonious and loving relationship with them. However, some parents do not know

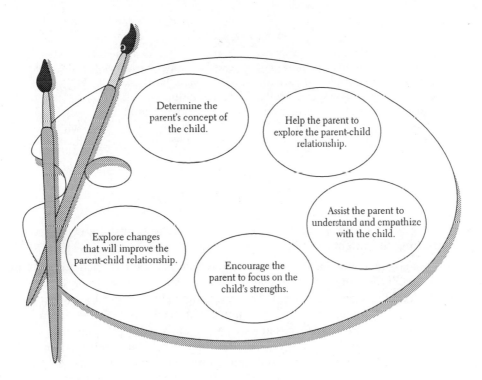

FIGURE 11-2 *Model for Counseling with Parents Individually*

how to achieve this relationship, and they may need someone who is not as close to the situation to help them see their behavior and the child's behavior more clearly. Because counselors can provide a more objective view, they are in a unique position to help parents improve the parent-child relationship by focusing on strengths and discovering ways to minimize weaknesses.

I originated the modified Adlerian model described in this chapter to help parents improve their relationship with their children. This model guides the counselor in a step-by-step procedure that allows for a great deal of individuality and flexibility and therefore appears to have universal application (see Figure 11-2). It has met with repeated success in my own practice and in the practice of other counselors with whom it has been shared.

The time needed to achieve each step is determined by the amount of rapport that has been established between the parent and counselor. The parent's readiness to work toward self-understanding and to gain insight into the dynamics of the parent-child interaction, as well as the degree of commitment to change, will also affect the time required.

This model is applicable to all parents, not just parents of children who are having problems. It can be used to develop or strengthen the parent-child relationship in preventive, developmental, or remedial counseling in school, private practice, clinic, or agency settings.

MODEL

1. Solicit information from the parent to determine his or her concept of the child.
2. Obtain an expression of the parent's feeling toward the child.
3. Help the parent explore the parent-child relationship.
4. Assist the parent to understand and empathize with the child.
5. Help the parent to emphasize the positive aspects of the child's personality.
6. Encourage the parent to formulate ways to improve and strengthen the parent-child relationship.

Determining the Parent's Concept of the Child

As a first step, the counselor solicits information from the parent to determine his or her concept of the child. The counselor's task is to gain insight into how the parent views the child as a person, not as a son or daughter. This is sometimes difficult for parents because although they are very familiar with their children, they often have not stopped to view them as persons in their own right. Now the parent is being asked to view the child in a different way. The following examples are leads that may help the parent accomplish this task without feeling threatened.

LEAD 1: Tell me a little bit about Jai from a mother's (father's) point of view.
LEAD 2: If Jai were someone else's child, a child of a friend of yours for instance, how would you describe him?

With either of these two leads, the counselor can help the parent (in this illustration, it is a mother) begin to view the child objectively. The following dialogue, in which CO indicates counselor and CL indicates client (mother), serves as an illustration.

CO: If Jai belonged to someone else, a friend of yours for instance, how would you describe him?
CL: Hmmm, like if he belonged to say my girlfriend, right?
CO: Yes.
CL: And he was acting like he does with me right now?
CO: Yes.
CL: Like a little boy who needs a lot of love…and who needs more attention than he is getting. I think he acts like he doesn't think anybody wants him, and I think he thinks he needs more attention than he is getting.
CO: You mentioned that he acts like a boy who needs a lot of love.
CL: I think he acts like a baby…I mean I think he acts younger than 9 to me…
CO: I see.
CL: I would never say that he is 9 the way he acts. I think he feels he is not getting as much love as he should get—or as much as he should get of anything—not just love…attention, toys, anything.

The mother's concept of the child at this point is one of a demanding little boy who is immature for his age. The mother is bothered by her son's demands on her and is unsure whether she is meeting his needs for love and attention; she suspects that she is not.

In the individual session, parents need an opportunity to vocalize these feelings so that they can come to understand them and gain insight into how they are affecting their relationship with their child. In addition, parents need a place where they can tell someone about thoughts and feelings that many be too threatening to reveal in groups.

Generally, parents are good observers of their child's behavior, and they can provide the counselor with clues that will help the counselor assess the relationship between the parent and child. The counselor needs to communicate to the parent that his or her knowledge of the child is valued and needed. Without this special parent/counselor relationship, rapport will dissipate quickly or will not become established, and the session will be of little value to the parent and will have little or no positive effect on the child's behavior.

An Expression of the Parent's Feeling

The counselor needs to get an expression of how the parent feels about the child in order to understand the parent-child relationship. The following dialogue is a continuation of the same session with Jai's mother. A great deal of rapport exists between this mother and the counselor, and the mother has been waiting for many years for someone to help her with her relationship with her son. Intuitively, she knows that something is wrong with how she feels, but she doesn't know what it is.

In the following dialogue, Jai's mother explores how she feels about Jai.

Co: You say that Jai demands a lot of attention. What might be some reasons a child would act like this?

Cl: I don't know...I think I give him as much attention as I do the other three...I try not to show any more love to the other three than I do him...I think I love him just as much as the other three.

Co: You think you love him as much as the other three. (Pause.) Are you not sure?

Cl: Well, there are times when I just don't know. I know I do because if I ever think of something happening to him, I just couldn't stand it....But there are times when that kid drives me till I could just...Oooooh....just shake him and if I ever do I think I'll forget to stop!

Co: So you feel there are times when you love him very much and other times when you don't.

Cl: Yes, I guess you could say that, uh-hum.

Co: Do you ever have any time in between when you just like him?

Cl: Yes, I think so...

Co: When?

The mother in this case has very graphically described her feelings toward the child. She thinks she loves him as much as her other children but is really not sure because he "drives her." Parents use different terms for this feeling such as "he gets to me" or "she gets under my skin."

It is valuable to assess how the parent feels about the child in relation to him- or herself and the other members of the family. It is very likely, as (Adler, Ansbacher, & Ansbacher, 1956) points out, that one child in the family may be viewed as doing everything "right," whereas another child is viewed as the "bad" one or the one who "gets under the parent's skin." Often the parent feels guilty about having mixed feelings for the child and wonders, like the mother in the previous illustration, whether the parent does love the troublesome child as much as the other children.

Often the troublesome child exhibits characteristics that remind parents of their own unwanted behaviors, and they don't recognize that the child is acting like them. They make an effort to rid the child of behavior they don't particularly like in themselves, often responding in ways that their parents responded to them. In other situations, the troublesome child may remind parents of a spouse or ex-spouse whom they no longer have good feelings toward. In most cases, parents are unaware of this and have to be helped to think about and express their true feelings regarding their child.

At this point, it may be valuable to talk a bit about maternal love. It is a rare mother who does not love her child. Occasionally, however, if the rapport with the counselor is great enough, a mother will confide that she does not love one or all of her children. This is an extremely difficult thing to do because she may fear the condemnation of her family, friends, community, and society if she admits to these feelings. In addition, she will, in all likelihood suffer from a great deal of guilt, which may manifest itself in many ways and cause the mother both physical and psychological harm. If the counselor finds this to be the case, she or he can help the mother explore her feelings in depth. If the mother seems unable to love and nurture the child, does not seem capable of introspection, feels that someone else is to blame for her lack of affection, or has suffered severe maternal deprivation in her own childhood, the counselor must recognize the seriousness of the problem; and after considering his or her own limitations, the counselor may choose to refer the mother for more intensive therapy.

This model is not intended to provide therapy for the parent but rather to improve the parent-child relationship. But one of the beneficial side effects of counseling with parents is that it does improve the parent's self-esteem and therefore has a positive effect on the entire family. Often in the course of the sessions with the parent, the counselor will see evidence of personal problems that the parent is wrestling with and may need to refer the parent for more intense personal counseling. This will ultimately benefit the child because the parents will be better able to cope with whatever is bothering them, which certainly affects the quality of their life and their parenting.

It is not often that a parent will express or imply a lack of love, but parents frequently do not like what their children do. Sometimes it is difficult for the parent to separate the doer from the deed. In these instances, a parent may focus his or her dislike on the child rather than on the behavior that is so irritating. Often helping parents understand that they can love the child as a person and still disapprove of some of the child's behavior relieves a great deal of the parent's guilt. It also may help to clarify the feelings that the parent has about the child and about him- or herself.

The counselor must follow the basic assumption of the parent-child relationship, namely that the child is a good person and the parent is a good person; the problem lies in the interaction between the two. The ability to capitalize on the strengths of both parent and child is very important to the counseling process. Of course, the counselor will help the parent and child recognize the weaknesses of their relationship and try to change them into strengths, but the primary focus is on strengths and how to use those strengths to minimize weaknesses.

In getting parents to express their feelings toward the child whose behavior is troublesome, the counselor will want to learn about the parents' perception of the other children in the family. This information will serve several functions: the parent will (1) have an opportunity to verbalize feelings about each child in the family, (2) gain insight into how he or she is reacting to each child, and (3) recognize the differences in his or her relationship with each child. The following leads might help parents express their feeling about the child with problematic behavior in relation to the other children in the family.

LEAD 1:   You say that Jai seems to want to "get under your skin." How is this different than the way his brother and sisters affect you?

LEAD 2:   You feel that Jay deliberately misbehaves to "get to you." Do you have these same feelings when your other children misbehave?

Some parents express frustration with a particular child who is viewed as especially troublesome. The identified child client may be perceived as different from the other children in the family, and the parent may have strong feelings about how the child's behavior affects the family. The counselor helps clarify the feelings that the parent has for the child. Providing an opportunity for the parent to express these feelings is often beneficial in itself. If success is achieved at this step, empathy may begin to develop.

Exploring the Parent-Child Relationship

The third step is an attempt to get the parent to explore the parent-child relationship as a "two-way street." The counselor assists the parent in discovering that feelings are often reciprocal. If the parent feels this way, what about the child?

LEAD 1:   Think of your best friend, someone you really like. How do you know that he or she likes you? Think of someone you dislike. How do you think he or she feels about you?

Using another lead, the dialogue with Jai's mother evolved as follows:

CO: If you feel that Jai bothers you and does these things just to get under your skin and you can't stand it any longer, how do you think he feels?

CL: I never really thought about it—how he feels.

CO: Do you think it would help if you thought about it?

CL: Yes, it probably would. I don't know...I just always think he's doing it to get to me.

CO: Is there a reason?

CL: Yes, there must be a reason.

CO: You think perhaps he may feel you haven't really accepted him?

CL: You think he knows...do you think he knows that?

CO: Do you think he knows it?

CL: He must...

In the previous dialogue, the counselor interpreted a possible reason for the child's behavior based on what the mother has said throughout the session. The important aspect of the dialogue is that the mother is thinking about how her son may be feeling, possibly for the first time. Up to this point, she has been concerned only about her own feelings. Second, the mother is reflecting on her son's purposes for behaving the way he does. This mother believes that her son deliberately misbehaves to get even with her, and this is probably true. Now the mother can begin to discover ways to change this pattern of behavior.

Most parents recognize the attention-seeking aspects of their children's behavior. However, motives often go beyond attention getting, and the counselor cannot stop at this level. Counselors must be prepared to explore Dreikurs' (Dreikurs & Soltz, 1964) four goals of misbehavior, which are attention, power, revenge, and withdrawal. By the time the parents seek a counselor's help, the child's goal for misbehavior may have gone beyond attention-seeking and developed into a power struggle, retaliation, or withdrawal.

The counselor can usually determine what the child's goals are by taking her or his clue from what the parents say about how the child's behavior affects them (Dreikurs & Soltz, 1964). The mother who says her son makes her so angry that she could "just shake him and if I ever do I think I'll forget to stop" or "I could just take that kid and choke him" is probably in a power struggle with the child. The parent who says, "he deliberately fights with his sisters to upset me," or "she just seems to do things to get to me," may be the object of the child's retaliatory behavior. The occasional parent who comes to the counselor with "I give up, I just can't reach him anymore" or "I just can't cope with her, nothing I do gets a response" may be experiencing the child's reaction to unsatisfied needs.

After having successfully developed rapport, gained insight into how the parent regards the child, and explored some possible purposes for the child's behavior, the counselor and the parent are ready to proceed to the fourth step.

Assisting the Parent to Empathize

The fourth step is a crucial one, for it is at this level that the parent (in this case the mother) begins to gain insight into how the child is feeling. She may begin to silently explore what the child may be needing from her. At the fourth step, the counselor assists the parent to empathize with the child.

> LEAD: Sometimes it is easier to understand kids and their feelings if we think back to our own childhood. Tell me a little bit about yourself when you were growing up, if you would like to.

Parents often go back to their own childhoods as they talk about their children. If this happens, the counselor can lead as follows:

Example 1:

> CL: My father used to beat me if I didn't do as I was told—not just spank , but really beat me. He just lost control, I guess.
> CO: Do you feel that you are in control of yourself now when you discipline your children?

Example 2:

CL: My grandmother raised me and she never let me out of the house. She never gave me any money to spend or told me about boys—afraid I'd get pregnant, I guess.

CO: As you think about your relationship with your own daughter, how would you say you are different from your grandmother?

Counselors need to give parents an opportunity to reflect on their interactions with their own parents. Because parenting behaviors can be modeled, many adults find themselves repeating some of the same interactional patterns that they disliked as children.

The following dialogue with Jai's mother illustrates how the parent can be helped to gain insight into the parent-child relationship and be gently encouraged to explore her feelings toward her own childhood.

CO: One time you told me that Jai was good in art.

CL: Usually, when he does draw something I tell him it's nice and that he should—I always have to add that—he should keep drawing and practicing so he can get...oh...better.

CO: You feel that he never comes up to your expectations.

CL: I never really thought about it until just now when I said it to you, but I'm always doing that to him. I say "It's nice, but keep trying so you can get better at it."

CO: So he feels that you are never really pleased with his work.

CL: No, I guess I never really thought about it until just this minute...Hmm, I'll be darned. It was the thing my father used to do to me too. When we would bring our report cards home, he used to say, "Well, that's good, but you could do better."

CO: How did you feel about not being able to get your father's approval?

CL: Not very good, really...like what's the sense of trying?...Well, I'll be darned...I never really thought about that, but I always do that to Jai.

CO: You think that makes him feel defeated?

CL: Yes, it probably does. He tried to draw the best picture he could at the time and I come along and say, "Well you could do better." I've done the same thing to him about report cards: "This is okay but you could do better." I know one time my mother mentioned it to me when she heard me say that. She said, "You know how you used to feel when your father said that to you."

At this point, the parent has had an opportunity to express his or her feelings, explore possible purposes for the child's behavior, examine the parent-child relationship, and develop some understanding of the child's feelings. Now if any positive change is to occur, the parent must be helped to recognize and build on the child's strengths.

Emphasizing the Positive Aspects of the Child's Personality

At the fifth step, the counselor helps the parent emphasize the positive aspects of the child's personality. Thinking of the child's strengths rather than his or her weaknesses can present a challenge to some parents. Remember that, for a long time, the focus has been on all the things that the child does wrong. Very little time and attention has been devoted to the positive aspects of the child's behavior and the qualities that endear the child to the family. Many times, the parent will have to rediscover these with the help of a patient and encouraging counselor. For example:

LEAD 1: Tell me what you like about Jai.
LEAD 2: Suppose you were to say, "I am proud of Jai
because_____." How would you complete that sentence?

Often, after being given Lead 2, the parent will pause for a long time and say, "I don't know." Allow plenty of time for the parent to think about the response. The parent may be proud of the child for many reasons but has paid so much attention to the child's negative qualities that a quick response is not forthcoming. If the parent says honestly, "Nothing," the counselor may ask the parent to discover some positive things about the child. The following dialogue from the counseling session with Jai's mother is an example:

CO: Suppose you were to say, "I am proud of Jai because _____." How would you finish that sentence?
CL: Hummm…I guess I couldn't.
CO: So, as of this moment, you have nothing that you feel you could be proud of Jai for?
CL: Not really…
CO: If you were to start building something, where would you begin?
CL: Humm… Where would I start building something between Jai and me? Well probably I have to try to find something good in him and just bring that out and not…you know…humm…I really don't know…I yell a lot.

Parents often express pride in their children by noting the absence of negative behavior rather than by accentuating the positive aspects of the child's personality. "He cleaned up his room and I only reminded him twice"or "She didn't fight with her sisters today" are examples of compliments that focus on the absence of negative behavior. In contrast, statements highlighting the positive aspects of a child's personality might include: "She brings smiles wherever she goes" or "He is so helpful and kind."

It is often difficult for parents to focus on the positive aspects of the child's personality and to perceive the child as a person to be valued and respected in his or her own right. This difficulty may be due to one of two reasons. First, the parent may not perceive the child as a distinct person, instead seeing the child as either behaving or misbehaving. Second, the parent is often overwhelmed by the child's problem behavior and that becomes the entire focus of parent-child relationship. In either case, the counselor may help the parent focus on the positive aspects of the child's personality, as in the following example.

CL: I'm proud of Jai when he's being good…when he's doing what he's supposed to.
CO: You're proud of Jai when he obeys you. Are there other times when you are proud of his accomplishments?

It's important to try to get the parent to view the child as a distinct personality with strengths as well as weaknesses and then focus on the strengths. The counselor could ask the parent to focus on the strengths of someone in the family other than the child, to elicit responses such as "He's kind," "We like the same things," or "She has a wonderful sense of humor." The counselor can then use these comments to lead back to the parent so the focus is on the child's strengths, whatever they may be.

Here, again, the basic assumption is that the child is a good person and the parent is a good person; it is the interaction between the two that blocks the parent from seeing the child's strengths and vice-versa. In the sample counseling session, Jai's mother has become so preoccupied with his disturbing behavior that she has ceased to see any of his strengths. At this point, the counselor can assist the parent in discovering the child's strengths and building on them in order to change the parent-child relationship.

Changing the Parent-Child Relationship

"Building something between Jai and me" is exactly what step six is all about. The parent (in this case, the mother) attempts to formulate some ways that she can change the mother-child relationship. Parents must decide for themselves what steps to take to restore a healthy relationship with the child. The following is another excerpt from the session with Jai's mother.

CO: Do you think you could find something that Jai does that would be worthy of praise?

CL: Oh, I think I probably could.

CO: And what would you do?

CL: Well, to start off, until I got the habit, I probably would have to remind myself quite often to praise him or mention something good that he has done. I just don't do this.

CO: If you begin to find some good in him and praise him, how will you go about it?

CL: Put my arm around him and tell him what a good job he's done.

CO: You think this is what he needs?

CL: Yes, I think more than material things, he needs that.

CO: What does his father find to build him up on?

CL: They spend time together building things. Alex finds more than I do. He takes to Jai more. He's not very affectionate, but he does mention what Jai does well. I don't even do that.

CO: You're not in the habit of mentioning what Jai does well or doing things with him. If you wanted to break some of these old habits, do you think it would take a lot of conscious effort on your part?

CL: Yes, I'll have to really try.

CO: Do you think it's worth trying?

CL: Oh, yes, I certainly do. I really think about it a lot. It does bother me. I never had anyone to really talk to about it before.

If parents are committed to improving the parent-child relationship, they may, over a period of weeks, institute subtle changes in the way they interact with the child.

These positives alterations in their attitude and behavior will likely result in increased communication and understanding. Once these changes have occurred, significant improvement in the child's behavior is often noted. In Jai's case, his mother's ability to help him feel accepted and valued resulted in the disappearance of his bowel control problem.

INSIGHTS AND IMPLICATIONS

The family is central to children's healthy development, and enlisting the parents' help to bring about changes in the family dynamic is an important part of child therapy. The counseling model presented in this chapter is an effective strategy for helping parents influence their children's behavior in positive rather than negative ways. In this approach, the goal is to provide empathy, understanding and support to parents as they discover new ways of relating to their children. Positive changes in the parent-child relationship are often the result of more positive communications between them, new ideas and techniques for resolving problems, and parents' corrective emotional experiences.

Practitioners in all settings are encouraged to involve parents as much as possible in their child's therapy. This includes providing parents with opportunities to explore their interactions with their children and to resolve current problems as well as prevent future ones. Counselors can help parent gain the skills of listening, communicating, and encouraging their children. In addition to providing assistance and encouragement, counscling can contribute to the parent's self-esteem. This enhanced self-esteem and heightened self-confidence has beneficial effects on parents, children, and families.

WISDOM ACCORDING TO ORTON

- *Remember that parents are "on call" for 24 hours a day for about 21 years, give or take a few. Try to have empathy.*
- *Parents respond positively to a counselor who listens and cares.*
- *Guilt is a wasted emotion that often plagues parents. Don't add to this guilt by intimating that the parent is somehow to blame for the child's behavior.*
- *Try to be the counselor that you would seek out for your own child.*
- *Accept parents just as they are and help them do the same for their children.*

ORTON'S PICKS

Dinkmeyer, D. C., Dinkmeyer, D. C., Jr., & Sperry, L. (1987). *Adlerian counseling and psychotherapy* (2nd ed.). Columbus, OH: Merrill.
   This text gives a good overview of basic Adlerian concepts. Special chapters explain the phases of the counseling process and provide examples of techniques

that Adlerians use in counseling children, adolescents, and families. Practical examples help the reader understand how the techniques might be used in counseling.

Huber, C. H. (1994). *Transitioning from individual to family counseling*. Alexandria, VA: American Counseling Association.

This book addresses some of the challenges that professional counselors face when changing from an individual orientation to a family systems perspective. The chapters of special interest to child counselors are those that focus on the young child in family counseling, family-school intervention, and family counseling that involves working with an individual client.

Walsh, W. M. and Gilblin, N. J. (Eds.). (1988). *Family counseling in school settings*. Springfield, IL: Charles C Thomas.

This book suggests that family counseling should be a part of the psychological services offered by schools. Chapters of interest include strategies for brief intervention in the school setting and ways to use parent conferences as "therapeutic moments." Specific strategies for counseling stepfamilies, single-parent families, and cooperative efforts to help children in alcoholic homes are all discussed.

CHAPTER 12   Child-Focused Parent Groups

> *Parents don't seem to have the time for children anymore. They give them material things hoping they'll get by with that. Parents push kids away at times. I know I do. I know I should take the time to do something with them, but I'm tired from working all day and I just don't.*
>
> —Father making an observation about his interaction with his children in a group discussion

A child-focused parent group helps parents of all ages, races, social classes, and levels of adjustment to feel accepted and valued as individuals who can contribute something worthwhile to others. In a well-functioning parent group, social, economic, racial, and age barriers diminish and often disappear as parents interact as equals, each bringing something valuable to the group interaction and taking something in return. Each parent has a different way of doing things—not necessarily a right way or a wrong way—and often, in the group, mothers and fathers find a better way.

Parents soon discover that everyone in the group faces the same developmental problems with their children and that differences are mostly a matter of degree. In the group, parents have an opportunity to explore their relationship with their children, to gain insight into what they want to change, if anything, and to talk about ways of accomplishing this change. Parents are encouraged and supported by the group members as they learn more about child development and learn new ways of interacting with their children. As parents improve and strengthen their relationship with their children, they begin to feel and to be more competent themselves. They gradually feel proud of their children, and parenting becomes more satisfying. In this way, the group nurtures each member's need to belong, to feel understood, and to gain competence and confidence in his or her parenting skills.

A BIT OF BACKGROUND

> *Parent education is essentially interaction among members, because its goal is to improve [the] interaction between parent and child.*
> —DINKMEYER, DINKMEYER, & SPERRY (1987, p. 319)

Alfred Adler was instrumental in developing the first professional model for family counseling and education (Sherman & Dinkmeyer, 1987). Adler, who began his work in 1922, established the first child guidance clinic in Vienna, Austria. By 1930, thirty-two clinics throughout Europe used an educational approach to both treatment and prevention. Later, Rudolf Dreikurs expanded Adler's work and developed educational demonstrations and written materials for use in parent discussion groups (Dinkmeyer, Dinkmeyer, & Sperry, 1987).

Early parent discussion groups involved mostly mothers, and the groups were either structured or unstructured. The first Adlerian parent study groups used a structured curriculum that involved outside readings based on the work of Adler and

Dreikurs. In contrast, the mothers' discussion groups, sponsored by the Child Study Association of America, used an unstructured approach, which enabled members to share their concerns and experiences with the group and to learn from one another. This approach "gives the group members a wider knowledge, which serves as a backdrop against which they can look at their own children and themselves" (Auerbach, as cited in Freeman, 1975, p. 38).

Historically, parent groups have revolved around educating and training parents to be more effective in promoting positive behavior in their children. Today, three basic models of parent group education are being used by counselors in a variety of settings with different populations. These models include the Adlerian approach, developed and articulated by Dreikurs and Soltz (1964) and expanded by Dinkmeyer and McKay (1976, 1983); the Rogerian approach, which forms the basis for Parent Effectiveness Training (Gordon, 1970); and the behavioral approach (Krumboltz & Krumboltz, 1972), which relies heavily on B. F. Skinner's theory of operant conditioning. Despite the differences in orientation and emphasis, these models of parent-group education share the common goal of assisting parents "who are attempting to change their method of interaction with their children for the purpose of encouraging positive behavior in their children" (Croake & Glover, 1977, p. 151).

Adlerian approach   The approach articulated by Dreikurs and Soltz (1964) uses a set curriculum to help parents understand children, learn how they think, and comprehend their motives and actions. In these groups, parents are often assigned outside readings, which are then used as a focal point for discussion. Currently, the most widely used Adlerian parent education programs are Systematic Training for Effective Parenting (STEP) and Systematic Training for Effective Parenting of Teens (STEP/Teen), developed by Dinkmeyer and McKay (1976, 1983). These highly systematic programs use some PET approaches such as active listening and "I" messages, as well as basic Adlerian concepts.

STEP groups are based on a three-step process in which parents discuss new ideas, practice the new ideas as a concrete skill within the group, and then apply the skill in the home with the children (Dinkmeyer, Dinkmeyer & Sperry, 1987). Participants are provided with a parents' handbook, discussion-guide cards, and taped exercises. A leader's manual guides the facilitator through the nine sessions that make up the program.

Humanistic approach   Parent Effectiveness Training (PET) developed by Thomas Gordon (1970), helps parents create an environment that fosters the child's growth without interfering with the parents' progress toward self-actualization. Parental honesty, acceptance, and open communication are emphasized. PET groups meet in eight 3-hour sessions, which include lectures, readings, role playing, and homework exercises. The emphasis of the training is on learning human relations strategies such as active listening, sending "I" messages, and using a "no lose" method of resolving conflicts by negotiating a solution that is satisfactory to both the parent and the child.

Behavioral approach   The proponents of behavior modification (Krumboltz & Krumboltz, 1972) believe that most behavior is learned from others and that parents and children each play a role in shaping and influencing each other's behavior. Parents provide opportunities for the child to learn and set up a system of rewards and punishments to influence the child's behavior. Behaviorally oriented parent education programs usually include an overview of behavioral concepts, the nature and use of social and nonsocial reinforcers, observation and recording procedures, and techniques for weakening undesirable behaviors and strengthening desirable ones (Dembo, Sweitzer, & Lauritzen, 1985).

A review of the literature indicates that there are few measurable differences among the different types of parenting programs with regard to positive outcomes and improvement (Beutler, Oró-Beutler, & Mitchell, 1979; Dembo et al., 1985). Researchers found that there is a need to understand the parents' perception of their roles, their child rearing practices, what they already know about child development, and how they are applying this knowledge to their interaction with their children. What seems to be critical to the success of parent groups is the active participation of the parents and programs designed to meet the parents' needs, abilities, interests, and goals (Dembo et al., 1985).

Structured parent support groups   Recently, practitioners have developed structured parent groups to help parents become partners in their children's educational development (see Mercer, Peterson, & Ross, 1988; Miller & Hudson, 1994). These recent parent-group approaches combine the best features of parent education with the opportunities for parental sharing that were inherent in the early mother discussion groups sponsored by the Child Study Association of America.

Miller and Hudson's (1994) model is designed to "(1) disseminate information and concrete suggestions to assist parents in the challenge of raising their children; (2) provide a forum for parents to share information and experiences with other parents; and (3) provide information that will help parents work more effectively as partners in the development of their child's educational program" (p. 151). Parents meet monthly to hear a guest speaker give a brief talk. Then the group is divided into smaller groups to address individual situations. Parents share suggestions and select one idea to try for the next month. This format is effective in helping parents who are raising children with disabilities or children at risk of school failure.

Unstructured parent support groups   Education has been a standard feature in parent groups since they began. However, simply knowing what children need at certain developmental stages and teaching parents how to meet these needs is often not enough to modify their behavior. Although education often paves the way, true change usually occurs as a result of seeing the need for it and developing one's own way to achieve it. Parents, like everyone else, need a compelling reason to change, insight into what needs to be changed, a strong desire to make the change, support and encouragement, and continued help to maintain the change. Therefore, parents need an opportunity to offer and receive support as they attempt to improve their relationship with their children. This climate for change characterizes the unstructured parent support group.

I first developed the format for the unstructured parent support group described in this chapter as part of an elementary school guidance program. It is designed to meet the emerging needs of the group participants. Ideas for each week's discussion are taken from the previous week's discussion and relate directly to the needs of the parents and the children. The group does not have a structured curriculum, and the facilitator does not teach or lecture, give reading assignments, or assign homework. Instead, the facilitator provides parents with an opportunity to share their ideas and their insights with other parents. This exchange enables parents to explore the parent-child relationship and to decide on what needs to be improved or strengthened. In the warm, accepting atmosphere of the parent group, group members can translate their insights into practice. The group can provide the support and encouragement that parents need to cherish the strengths of their relationship with their children, while at the same time, seeking to improve and strengthen it.

THE VALUE OF PARENT GROUPS

If you think of something as just your own problem, you sit and brood about it, but when you come here and talk it over, it's just like a big load has been lifted off.
—A grandmother's thoughts

The Child-Focused Parent Group

The child-focused parent group is designed to help parents find ways to improve and strengthen the parent-child relationship. Parents focus on maximizing the healthy growth and development of their children, encouraging positive behavior, and preventing behavior problems before they have a chance to develop. For those parents who have children who are already experiencing some problems, the group offers an opportunity to share their concerns with other parents and to discover ways that they can improve their interaction with their children.

Positive attitudes toward child rearing are fostered in parent group. Parents who lack a good parenting model can learn from other parents who are more effective models. Armed with knowledge about child development and with the support of a warm and caring group, parents are often able to function more effectively as parents and role models.

Value of Parent Groups

In addition to being less costly and less time-consuming for counselors, parent groups have many advantages over individual sessions. The following advantages have been identified by parents themselves and are outlined in Figure 12-1.

Parents have a forum to talk about their concerns   Generally, parents have few occasions to compare notes with other parents. Therefore, they need opportunities to express their concerns for their children and any doubts they may have about their parenting. In the group, members are able to discuss their hopes, fears, and joys with other parents who will listen, understand, and provide support.

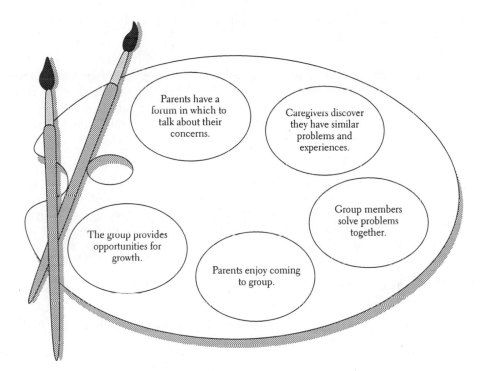

FIGURE 12-1 *The Value of Parent Groups*

"I don't think that parents are talking about the things that bother them the most. They can't talk about the things that we talk about here with their friends. We come here and we don't seem to be afraid to talk about anything. I think the counselor has created this atmosphere for us."

Caregivers discover that they have similar problems and experiences Group meetings provide parents with an opportunity to share their experiences with other parents who are having similar problems. The realization that other parents are facing similar challenges provides comfort. As parents listen to others, they often discover alternate ways of coping with their own difficult situations.

"It's a comfort to know that other people have the same problems that you do. It's interesting to know how they handle them."

Group members solve problems together In the group, parents are able to share their concerns and gain insight from the mutual discussion. No one gives them a pat "solution" or judges them as inadequate. Instead, each parent is encouraged to share his or her concerns, listen and learn from others, and decide what, if anything, she or he wishes to change. The strength is the group and the counselor is a facilitator, not a teacher.

> "We can really toss everything to the middle of the table, and no matter what we say there isn't going to be any judgment of us. There's not going to be any final solution by anybody, but everyone is going to start thinking and perhaps pursuing whatever insights they receive from the mutual discussion of the group. I think the important thing is that the group is doing this, not any individual."

Parents enjoy coming to group   The parent group provides members with an opportunity to socialize, to learn, and to have fun. In addition to finding solace and support in the parent group, members enjoy each other's company. Feelings are expressed freely and honestly, and parents often find humor in everyday situations, which adds to the enjoyment of the group.

> "I just enjoy the group. I think it's hard to explain just what you learn. You just go home with a better feeling."
>
> "The group gives us a chance to get out and talk over our problems but it also gives us a change to get away for a few hours."

The group provides opportunities for growth   Group meetings provide opportunities for parents to offer as well as receive support. The process of giving help, as opposed to continually receiving it, often enhances the parents' self-esteem and promotes healing. When growing self-confidence is coupled with newly acquired insight, parents often make positive changes in the parent-child relationship. This frequently results in improvements in the child's behavior.

> PARENT 1: I thought all of my problems were somebody else's fault. I laugh now when I think that I was willing to blame everything else and really, when it comes down to it, it was me.
>
> PARENT 2: Sometimes you don't see that until you hear someone else talking.
>
> PARENT 1: Yes, and you have to see it for yourself.

THE DEVELOPMENT OF THE PARENT GROUP

There are so many different parents represented—some with a lot of education, some without very much, some with eight children, some with only one—but everyone has problems. We're all willing to listen to what others have done with their problems so it will help us. I've gained a lot of insight from almost everyone here.

—A mother's view

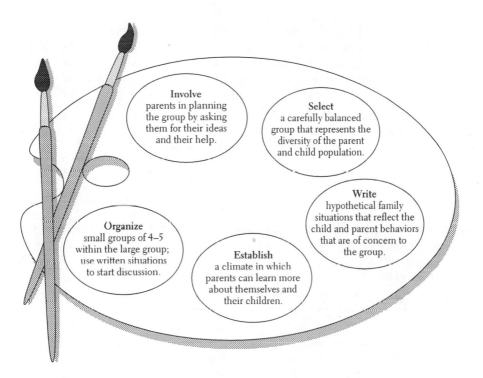

FIGURE 12-2 *The Development of Successful Parent Groups*

To have a successful parent group, counselors need to recognize the participants' needs, value each person's contribution to the group's planning and functioning, and enable parents to give and receive support within the group once it is developed. The counselor's positive attitude, enthusiasm, and commitment to the group will provide a good model for the members. Central to the success of the parent group is the belief that each member possesses the ability to grow as a person and as a parent. There are a number of steps in the development of successful parent groups. These steps are presented in Figure 12-2 and are explained in this chapter.

Keys to Forming a Successful Parent Group

Involve Parents as Partners in Preplanning

Historically, schools have educated children the way they saw fit without consulting parents or making them feel involved and important to the educational process. Many parents have never been asked their opinion by anyone involved with the school, and parents appreciate the fact that someone would value their opinion enough to ask for it. As the counselor talks with mothers and fathers about the possibility of forming a group, it is necessary to let the parents know that their help is needed, not only for their children and themselves, but for other parents as well.

It goes without saying that the counselor will learn a great deal about parents and children from the group members. The counselor cannot possibly know the solution to every child's problem, or the intricacies of every parent-child relationship. The only way to know and to help is to listen to parents when they talk about their children.

Listen to parents as they talk about their children   The key to a successful parent group is listening to the parents of well-adjusted children *and* to the parents of children who are experiencing difficulties. Well-adjusted children, according to Dreikurs and Soltz (1964), are tolerant, respectful, and courteous toward others; are willing to share; and have socially acceptable goals and a strong, positive self-concept. Children who are confident, self-disciplined, able to make decisions, and socially integrated with their peers are usually considered well-adjusted by their teachers. It is necessary to listen to the parents of these children to discover some of their approaches to child rearing before beginning the parent group.

Conversations with parents of well-adjusted children enable the counselor to discover some of the dynamics involved in positive parent-child relationships. The counselor can get a glimpse of the parenting style, the family atmosphere, the quality of the interaction between parent and child, and the parent's perception of the child. In my experience, parents of well-adjusted children generally begin with strengths when they talk about their children, and, although they see weaknesses, they put them in the proper perspective. Generally, parents of well-adjusted children do not desire a "perfect child" but rather accept their children as they are, emphasizing their strengths and minimizing their weaknesses. The interaction between the parent and child is characterized by understanding, acceptance, warmth, and the opportunity to develop confidence and decisiveness and to internalize discipline.

Parents of well-adjusted children represent many parenting philosophies and differ in their methods of discipline. However, parents of well-adjusted children are generally consistent in the type of discipline they use, and there is general agreement between the parents on matters of discipline The parents' socioeconomic status and amount of education do not seem to be as much of a factor as the quality of the relationship between the parent and child.

Occasionally, as a result of inherent differences in disposition and temperament, stresses in marriage, societal pressures, or learned attitudes toward parenting, the positive relationship between a parent and one or more of the children breaks down. In these situations, the child who is trying to find his or her place in the family may seek to meet these goals through misbehavior (see Chapter 11). Often the child's misbehavior results in increased frustration and misery for the parents, as their efforts to discipline the child are met with resistance and failure.

In the normal course of their work, counselors will have many opportunities to listen to parents talk about the difficulties they are experiencing in raising their children. Consistency of discipline, confidence building, opportunities for decision making, and self-discipline are often lacking in these parent-child relationships. In individual sessions, parents of children who are experiencing adjustment problems often focus on the child's weaknesses, instead of on the child's strengths. Many parents confess that they are totally defeated by their children and can no longer control them or get them to cooperate. The familiar lament is "nothing works."

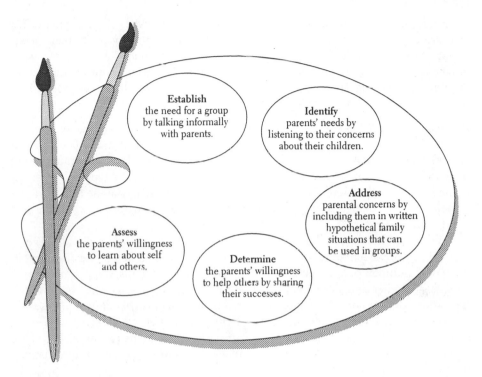

FIGURE 12-3 *Parents as Partners in Planning the Group*

The counselor's task is to get *all* the parents involved in planning the group so that they will become an integral part of the group. It is human nature that people whole-heartedly support projects they have had a part in developing. The counselor can begin by asking parents whether they would be willing to come to a group one day or evening a week, and, if so, what they would like to talk about. In many cases, the parents aren't sure what they would like to discuss, but they will relate some of their concerns about their children. This information can be used to develop open-ended hypothetical family situations for the group to use as a starting point for discussion.

As part of involving parents as partners in planning the group (see Figure 12-3), the counselor will be able to:

- Establish the need for a group.
- Identify the parents' needs by listening to their concerns about their children.
- Address parental needs and concerns by including them in written hypothetical family situations that can be used in group discussions.
- Determine the parents' willingness to help others by sharing their successful parenting experiences.
- Assess the parents' readiness to learn about themselves and their children.

Establish the need for a group To form a successful parent group, it is necessary to first establish a need for the group. This can be accomplished through a series of informal interviews with the parents of the children being served. Many of the parents who are experiencing problems with their children have already made their needs known through individual sessions with the counselor, and many, if asked, may want to take advantage of the help and support offered by the parent group. Parents, who are not experiencing any particular problems with their children may want to be involved in the group to strengthen their relationship with their children.

Identify the parents' needs   The counselor will be able to identity the parents' needs and goals by listening to the parents' concerns about the children in the family. Each family's needs and concerns will vary according to the age and developmental level of the child, the number of children in the family, differences in the type and intensity of the stressors each parent is experiencing, whether the parent is alone or has a mate to help with the demands of parenting, and the age of the parent(s) when the first child was born.

Although children need both parents as they are growing up, Gerler (1993) estimates that in some schools, 80% of the children come from broken homes. As a result, increasing numbers of children are being raised by single parents, stepparents, grandparents, and other caregivers. Many families led by one parent—whether as a result of separation, divorce, or widowhood—share similar concerns. According to research reported by Goldenberg and Goldenberg (1990, p. 89), single mothers report "feeling overburdened, unsupported, and guilty about not being up to the task of raising a family alone." These concerns need to be considered in forming parent groups that will meet the participants' needs and goals.

Address parental needs and concerns through hypothetical family situations   Most parents, if asked what they want for their children, will say that they want them to be able to make responsible decisions and to grow in independence, competence, and self-confidence. Above all, parents want their children to be happy. Some children are all these things, and counselors need to learn what parents do that promotes this kind of good adjustment. What is there about the parent-child relationship that nurtures the child's feelings of competence and self-acceptance? Parent's of well-adjusted children can contribute some of their positive parenting to the group situations. Consistency of discipline, confidence building, opportunities for decision-making, and self-discipline are common problems in parent-child relationships. These topics are often the first to be discussed in parent group.

Meeting and talking with parents informally at school and in their homes will provide opportunities for the counselor to listen and learn more about the parents' many concerns. These concerns can be incorporated into written hypothetical family situations that will help the parents focus on problem areas without having to identify them as their own. In this way, the parents do not have to share their own concerns until they feel ready.

Determine the parents' willingness to help others by sharing   It is the desire to help someone else and the knowledge that everyone can contribute something valuable as well as gain something from the group that will keep the parents coming week after week. Every parent can contribute something valuable that will heighten the knowledge and experiences of the others. In a balanced group, the counselor will not be placed in the position of giving advice, information, and solutions to the members. Rather, group members can help one another in a give-and-take process that promotes growth for all members of the group, including the counselor.

Assess the parents' readiness to learn   In discussions with parents, the counselor will want to determine the parents' willingness to learn more about themselves. Most parents, when asked to share their parenting experiences with the group, will express a desire to learn more about themselves and their relationship with their children. Occasionally, because of fear, depression, or extreme feelings of inferiority, a parent will not be ready for group work. However, this does not mean that the parent will never be ready. The counselor can work with this parent individually until the parent feels ready for group work. Parents who are not a part of a current group will have an opportunity to join a future group.

In summary, one of the most important keys to forming a successful parent group is preplanning. During the preplanning phase, the counselor meets and talks with the parents of well-adjusted and poorly adjusted children in order to establish a need for the group. Listening to parents helps the counselor assess the needs and goals of the parents who want to attend the group. These needs can then be used as a basis for written hypothetical family situations that address the parents' needs and can be used later to stimulate conversation in the group sessions. In addition to learning more about each parent's individual style of interacting with his or her children, the counselor is able to assess the parent's readiness for involvement in group work. Because the group involves sharing and commitment, the counselor must assess the parents' willingness to share their experiences and to learn more about themselves and their children.

Structuring the Group

Who's in a group?   A child-focused parent group embraces parents of all ages, races, ethnic backgrounds, religions, and social classes. It should include parents of well-adjusted children as well as parents who need to learn new ways of interacting with their children. In addition, parents who are talkative and outgoing should be included as well as those who are quiet and reserved. This mix is especially important if the meetings are to be interesting and fun. The group should be a microcosm of the larger society and its members should represent all the different types of family structures discussed in Chapter 1. The following people should be represented in the group:

- Parents who want to improve or strength their relationship with their children.
- Single parents, stepparents, grandparents, custodial parents, foster parents, adoptive parents, and biological parents.
- Parents with children of various ages.
- Caregivers who range in age from teen mothers to grandmothers.
- Parents representing all races, religions, and ethnic backgrounds.

- Talkative parents as well as those who are quiet and reserved.
- Parents with a sense of humor.

Achieving a balanced group   Selection is very important because it ensures that a correct balance will be established, which will make the group successful when it is formed. A carefully balanced group includes parents of well-adjusted children as well as parents who need to learn new ways of interacting with their youngsters. Having a balanced group also allows parents to avoid the stigma frequently attached to groups specifically designed for parents of children with behavior problems. Having a balanced group also allows parents to participate without fear of being labeled "dysfunctional." This is especially important when groups are conducted in conjunction with an elementary school guidance program. Developmental child-focused groups that include parents of all the children send the message that the guidance program is for everyone and not for just a few "problem children."

This balance is necessary for another very important reason. If only the parents of children with adjustment problems are invited, there is no one except the counselor to point out alternate ways of thinking and behaving. In a group that represents a broad cross section of parenting styles and temperament, the participants are able to share and learn from each other. Abusive parents can be helped by gentle parents; tense parents can be disarmed with humor; rigid disciplinarians can be influenced to "lighten up" by a parent who is flexible and fun to be around. This is generally a more effective way for parents to develop insight and experiment with different parenting styles. Counselors can then function as group facilitators, which is more in keeping with their role.

Parents with children at various age levels add variety and enhance the group's overall effectiveness. Mothers can relate some of the developmental stages that children pass through as a normal part of growing up and can share their experiences with other mothers. Some of the difficulties that everyone faces in raising children can be discussed, which helps remove some of the fear and apprehension about child rearing. The group also provides an opportunity for parents of various ages to get together to exchange thoughts and ideas. The young mother who rejected her mother-in-law's suggestion about consistency of discipline will listen intently in group as a middle-aged mother relates her own mistakes and how she did better with the second child.

A group that includes parents who are talkative and outgoing as well as quiet and shy keeps the discussion lively and interesting. Parents with a well-developed sense of humor are often able to disarm stressed and uptight parents, relieving some of the tensions and frustrations that parents frequently experience. A group that is interesting and fun to attend benefits the parents and the counselor, who enjoy each other as they learn and share.

In summary, the group setting provides an opportunity to cross the religious, economic, and racial barriers that so often divide people. Both mothers and fathers, from all walks of life and with divergent parenting philosophies, come together and share common experiences. In a well-functioning group, parents are accepted and understood whether they are young or old, rich or poor, black or white. A successful group helps parents feel valued as individuals who have a common desire to raise their children to be healthy, happy, and productive adults.

Preparation of the Group

Personal invitations Each parent should be extended a personal invitation each week. Sending invitations communicates to parents that they are needed and important to the success of the group. These invitations can be designed by the parents themselves, who can take turns doing them. The mothers in the group are usually pleased to help a busy counselor by making invitations, and a parent aide or a paraprofessional can address envelopes. Designing invitations, addressing envelopes, and preparing a special dessert for the meeting are ways that members can get involved and make a commitment to the group. This involvement by the parents of the children is important to the success of both the group and the guidance program.

Beginning and ending It is best to set a beginning and ending date for parent groups so that participants know that they are committed to the group for a specific length of time. Parent groups usually require a commitment of at least two hours a week for 8 to 10 weeks. Of course, there is a great deal of flexibility in the length of the session. Depending on the group's goals, the sessions could be limited to eight weeks or could last as long as 12 weeks. The number of weeks will be determined by the parents' and the counselor's goals, as well as by time constraints. Most counselors, particularly those in school settings, need to have a number of sessions throughout the year in order to accommodate the large number of parents who want to be involved.

Parent-group sessions usually last at least two hours and can be held in the daytime or in the evening. Some counselors may prefer to run two groups simultaneously, one in the daytime and one in the evening. In districts where evening work is discouraged for safety reasons or contract stipulations, groups can be conducted during school hours.

Number of participants The counselor may want to invite approximately 20 parents to the first group session. The group may be started with as few as 8 to 10 parents if the counselor feels more comfortable with a smaller number or if no more initially express an interest. The number of participants will also depend on the population the counselor is working with and the number of parents currently being counseled in individual sessions. Because the parent group is designed to help parents learn more about child development and to get helpful information and support from other parents, the initial groups may be small. However, as soon as the word is out about how helpful and enjoyable the groups are, many more parents will be asking to join the next session.

Structuring the session A large group is usually divided into smaller groups of four or five parents. Each group is given written hypothetical family situations that address the concerns of the majority of the parents. These situations usually serve as a springboard to more in-depth discussions of the participants' interaction with their own children. After the small group discussions are completed and parents have summarized their insights and suggestions, the group gets together for a large group discussion of their individual ideas. The group usually ends with coffee and dessert so parents can socialize for a few minutes before going home. The entire process can last up to two hours.

The length of the session depends on the group, the topic being discussed, and the counselor's available time. However, counselors should establish a specific length of time for the session so that parents will know how long to arrange for childcare, and so on. There should be a certain amount of flexibility, and the time may vary a little from week to week.

Open versus closed groups   Open groups generally allow new members in whenever they wish to join the group. This type of group is common in agency settings where the clientele is continually changing. In the child-focused parent group, it is recommended that membership be closed after the third meeting. The reason for closing the group is that new members who come in after the group has established trust and cohesion might be threatened by the level of emotional involvement that the group has attained. Also, introducing a new member after the group has developed rapport, trust, and cohesion might threaten original members and bring the group back to the starting point. In either case, the introduction of new members after the third week of any series of sessions should, in my opinion, be avoided.

Orientation to the Group

Create a climate for growing   First, the group must provide a climate that will enable the parents to develop a warm and accepting attitude toward each other. This will help them grow together for the duration of the group. The counselor sets the climate for this acceptance through example. The counselor, who looks on the group of mothers and fathers as equals, will be able to set the climate of friendship so that it spreads through the group. As the weeks progress, the parents gradually develop warmth, affection, and acceptance of each other. Even though they are from diverse backgrounds, they learn to trust each other. If the counselor cares about the parents as people and treats them as friends rather than as patients or clients that need help, the group can learn and grow together and the counselor will grow as a person also.

Establishing trust is critical to the continued development of the group (Corey, 1995) for without it, the parents would hide their feelings and would not be willing to explore their own interaction with their children in the group. The counselor helps establish trust by providing a basic structure that enables the parents to feel safe and secure within the group. This is accomplished by creating an atmosphere in which parents can reveal their innermost thoughts and feelings and feel secure that they will be accepted by the other group members. In addition, the parents must feel secure that their confidences will be kept by the counselor and by the other group members.

Four basic principles of behavior   At the very beginning of the group sessions, it is necessary to clarify a few principles of behavior that will serve as a structure for the group. Four basic tenets can guide the parents in their study of child behavior and assist them in examining their interaction with their own children. These basic Adlerian assumptions are:

1. Child behavior is purposive and goal directed, with the primary goal being to feel wanted and needed.

2. As children strive for acceptance in the family, they may misbehave to achieve their goals.
3. Child behavior is greatly influenced by adult behavior.
4. Behavior can be changed.

Individual counselors can structure the group according to their own theoretical orientation. In the child-focused parent group, the four goals of children's misbehavior (Dreikurs & Soltz, 1964) are used to explain the child's goals and his or her struggle to create solutions to problems (see Chapter 11). As the group progresses and the parents discuss the open-ended hypothetical family situations, these few principles of behavior will become clear. Therefore, there is no need for the counselor to "teach" them.

It is essential to keep the opening structure of the group simple because parents do not want to be treated as if they were students returning to school. Some of the parents in the group will not have pleasant memories of school. They may view it as a hostile place of failure, rejection, or humiliation. Therefore, the purpose of the group is not to teach parents what is best for them and their children but rather to create a climate of acceptance that frees the parents to grow in their understanding of their children. This understanding is often translated into action that improves and strengthens the parent-child relationship.

Rules to govern the group   The last task in group orientation is to establish three basic rules that are needed to build trust and to protect the group participants. These rules can be communicated verbally and informally to the group at the onset of the sessions. The explanations are intended to help the group members understand what is expected of them in terms of confidentiality. The counselor is also expected to abide by all the ethics of the profession and not divulge any information that is discussed in the group.

Ground Rules

1. The group must safeguard the participants' confidentiality by not repeating names and information that were discussed to anyone outside of the group. This pertains to information of a personal nature confided by an individual in the course of the group discussion.
2. The group is especially designed to improve the relationship between parents and children and not to improve teacher performance. If parents have questions or complaints about individual teachers, they are asked to discuss them with the teacher or administrator and not in the group.
3. Discussion of the performance of school administrators, social services workers, or any other school or community personnel working with the child or family would not be consistent with the goals of the group.

These ground rules are intended to be a guide to the counselor or facilitator and can be adapted to the particular concerns of the group. They are meant not to be read to the parents verbatim but rather to be discussed informally. For instance, the counselor will want to communicate to parents that such rules are intended to promote the kind of free exchange of ideas and feelings that can only take place when one feels secure that what is said will be held in confidence. The counselor will also want to emphasize that parents can talk about the group in the community to create enthusiasm among the people to be part of the continuing program and to create interest in the school and in the guidance program; but they are *not* to discuss what individuals in the group have disclosed.

The counselor has an obligation to help parents understand that they can discuss individual problematic situations with teachers or caseworkers in separate conferences but not in group meetings. If a parent should forget and begin a discussion about his or her child's teacher, other parents in the group will often remind the parent about the rule. If not, the counselor has an obligation to bring the conversation to a more productive topic. Allowing parents to displace blame on others only slows the growth process of the individual parent as well as of the group as a whole.

Establishing group goals Once the group has met, the counselor can help the group members decide just what it is that they want to accomplish in the parent group. In the beginning, some parents do not really know what they want to talk about, but as the group progresses and the parents begin to trust, they start to share their concerns. The counselor can then help the parents focus on these concerns, which can be done through the hypothetical situations in the early stage of the group. Using the hypothetical situations minimizes the threat until the parents trust enough to reveal their feelings and begin the self-exploration process. As the parents listen to and respond to one another with honesty and candor, they can develop insight, take risks, and challenge one another. Gradually they begin to examine their own relationship to their children and to act on these new insights. Finally, they become able to apply their newly learned behavior to their everyday interactions with their children.

THE OPERATION OF THE GROUP

A great deal of important work has already been accomplished by the time the group is at this stage of its development. The parents have been involved in planning the group, the counselor has done a needs assessment and has written a few open-ended hypothetical situations that address the common developmental problems. All the parents have been extended personal invitations to the group and have been given guidelines for its operation. The counselor has set the tone of the group and avoided assuming the role of teacher. The counselor's interaction with parents as equal partners has helped generate the warmth and support needed to develop trust and cohesion in the group.

Group Discussion Format

As discussed earlier, the counselor sets the climate of warmth and acceptance at the first meeting. After a period of introductions and informal conversation, the counselor divides the group into smaller groups of 4 to 5 members. Each smaller group should contain a mix of parents representing all ages and parenting styles, with introverts and extroverts, parents with a sense of humor, and others who are quiet and reserved. The small group technique has some distinct advantages over a large group of 20 parents:

1. Trust and cohesion develop rapidly when there are fewer people to relate to.
2. The group members, particularly those who are quiet and shy, have more opportunities to talk and be heard.
3. In a small group, all the participants' ideas are needed to solve the "problems" presented in the hypothetical family situations.
4. Parents are more likely to confide their concerns to a smaller group.
5. Each parent has an opportunity to give and receive feedback in the small group.

Following the small group discussions, the parents assemble into a large group to share their ideas. The counselor facilitates the large group discussion, encouraging the parents to contribute the insights that they have gained in the small group conversations. This sharing usually occurs after trust and cohesion have been developed. With a sense of trust established, parents feel comfortable enough to talk about themselves and their own children, rather than the people in the hypothetical situations. The facilitator can also use the large group as a means of increasing the depth of the discussion and encouraging parents to help and support one another as they work to improve and strengthen their relationship with their children.

Hypothetical Family Situations

Open-ended hypothetical family situations are used to assist parents to (1) empathize with the child in the situation, (2) identify with the parent in the situation, (3) relate their own experiences when they feel ready, (4) develop insight into their interaction with their own child, and (5) use strategies discussed in the group to improve and strengthen their relationship with their own child.

Initially, the counselor writes the hypothetical family situations on a variety of topics that are of interest to all parents, regardless of their age, ethnicity, or social class. These situations are used to get the discussion started on topics that are of general interest to all parents and that do not threaten anyone in any way. The open-ended hypothetical situation assists parents in considering what the children in a particular siltation might be thinking and feeling, which helps the parents consider the child's point of view and assists them in developing empathy for their own children. The hypothetical situation also enables the parents to contemplate, without threat, how they might feel if they were the adult in the situation, helping them develop insight into their actions with their own children. Hopefully, this insight can be translated into action, and the parents and children can interact in more positive ways.

As the sessions progress, the level of emotional involvement intensifies and the parents openly contribute their own concerns to the group discussion. The parents determine the content of each session through written and oral evaluation. As the participants relate what they would like to talk about, the counselor develops open-ended family situations to meet these needs. As the discussion progresses, usually in the course of one or two sessions, conversation gradually departs from the hypothetical situations and becomes personalized as parents relate their own situations and experiences.

Starting the group discussion A productive way to begin the initial group sessions is with situations that are commonly encountered in the course of all family interactions.

This procedure serves a dual purpose. First, it reduces the personal threat to each group member in the early weeks, when it is important for the participants to develop cohesion as a group; second, it helps the parents understand that all children go through certain developmental stages that need to be understood.

Several good topics for initial group interaction might relate to confidence building and decision making. The following is an example of an open-ended hypothetical family situation pertaining to confidence building.

"I KNOW...I'M STUPID"

Nisha's parents notice that she avoids certain activities that her brothers and sisters seem to be able to do. Nisha feels she can't do anything right. She tells her parents that she knows that she is "stupid" and when faced with a difficult situation she cries, "I can't do this!" or " I know...I'm stupid." Nisha's mother asks her to do things and ends up doing them herself because it is faster and easier. Her father helps Nisha with homework and when she cries that it is "too hard", he finishes it for her. Nisha's parents get very frustrated with her.

DISCUSS: *What is Nisha's behavior telling us?*
What is her parents' behavior telling us?
Outline some ways that you think a parent can help a child such as Nisha.

The advantage to beginning with topics such as confidence building and decision making is that they are common human experiences. Everyone has felt a lack of confidence or has had difficulty making a decision at some point in his or her life. Therefore, talking about these common developmental tasks usually does not pose as much of a threat to the parent group as other topics might, and so they help the group develop trust. A second advantage is that the parents can empathize with the child in these situations by relating their own feelings and experiences. As the parents recall times from their childhoods when they were unable to make a decision or lacked confidence, they begin to see the world through their children's eyes. These recollections not only help the parents develop empathy for their children but also help the group members begin to develop empathy for each other.

As parents disclose their own experiences and the thoughts and feelings that accompany them, they begin to develop a closeness with the group that gradually develops into intimacy. This intimacy enables the parents to share their thoughts, feelings, apprehensions, and fears. Later, as the level of the group deepens, parents begin to face and challenge their fears.

Decision making can be another important developmental topic to use with the group. Here is an example of an open-ended situation dealing with decision making.

"WHAT SHOULD I DO?"

Jane is 12 years old and her friends notice that she can never decide on anything. She seems to wait and follow others. She constantly asks her mother, "What should I do?" Her mother complains that Jane acts "babyish" and takes after her father.

At home, Mrs. K. selects Jane's clothes and lays them on her bed each morning. Jane's mother has her breakfast cereal all mixed for her when she sits down for breakfast. Jane is painfully slow getting ready for school, and this irritates her mother.

Jane can never decide anything on her own and depends on her mother to tell her what to do. Mrs. K. fears that "When Jane goes to college. I'll probably have to go with her!"

DISCUSS: *What is Jane's behavior telling us?*
What is her mother's behavior telling us?
What are some of the ways that parents can help children
like Jane?

Parents usually begin to talk about their interaction with their own children as they discuss these hypothetical situations in the group. They begin to express their feelings and give ideas that might help. The counselor gently encourages them to reflect on their children's behavior as well as on their own. The counselor then recaps the positive suggestions that have been made and allows the group to react.

Generally, depending on the amount of time allowed, the group will be able to discuss two topics at each session. Confidence building and decision making both encompass a great deal in terms of child development and should not be discussed in the same session. It is better to mix one of these topics with a lighter and less detailed situation, such as the following.

Sample Situation	Discussion Questions
SAM: "I give up!" I'm going to quit! "I just can't do the work that teacher gives."	*How do you think Sam feels?* *What is Sam's behavior telling us?*

Here is an example of a group discussion about the situation with Sam.

PARENT 1:   He's probably frustrated and doesn't know where to begin. I've felt that way before. (*Identifying with Sam, this father has felt the same way himself.*)

PARENT 2:   He feels like giving up. He doesn't have enough confidence in himself or he would try. So I guess he has to have help to gain this confidence. (*This grandmother gains insight into how Sam feels and guesses that he lacks confidence.*)

PARENT 3:   That's the basic thing. He's not confident. He feels stupid and he's blaming the teacher for his own inadequacy. (*Understanding how Sam feels, this mother recognizes that he is projecting his feelings on the teacher.*)

PARENT 1:   I know how he feels…It's too hard. It's too big a problem. You're not prepared emotionally and you don't have enough confidence to try. I think he needs to have help to gain this confidence. He needs some special help with his schoolwork. Then maybe he could tackle it. (*This father has empathy for Sam; notice the use of "you" and "you're."*)

PARENT 4: He needs to be helped to gain more confidence and that doesn't happen overnight. (*This mother focuses the discussion on how parents can contribute to the confidence of their own children.*)

In the following dialogue, the hypothetical situation involving Sam's discouragement with school has served as a springboard for parents to discuss their own children and their interaction with them.

PARENT 2: I think a kid like Sam would get depressed quite often.

PARENT 4: If you could make sure he was happy emotionally, maybe his work would come easier.

PARENT 5: I have one boy like this—my 10-year-old. If things don't go right at home, he goes to school and worries. (*Moving beyond the hypothetical situation, this mother is able to gain insight into her own son's behavior.*)

PARENT 4: My son worries a lot! He worries about our financial problems. He worries about a lot of things that aren't any of his business. (*This father is linking his own worries about the family's finances to his son's worries.*)

PARENT 3: That's true isn't it? Our kids do worry about our financial situation.

PARENT 2: You know, I wonder…I wonder if kids worry because we worry. I think they see us upset and it upsets them. (*This grandmother has insight into how a parent's behavior affects the child.*)

Role Playing

Role playing is another technique to help parents gain insight into their interaction with their children. To accompany the session on confidence building, the counselor can arrange a role-play situation that will help participants develop empathy for their children. This role play can be used when the group members come back to the large group after the small-group discussion.

Objective: To help parents understand how children feel when they are continually subjected to criticism while they are attempting to do something.

The counselor asks for a volunteer to play the part of a child and build a pyramid with ordinary building blocks. As the "child" tries to build the pyramid, the counselor offers no model, help, or encouragement. Instead, the counselor downgrades the effort, expects perfection, and otherwise seeks to frustrate the entire procedure and the parent player as well.

COUNSELOR: Who would like to play a game with me?

JUNE: I will.

COUNSELOR: Okay, here are some blocks. Pretend that you are a 10-year-old girl: "June, I want you to build a pyramid." (*The mother role plays the child and is offered no model or encouragement.*)

JUNE: Oh, No! How will I do that?

COUNSELOR: Just do it. It isn't hard (*Counselor displays no understanding of the "child's" fears or expressions of doubt.*)

JUNE: (*Attempts to build pyramid and begins with a square base.*)

COUNSELOR: No. Don't build a square. Build a pyramid! (*Instead of encouraging, the counselor demands perfection.*)

JUNE: (*Begins again.*)

COUNSELOR: Come on now, you've seen pyramids haven't you? Don't be so slow...Build a pyramid. (*Counselor deliberately frustrates the parent so that she and the group can experience how it feels to perform under pressure.*)

JUNE: (*Showing signs of frustration. She builds a structure that is block-like, but with some adjustments would be a good pyramid.*)

COUNSELOR: You've built a cube! I told you to build a pyramid. Can't you do anything right? Now do it again! (*The counselor is trying to help the group participants experience the effects of criticism.*)

JUNE: (*After a few more tries, and more criticism from the counselor, June takes the blocks and shoves them to the center of the table.*) You do it!

The frustration, anger, and defeat felt by the parent who is playing the child will often be shared by the others in the group. After a role-play experience such as this, the parents are better able to understand why a child says, "You do it!" or "I can't do it." After the parents have had the role-play experience, they are more likely to have empathy for children in a similar situation.

A second role play is then enacted with other participants. This time the role play is designed to show the adult instructing, guiding, and encouraging the child (played by a parent) to build a pyramid. It is a good idea to follow the role plays with a group discussion that compares the positive and negative approaches. The group can then discuss the concept of expectations, adequate models, and encouragement, and parents can see the effect of each on the group members' performance. These techniques help parents develop insight into how to build confidence in their children.

Follow-up and Evaluation

Follow-up Following up on individuals who may drop out of the group is essential for two reasons. First, it shows that the counselor misses that person and cares about him or her; and second, it gives some clues as to how the counselor may better meet that individual's needs. The dropout rate in a group that is functioning properly will be low, but a few individuals may leave early. Some of the reasons for dropping out may be completely unrelated to the functioning of the counselor or the content of the group.

Juanita was particularly interested in joining the group and inquired several times as to when the sessions would begin. She came to the first meeting and was a cheerful addition to the group. Juanita volunteered to bring the dessert for the following week but called in midweek to say she couldn't make it.

The next week Juanita was absent again, and the counselor added a personal note to the invitation telling her how much she was missed. After another session went by, the counselor phoned and Juanita said that she was sick but then suddenly confided that wasn't the real problem. Hilda, who had been her friend and had betrayed her confidence, had joined the group the second week and Juanita had learned about it. She didn't come to the group because she had reason not to trust Hilda and didn't feel she could confide in the group if Hilda were a participant.

The counselor handled the problem by assuring Juanita that if she would participate, she would not be in the same small-group session as Hilda. The result was that both Juanita and Hilda came to the rest of the group sessions and brought their husbands. The counselor was careful to arrange the small groups so that the two women were separated and did not press them to interact in the large group unless they wanted to.

If the counselor is aware of personality conflicts ahead of time, he or she can arrange to invite these parents to separate groups, thus avoiding the problem. However, the counselor will not always have advance notice and may have to work out a compromise, as in Juanita's case.

There are many other reasons people drop out of groups. Let's examine the case of Allison.

Allison had been in and out of psychiatric care for several years. When the counselor first met her, she was having periods of depression so severe that she didn't get off the couch for days. She definitely was not ready for group work during that time. However, the following year, Allison was quite improved and she and her husband attended the dinner held at the culmination of the 10-session parent group.

During the next session, Allison wanted to come. The counselor asked her to check with her psychiatrist about it and he encouraged her to participate. For several weeks Allison came and then abruptly quit. On follow-up, Allison related that her husband had to work the second shift and she was frightened to come without him.

This example illustrates that the counselor needs to be aware that factors such as fears, worries, prejudices, or insecurities may prevent a person from enjoying the benefits of the group. In these instances, the counselor may need to continue consulting with parents on an individual basis until they are ready for group. It is possible that some parents will not be able to participate in group at all.

Dropouts can also signal that the group is not functioning properly. In a parent group that is operating properly, the facilitator can expect to lose one or two participants during the 10-week session. If the early termination rate is higher than this, then the counselor should examine the group interaction and determine why the group is not meeting the participants' needs.

> *Well, I know one thing and I know by experience. The group has really helped me out a lot. It not only helped me, it helped my kids. By getting acquainted with the group, I now know that I wasn't the only one that was confused and discouraged with life.*
>
> —A mother commenting on her experiences in group

Evaluation   The counselor will want to devise some way of measuring the effectiveness of parent groups. A number of research studies have been conducted on the value of parent groups as both preventive and intervention strategies. Much of the evidence of the success of parent discussion groups is descriptive (Freeman, 1975), questionnaires and parent reports of change in individual children have been the most common forms of evaluation. The format used by Miller and Hudson (1994) to evaluate the structured parent support group consists of a seven-statement questionnaire. Other studies report using child-behavior rating scales to evaluate behavior change in children (Dembo, et al., 1985).

GROUP TOPICS: FROM SIBLING RIVALRY TO SEX

During the initial interviews and needs assessment, the counselor will learn about a variety of parental concerns that can be incorporated into the written hypothetical family situations. Most of the concerns that parents voice occur in the normal development of all children and revolve around a range of topics from sibling rivalry to sex. The following examples of open-ended hypothetical situations are intended as guides to help students and practitioners get started. However, each group leader will want to develop his or her own situations that address the particular concerns of the parents that are attending a specific group. The concerns expressed at each group meeting can be incorporated in the hypothetical family situations for the next week. Confidence building and decision making are two good starting topics, but the others should come from the parents themselves.

Special problems of a more serious nature, such as stealing, should be reserved for later sessions when parents have developed a great deal of trust and cohesion in the group. Revealing their own special problems with their children is often difficult for parents, and they need to feel accepted and secure in the group before they will self-disclose.

Hypothetical Family Situations

Sibling Rivalry

Sibling rivalry is a normal part of growing up for many children. Just as adults do not live without frictions in their interpersonal relationships, children cannot be expected to either. Sibling rivalry is present to some degree in all families with more than one child, but it is still a source of concern to parents. Although rivalry is common in all sibling relationships, intense rivalry (see Chapter 2) may be a warning signal that something is wrong with the parent-child relationship. For example, one child may perceive that another child is favored because of differences in the way the children are treated.

Parents need to be given an opportunity to discuss these sibling tensions, and the following example offers a good situation to get the discussion started.

"I'M TELLING!"

Mrs. T. is a single parent. She reports that her days are miserable because her children fight constantly. The toddler insists on playing with the other children's toys. The older children grab the things away from him, and he starts to scream and cry. The oldest two complain that they can't have anything of their own. The middle child runs to her every other minute and tattles on the older kids. Later, the older children beat him up for tattling, and the uproar continues. Mrs. T. is at the end of her rope and ends up screaming at them all to be quiet.

DISCUSS: *What are some possible reasons for this situation?*
           How can a parent help a child who tattles? What might be some
               purposes for his behavior?
           How should the matter of personal possessions be dealt with?

Discussing topics like sibling rivalry helps parents understand that their children aren't the only ones who behave like this. In sharing with the group, parents learn that they are not alone in thinking and feeling as they do. The group provides a way for parents to offer and receive support from each other as they explore alternative ways of interacting with their children.

Developing a Sense of Responsibility

Parents want their children to develop a sense of responsibility and to grow up strong and independent. Most parents recognize that their children need help to become more responsible, but many are at a loss as to how to accomplish this. Some parents work hard to raise responsible children, whereas others cultivate responsibility in their children without giving it too much thought. A few parents create a strong sense of responsibility in their children by accident. This can occur when parents lack initiative or have an overreliance on the child to accept adult responsibilities. All these parents will be represented in the group and can share their ideas and opinions for the benefit of everyone. Here is a situation to get them thinking.

THE "CAN'T DO IT!" KID

Lamont is 5 and is in an all-day kindergarten. Lamont took the school bus on the first day of school, but by the third day he refused to go anymore. He told his parents that he "hates kindergarten." Now his father drives him to school each day and picks him up.

On the first snowy day, while the other children scurried to clothespin their boots together and hang their mittens and coats on the hooks, Lamont sat in a chair. He had his arms and legs extended, waiting for the teacher to remove his mittens and his boots. At the end of the day, Lamont repeated the same behavior, waiting for the teacher to dress him.

Lamont spends a lot of the time in the bathroom. He stays there until his teacher misses him and hunts for him. He is used to his mom zipping up his pants and helping him wash his hands. Lamont wants the teacher to do these things for him.

Lamont's favorite phrase is, "Can't do it!" He is overweight for his age and gets no physical exercise. His mother says that he doesn't like to play outside and prefers to lie on the floor and watch television. He has never had any chores to do at home. He is an only child and is the center of his parents' lives. His mother and father spend their days "doing for Lamont."

DISCUSS: If you were Lamont's parents, what would be the first thing that you would do to help Lamont develop more responsibility?
How should Lamont's parents change their behavior so that Lamont can gradually be more independent and responsible?
How do you think Lamont's self-esteem is affected by his dependency?
What can his parents do to improve his self-esteem? What can his teachers do?

Respect and Cooperation

Parents want their children to respect them and cooperate with them. They know that discipline is necessary to achieve respect and cooperation, but there is often disagreement as to how and when to discipline. Many parents are confused as to the best way to handle their children. They know that all children are different and that one method may work with one of their youngsters but fail with another.

PARENT 1:   I think children should be seen and not heard! My mother used to say that, and I'm beginning to agree. My kids are too mouthy.

PARENT 2:   There was a lot more respect for our parents' generation than there is for us.

PARENT 3:   I think children like discipline.

PARENT 4:   I don't know if I agree that our parents had more respect. I dislike respect and discipline solely out of fear. I would like to think we could bring this about because the children would want to please and not because they're scared to death!

PARENT 1:   I think to myself, "You are living in my home, and I'm buying your clothes and your food and we all have to live here so you might as well do your part in gratitude for these things." But that might be wrong, because are we doing these things because we want the kids to be grateful or because we love them?

PARENT 4:   I don't want them to be grateful, but this is their home and they should be proud of it and have their friends in. If we treat them with respect, I think they will return it.

PARENT 5:	Parents don't seem to have the time for children anymore. They give them material things hoping they'll get by with that. Parents push kids away at times rather than do something with them. I know I do. I'm tired from working all day, and I just don't take the time with them that I should.
COUNSELOR:	Then you're saying if you give love and respect and time, you can expect it in return.
PARENT 1:	I think it would be nice if they would consider it once in a while! (*Laughter.*)

Consistency in Discipline

Consistency in discipline fosters respect. Some of the most disturbing behavior problems arise from the lack of consistency. Children never know what is expected of them. They can bounce the ball in the living room sometimes, and no one says a word; other times they get scolded and sent to their room.

Agreement between parents is also very important. Parents must agree on how to discipline their children and they must stick together. Children have an uncanny sense of "divide and conquer" and can use it to destroy family tranquility and even marriages. This is especially true in blended families where each parent has children from a previous marriage as well as children of their own. The following are hypothetical situations related to consistency in discipline that can be used to focus group discussion.

THE MERRIWEATHER MESS

Mr. and Mrs. Merriweather have two children. Both of their children do pretty much as they please, are rude and disrespectful, and always insist on their own way. They are very resentful of authority and are disliked by the parents and children in the neighborhood.

Mr. Merriweather has very little time to spend with the children because he is so busy, but he does feel they need to be punished for their misbehavior. He lets them get away with things as long as he can and then hits them anywhere he can reach.

Mrs. Merriweather doesn't like the way her husband hits the kids. She thinks he is too harsh. When the father tells the children that they can't do something, the mother later tells them that they can because she feels sorry for them. However, when the children get out of hand, she screams at the father to "do something."

DISCUSS: *What are the Merriweathers doing that may be contributing to their children's problems?*
Can you suggest some possible solutions to the "Merriweather Mess?"
Outline some more constructive ways of disciplining children.

Sometimes children can use a particular behavior as a weapon to divide their parents, as illustrated in the following situation.

MEALTIME IS MURDER AT THE HITCHCOCK'S!!

Mealtime is murder at the Hitchcock's. Allie Hitchcock is a very fussy eater. She dislikes more foods than she likes and lets her mother know it. Mrs. Hitchcock begins each meal by admonishing Allie to eat everything on her plate. When Allie refuses, her father gets up from the table and fixes her a dish of cereal or a sandwich. Mrs. Hitchcock fumes. Later Allie snacks.

DISCUSS: *What is Allie's behavior telling us?.*
What is Allie's parents' behavior telling us?
If you were Allie's parents, what would you do to help this situation?

Helping Parents Talk about Sexuality

Of the many topics discussed in parent groups, sex seems to be one of the most difficult ones for parents to discuss with their children, and for a variety of reasons. The primary reasons are the parent's lack of knowledge about sexual development and their fear that children will get involved early in sexual activity. Although there is more exposure to things sexual and more emphasis on sex on television and in films, many parents are still not communicating the basic facts of sexual development to their children through warm and empathic conversation.

Some parents find it difficult to communicate with their children about sex because their own parents were often silent on the subject. Consequently, parents often let the schools, television, or the children's peers do the educating for them. Most experts agree that the television is a poor substitute for the parent in sex education. Many parents want their children to be informed about sexual matters but find it difficult to help them acquire this knowledge. The parent group, through discussion and role play, can provide a model for parents who are struggling with these dilemmas. This is why role playing is such an integral part of the group process; it allows parents an opportunity to practice before a warm and understanding group of people who have the same difficulty.

Because sex education and the ability to discuss it encompasses so much, the counselor may want to have more than one session to address the various aspects of sex education. Some areas of sexual development that children might need to know are incorporated in the following open-ended hypothetical situations.

"WHERE DO BABIES COME FROM?"

Sally J. is in kindergarten. She has seen her neighbor's belly growing larger each day and has heard it mentioned that her neighbor is going to have a baby. Sally asks her mother, "Where do babies come from?"

DISCUSS: *If you were Sally's mother, how would you answer Sally?*
What would you say if your son, Stu, was asking similar questions?
(Keep in mind that Sally and Stu are in kindergarten.)

Often parents can get through the preceding situation without too much difficulty, but age-old fears and inhibitions cause this next situation to be much more difficult.

Josie is in the third grade and says, "Mom, I know that when two people love each other they have babies, but I don't understand how? I know that babies are in the mother's stomach, and I know how they get out but I don't know how they get there."

DISCUSS: *As a parent, how would you answer Josie's questions?*
   What would you say if your son Jose was asking similar questions.

This second situation lends itself particularly well to role playing. In the role play, the parent can actually assume the role of the mother or father in the situation and practice how they would discuss this important topic with their children. Often, one or two members of the group feel at ease with the topic and can get the role play started. A parent who is not comfortable with the topic might be willing to play the part of the child in the situation. Others should be encouraged, but not forced to participate. Topics of this nature should be reserved for the last several sessions, giving the group time to develop trust and rapport and the parents to feel secure in the group first.

Often parents will mention that their children do not come to them with questions about sex, particularly if the children sense that the parent is reluctant to talk about the subject. Occasionally a mother will say, "My Marcel could care less about girls! He is in the seventh grade and has yet to ask where babies come from." A father may confide that his child did ask about babies one time and it embarrassed him so much that he replied, "Go ask your mother!" and the child never mentioned the subject again.

The parent group is a safe place to discuss fears and misconceptions about sex and about child development. A parent's lack of knowledge about child development can lead to child abuse. Carmelita's mother did not understand that exploring the genital area is normal in small children. When the mother discovered 4-year-old Carmelita masturbating, she feared that the child had inherited her biological father's disposition and would grow up to be a "sex maniac like her father!" These fears magnified as Mrs. S. sought to cure the problem. Finally, she held the child's fingers over an open flame. If Carmelita's mother had been a participant in a parent group, her fears that her daughter's behavior was deviant would have been assuaged.

A discussion about AIDS will help dispel some of the misconceptions about the disease and will create a more tolerant atmosphere for children who are affected by it. Many children are affected by AIDS because a parent has it; or some have the disease themselves. Generally, it is fear of the unknown that leads to misconceptions.

Specific Problems

Parent groups can have a developmental, preventive, or remedial focus and can be held in any setting. Some groups are important to primary and secondary prevention efforts with parents and children (such as expectant teenage mothers, or parents of children at risk for school failure). These groups are designed to identify potential problems and lessen their severity and impact. Other groups have a remedial focus and address specific problems that are common to all the group members. For example, parents of children who are struggling with anorexia may meet to offer support and suggestions on how to cope with their child's illness.

Although unstructured support groups are developmental in nature, specific problems may arise that individual group members want to discuss. Initially, group members may make their needs known to the counselor who will include them in a written hypothetical situation. These hypothetical situations may reflect concerns about lying, stealing, peer rejection, bullying and other similar problems that children encounter as they are growing up. As rapport is established and trust builds, parents often discuss their specific concerns with the group.

The following example deals with stealing, a problem that is not uncommon among children and that causes most parents a great deal of concern.

"SEE WHAT MY MOTHER BOUGHT ME LAST NIGHT"

The Zoe family is very concerned about their daughter Renée, who is 9. Recently, Mr. Zoe was called by the manager of the local supermarket because Renée, in the company of several others, took several packs of gum and ran.

In school, Renée takes other children's pencils, crayons, and erasers when she sits in their desks during math and reading class. Often she will go to the teacher and say, "See my crayons" or "See what my mother bought me last night" and the teacher will recognize some item that belongs to another child.

Last night, Renée's mother noticed that $10 was missing from her purse. Today, the principal called to say that Jane was treating as many children as she could to ice cream at lunch and that she had a lot of money.

DISCUSS: *List all the reasons you can think of for Renée's stealing.*
If you were Renée's parents, how would you handle this problem?

The following dialogue was taken from the group discussion that followed this hypothetical situation. Notice that the parents have different ideas about why children take things. There is no way of knowing for sure what Renée's motives are, but the parents offer suggestions as to how Renée's parents might better meet her needs so that the stealing behavior can be eliminated.

COUNSELOR: Do all children take things that belong to someone else at some time during their life?

PARENT 1: Yes, but I think there are different types of stealing. Some kids take things that don't belong to them until they learn respect for property.

PARENT 3: Children have to learn not to take things just because they want them.

PARENT 1: I think this child has another reason. She knew her mother would find out.

COUNSELOR: What might be some possible reasons this child has for taking things?

PARENT 1: She wants to feel important.

PARENT 2: She needs friends.

PARENT 4: Maybe she is never allowed to go up town to buy something.

PARENT 3: She is trying to buy friendships because she doesn't have any.

COUNSELOR: Anything else she might need?

PARENT 1: She might need support, security,...love.

PARENT 5: Her parents should show their love more—provide her with more time and attention.

PARENT 3: What would you do about the money?

PARENT 1: There's a sense of responsibility that comes in here too. You have to love them, but you have to show them that they are responsible for their actions too. I'm not exactly sure how to do that.

COUNSELOR: You are saying that Renée's parents need to show her love and help her accept responsibility for her actions.

The preceding dialogue illustrates how parents view a problem situation from a variety of perspectives and contribute to each other's understanding. Parents who are experiencing specific problems with their children can analyze their own behavior and project themselves into the solution without threat. This helps parents explore possible ways that they can improve the parent-child relationship and help their children overcome some of the difficulties of childhood.

In summary, the parent group serves a developmental, preventive, and remedial function. Prevention relies heavily on developing a positive interaction between parent and child. Remediation involves improving and strengthening the parent-child interaction so that children can get back on track. In the broadest sense, the entire ten-session parent group is devoted to developing the kinds of attitudes, feelings and positive interaction between parent and child that will help to prevent problems from developing and resolve those problems that already exist.

Positive attitudes toward child rearing can be fostered in parent group. Parents who lack a good role model in their own parenting can learn from other parents who are more effective models. Armed with knowledge about child development and encouraged and supported by the group, parents gain confidence and competence in their parenting skills.

PARENT-CHILD GROUPS

Parents sometimes don't understand kids as much as some kids wish they could.
—JOSH, age 12

Increased positive communication and mutual understanding help improve the parent-child relationship. However, simply helping parents understand that communication is needed and then presenting some techniques for improving that communication is not enough. Parents need an opportunity to practice talking with children and sharing ideas and feelings.

After parents have met together as a group for eight or ten weeks, they may decide to form a parent-child group. In this group, each parent will have an opportunity to interact with the children of other parents in the group. This interaction provides the parent with an objective view of children as individuals, and gives the parent an opportunity to develop insight into the dynamics of the parent-child relationship and to understand how important it is to the child. The child, on the other hand, develops an understanding of parents and sees them as people with thoughts and feelings.

> ## KEYS TO A SUCCESSFUL PARENT-CHILD GROUP
>
> - Ascertain the need for a parent-child group.
> - Train parents to communicate with children.
> - Involve children in planning and setting goals.
> - Select a diverse group of parents and children.
> - Arrange small discussion groups of parents and children from different families.
> - Send invitations to children asking them to bring their parent(s).
> - Use open-ended hypothetical situations to start small-group discussions.
> - Use a large-group format for follow-up discussion.
> - Evaluate group effectiveness at the end of the six sessions.

Structuring the Group

If a parents' group has met successfully for eight or ten weeks, certain attitudes will have developed among the participants that are prerequisites for a parent-child group. These attitudes encompass such things as warmth, acceptance, and trust, which have enabled the parents to share a great deal about themselves and their families. Hopefully, this atmosphere of warmth and trust will carry over into the parent-child group and will help allay any fears the parents have about what their children may reveal in the group .

Ascertain the Need for a Parent-Child Group

After a parent group has ended, the counselor can help the parents explore the need for a parent-child group. For weeks, the group members have focused on how better to understand and communicate with their children. Because it is difficult for many parents to put their knowledge into practice with their own children, the parents may want to form a group that includes each other's children. This group will provide them with an opportunity to practice what they have been discussing in the parent group.

As a first step in the group's development, the counselor invites the parents to a special planning session. The purpose of this session is to get the parents' ideas about forming a parent-child group and to determine what they hope to accomplish. Many suggestions will be given, some of them conflicting. One parent may conceive of the sessions as give-and-take relationships, whereby children learn that adults are human and capable of mistakes. Another parent may want his or her child to realize that adults are usually right and may want someone to explain this to the child. Usually, a good discussion coupled with the counselor's gentle reinforcement of the positive aspects of communication offered by the group members will help the group reach some workable conclusions.

If parents are encouraged to express any reservations they may have, these doubts can be taken into account or dispelled by the group. Some parents may be reluctant to have their children exposed to someone else's viewpoint for fear that it might be more liberal than their own. For example, one mother may think that sixth-grade girls should be allowed to wear nylons and light makeup, whereas another mother may think that these things should be reserved until her daughter is older. Counselors can help assure parents that their values will be respected in the group.

Train Parents to Communicate with Children

The conclusion that most often emerges from such a group discussion is that parents want to communicate better with their own children but they are not sure of how to attain this goal. The counselor can help prepare the parents for talking with children. The following is a good open-ended hypothetical situation to stimulate discussion of this important topic.

Justin J. feels that he cannot talk with his parents. When he and his father talk his dad asks him a lot of questions like, "How was school today?" or "Did you eat your lunch?" or "Why did you get a D in arithmetic?

When he talks with his mother, she offers all kinds of advice like, "Well, you should have done it this way, don't you think?" or "You'll understand when you grow up." Sometimes his mom gets bogged down with her own work and worry and says, "You don't know what problems are. Wait until you have mine!" or "I'm busy right now, I'll talk to you later."

Justin's parents complain that he never talks to them. Instead, he answers them with a "yes," "no," "fine," or "O,K." They really are interested in him and would like to share his life. They don't understand him very well and he doesn't understand them.

Justin says that his mother and dad don't listen to him when he tells them about things he is interested in. He claims that his parents are so busy that they forget what he tells them.

DISCUSS: What is Justin's behavior telling us?
What is Justin's parents' behavior telling us?
What are some ways to improve communication between parents and children?

The following dialogue illustrates how parents can develop insight by discussing this open-ended situation:

PARENT 1: When my kids were younger and I wasn't working, I used to try to get time when I could be alone with each one at a different time.
PARENT 2: Yes, but I have six kids and it just seems impossible.
PARENT 1: I know it's hard, but if you can, just find the time to talk or just listen to the one that needs you the most that day. It's good to try to give one a chance each day, but I know it's hard.
PARENT 3: I try to listen to each child as he comes home and take the youngest one first because he can't wait as long. Some days they all don't want to talk so I have a conversation with the one that wants to talk.
PARENT 5: It's good to just listen if you have a child who will talk. My grandson won't talk to me.
PARENT 6: I have a teenager who won't talk but I discovered something as I was driving him home from the game. I was telling him what we had been talking about at our meeting and he started to tell me

about the game and we actually had a conversation. Before I used to ask him questions, questions, questions! The reason he doesn't talk to me enough is that I don't talk to him on an equal basis. When I started to just discuss my feelings about the group, he told me what the coach said and all about the game. I never had to ask a single question!

The case of Justin J. can be used to help parents learn some of the techniques of good conversation. Conversation seems so simple between friends, but it takes on many different forms with children. Parents often resort to probing, advising, ordering, admonishing, not listening, or dismissing what the child has to say as unimportant or foolish. The purpose of the preceding hypothetical situation is to assist the parents in developing insight into the ways that they may be blocking communication with their children.

Role playing Role playing can be used to supplement the written situations as a means of helping parents learn some productive communication techniques. Parents, by assuming the roles of the children, can demonstrate ways to communicate with children more effectively. Role playing also helps the parents develop empathy for the child.

The following role-play situations can be used to help prepare parents for the parent-child group.

1. Pretend you are a child coming home, and you are greeted by your mother. Today was report card day at school.
2. Pretend you are a child and you have gotten into trouble for accidently breaking a neighbor's window. Your mother does not know about the window, but you come to the house crying.
3. Pretend you are a child and it is a rainy day and you have nothing to do. You notice that your mother looks lonely.

Involve Children in Planning and Setting Goals

Children who participate in the group should also be involved in the planning. Children enjoy this activity for many of the same reasons that adults do. The fact that someone asks their opinion makes them feel valued and understood. It also contributes to increased self-confidence and enhances self-esteem.

Children are especially valuable to the planning process for they are the main source of ideas for the topics they would like to discuss with a caring and concerned adult. Children can also help the counselor arrange the groups so that they will operate successfully.

The children will be somewhat less able than adults to set long-range goals for the group, but they can tell the counselor what seem to be the most difficult subjects to discuss with grown-ups and give their point of view. This input helps the counselor develop open-ended hypothetical situations that express both the parent's and the child's viewpoint.

Selection of Participants

Because the parents group is a prerequisite to the parent-child group, both groups will represent a diverse cross section of the population. The parent-child group will include children who are well-adjusted as well as those who are currently struggling with problems that need attention. The group will also include parents and children from varying socioeconomic backgrounds, race, ethnicity, age levels and will include extroverts as well as introverts. The more diverse the group, the more interesting it is.

Children from grades 4 through 6 function well in this type of group situation. Most children age 8 and older are able to conceptualize, and they can sit and engage in productive conversation. Some children, particularly those with adjustment problems, may not be able to be attentive and concentrate. However, the counselor can arrange to put them with adults who can help them develop as much control as possible. Often just the extra attention and the knowledge that they are doing something special with their parents helps their behavior improve.

Children who are below the fourth-grade level may also be able to benefit from the group. A child's readiness to participate would depend on his or her maturity, adjustment, and ability to conceptualize. The counselor should not be put in the position of judging which children of this age can and cannot attend. The group can be structured so that only children in grades 4 through 6 can attend, or it can be designed for children in this age bracket but include younger children if their parents feel the children are mature enough to benefit from the group. Here again, the counselor is demonstrating his or her faith in the parent's judgment. Parents are usually very good judges of their children's behavior and will bring younger children only if they think that the children will enjoy the experience and be able to profit from it. The parents are just as likely to leave a younger child at home because they recognize that the child is not quite mature enough for this type of group work.

It is up to the counselor and the group members to decide when the group should begin and end. However, because the parent group is a prerequisite for the parent-child group, it usually starts a few weeks after the first parent group ends. The parent-child group should run at least 6 weeks for about 1 1/2 hours each session. About 1 hour of this time is spent in group work, and the remainder is for snacking and socializing. This still leaves plenty of time for children to do homework and get to bed early enough.

Operation of the Group

This group helped me realize that I need to listen more to my children's problems. They are just as big as my own.
—Parent's comment in a group

Preliminary Activities

Each child attending the group receives a personal invitation in the mail, asking the child to bring his or her parents rather than vice versa. Receiving a personal invitation surprises and delights children, enhances their self-esteem, and makes them eager to attend the parent-child group. In each weekly invitation, a different child is asked to arrange for the snack. Parents generally take turns providing a treat for the group to enjoy at the end of the evening's activities.

Considering that children have shorter attention spans than adults do, the counselor will want to have many different types of activities planned. Open-ended hypothetical situations representing various points of view can be used along with other methods of stimulating conversation. Role plays can be interspersed to provide variety and hold the children's interest. Examples of activities that can be used with groups of children and adults are included in this chapter.

Small Discussion Groups of Children and Adults

In advance of the first meeting, the counselor will want to divide the participants into carefully balanced small groups of four or five children and adults. Initially, the groups are arranged to meet the needs and goals that have been expressed by the participants in the preplanning phase of the group process. The counselor, through careful observation and evaluation of each session, can arrange the groups to meet the individual needs of each participant as the sessions progress. For example, a shy child could be put in a group with a friend so that he or she would be more comfortable and able to converse. On certain topics, it might prove valuable to have all girls or all boys in a group.

These groups may vary in size according to the members' needs. One group may require 5 or 6 people to keep the conversation going, whereas another group may need fewer. A group of three members can give a particularly active child a chance to be heard and responded to by two caring adults. Perhaps one group will have only one adult whereas another has three. Sometimes a shy, retiring parent can relate better to children than to adults and can gain confidence if he or she is the only adult in a small group of children.

The counselor needs to know as much about the personalities of the participants as possible. This is not as difficult as it sounds, because the parents have already spent eight or ten weeks in group sessions and the counselor knows them all very well. The counselor also understands a great deal about the positive as well as the negative aspects of their individual parenting. Most of the children will also be well known to the counselor, but if they are not, careful observation and evaluation will assist the counselor in meeting each child's individual needs within the group.

The children are grouped so that they are interacting with adults other than their own parents so that both adults and children can view each other more objectively. This combination has yielded some surprising insights on the part of both adult and child participants. Some of these are shared under the section on evaluation.

Open-Ended Hypothetical Situations

> *I found out that my kid's bedrooms aren't the only messy ones in town.*
> —Mother's reaction to group discussion

In discussions with the counselor, the children provide real-life parent-child struggles that can then be woven into hypothetical open-ended situations for the group to address. There may be no real solution to some of the difficulties the children present—other than just growing up—but it is beneficial for the children to express them and to have them taken seriously by adults, especially their parents.

SIBLING RIVALRY

Polly is in the sixth grade and she has a younger brother who thinks that it's not fair that Polly gets to stay up later than he does. He is a little frightened to go to bed alone so he complains loudly to his mother. Polly needs extra time for homework and feels that older kids should have more privileges. The children exchange words, argue, and begin to fight. Finally, their angry father says, "Okay, everybody. Get to bed!"

DISCUSS: Consider each person's side of the story. What might be an acceptable solution to this problem?

DEVELOPING RESPONSIBILITY

Melina, age 10, is in constant trouble over her room. Her mother tells her to make her bed, pick up her clothes, dust, sweep the floor, straighten the shelves, and keep things neat. Melina doesn't do it. She reads a book, turns on her radio, calls her friends to have ice cream, and watches television. She says, "I'll do it later." Her mother yells at her, calls her dad to hit her, threatens to ground her, and tells her she can't see her friends anymore. Her mother tells Melina that she is irresponsible.

DISCUSS: Consider each person's side of the story and give your thoughts, feelings, and opinions.
What would be some ways to handle this situation?

TEASING AND TATTLING

Alex is 9 years old and enjoys teasing his 11-year-old sister, Prudence. He plops himself smack in front of the T.V. and blocks her view. She says, "Alex, move out of the way." He continues to sit there, smirking. She screams, "Mother! He's bugging me."

Alex's mother says, "Quit screaming." She finally gets angry and says, "Okay, go to your room."

DISCUSS: Give some reasons kids tease and tattle.
What would be some ways that you might handle this situation?

FIGHTING

Enrique, age 6, teased his sister, made faces, and called her names until she couldn't take it anymore. Frustrated, she slapped him in the face. Just as she was slapping him, her father came in the room and saw her. He got angry and sent her to bed. She screamed, "I didn't start it!" Enrique answered, "She's always picking on me."

DISCUSS: What do you think will happen?
Consider each person's side of the story. What should be done?

These open-ended hypothetical situations were developed after talking with parents and children about some of the common situations that occur in their interaction's with each other. However, these situations may not always address the concerns that children have. To allow children to express their concerns, the counselor can arrange to have words printed on cards and left at each table. The group can then choose the topic they want to discuss. This technique is more workable after the group has developed trust and cohesion, and should not be used in the first few sessions. Examples of words that indicate ideas for discussion might include *lonely, sad, scared, happy, glad, hurt,* and *upset.*

Large-Group Discussion

As trust develops and children and adults become more comfortable, the discussion in the small groups focuses on the thoughts and feelings that children and parents commonly experience in their relationship with one another. These insights are then brought to the large group where children and their own parents interact. Initially, the large-group discussions focus on the hypothetical situations. This provides a non-threatening way for parents and children to talk about issues that may be affecting their own relationship. Even if children and adults do not verbalize the difficulties in their relationship, they are gaining insight as they sit and discuss these parent-child interactions with their own parents and with the parents of others in the group.

Evaluation

The counselor will want to evaluate the group's effectiveness in addressing the participants' needs and goals. This can be done in the form of a questionnaire given to the children and their parents at the end of the six-week session. The child's questionnaire simply asks children what they learned about themselves and their parents. The parent questionnaire asks parents for their assessment of the group experience and whether it had any effect on their interaction with their children. Both questionnaires are provided in Appendix C.

The following comments, taken from parent and child evaluations, are some of the most entertaining and insightful. In response to the question, "What did you learn about parents?" some children had these bits of wisdom.

"Parents aren't as bad as I thought."

"Parents misunderstand us! It's not fair that parents don't think the way we do but, we should go the way they do because they need more help than we do. They're way back then and its a whole knew [sic] generation. They need help!"

"I learned that nobody's perfect, and that the parents have it just as bad as we have it. We ought to be fair to parents."

"Parents are not always wright [sic]."

Parents gained insight into themselves and their children. Here are some of their answers to "What did you learn about children?"

"I didn't realize just how important it is to talk to a child. I guess I didn't realize just how much a child is a person with thoughts and feelings of their very own."

"Children are smarter than we give them credit for."

"Children think that parents don't understand them."

In summary, the parent-child group is a way to help parents practice what they have learned in the child-focused parent group. After the parents develop trust in each other and in the counselor, they are involved in planning and then in practicing interactions with each other's children. An equally important part of the planning process is the children's involvement. In informal conversations with the children of the identified parents, the counselor is often able to determine what the children would like to talk to adults about. These concerns are incorporated into written hypothetical situations that are used as a starting point for the parent-child discussions. Eventually, the discussion departs from the hypothetical situation and becomes more personalized as the parents and children develop trust in each other and cohesion as a group. After the small-group discussions have concluded, parents and children can interact together in a large group. The parent-child group usually lasts about $1\frac{1}{2}$ hours and includes a time for socializing and snacking.

INSIGHTS AND IMPLICATIONS

The dramatic changes in home and family life discussed in Chapter 1 have increased the need for counselors to develop collaborative strategies with parents. Members of the helping professions have responded to this need with a variety of parent education and training programs designed to encourage parent involvement. Another way to help and encourage parents is to involve them in a parent support group. This group provides parents with an opportunity to talk about their concerns, learn from others, and discover solutions to problems together. Additional benefits include improved parent-child communication, prevention and resolution of problems, and increased parenting skill and confidence. Understanding and communication between children and parents is enhanced when parent-child groups are part of the program. Such groups give parents actual practice in listening and responding to each other's children. These experiences often help parents improve and strengthen the relationships that they have with their own children.

WISDOM ACCORDING TO ORTON

- *Be as warm and welcoming to parents as you would be to your friends.*
- *Let parents know that you value their opinion, and include them in planning.*
- *Respect and guard confidences, and help parents do the same.*
- *Write or phone anyone who drops out to let them know they are missed.*
- *When children come to the group, help them feel special.*
- *Relax, have fun, and enjoy the group!*

ORTON'S PICKS

Elkind, D. (1990). *Grandparenting: Understanding today's children.* Glenview, IL: Scott, Foresman.

This book is recommended reading for all grandparents but especially for those who are raising their grandchildren. It addresses ways that grandparents can offer their grandchildren the love and support that they need to become healthy, happy adults.

Grunwald, B. B., & McAbee, V. (1985). *Guiding the family: Practical counseling techniques.* Muncie, IN: Accelerated Development.

This text gives a good overview of Adlerian theory as it applies to families. Specific problem situations that are of concern to most parents are addressed. Helpful vignettes offer concrete suggestions for improving relationships between parents and their children. The concerns of single-parent families, blended families, and extended families are addressed, and case studies that illustrate the principles and techniques delineated throughout the book are offered.

Main, F. (1986). *Perfect parenting and other myths.* Minneapolis, MN: Compcare Publications.

This delightful book, written in easy-to-understand language and sprinkled with humor, is recommended for parents and professionals who want to know more about the intricacies of child rearing. It offers commonsense solutions to parents who are dealing with specific problems and offers counselors a rich source of information for parent group discussions.

Assessment Forms and Conference Procedures

CHILD INFORMATION FORM

IDENTIFYING INFORMATION

Child's Name _____ Nickname _____

Date of Birth _____ Sex: M F Present Age _____

School Attending _____ Grade _____ Teacher _____

Birth Order: 1st 2nd 3rd 4th 5th 6th of 1 2 3 4 5 6 children

Child lives with _____

Name of Parents/Guardians _____

Address _____

Home Phone _____ Work Phone(s) _____

MAJOR CONCERNS

Please describe, in your own words, your concerns about your child and the reasons

that you are seeking help _____

_____

_____

_____

_____

When were these difficulties first noticed? Please explain as fully as you can. _____

_____

_____

Has this child had any previous professional assistance with the problems stated
here? If so, please provide information.

Agency/professional   Approximate dates   What was done?

_____

_____

MEDICAL HISTORY

Please describe this child's general health. _____

_____

_____

Has he/she had any serious illnesses, accidents, or injuries? _____

_____

_____

Please give reasons and approximate dates for any hospitalizations._____

_____

_____

Are there any conditions that require regular medical care _____

_____

_____

Does this child take any medications on a regular basis? If so, please note type of medication and frequency of use. _____

_____

_____

Does the child have any difficulties with vision or hearing? Note date and results of any previous vision or hearing examinations. _____

_____

_____

Does the child have any allergies? If yes, please identify. _____

_____

_____

Name of pediatrician/family physician _____

Date of last physical examination _____

DEVELOPMENTAL HISTORY

Please note any complications during pregnancy with this child (such as, illness, accidents, prolonged emotional stress, etc.). _____

_____

_____

Delivery was: on time _____ early _____ late _____

Length of labor _____

Any complications? _____

Birth weight _____ Incubator? _____ Need oxygen? _____

How would you describe your child as an infant? _____

_____

Has this child had any problems with motor development (such as difficulty learning
to walk; poor coordination; difficulty coloring, cutting, or drawing)? _____

_____

At what age was the child able to:

Smile and recognize people _____ Feed self with spoon _____

Sit up without support _____ Drink from glass/cup _____

Stand alone _____ Ride a tricycle _____

Walk alone _____ Tie shoes _____

Has this child had any problems with understanding or speaking language? _____

_____

_____

At what age (months/years and months) was this child able to:

Coo and babble _____ Combine two words _____

Say first words _____ Follow simple directions _____

Name people and things _____ Use short sentences _____

Does this child have current problems with soiling or wetting during the day or at
night?

If so, explain _____

_____

At what age did this child:

Begin toilet training _____ Complete toilet training _____

Remain dry during the day _____ Remain dry during the night _____

Does this child have current sleep disturbances, such as difficulty falling asleep, getting up in the middle of the night, or being difficult to wake? _____

_____

_____

LEARNING DEVELOPMENT

Compared to other children you know, this child did/does have difficulty with:

	Did	Does		Did	Does
Identifying basic colors	___	___	Telling time	___	___
Learning the alphabet	___	___	Adding numbers	___	___
Learning to count	___	___	Subtracting	___	___
Recognizing numbers	___	___	Multiplying	___	___
Reading	___	___	Dividing	___	___
Printing	___	___	Cursive writing	___	___
Spelling correctly	___	___	Retaining information	___	___
Understanding what is read	___	___			

Please note the grades and explain the circumstances if this child has:

(1) Had extended or frequent absences _____

(2) Had to repeat the year _____

(3) Changed schools in mid-year _____

(4) Began school year at a new school _____

Briefly describe how this child is doing in school. Note current marks and areas of strength or weakness in school work. _____

_____

Has he/she had any remedial help or special education services in school or privately?

If so, please describe and give approximate dates. _____

_____

_____

Please describe this child's attitude toward school. Note any special interests or dislikes he/she has in school. _____

_____

How does this child get along with the teacher and other students in school? _____

_____

_____

_____

SOCIAL DEVELOPMENT AND PEER RELATIONSHIPS

What special interests, hobbies, sports, and games does the child enjoy both in and after school? _____

_____

When this child chooses playmates, are they:

older   younger   own age   all ages

boys   girls   both boys and girls

In play activities, is the child a leader, a follower, or a loner? _____

Does the child prefer the company of adults to other children? Yes _____ No _____

Does the child have at least one best friend? Yes _____ No _____

What is the friend's age? _____

EMOTIONAL DEVELOPMENT

Has your child ever been characterized by family members, teachers or others as being:

	Yes	No		Yes	No
Restless/ inattentive	___	___	Forgetful	___	___
Humorous/ fun	___	___	Quick to anger	___	___
Cheerful	___	___	Depressed/sad	___	___
Daydreamer	___	___	Disruptive	___	___
Immature	___	___	Happy	___	___
Aggressive	___	___	Nervous/ tense	___	___

Does this child have a great many fears or worries? If so, what are they? _____

_____

Does the child have unusual or persistent nightmares? If so, what are they about?

_____

_____

SPECIAL CONCERNS

Briefly describe this child's behavior at home. _____

_____

_____

Please check below any past or present concerns; then give the age during which they occurred. (*Example*: Eating...from 4–6 years)

Area of Difficulty	Age		Area of Difficulty	Age	
	From	*To*		*From*	*To*
___ Speech	___	___	___ Destructiveness	___	___
___ Eating	___	___	___ Physical health	___	___
___ Sleeping	___	___	___ Fears	___	___
___ Activity level	___	___	___ Bladder control	___	___
___ Coordination	___	___	___ Bowel function	___	___
___ Aggressiveness	___	___	___ Temper tantrums	___	___
___ Sexual activity	___	___	___ Lying	___	___
___ Response to discipline	___	___	___ Stealing	___	___
___ Relationship to peers	___	___	___ Firesetting	___	___
___ Ability to learn	___	___	___ Thumb sucking	___	___
___ School adjustment	___	___	___ Tics	___	___
___ Play behavior	___	___	___ Drugs	___	___
___ Anxiety	___	___	___ Truancy	___	___
___ Degree of responsibility	___	___	___ Other	___	___

Please elaborate on any concerns that you have about any of the difficulties listed.

_____

_____

Describe special strengths the child has shown in his or her overall adjustment to past difficulties. _____

_____

FAMILY RELATIONSHIPS/HISTORY

Please list all family members currently living at home or closely connected with the family. Indicate their ages, relationship to this child (sister, stepbrother, aunt, etc.), and their school grade or occupation. Include parents who are currently living with the child.

Name	Age	Relationship	Grade or Occupation
_____	____	_____	_____
_____	____	_____	_____
_____	____	_____	_____
_____	____	_____	_____

Have any of the following potential problems been present in your (the parents') original families, previous family if remarried, and/or your current family? If so, state which family unit(s) experienced the problem [mother's (M), father's (F), previous family (P), and/or current family (C)].

_____ Career involvement, father   _____ Multiple moves

_____ Career involvement, mother   _____ Financial pressures

_____ Physical health of family member(s)   _____ Marital problems

_____ Mental health of family member(s)   _____ Separation or divorce

_____ Death of special family member   _____ Prolonged absence

_____ Differences in child rearing   _____ Drinking

RELATIONSHIPS

How does this child get along with his/her brothers and/or sisters? _____

_____

_____

Describe any special activities that you do with this child. _____

_____

_____

If you were to describe your child as a person and not as a son or daughter, what would you say about him or her? _____

_____

_____

SIGNATURE(S) OF PARENT OR PARENTS WHO COMPLETED THIS FORM

Father: _____ Date _____

Mother: _____ Date _____

BEHAVIOR OBSERVATION FORM

Name of Child _____ School _____ Grade _____

Dear _____,
　　　　(Name of teacher)

We are evaluating the psychological and neurological status of this child. Your judgments about his or her behavior functioning are indispensable to us in interpreting our own observations and tests. Please rate this child on each statement. You may use the space provided for comments about each item.

Thank you _____
　　　　　　　　　　　　　(Name of clinician)

BEHAVIOR	FREQUENCY			
	Seldom	*Sometimes*	*Often*	*Always*
1. Is restless or fidgety	____	____	____	____
2. Speaks out or jumps out of seat	____	____	____	____
3. Seems overwhelmed by group activities	____	____	____	____
4. Interrupts, has difficulty waiting turn	____	____	____	____
5. Avoids tasks that require sustained effort	____	____	____	____
6. Is easily distracted	____	____	____	____
7. Doesn't seem to hear directions	____	____	____	____
8. Is fearful of being wrong, indecisive	____	____	____	____
9. Makes many careless mistakes in written work	____	____	____	____
10. Paperwork is messy, disorganized, or incomplete	____	____	____	____
11. Has daily fluctuations in performance	____	____	____	____
12. Is upset by changes in routine	____	____	____	____
13. Is confused by number process	____	____	____	____
14. Has difficulty in reading/spelling	____	____	____	____
15. Is aggressive or destructive	____	____	____	____
16. Gives up easily	____	____	____	____
17. Tells strange stories or makes peculiar comments	____	____	____	____
18. Cries often and easily	____	____	____	____
19. Seeks or demands a lot of attention	____	____	____	____
20. Acts without thinking of consequences	____	____	____	____

Date Completed _____

CASE CONFERENCE PROCEDURE

I. Collect information

II. Invite appropriate people

III. Conduct meeting

    A. State reasons for the meeting

    B. Identify behaviors of concern

    C. Present factual data

    D. Solicit factual information from participants

    E. Encourage participants to react to what has been presented and collect additional data

    F. Seek interpretation of data from each participant's perspective

    G. Develop a plan of intervention

IV. Organize intervention strategies and activities

V. Follow-up

WORKSHEET FOR CASE CONFERENCE

I. Data presented by each participant:

II. Reactions to data presented:

III. Interpretation of data:

    A. Child strengths/potential strengths

        1. Positive aspects of child's behavior

        2. Positive aspects of family behavior/background

        3. Positive impact of significant others

        4. Positive impact of school and community

B. Negative factors/potential negative factors

    1. Potential consequences of child's negative behavior

    2. Family behavior/background liabilities

    3. Negative impacts of school and community

Conclusions

IV. Intervention strategies/activities

    A. Home

    B. School

    C. Community

V. Suggestions for intervention follow-up

Consent Forms and Reporting Procedures

CHILD'S INFORMED CONSENT FORM

PRIVATE PRACTICE OR CLINIC SETTING

I understand that when I come to this office I will be playing, drawing, and talking. I can talk about anything that I want to. I can talk about myself and my family. I can even talk about my worries, if I want to. If I don't feel like talking, I don't have to. Sometimes when I come here, I will feel a lot better. Sometimes I might feel a lot worse. I am allowed to come often, but if I don't want to come, I don't have to.

During play, I can do anything I want if I follow three rules. I can't hurt myself or the other kids. I can't hurt my counselor. I can't break any of the toys on purpose.

Sometimes my counselor uses a video camera to tape when we talk and play. I know these tapes are to help my counselor learn more about me and how I am doing.

My counselor won't tell my parents if I talk about them or my family. My parents will know only if I am doing better or not. My counselor might give my parents ideas on how to help me with problems. If my counselor wants to talk about me with another person, my counselor will ask my parents and me for our permission.

My counselor will have to talk to other people if I say that someone is hurting me or doing things to me that they shouldn't. Also, if I say that I want to hurt myself, then my counselor will have to tell someone.

I am signing my name on this paper to show that I agree to talk and play with my counselor.

Child's Signature _____ Date _____

FORMA DE AUTORIZACIÓN, CON PREVIO AVISO, PARA EL NIÑO

PRÁCTICA PARTICULAR O CLÍNICA

Yo comprendo que cuando venga a esta oficina voy a jugar, dibujar y hablar. Puedo hablar sobre cualquier cosa. Puedo hablar de mi familia y de mí mismo. Si quiero, puedo hablar de mis preocupaciones. Si no quiero, no tengo que hablar. A veces cuando venga aquí, voy a sentirme mucho mejor. A veces puedo sentirme peor. Puedo venir con frecuencia pero si no quiero, no tengo que venir.

Cuando juegue podré hacer todo lo que quiera si sigo tres reglas. No puedo lastimarme ni lastimar a los otros niños. No puedo lastimar a mi consejero. No puedo romper ningún juguete a propósito.

A veces, mi consejero va a usar una camara de video para grabar cuando hablemos o juguemos. Yo sé que estas cintas van a ayudar a mi consejero a aprender más sobre mí y sobre cómo estoy.

Mi consejero no les va a contar a mis padres si yo hablo de ellos o de mi familia. Ellos sabrán sólo si estoy mejorando o no. Mi consejero podría aconsejar a mis padres como ayudarme con mis problemas. Si mi consejero quiere hablar sobre mí con otra persona, mi consejero nos pedirá el permiso a mí y a mis padres.

Mi consejero tendrá que hablar con otras personas si yo digo que alguien me está haciendo daño o me está haciendo cosas que no debe. Si yo quiero lastimarme, mi consejero también tendrá que informarle a alguien.

Voy a firmar mi nombre en este papel para demostrar que estoy de acuerdo en hablar y jugar con mi consejero.

_____   _____
            Firma del niño   Fecha

Traducido por el Prof. Carlos Mamani y la Prof. Mary Lou Scalise de Gannon University.

ADULT'S INFORMED CONSENT FORM

PRIVATE PRACTICE/CLINIC SETTING

I/We _____ voluntarily consent to services provided
  (parent/guardian)

by this clinic/clinician(s) on behalf of _____
                    (Name of child/children)

These services, which will be explained to me, may include individual, group, play, marital and family therapy, consultation, and psychological testing. I realize that psychology is an imperfect science and that a particular benefit or outcome cannot be guaranteed. I understand that to achieve the best results, I may need to confront troubling feelings. I may feel worse before I start to feel better, and I may experience emotional strain or make distressing life changes. I am seeking this treatment of my own accord and am free to discontinue counseling at any time.

I understand and agree to the following terms:
- Confidentiality will be maintained and information will be released only to qualified professionals and only with my explicit written permission, *except* in certain situations where maintaining confidentiality would result in clear and imminent danger to myself or others, or as otherwise provided by state law.
- The therapist is required by law to report to the appropriate authorities any suspected child abuse, elder abuse, or abuse of people with disabilities. When a threat of bodily harm to myself or others is present, the therapist may break the confidentiality of our communications. I understand that the therapist will make reasonable efforts to resolve these situations before breaking confidentiality.
- I may be cared for by a therapist who is completing an advanced degree or doing an internship. In all such instances, counseling sessions are supervised by a licensed psychologist or by a counselor with the appropriate credentials.
- Sessions may be audiotaped or videotaped and may be used in supervision or to record client progress. All tapes, records, and materials concerning clients are confidential and are not released to nor shared with any other agency or individual without the client's specific written permission.
- Authorization will be obtained in writing, and my signature required, before the therapist will consult with other professionals.
- Information obtained in counseling sessions may be used for research purposes, presented anonymously at professional meetings, and/or published in journals or textbooks. At no time will the child's/client's name or identifying information be used.
- I understand that therapy is $ _____ per hour.

_____   and/or   _____
          Client   Parent or Legal Guardian
      (if 18 or older)   (if client is under 18)

Date: _____

AUTORIZACIÓN, CON PREVIO AVISO, PARA ADULTOS

PRÁCTICA PARTICULAR/CLÍNICA

Yo/Nosotros _____ voluntariamente
(padre/tutor o guardian legal)

consiento/consentimos a los servicios proveídos por esta clínica y/o clínico(s) en beneficio de _____
[Nombre(s): niño(s)]

Estos servicios, que me serán explicados, pueden incluir terapia individual, de grupo, de juego, de matrimonio, de familia; consulta y examen psicológico. Yo comprendo que la psicología es una ciencia imperfecta y que no se puede garantizar un beneficio o resultado específico. Yo comprendo que para lograr los mejores resultados, quizás tenga que confrontar sentimientos inquietantes. Quizás me sienta peor antes de empezar a sentirme mejor, y puede ser que experimente tensiones emocionales o efectúe cambios que me pueden causar angustia. Estoy solicitando este tratamiento de mi propia voluntad y soy libre de descontinuarlo en cualquier momento.

Yo comprendo y estoy de acuerdo con las siguientes condiciones:

- Se protegerá la confidencialidad y la información será proporcionada solamente a profesionales competentes y sólo con mi permiso explícito y por escrito, excepto en ciertas situaciones en que el mantener la confidencialidad resultaría en un claro e inminente peligro para mi persona u otros, o en casos como lo manda la ley estatal.
- El terapeuta está obligado por ley a informar a las autoridades apropiadas, sus sospechas de abuso: de niños, de ancianos o de personas con incapacidades. Cuando hay peligro de daño corporal a mi persona u otros, el terapeuta puede violar la confidencialidad de nuestras comunicaciones si surgiera tal situación. Yo comprendo que el terapeuta hará un esfuerzo razonable para resolver dichas situaciones antes de violar la confidencialidad.
- Puedo estar bajo cuidado de un terapeuta que está terminando un título avanzado o que está realizando un internado. En estos casos, las conferencias de consulta serán supervisadas por un psicólogo licenciado o un consejero con las credenciales pertinentes.
- Las conferencias pueden ser grabadas en audio o video, y pueden ser utilizadas como control o como registro del progreso del cliente. Todas las cintas, documentos y materiales concernientes al cliente son confidenciales y no serán proporcionados a ni compartidos con ninguna otra agencia o individuo sin el permiso explícito y por escrito del cliente.
- Mi autorización tendrá que obtenerse por escrito y con mi firma antes que el terapeuta consulte con otros profesionales.
- La información obtenida en las sesiones de consulta pueden ser utilizadas para propósitos de estudio, o presentadas de forma anónima en reuniones profesionales, y/o publicadas en revistas o libros académicos. En ningún momento se usará el nombre del niño o del cliente o ninguna otra información que los pueda identificar.

• Yo comprendo que la terapia cuesta $_____ por hora.

_____ Y/O _____
Cliente   Padre o Guardian Legal
(si es de 18 años o mayor)   (si el cliente es menor de 18 años)

Fecha: _____

EXCERPTS FROM PENNSYLVANIA CHILD PROTECTIVE SERVICES LAW

LEGAL DEFINITIONS OF CHILD ABUSE

"Serious bodily injury." Bodily injury which creates a substantial risk of death or which causes serious permanent disfigurement or protracted loss or impairment of function of any bodily member or organ.

"Serious mental injury." A psychological condition, as diagnosed by a physician or licensed psychologist, including the refusal of appropriate treatment, that:

(1) Renders a child chronically and severely anxious, agitated, depressed, socially withdrawn, psychotic or in reasonable fear that the child's life or safety is threatened; or
(2) Seriously interferes with a child's ability to accomplish age-appropriate developmental and social tasks.

"Serious physical injury." An injury that:

(1) Causes a child severe pain; or
(2) Significantly impairs a child's physical functioning, either temporarily or permanently.

"Sexual abuse or exploitation." The employment, use, persuasion, inducement, enticement or coercion of any child to engage in or assist any other person to engage in any sexually explicit conduct for the purpose of producing any visual depiction, including photographing, videotaping, computer depicting or filming, of any sexually explicit conduct or the rape, sexual assault, involuntary deviate sexual intercourse, aggravated indecent assault, molestation, incest, indecent exposure, prostitution, statutory sexual assault or any other form of sexual exploitation of children....

(1) The term "child abuse" shall mean any of the following:

(i) Any recent act or failure to act by a perpetrator which causes nonaccidental physical injury to a child under 18 years of age.

(ii) An act or failure to act by a perpetrator which causes nonaccidental serious mental injury or sexual abuse or exploitation of a child under 18 years of age.

(iii) Any recent act, failure to act or series of such acts or failures to act by a perpetrator which creates an imminent risk of serious physical injury to or sexual abuse or sexual exploitation of a child under 18 years of age.

(iv) Serious physical neglect by a perpetrator constituting prolonged or repeated lack of supervision or the failure to provide the essentials of life, including adequate medical care, which endangers a child's life or development or impairs the child's functioning.

(2) No child shall be deemed to be physically or mentally abused based on injuries that result solely from environmental factors that are beyond the control of the parent or person responsible for the child's welfare, such as inadequate housing, furnishings, income, clothing and medical care.

(3) If, upon investigation, the county agency determines that a child has not been provided needed medical or surgical care because of seriously held religious beliefs of the child's parents, guardian or person responsible for the child's welfare, which beliefs are consistent with those of a bona fide religion, the child shall not be deemed to be physically or mentally abused. The county agency shall closely monitor the child and shall seek court-ordered medical intervention when the lack of medical or surgical care threatens the child's life or long-term health....

PERSONS REQUIRED TO REPORT SUSPECTED CHILD ABUSE

(a) General rule.—Persons who, in the course of their employment, occupation or practice of their profession come into contact with children shall report or cause a report to be made...when they have reasonable cause to suspect on the basis of their medical, professional or other training and experience, that a child coming before them in their professional or official capacity is an abused child. Except with respect to confidential communications made to an ordained member of the clergy...,the privileged communication between any professional person shall not apply to situations involving child abuse and shall not constitute grounds for failure to report....

IMMUNITY FROM LIABILITY

(a) General rule.—A person, hospital, institution, school facility, agency or agency employee that participates in good faith in making a report, cooperating with an investigation, testifying in a proceeding arising out of an instance of suspected child abuse, the taking of photographs or the removal or keeping of a child (in protective custody),...shall have immunity from any liability civil and criminal, that might otherwise result by reason of those actions.

PENALTIES FOR FAILURE TO REPORT

A person or official required to report a case of suspected child abuse who willfully fails to do so commits a summary offense for the first violation and a misdemeanor of the third degree for a second and subsequent violation....

INSTRUCTIONS FOR REPORTING

Reports from persons required to report suspected child abuse shall be made immediately by telephone and in writing within 48 hours after the *oral report*.

Written reports shall include the following information if available:

1. The names and addresses of the child and the parents or other person responsible for the care of the child if known.
2. Where the suspected abuse occurred.
3. The age and sex of the subjects of the report.
4. The nature and extent of the suspected child abuse including any evidence of prior abuse to the child or siblings of the child.
5. The name and relationship of the person or persons responsible for causing the suspected abuse, if known, and any evidence of prior abuse by that person or persons.
6. Family composition.
7. The source of the report.
8. The person making the report and where that person can be reached.
9. The actions taken by the reporting source, including the taking of photographs and X-rays, removal or keeping of the child or notifying the medical examiner or coroner.
10. Any other information which the department may require by regulation.

This information is quoted from Chapter 63 of the Pennsylvania Child Protection Services Law, ACT 124 of 1975, as amended by Act 10 of 1995.

CHILD EVALUATION OF THE PARENT-CHILD GROUP

1. What did you learn about yourself?

2. What did you learn about parents (and or) children?

3. Did the situations have meaning to you?   Yes _____ No _____

   If not, what would you like to talk about? _____

   _____

   _____

   Did your group work successfully?   Yes _____ No _____

   If not, what changes would you make? _____

   _____

   _____

PARENT EVALUATION OF THE PARENT-CHILD SESSIONS

1. What effect would you say this experience has had on your child?

2. What effect has this experience had on you as a parent?

3. How did this experience affect your relationship with your child?

4. Do you think there were advantages to this group session that were not available to you otherwise?   Yes _____ No _____ If yes, please explain.

5. Do you believe that there were any disadvantages to the parent-child sessions? Yes _____ No _____ If yes, please explain and give a possible way to overcome the disadvantages.

6. Would you recommend that we continue this type of group next year? Yes _____ No _____ If yes, what ages and/or grade levels of children should be included?

REFERENCES

Abramovitch, R., Corter, C., Pepler, D. J., & Stanhope, L. (1986). Sibling and peer interaction: A final follow-up and comparison. *Child development, 47*, 217–229.

Achenbach, T. M., & Edelbrock, C. S. (1983). *Manual for the Child Behavior Checklist and Revised Child Behavior Profile*. Burlington: University of Vermont.

Ainsworth, M. D. S. (1979). Infant-mother attachment. *American Psychologist, 34*, 932–937.

Alexander, H. (1972). The social worker and the family. In C. H. Kempe & R. E. Helfer, (Eds.), *Helping the battered child and his family* (pp. 22–40). Philadelphia: Lippincott.

Allan, J., & Berry, P. (1987, April). Sand play. *Elementary School Guidance and Counseling, 21*(4), 300–306.

Allen, F. (1942). *Psychotherapy with children*. New York: Norton.

Almeida, D. M., Maggs, J. L., & Galambos, N. L. (1993). Wives' employment hours and spousal participation in family work. *Journal of Family Psychology, 7*, 233–244.

American Counseling Association. (1995). *Code of ethics and standards of practice*. Alexandria, VA: Author.

American Psychiatric Association. (1994). *Diagnostic and statistical manual of mental disorders* (4th ed.). Washington, DC: Author.

American Psychological Association. (1992). *Ethical principles of psychologists and code of conduct*. Hyattsville, MD: Author.

American School Health Association. (1992). *National adolescent student health survey: A report on the health of America's youth* (1987–88). Washington, DC: Author.

Ames, L. B., & Learned, J. (1946). The development of verbalized space in the young child. *Journal of Genetic Psychology, 68*, 97–125.

Ansbacher, H. L., & Ansbacher, R. R. (Eds.) (1956). *The individual psychology of Alfred Adler*. New York: Harper & Row.

Aries, P. (1962). *Centuries of childhood: A social history of family life* (R. Baldrick, Trans.). New York: Knopf. (Original work published 1960.)

Artlip, M. A., Artlip, J. A., & Saltzman, E. S. (1993). *The new American family*. Lancaster, PA: Starburst.

Axline, V. M. (1947). *Play therapy*. Cambridge, MA: Houghton Mifflin.

Axline, V. M. (1950). Play therapy experiences as described by child participants. *Journal of Consulting Psychology, 14*, 53–63.

Bandura, A. (1969). *Principles of behavior modification*. New York: Holt, Rinehart & Winston.

Bandura, A. (1977). *Social learning theory*. Englewood Cliffs, NJ: Prentice-Hall.

Barker, P. (1990). *Clinical interviews with children and adolescents*. New York: Norton.

Beer, W. R. (1989). *Strangers in the house: The world of stepsiblings and half-siblings*. New Brunswick, NJ: Transaction.

Bender, L. (1946). *Bender Visual Motor Gestalt Test: Cards and manual of instructions*. The American Orthopsychiatric Association.

Bergin, J. J. (1989). Building group cohesiveness through cooperation activities. *Elementary School Guidance and Counseling, 24*, 90–94.

Berry, F. (1978). Contemporary bibliotherapy: Systematizing the field. In R. Rubin (Ed.), *Bibliotherapy sourcebook* (pp. 185–190). Phoenix, AZ: Oryz Press.

Berry, J. (1987). *Every kid's guide to handling feelings*. Chicago: Children's Press.

Bertoia, J., & Allan, J. (1988). School management of the bereaved child. *Elementary School Guidance and Counseling, 23*, 30–38.

Bettleheim, B. (1987, March). The importance of play. *The Atlantic Monthly*, pp. 35–46.

Beutler, L. E., Oró-Beutler, M. E., & Mitchell, R. (1979). Systematic comparison of two parent training programs in child management. *Journal of Counseling Psychology, 26* (6), 531–533.

Bjorklund, D. F. (1995). *Children's thinking: Developmental function and individual differences* (2nd ed.). Pacific Grove, CA: Brooks/Cole.

Black, C. (1984). Children of alcoholics: The clinical profile. In *Changing legacies: Growing up in an alcoholic home* (pp.73–75). Pompano Beach, FL: Health Communications.

Black, C. (1986). Claudia Black: Children of alcoholics. *Journal of Child and Adolescent Psychotherapy, 3*, (4), 311.

Black, C. (1987). Introduction. In V. Rachel, *Family Secrets: Life stories of adult children of alcoholics*. New York: Harper & Row.

Blau, M.,(1996). *Loving and listening: A parent's book of daily inspirations for rebuilding the family after divorce*. New York: Berkley Publishing.

Blocher, D. H. (1987). *The professional counselor*. New York: Macmillan.

Bluestone, J. (1991). School-based peer therapy to facilitate mourning in latency-age children following sudden paternal death. In N. B. Webb (Ed.), *Play therapy with children in crisis* (pp. 254–275). New York: Guilford Press.

Blume, E. S. (1990). *Secret survivors: Uncovering incest and its aftereffects in women*. New York: Wiley.

Boat, B. W., & Everson, M. D. (1993). The use of anatomical dolls in sexual abuse evaluations: Current research and practice. In G. S. Goodman & B. L. Bottoms (Eds.), *Child victims, child witnesses: Understanding and improving testimony* (pp. 47–70). New York: Guilford Press.

Borke, H. (1973). The development of empathy in Chinese and American children between three and six years of age: A cross-culture study. *Developmental Psychology, 9*, 102–108.

Borke, H. (1975). Piaget's mountains revisited: Changes in the egocentric landscape. *Developmental Psychology, 11*, 240–243.

Bowlby, J. (1969). *Attachment and loss. Vol. 1: Attachment*. London: Hogarth.

Bowlby, J. (1973). *Attachment and loss. Vol. 2: Separation: anxiety and anger*. London: Hogarth.

Bowlby, J. (1980). *Attachment and loss. Vol. 3: Loss: sadness and depression*. New York: Basic Books.

Bowlby, J. (1988). *A secure base: Parent-child attachment and healthy human development*. New York: Basic Books.

Bracken, B. A. (1992). *Multidimensional Self-Concept Scale*. Austin, TX: Pro-Ed.

Brake, K. (1988). Counseling young children of alcoholics. *Elementary School Guidance and Counseling, 23*, 106–111.

Brandt, F., & Pollock, C. B. (1974). A psychiatric study of parents who abuse infants and small children. In R. E. Helfer & C. H. Kempe (Eds.), *The battered child* (2nd ed.) (pp. 89–133). Chicago, IL: University of Chicago Press.

Bremner, R. (1970–1974). *Children and youth in America: A documentary history*. (Vols: I–IV). Cambridge: Harvard University Press.

Brems, C. (1993). *A comprehensive guide to child psychotherapy*. Boston: Allyn & Bacon.

Broken Nose, M. A. (1992, June). Working with the Oglala Lakota: An outsider's perspective. *Families in Society: The Journal of Contemporary Human Services*, 380–384.

Brown, L., & Brown, M. (1986). *Dinosaurs divorce: A guide for changing families*. Boston, MA: Little, Brown.

Buck, J. N. (1948). The H-T-P Test. *Journal of Clinical Psychology, 4*, 151–159.

Burns, R. C. (1982). *Self-growth in families: Kinetic family drawing (K-F-D) research and application*. New York: Brunner/Mazel.

Burns, R. C. (1987). *Kinetic-house-tree-person drawings (K-H-T-P): An interpretative manual*. New York: Brunner/Mazel.

Burns, R. C., & Kaufman, S. H. (1970). *Kinetic family drawings (K-F-D): An introduction to understanding children through kinetic drawings*. New York: Brunner/Mazel.

Burns, R. C., & Kaufman, S. H. (1972). *Actions, styles and symbols in kinetic family drawings (K-F-D): An interpretative manual*. New York: Brunner/Mazel.

Buwick, A., Martin, D., & Martin, M. (1988). Helping children deal with alcoholism in their families. *Elementary School Guidance and Counseling, 23*, 112–117.

Canter, A. (1996). The Bender-Gestalt Test (BGT). In C. S. Newmark (Ed.), *Major psychological assessment instruments*. (2nd ed.), (pp. 400–430). Boston: Allyn & Bacon.

Carkhuff, R. R. (1969). *Helping and human relations: A primer for lay and professional helpers* (Vols. 1 & 2) New York: Holt, Rinehart & Winston.

Carkhuff, R. R. (1987). *The art of helping* (6th ed.). Amherst, MA: Human Resource Development Press.

Casey, R. J., & Berman, J. S. (1985). The outcome of psychotherapy with children. *Psychological Bulletin, 98*, 388–400.

Cassel, R. N. (1962). *The Child Behavior Rating Scale: Manual*. Los Angeles: Western Psychological Services.

Center for the Study of Social Policy. (1993). *Kids count data book*. Washington, DC: Author.

Chase, N. F. (1975–1976). *A child is being beaten*. New York: McGraw-Hill.

Children's Defense Fund (CDF). (1994). *The state of America's children yearbook*. Washington, DC: Author

Clarizio, H. F., & McCoy, G. F. (1983). *Behavior disorders in children* (3rd ed.). New York: Harper & Row.

Cohen, C. P., & Naimark, H. (1991). United Nations Convention on the Rights of the

Child: Individual rights concepts and their significance for social science students. *American Psychologist, 46,* 60–65.

Cohen, F. L. (1993). Epidemiology of HIV infection and AIDS in children. In F. L. Cohen & J. D. Durham (Eds.) *Women, children and HIV/AIDS.* (pp. 137–155). New York: Springer.

Cohen, F. L., & Durham, J. D. (Eds.). (1993). *Women, children, and HIV/AIDS.* New York: Springer.

Collins, G. (1993, November). Where we are now. *Ladies' Home Journal, 110* (11), 198.

Coontz, S. (1992). *The way we never were: American families and the nostalgia trap.* New York: Basic Books.

Corey, G. (1995). *Theory and practice of group counseling* (4th. ed.). Pacific Grove, CA: Brooks/Cole.

Corey, G., Corey, M., & Callanan, P. (1993). *Issues and ethics in the helping professions* (4th ed.). Pacific Grove, CA: Brooks/Cole.

Corey, M. S., & Corey, G. (1992). *Groups: Process and practice* (4th ed.). Pacific Grove, CA: Brooks/Cole.

Cork, M. (1969). *The forgotten children: A study of children with alcoholic parents.* Toronto: Alcoholism and Drug Addiction Research Foundation.

Croake, J. W., & Glover, K. E. (1977, April). A history and evaluation of parent education. *The Family Coordinator, 26,* 151–158.

Crutcher, D. M. (1991). Family support in the home: Home visiting and Public Law 99-457. *American Psychologist, 46* (2), 138–140.

Dale, P. S. (1972). *Language development: Structure and function.* Hinsdale, IL: Dryden Press.

Dembo, M. H., Sweitzer, M., & Lauritzen, P. (1985, Summer). An evaluation of group parent education: Behavioral, PET and Adlerian programs. *Review of Educational Research, 55* (2), 155–200.

Denny, J. M. (1977). Techniques for individual and group art therapy. In E. Ulman & P. Dachinger (Eds.), *Art therapy: In theory and practice* (2nd ed.) (pp. 132–149). New York: Schocken Books.

Di Leo, J. H. (1970). *Young children and their drawings.* New York: Brunner/Mazel.

Di Leo, J. H. (1973). *Children's drawings as diagnostic aids.* New York: Bunner/Mazel.

Di Leo, J. H. (1983). *Interpreting children's drawings.* New York: Brunner/Mazel.

Dinkmeyer, D. (1966). Developmental counseling in the elementary school. *Personnel and Guidance Journal, 45,* 262–266.

Dinkmeyer, D. C., Dinkmeyer, D. C., Jr., & Sperry, L. (1987). *Adlerian counseling and psychotherapy* (2nd ed.). Columbus, OH: Merrill.

Dinkmeyer, D. C., & Dreikurs, R. (1963). *Encouraging children to learn: The encouragement process.* Englewood Cliffs, NJ: Prentice-Hall.

Dinkmeyer, D. C., & McKay, G. D. (1976). *Systematic Training for Effective Parenting* (STEP). Circle Pines, MN: American Guidance Services.

Dinkmeyer, D. C., & McKay, G. D. (1983). *Systematic Training for Effective Parenting of Teens.* (STEP/Teen). Circle Pines, MN: American Guidance Service.

Dinkmeyer, D. C., Pew, W. L., & Dinkmeyer, D.C., Jr. (1979). *Adlerian counseling and psychotherapy.* Pacific Grove, CA: Brooks/Cole.

Donaldson, M. (1978). *Children's minds.* New York: Norton.

Dorfman, E. (1951). Play therapy. In C. R. Rogers, *Client-centered therapy: Its current practice, implications, and theory* (pp. 235–277). Boston: Houghton Mifflin.

Dougherty, A. M. (1992). Ethical issues in consultation. *Elementary School Guidance and Counseling, 26*, 214–220.

Dreikurs, R. (1958). *The challenge of parenthood*. New York: Meredith Press.

Dreikurs, R., & Grey, L. (1968). *A new approach to discipline*. New York: Hawthorne Books.

Dreikurs, R., & Soltz, V. (1964). *Children: The challenge*. New York: Hawthorne Books.

Dunn, J., & Munn, P. (1985). Becoming a family member: Family conflict and the development of social understanding in the second year. *Child Development, 56*, 480–492.

Dunn, J., & Kendrick, C. (1982). *Siblings: Love, envy and understanding*. Cambridge, MA: Harvard University Press.

Dvorchak, R. (1994, September, 6). Back to school: Districts try to get guns out of the classrooms. *Erie Morning News*, pp. 1A–2A.

Eddy, B. (1988, April). Quiet rebirth. *Elementary School Guidance and Counseling, 22*, 313.

Egan, G. (1994). *The skilled helper: A problem-management approach to helping* (5th ed.). Pacific Grove, CA: Brooks/Cole.

Elkind, D. (1988). *The hurried child: Growing up too fast too soon* (Rev. ed.). New York: Addison-Wesley.

Elkind, D. (1990). *Grandparenting: Understanding today's children*. Glenview, IL: Scott, Foresman.

Erikson, E. (1950). *Childhood and society*. New York: Norton.

Eysenck, H. J. (1952). The effects of psychotherapy: An evaluation. *Journal of Consulting Psychology, 16*, 319–324.

Fassler, D., Lash, M., & Ives, S. (1988). *Changing families: A guide for kids and grown-ups*. Burlington, VT: Waterford Books.

Federal Educational Rights and Privacy Act of 1974, P.L. 93-380, 788 Stat. 484.

Finney, P. B. (1993, May 17). The PTA/Newsweek National Education Survey. *Newsweek*, pp. 10-14.

Flavel, J. H. (1985). *Cognitive development* (2nd ed.). Englewood Cliffs, NJ: Prentice Hall.

Fontana, V. J. (1984, October). Introduction: The maltreatment syndrome of children. *Pediatric Annals, 13*, 736–744.

Frank, J. (1961). *Persuasion and healing: A contemporary study of psychotherapy* (rev. ed.). Baltimore, MD: John Hopkins University Press.

Freeman, C. W. (1975). Adlerian mother study groups: Effects on attitudes and behaviors. *Journal of Individual Psychology, 31*, 37–50.

Freud, A. (1946). *Psychoanalytic treatment of children*. London: Imago Press. (Original work published 1926.)

Frey, D. E. (1986). Communication boardgames with children. In C. E. Schaefer & S. E. Reid (Eds.), *Game play: Therapeutic use of childhood games* (pp. 21–39). New York: Wiley.

Frey, D. H. (1972). Conceptualizing counseling theories: A content analysis of process and goal statements. *Counselor Education and Supervision, 11* (4), 243–250.

Furman, W., & Buhrmester, D. (1985). Children's perceptions of the qualities of sibling relationships. *Child Development, 56,* 448–461.

Garbarino, J., Kostelny, K., & Dubrow, N. (1991, April). What children can tell us about living in danger. *American Psychologist, 46,* (4), 376–383.

Gardner, R. A. (1971). *Therapeutic communication with children: The mutual story-telling technique.* New York: Science House.

Gardner, R. A. (1993). Mutual Storytelling. In C. E. Schaefer & D. M. Cangelosi (Eds.), *Play therapy techniques* (pp. 199–209). Northvale, NJ: Aronson.

Garner, D. M. (1991). *Eating Disorder Inventory-2.* Odessa, FL: Psychological Assessment Resources, Inc.

Gately, D., & Schwebel, A. I. (1992). Favorable outcomes in children after parental divorce. *Journal of Divorce and Remarriage, 18,* (3), 4, 57–78.

Gazda, G., Duncan, J., & Meadows, M. (1967). Group counseling and group procedures: Report of a survey. *Counselor Education and Supervision, 9,* 305–310.

Gelman, R. (1982). Basic numerical abilities. In R. J. Sternberg (Ed.), *Advances in psychology of human intelligence* (Vol. 1). Hillsdale, NJ: Erlbaum.

Gelman, R., Meck, E., & Merkin, S. (1986). Young children's numerical competence. *Cognitive Development, 1,* 1–29.

Gerler, E. R. (1993). Parents, families and the schools. *Elementary School Guidance and Counseling, 27,* 243.

Gibson, J. (1978). *Growing up: A study of children.* Reading, MA: Addison-Wesley.

Gil, E. (1991). *The healing power of play: Working with abused children.* New York: Guilford Press.

Gilmore, M. (1994a). *Shot in the heart.* New York: Doubleday.

Gilmore, M. (1994b). *Shot in the heart: Book group companion.* (pp. 5–24). New York: Doubleday.

Ginott, H. G. (1960). A rationale for selecting toys in play therapy. *Journal of Consulting Psychology, 24* (3), 243–246.

Ginott, H. G. (1979). Therapeutic intervention in child treatment. In C. E. Schaefer (Ed.), *The therapeutic use of child's play* (pp. 279–290). Northvale, NJ: Aronson.

Glenwick, D. S, & Mowrey, J. D. (1986). When parent becomes peer: Loss of intergenerational boundaries in single parent families. *Family Relations, 35,* 57–62.

Glick, P. C. (1989). Remarried families, stepfamilies, and stepchildren: A brief demographic profile. *Family Relations, 38,* 24–27.

Goldenberg, H., & Goldenberg, I. (1990). *Counseling today's families.* Pacific Grove, CA: Brooks/Cole

Goldstein, S. L. (1987). *The sexual exploitation of children: A practical guide to assessment, investigation and intervention.* New York: Elsevier Science Publishing.

Goodenough, F. L. (1931). *Anger in young children.* Minneapolis: University of Minnesota Press.

Goodman, E. (1995, September 20). End of "motherhood" ideal. *Erie Morning News,* p. 2B.

Gordon, T. (1970). *PET: Parent effectiveness training.* New York: Wyden.

Gordon, T., & Sands, J. (1978). *P.E.T. in action.* New York: Bantam.

Greenspan, S. I., with Greenspan, N. T. (1981). *The clinical interview of the child.* New York: McGraw-Hill.

Greenspan, S. I., with Greenspan, N. T. (1991). *The clinical interview of the child.* (2nd ed.). New York: American Psychiatric Press.

Griff, M. D. (1983). Family play therapy. In C. E. Schaefer & K. J. O'Connor (Eds.), *Handbook of play therapy* (pp. 65–75). New York: Wiley.

Griffin, J. L., & Waltz, T. (1991, December). Schools offer hope for cocaine babies. *Chicago Tribune.*

Grisso, T., & Vierling, L. (1978). Minors' consent to treatment. A developmental perspective. *Professional Psychology, 9* (3), 412–425.

Group for the Advancement of Psychiatry. (1982). *The process of child therapy.* New York: Brunner/Mazel

Grunwald, B. B., & McAbee, H. V. (1985). *Guiding the family: Practical counseling techniques.* Muncie, IN: Accelerated Development.

Guerney, B. (1964). Filial therapy: Description and rationale. *Journal of Counseling Psychology, 28,* 304–310.

Gumaer, J. (1984). *Counseling and therapy for children.* New York: Free Press.

Gustafson, K. E., & McNamara, J. R. (1987). Confidentiality with minor clients: Issues and guidelines for therapists. *Professional Psychology: Research and Practice, 18,* 503–508.

Halperin, E. N. (1993). Denial in children whose parents died of AIDS. *Child Psychiatry and Human Development, 23* (4), 249–257.

Hambridge, G. (1955). Structured play therapy. *American Journal of Orthopsychiatry, 25,* 601–617.

Hambridge, G. (1979). Structured play therapy. In C. E. Schaefer (Ed.), *Therapeutic use of child's play* (pp. 187–206). Northvale, NJ: Aronson.

Hamman v. County of Maricopa, 775 P. 2d 1122 (Ariz. 1990).

Hammer, E. F. (1971). *The clinical application of projective drawings.* Springfield, IL: Charles C Thomas.

Handler, L. (1996). The clinical use of drawings: Draw-A-Person, House-Tree-Person, and Kinetic Family Drawings. In C. S. Newmark (Ed.). *Major psychological assessment instruments* (2nd ed.) (pp. 206–293). Boston: Allyn & Bacon.

Hansen, J. C., Rossberg, R. H., & Cramer, S. H. (1994). *Counseling: Theory and process* (5th ed.). Boston: Allyn & Bacon.

Hansen, J. C., Warner, R. W., & Smith, E. M. (1980). *Group counseling: Theory and process* (2nd ed.). Chicago: Rand McNally.

Hardy, K. V., & Laszloffy, T. A. (1992, June). Training racially sensitive family therapists: Context, content and contact. *Families in Society: The Journal of Contemporary Human Services,* 364–370.

Hart, S. N. (1991). From property to person status. Historical perspective on children's rights. *American Psychologist, 46,* 53–59.

Hartup, W. W. (1974). Aggression in childhood: Developmental perspectives. *American Psychologist, 29,* 236–341.

Hayes, R. (1989). Homeless children. In F. Macchiarola and A. Gartner (Eds.) *Caring for America's Children.* New York: Academy of Political Science.

Heitler, S. (1985). *David decides: No more thumb-sucking.* Denver, CO: Reading Matters.

Helfer, R. E. (1980). Developmental deficits which limit interpersonal skills. In C. E. Kempe & R. E. Helfer (Eds.), *The battered child* (3rd ed.) (pp. 36–48). Chicago: University of Chicago Press.

Helfer, R. E., & Kempe, R. S. (1987). *The battered child* (4th ed.). Chicago: University of Chicago Press.

Henry, P. (1993, May 17). Finally: Children first. *Newsweek*, pp. 4–5.

Herman-Giddens, M. (1984, November). Diagnosing and treating sexually abused children. *PA Consultations*, 12–15.

Hewlitt, S. A. (1991) *When the bough breaks: The cost of neglecting our children*. New York: Basic Books.

Hochschild, A., with Machung, A. (1989). *The second shift: Working parents and the revolution at home*. New York: Viking Press.

Hollander, S. K. (1989, February). Coping with child sexual abuse through children's books. *Elementary School Guidance and Counseling, 23*, 183–193.

Horwitz, L. (1974). *Clinical prediction and psychotherapy*. New York: Aronson.

Huber, C. H. (1994). *Transitioning from individual to family counseling*. Alexandra, VA: American Counseling Association.

Hurlock, E. (1978). *Child development* (6th ed.). New York: McGraw-Hill.

Information Legislative Service (ILS). (1995, February 10) *Federal act requires states to pass gun-free schools laws*. (Vol. 33, No. 6, p. 9). Harrisburg, PA: Author.

Irwin, E. C. (1983). The diagnostic and therapeutic use of pretend play. In C.E. Schaefer & K. J. O'Connor (Eds.), *Handbook of play therapy* (pp. 148–173). New York: Aronson.

Irwin, E. C. (1993). Using puppets for assessment. In C. E. Schaefer & D. M. Cangelosi (Eds.), *Play therapy techniques* (pp. 69–81). Northvale, NJ: Aronson.

Irwin, E. C., & Malloy, E. S. (1975). Family puppet interview. *Family Process, 14*, 179–191.

Ives, S., Fassler, D., & Lash, M. (1985). *The divorce workbook: A guide for kids and families*. Burlington, VT: Waterford Books.

Jagim, R. D., Wittman, W. D., & Noll, J. O. (1978). Mental health professionals' attitudes toward confidentiality, privilege and third-party disclosures. *Professional Psychology, 9* (3), 458–66.

Jenkins, R. L., & Beckh, E. (1993). Finger puppets and mask making. In C. E. Schaefer & D. M. Cangelosi (Eds.), *Play therapy techniques* (pp. 83–90). Northvale, NJ: Aronson.

Jenson, W. R., Rhode, G., & Reavis, H. K. (1996). *What, me worry?: Practical solutions to everyday parenting problems*. Longmont, CO: Sopris West.

Jernberg, A. M. (1983). Therapeutic use of sensory-motor play. In C. E. Schaefer & K. J. O'Connor (Eds.), *Handbook of play therapy* (pp. 128–147). New York: Wiley.

Jersild, A. T. (1960). *Child psychology*. Englewood Cliffs, NJ: Prentice-Hall.

Jersild, A. T., & Holmes, F. B. (1935). Children's fears. *Child Development Monographs*, No. 20. New York: Teachers College, Columbia University.

Johnston, S. A. (1987, February). The mind of a molester. *Psychology Today, 21*, pp. 60–63.

Jones, D., & Alexander, H. (1987). Treating the abusive family. In R. E. Helfer & R. S. Kempe (Eds.), *The battered child* (4th ed.) (pp. 339–359). Chicago: University of Chicago Press.

Kantrowitz, B., & Wingert, P. (1990, Feb.). The crack children: Their troubles don't end in infancy. *News Monitor*, pp. 18–19.

Kazdin, A. E. (1978). *History of behavior modification: Experimental foundations of contemporary research*. Baltimore: University Park Press.

Kazdin, A. E. (1994). *Behavior modification in applied settings* (5th ed.). Pacific Grove, CA: Brooks/Cole.

Kazdin, A. E. (1995). Scope of child and adolescent psychotherapy research: Limited sampling of dysfunction, treatments, and client characteristics. *Journal of Clinical Child Psychology, 24*, 125–140.

Kellogg, R., with O'Dell, S. (1967). *The psychology of children's art*. New York: CRM-Random House.

Kempe, C. H. (1980). Incest and other forms of sexual abuse. In C. H. Kempe & R. E. Helfer (Eds.), *The battered child* (3rd ed.), (pp. 198–214). Chicago: University of Chicago Press.

Kempe, C. H., & Helfer, R. E. (1972). Innovative therapeutic approaches. In C. H. Kempe & R. E. Helfer (Eds.), *Helping the battered child and his family* (pp. 41–54). Philadelphia: Lippincott.

Kempe, C. H., & Helfer, R. E. (Eds.) (1980). *The battered child* (3rd ed.). Chicago: University of Chicago Press.

Kempe, C. H., Silverman, F. N., Steele, B. F., Droegemueller, W., & Silver, H. K. (1962). The battered child syndrome. *Journal of the American Medical Association, 181*, 105–112.

Kempe, R. S., & Kempe, C. H. (1978). *Child abuse*. Cambridge, MA: Harvard University Press.

Kendall, P. C., & Panichelli-Mindel, S. M. (1995). Cognitive-behavioral treatments. *Journal of Abnormal Child Psychology, 23*, 107–123.

Kern, R. M., & Carlson, J. (1981, April). Adlerian family counseling. *Elementary School Guidance and Counseling, 15*, 301–306.

Klein, M. (1932). *The psychoanalysis of children*. London: Hogarth.

Kluft, K. P. (1984). Child abuse in eight cases of multiple personality. *Psychiatric Clinics of North America, 7*, 37–49.

Kohn, A. (1987, February). Shattered innocence. *Psychology Today, 21*, pp. 54–58.

Koocher, G. P. (1973). Childhood, death, and cognitive development. *Developmental Psychology, 9*, 369–375.

Kopp, C., & Krakow, J. (1982). *The child: Development in a social context*. Reading, MA: Addison-Wesley.

Koppitz, E. M. (1963). *The Bender Gestalt Test for young children*. New York: Grune & Stratton.

Korner, A. (1974). The effects of the infant's level of arousal, sex and ontogenetic stage on the caregiver. In M. Lewis & L. Rosenblum (Eds.), *The effect of the infant on its caregiver*. New York: Wiley.

Kottman, T. (1993). The king of rock and roll: An application of Adlerian play therapy. In T. Kottman & C. Schaefer (Eds.), *Play therapy in action: A casebook for practitioners* (pp. 133–167). Northvale, NJ: Aronson.

Kottman, T., & Johnson, V. (1993, October). Adlerian play therapy: A tool for school counselors. *Elementary School Guidance and Counseling, 28*, 42–51.

Kottman, T., & Schaefer, C. (Eds.). (1993). *Play therapy in action: A casebook for practitioners*. Northvale, NJ: Aronson.

Kottman, T., & Stiles, K. (1990). The mutual storytelling technique: An Adlerian application in child therapy. *Individual Psychology, 46*(2), 148–156.

Kramer, E. (1958). *Art therapy in a children's community*. Springfield, IL: Charles C Thomas.

Kramer, E. (1971). *Art as therapy with children*. New York: Schocken Books.

Kramer, E. (1979). *Childhood and art therapy*. New York: Schocken Books.

Kramer, E., & Schehr, J. (1983). An art therapy evaluation session for children. *American Journal of Art Therapy, 23*, 3–12.

Krementz, J. (1988). *When a parent dies*. New York: Knopf.

Krumboltz, J. D., & Krumboltz, H. B. (1972). *Changing children's behavior*. Englewood Cliffs, NJ: Prentice-Hall.

Kübler-Ross, E. (1983). *On children and death*. New York: Macmillan.

Kuhli, L. (1979). The use of two houses in play therapy. *American Journal of Orthopsychiatry, 49*(3), 431–435.

Kuhli, L. (1993). The use of two houses in play therapy. In C. E. Schaefer & D. M. Cangelosi (Eds.), *Play therapy techniques* (pp. 63–68). Northvale, NJ: Aronson.

Kwiatkowska, H. Y. (1977). Family art therapy: Experiments with a new technique. In E. Ulman & P. Dachinger (Eds.), *Art therapy: In theory and practice* (2nd ed.) (pp. 113–125). New York: Schocken Books.

Kwiatkowska, H. Y. (1978). *Family therapy and evaluation through art*. Springfield: IL: Charles C Thomas.

LaGrange, R. L. (1993). *Policing American society*. Chicago: Nelson-Hall.

Landau-Stanton, J., & Clements, C. D., and Associates. (1993). *AIDS, health, and mental health: A primary sourcebook*. New York: Brunner/Mazel.

Landgarten, H. B. (1981). *Clinical art therapy: A comprehensive guide*. New York: Brunner/Mazel.

Landreth, G. L. (1987). Play therapy: Facilitative use of child's play in elementary school counseling. *Elementary School Guidance and Counseling, 2* (4), 253–261.

Landreth, G. L. (1991). *Play therapy: The art of the relationship*. Muncie, IN: Accelerated Development, Inc.

Lane, R. D., & Swartz, G. E. (1987). Levels of emotional awareness: A cognitive-developmental theory and its application to psychopathology. *American Journal of Psychiatry, 144* (2), 133–143.

Lauter-Klattell, N. (Ed.). (1991). *Readings in child development*. Mountain View, CA: Mayfield.

Lefrancois, G. R. (1990). *The lifespan* (3rd ed.). Belmont, CA: Wadsworth.

Lehrmann, E. (1995, March-April). Help for the caregiving grandparent. *Modern Maturity*, pp. i-iii.

Levin, D. S. (1985). *Developmental experiences: Treatment of developmental disorders in children*. New York: Aronson.

Levy, D. (1939). Release therapy. *American Journal of Orthopsychiatry, 9*, 713–736.

Levy, D. (1979). Release therapy. In C. E. Schaefer (Ed.), *The therapeutic use of child's play* (pp. 173–186). Northvale, NJ: Aronson.

In re Lifschutz, 476 P. 2d 577 (Cal. 1970).

Linesch, D. (Ed.). (1993). *Art therapy with families in crisis: Overcoming resistance through nonverbal expression*. New York: Brunner/Mazel.

Lowenfeld, V. (1957). *Creative and mental growth* (3rd ed.). New York: Macmillan.

Lowenfeld, V., & Brittain, W. L. (1987). *Creative and mental growth* (8th ed.). New York: Macmillan.

Lüscher, M. (1969). *The Lüscher color test* (I. Scott, Ed. and Trans.). New York: Random House.

Machover, K. (1949). *Personality projection in the drawing of the human figure.* Springfield, IL: Charles C Thomas.

Mahler, C. Q. (1969). *Group counseling in the schools.* Boston: Houghton Mifflin.

Main, F. (1986). *Perfect parenting and other myths.* Minneapolis, MN: CompCare Publications.

Massachusetts Mutual American Family Values Study. (1989). Washington, DC: Mellman & Lazarus.

McGrath, L. P., & Scobey, J. (Eds.). (1970a) *What is a brother?* New York: Simon & Schuster.

McGrath, L. P., & Scobey, J. (Eds.). (1970b) *What is a sister?* New York: Simon & Schuster.

Melton, G. B. (1991). Socialization in the global community: Respect for the dignity of children. *American Psychologist, 46,* 66–71.

Menendez v. Superior Court, 834 P.2d 786, (Cal.1992).

Mercer, C. D., Peterson, S. K., & Ross, J. (1988). A university-based model of multi-disciplinary services to exceptional students and related professionals. *Focus on Exceptional Children, 2* (2), 1–12.

Miles, B. (1975). *Around and around love.* New York: Knopf.

Miller, A. (1990). *For your own good: Hidden cruelty in child-rearing and the roots of violence* (H. & H. Hannun, Trans.). New York: Noonday Press. (Original work published 1980.)

Miller, G. A. (1981). *Language and speech.* New York: W. H. Freeman.

Miller, S. P., & Hudson, P. (1994). Using structured parent groups to provide parental support. *Intervention in School and Clinic, 29* (3), 151–155.

Minton, L. (1994, October 2). Fresh voices: A teenager copes with being homeless. *Parade Magazine,* p. 32.

Morris-Vann, A. M. (1979). *Once upon a time...A guide to the use of bibliotherapy.* Oak Park, MI: Aid-U Publishing Co.

Moses, H., & Zaccaria, J. (1978). *Bibliotherapy in rehabilitation, educational, and mental health settings.* Champaign, IL: Stripes.

Moustakas, C. (1959). *Psychotherapy with children.* New York: Harper & Row

National Association of Social Workers. (1990). *Code of ethics.* Silver Spring, MD: Author.

National Center for Injury Prevention and Control (NCIPC). (1995, March. 24) *Youth risk behavior surveillance—United States, 1993* (Vol. 44, No. SS-1, pp. 5–34). Atlanta, GA: Centers for Disease Control and Prevention.

National Commission on Children. (1991). *Beyond rhetoric: A new American agenda for children and families.* Washington, DC: U.S. Government Printing Office.

National Research Council. (1993). *Understanding child abuse and neglect.* Washington, DC: Author.

Naumburg, M. (1966). *Dynamically oriented art therapy: Its principles and practice.* New York: Grune & Stratton.

Newmark, C. (Ed.). (1996). *Major psychological assessment instruments*. (2nd ed.). Boston: Allyn & Bacon.

Niles, F. S. (1993, January). Issues in multicultural counselor education. *Journal of Multicultural Counseling and Development, 21,* 14–21.

O'Connor, K. J. (1991). *The play therapy primer: An integration of theories and techniques*. New York: Wiley.

O'Connor, K. J., & Schaefer, C. E. (Eds.). (1994). *Handbook of play therapy: Vol. 2: Advances and innovations*. New York: Wiley.

O'Rourke, K. (1990). Recapturing hope: Elementary school support groups for children of alcoholics. *Elementary School Guidance and Counseling, 25,* 107–115.

Orton, G. L. (1982). A comparative study of children's worries. *Journal of Psychology 110,* 153–162.

Oster, G. D., & Gould, P. (1987). *Using drawings in assessment and therapy: A guide for mental health professionals*. New York: Brunner/Mazel.

Padilla, M. L., & Landreth, G. L. (1989). *Latchkey children: A review of the literature*. Washington, DC: Child Welfare League of America.

Papalia, D. E., & Olds, S. W. (1996). *A child's world: Infancy through adolescence* (7th ed.). New York: McGraw-Hill.

Pardeck, J. T., & Pardeck, J. A. (1984). *Young people with problems: A guide to bibliotherapy*. Westport, CT: Greenwood Press.

Pardeck, J. T., & Pardeck, J. A. (1986). *Books for early childhood: A developmental perspective*. Westport, CT: Greenwood Press.

Pardeck, J. T., & Pardeck, J. A. (1993). *Bibliotherapy: A clinical approach for helping children*. Landhorne, PA: Gordon & Breach Science Publishers.

Pearce, J. C. (1992). *Evolutions end*. San Francisco, CA: HarperCollins.

Peck v. Counseling Services of Addison County, 499 A.2d 422 (Vt. 1985).

Pennsylvania Dept. of Public Welfare. (1993). *Child abuse report*. Harrisburg, PA: Office of Children and Youth.

Peterson, L. (1989). Latchkey children's preparation for self-care: Overestimated, underrehearsed, and unsafe. *Journal of Clinical Child Psychology, 18,* 36–43.

Phelps, L., Augustyniak, K., Nelson, L. D., & Nathanson, D. S. (in press). Adolescent eating disorders: Chronic dieting and body dissatisfaction. In G. Bear & K. Minke (Eds.), *Children's Needs II*. Bethesda, MD: National Association of School Psychologists.

Piaget, J. (1950). *The psychology of intelligence*. San Diego, CA: Harcourt, Brace & Jovanovich.

Piaget, J. (1962). *Play, dreams and imitation in childhood*. New York: Norton.

Piaget, J., & Inhelder, B. (1969). *The psychology of the child*. New York: Basic Books.

Pill, C. J. (1990). Stepfamilies: Redefining the family. *Family Relations, 39,* 188–193.

Platt, A. (1969). *The child savers*. Chicago: University of Chicago Press.

Popenoe, D. (1993, August). American family decline, 1960–1990: A review and appraisal. *Journal of Marriage and the Family, 55,* 527–545.

Postman, N. (1991). The disappearance of childhood. In N. Lauter-Klatell (Ed.), *Readings in child development* (pp. 109–114). Mountain View, CA: Mayfield.

Radbill, S. X. (1980). Children in a world of violence: A history of child abuse. In C.

H. Kempe & R. E. Helfer (Eds.), *The battered child* (3rd ed.) (pp. 3–20). Chicago: University of Chicago Press.

Reid, S. E. (1991). AIDS in the family. In Nancy B. Webb (Ed.), *Play therapy with children in crisis* (pp. 333–352). New York: Guilford Press.

Reynolds v. State, 633 A.2d 455 (Md. Ct. Spec. App.1993).

Rhyne, J. (1973). *The Gestalt art experience*. Pacific Grove, CA: Brooks/Cole.

Rhyne, J. (1987). Gestalt art therapy. In J. A. Rubin (Ed.), *Approaches to art therapy: Theory and technique* (pp. 167–187). New York: Brunner/Mazel.

Richardson, J. L., Dwyer, K., McGrugan, K., Hansen, W. B., Dent, C., Johnson, C.A., Sussman, S.Y., Brannon, B., & Glay, B. (1989). Substance use among eighth grade students who take care of themselves after school. *Pediatrics, 84*, 556–566.

Rinas, J., & Clyne-Jackson, S. (1988). *Professional conduct and legal concerns in mental health practice*. Norwalk, CT: Appleton & Lange.

Robbins, A., & Sibley, L. B. (1976). *Creative art therapy*. New York: Brunner/Mazel.

Roberts, R. N., Wasik, B. H., Casto, G., & Ramey, C. T. (1991). Family support in the home: Programs, policy and social change. *American Psychologist, 46* (2), 131–137.

Roberts, S. (1993). *Who we are: A portrait of America*. New York: Random House.

Rogers, C. R. (1951). *Client-centered therapy: Its current practice, implications, and theory*. Boston: Houghton Mifflin.

Rogers, C. R. (1957). The necessary and sufficient conditions of therapeutic personality change. *Journal of Counseling Psychology, 21*, 95–103.

Rogers, C. R. (1961). *On becoming a person: A therapist's view of psychotherapy*. Boston: Houghton Mifflin.

Rosewater, A. (1989). Child and family trends: Beyond the numbers. In F. Macchiarola & A. Gartner (Eds.), *Caring for America's children* (pp. 4–19). New York: Academy of Political Science.

Rowan, C. (1993, July 13). Blaming TV for violence too easy. *Erie Daily Times*, p. 2B.

Rubin, J. A. (1984). *Child art therapy: Understanding and helping children grow through art* (2nd ed.). New York: Van Nostrand Reinhold.

Rubin, J. A. (Ed.). (1987). *Approaches to art therapy: Theory and technique*. New York: Brunner/Mazel.

Rubin, J. A. (1988). Art counseling: An alternative. *Elementary School Guidance and Counseling, 22*, 180–185.

Rubin, J. A., & Magnussen, M. G. (1974). A family art evaluation. *Family Process, 13*, 185–200.

Rubin, L. J., & Borgers, S. B. (1991, September). The changing family: Implications for education. *Principal*, 11–13.

Ryan, M. (1995, Aug. 6). There's nothing better than a big brother or a big sister. *Parade Magazine*, pp. 8–10.

Sandberg, D. N., Crabbs, S. K., & Crabbs, M. A. (1988, April). Legal issues in child abuse: Questions and answers for counselors. *Elementary School Guidance and Counseling, 22*, 268–274.

Sanford, D. (1986). *I can't talk about it*. Portland, OR: Multnamah Press.

Santrock, J. W. (1994). *Child development* (6th ed). Dubuque, IA: Wm. C. Brown.

Saravay, B. (1991). Short-term play therapy with two preschool brothers following sudden paternal death. In N. B. Webb (Ed.), *Play therapy with children in crisis* (pp. 177–201). New York: Guilford Press.

Schaefer, C. E., (Ed.). (1988). *Innovative interventions in child and adolescent therapy.* New York: Wiley.

Schaefer, C. E., & Briesmeister, J. M. (Eds.). (1989). *Handbook of parent training: Parents as co-therapists for children's behavior problems.* New York: Wiley.

Schaefer, C. E., & Cangelosi, D. M. (Eds.). (1993). *Play therapy techniques.* Northvale, NJ: Aronson.

Schaefer, C. E., & O'Connor, K. J. (Eds.). (1983). *Handbook of play therapy.* New York: Wiley.

Schaefer, C. E., & Reid, S. E. (Eds.). (1986). *Game play: Therapeutic use of childhood games.* New York: Wiley.

Schor, J. (1992). *The overworked American.* New York: Basic Books.

Schrank, F. (1982, February). Bibliotherapy as an elementary school counseling tool. *Elementary School Guidance and Counseling, 16,* 218–227.

Schrank, F. A., & Engels, D. W. (1981, November). Bibliotherapy as a counseling adjunct: Research findings. *The Personnel and Guidance Journal, 60,* 143–147.

Schutz, B. M. (1982). *Legal liability in psychotherapy.* San Francisco: Jossey-Bass.

Selman, R. L. (1980). *The growth of interpersonal understanding.* New York: Academic Press.

Selman, R. L. (1981). The child as friendship philosopher. In S. R. Asher & J. M. Gottman (Eds.), *The development of children's friendships.* New York: Cambridge University Press.

Shaffer, D. R. (1989). *Developmental psychology: Childhood and adolescence.* (2nd ed.). Pacific Grove, CA: Brooks/Cole.

Shamroy, J. A. (1987). Interviewing the sexually abused child with anatomically correct dolls. *Social Work, 32,* 165–166.

Shaw v. Glickman, 415 A. 2nd 625 (Md. Ct. Spec. App. 1980).

Sherman, R., & Dinkmeyer, D. (1987). *Systems of family therapy: An Adlerian integration.* New York: Brunner/Mazel.

Sidel, R. (1973). *Women and child care in China.* Baltimore: Penguin Books.

Simon, R. (1972). Sculpting the family. *Family Process, 11,* 49–59.

Skinner, B. F. (1971). *Beyond freedom and dignity.* New York: Free Press.

Smart, M. S., & Smart, R. C. (1977). *Children: Development and relationships* (3rd ed.). New York: Macmillan.

Smilansky, S. (1968). *The effects of sociodramatic play on disadvantaged preschool children.* New York: Wiley.

Smith, C. A. (1989). *From wonder to wisdom: Using stories to help children grow.* New York: New American Library.

Solomon, A. (1992, June). Clinical diagnosis among diverse populations: A multicultural perspective. *Families in Society: The Journal of Contemporary Human Services,* 371–377.

Spielberger, C. D. (Ed.). (1972). *Anxiety: Current trends in theory and research.* (Vol. 1 and 2). New York: Academic Press.

Steele, B. (1980). Psychodynamic factors in child abuse. In C. H. Kempe & R. E. Helfer (Eds.), *The battered child.* (3rd ed.) (pp. 49–85). Chicago:University of Chicago Press.

Steele, B. (1987). Psychodynamic factors in child abuse. In R. E. Helfer & R. S.

Kempe (Eds.), *The battered child* (4th ed.) (pp. 81–114). Chicago: University of Chicago Press.

Stone, N. (1993). Parental abuse as a precursor to childhood onset depression and suicidality. *Child Psychiatry and Human Development, 24* (1), 13–24.

Strangeland, C. S., Pellegreno, D. D., & Lundholm, J. (1989). Children of divorced parents: A perceptual comparison. *Elementary School Guidance and Counseling, 23,* 167–173.

Sutton-Smith, B. (1976). A developmental structural account of riddles. In B. Kirschenblatt-Gimblett (Ed.), *Speech play.* Philadelphia, PA: University of Pennsylvania Press.

Swenson, L. C. (1993). *Psychology and law for the helping professions.* Pacific Grove, CA: Brooks/Cole.

Tarasoff v. Regents of the University of California, 551 P.2d 334 (Cal., 1976).

Tavantzis, T. (1984), Family therapy: An introduction to a structural perspective. In J. Gumaer, *Counseling and therapy for children* (pp. 287–314). New York: Free Press.

Terry, S. (October, 1991). Children are falling victim to a new kind of sexual offender—other children. *Rolling Stone,* pp. 67–72.

Thompson, C. L., & Rudolph, L. B. (1996). *Counseling children* (4th ed.). Pacific Grove, CA: Brooks/Cole.

Thorndike, R. L., Hagan, E. P., & Sattler, J. M. (1986). *Guide for administering and scoring the Stanford-Binet Intelligence Scale: Fourth edition.* Chicago: Riverside Publishing.

Tuma, J. (1989). Mental health services for children: The state of the art. *American Psychologist, 44* (2), 188–199.

Ulman, E., Kramer, E., & Kwiatkowska, H. (1978). *Art therapy in the United States.* Craftsbury Common, VT: Art Therapy Publications.

United Nations General Assembly. (1989). *Adoption of a convention on the rights of the child.* New York: Author.

U.S. Bureau of the Census (1989). *Studies in marriage and the family.* Current Population Reports (Series P-23, No. 162). Washington, DC: U.S. Government Printing Office.

U.S. Bureau of the Census (1994a). *The diverse living arrangements of children: Summer, 1991.* Current Population Reports (Series P-70, No. 38). Washington, DC: U.S. Government Printing Office.

U.S. Bureau of the Census (1994b). *Who's minding the kids? Child care arrangements: Fall, 1991.* Current Population Reports (Series P-70, No. 36). Washington, DC: U.S. Government Printing Office.

U.S. Department of Justice. (1991) *Uniform crime reports for the United States.* Washington, DC: U.S. Government Printing Office.

V., Rachel (1987). *Family secrets: Life stories of adult children of alcoholics.* San Francisco: Harper & Row.

Vasta, R., Haith, M. M., & Miller, S. A. (1995). *Child psychology: The modern science* (2nd ed.). New York: Wiley.

Vinturella, L., & James, R. (1987, February). Sand play: A therapeutic medium with children. *Elementary School Guidance and Counseling, 21*(3), 229–238.

Waldman, S. (1994, June 20). Taking on the welfare dads: Teen parenthood. *Newsweek,* pp. 34–38.

Walker, C. E., Bonner, B. L., & Kaufman, K. L. (1988). *The physically and sexually abused child: Evaluation and treatment.* New York: Pergamon Press.

Walker, D., & Hulecki, M. (1989). Is AIDS a biasing factor in teacher judgment? *Exceptional Children, 55* (4), 342–345.

Wallerstein, J. S. (1983). Children of divorce: The psychological tasks of the child. *American Journal of Orthopsychiatry, 53,* 230–243.

Wallerstein, J. S., & Blakeslee, S. (1989). *Second chances: Men, women and children a decade after divorce.* New York: Ticknor & Fields.

Wallerstein, J. S., & Kelly, J. B. (1980). *Surviving the breakup: How children and parents cope with divorce.* New York: Basic Books.

Walsh, W. M., & Gilblin, N. J. (Eds.). (1988). *Family counseling in school settings.* Springfield, IL: Charles C Thomas.

Watson, R. I., & Lindgren, H. C. (1979). *Psychology of the child and the adolescent* (4th ed.). New York: Macmillan.

Webb, N. B. (Ed.). (1991). *Play therapy with children in crisis: A casebook for practitioners.* New York: Guilford Press.

Weisz, J. R., Weiss, B., Alicke, M. D., & Klotz, M. L. (1987). Effectiveness of psychotherapy with children and adolescents: Meta-analytic findings for clinicians. *Journal of Consulting and Clinical Psychology, 55,* 542–549.

Weisz, J. R., Weiss, B., Han, S. S., Granger, D. A., & Morton, T. (1995). Effects of psychotherapy with children and adolescents revisited: A meta-analysis of treatment outcome studies. *Psychological Bulletin, 117,* 450–468.

Westwood, M. J., & Ishiyama, F. I. (1990, October). The communication process as a critical intervention for client change in cross-cultural counseling. *Journal of Multicultural Counseling and Development, 18,* 163–171.

Wicks-Nelson, R., & Israel, A. C. (1991). *Behavior disorders of childhood* (2nd ed.). Englewood, Cliffs, NJ: Prentice-Hall.

Wiener, L. S., Best, A., & Pizzo, P. A. (Eds.). (1994). *Be a friend: Children who live with HIV speak.* Morton Grove, IL: Albert Whitman.

Wilbur, C. B. (1984). The etiology of multiple personalities: Multiple personality and child abuse, *Psychiatric Clinics of North America, 7,* 3–7.

Wilcox, B. L., & Naimark, H. (1991). The rights of the child: Progress toward human dignity. *American Psychologist, 46,* 49–52.

Williams, B. F. (1992). Changing demographics: Challenges for educators. *Intervention in School and Clinic, 27* (3), 157–163.

Wilson, J., & Blocher, L. (1990). The counselor's role in assisting children of alcoholics. *Elementary School Guidance and Counseling, 25,* 98–106.

Wilson, L. L., & Stith, S. M. (1991, January). Culturally sensitive therapy with black clients. *Journal of Multicultural Counseling and Development, 19,* 32–43.

Zastrow, C. (1995). *The practice of social work* (5th ed.). Pacific Grove, CA: Brooks/Cole.

Ziegler, R. G. (1980). Task-focused therapy with children and families. *American Journal of Psychotherapy, 34,* 107–118.

Zigler, E., Taussig, C., & Black, K. (1992, August). Early childhood intervention: A promising preventative for juvenile delinquency. *American Psychologist, 47* (8), 997–1006.

NAME INDEX

SUBJECT INDEX

CREDITS

This page constitutes an extension of the copyright page. We have made every effort to trace the ownership of all copyrighted material and to secure permission from copyright holders. In the event of any question arising as to the use of any material, we will be pleased to make the necessary corrections in future printings. Thanks are due to the following authors, publishers, and agents for permission to use the material indicated.

Chapter 1: 22: Excerpt from "A Teenager Copes with Being Homeless," by Lynn Minton, Fresh Voices, *Parade Magazine*, October 2, 1994. Reprinted with permission from Parade. Copyright © 1994.

Chapter 2: 37: *Around and Around—Love*, by B. Miles, Alfred A. Knopf, 1975. Copyright 1975 by Betty Miles. Used by permission of the author.

Part II: 131: *Quiet Rebirth*, by B. Eddy, reprinted from *Elementary School Guidance and Counseling*, 22, April, 1988, p. 313. © ACA. Reprinted with permission. No further reproduction authorized without written permission of the American Counseling Association.

TO THE OWNER OF THIS BOOK:

I hope that you have found *Strategies for Counseling with Children and Their Parents* useful. So that this book can be improved in a future edition, would you take the time to complete this sheet and return it? Thank you.

School and address: ─────────────────────────────

Department: ──────────────────────────────────

Instructor's name: ──────────────────────────────

1. What I like most about this book is: ───────────────

───

───

2. What I like least about this book is: ───────────────

───

───

3. My general reaction to this book is: ───────────────

───

4. The name of the course in which I used this book is: ─────────

───

5. Were all of the chapters of the book assigned for you to read? ───────

   If not, which ones weren't? ──────────────────────

6. In the space below, or on a separate sheet of paper, please write specific suggestions for improving this book and anything else you'd care to share about your experience in using the book.

───

───

───

───

───

Optional:

Your name: _____ Date: _____

May Brooks/Cole quote you, either in promotion for *Strategies for Counseling with Children and Their Parents* or in future publishing ventures?

Yes: _____ No: _____

Sincerely,

Geraldine Orton

FOLD HERE

- -

BUSINESS REPLY MAIL

FIRST CLASS   PERMIT NO. 358   PACIFIC GROVE, CA

POSTAGE WILL BE PAID BY ADDRESSEE

ATT: *Geraldine Orton* _____

**Brooks/Cole Publishing Company
511 Forest Lodge Road
Pacific Grove, California 93950-9968**

FOLD HERE